lonely planet

New Zealand's South Island
(Te Waipounamu)

Marlborough
& Nelson
(p50)

The
West
Coast
(p95)

Christchurch
& Canterbury
(p128)

Queenstown
& Wanaka
(p214)

Dunedin
& Otago
(p181)

Fiordland &
Southland
(p251)

THIS EDITION WRITTEN AND RESEARCHED BY

Brett Atkinson,
Sarah Bennett, Peter Dragicevich,
Charles Rawlings-Way, Lee Slater

PLAN YOUR TRIP

PETE SEAWARD/LONELY PLANET ©

MARLBOROUGH
WINE REGION P64

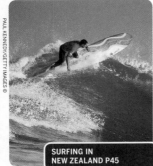

PAUL KENNEDY/GETTY IMAGES ©

SURFING IN
NEW ZEALAND P45

ON THE ROAD

Contents

VIEW FROM THE
REMARKABLES P215

Welcome to the South Island

Welcome to possibly the world's most scenically diverse island; with lakes, mountains and beaches, often incorporating quintessentially Kiwi ways to get active and adventurous.

Walk on the Wild Side

With just a million people scattered across 151,215 sq km, the South Island has a population density smaller than Tasmania, Australia. Filling in the gaps are the sublime forests, mountains, lakes, beaches and fiords that have made New Zealand's 'Mainland' one of the best hiking (locals call it tramping) destinations on the planet. Tackle one of the six epic 'Great Walks' or just spend a few dreamy hours wandering through some easily accessible wilderness.

Action Aplenty

The easygoing heritage charms of Arrowtown, Dunedin and Oamaru are undoubted, but the South Island's most iconic experiences are best enjoyed with a healthy sense of adventure. Kayak in the meandering coves of the Marlborough Sounds or amid Fiordland's remote isolation, scare yourself silly with Queenstown's gravity-defying menu of bungy options, or take to two wheels through stunning scenery on the Otago Central Rail Trail. During winter, squeeze in a short ski-field break around Wanaka, Queenstown or Mt Hutt, before adjourning to cosy bars and cafes to watch NZ's rugby legends take on the best of Australia and South Africa.

Food, Wine & Beer

After all this exercise, visitors can ease into the local eating and drinking scene. NZ food was once a bland facsimile of a British Sunday dinner, but these days Kiwi chefs dip into new-world culinary oceans for inspiration. Expect a tasty focus on local and seasonal produce, especially around the stone-fruit orchards of Otago and the salty marine larder surrounding Kaikoura.

Thirsty? NZ's cool-climate wineries have been collecting trophies for decades now, and Marlborough, Christchurch and Dunedin are all hoppy hubs for the country's emerging craft beer movement.

Meet the Locals

Prepare to meet the South Island's idiosyncratic wildlife: whales, fur seals, dolphins and penguins frequent the waters around Kaikoura, partnered by an armada of pelagic bird species; NZ's endangered Hector's dolphins cavort in the waters of Banks Peninsula and the Catlins; and the Otago Peninsula has penguins, royal albatross and sea lions. Further south, battered by Southern Ocean winds, Stewart Island presents opportunities to spy NZ's iconic but shy kiwi. More bolshy avian species include the kea, NZ's native alpine parrot. Keep a close eye on your rental car's aerial if they're hanging around.

Why I Love the South Island

By Brett Atkinson, Coordinating Author

Although I'm a born and bred North Islander, I'm a huge fan of the South Island. Kayaking around Abel Tasman National Park is truly special – include time to explore Marlborough's craft beer scene – and further south at Kaikoura and Akaroa I've loved swimming with fur seals and dolphins. Historic Dunedin and Oamaru are packed with heritage architecture (and great pubs), and Christchurch's post-earthquake creativity and energy are contagious. Beautiful Central Otago, the sleepy Catlins coast, and wildlife-watching on the Otago Peninsula are all special memories.

For more about our authors, see page 360

Above: Lake Tekapo (p172)

New Zealand – South Island

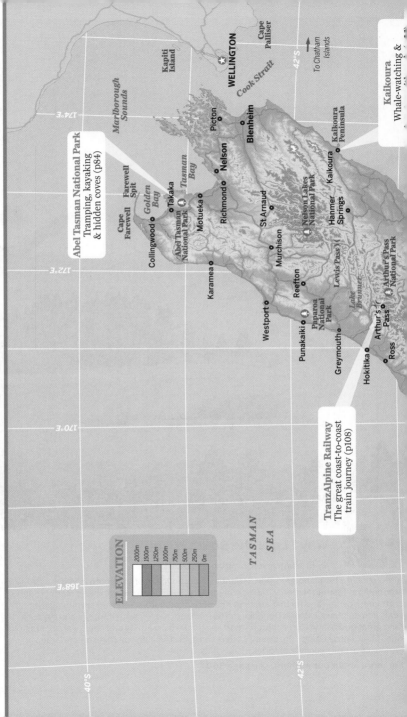

N

0   200 km
0   100 miles

Abel Tasman National Park
Tramping, kayaking
& hidden coves (p84)

Marlborough
Sounds

Cape   Farewell
Farewell   Spit

Golden
Bay

Tasman
Bay

Takaka

Collingwood

Abel Tasman
National Park

Motueka

Richmond

Nelson

Picton

Blenheim

WELLINGTON

Kapiti
Island

Cook Strait

Cape
Palliser

To Chatham
Islands

Karamea

Murchison

St Arnaud

Nelson Lakes
National Park

Hanmer
Springs

Lewis Pass

Kaikoura

Kaikoura
Peninsula

Kaikoura
Whale-watching &

Reefton

Westport

Punakaiki

Paparoa
National
Park

Lake
Brunner

Arthur's
Pass

Arthur's Pass
National Park

Greymouth

Hokitika

Ross

TranzAlpine Railway
The great coast-to-coast
train journey (p108)

TASMAN
SEA

ELEVATION

2000m
1500m
1250m
1000m
750m
500m
250m
0m

174°E

172°E

170°E

168°E

40°S

42°S

42°S

Banks Peninsula
French history &
coastal landscapes (p150)

To Bounty Islands;
Antipodes Islands

Oamaru
Victorian heritage &
steampunk culture (p185)

Central Otago
History, cycling &
summer fruit (p205)

Otago Peninsula
Welcoming wildlife amid
coastal grandeur (p203)

The Catlins
Wildlife on the
scenic route (p271)

Queenstown
Action aplenty meets
alpine vistas (p215)

Stewart Island
Up close with
NZ's kiwi (p275)

Glacial thrills adjoining
rugged rainforest (p118)

Milford Sound
Peaks soaring from
indigo depths (p262)

SOUTH PACIFIC

OCEAN

To Campbell
Island

To Snares Islands;
Auckland Islands

44°S

46°S

174°E

172°E

Christchurch
Lyttelton
Banks Peninsula
Akaroa

Canterbury
Bight

Ashburton

Methven

Timaru

Temuka

Waimate

Oamaru

Palmerston

Otago Peninsula

Dunedin

Milton

Balclutha

Chaslands Mistake

Lake
Mahinerangi

Mt Cook ▲ (3724m)
Mt Cook Village
Aoraki/Mt Cook
National Park
Lake
Tekapo

Westland
National
Park
Lake
Pukaki

Twizel

Alexandra

Cromwell

Arrowtown

Lumsden

Gore

Catlins
Conservation
Park

Haast

Haast
Pass

Jackson
Bay

Mt Aspiring
(3035m) ▲
Lake
Wanaka

Wanaka

Queenstown
Lake
Wakatipu

Te Anau

Manapouri

Winton

Invercargill

Bluff

Oban

Foveaux Strait

Fiordland
National Park

Glenorchy

Lake Te Anau

Milford
Sound

Milford
Sound

George
Sound

Tuatapere

Lake
Manapouri

Doubtful
Sound

Dusky
Sound

West
Cape

Stewart
Island
(Rakiura)

The South Island's
Top 15

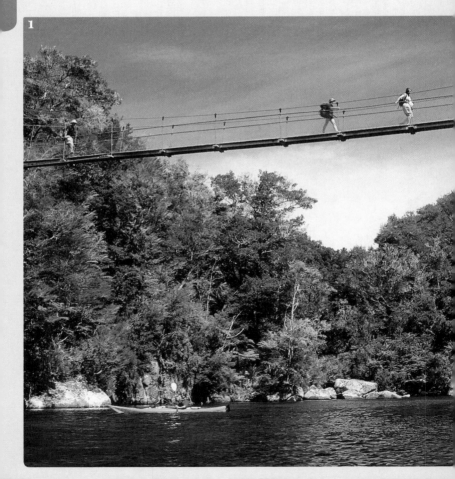
1

Abel Tasman National Park

1 Here's New Zealand nature at its most glorious and seductive: lush green hills fringed with golden sandy coves, slipping gently into warm shallows before meeting a crystal-clear sea of cerulean blue. Abel Tasman National Park (p84) is the quintessential postcard paradise, where you can put yourself in the picture, assuming an endless number of poses: tramping, kayaking, swimming, sunbathing, or even makin' whoopee in the woods. This sweet-as corner of NZ's South Island raises the bar and effortlessly keeps it there.

Kaikoura

2 First settled by Maori with their keen nose for seafood, Kaikoura (p66) – meaning 'eat crayfish' – is now NZ's best spot for both consuming and communing with marine life. Whales are definitely off the menu, but you're almost guaranteed a good gander at Moby's mates on a whale-watching tour. There's also swimming with seals and dolphins, or bird-watching including albatross. When it comes to 'sea food and eat it', crayfish is still king, but on fishing tours you can hook into other edible wonders of the unique Kaikoura deep.

DAVID WALL/GETTY IMAGES ©

DAVID WALL/GETTY IMAGES ©

2

karoa &
anks Peninsula

Infused with a healthy
dash of Gallic ambi-
ce, French-themed
aroa (p150) bends
nguidly around one of
e prettiest harbours on
nks Peninsula. Sleek
lphins and plump pen-
ins inhabit clear waters
rfect for sailing and
ploring. Elsewhere on
e peninsula, the spidery
mmit Rd prescribes the
n of an ancient volcano,
ile winding roads
scend to hidden bays
d coves. Spend your
ys tramping and kayak-
amid the improbably
autiful land- and sea-
ape, while relaxing at
ght in chic bistros or cosy
B accommodation.

Franz Josef
& Fox Glaciers

The spectacular
glaciers of Franz Josef
(p118) and Fox (p122)
are remarkable for many
reasons, including their
rates of accumulation and
descent, and their proximity to both the loftiest peaks
of the Southern Alps and
the Tasman Sea around
10km away. Get almost
face-to-face with them on
a short walk, or take a hike
on the ice with Franz Josef
or Fox Glacier Guides. The
ultimate encounter is on a
scenic flight, which often
also provides grandstand
views of Aoraki/Mt Cook,
Westland forest, and a
seemingly endless Tasman
Sea. Trampers on Franz Josef
Glacier (p118)

Central Otago

Here's your chance
to balance virtue and
vice, all with a background
of some of NZ's most
starkly beautiful land-
scapes. Take to two wheels
to negotiate the easygoing
Otago Central Rail Trail
(p206), cycling into heritage South Island towns
such as Clyde (p210) and
Naseby (p207). Tuck into
well-earned beers in laid-
back country pubs, or
linger for a classy lunch in
the vineyard restaurants
of Bannockburn. Other
foodie diversions include
Cromwell's weekly farmers
market, and the summer
stone-fruit harvest of the
country's best orchards.

Queenstown

6 Queenstown (p215) may be the birthplace of bungy jumping, but there's more to NZ's adventure hub than leaping off a bridge wearing a rubber band. Against the scenic backdrop of the jagged indigo profile of the Remarkables, travellers can spend days skiing, hiking or mountain biking, before dining in cosmopolitan restaurants or partying in some of NZ's best bars. Next-day options include hang gliding, kayaking or river rafting, or easing into holiday mode with sleepier detours to Arrowtown or Glenorchy. View from the Remarkables (p39)

Otago Peninsula

7 The Otago Peninsula (p203) is proof there's more to the South Island's outdoor thrills than heart-stopping alpine and lake scenery. Amid a backdrop of coastal vistas combining rugged, hidden beaches with an expansive South Pacific horizon, it's easy to spot penguins, seals and sea lions. Beyond the rare yellow-eyed penguin or hoiho, other fascinating avian residents include the royal albatross. Taiaroa Head is the world's only mainland royal albatross colony: visit in January or February to see these magnificent ocean-going birds.

6

DAVID WALL/GETTY IMAGES ©

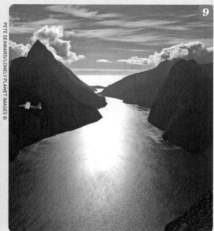

PETE SEAWARD/LONELY PLANET IMAGES ©

TranzAlpine

8 In less than five hours the *TranzAlpine* (p108) crosses from the Pacific Ocean to the Tasman Sea. Leaving Christchurch it speeds across the Canterbury Plains to the foothills of the Southern Alps. After negotiating tunnels and viaducts, the train enters the broad expanse of the Waimakariri Valley. A stop at Arthur's Pass Village is followed by the 8.5km-long Otira tunnel, burrowing right through the bedrock of New Zealand's alpine spine. Then it's all downhill: through the Taramakau River valley, past Lake Brunner, and finally into sleepy Greymouth.

Milford Sound

9 Fingers crossed you'll be lucky enough to see Milford Sound (p262) on a clear, sunny day. That's definitely when the world-beating collage of waterfalls, verdant cliffs and peaks, and dark cobalt waters is at its best. More likely though is the classic Fiordland combination of mist and drizzle, with the iconic snowcapped profile of Mitre Peak revealed slowly through shimmering sheets of precipitation. Either way, keep your eyes peeled for seals and dolphins, especially if you're exploring NZ's most famous fiord by kayak.

Skiing & Snowboarding

10 You're guaranteed to find decent South Island snow right through the winter season (June to October). The most famous slopes are around hip Queenstown (p215) and laid-back Wanaka (p241), with iconic ski runs such as Coronet Peak, the Remarkables and Treble Cone close at hand. There are also dedicated snowboarding and cross-country (Nordic) snow parks here. Further north the smaller club-operated ski fields of Canterbury offer a more local experience. And when it comes to après-ski time, a cosy bar or restaurant is never far away. Skiing Coronet Peak (p37)

Stewart Island

11 Stewart Island (p275), the country's rugged southern addendum, is paradise for trampers, bird-watchers and travellers seeking an authentic NZ experience. Test yourself on the North West Circuit Track or spend three days on the easier, but still spectacular, Rakiura Track. Join the friendly locals at NZ's southern-most pub quiz at the South Sea Hotel in Oban, before making plans to explore the abundant bird life on nearby Ulva Island, or join a kiwi-spotting tour to see NZ's shy feathered icon mooching around at twilight on isolated beaches. Ulva Island (p277)

10

Oamaru

12 A wonderfully restored Victorian townscape, the quirky celebration of Steampunk culture, or the nightly arrival of hundreds of little blue penguins: surprising Oamaru (p185) has plenty of reasons for a mandatory inclusion on your South Island itinerary. Explore the town's harbourside historic precinct on a penny-farthing bicycle before adjourning for Earl Grey or something stronger in heritage cafes and restaurants. At dusk, grab a grandstand seat to say g'day to penguins returning home after a day's fishing, before toasting their ocean-going bravery with a beer at a corner pub.
Bank of NSW building, Thames St (p187)

The Catlins

13 Even for many New Zealanders the rugged Catlins coast (p271) is unknown territory. Avoid the speedy but functional inland route linking Dunedin and Invercargill, and traverse through the Catlins' more diverse and interesting procession of isolated bays and coves, sweeping coastal scenery, and opportunities to meet the locals and the local wildlife. Catlins' highlights include Blair Sommerville's quirky Lost Gypsy Gallery at Papatowai, swimming (or surfing) with dolphins at Curio Bay, and the windswept environs of Slope Point, the southernmost tip of the South Island.

Rugby

14 Rugby Union (p314) is New Zealand's national game and governing preoccupation. If your timing's good you might catch the revered national team (and reigning world champions) the All Blacks in action. The 'ABs' are resident gods: mention Richie McCaw or Dan Cart in any conversation and you'll win friends for life! Or just watch some kids chasing a ball around a suburban field on a Saturday morning, or yell along with the locals in a small-town pub as the big men collide on the big screen.

13

Maori Culture

15 New Zealand's indigenous Maori culture (p303) is accessible and engaging: join in a *haka* (war dance); chow-down at a traditional *hangi* (Maori feast cooked in an earth oven); carve a pendant from bone or *pounamu* (greenstone); learn some Maori language; or check out an authentic cultural performance with song, dance, legends, arts and crafts. Big-city and regional museums around the South Island are crammed with Maori artefacts and historical items, and Timaru's excellent Te Ana Maori Rock Art Centre showcases the fascinating story of NZ's indigenous rock art. Maori carving, Otago Museum

Need to Know

For more information, see Survival Guide (p321)

Currency
New Zealand dollars ($)

Language
English, Maori

Visas
Citizens of Australia, the UK and 56 other countries don't need visas for NZ (length of stay allowances vary). Other countries' citizens require visas. See www.immigration.govt.nz.

Money
ATMs are widely available, especially in larger cities and towns. Credit cards accepted in most hotels and restaurants.

Mobile Phones
Australian and European phones will work on NZ's networks, but not most American or Japanese phones. Use global roaming or a local SIM card and pre-pay account.

Time
New Zealand time is GMT/UCT plus 12 hours (two hours ahead of Australian Eastern Standard Time).

When to Go

Nelson
GO Jan–Mar

Franz Josef
GO Feb–Mar

Christchurch
GO Jan–Mar

Queenstown
GO Jun–Aug

Te Anau
GO Oct–Apr

High Season
(Dec–Feb)

➡ Summer: busy beaches, outdoor explorations, festivals and sporting events. City accommodation increases up to 25%.

➡ High season in the ski towns is during winter (Jun–Aug): chilly days, cold nights and deep powder.

Shoulder
(Mar–Apr)

➡ Prime travelling time: fine weather, short queues, kids in school and warm(ish) ocean.

➡ Long evenings supping Kiwi wines and craft beers.

➡ Spring (Sep–Nov) is spring shoulder season too.

Low Season
(May–Aug)

➡ Head for the slopes of the Southern Alps for some brilliant southern hemisphere skiing.

➡ No crowds, good accommodation deals and a seat in any restaurant.

Useful Websites

100% Pure New Zealand (www.newzealand.com) Official tourism site.

Department of Conservation (www.doc.govt.nz) DOC parks and camping info.

Destination New Zealand (www.destination-nz.com) Resourceful tourism site.

Lonely Planet (www.lonely planet.com/new-zealand) Destination information, hotel bookings, traveller forum and more.

Te Ara (www.teara.govt.nz) Online encyclopedia of NZ.

DineOut (www.dineout.co.nz) Restaurant reviews.

Important Numbers

Regular NZ phone numbers have a two-digit area code followed by a seven-digit number. When dialling within a region, the area code is still required. Drop the initial 0 if dialling from abroad.

NZ country code	64
International access code from NZ	00
Emergency (fire, ambulance, police)	111
Directory assistance	018
International directory	0172

Exchange Rates

Australia	A$1	NZ$1.09
Canada	C$1	NZ$1.08
China	Y10	NZ$1.89
Euro zone	€1	NZ$1.61
Japan	¥100	NZ$1.15
Singapore	S$1	NZ$0.94
UK	UK£1	NZ$1.97
US	US$1	NZ$1.18

For current exchange rates see www.xe.com

Daily Costs

**Budget:
Less than $130**

➡ Dorm beds or campsites: $25–$35 per night

➡ Big-city food markets for self-catering bargains

➡ Explore NZ with a money-saving bus pass

**Midrange:
$130–$250**

➡ Double room in a midrange hotel/motel: $100–$200

➡ Midrange restaurant, a movie or a live band, and a few beers at a pub

➡ Hire a car and explore further

**Top End:
More than $250**

➡ Double room in top-end hotel: from $200

➡ Three-course meal in a classy restaurant: $70

➡ Take a guided tour, go shopping or hit some ritzy bars

Opening Hours

Opening hours vary seasonally, but use the following as a general guide:

Banks 9.30am–4.30pm Monday to Friday; some 9am–noon Saturday

Cafes 7am–4pm

Pubs & Bars noon–late

Restaurants noon–2.30pm and 6.30–9pm

Shops 9am–5.30pm Monday to Friday; 9am to 12.30pm or 5pm Saturday

Supermarkets 8am–7pm, often 9pm or later in cities

Arriving in the South Island

Christchurch Airport (p335)
Metro Bus 3 and 29 run into the city regularly from 7am to 11pm. The pre-booked shuttle bus provides 24-hour door-to-door services. Taxis cost around $50-60 and take around 20 minutes to the city.

Queenstown Airport (p335)
Connectabus buses run every 15 minutes from 6.50am to 10.20pm. The pre-booked shuttle bus provides 24-hour door-to-door services. Taxis cost around $35 and will take approximately 15 minutes to the city.

Getting Around

The South Island is long and skinny, and many roads are two-lane country byways: getting from A to B requires some thought.

Car Travel at your own tempo, explore remote areas and visit regions with no public transport. Hire cars in major towns. Driving is on the left; the steering wheel is on the right.

Bus Reliable, frequent services around the country (usually cheaper than flying).

Plane Fast-track your holiday with affordable, frequent, fast internal flights.

Train Two scenic routes through the Southern Alps, and along the coast linking Picton and Christchurch.

For much more on **getting around**, see p336

PLAN YOUR TRIP NEED TO KNOW

If You Like...

Cities

Christchurch Re-emerging from recent earthquakes with energy and verve largely due to the determination and resilience of proud locals. Stay longer than you planned to fully experience the city's renaissance. (p129)

Dunedin Exuding history and an artsy, boozy ambience (so many students), and surprisingly close to superb wildlife-viewing opportunities on the Otago Peninsula. (p192)

Queenstown Maybe only a town in an international sense, but a global posse of travellers and adventure seekers ensures New Zealand's most scenic alpine resort exudes a cosmopolitan vibe year round. (p215)

Beaches

Wharariki No car park, no ice-cream van, no swimsuits... This isolated stretch near sweeping Farewell Spit is for wanderers and ponderers. (p91)

Abel Tasman Coast Track No need to Photoshop this postcard paradise. These golden beaches, blue bays and verdant hills are for real. (p84)

Kaiteriteri Wildly popular, and for good reason, Kaiteriteri's gorgeous, golden stretch of sand is the gateway to the beautiful Abel Tasman National Park. That's where you can kayak or tramp to more isolated beachy spots such as Onetahuti. (p83)

History

Dunedin Railway Station One hundred or so years old, trimmed with mosaic tiles and stained-glass windows. One of NZ's most-photographed buildings, and the starting point for the spectacular Taieri Gorge Railway. (p193)

Oamaru Historic Precinct Beautifully restored whitestone buildings and warehouses, now house galleries, restaurants and artisan workshops. Pack your sense of balance to ride a penny-farthing bicycle. (p187)

Christchurch The earthquakes damaged much of the southern capital's architectural heritage, but some essential historic experiences remain. Punt slowly down the Avon River and explore the excellent Canterbury Museum. (p129)

Denniston Plateau Explore this ghostly former coal-mining town near Westport, once home to 1500 sooty locals. (p100)

Akaroa Discover the French colonial history of the pretty seaside village of Akaroa. The French Fest held in late October every two years is a great time to visit. (p150)

Maori Culture

Te Ana Maori Rock Art Centre Learn about traditional Maori rock art in Timaru before exploring remote sites around South Canterbury. (p169)

Okains Maori & Colonial Museum Tucked away in sleepy Okains Bay on the Banks Peninsula, this community-run museum is a surprising storehouse of heritage treasures including a *waka taua* (war canoe). (p152)

Hokitika The primary source of NZ *pounamu* (greenstone) and home to numerous master carvers of stone, bone and paua in traditional designs. (p112)

Ko Tane Visit the Willowbank Wildlife Reserve in Christchurch for a replica Maori village and an excellent cultural show. (p135)

Museums & Galleries

Otago Museum Harnessing Dunedin's academic firepower, the Otago Museum presents an overview of the region's history, flora and fauna – an excellent primer before wildlife-watching on the Otago Peninsula. (p195)

Canterbury Museum One of the few heritage buildings to survive the Christchurch earthquakes unscathed: a fascinating showcase of Maori culture and natural history. (p132)

World of Wearable Art & Classic Cars Museum Nelson's WOW remains as popular as ever, with the added (though incongruous) bonus of a classic cars display out the back. (p76)

Eastern Southland Gallery A real surprise in sleepy Gore, a town more known for moonshine whiskey, country music and trout fishing, this erudite establishment features works by iconic NZ artists Ralph Hotere and Rita Angus. (p270)

Tramping

Milford Track Justifiably famous, Milford is our pick of the 'Great Walks': 53.5km of gorgeous fiords, sounds, peaks and raindrops. Good luck dealing with the challenging Mackinnon Pass and a few pesky sandflies. (p262)

Routeburn Track Those with plenty of 'Great Walk' kilometres in their boots rate the Routeburn as the best of the bunch. (p234)

Banks Peninsula Track The peninsula's rolling hills and picturesque bays might not look like the eroded remains of twin volcanoes. Geology lesson, anyone? (p153)

Lake Angelus Track Yes, the zigzag up Pinchgut Track is a bit of a rude awakening, but the views along Mt Robert Ridge last all day. (p94)

Pubs, Bars & Beer

Nelson Craft Beer Home of NZ hops, Nelson boasts a craft-beer trail featuring a host of breweries and legendary inns. (p78)

Christchurch Craft-beer hubs such as Pomeroy's Old Brewery Inn and The Brewery present the

op) Trampers in the Clinton Valley, along the Milford Track (p258)
ottom) Vineyard in the Marlborough wine region (p64)

absolute best of Kiwi brews from around the country. (p145)

Dunedin There are plenty of great bars to keep you off the streets in NZ's best university town. (p200)

Queenstown Kick back after a day of mountain biking, bungy jumping or skiing with a few not-so-quiet ones in the resort town's happening bars. (p231)

Invercargill Brewery This workhorse not only produces its own range but also brews on behalf of some of NZ's best small producers. (p267)

Foodie Experiences

Central Otago wineries Eye-popping Central Otago scenery combined with the best of NZ food and wine. Don't miss excellent restaurants in nearby Queenstown and Arrowtown. (p205)

Central Otago orchards Drift by the orchards around Alexandra, Cromwell and Roxburgh in February and March for juicy stone fruit. Apricots, peaches, plums and nectarines – anything goes. (p210)

Wildfoods Festival (Hokitika) You're a big baby, Bear Grylls – eating insects can be fun – especially washed down with Monteith's beers. (p114)

Kaikoura Seafood BBQ Swing by this fabulous outdoor fish shack for some whitebait, mussels, paua or crayfish, cooked hot and fresh. (p71)

West Coast whitebait Have a pattie and a pint at a country pub, or buy a half-pound from an old-timer's back door. (p114)

Stewart Island Good cod! Is everyone on this island a fisherman? (Answer: yes. Bring lemons.) (p275)

Skiing

Treble Cone 26km from Wanaka, with everything from challenging downhill terrain to snowboard half-pipes and cross-country skiing at the nearby Cardrona Snow Farm. (p39)

Canterbury From Mt Hutt and Methven's après-ski buzz, to smaller fields such as Ohau, Round Hill, Porters and Broken River. (p39)

Coronet Peak The Queenstown area's oldest ski field, just 18km from town. Night skiing on Friday and Saturday gives you time to hit the slopes before hitting the bars and clubs back in town. (p37)

Cardrona More great skiing in the Wanaka area, with slopes to suit all levels of experience. (p249)

Wine Regions

Marlborough The country's biggest and best wine region keeps on turning out superb sauvignon blanc. Don't be picky – just drink some and see what the fuss is about. (p64)

Waitaki Valley In a quiet back road linking Canterbury and North Otago, the South Island's newest wine region produces excellent pinot gris. It's where All Blacks legend Richie McCaw was born, so please pay your respects. (p184)

Gibbston Valley Negotiate a tasty pathway through the vineyards of this meandering river valley near Queenstown, You can even visit on a retro bicycle. (p223)

Waipara Valley A short hop north of Christchurch are spectacular vineyards producing equally spectacular riesling. (p161)

Markets

Otago Farmers Market Organic fruit and veg, Dunedin's own Green Man beer, robust coffee and homemade pies – stock up for life on the road. (p198)

Nelson Market A big, busy weekly market featuring everything from Doris' traditional bratwursts to New Age clothing. (p73)

Cromwell Central Otago's best farmers market takes place Sunday morning in Cromwell's small but perfectly formed historic precinct. Come hungry as there are plenty of free samples. (p211)

Christchurch Farmers' Market The historic surroundings of Riccarton Bush are transformed every Saturday with artisan cheeses, craft beer and international street food. On Sundays an arts and crafts market takes centre stage. (p145)

Extreme Activities

Queenstown Bungy Strap yourself into the astonishing Shotover Canyon Swing or Nevis Bungy and be propelled into the void. (p218)

Skydive Franz If you're really up for some super-human thrills, this is the highest skydiving in NZ at 18,000 ft. (p119)

U-fly Extreme Yes, YOU fly – a stunt plane, no less – across the clear blue skies above Motueka. (p81)

Buller River Look forward to a combo of stunning West Coast scenery and exciting river rafting through tight spots such as 'Earthquake Rapids'. Jetboating the Buller is reputed to be NZ's best – sorry Queenstown. (p97)

Month by Month

January

New Zealand peels its eyes open after New Year's Eve, gathers its wits and gets set for another year. Great weather, the cricket season in full swing and it's happy holidays for the locals.

☆ World Buskers Festival

Christchurch could use a little cheering up: jugglers, musos, tricksters, puppeteers, mime artists, dancers... Shoulder into the crowd, see who's performing in the middle and maybe leave a few dollars (www.worldbuskers festival.com). Avoid if you're scared of audience participation.

☆ Nelson Jazz & Blues Festival

Get your groove on at rockin' venues and ad hoc street corner stages (www. nelsonjazzfest.co.nz). Acts range from international funkateers through to Kiwi hipsters, and Nelson's reputation for great wine and beer makes it very easy to enjoy the diverse beats.

February

The sun is shining, the nights are long, and the sauv blanc and pale ale are chillin' in the fridge: this is prime party time across NZ. Book your festival tickets (and beds) in advance.

🍷 Marlborough Wine & Food Festival

NZ's biggest and best wine festival (www.marlborough winefestival.co.nz) features tastings from around 50 Marlborough wineries (also NZ's biggest and best), plus fine food and entertainment. It's mandatory over-indulgence; remember to keep quiet if you don't like sauvignon blanc.

☆ Rippon Festival

Wanaka's alternative music festival (www.rippon festival.co.nz) – held in a gently sloping lakeside vineyard – features cool sounds with a dance, reggae, rock and electronica spin. It's an uber-relaxed opportunity to listen to the finely curated best of the NZ music scene.

March

March brings a hint of autumn, and it's harvest time in the vineyards of Marlborough and orchards of Central Otago. Expect long dusky evenings and plenty of festivals plumping out the calendar.

🍴 Wildfoods Festival

Eat worms, hare testicles or crabs at Hokitika's comfort-zone-challenging food fest (www.wildfoods.co.nz). Not for the mild-mannered or weak-stomached... But even if you are, it's still fun to watch! There are plenty of fine quality NZ brews to help subdue any difficult tastes.

✨ Ellerslie Flower Show

Christchurch's glorious Hagley Park is made even more spectacular by the lovingly crafted introduction of beautiful gardens (www.ellerslie flowershow.co.nz). Don't come expecting a haven for fuddy-duddy gardeners, as many of the colourful, floral additions are also bold, modern and innovative.

🍷 Gibbston Wine & Food Festival

Head to the Queenstown Gardens in mid-March to try wines and produce from the rugged and meandering river valley to the east of Queenstown. Look forward to award-winning wines from 10 vineyards, local cheese and chocolate, and cooking masterclasses from celebrated NZ chefs (www. gibbstonwineandfood. co.nz).

April

April is when canny travellers hit NZ: the ocean is swimmable and the weather still mild, with nary a tourist or queue in sight. Easter equals pricey accommodation everywhere.

✈️ Warbirds Over Wanaka

Held every second Easter in even-numbered years, Warbirds Over Wanaka (www. warbirdsoverwanaka.com) is an internationally renowned airshow set against rugged Central Otago scenery. Heritage and iconic aircraft pull crazy manoeuvres for up to 50,000 spectators. Tally ho chaps, and BYO Biggles goggles.

🍷 Clyde Wine & Food Festival

Sleepy Clyde is well-known as the northern terminus of the Otago Central Rail Trail, but the cool-climate pinots and rieslings of local vineyards are also damn fine. Keep an eye out for Two Paddocks, Kiwi actor Sam Neill's vineyard. Held annually on Easter Sunday.

May

The nostalgia of autumn runs deep: party nights are long gone and a chilly NZ winter beckons. Thank goodness for the Comedy Festival. It's your last chance to explore Fiordland and Southland in reasonable weather.

🍴 Bluff Oyster & Food Festival

Bluff and oysters go together like, well, like a bivalve. Truck down to the deep south for some slippery, salty specimens (www.bluff oysterfest.co.nz). It's chilly down here in May, but the live music and oyster eating/opening competitions warm everybody up.

☆ New Zealand International Comedy Festival

This three-week laughfest (www.comedyfestival. co.nz) in May kicks off in the North Island, but then hits the South Island with the on-the-road Comedy Convoy. International gagmerchants (such as Arj Barker and Danny Bhoy) line up next to home-grown talent.

June

Time to head south: it's ski season. Queenstown and Wanaka hit their strides, and international legions of skiers and snowboarders hit the slopes at Coronet Peak, the Remarkables and Cardrona.

☆ New Zealand Gold Guitar Awards

We like both kinds of music: country and western! With niche-market appeal, these awards (www. goldguitars.co.nz) in Gore cap off a week of everlovin' country twang and bootscootin' good times, with plenty of concerts and buskers.

July

Queenstown gets more than a little crazy with the annual winter festival. Expect increases in accommodation prices while it's happening. If you're feeling less active, combine cinema, Cadbury chocolate and craft beer in Dunedin.

❄️ Queenstown Winter Festival

This southern snow-fest (www.winterfestival.co.nz) has been running since 1975, and now attracts around 45,000 snowbunnies. It's a 10-day party, studded with fireworks, jazz, street parades, comedy, a Mardi Gras, masquerade ball and lots of snow-centric activities on the mountain slopes.

☆ **New Zealand International Film Festivals**

After separate film festivals (www.nzff.co.nz) in Dunedin (July–August) and Christchurch (August), a selection of flicks hits the road for screenings in regional towns from July to November. Film buffs in Greymouth and Invercargill get very excited at the prospect.

August

Land a good deal on accommodation pretty much anywhere except the ski towns. Winter is almost spent, but there's still not much happening outside: music and art are your saviours...or watch some rugby.

🎭 Christchurch Arts Festival

The South Island's biggest arts festival (www.arts festival.co.nz) takes place in odd-numbered years. Celebrate with resilient Cantabrians at a wide array of venues right across the city. Music, theatre and dance all feature.

September

Spring has sprung, and baby lambs are running amok on the South Island. There are good accommodation bargains to be had, but definitely be ready for four seasons in one day. The snow season often lingers.

Top) Views across the Marlborough wine region (p64)
Bottom) French street signs in Akaroa (p150)

🏃 Snowsports

Forget flying off to Europe or South America. Here's your chance to experience the widest range of snow-sports activities in the southern hemisphere. Focus on your downhill at Coronet Peak, achieve snowboarding nirvana at Cardrona, or go Nordic at Snow Farm New Zealand.

October

Post-rugby and pre-cricket sees sports fans twiddling their thumbs: a trip to Kaikoura, Akaroa or Nelson perhaps? October is 'shoulder season' with reasonable accommodation rates, minimal crowds and no competition for the good campsites.

🎭 Nelson Arts Festival

Sure, Nelson is distractingly sunny, but that doesn't mean the artsy good stuff isn't happening inside and out. Get a taste of the local output over two weeks in October (www.nelsonfestivals.co.nz).

🎭 Kaikoura Seafest

Kaikoura is a town built on crayfish. Well, not literally, but there sure are plenty of crustaceans in the sea here, many of which find themselves on plates at Seafest (www.seafest.co.nz),

which is also a great excuse to drink a lot and dance around.

🎭 French Fest

Allez très vite to Akaroa's French Fest (www.french-fest.co.nz) – held in odd-numbered years in late October to celebrate the harbour town's Gallic heritage. Quirky events include a waiters' race and a French cricket tournament. Sorry Aussies, underarm bowling is not allowed.

🍴 Wanaka Fest

Wanaka's normally all about exploring the alpine vistas on two legs or two knobbly mountain-bike tyres, but the lakeside town's emerging gourmet side is also showcased at the annual Wanaka Fest (www.wanakafest.co.nz). Come along and tuck into lots of local produce.

November

Another NZ summer threatens as days get longer following the introduction of daylight saving. Now's a good time to be doing the Milford or Routeburn Tracks, but you'll need to book ahead.

🎭 Oamaru Victorian Heritage Celebrations

Ahhh, the good old days: when Queen Vic sat dourly on the throne, the hems were low, collars were

high, and civic decency was a matter of course. Old Oamaru thoroughly enjoys this tongue-in-cheek historic homage (www.historicoamaru.co.nz) with dress-ups, penny-farthing races, choirs, guided tours etc.

🎭 NZ Cup & Show Week

Christchurch's annual NZ Cup & Show Week (www.nzcupandshow.co.nz) is an iconic Canterbury event, and it's a great opportunity for the good people of Christchurch to celebrate with fashion shows, horse racing and the country-comes-to-town appeal of the A&P (agricultural and pastoral) Show.

December

Summertime! The crack of leather on willow resounds across the nation's cricket pitches and office workers surge towards the finish line. Everyone gears up for Christmas: avoid shopping centres like the plague.

🏃 Queen Charlotte Track

Beat the summer rush with a December departure on the hugely popular Queen Charlotte Track. Cover the coastal track's spectacular 71km on two legs or two wheels, or even integrate a spot of sea kayaking into your stunning journey.

Itineraries

 Southern Circuit

Head to **Christchurch** and see how the city is rebuilding post-earthquakes. Grab a kick-ass coffee at C1 Espresso or the Addington Coffee Co-op, then visit the Canterbury Museum and Transitional Cathedral. The Avon River cuts a lazy ribbon through town. Check it out in the Botanic Gardens, and then ride the historic tram around the city, and ascend in the Gondola for excellent views.

City saturated? Drive out to Banks Peninsula and the French-colonial settlement of **Akaroa**, then head north for whale-watching in **Kaikoura**. Continue to the famous **Marlborough wine region** and pretty harbour town of **Picton** to lose a day in the waterways of the **Marlborough Sounds**.

Detour west past artsy **Nelson** to ecofriendly **Golden Bay**. Heading along the West Coast there's time to check out the town of **Franz Josef** and visit the Franz Josef Glacier and **Fox Glacier** before continuing to ski-central **Queenstown**, the desolate and mesmerising **Doubtful Sound** and the overgrown **Catlins**. Back up the East Coast, drop in to Scottish-flavoured **Dunedin**, then detour through Central Otago to the snowy heights of **Aoraki/Mt Cook** and **Lake Tekapo**, before rolling back into Christchurch.

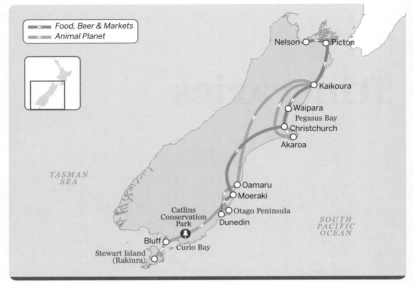

Food, Beer & Markets

10 DAYS

Fire up your tastebuds around Marlborough, widely regarded as the nation's craft-brewing capital and home to microbreweries such as Renaissance, Hop Federation and Golden Bear. Loop east from **Nelson** to **Picton** and down the South Island's rugged East Coast to **Kaikoura** for delicious seafood. Graduate from Kaikoura's rustic seafood eateries to classier dining at vineyard restaurants in the wine region around **Waipara**, north of Christchurch. Pegasus Bay and Waipara Hills are both great for leisurely lunches.

Journey to **Christchurch** to sample the restaurants of Victoria St, Sumner and Lyttelton, and don't miss Christchurch Farmers Market on Saturday morning. Craft-beer heaven awaits beer buffs at Pomeroy's Old Brewery Inn and The Brewery.

Continue south to North Otago and award-winning eateries such as Oamaru's Riverstone Kitchen and Fleur's Place in **Moeraki**. Emerson's and Green Man are the microbreweries to check out further south in **Dunedin** – sample a few at Albar or Tonic – before loading up the car with organic, free-range and locavore goodies at Dunedin's Otago Farmers Market.

Animal Planet

10 DAYS

From **Christchurch**, travel to **Akaroa** to swim with Hector's dolphins, New Zealand's smallest and rarest. Squeeze in a return trip up the coast to **Kaikoura** for whale-watching and swimming with NZ fur seals, before travelling south to **Oamaru**. There's a fascination with Steampunk culture and a wonderful historic precinct, but nature buffs are in town to meet the little blue penguins that swim ashore every night at dusk.

From Oamaru, travel to the **Otago Peninsula** for more little blue penguins, and their extremely rare, shuffling cousin, the yellow-eyed penguin, or hoiho. Join a tour with Nature's Wonders Naturally to get close up to seals and sea lions before admiring the royal albatross colony on nearby Taiaroa Head. A sea journey with Elm Wildlife Tours is another essential experience.

Continue south to the rugged and isolated **Catlins**. Little blue penguins, yellow-eyed penguins and Hector's dolphins are all regular visitors to **Curio Bay**. Head further south and leave the South Island at **Bluff** for kiwi-spotting on wild and idiosyncratic **Stewart Island**. Now you can really say you've met a kiwi.

Plan Your Trip

Hiking in the South Island

Hiking (aka bushwalking, trekking or tramping, as the Kiwis call it) is the perfect vehicle for a close encounter with the South Island's natural beauty. There are thousands of kilometres of wilderness tracks here (some well marked, including six of New Zealand's celebrated 'Great Walks', some barely a line on a map) plus an excellent network of huts and campgrounds.

Planning Your Tramp

When to Go

Mid-December–late January Tramping high season is during the school summer holidays, starting a couple of weeks before Christmas – avoid it if you can.

January–March The summer weather lingers into March: wait until February if you can, when tracks are (marginally) less crowded. Most nonalpine tracks can be walked enjoyably at any time from about October through to April.

June–August Winter is not the time to be out in the wild, especially at altitude – some paths close in winter because of avalanche danger and reduced facilities and services.

What to Bring

Primary considerations: your feet and your shoulders. Make sure your footwear is tough and well worn-in, and your pack isn't too heavy. Wet-weather gear is essential, especially on the South Island's waterlogged West Coast. If you're camping or staying in huts without stoves, bring a camping stove. Also bring insect repellent to keep sandflies away, and don't forget your 'scroggin' – a mixture of dried fruit and nuts (and sometimes chocolate) for munching en route.

Best Walks

Top Long Tramps
Heaphy Track (p92), Kahurangi National Park

Abel Tasman Coast Track (p84), Abel Tasman National Park

Milford Track (p258), Fiordland

Top Short Tramps
St Arnaud Range Track (p93), Nelson Lakes National Park

Avalanche Peak (p163), Canterbury

Top Wildlife Encounters
Birdlife St Arnaud Range Track (p93), West Coast

Seals Cape Foulwind Walkway (p100), West Coast

Kiwi Rakiura Track (p279), Stewart Island

Best for Beginners
Queen Charlotte Track (p58), Marlborough Sounds

Banks Peninsula Track (p153), Canterbury

Books & Resources

Before plodding off into the forest, get up-to-date information from the appropriate authority – usually the **DOC** (Department of Conservation; www.doc.govt.nz) or regional i-SITE visitor information centres. As well as current track condition and weather info, DOC supplies detailed books on the flora, fauna, geology and history of NZ's national parks, plus leaflets (mostly $2 or less) detailing hundreds of NZ walking tracks.

➡ Lonely Planet's *Hiking & Tramping in New Zealand* describes around 50 walks of various lengths and degrees of difficulty.

➡ *101 Great Tramps,* by Mark Pickering and Rodney Smith, has suggestions for two- to six-day tramps around the country. The companion guide, *202 Great Walks: The Best Day Walks in New Zealand,* by Mark Pickering, is handy for shorter, family-friendly excursions.

➡ *Accessible Walks,* by Anna and Andrew Jameson, is an excellent guide for elderly, disabled and family trampers, with detailed access information on more than 100 South Island walks.

➡ *New Zealand Tramper's Handbook,* by Sarah Bennett and Lee Slater, is all about being safe and happy on the track, perfect for new trampers.

➡ *Shelter from the Storm,* by Shaun Barnett, Rob Brown and Geoff Spearpoint, is a meticulously researched history of NZ's backcountry huts (you'll no doubt stay in a few if you're planning on doing any serious hiking).

➡ Bird's Eye Tramping Guides from Craig Potton Publishing have fab topographical maps, and there are countless books covering tramps and short urban walks around NZ – scan the bookshops.

Maps

The topographical maps produced by **Land Information New Zealand** (LINZ; www.linz.govt.nz) are a safe bet. Bookshops don't often have a good selection of these, but LINZ has map-sales offices in major cities and towns, and DOC offices often sell LINZ maps for local tracks. Outdoor stores also stock them. LINZ map series includes 1:250,000 'Topo250' regional maps and more detailed 'Topo50' maps (you may need two or three of these per track).

Websites

www.trampingtracks.co.nz Descriptions, maps and photos of long and short tramps all over NZ.

www.tramper.co.nz Articles, photos, forums and excellent track and hut information.

www.trampingnz.com Region-by-region track info with readable trip reports.

www.topomap.co.nz Online topographic map of the whole country.

www.mountainsafety.org.nz Safety tips, gear advice and courses.

www.peakbagging.org.nz Find a summit and get up on top of it.

Track Classifications

Tracks in NZ are classified according to various features, including level of difficulty. We loosely refer to the level of difficulty as easy, medium, hard or difficult. The widely used track classification system is as follows:

Short Walk Well formed; possibly allows for wheelchair access or is constructed to 'shoe' standard (ie walking boots not required). Suitable for people of all ages and fitness levels.

TRACK SAFETY

Thousands of people tramp across NZ without incident, but every year a few folks meet their maker in the mountains. Some trails are only for the experienced, fit and well equipped – don't attempt these if you don't fit the bill. Ensure you are healthy and feel comfortable walking for sustained periods.

NZ's climatic changeability subjects high-altitude walks to snow and ice, even in summer: always check weather and track conditions before setting off, and be ready for them to change rapidly. Resources:

Department of Conservation (DOC; www.doc.govt.nz) Weather and track info.

www.adventuresmart.org.nz Log your walk intentions online (and tell a friend!).

www.mountainsafety.org.nz Tramping safety tips.

www.metservice.co.nz Weather.

Top: Road leading towards Aoraki/Mt Cook (p174)

Bottom: A cloud-filled valley along the Milford Track (p258)

COLIN MONTEATH / GETTY IMAGES ©

Walking Track Easy and well-formed longer walks; constructed to 'shoe' standard. Suitable for people of most ages and fitness levels.

Easy Tramping Track or **Great Walk** Well formed; major water crossings have bridges and track junctions have signs. Light walking boots required.

Tramping Track Requires skill and experience; constructed to 'boot' standard. Suitable for people of average physical fitness. Water crossings may not have bridges.

Route Requires a high degree of skill, experience and navigation skills. Well-equipped trampers only.

Great Walks

Six of NZ's nine official 'Great Walks' are on the South Island. Natural beauty abounds, but prepare yourself for crowds, especially over summer.

All six of the South Island's Great Walks are described in Lonely Planet's *Hiking & Tramping in New Zealand,* and are detailed in pamphlets provided by DOC visitor centres and online at www.greatwalks.co.nz.

Tickets & Bookings

To tramp these tracks you'll need to buy **Great Walk Tickets** before setting out. These track-specific tickets cover you for hut accommodation (from $22 to $54 per adult per night, depending on the track) and/or camping ($6 to $18 per adult per night). You can camp only at designated camping grounds; note there's no camping on the Milford Track. In the off-peak season (May to September) you can use Backcountry Hut Passes or pay-as-you-go Hut Tickets instead of Great Walk Tickets on all South Island Great Walks except for the Heaphy Track, Abel Tasman Coast Track and Rakiura Track (Great Walk Tickets required year-round). Kids under 17 stay in huts and camp for free on all Great Walks. (Note: we hear whispers of hut tickets being phased out over coming years: Backcountry Hut Passes are the way of the future).

For bookings see www.greatwalks.co.nz, email greatwalksbookings@doc.govt.nz, phone 🕾0800 694 732, or visit DOC offices close to the tracks. Trampers must book and pay for their chosen accommodation in advance and specify dates. Book as far in advance as possible, especially if you're planning on walking during summer.

Other Tracks

Of course, there are a lot more walks in the South Island than just the Great ones! Try these selections on for size:

Banks Peninsula Track A 35km, two-day (medium) or four-day (easy) walk over the hills and along the coast of Banks Peninsula.

Hollyford Track A typically hair-brained scheme of the era, the settlement of Jamestown was always a long shot. Cue: colourful characters and a dash of drama. A four- to five-day tramping track over 56km in Fiordland.

Kaikoura Coast Track An easy three-day, 40km walk over private and public land along the spectacular coastline 43km south of Kaikoura.

Mueller Hut Route Yes, it's a hardcore 1040m, eight-hour return climb on the Sealy Range near Aoraki/Mt Cook, but this is a quintessential alpine

THE SOUTH ISLAND'S SIX 'GREAT WALKS'

WALK	DISTANCE	DURATION	DIFFICULTY	DESCRIPTION
Abel Tasman Coast Track	54km	3-5 days	Easy to medium	NZ's most popular walk (or sea kayak); beaches and bays in Abel Tasman National Park
Heaphy Track	78km	4-6 days	Medium to hard	Forests, beaches and karst (limestone) landscapes in Kahurangi National Park
Kepler Track	60km	3-4 days	Easy to medium	Lakes, rivers, gorges, glacial valleys and beech forest in Fiordland National Park
Milford Track	53.5km	4 days	Easy	Rainforest, crystal-clear streams and 630m-high Sutherland Falls in Fiordland National Park
Rakiura Track	39km	3 days	Medium	Bird life (kiwi!), beaches and lush bush on remote Stewart Island (Rakiura)
Routeburn Track	32km	2-4 days	Medium	Eye-popping alpine scenery around Mt Aspiring and Fiordland National Parks

experience: geological wonders, fascinating plant life and an amazing hut.

Pelorus Track So scenic it starred in *The Hobbit*, the gorgeous Pelorus Valley – a boulder-lined gorge with deep green pools – is followed for two days on this three-day, 28km tramp.

Queen Charlotte Track A 71km, three- to five-day medium walk in the Marlborough Sounds, affording great water views. Top-notch accommodation and water transport available.

Rees-Dart Track A 70km, four- to five-day hard tramping track in Mt Aspiring National Park, through river valleys and traversing an alpine pass.

St James Walkway This tramping track passes through a significant conservation area, home to some 430 species of flora from lowland grasses to mountain beech and alpine herbs. Five days over 66km around Lewis Pass.

Tuatapere Hump Ridge Track An excellent three-day, 53km circuit beginning and ending at Bluecliffs Beach on Te Waewae Bay, 20km from Tuatapere.

Backcountry Huts & Campsites

In addition to Great Walk huts, DOC maintains more than 950 Backcountry Huts in

Great Walks

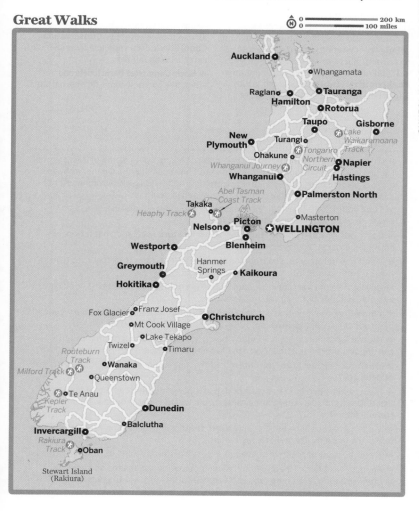

NZ's national and forest parks. Hut categories are as follows:

➡ **Basic Huts** Just a shed; free.

➡ **Standard Huts** No cooking equipment and sometimes no heating, but mattresses, water supply and toilets. Fees are $5 per adult per night.

➡ **Serviced Huts** Mattress-equipped bunks or sleeping platforms, water supply, heating, toilets and sometimes cooking facilities. Fees are $15 per adult per night.

Note that bookings are required for some huts (see the website for listings): book online at https://booking.doc.govt.nz or at DOC visitor centres. Prices for kids aged 11 to 17 are half those listed here; kids 10 and under stay free. For comprehensive hut details see www.doc.govt.nz/parks-and-recreation/places-to-stay.

If you do a lot of tramping, a six-month **Backcountry Hut Pass** ($92 per adult) might be a good idea; otherwise use or pay-as-you-go **Hut Tickets** ($5: you'll need to use three of these for a Serviced Hut). Date your tickets and put them in the boxes provided at huts. Accommodation is on a first-come, first-served basis. In the low season (May to September), Backcountry Hut Tickets and Passes can also be used to procure a bunk or campsite on some Great Walks.

Backcountry Campsites are often nearby the huts, and usually have toilets and fresh water; possibly picnic tables, fire places and/or cooking shelters. Prices vary from free to $8 per person per night.

Conservation Campsites

Aside from Great Walk campsites, DOC also manages 250-plus 'Conservation Campsites' (often vehicle-accessible) with categories as follows:

➡ **Basic Campsites** Basic toilets and fresh water; free on a first-come, first-served basis.

RESPONSIBLE TRAMPING

If you went straight from the cradle into a pair of hiking boots, some of these tramping tips will seem obvious; others you mightn't have considered. Online, www.lnt.org is a great resource for low-impact tramping, and DOC (www.camping.org.nz) has plenty more responsible camping tips. When in doubt, ask DOC or i-SITE staff.

➡ Time your tramp to avoid peak season: less people equals less stress on the environment and fewer snorers in the huts.

➡ Carry out *all* your rubbish. Burying rubbish disturbs soil and vegetation, encourages erosion, and animals will probably dig it up anyway.

➡ Don't use detergents, shampoo or toothpaste in or near watercourses (even if they're biodegradable).

➡ Use lightweight kerosene, alcohol or Shellite (white gas) stoves for cooking; avoid disposable butane gas canisters.

➡ Where there's a toilet, use it. Where there isn't one, dig a hole and bury your by-product (at least 15cm deep, 100m from any watercourse).

➡ If a track passes through a muddy patch, just plough straight on through – skirting around the outside increases the size of the bog.

➡ Wash your dishes 50m from watercourses; use a scourer, sand or snow instead of detergent.

➡ If you *really* need to scrub your bod, use biodegradable soap and a bucket, at least 50m from any watercourse. Spread the waste water around widely to help the soil filter it.

➡ If open fires are allowed, use only dead, fallen wood in existing fireplaces. Leave any extra wood for the next happy camper.

➡ Keep food out of reach of scavengers by tying storage bags to rafters or trees.

➡ Feeding wildlife can lead to unbalanced populations, diseases and animals becoming dependent on handouts. Keep your dried apricots to yourself.

➡️ **Standard Campsites** Toilets and water supply, and perhaps barbecues and picnic tables; $6 on a first-come, first-served basis.

➡️ **Scenic Campsites** High-use coastal sites with toilets and tap water, and sometimes barbeques, fireplaces, cooking shelters, showers, picnic tables and rubbish bins. Fees are $10 per night.

➡️ **Serviced Campsites** Full facilities: flush toilets, tap water, showers and picnic tables. They may also have barbecues, a kitchen and a laundry; $15 per night.

Note that bookings are necessary for all Serviced Campsites, plus some Scenic and Standard Campsites in peak season (October to April).

Book online – https://booking.doc.govt.nz – or at DOC visitor centres. Kids' prices are half those listed here.

DOC publishes free brochures with detailed descriptions and instructions to find every campsite (even GPS co-ordinates). Pick up copies from DOC offices before you hit the road, or visit the website.

Guided Walks

If you're new to tramping or just want a more comfortable experience than the DIY alternative, several companies can escort you through the wilds, usually staying in comfortable huts (showers!), with meals cooked and equipment carried for you.

On the South Island try Kaikoura, the Banks Peninsula, Milford Track, Queen Charlotte Track, Heaphy Track or Hollyford Track. Prices for a five-day/four-night guided walk start at around $1800,

---

TE ARAROA

Epic! **Te Araroa** (The Long Pathway; www.teararoa.org.nz) is a 3000km tramping trail from Cape Reinga in NZ's north to Bluff in the south (or the other way around). The route links existing tracks with new sections. Built over a decade, mostly by volunteers, it's one of the longest tramps in the world: check the website for maps and track notes, plus blogs and videos from hardy types who have completed the end-to-end epic.

---

and rise towards $2200 for deluxe guided experiences.

Getting To & From

Getting to and from trailheads can be problematic, except for popular trails serviced by public and dedicated trampers' transport. Having a vehicle only helps with getting to one end of the track (you still have to collect your car afterwards). If the track starts or ends down a dead-end road, hitching will be difficult.

Of course, tracks accessible by public transport or shuttle bus services (eg Abel Tasman Coast Track) are also the most crowded. An alternative is to arrange private transport, either with a friend or by chartering a vehicle to drop you at one end then pick you up at the other. If you intend to leave a vehicle at a trailhead, don't leave anything valuable inside – theft from cars in isolated areas is a significant problem.

Plan Your Trip

Skiing & Snowboarding in the South Island

New Zealand's South Island is an essential southern-hemisphere destination for snow bunnies, with downhill skiing, cross-country (Nordic) skiing and snowboarding all passionately pursued. The South Island ski season is generally June to October, though it varies considerably from one ski area to another, and can run as late as November.

Best on the Slopes

Best Extreme Skiing
Heliskiing on the South Island is big fun (and big money): if you can afford it, spin your rotor blades up to the high, pristine slopes of Coronet Peak, Cardrona, Mt Hutt, Treble Cone or Mt Potts.

Best for Beginners
Coronet Peak (p221), Queenstown

Mt Hutt (p165), Central Canterbury

Mt Dobson (p39), South Canterbury

Roundhill (p39), South Canterbury

Best Snowboarding
Mt Hutt (p165), Central Canterbury

Treble Cone (p39), Wanaka

Cardrona (p39), Wanaka

Best Après-Ski Watering Holes
Cardrona Hotel (p249), Cardrona

Blue Door (p240), Arrowtown

Blue Pub (p166), Methven

Ballarat Trading Company (p231), Queenstown

Planning

Where to Go

The variety of locations and conditions makes it difficult to rate the South Island's ski fields in any particular order. Some people like to be near Queenstown's party scene or Wanaka's snowboarding hub; others prefer the quality high-altitude runs on Mt Hutt, uncrowded Rainbow or less-stressed club skiing areas. Club areas are publicly accessible and usually less crowded and cheaper than commercial fields, even though nonmembers pay a higher fee.

Practicalities

The South Island's commercial ski areas are not generally set up as resorts with chalets, lodges and hotels. Rather, accommodation and après-ski carousing are often in surrounding towns, connected with the slopes via daily shuttles. Many club areas have lodges where you can stay, subject to availability.

Visitor information centres in NZ, and **Tourism New Zealand** (www.new-zealand.com) internationally, have info

Ski Areas

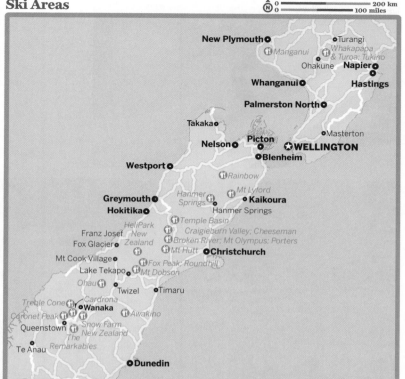

on the various ski areas and can make bookings and organise packages. Lift passes usually cost between $50 and $100 per adult per day (half-price for kids). Lesson-and-lift packages are available at most areas. Ski and snowboard equipment rental starts at around $50 a day (cheaper for multiday hire). Private/group lessons start at around $130/60 per hour.

Websites

www.brownbearski.co.nz Brilliant reference detailing all of NZ's ski areas.

www.snow.co.nz Reports, cams and ski info across the country.

www.nzski.com Reports, employment, passes and webcams for Mt Hutt, Coronet Peak and the Remarkables.

www.chillout.co.nz Info on Mt Lyford, Awakino, Hanmer Springs, Cheeseman, Roundhill, Rainbow,

Temple Basin, Treble Cone, Fox Peak, Mt Dobson, Mt Olympus, Porters, Craigieburn Valley and Broken River ski areas.

www.nzsnowboard.com Snowboarding info around NZ.

South Island Ski Regions

Queenstown & Wanaka

Coronet Peak (☎03-450 1970, snow-phone 03-442 4620; www.nzski.com; daily lift pass adult/child $97/54) At the Queenstown region's oldest ski field, snow-making systems and treeless slopes provide excellent skiing and snowboarding for all levels. There's night skiing Friday and Saturday from July to September. Shuttles run from Queenstown, 18km away.

WILL SALTER / GETTY IMAGES ©

Top: Snowboarding at Coronet Peak (p37)

Bottom: A ski jumper takes flight in the Treble Cone area

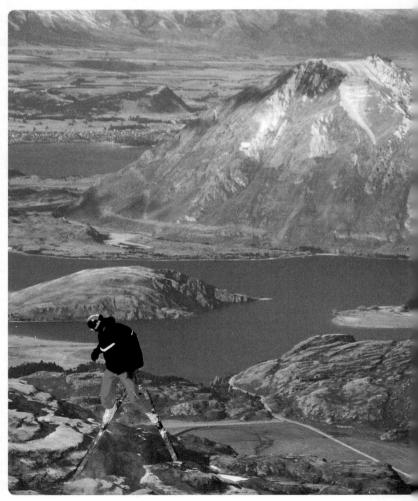

Remarkables (03-450 1970, snowphone 03-442 4615; www.nzski.com; daily lift pass adult/child $97/54) Visually remarkable, this ski field is also near Queenstown (28km away) – shuttle buses run during ski season. It has a good smattering of intermediate, advanced and beginner runs (kids under 10 ski free). Look for the sweeping 'Homeward Bound' run.

Treble Cone (03-443 7443, snow-phone 03-443 7444; www.treblecone.com; daily lift pass adult/child $97/49) The highest and largest of the southern lakes ski areas is in a spectacular location 26km from Wanaka, with steep slopes suitable for intermediate to advanced skiers (a rather professional vibe). There are also half-pipes and a terrain park for boarders.

Cardrona (03-443 7007, snow-phone 03-443 7341; www.cardrona.com; daily lift pass adult/child $97/54) Around 34km from Wanaka, with several high-capacity chairlifts, beginners tows and extreme snowboard terrain (including the 'Heavy Metal' snowboard park). Buses run from Wanaka and Queenstown during ski season. A friendly scene with good services for skiers with disabilities, plus an on-field crèche.

Snow Farm New Zealand (p249) NZ's only commercial Nordic (cross-country) ski area is 35km from Wanaka on the Pisa Range, high above Lake Wanaka. There are 50km of groomed trails, huts with facilities, and thousands of hectares of open snow. Plus full-moon fondue!

South Canterbury

Ohau (03-438 9885; www.ohau.co.nz; daily lift pass adult/child $79/32) This commercial ski area is on Mt Sutton, 42km from Twizel. There are plenty of intermediate and advanced runs, excellent snowboarding/cross-country terrain, and a ski lodge.

Mt Dobson (03-685 8039; www.dobson.co.nz; daily lift pass adult/child $75/44) The 3km-wide basin here, 26km from Fairlie, caters for learners and intermediates, and has a terrain park and famously dry powder. On a clear day you can see Aoraki/Mt Cook and the Pacific Ocean from the summit.

Fox Peak (03-685 8539, snow-phone 03-688 0044; www.foxpeak.co.nz; daily lift pass adult/child $50/10) An affordable club ski area 40km from Fairlie in the Two Thumb Range. Expect rope tows, good cross-country skiing and dorm-style accommodation.

Roundhill (021 680 694, snow-phone 03-680 6977; www.roundhill.co.nz; daily lift pass adult/

child $75/46) A small field with wide, gentle slopes, perfect for beginners and intermediates. It's 32km from Lake Tekapo village. 'Ski Tekapo!'.

Central Canterbury

Mt Hutt (03-302 8811; www.nzski.com; day lift pass adult/child $95/53; 9am-4pm) One of the highest ski areas in the southern hemisphere, as well as one of NZ's best. It's close to Methven; Christchurch is 118km to the west – ski shuttles service both towns. Road access is steep – be extremely cautious in lousy weather. Plenty of beginner, intermediate and advanced slopes, with chairlifts, heliskiing and wide-open faces that are good for learning to snowboard.

HeliPark New Zealand (03-303 9060; www.snow.co.nz/helipark; access incl 1st run $325, per subsequent run $75) One of NZ's snow-white gems, sitting on Mt Potts above the headwaters of the Rangitata River, 75km from Methven. It offers a helicopter-accessed skiing experience. Accommodation and meals are available at a lodge 8km from the ski area.

Porters (03-318 4002, snow-phone 03-379 9931; www.skiporters.co.nz; daily lift pass adult/child $84/44) The closest commercial ski area to Christchurch (96km away on the Arthur's Pass road). 'Big Mama', at 620m, is one of the steepest runs in NZ, but there are wider, gentler slopes, too. There's a half-pipe for snowboarders, good cross-country runs along the ridge, and lodge accommodation.

Temple Basin (03-377 7788; www.temple basin.co.nz; daily lift pass adult/child $68/37) A club field 4km from the Arthur's Pass township. It's a 40-minute walk uphill from the car park to the ski-area lodges. There's floodlit skiing at night and excellent backcountry runs for snowboarders.

Craigieburn Valley (03-318 8711; www.craigieburn.co.nz; daily lift pass adult/child $72/35) Centred on Hamilton Peak, Craigieburn Valley is 40km from Arthur's Pass. It's one of NZ's most challenging club areas, with intermediate and advanced runs (no beginners). Accommodation in please-do-a-chore lodges.

Broken River (03-318 8713; www.broken river.co.nz; daily lift pass adult/child $70/35) Not far from Craigieburn Valley is another club field, with a 15- to 20-minute walk from the car park and a real sense of isolation. Reliable snow; laid-back vibe. Catered or self-catered lodge accommodation available.

Cheeseman (03-344 3247, snow-phone 03-318 8794; www.mtcheeseman.co.nz; daily lift pass

PLAN YOUR TRIP SKIING & SNOWBOARDING IN THE SOUTH ISLAND

HELISKIING

NZ's remote heights are tailor-made for heliskiing, with operators covering a wide off-piste area along the Southern Alps. Costs range from around $825 to $1450 for three to eight runs. HeliPark New Zealand (p39) at Mt Potts is a dedicated heliski park. Resort-run heliskiing is also available at Coronet Peak, Treble Cone, Cardrona, Mt Hutt, Mt Lyford, Ohau and Hanmer Springs. Alternatively, independent operators include the following:

Alpine Heli-Ski (☏03-441 2300; www.alpineheliski.com; Queenstown)

Harris Mountains Heli-Ski (☏03-442 6722; www.heliski.co.nz; Queenstown, Wanaka & Aoraki/Mt Cook)

Methven Heliskiing (☏03-302 8108; www.methvenheli.co.nz; Methven)

Over The Top (☏0800 123 359, 03-442 2233; www.flynz.co.nz; Queenstown)

Southern Lakes Heliski (☏03-442 6222; www.heliskinz.com; Queenstown & Wanaka)

Wilderness Heliski (☏03-435 1834; www.wildernesheli.co.nz; Aoraki/Mt Cook)

adult/child $79/39) Another cool club area in the Craigieburn Range, this family-friendly operation is 99km from Christchurch (the closest club to the city). Based on Mt Cockayne, it's a wide, sheltered basin with drive-to-the-snow road access. Lodge accommodation available.

Mt Olympus (☏03-318 5840; www.mtolympus.co.nz; daily lift pass adult/child $70/35) Difficult to find (but worth the search), 2096m Mt Olympus is 58km from Methven and 12km from Lake Ida. This club area has intermediate and advanced runs, and there are solid cross-country trails to other areas. Access is sometimes 4WD-only, depending on conditions. Lodge accommodation available.

Northern South Island

Hanmer Springs (p158) A commercial field based on Mt St Patrick, 17km from Hanmer Springs township, with mostly intermediate and advanced runs. There are pipe-rides for snow-boarders, a new beginners tow and family lodge accommodation.

Mt Lyford (p159) Around 60km from both Hanmer Springs and Kaikoura, and 4km from Mt Lyford village, this is more of a 'resort' than most NZ ski fields, with accommodation and eating options. There's a good mix of runs and a terrain park.

Rainbow (☏03-521 1861, snow-phone 0832 226 05; www.skirainbow.co.nz; daily lift pass adult/child $70/35) Borders Nelson Lakes National Park (100km from Nelson, a similar distance from Blenheim), with varied terrain, minimal crowds and good cross-country skiing. Chains are often required. St Arnaud is the closest town (32km).

Otago

Awakino (☏021 890 584; www.skiawakino.com; daily lift pass adult/child $50/25) A small player in North Otago, but worth a visit for intermediate skiers. Oamaru is 45km away; Omarama is 66km inland. Weekend lodge-and-ski packages available.

Plan Your Trip

Extreme South Island

The South Island's astounding natural assets tempt even the laziest lounge lizards outside to get active. 'Extreme' sports are abundant and supremely well organised here. Mountaineering is part of the national psyche; skydiving, mountain biking, jetboating and rock climbing are well established; and pant-wetting, illogical activities like bungy jumping are everyday pursuits.

On the Land
Bungy Jumping

Bungy jumping was made famous by Kiwi AJ Hackett's 1986 plunge from the Eiffel Tower, after which he teamed up with champion New Zealand skier Henry van Asch to turn the endeavour into a profitable enterprise. Now you can get crazy too!

Queenstown is a spiderweb of bungy cords, including Hackett's triad: the 134m Nevis Bungy (the highest); the 43m Kawarau Bungy (the original); and the Ledge Bungy (the highest altitude – diving off a platform 400m above Queenstown). Other South Island bungy jumps include above the Waiau River near Hanmer Springs, and Mt Hutt ski field. Varying the theme, try the 109m-high Shotover Canyon Swing or Nevis Swing in Queenstown, both seriously high rope swings: *swooosh...*

Caving

Caving (aka spelunking) opportunities abound in NZ's honeycombed karst (limestone) regions. In the South Island, you'll find clubs and tours around Westport and Karamea. Golden Bay also has some mammoth caves. Useful resources:

New Zealand Speleological Society (www.caves.org.nz)

Top Extreme Experiences

Top Anti-Gravity Action
Queenstown There are plenty of places in New Zealand where you can hurl yourself into oblivion attached to a giant rubber band, but why mess around: head straight to Queenstown for the biggest and the best bungy jumping.

Top White-Water Rafting
Buller Gorge (p97), Murchison

Kawarau River (p219), Queenstown

Shotover Canyon (p219), Queenstown

Top Surfing
Taylors Mistake (p138), Christchurch

St Clair Beach (p196), Dunedin

Top Mountain-Biking Tracks
Nga Haerenga, New Zealand Cycle Trail (p42), 12 South Island trails

Queenstown Bike Park (p221), Queenstown

Hanmer Springs (p157), Canterbury

Hang Gliding & Paragliding

Suspend yourself below an enormous fake wing – either rigid (hang gliding) or frameless (paragliding) – and set sail from a hillside or clifftop. Tandem flights happen in Queenstown, Wanaka and Nelson, or after a half-day of instruction you should be able to do limited solo flights. The New Zealand Hang Gliding and Paragliding Association (www.nzhgpa.org.nz) rules the roost.

Horse Trekking

Unlike some other parts of the world where beginners are led by the nose around a paddock, horse trekking in NZ lets you out into the countryside, on a farm, in the forest or along a beach. Rides range from one-hour jaunts (from around $60) to week-long, fully catered treks.

All-day horseback adventures happen around Kaikoura, Nelson, Mt Cook, Lake Tekapo, Hanmer Springs, Queenstown, Glenorchy, Methven, Mt Hutt, Cardrona, Te Anau and Dunedin. Treks are also offered alongside Paparoa National Park on the West Coast. For details, see the following:

100% Pure New Zealand (www.newzealand.com)

True NZ Horse Trekking (www.truenz.co.nz/horsetrekking)

Mountain Biking

Aside from the New Zealand Cycle Trail, NZ is laced with quality mountain-biking opportunities. Mountain bikes can be hired in major towns or adventure-sports centres like Queenstown, Wanaka, Nelson and Picton which also have repair shops.

Key South Island mountain-biking meccas include the Alexandra goldfield trails in Central Otago, the Queenstown Bike Park, and Twizel near Mt Cook. Also good on the South Island are the Waitati Valley and Hayward Point near Dunedin, Canaan Downs near Abel Tasman National Park, and Mt Hutt, Methven and the Banks Peninsula.

Not feeling so energetic? Various companies will take you up to the tops of mountains and volcanoes (eg Christchurch's Port Hills, Cardrona and the Remarkables) so you can hurtle down without the gruntwork of getting to the top first.

Some tramping tracks are open to mountain bikes, but the Department of Conservation (DOC; p30) has restricted access in many cases due to track damage and inconvenience to walkers, especially at busy times. Never cycle on walking tracks in national parks unless it's permissible (check with DOC), or risk heavy fines and the unfathomable ire of trampers. The Queen Charlotte Track is a good one to bike, but part of it is closed in summer. Resources include *Classic New Zealand Mountain Bike Rides* (www.kennett.co.nz) and *New Zealand Mountain Biker* (www.nzmtbr.co.nz).

Cycle Touring

OK, so cruising around the country on a bicycle isn't necessarily 'extreme', but it is super-popular in NZ, especially during summer. Most towns offer bike hire, at either backpacker hostels or specialist bike shops, with bike repair shops in bigger towns.

If you're not after altitude, the **Otago Central Rail Trail** between Middlemarch and Clyde is a winner. The **Little River Rail Trail** in Canterbury (en route to Banks Peninsula) is also fabulous. For an off-the-beaten-highway option, try the **Southern Scenic Route** from Invercargill round Tuatapere to Te Anau. For detailed touring info, see Lonely Planet's *Cycling New Zealand*. Online resources:

Independent Cycle Tours (www.cyclehire.co.nz)

Paradise Press (www.paradise-press.co.nz) *Pedallers' Paradise* booklets by Nigel Rushton.

NGA HAERENGA, NEW ZEALAND CYCLE TRAIL

The Nga Haerenga, New Zealand Cycle Trail (www.nzcycletrail.com) is a major nationwide project that has been in motion since 2009, expanding and improving NZ's extant network of bike trails. Funded to the tune of around NZ$50 million, the project currently has 22 'Great Rides' up and running across both islands (10 in the North Island and 12 in the South Island), all of which are either fully open to cyclists or have sections open in some capacity. The network is proving to be extremely popular: the West Coast Wilderness Trail is an easy trail winning plenty of fans, as is the Great Taste Trail in Nelson. See the website for info, maps and updates, including grades and durations, photos, videos and weather and accommodation links.

Top: Jetboating through a canyon along Shotover River (p219)

Bottom: Cyclists on the Otago Central Rail Trail (p206)

MATTHEW MICAH WRIGHT / GETTY IMAGES ©

Top: Climber in an ice cave, Fox Glacier (p122)

Bottom: Surfer catching a wave

Mountaineering

NZ has a proud mountaineering history – this was, after all, the home of Sir Edmund Hillary (1919–2008), who, along with Tenzing Norgay, was the first to reach the summit of Mt Everest. When he came back down, Sir Ed famously uttered to friend George Lowe, 'Well, George, we knocked the bastard off!'

The Southern Alps are studded with impressive peaks and challenging climbs. The Aoraki/Mt Cook region is outstanding; other mountaineering areas extend along the spine of the South Island from Tapuaenuku (in the Kaikoura Ranges) and the Nelson Lakes peaks in the north to the rugged southern mountains of Fiordland. Another area with climbs for all levels is Mt Aspiring National Park. To the south in the Forbes Mountains is Mt Earnslaw, flanked by the Rees and Dart Rivers.

The Christchurch-based New Zealand Alpine Club (www.alpineclub.org.nz) proffers professional information and produces the annual *NZAC Alpine Journal* and the quarterly *The Climber* magazine. Outfits for training, guiding and advice can be found at Wanaka, Aoraki/Mt Cook, Lake Tekapo, and Fox and Franz Josef Glaciers.

Rock Climbing

Time to chalk-up your fingers and don some natty little rubber shoes. On the South Island, try the Port Hills area above Christchurch or Castle Hill on the road to Arthur's Pass. West of Nelson, the marble and limestone mountains of Golden Bay and Takaka Hill provide prime climbing. Other options are Long Beach (north of Dunedin), and Mihiwaka and Lovers Leap on the Otago Peninsula. Raining? You'll find indoor climbing walls in Wanaka and Christchurch.

Climb New Zealand (www.climb.co.nz) has the low-down on the gnarliest overhangs, plus access and instruction info.

Skydiving

For most first-time skydivers, a tandem skydive will help you make the leap, even if common sense starts to get the better of you. Tandem jumps involve training with a qualified instructor, then experiencing

---

SURFING IN NZ

As a surfer I feel particularly guilty in letting the reader in on a local secret – NZ has a sensational mix of quality waves perfect for beginners and experienced surfers. As long as you're willing to travel off the beaten track, you can score some great, un-crowded waves. The islands of NZ are hit with swells from all points of the compass throughout the year. So, with a little weather knowledge and a little effort, numerous options present themselves. Point breaks, reefs, rocky shelves and hollow sandy beach breaks can all be found – take your pick!

Surfing has become increasingly popular in NZ and there are surf schools up and running at most premier surf beaches. It's worth doing research before you arrive: Surfing New Zealand (www.surfingnz.co.nz) recommends a number of schools. If you're on a surf holiday in NZ, consider purchasing a copy of the *New Zealand Surfing Guide* by Mike Bhana. Surf.co.nz provides info on many great surf spots, but most NZ beaches hold good rideable breaks. Some I particularly enjoy on the South Island are:

➡ **Marlborough & Nelson** Kaikoura Peninsula, Mangamaunu and Meatworks

➡ **Canterbury** Taylors Mistake and Sumner Bar

➡ **Otago** Dunedin is a good base for surfing on the South Island, with access to a number of superb breaks, such as St Clair Beach

➡ **West Coast** Punakaiki and Tauranga Bay

➡ **Southland** Porridge and Centre Island

NZ water temperatures and climate vary greatly from north to south. For comfort while surfing, wear a wetsuit. In summer on the North Island you can get away with a spring suit and boardies; on the South Island, a 2mm–3mm steamer. In winter on the South Island use a 3mm–5mm steamer with all the extras.

By Josh Kronfeld, surfer and former All Black

up to 45 seconds of free fall before your chute opens. The thrill is worth every dollar (around $250/300/350 for an 8000/10,000/12,000ft jump; extra for a DVD/photograph). The New Zealand Parachute Federation (www.nzpf.org) is the governing body. Ask your operator if it has Civil Aviation Authority (CAA) accreditation before you take the plunge.

On the Water

Jetboating

Hold onto your breakfast: passenger-drenching 360-degree spins ahoy! On the South Island, the Shotover and Kawarau Rivers (Queenstown) and the Buller River (Westport) have fab jetboating. The Dart River (Queenstown) is less travelled but also good, while the Waiatoto River (Haast) and Wilkin River (Mt Aspiring National Park) are superb wilderness experiences. Try also the Kawarau River (Cromwell), Waiau River (Te Anau), Wairahurahiri River (Tuatapere) and the Waiau River at Hanmer Springs.

Parasailing & Kiteboarding

Parasailing (dangling from a modified parachute that glides over the water while being pulled along by a speedboat or jet ski) is perhaps the easiest way for humans to achieve assisted flight. There are South Island operators in Wanaka and Queenstown.

Kiteboarding (aka kitesurfing), where a mini parachute drags you across the ocean on a mini surfboard, can be attempted at Nelson. Lessons are also available if you're new to the sport.

Sea Kayaking

Sea kayaking is a fantastic way to see the coast, and get close to wildlife you'd otherwise never see.

Highly rated sea-kayaking areas around the South Island include the Marlborough Sounds (Picton) and along the coast of Abel Tasman National Park. Fiordland is also a hot spot, with a heap of tour operators in Te Anau, Milford, Doubtful Sound and Manapouri. Also try the Otago Peninsula, Stewart Island and Kaikoura down south. Useful resources:

Kiwi Association of Sea Kayakers (www.kask.org.nz)

Sea Kayak Operators Association of New Zealand (www.skoanz.org.nz)

Scuba Diving

NZ is prime scuba territory, with warm waters in the north, brilliant sea life and plenty of interesting sites.

Down south, the Marlborough Sounds Maritime Park hosts the *Mikhail Lermontov,* the largest diveable cruise-ship wreck in the world. In Fiordland head for Dusky Sound, Milford Sound and Doubtful Sound, which offer amazingly clear pseudo-deep-water conditions not far below the surface. Invercargill, with its Antarctic waters, also has a diving club.

Expect to pay anywhere from $180 for a short, introductory, pool-based scuba course, and around $600 for a four-day, PADI-approved, ocean dive course. One-off organised boat- and land-based dives start at around $170.

Resources include:

New Zealand Underwater Association (www.nzu.org.nz)

Dive New Zealand (www.divenewzealand.com)

White-Water Rafting, Kayaking & Canoeing

There are almost as many white-water rafting and kayaking possibilities as there are rivers in NZ. Rivers are graded from I to VI, with VI meaning 'unraftable'. On the rougher stretches there's usually a minimum age limit of 12 or 13 years.

Popular rafting rivers include the Shotover and Kawarau Rivers (p219), Rangitata River (p167), Buller River (p97) and the Arnold (p111) and Waiho Rivers (p119). The grading of the Shotover Canyon varies from III to V+, depending on the time of year. The Kawarau River is rated IV; the Rangitata River has everything from I to V.

Canoeing is popular on freshwater lakes. Many backpacker hostels close to canoe-friendly waters have Canadian canoes and kayaks for hire (or free), and commercial operators run guided trips. Resources:

New Zealand Rafting Association (www.nz-rafting.co.nz)

Whitewater NZ (www.rivers.org.nz)

New Zealand Kayak (see www.kayaknz.co.nz)

Regions at a Glance

Get ready for an oft-changing selection of some of the planet's most surprising scenery. From the marine labyrinth of the Marlborough Sounds to the craggy volcanic legacy of Banks Peninsula, the South Island packs a stunning scenic punch. Along the way, taste test the best of the country's emerging gourmet scene, balancing enjoyment of excellent wine and craft beer with active adventure amid the great outdoors. Kayak through the mist of Doubtful Sound or test yourself on the Milford or Routeburn Tracks – often in the company of New Zealand's quirky wildlife – before experiencing colonial history around the heritage streets of Dunedin and Oamaru.

Marlborough & Nelson

Wilderness
Wine
Wildlife

National Parks

Not satisfied with just one national park, the Nelson region has three – Nelson Lakes, Kahurangi and the Abel Tasman. You could tramp in all three over a week.

Marlborough Wine Region

Bobbing in Marlborough's sea of sauvignon blanc, riesling, pinot noir and bubbly are barrel loads of quality cellar-door experiences and some fine regional food.

Kaikoura

The top of the South Island is home to myriad creatures, both in the water and on the wing. Kaikoura is a great one-stop shop for spotting a whale or swimming with dolphins and seals.

p50

The West Coast

Wilderness
Outdoor Activities
History

Natural Wonders

This area has many natural wonders: around 90% of the land lies within a conservation estate. Don't miss Oparara's famous arch and Punakaiki's Pancake Rocks.

Tramping

The West Coast offers tracks from an easy hour through to hardcore epics. Old mining and milling routes like Charming Creek Walkway and Mahinapua Walkway entice beginners and history buffs.

History

The West Coast's pioneering history comes vividly to life at places such as Denniston, Shantytown, Reefton and Jackson Bay.

p95

Christchurch & Canterbury

History
Outdoor Activities
Scenery

Christchurch & Akaroa

Earthquakes have damaged Christchurch's architecture, but the Canterbury Museum, Botanic Gardens and New Regent St still showcase the city's proud history. Nearby, Akaroa celebrates its French heritage.

Tramping & Kayaking

Hike the alpine valleys around Arthur's Pass, kayak with dolphins on pristine Akaroa Harbour, or head inland to hike and kayak amid the glacial lakes of the Aoraki/Mt Cook National Park.

Banks Peninsula

Descend Summit Rd to explore hidden coves and experience nature's grand scale: river valleys, soaring peaks and glaciers of the Southern Alps.

p128

Dunedin & Otago

Wildlife
Wine
History

Birds, Seals & Sea Lions

Otago Peninsula's wild menagerie – seals, sea lions and penguins – patrols the rugged coastline, while rocky Taiaroa Head is the world's only mainland breeding location for the royal albatross.

Bannockburn & the Waitaki Valley

Barrel into the craggy valleys of Bannockburn for excellent vineyard restaurants and the world's best pinot noir, or delve into the up-and-coming Waitaki Valley wine scene for riesling and pinot gris.

Victoriana

Explore the arty and storied streets of Dunedin, or escape by foot or penny-farthing bicycle into the heritage ambience of Oamaru's restored Victorian Precinct.

p181

Queenstown & Wanaka

Outdoor Activities
Scenery
Wine

Extreme Queenstown

Nowhere else on earth offers so many adventurous activities: bungy jumping, river rafting and mountain biking only scratch Queenstown's adrenaline-fuelled surface.

Mountains & Lakes

Queenstown's combination of Lake Wakatipu and the soaring Remarkables is a real jaw-dropper, or venture into prime NZ wilderness around Glenorchy and Mt Aspiring National Park.

Wine Regions

Start with lunch at Amisfield Winery's award-winning restaurant, then explore the Gibbston subregion and finish with a riesling tasting at Rippon, overlooking gorgeous Lake Wanaka.

p214

Fiordland & Southland

Scenery
Wilderness
Outdoor Activities

Epic Landscapes

The star of the show is remarkable Milford Sound, but take time to explore the rugged Catlins coast or experience the remote, end-of-the-world appeal of Stewart Island.

National Parks

Fiordland National Park comprises much of New Zealand's precious Southwest New Zealand (Te Wahipounamu) World Heritage Area. Further south, Rakiura National Park showcases Stewart Island's beauty.

Tramping & Sea Kayaking

Test yourself by tramping the Milford or Humpridge Tracks or negotiating a sea kayak around gloriously isolated Doubtful Sound.

p251

On the Road

Marlborough & Nelson (p50)

The West Coast (p95)

Christchurch & Canterbury (p128)

Queenstown & Wanaka (p214)

Dunedin & Otago (p181)

Fiordland & Southland (p251)

Marlborough & Nelson

Best Places to Eat

➡ Rock Ferry (p64)

➡ Hopgood's (p77)

➡ Green Dolphin (p72)

➡ Sans Souci Inn (p90)

Best Places to Stay

➡ Te Mahia Bay Resort (p60)

➡ Watson's Way (p63)

➡ South Street Cottages (p77)

➡ Kerr Bay Campsite (p94)

Why Go?

For many travellers, Marlborough and Nelson will be their introduction to what South Islanders refer to as the 'Mainland'. Having left windy Wellington, and made a white-knuckled crossing of Cook Strait, folk are often surprised to find the sun shining and the temperature up to 10 degrees warmer.

These top-of-the-south neighbours have much in common beyond an amenable climate: both boast renowned coastal holiday spots, particularly the Marlborough Sounds, Abel Tasman National Park and Kaikoura. There are two other national parks (Kahurangi and Nelson Lakes) amid more mountain ranges than you can poke a walking pole at.

And so it follows that these two regions have an abundance of produce, from game and seafood to summer fruits, but most famously the grapes that work their way into the wineglasses of the world's finest restaurants. Keep your penknife and picnic set at the ready.

When to Go

➡ The forecast is good: Marlborough and Nelson soak up some of New Zealand's sunniest weather, with January and February the warmest months when daytime temperatures average 22°C.

➡ July is the coldest, averaging 12°C. However, the top of the South sees some wonderful winter weather, with frosty mornings often giving way to sparklingly clear skies and T-shirt temperatures.

➡ The rumours are true: it *is* wetter and more windswept the closer you get to the West Coast.

➡ From around Christmas to mid-February, the top of the South teems with Kiwi holidaymakers, so plan ahead during this time and be prepared to jostle for position with a load of jandal-wearing families.

Marlborough & Nelson Highlights

1 Getting up close to wildlife, including whales, seals, dolphins and albatross, in **Kaikoura** (p84)

2 Nosing your way through the **Marlborough Wine Region** (p64)

3 Tramping or biking the **Queen Charlotte Track** (p58) in the Marlborough Sounds

4 Eating and drinking your way along Nelson's **Great Taste Trail** (p79)

5 Sea kayaking in postcard-perfect **Abel Tasman National Park** (p86)

6 Getting blown away at Blenheim's **Omaka Aviation Heritage Centre** (p62), one of New Zealand's best museums

7 Driving through a dunescape to **Farewell Spit** (p91), where there'll be gannets and godwits for company

8 Reaching the wild West Coast on foot, across Kahurangi National Park on the **Heaphy Track** (p92)

ℹ️ Getting There & Around

Cook Strait can be crossed slowly and scenically on the ferries between Wellington and Picton, and swiftly on flights servicing key destinations.

InterCity is the major bus operator, but there are also local shuttles. From October to May, KiwiRail's *Coastal Pacific* train takes the scenic route from Picton to Christchurch, via Blenheim and Kaikoura.

Renting a car is easy, with a slew of car-hire offices in Picton and depots throughout the region.

Popular coastal areas such as the Marlborough Sounds and Abel Tasman National Park are best navigated on foot or by kayak, with water-taxi services readily available to join the dots.

MARLBOROUGH REGION

Picton is the gateway to the South Island and the launching point for Marlborough Sounds exploration. A cork's pop south of Picton is Blenheim and its world-famous wineries, and further south still is Kaikoura, the whale-watching town.

History

Long before Abel Tasman sheltered on the east coast of D'Urville Island in 1642 (more than 100 years before James Cook blew through in 1770), Maori knew the Marlborough area as Te Tau Ihu o Te Waka a Maui (the prow of Maui's canoe). It was Cook who named Queen Charlotte Sound; his reports made the area

ESSENTIAL MARLBOROUGH & NELSON

....

Eat Doris' bratwurst at the weekend markets in Nelson and Motueka

Drink A pint of Captain Cooker at Golden Bay's Mussel Inn (p89)

Read *How to Drink a Glass of Wine* by John Saker

Listen to The dawn chorus in Nelson Lakes National Park

Watch The tide roll in, and then watch it roll away again...

Festival Marlborough Wine Festival

Go Green On the Heaphy Track a hot-bed of ecological wonderment

Online www.lovemarlborough.co.nz; www.nelsonnz.com; www.kaikoura.co.nz

Area code 📞 03

the best-known sheltered anchorage in the southern hemisphere. In 1827 French navigator Jules Dumont d'Urville discovered the narrow strait now known as French Pass. His officers named the island just to the north in his honour. In the same year a whaling station was established at Te Awaiti in Tory Channel, which brought about the first permanent European settlement in the district.

Picton

POP 2750

Half asleep in winter, but hyperactive in summer (with up to eight fully laden ferry arrivals per day), boaty Picton clusters around a deep gulch at the head of Queen Charlotte Sound. It's the main traveller port for the South Island, and the best base for tackling the Marlborough Sounds and Queen Charlotte Track. Over the last few years this little town has really bloomed, and offers visitors plenty of reason to linger even after the obvious attractions are knocked off the list.

⊙ Sights & Activities

The majority of activity happens around the Marlborough Sounds, but landlubbers will still find plenty to occupy themselves.

The town has some very pleasant walks. A free i-SITE map details many of these, including an easy 1km track to Bob's Bay. The Snout Track (three hours return) continues along the ridge offering superb water views. Climbing a hill behind the town, the Tirohanga Track is a two-hour leg-stretching loop offering the best view in the house. For town explorations, hire bikes for the whole family from Wilderness Guides (p57).

Edwin Fox Maritime Museum   MUSEUM
(www.edwinfoxsociety.co.nz; Dunbar Wharf; adult/child $10/4; ⊙9am-5pm) Purportedly the world's third-oldest wooden ship, the *Edwin Fox* was built in Calcutta and launched in 1853. During its career it carried troops to the Crimean War, convicts to Australia and immigrants to NZ. This museum has maritime exhibits, including the venerable old dear herself.

Eco World Aquarium   WILDLIFE CENTRE
(www.ecoworldnz.co.nz; Dunbar Wharf; adult/child/family $22/10/55; ⊙10am-5.30pm Oct-Apr, 10am-4pm May-Sep) 🐾 The primary purpose of this centre is animal rehabilitation: all sorts of critters come here for fix-ups and rest-ups, and the odd bit of hanky panky! Special specimens include NZ's 'living dinosaur' – the tuatara –

as well as blue penguins, gecko and giant weta. Fish-feeding time (11am and 2pm) is a splashy spectacle. Sharing the ageing building is the **Picton Cinema** (☑ 03-573 6030; www.pictoncinemas.co.nz; Dunbar Wharf; adult/child $15/9), screening mainstream and edgy flicks.

Picton Museum   MUSEUM
(London Quay; adult/child $5/1; ☺ 10am-4pm) If you dig local history – whaling, sailing and the 1964 Roller Skating Champs – this will float your boat. The photo displays are well worth a look, especially for five bucks.

🛏 Sleeping

Tombstone Backpackers   HOSTEL $
(☑ 03-573 7116, 0800 573 7116; www.tombstonebp.co.nz; 16 Gravesend Pl; dm $28-29, d with/without bathroom $85/78; @ ☎) Rest in peace in smart dorms, double rooms or a self-contained apartment ($118). Also on offer is a spa overlooking the harbour, free breakfast, sunny reading room, pool table, free internet, ferry pick-up and drop-off... The list goes on.

Jugglers Rest   HOSTEL $
(☑ 03-573 5570; www.jugglersrest.com; 8 Canterbury St; campsites from $19, dm $32, d $70-75; ☺ closed Jun-Sep; @ ☎) 🏄 Jocular hosts keep all their balls up in the air at this well-run, ecofriendly, bunk-free backpackers. Peacefully located 10 minutes' walk from town or even less on a free bike. Cheery, private gardens are a good place to socialise with fellow travellers, especially during the occasional fire shows.

Sequoia Lodge Backpackers   HOSTEL $
(☑ 03-573 8399, 0800 222 257; www.sequoialodge.co.nz; 3a Nelson Sq; dm $26-29, d with/without bathroom $78/68; @ ☎) A well-managed backpackers in a colourful, high-ceilinged Victorian house. It's a little out of the centre, but has bonuses including free wi-fi, hammocks, barbecues, a hot tub and nightly pudding. Complimentary breakfast May to October.

Buccaneer Lodge   LODGE $
(☑ 03-573 5002; www.buccaneerlodge.co.nz; 314 Waikawa Rd; s/d/tr $75/85/110; @ ☎) The owners have spruced up this Waikawa Bay lodge to offer good en suite rooms, many with expansive views from the 1st-floor balcony. Courtesy town transfers, free bike hire and the pretty foreshore just five minutes' walk away.

**Parklands Marina
Holiday Park**   HOLIDAY PARK $
(☑ 03-573 6343, 0800 111 104; www.parktostay.co.nz; 10 Beach Rd, Waikawa; campsites from $30, units

MAORI NZ: MARLBOROUGH & NELSON
....
While Maori culture on the South Island is much less evident than in the north, it can still be found in pockets, and particularly around coastal Marlborough.

Kaikoura is rich in Maori history, into which Maori Tours Kaikoura (p70) can offer an insight. The Marlborough Sounds, too, has some stories to tell. Plug into them on eco-oriented tours and wildlife cruises with Myths & Legends Eco-Tours (p57).

$55-95; @ ☎ 🏊) Large, leafy campground with grassy sites, satisfactory cabins, plus ready access to boat-ilicious Waikawa Bay and Victoria Domain. It's a pleasant 3km walk/cycle to town. Courtesy transfers available.

Picton Top 10 Holiday Park   HOLIDAY PARK $
(☑ 03-573 7212, 0800 277 444; www.pictontop10.co.nz; 70 Waikawa Rd; campsites from $21, units $75-160; @ ☎ 🏊) About 500m from town, this compact, well-kept place has plenty of lawn and picnic benches, plus crowd-pleasing facilities including playground, barbecue area and swimming pool.

Harbour View Motel   MOTEL $$
(☑ 03-573 6259, 0800 101 133; www.harbourviewpicton.co.nz; 30 Waikawa Rd; d $125-200; ☎) The elevated position of this motel commands good views of Picton's mast-filled harbour from its tastefully decorated, self-contained studios with timber decks.

Bay Vista Waterfront Motel   MOTEL $$
(☑ 03-573 6733; www.bayvistapicton.co.nz; 303 Waikawa Rd, Waikawa; d $130-185; ☎) This motel enjoys an enviable position on Waikawa foreshore, with views down Queen Charlotte Sound. All units have their own patio and share a big, lush lawn. Located 4km from Picton (courtesy transfer available by request).

Gables B&B   B&B $$
(☑ 03-573 6772; www.thegables.co.nz; 20 Waikawa Rd; s $100, d $140-170, units $155-200, all incl breakfast; @ ☎) This historic B&B (once home to Picton's mayor) has three individually styled en suite rooms in the main house and two homely self-contained units out the back. Prices drop if you organise your own breakfast. Lovely hosts show good humour (ask about the Muffin Club).

Picton

Whatamonga Homestay HOMESTAY **$$**
(☎03-573 7192; www.whsl.co.nz; 425 Port Under-
wood Rd; d incl breakfast $175; @☎) Follow
Waikawa Rd, which becomes Port Under-
wood Rd, for 8km and you'll bump into this
classy waterside option – two self-contained
units with king-sized beds and balconies
with magic views. Two other rooms under
the main house (also with views) share a
bathroom. Free kayaks, dinghies and fishing
gear are available.

Picton

✖ Eating & Drinking

Picton Village Bakkerij BAKERY **$**
(cnr Auckland & Dublin Sts; items $3-8; ☉6am-4pm) Dutch owners bake trays of European goodies here, including interesting breads, filled rolls, cakes and custardy, tarty treats. An excellent stop before or after the ferry.

Gusto CAFE **$**
(33 High St; meals $14-20; ☉7.30am-2.30pm; 🖉) This friendly and hard-working joint does beaut breakfasts including first-class salmon-scrambled egg and a 'Morning Glory' fry-up worth the calories. Lunch options include local mussels or a steak sandwich.

Fresh Choice Supermarket SUPERMARKET **$**
(Mariners Mall, 100 High St; ☉7am-9pm) Pretty much the only choice, and fortunately a good one.

Le Café CAFÉ **$$**
(www.lecafepicton.co.nz; London Quay; lunch $12-24, dinner $20-34; ☉7.30am-10.30pm; 🖉) A perennially popular spot for its quayside location, dependable food and Havana coffee. The likes of salami sandwiches and sweets are in the cabinet, while a good antipasto platter, generous pasta, local mussels, lamb and fish dishes feature à la carte. Laidback atmosphere, craft beer and occasional live gigs make this a good evening hang-out.

Café Cortado CAFE **$$**
(www.cortado.co.nz; cnr High St & London Quay; mains $17-36; ☉8am-late) A pleasant corner cafe and bar with sneaky views of the harbour through the foreshore's pohutukawa and palms. This consistent performer turns out fish dishes, good cheeseburgers and decent pizza.

Seamus's PUB
(25 Wellington St; meals $20-24; ☉noon-1am) A snug drinking den, pouring a reliable Guinness and a good selection of whiskies. Mix this up with hearty food, regular live music and a sunny garden bar, and you've got the liveliest joint in town.

❶ Information

Picton i-SITE (☎03-520 3113; www.lovemarlborough.co.nz; Foreshore; ☉9am-5pm Mon-Fri, to 4pm Sat & Sun) All vital tourist guff including maps, Queen Charlotte Track information, lockers and transport bookings. Dedicated Department of Conservation (DOC) counter.
Picton Library (67 High St; ☉8am-5pm Mon-Fri, 10am-1pm Sat; 🛜) Free wi-fi.
Post Office (Mariners Mall, 72 High St)

❶ Getting There & Away

Make bookings for nationwide transport at Picton i-SITE.

AIR

Soundsair (☎03-520 3080, 0800 505 005; www.soundsair.co.nz) Flies daily between Picton and Wellington (adult/child from $95/85); a shuttle bus to/from the airstrip at Koromiko, 8km south, costs $7.

BOAT

There are two operators crossing Cook Strait between Picton and Wellington, and, although all ferries leave from more or less the same place, each has its own terminal. The main transport hub (with car-rental depots) is at the Interislander Terminal, which also has public showers, a cafe and internet facilities.
Bluebridge Ferries (☎0800 844 844, in Wellington 04-471 6188; www.bluebridge.co.nz; adult/child from $51/26; 🛜) crossings takes 3½ hours, and the company runs up to four sailings in each direction daily. Cars and campervans from $118, motorbikes $51,

MARLBOROUGH & NELSON PICTON

bicycles $10. The sleeper service arrives in Picton at 6am.

Interislander (☑0800 802 802; www.inter-islander.co.nz; adult/child $55/28) Crossings take three hours 10 minutes; up to five sailings in each direction daily. Cars are priced from $118, campervans (up to 5.5m) from $133, motorbikes $56, bicycles $15.

BUS

Buses serving Picton depart from the Inter-islander terminal or nearby i-SITE.

InterCity (☑03-365 1113; www.intercity.co.nz) runs south to Christchurch (5½ hours) via Blenheim (30 minutes) and Kaikoura (2½ hours), with connections to Dunedin, Queenstown and Invercargill. Services also run to/from Nelson (2¼ hours), with connections to Motueka and the West Coast. At least one bus daily on each of these routes connects with a Wellington ferry service.

Smaller shuttle buses running from Picton to Christchurch include **Atomic Shuttles** (☑03-349 0697, 0508 108 359; www.atomictravel.

EXPLORING THE MARLBOROUGH SOUNDS

The Marlborough Sounds are a maze of peaks, bays, beaches and watery reaches, formed when the sea flooded deep river valleys after the last ice age. They are very convoluted: Pelorus Sound, for example, is 42km long but has 379km of shoreline.

Many spectacular locations can be reached by car. The wiggly 35km drive along Queen Charlotte Drive from Picton to Havelock is a great Sounds snapshot, but if you have a spare day, head out to French Pass (or even D'Urville Island) for some big-picture framing of the Outer Sounds. Roads are predominantly narrow and occasionally unsealed; allow plenty of driving time and keep your wits about you.

Sounds travel is invariably quicker by boat (for example, Punga Cove from Picton by car takes two to three hours, but just 45 minutes by boat). Fortunately, an armada of vessels offer scheduled and on-demand boat services, with the bulk operating out of Picton for the Queen Charlotte Sound, and some from Havelock for Kenepuru and Pelorus Sounds.

There are walking, kayaking and biking opportunities, but there's diving as well – notably the wreck of the *Mikhail Lermontov,* a Russian cruise ship that sank in Port Gore in 1986.

From Picton

Most of Picton's boat operators depart from the smart Town Wharf. They offer everything from direct lodge transfers to cruises taking in sites such as Ship Cove and Motuara Island bird sanctuary, to round-trip Queen Charlotte Track transport and pack transfers that allow trampers to walk without a heavy burden. Bikes and kayaks can also be transported.

Cougar Line (☑03-573 7925, 0800 504 090; www.cougarlinecruises.co.nz; Town Wharf; track round trip $105, full-day tour from $80) Queen Charlotte Track transport, plus various half- and full-day cruise/walk trips, including the rather special (and flexible) ecocruise to Motu-ara Island and a Ship Cove picnic.

Beachcomber Fun Cruises (☑03-573 6175, 0800 624 526; www.beachcombercruises.co.nz; Town Wharf; mail run $93, cruises from $35, track round trip $99) Two- to four-hour cruises, some with resort lunches. Cruise/walk, cruise/bike and Queen Charlotte Track options available.

Wilderness Guides (☑03-573 5432, 0800 266 266; www.wildernessguidesnz.com; Town Wharf; 1-day trip from $120, kayak/bike hire per day $60) Host of the popular and flexible one- to three-day 'multisport' trips (kayak/walk/cycle) plus many other guided and independent biking, tramping and kayaking tours including a remote Ship Cove paddle. A good range of bicycles also available for hire.

Marlborough Sounds Adventure Company (☑03-573 6078, 0800 283 283; www.marl-boroughsounds.co.nz; Town Wharf; half- to 3-day packages $85-545) Bike-walk-kayak trips, with options to suit every inclination and duration. A top day option is the kayak and hike ($175). Gear rental (bikes, kayaks and camping equipment) also available.

Dolphin Watch Nature Tours (☑03-573 8040, 0800 945 354; www.naturetours.co.nz; Town Wharf; dolphin swimming/viewing $165/99, other tours from $75) Half-day 'swim with dolphins' and wildlife tours including trips to Motuara Island.

Myths & Legends Eco-Tours (☑03-573 6901; www.eco-tours.co.nz; half-/full-day cruises $200/250) A chance to get out on the water with a local Maori family – longtime locals, co.nz), which can also be booked via **Naked Bus** (www.nakedbus.com).

TRAIN

KiwiRail Scenic (☑ 04-495 0775, 0800 872 467; www.kiwirailscenic.co.nz) Runs the *Coastal Pacific* service daily (October to May) each way between Picton and Christchurch via Blenheim and Kaikoura (and 22 tunnels and 175 bridges!), departing Christchurch at 7am, Picton at 1pm. Adult one-way Picton–Christchurch fares range from $79 to $159. The service connects with the Interislander ferry.

❶ Getting Around

Shuttle services around town and beyond are offered by **Picton Shuttles** (☑ 027 696 5207). Cheap transport along the Queen Charlotte Drive between Picton and Havelock is offered by **Coleman Post** (☑ 027 255 8882; $15).

Renting a car in Picton is easy and competitively priced (as low as $35 per day), with

MARLBOROUGH & NELSON PICTON

storytellers and environmentalists. There are six different trips to choose from, including bird-watching and visiting Ship Cove.

Marlborough Travel (☑ 03-577 9997, 0800 990 800; www.marlboroughtravel.co.nz; Town Wharf; adult/child $135/55; ⊙ departs 1.30pm) Runs the 3½-hour 'Seafood Odyssea' cruise to a salmon farm, complete with salmon snack and sauvignon blanc.

Dive Boat Picton (☑ 03-573 7199, 0800 934 837; www.ninedives.co.nz; 6hr trip $195) Offers dive trips around the Sounds taking in marine reserves and various wrecks including the *Mikhail Lermontov*, plus diver training. Snorkelling and seal-swims also available.

Arrow Water Taxis (☑ 027 444 4689, 03-573 8229; www.arrowwatertaxis.co.nz; Town Wharf) Pretty much anywhere, on demand, for groups of four or more.

Picton Water Taxis (☑ 027 227 0284, 03-573 7853; www.pictonwatertaxis.co.nz) Water taxi and sightseeing trips around Queen Charlotte, on demand.

Float Plane (☑ 03-573 6866, 021 704 248; www.nz-scenic-flights.co.nz; Ferry Terminal; flights from $75) Offers Queen Charlotte Track and Sounds accommodation transfers, scenic flights, and flights and trips to Nelson, the Abel Tasman National Park and to the lower North Island.

From Anakiwa

Sea Kayak Adventures (☑ 03-574 2765, 0800 262 5492; www.nzseakayaking.com; cnr Queen Charlotte Dr & Anakiwa Rd; half-/two-day guided paddle $85/190) Guided and 'guided then go' kayaking with bike/hike options around Queen Charlotte, Kenepuru and Pelorus Sounds plus freedom kayak and mountain-bike rental (half-/full-day $40/60).

From Havelock

Pelorus Mail Boat (☑ 03-574 1088; www.mail-boat.co.nz; Jetty 1; adult/child $128/free; ⊙ departs 9.30am Tue, Thu & Fri) Popular full-day boat cruise through the far reaches of Pelorus Sound on a genuine NZ Post delivery run. Bookings essential; BYO lunch. Picton and Blenheim pick-up and drop-off available.

Greenshell Mussel Cruise (☑ 0800 990 800, 03-577 9997; www.greenshellmusselcruise. co.nz; adult/child $115/39; ⊙ departs 1.30pm) Three-hour cruise on a catamaran to mussel in on Kenepuru's aquaculture. Includes a tasting of steamed mussels and a glass of wine. Bookings essential.

Waterways Boating Safaris (☑ 03-574 1372; www.waterways.co.nz; 745 Keneperu Rd; half-/full-day $110/150) Be guided around Kenepuru Sound while piloting your own zippy boat. A unique and fun way to get out on the water, see the scenery and learn about the area's ecology and history. BYO lunch. Local pick-up and drop-offs.

Pelorus Sound Water Taxi (☑ 03-574 2151, 027 444 2852; www.pelorussoundwatertaxis. co.nz; Jetty 1a) Taxi and sightseeing trips from Havelock, around Pelorus, on demand.

Kenepuru Water Taxi (☑ 03-573 4344, 021 455 593; www.kenepuru.co.nz; 7170 Kenepuru Rd) Taxi and sightseeing trips around Kenepuru Sound, on demand.

numerous rental companies based at the Interislander ferry terminal and many others within a short walk. **Ace** (☑ 03-573 8939; www.acerentalcars.co.nz; Ferry Terminal), **Omega** (☑ 03-573 5580; www.omegarentalcars.com; 1 Lagoon Rd) and **Pegasus** (☑ 03-573 7733; www.carrentalspicton.co.nz; 1 Auckland St) are reliable local operators. Most agencies allow drop-offs in Christchurch; if you're planning to drive the North Island, most companies suggest you leave your car at Picton and pick up another one in Wellington after crossing Cook Strait.

Queen Charlotte Track

The hugely popular, meandering, 70km Queen Charlotte Track offers gorgeous coastal scenery on its way from historic Ship Cove to Anakiwa, passing through a mixture of privately owned land and DOC reserves. Access depends on the cooperation of local landowners; respect their property by utilising designated campsites and toilets, and

carrying out your rubbish. Your purchase of the Track Pass ($15 to $18), available from operators in town and on the track, provides the co-op with the means to maintain and enhance the experience for all.

Queen Charlotte is a well-defined track, suitable for people of average fitness. Numerous boat and tour operators service the track, allowing you to walk the whole three-to five-day journey, or start and finish where you like, on foot or by kayak or bike. We're talking mountain biking here, and a whole lot of fun for fit, competent off-roaders. Part of the track is off-limits to cyclists from 1 December to the end of February, but there is still good riding to be had during this time.

Ship Cove is the usual (and recommended) starting point – mainly because it's easier to arrange a boat from Picton to Ship Cove than vice versa – but the track can be started from Anakiwa. There's a public phone at Anakiwa but not at Ship Cove.

Estimated walk times:

TRACK SECTION	DISTANCE (KM)	DURATION (HR)
Ship Cove to Resolution Bay	4.5	1½-2
Resolution Bay to head of Endeavour Inlet	10.5	2½-3
Endeavour Inlet to Camp Bay/Punga Cove	12	3-4
Camp Bay/Punga Cove to Torea Saddle/Portage	24	6-8
Torea Saddle/Portage to Te Mahia Saddle	7.5	3-4
Te Mahia Saddle to Anakiwa	12.5	3-4

🛏 Sleeping & Eating

The beauty of the Queen Charlotte Track is that there are plenty of great day-trip options, allowing you to base yourself in Picton. However, there is also plenty of accommodation, nicely spaced along the way, and boat operators will transport your luggage along the track for you.

At the self-sufficient end of the scale are six DOC campsites: Schoolhouse Bay, Camp Bay, Bay of Many Coves, Black Rock, Cowshed Bay and Davies Bay. All have toilets and a water supply but no cooking facilities. There's also a variety of resorts,

Marlborough Sounds

lodges, backpackers and guesthouses, of which our picks follow below, ordered from Ship Cove to Anakiwa. Unless you're camping, it pays to book your accommodation waaay in advance, especially in summer.

Numerous cafes are also dotted along the track, the majority of which will only be in full swing during high summer. Some – namely those at Furneaux Lodge (www.furneaux.co.nz), Punga Cove Resort (www.pungacove.co.nz; @ 🕿) and Portage Resort Hotel (www.peppers.co.nz/portage; 🕿 🕿) – are the in-house eateries of long-standing but not necessarily shipshape Sounds resorts. We recommend restricting your financial outlay to cold beer and bar snacks at these destinations.

A list of sleeping and eating options can be found in the official Queen Charlotte Track Directory (www.qctrack.co.nz).

Cnoc Na Lear GUESTHOUSE $$
(⌨ 03-579 8444; www.cnocnalear.co.nz; Endeavour Inlet; d/tr incl breakfast $195/255; 🕿) Sitting just above the track with bay views, this modern guesthouse offers plenty of home comforts including dinner and packed lunches by arrangement, as well as continental breakfast.

Mahana Lodge LODGE $$
(⌨ 03-579 8373; www.mahanalodge.co.nz; Endeavour Inlet; d $195; ⊙ closed Jun-Aug) 🍃 This beautiful property features a pretty waterside lawn and purpose-built lodge with four en suite doubles. Ecofriendly initiatives include bush regeneration, pest trapping and organic veggie patch. In fact, feel-good factors abound: free kayaks, home baking and a blooming conservatory where the evening meal is served (three courses $55).

Noeline's Homestay HOMESTAY $
(⌨ 03-579 8375; Endeavour Inlet; dm $35-40) Follow the pink arrows from Camp Bay to this relaxed homestay and be greeted by 70-something Noeline, 'the Universal Grandma', and her home-baked treats. It's a friendly arrangement with beds for five people, cooking facilities and great views.

Bay of Many Coves Resort RESORT $$$
(⌨ 03-579 9771, 0800 579 9771; www.bayofmanycoves.co.nz; Bay of Many Coves; 1-/2-/3-bedroom apt $640/845/995; 🕿 🕿) These plush and secluded apartments feature all mod cons and private balconies overlooking the water. As well as upmarket cuisine, there are various indulgences such as room service, massage, spa and hot tub.

DeBretts   GUESTHOUSE $
(☑03-573 4522; www.stayportage.co.nz; s with/
without linen $50/45) The family-run duo of
DeBretts and Treetops (☑03-573 4404) offers a combined total of six bedrooms in two
homely backpackers on the hill behind Portage Resort. Torea Bay bag transfers included.

Lochmara Lodge   RESORT $$
(☑03-573 4554; www.lochmaralodge.co.nz; Loch-
mara Bay; units $95-295; ☎) 🖉 This arty,
ecoretreat can be reached via the Queen
Charlotte Track or direct from Picton aboard
the lodge's water taxi ($55 return). There are
en suite doubles, units and chalets, all set in
lush surroundings, and a fully licensed cafe
and restaurant, plus a bathhouse where you
can indulge in a spa or massage.

Mistletoe Bay   HOLIDAY PARK $
(☑03-573 4048; www.mistletoebay.co.nz; Mistle-
toe Bay; unpowered sites $32, dm/d $30/70, cabins
$140, linen $7.50; ☎) 🖉 Surrounded by bushy
hills, Mistletoe Bay offers attractive camp-
ing with no-frills facilities. There are eight
modern cabins sleeping up to six, plus a
bunkhouse. Environmental sustainability
abounds, as does the opportunity to jump
off the jetty, kayak in the bay or walk the
Queen Charlotte Track.

★ **Te Mahia Bay Resort**   RESORT $$
(☑03-573 4089; www.temahia.co.nz; d $148-248;
☎) This lovely low-key resort is within cooee
of the Queen Charlotte Track in a picturesque bay on Kenepuru Sound. It has a range
of delightful rooms-with-a-view, our pick of
which is the great-value heritage units. The
on-site store has pre-cooked meals, pizza,
cakes, coffee and camping supplies (wine!),
plus there is kayak hire and massage.

Anakiwa Backpackers   HOSTEL $
(☑03-574 1388; www.anakiwabackpackers.co.nz;
401 Anakiwa Rd; dm $35, d $85-105; ☎) At the
southern end of the track, this former
schoolhouse is a soothing spot to rest and
reflect. There are two doubles (one with en
suite), a three-bed dorm and a beachy self-
contained unit. Jocular owners will have you
jumping off the jetty for joy and imbibing espresso and ice cream (hallelujah) from their
little green caravan (open summer afternoons). Provisions available by arrangement
and free kayak hire.

Smiths Farm Holiday Park   HOLIDAY PARK $
(☑03-574 2806, 0800 727 578; www.smithsfarm.
co.nz; 1419 Queen Charlotte Dr, Linkwater; campsites from $16, cabins $60-130, units $130; @☎)
🖉 Located on the aptly named Linkwater
flat between Queen Charlotte and Pelorus,
friendly Smiths makes a handy base camp
for the track and beyond. Well-kept cabins
and motel units face out onto the bushy
hillside, while livestock nibble around the
lush camping lawns. Short walks extend to a
waterfall and magical glow-worm dell.

❶ Information

The best place to get track information and
advice is Picton i-SITE (p55), which also handles
bookings for transport and accommodation. See
also the online **Queen Charlotte Track Directory** (www.qctrack.co.nz).

Kenepuru &
Pelorus Sounds

Kenepuru and Pelorus Sounds, to the west of
Queen Charlotte Sound, are less populous and
therefore offer fewer traveller services, including transport. There's some cracking scenery,
however, and those with time to spare will be
well rewarded by their explorations.

Havelock is the hub of this area, the western bookend of the 35km Queen Charlotte
Drive (Picton being the eastern) and the
self-proclaimed 'Greenshell Mussel Capital
of the World'. While hardly the most rock-
and-roll of NZ towns, Havelock offers most
necessities, including accommodation, fuel
and food. As you get out into the Sounds be
prepared to encounter scant fuel and only
the occasional shop, which *may* have frozen
bread and out-of-date popsicles.

For finer detail, including a complete
list of visitor services, visit www.pelorusnz.
co.nz, which covers Havelock, Kenepuru
and Pelorus Sounds, and the extremities of
French Pass and D'Urville Island.

◉ Sights & Activities

If a stroll through the streets of Havelock
leaves you thinking that there *must* be more
to this area, you're right – and to get a taste
of it you need go no further than the Cul-
len Point Lookout, 10 minutes' drive from
Havelock along the Queen Charlotte Drive.
A short walk leads up and around a headland overlooking Havelock, the surrounding
valleys and Pelorus Sound. Look out for the
Havelock Map & Walkway Guide which details more walks in the area.

To venture out into the sounds themselves, see p57.

fished the North Island up from the depths. The area was heavily settled by Maori, with excavations showing that the area was a moa-hunter settlement about 800 to 1000 years ago. The name Kaikoura comes from 'Kai' (food) and 'koura' (crayfish).

James Cook sailed past the peninsula in 1770, but didn't land. His journal states that 57 Maori in four double-hulled canoes came towards the *Endeavour,* but 'would not be prevail'd upon to put along side'.

In 1828 Kaikoura's beachfront was the scene of a tremendous battle. A northern Nga-ti Toa war party, led by chief Te Rauparaha, bore down on Kaikoura, killing or capturing several hundred of the local Ngai Tahu tribe.

Europeans established a whaling station here in 1842, and the town remained a whaling centre until 1922 after which arming and fishing sustained the community. It was in the 1980s that wildlife tours began to transform the town into the tourist mecca it is today.

⊙ Sights

Point Kean Seal Colony   WILDLIFE RESERVE
At the end of the peninsula seals laze around in the grass and on the rocks, lapping up all the attention. Give them a wide berth (10m), and never will get between them and the sea – they will attack if they feel cornered and can move surprisingly fast.

Fyffe House   HISTORIC BUILDING
(www.fyffehouse.co.nz; 62 Avoca St; adult/child $10/free; ◉10am-5.30pm daily Nov-Apr, to 4pm Thu-Mon May-Oct) Kaikoura's oldest surviving building, Fyffe House's whale-bone foundations were laid in 1844. Proudly positioned and fronted with a colourful garden, the little two-storey cottage offers a fascinating insight into the lives of colonial settlers. Interpretive displays are complemented by historic objects, while peeling wallpaper and the odd cobweb lend authenticity. Cute maritime-themed shop.

Kaikoura Museum   MUSEUM
(www.kaikoura.govt.nz; West End; adult/child $5/1; ◉10am-4.30pm Mon-Fri, 2-4pm Sat & Sun) Housed in the new council building along with the library, this provincial museum displays historical photographs, Maori and colonial artefacts, a huge sperm-whale jaw and the fossilised remains of a plesiosaur.

Point Sheep Shearing Show   FARM
(www.pointsheepshearing.co.nz; Fyffe Quay; adult /child $10/5; ◉shows 1.30pm & 4pm) The

30-minute Point Sheep Shearing Show at the Point B&B is fun and educational. You can feed a ram, and lambs between September and February. Classic NZ!

🏃 Activities

There's a safe swimming **beach** in front of the Esplanade, alongside which is a **pool** (adult/child $3/2; ◉10am-5pm Nov-Mar) if you have a salt aversion.

Decent **surfing** can be found in the area, too, particularly at **Mangamaunu Beach** (15km north of town), where there's a 500m point break, which is fun in good conditions. Get the low-down, organise transport, learn to surf or hire gear from **Board Silly Surf Adventures** (📋0274 188 900, 0800 787 352; 134 Southbay Pde; 3hr lesson $75, board & suit from $45) based at South Bay. Gear hire and advice is also available from **R&R Sport** (www.rrsport.co.nz; 14 West End) and **Surf Kaikoura** (www.surfkaikoura.co.nz; 4 Beach Rd).

Kaikoura Peninsula Walkway   WALKING
A foray along this walkway is a must-do. Starting from the town, the three- to four-hour loop heads out to Point Kean, along the cliffs to South Bay, then back to town over the isthmus (or in reverse, of course). En route you'll see fur seals and red-billed seagull and shearwater colonies. Lookouts and interesting interpretive panels abound. Collect a map at the i-SITE or follow your nose.

Dive Kaikoura   DIVING
(📋03-319 6622, 0800 348 352; www.divekaikoura. co.nz; Yarmouth St; half-day $250) With its rocky formations and abundant marine life, the Kaikoura coast offers rewarding diving and snorkelling. Dive Kaikoura runs small-group trips and diver training.

Clarence River Rafting   RAFTING
(📋03-319 6993; www.clarenceriverrafting.co.nz; 3802 SH1, at Clarence Bridge; half-day trip adult/ child $120/80) Raft the bouncy Grade II rapids of the scenic Clarence River on a half-day trip (two hours on the water), or on longer journeys including a five-day trip with wilderness camping ($1350). Based on SH1, 40km north of Kaikoura near Clarence Bridge.

☞ Tours

Wildlife tours are Kaikoura's speciality, particularly those involving whales (including sperm, pilot, killer, humpback and southern right), dolphins (Hector's, bottlenose and

Kaikoura

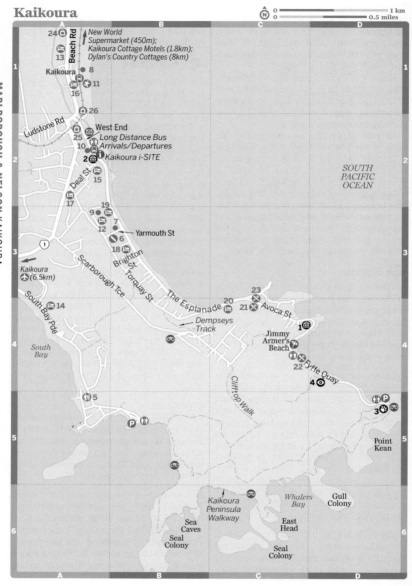

MARLBOROUGH & NELSON KAIKOURA

0 — 1 km
0 — 0.5 miles

24
13
Beach Rd

New World Supermarket (450m);
Kaikoura Cottage Motels (1.8km);
Dylan's Country Cottages (8km)

Kaikoura
8
16
11
26
Ludstone Rd
West End
25
Long Distance Bus Arrivals/Departures
10
2
Kaikoura i-SITE
15
Deal St
17
19
9
7
12
Yarmouth St
6
18
Brighton St
Scarborough Tce
Torquay St

1
Kaikoura
(6.5km)

South Bay Pde
14
South Bay

The Esplanade
Dempseys Track

23
20
21
Avoca St
1
Jimmy Armer's Beach
22
Fyffe Quay
4

5
P
3

Clifftop Walk

Point Kean

Kaikoura Peninsula Walkway
Whalers Bay
Gull Colony

Sea Caves
Seal Colony
East Head
Seal Colony

SOUTH PACIFIC OCEAN

dusky) and NZ fur seals. There's also plenty of birdlife, including albatross and blue penguins. During summer, book your tour a few weeks ahead, and allow some leeway for lousy weather.

Whale-Watching

Your choices are boat, plane or helicopter. Aerial options are shorter and pricier, but allow you to see the whole whale, as opposed to just a tail, flipper or spout.

Kaikoura

◎ **Sights**
  1 Fyffe House..C4
  2 Kaikoura Museum..................................A2
  3 Point Kean Seal Colony.........................D5
  4 Point Sheep Shearing Show..................D4

◯ **Activities, Courses & Tours**
    Albatross Encounter ....(see 7)
  5 Board Silly Surf Adventures.................A5
  6 Dive Kaikoura B3
  7 Dolphin Encounter B3
  8 Kaikoura Helicopters.............................A1
  9 Kaikoura Kayaks A3
 10 Seal Swim Kaikoura...............................A2
 11 Whale Watch Kaikoura..........................A1

◯ **Sleeping**
 12 Albatross Backpacker Inn A3
 13 Alpine Pacific Holiday Park...................A1

 14 Bay Cottages...A4
 15 Dolphin Lodge...A2
 16 Kaikoura Top 10 Holiday Park A1
 17 Nikau Lodge..A2
 18 Sails Motel..B3
 19 Waves on the Esplanade A3
 20 YHA Kaikoura Maui C4

◯ **Eating**
    Cafe Encounter............................. (see 7)
 21 Green Dolphin C4
 22 Kaikoura Seafood BBQ...........................C4
 23 Pier Hotel..C4
    Reserve Hutt .... (see 10)

◯ **Shopping**
 24 Cods & Crayfish......................................A1
 25 R&R Sport A2
 26 Surf Kaikoura A1

Whale Watch Kaikoura ECOTOUR
(☑ 03-319 6767, 0800 655 121; www.whale-watch.co.nz; Railway Station; 3hr tour adult/child $145/60) ✎ With knowledgeable guides and fascinating 'world of whales' on-board animation, Kaikoura's biggest operator heads out on boat trips (with admirable frequency) to introduce you to some of the big fellas. It'll refund 80% of your fare if no whales are sighted (success rate: 98%). If this trip is a must for you, allow a few days flexibility in case the weather turns to custard.

Kaikoura Helicopters SCENIC FLIGHTS
(☑ 03-319 6609; www.worldofwhales.co.nz; Railway Station; 15-60min flight from $100-490) Reliable whale-spotting flights (standard 30-minute tour $220 each for three or more people), plus jaunts around the peninsula, Mt Fyffe and peaks beyond.

Wings over Whales ECOTOUR
(☑ 0800 226 629, 03-319 6580; www.whales.co.nz; 30min flight adult/child $180/75) Light-plane flights departing from Kaikoura Airport, 7km south of town. Spotting success rate: 95%.

Dolphin- & Seal-Spotting

★**Seal Swim Kaikoura** ECOTOUR
(☑ 03-319 6182, 0800 732 579; www.sealswimkaikoura.co.nz; 58 West End; tours $70-110, viewing adult/child $55/35; ☺ Oct-May) Take a (warmly wetsuited) swim with Kaikoura's healthy population of playful seals – including very cute pups – on two-hour guided snorkelling tours run by the Chambers family. Shore or boat options available.

Dolphin Encounter ECOTOUR
(☑ 0800 733 365, 03-319 6777; www.encounterkaikoura.co.nz; 96 Esplanade; swim adult/child $175/155, observation $90/45; ☺ tours 8.30am & 12.30pm year-round, plus 5.30am Nov-Apr) Here's your chance to rub shoulders with pods of dusky dolphins on three-hour tours. Limited numbers, so book in advance.

Kaikoura Kayaks KAYAKING
(☑ 03-319 7118, 0800 452 456; www.kaikourakayaks.co.nz; 19 Killarney St; 3hr tours adult/child $95/70; ☺ tours 8.30am, 12.30pm & 4.30pm Nov-Apr, 9am & 1pm May-Oct) Excellent guided sea-kayak tours to view fur seals and explore the peninsula's coastline. Family-friendly, kayak fishing and other on-demand trips available, plus freedom kayak and paddle-board hire.

Bird-watching

Albatross Encounter BIRD-WATCHING
(☑ 03-319 6777, 0800 733 365; www.encounterkaikoura.co.nz; 96 Esplanade; adult/child $115/55; ☺ tours 9am & 1pm year-round, plus 6am Nov-Apr) Kaikoura is heaven for bird-nerds, who fly at the opportunity for a close encounter with pelagic species such as shearwaters, shags, mollymawks, petrels and the inimitable albatross.

Fishing

Fishing is a common obsession in Kaikoura, with local boaties angling for any excuse to go out for a little look-sea. It's a good opportunity to *kai koura* (eat crayfish). Trips start from around $60; the **i-SITE** (☑ 03-319 5641; www.kaikoura.co.nz; West End; ☺ 9am-5pm Mon-Fri, to 4pm Sat & Sun, extended hours Dec-Mar) has a full list of operators.

Fishing at Kaikoura FISHING

(☑ 03-319 3003; gerard.diedrichs@xtra.co.nz) Fishing, crayfishing, scenic tours and water-skiing, on the 6m *Sophie-Rose*.

Kaikoura Fishing Charters FISHING

(☑ 03-319 6888; www.kaikourafishing.co.nz) Dangle a line from the 12m *Takapu,* then take your filleted, bagged catch home to eat.

Kaikoura Fishing Tours FISHING

(☑ 0800 246 6597; www.kaikoura-fishing-tours.co.nz) Serious about scenery and seafood. Your catch is filleted ready for dinner.

Tramping & Cycling

For town riding, hire bicycles from R&R Sport (p67) and Surf Kaikoura (p67). While you're there, ask about the trail to the foot of Mt Fyffe.

Walks Kaikoura WALKING

(☑ 027 473 2659, 027 437 2426; www.walkskaikoura.com; half-/full day from $75/145) Experienced local guides offer tailored walks around the area, from mountains to coast with heli options, plus cycle tours on quiet sealed roads and the newly developed riverside trail.

Kaikoura Coast Track TRAMPING

(☑ 03-319 2715; www.kaikouratrack.co.nz; $230) This easy three-day, 37km, self-guided walk across private farmland combines coastal and alpine views. The price includes three nights' farm-cottage accommodation and pack transport; BYO sleeping bag and food. Starts 45km south of Kaikoura.

Kaikoura Wilderness Walks TRAMPING

(☑ 03-319 6966, 0800 945 337; www.kaikourawilderness.co.nz; 1-/2-night package $1195/1595) 🔊 Two- or three-day guided walks through the privately owned Puhi Peaks Nature Reserve high in the Seaward Kaikoura Range. Package includes accommodation and sumptuous meals at the luxurious Shearwater Lodge.

Other Tours

Kaikoura Mountain Safaris DRIVING TOUR

(☑ 03-319 6424, 021 869 643; www.kaikouramountainsafaris.co.nz; half-day tour adult/child $100/55, 1-day tour adult/child $165/100) Journey into the backcountry in a 4WD or Unimog – three different tours (departing from the i-SITE) take in alpine vistas, remote farms and the Clarence River valley.

Maori Tours Kaikoura CULTURAL TOUR

(☑ 03-319 5567, 0800 866 267; www.maoritours.co.nz; 3½hr tour adult/child $134/74; ⊙ tours 9am

& 1.30pm) Fascinating half-day, small-group tours laced with Maori hospitality and local lore. Visit historic sites, hear legends and learn indigenous use of trees and plants. Advance bookings required.

🛏 Sleeping

Summer sees accommodation fill up, so book in advance or save your visit for the off-season when reduced rates are in the offing.

Albatross Backpacker Inn HOSTEL $

(☑ 03-319 6090, 0800 222 247; www.albatross-kaikoura.co.nz; 1 Torquay St; dm $29-32, tw/d $69/74; @ 🛜) 🔊 This arty backpackers resides in three sweet buildings, one a former post office. It's colourful and close to the beach but sheltered from the breeze. As well as a laid-back lounge with musical instruments for jamming, there are decks and verandahs to chill out on.

Dolphin Lodge HOSTEL $

(☑ 03-319 5842; www.dolphinlodge.co.nz; 15 Deal St; dm $28, d with/without bathroom $69/62; @ 🛜) This small home-away-from-home has green-thumbed owners who fuss over their lovely scented garden. Inside is a bit squeezed, but on dry days most of the action will be out on the fantastic deck, around the barbecue, or in the spa pool.

Alpine Pacific Holiday Park HOLIDAY PARK $

(☑ 03-319 6275, 0800 692 322; www.alpine-pacific.co.nz; 69 Beach Rd; campsites from $46, cabins $78, units $130-195; @ 🛜 ⊛) This compact and proudly trimmed park copes well with its many visitors, and offers excellent facilities, including a shiny kitchen, resorty pool area and barbecue pavilion. Rows of cabins and units are slightly more stylish than average, and mountain views can be had from many angles.

Kaikoura Top 10 Holiday Park HOLIDAY PARK $

(☑ 03-319 5362, 0800 363 638; www.kaikouratop10.co.nz; 34 Beach Rd; campsites $42-52, cabins $70-95, units $110-160; @ 🛜 ⊛) Hiding from the highway behind a massive hedge, this busy, well-maintained campground offers family-friendly facilities (heated pool, hot tub, trampoline) and cabins and units to the usual Top 10 standard.

YHA Kaikoura Maui HOSTEL $

(☑ 03-319 5931, 0800 278 299; www.yha.co.nz; 270 Esplanade; dm $33, d $89-110, tr $102; @ 🛜) A 15-minute walk to town, this oceanside YHA boasts unobstructed views across the bay to the pine-lined esplanade and mighty peaks beyond. Many rooms enjoy similar views, as does the big-windowed dining room. Communal areas in this purpose-built (1962) hostel are tidy and functional, but a little rough around the edges.

★ **Dylan's Country Cottages**   COTTAGES $$
(☑ 03-319 5473; www.lavenderfarm.co.nz; 268 Postmans Rd; d $195; ⊗ closed May-Aug; ☎) On the grounds of the delightful Kaikoura Lavender Farm, northwest of town, these two self-contained cottages make for an aromatic escape from the seaside fray. One has a private outdoor bath and a shower emerging from a tree; the other an indoor spa and handkerchief lawn. Homemade scones, preserves and free-range eggs for breakfast. Sweet, stylish and romantic.

Kaikoura Cottage Motels   MOTEL $$
(☑ 03-319 5599, 0800 526 882; www.kaikoura-cottagemotels.co.nz; cnr Old Beach & Mill Rds; d $140-160; ☎) This enclave of eight modern tourist flats looks mighty fine, surrounded by attractive native plantings. Oriented for mountain views, the self-contained units sleep four between an open-plan studio-style living room and one private bedroom. Soothing sand-and-sky colour scheme and quality chattels.

Bay Cottages   MOTEL $$
(☑ 03-319 5506; www.baycottages.co.nz; 29 South Bay Pde; cottages/motels $100/130; ☎) Here's a great-value option on South Bay, a few kilometres south of town: five tourist cottages with kitchenette and bathroom that sleep up to four, and two slick motel rooms with stainless-steel benches, a warm feel and clean lines. The cheery owner may even take you crayfishing in good weather.

Sails Motel   MOTEL $$
(☑ 03-319 6145; www.sailsmotel.co.nz; 134 Esplanade; d $120-140, q $170; ☎) There are no sea views (nor sails) at this motel, so the cherubic owners have to impress with quality. Their four secluded, tastefully appointed self-contained units are down a driveway in a garden setting (private outdoor areas abound).

Nikau Lodge   B&B $$$
(☑ 03-319 6973; www.nikaulodge.com; 53 Deal St; d $190-260; @☎) A waggly-tailed welcome awaits at this beautiful B&B high on the hill with grand-scale vistas. Five en suite rooms are plush and comfy, with additional satisfaction arriving in the form of cafe-quality breakfasts accompanied by fresh local coffee. Good humour, home baking, free wi-fi, complimentary drinks, a hot tub and blooming gardens: you may want to move in.

Waves on the Esplanade   APARTMENTS $$$
(☑ 03-319 5890, 0800 319 589; www.kaikoura-apartments.co.nz; 78 Esplanade; apt $240-350; ☎) Can't do without the comforts of home? Here you go: spacious, luxury two-bedroom apartments with Sky TV, DVD player, two bathrooms, laundry facilities and full kitchen. Oh, and superb ocean views from the balcony. Rates are for up to four people.

✖ Eating & Drinking

Kaikoura has a few swell cafes and restaurants, and many that plumb the depths.

Kaikoura Seafood BBQ   SEAFOOD $
(Fyffe Quay; $5-9; ⊗ 10.30am-7pm) Conveniently located on the way to the Point Kean seal colony, this long-standing roadside barbecue is a great spot to sample local seafood, including crayfish and scallops, at an affordable price.

Reserve Hutt   CAFE $
(72 West End; meals $10-20; ⊗ 9am-3pm) The best coffee in the town centre, roasted on site and espressed by dedicated baristas in Kaikoura's grooviest cafe. Puttin' out that rootsy retro-Kiwiana vibe we love so much, this is a neat place to linger over a couple of flatties and down a muffin, delicious ham croissant or the full eggy brunch.

CRAY CRAZY

Among all of Kaikoura's munificent marine life, the one species you just can't avoid is the crayfish, whose delicate flesh dominates local menus. Unfortunately (some say unnecessarily), it's pricey – at a restaurant, you'll (pardon the pun) shell out around $55 for half a cray or over $100 for the whole beast. You can also buy fresh, cooked or uncooked crays from **Cods & Crayfish** (81 Beach Rd; ⊗ 8am-6pm) and iconic **Nins Bin** (SH1; ⊗ 8am-6pm), a surf-side caravan 23km north of town. Upwards of $50 should get you a decent specimen. Alternatively, go out on a fishing tour, or simply head to the Kaikoura Seafood BBQ roadside stall near the peninsula seal colony where cooked crays can be gobbled in the sunshine, by the sea.

Cafe Encounter CAFE $
(96 Esplanade; meals $8-23; ⊗7am-5pm; 🛜🖉)
This cafe in the Encounter Kaikoura complex is more than just somewhere to wait
for your trip. The cabinet houses respectable sandwiches, pastries and cakes, plus
there's a tasteful range of daily specials such
as pork schnitzel and fennel slaw. A sunny
patio provides sea views.

New World Supermarket SUPERMARKET $
(124-128 Beach Rd; ⊗7.30am-9pm) Ten minutes'
walk from the town centre.

Pier Hotel PUB $$
(📋03-319 5037; www.thepierhotel.co.nz; 1 Avoca St;
lunch $15-23, dinner $27-38; ⊗11am-late) Situated
in the town's primo seaside spot, with pano-
ramic views, the historic Pier Hotel is a friend-
ly and inviting place for a drink or a meal,
whether outside or inside the character-filled
public bar or dining rooms. Upstairs lodgings
are worn and creaky, but good value (double
room, including breakfast, from $90).

⭐ **Green Dolphin** MODERN NZ $$$
(📋03-319 6666; www.greendolphinkaikoura.com;
12 Avoca St; mains $25-39; ⊗5-11pm) Kaikoura's
consistent top-end continues to dish up
high-quality produce including seafood,
beef, lamb and venison, as well as seasonal
flavours such as fresh tomato soup. There
are lovely homemade pasta dishes, too. The
hefty drinks list demands attention, featuring exciting aperitifs, craft beer, interesting
wines and more. Booking ahead is advisable,
especially if you want to secure a table by the
window and watch the daylight fade.

ℹ **Information**

Kaikoura i-SITE (📋03-319 5641; www.kaikoura.
co.nz; West End; ⊗9am-5pm Mon-Fri, to 4pm
Sat & Sun, extended hours Dec-Mar) Helpful
staff make tour, accommodation and transport
bookings, and help with DOC-related matters.
Paperplus/Post Office (📋03-319 6808; 41
West End) Postal agent.

ℹ **Getting There & Away**

BUS

Atomic Shuttles (📋0508 108 359, 03-349
0697; www.atomictravel.co.nz) Also services
Kaikoura on its Christchurch to Picton run,
which links with destinations as far afield as
Nelson, Queenstown and Invercargill.
InterCity (📋03-365 1113; www.intercity.co.nz)
Buses run between Kaikoura and Nelson (3½
hours), Picton (2¼ hours) and Christchurch

(2¾ hours). The bus stop is at the car park next
to the i-SITE (tickets and info inside).
Naked Bus (📋0900 625 33; www.nakedbus.
com) Tickets bargain seats on its own buses on
major routes, and on other services dependent
on capacity.

TRAIN

KiwiRail Scenic (📋0800 872 467; www.
kiwirailscenic.co.nz) Runs the daily *Coastal
Pacific* service, stopping at Kaikoura en route
to Picton (from $59, 2¼ hours; runs October to
May), and Christchurch (from $49, three hours).
The northbound train departs Kaikoura at
9.54am; the southbound at 3.28pm.

ℹ **Getting Around**

Kaikoura Shuttles (📋03-319 6166; www.kai-
kourashuttles.co.nz) will run you around the
local sights as well as to and from the airport.

NELSON REGION

The Nelson region is centred upon Tasman
Bay but stretches north to Golden Bay and
Farewell Spit, and south to Nelson Lakes. It's
not hard to see why it's such a popular travel
destination for both international and domestic traveller alike: not only does it boast
three national parks (Kahurangi, Nelson
Lakes and Abel Tasman), but it can also sat-
isfy nearly every other whim, from food, wine
and beer, art, craft and festivals, to that most
precious of pastimes for which the region is
well known: lazing about in the sunshine.

Nelson
POP 46,440

Dishing up a winning combination of great
weather and beautiful surroundings, Nelson
is hailed as one of NZ's most 'liveable' cities.
In summer it fills up with visitors, who lap
up its diverse offerings.

◎ **Sights**

Nelson has an inordinate number of galleries, most of which are listed in the *Art &
Crafts Nelson City* brochure (with walking-
trail map) available from the i-SITE. A fruitful
wander can be had by starting at the **Fibre
Spectrum** (www.fibrespectrum.co.nz; 280 Trafalgar St), where you can pick up hand-woven
woollens, before moving on to 'Lord of the
Ring' jeweller **Jens Hansen** (www.jenshansen.
com; 320 Trafalgar Sq), glassblower **Flamedaisy**
(www.flamedaisy.com; 324 Trafalgar Sq), then

around the corner to the home of Nelson pottery, **South Street Gallery** (www.nelsonpottery.co.nz; 10 Nile St W). More interesting local creations can be found at the **Nelson Market** (Montgomery Sq; ⊘ 8am-1pm Sat) on Saturday.

★ **Christ Church Cathedral** CHURCH
(www.nelsoncathedral.org; Trafalgar Sq; ⊘ 8am-7pm Nov-Mar, to 5pm Apr-Oct) `FREE` The enduring symbol of Nelson, the art deco Christ Church Cathedral lords it over the city from the top of Trafalgar St. The best time to visit is during the 10am and 6pm Sunday services when you can hear the organist and choir on song.

Nelson Provincial Museum MUSEUM
(www.nelsonmuseum.co.nz; cnr Hardy & Trafalgar Sts; adult/child $7/5; ⊘ 10am-5pm Mon-Fri, 10am-4.30pm Sat & Sun) This modern museum space is filled with cultural heritage and natural history exhibits which have a regional bias, as well as regular touring exhibitions (for which admission fees vary). It also features a great rooftop garden.

★ **Suter Art Gallery** GALLERY
(www.thesuter.org.nz; 208 Bridge St; adult/child $3/50c, free Sat; ⊘ 10.30am-4.30pm) Adjacent to Queen's Gardens, Nelson's public art gallery presents changing exhibitions, floor talks, musical and theatrical performances, and films. The Suter undergoes a major renovation from August 2014, so check the website for the reopening date and details of relocated exhibits.

Founders Heritage Park MUSEUM
(www.founderspark.co.nz; 87 Atawhai Dr; adult/child/family $7/5/15; ⊘ 10am-4.30pm) Two kilometres from the city centre, this park comprises a replica historic village with museum and gallery displays, and artisan products such as chocolate and clothing. It makes for a fascinating wander, which you can augment with a visit to the on-site **Founders Brewery & Café** (www.foundersbrewery.co.nz; meals $11-20; ⊘ 10am-6pm Sun-Thu, 10am-9pm Fri & Sat). With a sun-drenched hop garden and a range of freshly brewed beers arrayed on a $10 tasting tray, this is a lovely place for a leisurely meal or light snack. The beef burger is scrumptious!

Queens Gardens GARDENS
(Bridge St) Immerse yourself in more than 120 years of botanical history in this ornamental garden, which commemorates the 50th jubilee of Queen Victoria's coronation. Great for a picnic or lawny lie-down.

Tahuna Beach BEACH
Nelson's primo playground takes the form of an epic sandy beach (with lifeguards in summer), backed by a large grassy parkland with a playground, espresso cart, swimming pool, various other recreational facilities and an adjacent restaurant strip. Weekends can get veerrrrry busy around here!

🏃 Activities

Nelson offers plenty of opportunity to embrace the great outdoors.

Tramping & Cycling

There's plenty of walking and cycling to be enjoyed in and around the town, for which the i-SITE has maps. The classic walk from town is to the **Centre of NZ** atop the **Botanical Reserve** (Milton St), and if you enjoy that then ask about the **Grampians**. The **Dun Mountain Trail** network ranging over the hills to the south of the city centre has lots of interesting options for fit, keen mountain bikers, as does **Codgers MTB Park**. The new Great Taste Trail (p79) offers flat riding through the craft-beer- and wine-soaked countryside.

UBike CYCLING
(📞 0800 282 453; www.ubike.co.nz; Collingwood St Bridge; hire half-/full day $40/60) A short walk from the i-SITE, UBike hires city and mountain bikes from its riverside caravan. Trail maps and tips, plus espresso to get you going.

Gentle Cycling Company CYCLING
(📞 03-929 5652, 0800 932 453; www.gentlecycling.co.nz; 5/8hr tours $75/80) Self-guided cycle tours along the Great Taste Trail, with drop-ins (and tastings) at wineries, breweries, cafes and occasional galleries. Freedom bike hire (per day $45) and shuttles also available.

Biking Nelson MOUNTAIN BIKING
(📞 021 861 725, 0800 224 532; www.bikingnelson.co.nz; 3hr guided rides $115, bike hire half-/full day $45/65) Hit Nelson's mountain-bike trails with Dave and crew, who run entry-level to hard-core guided rides (all gear provided) and offer freedom rental and advice.

Bike Barn CYCLING
(www.bikebarn.co.nz; 114 Hardy St; hire per day from $40) Bike hire in the central city, plus servicing and repairs.

Paragliding, Kitesurfing & Paddle Boarding

Nelson is a great place to get high or undry, with plenty of action in summer, particularly around the rather divine Tahuna Beach.

Central Nelson

Tandem paragliding costs around $180, introductory kitesurfing starts at $150, and paddleboard hire is around $25 per hour.

Nelson Paragliding PARAGLIDING
(☎ 03-544 1182; www.nelsonparagliding.co.nz)

Kitescool KITESURFING, PADDLE BOARDING
(☎ 021 354 837; www.kitescool.co.nz)

Kite Surf Nelson KITESURFING
(☎ 0800 548 363; www.kitesurfnelson.co.nz)

Supstar PADDLE BOARDING
(☎ 021 0268 5552; www.supstarboards.co.nz)

Other Activities

★**Nelson Bonecarving** CARVING
(☎ 03-546 4275; www.carvingbone.co.nz; 87 Green St, Tahunanui; full-day course $79) Admirers of Maori design will love Stephan's acclaimed bonecarving course. He'll supply materials, tools, instruction, encouragement and cups of tea (plus free pick-up/drop-off in town);

you supply inspiration and talent, and you'll emerge with your very own bone carving.

Happy Valley Adventures ADVENTURE SPORTS
(☎ 03-545 0304, 0800 157 300; www.happyvalley-adventures.co.nz; 194 Cable Bay Rd; Skywire adult/child $85/55, quad-bike tours from $95, horse trek $75) Dangle 150m above the forest in the 'Skywire' (a chairlift/flying-fox hybrid), then soar through the air for its 1.65km length. If that ain't enough, take a quad-bike tour, or if it's too much, try a horse trek. Located 15-minute drive northeast of Nelson along SH6; on-site cafe.

Cable Bay Kayaks KAYAKING
(☎ 03-545 0332, 0508 222 532; www.cablebaykayaks.co.nz; Cable Bay Rd; half-/full day guided trip $85/145) Fifteen minutes' drive from Nelson city, Nick and Jenny offer guided sea-kayaking trips exploring the local coastline where you'll likely meet marine life (snorkelling gear on board) and may even enter a cave.

Central Nelson

MARLBOROUGH & NELSON NELSON

⌖ Tours

Bay Tours GUIDED TOUR
(☑ 03-548 6486, 0800 229 868; www.baytoursnelson.co.nz; half-/full-day tours from $75/144) Nelson city, region, wine, beer, food and art tours. The full-day scenic tour includes a visit to Kaiteriteri and a cruise in Abel Tasman National Park.

Nelson Tours & Travel GUIDED TOUR
(☑ 0272 375 007, 0800 222 373; www.nelsontoursandtravel.co.nz) CJ and crew run various small-group, flexible tours honing in on Nelson's edible, drinkable elements. The five-hour 'Best of Both Worlds' visits wineries and breweries ($95), or venture over to the Marlborough wineries on a day-long tour ($160).

✸ Festivals & Events

For current info on Nelson's active events program, visit www.itson.co.nz and www.nelsonfestivals.co.nz.

Nelson Jazz & Blues Festival MUSIC
(www.nelsonjazzfest.co.nz) More than 50 scoobedoobop events over a week in January. Features local and international acts in halls and on street corners, regionwide.

Nelson Arts Festival ARTS
(www.nelsonfestivals.co.nz) Over two weeks in October; events include a street carnival, exhibitions, cabaret, writers, theatre and music.

⌂ Sleeping

Accents on the Park HOSTEL $
(☑ 03-548 4335, 0800 888 335; www.accentsonthepark.com; 335 Trafalgar Sq; campsites from $15, dm $20-28, d with/without bathroom from $92/60; @ 🛜) This perfectly positioned hostel has a hotel feel with its professional staff, balconies, movie nights with free popcorn, free daily bread, wi-fi, soundproofed rooms, quality linen, fresh bathrooms and bikes for hire. On site, there's also **East St**, a groovy vegetarian cafe and bar.

Shortbread Cottage HOSTEL $
(☑ 03-546 6681; www.shortbreadcottage.co.nz; 33 Trafalgar St; dm $26, s & d $58; @ 🛜) This renovated 100-year-old villa has room for only a dozen or so beds but it's packed with charm and hospitality. It offers free internet, fresh-baked bread, and shortbread on arrival. It's also only a stone's throw from the town centre.

Tasman Bay Backpackers HOSTEL $
(☑ 03-548 7950, 0800 222 572; www.tasmanbaybackpackers.co.nz; 10 Weka St; campsites from $18, dm $26-28, d $70-85; @ 🛜) This well-designed, friendly hostel has airy communal spaces, hyper-coloured rooms, a sunny outdoor deck and a well-used hammock. Good freebies: wi-fi, bikes, breakfast during winter, and chocolate pudding and ice cream year-round.

Trampers Rest
HOSTEL $

(☑ 03-545 7477; 31 Alton St; dm/s/d $28/46/66; ⊙ closed Jun-Sep; @ 🛜) With just seven beds (no bunks), the tiny but much-loved Trampers is hard to beat for a homely environment. The enthusiastic owner is a keen tramper and cyclist, and provides comprehensive local information and free bikes. It has a small kitchen, a book exchange, and a piano for evening singalongs.

Bug Backpackers
HOSTEL $

(☑ 03-539 4227; www.thebug.co.nz; 226 Vanguard St; dm $25-28, d $66-100; @ 🛜) A well-kept hostel about 15 minutes' walk from town, occupying a converted villa, modern building next door and self-contained, well-priced unit sleeping up to five. The Bug emits *joie de vivre*, with an unashamedly bold colour scheme, quality beds, homely backyard and jovial owners. Free bikes, wi-fi and pick-ups/drop-offs.

Almond House
HOSTEL $

(☑ 03-545 6455; www.almondbackpackers.co.nz; 63 Grove St; dm/s/d $29/46/68; @ 🛜) Spread across a house and garden close to the city centre, four-bed dorms and double rooms at this hostel are decked out with colourful local art and quality linen, while the friendly vibe makes you feel like part of the family. Free internet and bikes.

Nelson YHA
HOSTEL $

(☑ 03-545 9988; www.yha.co.nz; 59 Rutherford St; dm/s/d from $33/66/87, d with bathroom $110; @ 🛜) A tidy, well-run, central hostel with high-quality communal areas including a soundproof TV room (including free DVDs), two well-organised kitchens and a sunny outdoor terrace. Excellent local knowledge for tours and activities, plus bookings.

Tahuna Beach Kiwi Holiday Park
HOLIDAY PARK $

(☑ 03-548 5159, 0800 500 501; www.tahuna-beach.co.nz; 70 Beach Rd; sites/cabins/units from $18/55/100; @ 🛜) Close to Tahuna beach, 5km from the city, this mammoth park is home to thousands in high summer, which you'll either find hellish or bloody brilliant, depending on your mood. Off season, you'll have the minigolf mostly to yourself.

Te Maunga House
B&B $$

(☑ 03-548 8605; www.nelsoncityaccommodation.co.nz; 15 Dorothy Annie Way; s $90, d $125-140; ⊙ closed May-Sep; 🛜) Aptly named ('the mountain'), this grand old family home has exceptional views. Two doubles and a single, with their own bathrooms, are filled with characterful furniture and made up with good linens. Your hearty breakfast can be walked off up and down *that* hill. It's only a 10-minute climb (15 minutes in all, from town), but only the leggy ones will revel in it.

Palazzo Motor Lodge
MOTEL $$

(☑ 0800 472 5293, 03-545 8171; www.palazzomotorlodge.co.nz; 159 Rutherford St; studios $130-225, apt $230-390; @ 🛜) Hosts with the most offer a cheerful welcome at this popular, modern, Italian-tinged motor lodge. The stylish studios and one- and two-room apartments feature enviable kitchens with decent cooking equipment, classy glassware and a dishwasher. The odd bit of dubious art is easily forgiven, particularly as Doris' sausage is available for breakfast.

Cedar Grove Motor Lodge
MOTEL $$

(☑ 0800 233 274, 03-545 1133; www.cedargrove.co.nz; cnr Trafalgar & Grove Sts; d $155-210; @ 🛜) A big old cedar landmarks this smart, mod-

---

THE WONDROUS WORLD OF WEARABLE ART

Nelson exudes creativity, so it's hardly surprising that NZ's most inspiring fashion show was born here. It began humbly in 1987 when creator Suzie Moncrieff held a local off-beat fashion show. The concept was to create a piece of art that could be worn and modelled. The idea caught on, and the World of WearableArt Awards Show became an annual event. Wood, papier mâché, paua shell, earplugs, soft-drink cans, ping-pong balls and more have been used to create garments; 'Bizarre Bra' entries are showstoppers.

The awards show has been transplanted to Wellington, but you can ogle entries at Nelson's **World of WearableArt & Classic Cars Museum** (WOW; www.wowcars.co.nz; 1 Cadillac Way; adult/child $22/8; ⊙ 10am-5pm). High-tech galleries include a carousel mimicking a catwalk, and a glow-in-the-dark room.

More car than bra? Under the same roof are around 50 mint-condition classic cars and motorbikes. Exhibits change, but may include a 1959 pink Cadillac, a yellow 1950 Bullet Nose Studebaker convertible and a BMW bubble car. You can view another 70 vehicles in *The Classic Collection* next door ($8 extra). Cafe and art gallery on site.

ern block of spacious apartments just three minutes' walk to town. Its range of studios and doubles are plush and elegant, with full cooking facilities.

★ **South Street Cottages**   RENTAL HOUSE **$$$**
(🖰 03-540 2769; www.cottageaccommodation. co.nz; South St; d from $230; 🕿) Stay on NZ's oldest preserved street in one of three elegant, two-bedroom self-contained cottages built in the 1860s. Each has all the comforts of home, including kitchen, laundry and courtyard garden; breakfast provisions supplied. There is a two-night minimum stay.

🍴 Eating

Nelson has a lively cafe scene as well as a varied array of restaurants. Self-caterers should steer resolutely towards the fruitful Nelson Market (p73) on Saturday and the **farmers market** (Morrison Sq, cnr Morrison & Hardy Sts ; ⊙11pm–4pm Wed) on Wednesday.

Falafel Gourmet   MIDDLE EASTERN **$**
(195 Hardy St; meals $8-18; ⊙9.30am-5.30pm Mon-Sat, to 8pm Fri; 🖰) A cranking joint dishing out the best kebabs for miles around. They're healthy, too!

Swedish Bakery & Café   BAKERY **$**
(www.theswedishbakery.co.nz; 54 Bridge St; snacks $2-8; ⊙8.30am-4pm Mon-Fri, 9am-2pm Sat) Delicious breads, pastries, cakes and small chocolate treats from the resident Scandinavian baker. Freshly filled rolls, bagels and croissants, too. Take your goodies away or eat in the bijou cafe.

Fish Stop   FISH & CHIPS **$**
(24 Alton St; fish & chips $5-9; ⊙11am-8pm) Five minutes' walk from the cathedral steps, this cracker chippy wraps up tasty fried treats with a smile. Small eat-in area.

Stefano's   PIZZERIA **$**
(91 Trafalgar St; pizzas $6-29; ⊙10am-late; 🖰) Located upstairs in the State Cinema complex, this Italian-run joint turns out some of NZ's best pizza. Thin, crispy and delicious, with some variations an absolute bargain. Wash it down with a beer and chase it with a creamy dessert.

Penguino Ice Cream Café   ICE CREAM **$**
(Montgomery Sq; ice creams $4-7; ⊙11am-5pm) Indulge yourself with superb gelato and sorbet, from vanilla and boysenberry to manuka honey and beyond. Next day, visit for a shake, fruit smoothie, sundae, or *stroopwafels...*

Organic Greengrocer   ORGANIC **$**
(www.organicgreengrocer.co.nz; cnr Tasman & Grove Sts; ⊙9am-5.30pm Mon-Fri, 10am-4pm Sat & Sun; 🖰) 🍃 Stocks foods for the sensitive, plus produce, organic tipples and natural bodycare. Food to go and coffee also on offer.

DeVille   CAFE **$$**
(22 New St; meals $11-20; ⊙9am-4pm Mon-Sat; 🖰) Most of DeVille's tables lie in its sweet walled courtyard, a hidden boho oasis in the inner city and the perfect place for a meal or morning tea. The food's good – from fresh baked goods to a chorizo-burrito brunch, caesar salad and sticky pork sandwich. Open late for live music Friday and Saturday in summer.

Indian Café   INDIAN **$$**
(🖰 03-548 4089; www.theindiancafe.com; 94 Collingwood St; mains $15-23; ⊙noon-2pm Mon-Fri, 5pm-late daily; 🖰) This saffron-coloured Edwardian villa houses an Indian restaurant that keeps the bhajis raised with impressive interpretations of Anglo-Indian standards, such as chicken tandoori, rogan josh and beef madras. Share the mixed platter to start, then mop up your mains with one of 10 different breads.

Ford's   MODERN NZ **$$**
(🖰 03-546 9400; www.fordsnelson.co.nz; 276 Trafalgar St; lunch $16-22; ⊙8am-late) Sunny pavement tables at the top of Trafalgar St make this a popular lunchtime spot, as does a menu of modern classics such as the excellent seafood chowder, steak sandwich and tuna niçoise. Make a short stop for coffee and a scone, or linger over dinner which leaps up a tenner or so.

★ **Hopgood's**   MODERN NZ **$$$**
(🖰 03-545 7191; www.hopgoods.co.nz; 284 Trafalgar St; mains $34-38; ⊙5.30pm-late Mon-Sat, 11.30am-2pm Fri) Tongue-and-groove-lined Hopgood's is perfect for a romantic dinner or holiday treat. The food is decadent and skilfully prepared but unfussy, allowing quality local ingredients to shine. Try Asian crispy duck, or aged beef fillet with wild mushroom gratin. Desirable, predominantly Kiwi wine list. Bookings advisable.

🍸 Drinking & Nightlife

Nelson's got a bad (read: good) case of craft-beer fever, so if your budget allows it, hoppiness awaits. Cheaper thrills can be found at numerous establishments clustered on Bridge St towards the intersection with Collingwood.

MARLBOROUGH & NELSON NELSON

IN PURSUIT OF HOPPINESS

The Nelson region lays claim to the title of craft-brewing capital of New Zealand. World-class hops have been grown here since the 1840s, and a dozen breweries are spread between Nelson and Golden Bay. One is **McCashin's** (www. mccashins.co.nz; 660 Main Rd, Stoke), a ground-breaker in the new era of craft brewing in NZ. Visit their historic cider factory for a tasting or tour.

Pick up a copy of the **Nelson Craft Beer Trail** map (available from the i-SITE and other outlets, and online at www.craftbrewingcapital.co.nz) and wind your way between brewers and pubs. Top picks for a tipple include the Free House Brewing Company, Mc-Cashins, the Moutere Inn (p80), Golden Bear (p80) and the Mussel Inn (p89).

Free House   CRAFT BEER
(www.freehouse.co.nz; 95 Collingwood St) Come rejoice at this church of ales. Tastefully converted from its original, more reverent purpose, it's now home to an excellent, oft-changing selection of NZ craft beers. You can imbibe inside, out, or even in a yurt, where there's regular live music. Hallelujah.

Sprig & Fern   CRAFT BEER
(www.sprigandfern.co.nz; 280 Hardy St) This outpost of Richmond's Sprig & Fern brewery offers 18 brews on tap, from lager through to doppelbock and berry cider. No pokies, no TV, just decent beer, occasional live music and a pleasant outdoor area. Pizzas can be ordered in. Look for a second Sprig at 143 Milton St, handy to Founders Park.

Vic   PUB
(www.vicbrewbar.co.nz; 281 Trafalgar St; noon-late) A commendable example of a Mac's Brewbar, with trademark, quirky Kiwiana fit-out, including a knitted stag's head. Quaff a handle of ale, dine on honest pub grub (mains $12 to $33) and tap a toe to regular live music, including open-mike Mondays. Good afternoon sun and people-watching from streetside seating.

⭐ Entertainment

Theatre Royal   THEATRE
(www.theatreroyalnelson.co.nz; 78 Rutherford St) State-of-the-art theatre in a charmingly re-stored heritage building. This 'grand old lady of Nelson' (aged 136) boasts a full program of local and touring drama, dance and musical productions. Check the website for what's on and book online at www.ticketdirect.co.nz, or in person at the **box office** (10am-4pm Mon-Fri, 10am-noon Sat)! Encore!

State Cinemas   CINEMA
(03-548 3885; www.statecinemas.co.nz; 91 Trafalgar St) This is the place to see mainstream, new-release flicks.

ℹ Information

Banks and ATMs pepper Trafalgar St.
After Hours & Duty Doctors (03-546 8881; 96 Waimea Rd; 8am-10pm)
Nelson Hospital (03-546 1800; www.nmdhb.govt.nz; Waimea Rd)
Nelson i-SITE (03-548 2304; www.nelsonnz.com; cnr Trafalgar & Halifax Sts; 8.30am-5pm Mon-Fri, 9am-4pm Sat & Sun) A slick centre complete with DOC information desk for the low-down on national parks and walks (including Abel Tasman and Heaphy tracks). Pick up a copy of the *Nelson Tasman Visitor Guide*.
Post Office (209 Hardy St)

ℹ Getting There & Away

AIR
Air New Zealand (0800 737 000; www.airnewzealand.co.nz) Direct flights to/from Wellington, Auckland, Christchurch and Palmerston North.

Soundsair (0800 505 005, 03-520 3080; www.soundsair.com) Flies daily between Nelson and Wellington.

BUS
Book Abel Tasman Coachlines, InterCity, KiwiRail Scenic and Interisland ferries at the **Nelson SBL Travel Centre** (03-548 1539; www.nelson-coachlines.co.nz; 27 Bridge St) or the i-SITE.

Abel Tasman Coachlines (03-548 0285; www.abeltasmantravel.co.nz) operates bus services to Motueka (one hour), Takaka (two hours), Kaiteriteri and Marahau (both two hours). These services also connect with Golden Bay Coachlines (p90) services for Takaka and around. Transport to/from the three national parks is provided by **Trek Express** (027 222 1872, 0800 128 735; www.trekexpress.co.nz).

Atomic Shuttles (03-349 0697; www.atomictravel.co.nz) runs from Nelson to Motueka (one hour), Picton (2¼ hours), Christchurch (7¾ hours) with a Greymouth connection, plus other southern destinations as far as Queenstown, Dunedin and Invercargill. Services can be booked at (and depart from) Nelson i-SITE.

InterCity (☏ 03-548 1538; www.intercity.co.nz; Bridge St, departs SLB Travel Centre) runs from Nelson to most key South Island destinations including Picton (two hours), Kaikoura (3½ hours), Christchurch (seven hours) and Greymouth (six hours).

❶ Getting Around

TO/FROM THE AIRPORT

Nelson Airport is 6km southwest of town, near Tahunanui Beach. A taxi from there to town will cost around $25, or **Super Shuttle** (☏ 0800 748 885; www.supershuttle.co.nz) offers door-to-door service for $21 (additional passengers $17).

BICYCLE

Hire a bike from Stewarts Avanti Plus Nelson or UBike (p73).

BUS

Nelson Suburban Bus Lines (SBL; ☏ 03-548 3290; www.nelsoncoachlines.co.nz; 27 Bridge St) operates NBUS, the local service between Nelson and Richmond via Tahunanui and Bishopdale until about 7pm weekdays and 4.30pm on weekends. It also runs the **Late Late Bus** (☉ hourly 10pm-3am Fri & Sat) from Nelson to Richmond via Tahunanui, departing from the Westpac Bank on Trafalgar St. Maximum fare for these services is $4.

TAXI

Nelson City Taxis (☏ 03-548 8225)
Sun City Taxis (☏ 03-548 2666)

Nelson to Motueka

From Richmond, south of Nelson, there are two routes to Motueka: the busier, more populated coastal highway (SH60) and the inland Moutere Hwy, a pleasant alternative and a nice way of making a loop. Either way, this area is generously sprinkled with attractions, so allow enough time to pull off the road. The area can be explored by bicycle on the Great Taste Trail.

There are numerous **wineries** in this area; the *Nelson Wine Guide* pamphlet (www.wineart.co.nz) will help you find them.

Art and **craft galleries** are also in the vicinity. Find these in the *Nelson Art Guide* or *Nelson's Creative Pathways* pamphlets, both available from local i-SITEs, where you can also get information on accommodation around these parts.

SH60 via Mapua

Skirting around Waimea Inlet and along the Ruby Coast, this is the quickest route from Nelson to Motueka (around 45 minutes' drive), although there are various distractions to slow you down.

Just 10km from Richmond you'll hit **Waimea** (www.waimeaestates.co.nz; SH60; ☉ 10am-6pm) winery, where a diverse range of interesting wines is available to taste. The on-site **Cellar Door** (www.thecellardoor.net.nz; mains $16-29) is a stylish conservatory cafe with vine views and a tapas-style menu.

Masterpiece glass is blown at **Höglund Glass Art** (www.hoglundartglass.com; 52 Lansdowne Rd, Appleby; ☉ 10am-5pm), where you can watch Ola the master and his colleagues working the furnace.

Just up the road is the turn-off to **Rabbit Island**, a recreation reserve offering estuary views from many angles, sandy beaches and plenty of quiet pine forest. The bridge to the island closes at sunset; overnight stays are not allowed.

Seifried (www.seifried.co.nz; cnr SH60 & Redwood Rd; ☉ 10am-5pm) winery sits at the Rabbit Island turn-off. It's one of the region's biggest,

MARLBOROUGH & NELSON NELSON TO MOTUEKA

WORTH A TRIP

GREAT TASTE TRAIL

In a stroke of genius propelled by great weather and easy topography, Nelson has developed what is destined to be one of NZ's most popular cycle trails. Why? Because no other is so frequently punctuated by stops for food, wine, craft beer and art, as it passes through a range of landscapes from rolling countryside to estuary boardwalk.

The full 175km trail is due for completion in 2016, but there's plenty of track ready for riding now, including the 69km Coastal Route from Nelson to Kaiteriteri. This can be ridden over two days (there's plenty of accommodation along the way) or you can just bite off a little chunk such as a ride to lunch. A good taster would be the 14km section from Stoke (near Nelson city) to the wineries around Brightwater.

The cycle companies on p73 can help you with bike hire and advice; see also the trail site, **Great Taste Trail** (www.heartofbiking.org.nz).

and is home to a pleasant garden restaurant and the delicious Sweet Agnes riesling.

As you reach the end of the inlet, you can either continue along SH60 or detour along the original coast road, now named the **Ruby Bay Scenic Route**. Along it lies the settlement of **Mapua** at the mouth of the Waimea River, home to arty shops and eateries including the **Smokehouse** (www. smokehouse.co.nz; Mapua Wharf; fish & chips $8-12; ⊙11am-8pm), where you can get fish and chips to eat on the wharf in the company of seagulls, as well as delicious wood-smoked fish and pâté to go. There's also delightful indoor dining at **Jellyfish** (www.jellyfishmapua. co.nz; Mapua Wharf; lunch $13-20, dinner $25-35; ✐), where fishy dishes sit amid an inspiring menu of fusion cuisine.

In the same wharfside cluster you will undoubtedly sniff out the **Golden Bear Brewing Company** (www.goldenbearbrewing.com; Mapua Wharf; meals $10-20), a microbrewery with tons of stainless steel out back and a dozen or so brews out front. Authentic Mexican food will stop you from getting a sore head. Occasional live music, takeaway beers and tours.

A few kilometres before the scenic route rejoins SH60 is **Jester House** (www.jester-house.co.nz; 320 Aporo Rd, Tasman; meals $13-23; ⊙9am-5pm). It alone is a good reason to take this detour, as much for its tame eels as for the peaceful sculpture gardens that encourage you to linger over lunch. A short, simple menu puts a few twists into staples (wild pork burger, lavender shortbread), and there is local beer and wines. It's 8km to Mapua or Motueka.

Moutere Hwy

This road traverses gently rolling countryside, dotted with farms, orchards and lifestyle blocks. Visitor attractions are fewer and far between, but it's a scenic, bucolic drive nonetheless, particularly fruitful in high summer when the berry farms are on song. Local producers and artists are listed at www.mouterartisans.co.nz.

The turn-off to the Moutere is signposted at Appleby on SH60. Not far along is the turn-off to Old Coach Rd, from where you can follow the signs to **Woollaston** (www.woollaston.co.nz; School Rd, Upper Moutere; ⊙11am-4.30pm), a flash hilltop winery complete with tasting room and contemporary art gallery. The patio is a spectacular place to enjoy a platter for lunch.

Upper Moutere is the main settlement along this route. First settled by German immigrants and originally named Sarau, today it's a sleepy hamlet with a shop, cafe and allegedly NZ's oldest pub, the **Moutere Inn** (www. mouterinn.co.nz; 1406 Moutere Hwy; meals $12-30), complete with retro, workaday interior to match. This welcoming establishment serves honest meals (pizza, burgers and fish 'n' chips) and quality, predominantly local craft beer. Pull up a pew with a beer-tasting platter, sit outside on the sunny patio, or come along at night to hear regular live music.

Continuing along the Moutere Hwy, Neudorf Rd is well signposted, leading as it does to various delectables. Call into **Neudorf Dairy** (www.neudorfdairy.co.nz; 226 Neudorf Rd; 10am-5pm Wed-Sun) for award-winning handcrafted sheeps-milk cheeses and a picnic, or **Neudorf** (www.neudorf.co.nz; 138 Neudorf Rd; ⊙10am-5pm, closed weekends May-Oct) winery for gorgeous pinot noir and some of the country's finest chardonnay.

Motueka
POP 7600

Motueka (pronounced 'mott-oo-ecka', meaning 'Island of Weka') is a bustling agricultural hub, and a great base from which to explore the region. It has all the vital amenities, ample accommodation, cafes, roadside fruit stalls, and a clean and beautiful river offering swimming and fishing. Stock up here if you're en route to Golden Bay or the Abel Tasman and Kahurangi National Parks.

⊙ Sights & Activities

While most of Mot's drawcards are out of town, there are a few attractions worth checking out, the buzziest of which is the active aerodrome, home to several air-raising activities. With a coffee cart on site, it's a good place to soak up some sun and views, and watch a few folks drop in.

While you might not realise it from the high street, Motueka is just a stone's throw from the sea. Eyeball the waters (with birds and saltwater baths) along the **estuary walkway**. Ask a local for directions or obtain a town map from the i-SITE.

To get a handle on the town, visit the i-SITE and collect the *Motueka Art Walk* pamphlet, detailing sculpture, murals and occasional peculiarities around town.

Motueka District Museum   MUSEUM
(140 High St; admission by donation; ⊙10am-4pm Mon-Fri Dec-Mar, 10am-3pm Tue-Fri Apr-Nov) An

interesting collection of regional artefacts, housed in a dear old school building.

Hop Federation
BREWERY

(☐ 03-528 0486; www.hopfederation.co.nz; 483 Main Rd, Riwaka) Pop in for tastings and take-aways (fill a flagon), or phone ahead to arrange a tour, at this teeny-weeny but ter-rific craft brewery 5km from Mot. Our pick of the ales is the hoppy, sessionable pale ale, ideal for a summer's day.

Skydive Abel Tasman
SKYDIVING

(☐ 03-528 4091, 0800 422 899; www.skydive. co.nz; Motueka Aerodrome, College St; jumps 13,000/16,500ft $299/399) Move over Taupo: we've jumped both and think Mot takes the cake (presumably so do the many sports jumpers who favour this drop zone, some of whom you may see rocketing in). DVDs and photos cost extra, but pick-up/drop-off from Motueka and Nelson are free.

Tasman Sky Adventures
SCENIC FLIGHTS

(☐ 027 229 9693, 0800 114 386; www.skyadven-tures.co.nz; Motueka Aerodrome, 60 College St; 30min flight $205) A rare opportunity to fly in a microlight. Keep your eyes open and blow your mind on a scenic flight above Abel Tasman National Park. Wow. And there's tandem hang gliding for the brave (15/30 minutes, 2500/5280ft $195/275).

Motueka

U-fly Extreme
AEROBATICS

(☐ 03-528 8290, 0800 360 180; www.uflyextreme. co.nz; Motueka Aerodrome, College St; 15/20min $345/445) You handle the controls in an open-cockpit Pitts Special stunt biplane. No experience necessary, just a stomach for loop the loops and barrel rolls. Roger wilco!

🛏 Sleeping

Be warned: Mot's population doubles in summer. The i-SITE (p83) can help you squeeze in somewhere if you get stuck.

★ Motueka Top 10 Holiday Park
HOLIDAY PARK $

(☐ 03-528 7189, 0800 668 835; www.motu-ekatop10.co.nz; 10 Fearon St; campsites from $40, cabins $55-130, units $99-350; @ 🛜 🏊) 🚲 A holiday park packed with plenty of grassy, green charm. Love those lofty kahikatea trees! Amenities are plentiful and shipshape including the family-friendly swimming pool and jumping pillow. Quality accommo-dation from tidy cabins through to a deluxe family unit sleeping up to 11. Local wine and bike tours by arrangement.

Eden's Edge Lodge
HOSTEL $

(☐ 03-528 4242; www.edensedge.co.nz; 137 Lod-der Lane, Riwaka; campsites from $17, dm $28, d with/without bathroom $82/76; @ 🛜 🏊) Sur-rounded by orchards, 4km from Motueka, this purpose-built lodge comes pretty close to backpacker heaven. Well-designed facilities include a gleaming kitchen and inviting communal areas. There's a rainwater pool in summer and bikes for hire, and it's all within walking distance of beer, ice cream and coffee.

Hat Trick Lodge
HOSTEL $

(📞 03-528 5353; www.hattricklodge.co.nz; 25 Wallace St; d with/without bathroom $70/62; @🛜) A purpose-built lodge right in the middle of town. What it lacks in personality it makes up for in cleanliness, boasting ample off-street parking, a friendly tourist-oriented atmosphere and sunny balconies.

Laughing Kiwi
HOSTEL $

(📞 03-528 9229; www.laughingkiwi.co.nz; 310 High St; dm $28, d with/without bathroom $74/66; 🛜) Compact, low-key YHA hostel with rooms spread between an old villa and a purpose-built backpacker lodge with a smart kitchen/lounge. The self-contained bach is a good option for groups (double $130).

Equestrian Lodge Motel
MOTEL $$

(📞 03-528 9369, 0800 668 782; www.equestrianlodge.co.nz; Avalon Ct; d $120-156, q $165-220; @🛜) No horses, no lodge, but no matter. This motel complex is close to town (off Tudor St), with expansive lawns, rose gardens, and a heated pool and spa. Rooms are plainly dressed but immaculate, and many have ovens. Cheerful owners will hook you up with local activities.

Nautilus Lodge
MOTEL $$

(📞 03-528 4658, 0800 628 845; www.nautiluslodge.co.nz; 67 High St; d $162-225; @🛜) A top-notch motel complex with 12 units decorated in neutral tones with low-profile furniture including European slatted beds. There are classy bathrooms and cooking facilities in all units, spa baths in some, Sky TV, and balconies and patios that collect afternoon sun.

Avalon Manor Motel
MOTEL $$

(📞 03-528 8320, 0800 282 566; www.avalonmotels.co.nz; 314 High St; d $150-215; 🛜) Prominent L-shaped motel with spacious rooms, five minutes' walk from the town centre. All rooms have a contemporary vibe, with cooking facilities, while the sumptuous studios have king-size beds and large flat-screen TVs. There's also a guest barbecue, laundry and views of Mt Arthur.

Resurgence
LODGE, CHALETS $$$

(📞 03-528 4664; www.resurgence.co.nz; Riwaka Valley Rd; d lodge from $625, chalets from $525; @🛜🌊) 🥂 Choose a luxurious en suite lodge room or self-contained chalet at this magical green retreat 15 minutes' drive south of Abel Tasman National Park, and 30 minutes' walk from the picturesque source of the Riwaka River. Lodge rates include aperitifs and a four-course dinner, as well as breakfast; chalet rates are for B&B, with dinner an extra $100.

🍴 Eating & Drinking

Patisserie Royale
BAKERY $

(152 High St; baked goods $2-8; ⏰6am-4.30pm Mon-Sat, 6am-2pm Sun) The best of several Mot bakeries and worth every delectable calorie. Lots of French fancies and darn good pies.

Up the Garden Path
CAFE $$

(www.upthegardenpath.co.nz; 473 High St; meals $15-24; ⏰9am-4pm; 🚗) Perfect for lunch or a coffee break, this licensed cafe-gallery kicks back in an 1890s house amid idyllic gardens. Unleash the kids in the playroom and linger over your blueberry pancakes, chicken burger, lamb souvlaki, pasta or lemon tart. Vegetarian, gluten- and dairy-free options available.

Simply Indian
INDIAN $$

(130 High St; mains $16-24; ⏰11am-10pm Mon-Sat, 5-10pm Sun; 🚗) As the name suggests: no-nonsense curry in a no-frills setting. The food, however, is consistently good and relatively cheap. Expect the usual suspects such as tikka, tandoori, madras and vindaloo, and the ubiquitous naan prepared eight different ways. Takeaways available.

Sprig & Fern
CRAFT BEER

(www.sprigandfern.co.nz; Wallace St; meals $14-19; ⏰2pm-late) A member of the Sprig & Fern family of taverns, this back-street tavern ups the ante among Motueka's drinking holes. Small but pleasant, it offers 20 hand-pulled brews, simple food (burgers, pizza, platters) and occasional live music.

☆ Entertainment

Gecko Theatre
CINEMA

(www.geckotheatre.co.nz; 23b Wallace St; tickets $9-13) Pull up an easy chair at this wee, independent theatre for interesting art-house flicks.

🛍 Shopping

Motueka Sunday Market
MARKET

(Wallace St; ⏰8am-1pm) On Sunday the car park behind the i-SITE fills up with trestle tables for the Motueka Sunday Market:

produce, jewellery, buskers, arts, crafts and Doris' divine bratwurst.

ℹ Information

Motueka i-SITE (📞03-528 6543; www.motuekaisite.co.nz; 20 Wallace St; ⏰8.30am-5pm Mon-Fri, 9am-4pm Sat & Sun) An excellent centre with helpful staff who handle bookings from Kaitaia to Bluff and provide local national-park expertise and necessaries.

Take Note/Post Office (207 High St) Bookshop moonlighting as a post office.

ℹ Getting There & Away

Bus services depart from Motueka i-SITE.

Abel Tasman Coachlines (📞03-528 8850; www.abeltasmantravel.co.nz) Runs daily from Motueka to Nelson (one hour), Kaiteriteri (25 minutes) and Marahau (30 minutes). These services connect with Golden Bay Coachline services to Takaka (1¼ hours) and other Golden Bay destinations including Totaranui in Abel Tasman National Park, Collingwood, and on to the Heaphy Track trailhead. Note that from May to September all buses run less frequently.

Atomic Shuttles (📞03-349 0697, 0508 108 359; www.atomictravel.co.nz) Run from Motueka to Nelson, connecting with further services via Christchurch over to Greymouth and down to Queenstown and Dunedin.

Motueka to Abel Tasman

Kaiteriteri

Known simply as 'Kaiteri', this seaside hamlet 13km from Motueka is the most popular resort town in the area. During the summer holidays its gorgeous, golden, safe-swimming beach feels more like Noumea than NZ, with more towels than sand. The beach is also a major departure point for Abel Tasman National Park transport, although Marahau is the main base. The village is also home to **Kaiteriteri Mountain Bike Park** (www.kaiteriterimtbpark.org.nz) with tracks to suit all levels of rider.

🛏 Sleeping & Eating

Kaiteriteri Beach Motor Camp HOLIDAY PARK $ (📞03-527 8010; www.kaiteriteribeach.co.nz; Sandy Bay Rd; campsites from $19, cabins $45-85; @🛜) A gargantuan park in pole position across from the beach. It's hugely popular, so book in advance. The on-site general store is very well stocked, as is the ice-cream hatch where a queue often forms.

Kaiteri Lodge LODGE $ (📞03-527 8281; www.kaiterilodge.co.nz; Inlet Rd; dm $30-35, d $80-160; @🛜) Modern, purpose-built lodge with small, simple dorms and en suite doubles. The nautical decor adds some cheer to somewhat lazily maintained communal areas. The sociable on-site **Beached Whale** (dinner $18-28; ⏰4pm-late) bar serves wood-fired pizza, steak, and the like, while the host busts out a few tunes on his guitar. The Whale will be open when the big bus pulls in.

Torlesse Coastal Motels MOTELS $$ (📞03-527 8063; www.torlessemotels.co.nz; 8 Kotare Pl, Little Kaiteriteri Beach; d $130-180, q & f $180-280; 🛜) Just 200m from Little Kaiteriteri Beach (around the corner from the main beach) is this congregation of roomy hillside units with pitched ceilings, full kitchens and laundries. Most have water views, and there's a barbecue deck and spa.

Bellbird Lodge B&B $$$ (📞03-527 8555; www.bellbirdlodge.co.nz; Kaiteriteri-Sandy Bay Rd; d $275-350; @🛜) An upmarket B&B 1.5km up the hill from Kaiteri Beach, offering two en suite rooms, bush and sea views, extensive gardens, spectacular breakfasts (featuring homemade muesli and fruit compote), and gracious hosts. Dinner by arrangement in winter, when local restaurant hours are irregular.

Shoreline RESTAURANT $$ (www.shorelinekaiteriteri.co.nz; cnr Inlet & Sandy Bay Rds; meals $15-24; ⏰8am-9pm, reduced hours Apr-Nov) A modern, beige cafe-bar-restaurant right on the beach. Punters chill out on the sunny deck, lingering over sandwiches, pizzas, burgers and other predictable fare, or pop in for coffee and cake. Erratic winter hours; burger booth out the back.

ℹ Getting There & Away

Kaiteriteri is serviced by Abel Tasman Coachlines (p87).

Marahau

POP 200

Further along the coast from Kaiteriteri and 18km north of Motueka, Marahau is the main gateway to Abel Tasman National Park. It's less of a town, more like a procession of holiday homes and tourist businesses.

If you're in an equine state of mind, **Pegasus Park** (📞03-526 8050; www.pegasuspark.co.nz) and **Marahau Horse Treks** (📞03-527 8425), both along Marahau–Sandy Bay

MARLBOROUGH & NELSON MOTUEKA TO ABEL TASMAN

Rd, offer the chance to belt along the beach on a horse, your hair streaming behind you (children's pony rides $35, two-hour rides $90).

🛏 Sleeping & Eating

Barn   HOSTEL $
(☑03-527 8043; www.barn.co.nz; 14 Harvey Rd; unpowered/powered sites per person $14/16, dm $28, d $55-70; @🛜) This backpackers has hit its straps with comfortable new dorms, a fresh toilet block and grassy camping field added to a mix of micro-cabins, alfresco kitchens and barbecue areas. The barn itself is the hub – a communal kitchen and lounge area good for socialising, as is the central deck which has a fireplace. Activity bookings and secure parking available.

Kanuka Ridge   HOSTEL $
(☑03-527 8435; www.abeltasmanbackpackers.co. nz; Moss Rd, off Marahau-Sandy Bay Rd; dm $29, d & tw with/without bathroom $89/64; 🛜) Five minutes' drive from Marahau, this purpose-built cottage arrangement is ringed by forest, offering birdy, bushy surroundings for a bit of peace and quiet. Active hosts are willing and able to hook you up with activities inside and outside of the national park. Secure car parking available.

Ocean View Chalets   CHALET $$
(☑03-527 8232; www.accommodationabeltasman. co.nz; 305 Sandy Bay-Marahau Rd; d $145-235, q $290; 🛜) Positioned on a leafy hillside affording plenty of privacy, these cheerful, cypress-lined chalets are 300m from the Abel Tasman Track with views across Tasman Bay to Fisherman Island. All are self-contained; breakfast and packed lunches available.

Abel Tasman Marahau Lodge   MOTEL $$
(☑03-527 8250; www.abeltasmanmarahaulodge. co.nz; Sandy Bay-Marahau Rd; d $135-255; @🛜) 🏊 Enjoy halcyon days in this arc of 12 lovely studios and self-contained units with cathedral ceilings, opening out on to landscaped gardens with lush lawns. There's also a fully equipped communal kitchen for self-caterers, plus spa and sauna. Cuckoos, tui and bellbirds squawk and warble in the bushy surrounds.

★ Fat Tui   BURGERS $
(cnr Marahau-Sandy Bay & Marahau Valley Rds; burgers $13-16; ⊙noon-8.30pm daily summer, Wed-Sun winter; ☑) Everyone's heard about this bird, based in a caravan that ain't rollin' anywhere fast. Thank goodness. Superlative burgers, such as the Cowpat (beef), the Ewe Beaut (lamb) and the Sparrow's Fart breakfast burger. Fish and chips, and coffee, too.

Park Cafe   CAFE $$
(www.parkcafe.co.nz; Harvey Rd; lunch $9-22, dinner $16-30; ⊙8am-late mid-Sep–May; ☑) Sitting at the Abel Tasman Track trailhead, this breezy cafe is perfectly placed for fuelling up or restoring the waistline. High-calorie options include the big breakfast, pizzas, burgers and cakes, but there are also seafood and salad options. Enjoy in the room with a view or in the sunny courtyard garden. Live music on occasion.

Hooked on Marahau   CAFE $$
(☑03-527 8576; Marahau-Sandy Bay Rd; lunch $15-19, dinner $24-29; ⊙hours vary) This popular place certainly reels them in, so reservations are advisable for dinner. The art-bedecked interior opens onto an outdoor terrace with distracting views. Lunch centres on salads, chowder and wraps, while the dinner menu boasts fresh fish of the day, green-lipped mussels and NZ lamb shanks.

ℹ Getting There & Away

Marahau is serviced by Abel Tasman Coachlines (p87).

Abel Tasman National Park

Coastal Abel Tasman National Park blankets the northern end of a range of marble and limestone hills that extend from Kahurangi National Park. Various tracks in the park include an inland route, although the coast track is what everyone is here for – it's NZ's most popular Great Walk.

Abel Tasman Coast Track

This is arguably NZ's most beautiful Great Walk – 51km of sparkling seas, golden sand, quintessential coastal forest, and hidden surprises such as Cleopatra's Pool. Such pulling power attracts nearly 30,000 overnight trampers and kayakers per year, who all stay at least one night in the park. A major attraction is the terrain: well cut, well graded and well marked. It's almost impossible to get lost and can be tramped in sneakers.

You will, however, probably get your feet wet, as this track features long stretches of beach and crazy tides. In fact the tidal differences in the park are among the greatest in

Abel Tasman National Park

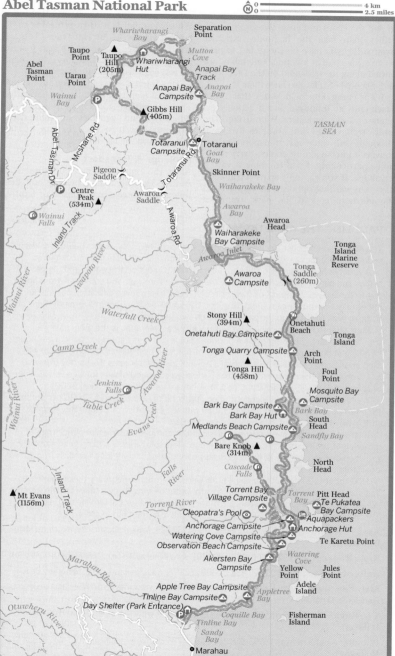

the country, up to a staggering 6m. At Torrent and Bark Bays, it's much easier and more fun to doff the shoes and cross the soggy sands, rather than take the high-tide track. At Awaroa Bay you have no choice but to plan on crossing close at low tide. Tide tables are posted along the track and on the DOC website; regional i-SITEs also have them.

It's a commonly held belief that Coast Track ends at Totaranui, but it actually extends to a car park near Wainui Bay. The entire tramp takes only three to five days, although with water taxi transport you can convert it into an almost endless array of options, particularly if you combine it with a kayak leg. If you can only spare a couple of days, a rewarding option is to loop around the northern end of the park, tramping the Coast Track from Totaranui, passing Anapai and Mutton Cove, overnighting at Whariwharangi Hut, then returning to Totaranui via the Gibbs Hill Track. This will give you a slice of the park's best features (beaches, seals, coastal scenery) while being far less crowded than other segments.

This track is so well trodden that a topographical map isn't essential for navigation. The map within DOC's *Abel Tasman Coast Track* brochure provides sufficient detail. However, NewTopo *Abel Tasman* 1:55,000 will give you the lay of the land.

Bookings & Transport

Along the Coast Track are four Great Walk huts ($32) with bunks, heating and flush toilets but no cooking facilities or lighting.

PADDLING THE ABEL TASMAN

The Abel Tasman Coast Track has long been trampers' territory, but its beauty makes it seductive spot for sea kayaking, which can be combined with walking and camping.

A variety of professional outfits are able to float you out on the water, and the possibilities and permutations for guided or freedom trips are vast. You can kayak from half a day to three days, camping, or staying in DOC huts, bachs, even a floating backpackers, either fully catered for or self-catering. You can kayak one day, camp overnight then walk back, or walk further into the park and catch a water taxi back.

Most operators offer similar trips at similar prices. Marahau is the main base, but trips also depart from Kaiteriteri. A popular choice if time is tight is to spend a few hours kayaking in the Tonga Island Marine Reserve, followed by a walk from Tonga Quarry to Medlands Beach. This will cost around $195 including water taxis. Three-day trips usually drop you at the northern end of the park, then you paddle back (or vice versa); they cost from around $620 including food. One-day guided trips are around $200.

Freedom rentals (double-kayak and equipment hire) are around $70/110 per person for one/two days; all depart from Marahau with the exception of Golden Bay Kayaks (p90), which is based at Tata Beach in Golden Bay.

Instruction is given to everyone, and most tour companies have a minimum age of either eight or 14 depending on the trip. None allow solo hires. Camping gear is usually provided on overnight trips; if you're disappearing into the park for a few days, most operators provide free car parking.

November to Easter is the busiest time, with December to February the absolute peak. You can, however, paddle all year round, with winter offering its own rewards. The weather is surprisingly amenable, the seals are more playful, there's more bird life and less haze.

Following are the main players in this competitive market (shop around):

Abel Tasman Kayaks (☑ 03-527 8022, 0800 732 529; www.abeltasmankayaks.co.nz; Main Rd, Marahau)

Kahu Kayaks (☑ 03-527 8300, 0800 300 101; www.kahukayaks.co.nz; cnr Marahau Valley Rd)

Kaiteriteri Kayaks (☑ 03-527 8383, 0800 252 925; www.seakayak.co.nz; Kaiteriteri Beach)

Marahau Sea Kayaks (☑ 03-527 8176, 0800 529 257; www.msk.co.nz; Abel Tasman Centre, Franklin St, Marahau)

Sea Kayak Company (☑ 03-528 7251, 0508 252 925; www.seakayaknz.co.nz; 506 High St, Motueka)

Wilsons Abel Tasman (☑ 03-528 2027, 0800 223 582; www.abeltasman.co.nz; 25 High St, Motueka)

There are also 19 designated **Great Walk campsites** ($14). As the Abel Tasman Track is a Great Walk, all huts and campsites must be booked in advance year-round, either online through **Great Walks Bookings** (☑0800 694 732; www.greatwalks.co.nz) or at DOC visitor centres, nationwide. Hut tickets and annual passes cannot be used on the track, and there is a two-night limit on staying in each hut or campsite, except for Totaranui campsite which has a one-night limit. Penalty fees apply to those who do not have a valid booking, and you may be required to leave the park.

Moored permanently in Anchorage Bay, **Aquapackers** (☑0800 430 744; www.aquapackers.co.nz; dm/d incl breakfast $75/195) is a converted 13m catamaran providing unusual but buoyant backpacker accommodation. Facilities are basic but decent; prices include bedding, dinner and breakfast. Bookings are essential. **Totaranui Campsite** (☑03-528 8083; www.doc.govt.nz; summer/winter $15/10) is an extremely popular facility with a whopping capacity (850 campers) and a splendid setting next to the beach backed by some of the best bush in the park. A staffed DOC office has interpretive displays, flush toilets, cold showers and a public phone.

The closest big town to Abel Tasman is Motueka, with nearby Marahau the southern gateway. Although Wainui is the official northern trailhead, it is more common to finish in Totaranui, either skipping the northernmost section or looping back to Totaranui over Gibbs Hill Track. All gateways are serviced between **Abel Tasman Coachlines** (☑03-548 0285; www.abeltasmantravel.co.nz) and **Golden Bay Coachlines** (☑03-525 8352; www.gbcoachlines.co.nz).

Once you hit the park, it is easy to get to/from any point on the track by water taxi, from Kaiteriteri or Marahau. Typical one-way prices from either: Anchorage and Torrent Bay ($33), Bark Bay ($38), Tonga ($40), Awaroa ($43) and Totaranui ($45). The following are key operators:

Abel Tasman Sea Shuttle BOAT
(☑03-527 8688, 0800 732 748; www.abeltasmanseashuttles. co.nz; Kaiteriteri) Scheduled services with cruise/walk options. Also runs between Nelson and Kaiteriteri from 1 December to 31 March (adult/child return $40/20).

Abel Tasman Aqua Taxi BOAT
(☑03-527 8083, 0800 278 282; www.aquataxi.co.nz; Marahau-Sandy Bay Rd, Marahau) Scheduled and on-demand services as well as boat/walk options.

Wilsons Abel Tasman BOAT
(☑03-528 2027, 0800 223 582; www.abeltasman.co.nz; 265 High St, Motueka; pass adult/child $150/75) Offers an explorer pass for unlimited taxi travel on three days over a five-day period, plus backpacker specials and an array of tours.

Marahau Water Taxis BOAT
(☑03-527 8176, 0800 808 018; Abel Tasman Centre, Franklin St, Marahau) Scheduled services plus boat/walk options.

👉 Tours

Tour companies usually offer free Motueka pick-up/drop-off, with Nelson pick-up available at extra cost.

Abel Tasman Sailing Adventures SAILING
(☑03-527 8375, 0800 467 245; www.sailingadventures.co.nz; Kaiteriteri; day trip $179) Scheduled and on-demand catamaran trips, with sail/walk/kayak combos available. The popular day trip includes lunch on Anchorage Beach.

Abel Tasman Tours & Guided Walks GUIDED HIKE
(☑03-528 9602; www.abeltasmantours.co.nz; from $220) Small-group, day-long walking tours (minimum two people) that include packed lunch and water taxis.

Wilsons Abel Tasman WALKING, KAYAKING
(☑03-528 2027, 0800 223 582; www.abeltasman.co.nz; 265 High St, Motueka; half-day cruise $78, cruise & walk $60-78, kayak & walk $80-195) Impressive array of cruises, walking, kayaking and combo tours, including a $35 backpacker day-walk and a barbecue cruise (great winter option). Luxurious beachfront lodges at Awaroa and Torrent Bay for guided-tour guests.

Abel Tasman Canyons CANYONING
(☑03-528 9800, 0800 863 472; www.abeltasmancanyons.co.nz; full-day trip $250) Few Abel Tasman visitors explore the beautiful Torrent River. Here's your chance to journey down its staggeringly beautiful granite-lined canyon, via a fun-filled combination of swimming, sliding, abseiling and big leaps into jewel-like pools.

Golden Bay

Motueka to Takaka

From Motueka, SH60 takes a stomach-churning meander over Takaka Hill. On the way it passes dramatic lookouts over Tasman Bay and Abel Tasman National Park before swooping down towards Takaka and Collingwood. The best way to tackle this region is with your own wheels.

Takaka Hill (791m) butts in between Tasman Bay and Golden Bay. Just below the summit (literally) are the **Ngarua Caves** (SH60; adult/child $15/7; ⏱45min tours hourly 10am-4pm Sep-May, open Sat & Sun only Jun-Aug), a rock-solid attraction karst in stone, where you can see myriad subterranean delights including moa bones. Access is restricted to tours – you can't go solo spelunking.

Also just before the summit is the turn-off to **Canaan Downs Scenic Reserve**, reached at the end of an 11km gravel road. This area stars in both the *Lord of the Rings* and *Hobbit* movies, but **Harwood's Hole** is the most famous feature here. It's one of the largest *tomo* (caves) in the country at 357m deep and 70m wide, with a 176m vertical drop. It's a 30-minute walk from the car park. Allow us to state the obvious: the cave is off-limits to all but the most experienced cavers. Mountain bikers with intermediate-level skills can venture along a couple of new loop tracks, or head all the way down to Takaka via the famous **Rameka Track**. There's a basic **DOC Campsite** (per person $6) here too.

Close to the zenith also lies the **Takaka Hill Walkway**, a three-hour loop walk through marble karst rock formations, native forest and farmland, and **Harwood Lookout**, affording fine views down the Takaka River Valley to Takaka and Golden Bay. For more walks on the sunny side of the hill, see DOC's brochure *Walks in Golden Bay*.

Takaka & Around

Boasting NZ's highest concentration of yoga pants, dreadlocks and alternative life-stylers, Takaka (population 1240) is nevertheless a largely down-to-earth town and the last 'big' centre before the road west ends at Farewell Spit. You'll find most things you need here, and a few things you don't, but we all have an unworn tie-dye tanktop in our wardrobe, don't we?

◉ Sights & Activities

Many of Takaka's sights can readily be reached via bicycle, with hire and maps available from the time-warped **Quiet Revolution Cycle Shop** (☑03-525 9555; www.quiet-revolution.co.nz; 11 Commercial St; bike hire per day $25-65) on the main street.

Te Waikoropupu Springs   SPRING
'Pupu Springs' are the largest freshwater springs in Australasia and reputedly the clearest in the world. About 14,000 litres of water per second surges from underground vents, creating 'dancing sands' and swirling curious plantlife throughout colourful pools, which are viewed from a network of tracks and are off-limits for swimming. From Takaka, head 4km northwest on SH60 and follow the signs inland for 3km from Waitapu Bridge.

Grove Scenic Reserve   LOOKOUT
Around 10 minutes' drive from Takaka (signposted down Clifton Rd) you will find this crazy limestone maze punctuated by gnarled old rata trees. The walkway takes around 10 minutes and passes an impressive lookout.

Rawhiti Cave   CAVE
(www.doc.govt.nz) The ultimate in geological eye candy around these parts are the phytokarst features of Rawhiti Cave, 15 minutes' drive from Takaka (reached via Motupipi, turning right into Glenview Rd, then left into Packard Rd and following the signs). The rugged two-hour-return walk (steep in places; dangerous in the wet) may well leave you speechless (although we managed 'monster', 'fangs', and even 'Sarlacc').

Golden Bay Museum & Gallery   MUSEUM
(Commercial St; admission by donation; ⏱10am-4pm) This small museum's standout exhibits include a diorama depicting Abel Tasman's 1642 landing, and some dubious human taxidermy. Ask about the albatross. The adjoining gallery offers satisfying browsing of local and national knick-knackery and quite possibly the purchase of a quality souvenir. For additional arty ambling, look for the free *Artists in Golden Bay* and *Arts Trail* pamphlets.

Pupu Hydro Walkway   WALKING
This enjoyable two-hour circuit passes through beech forest, past engineering and gold-mining relics to the restored (and operational) Pupu Hydro Powerhouse, built in 1929. To get here, take the 4km gravel road signposted from Pupu Springs Rd.

Adventure Flights Golden Bay
SCENIC FLIGHTS

(☑ 03-525 6167, 0800 150 338; www.adventure-flightsgoldenbay.co.nz; Takaka Airfield) Scenic and charter flights around Golden Bay and surrounds; from $40.

Golden Bay Air
SCENIC FLIGHTS

(☑ 03-525 8725, 0800 588 885; www.goldenbayair.co.nz; Takaka Airfield) Scenic and charter flights around Golden Bay and surrounds; from $49.

🛏 Sleeping

Kiwiana
HOSTEL $

(☑ 03-525 7676, 0800 805 494; www.kiwianaback-packers.co.nz; 73 Motupipi St; tent sites per person $18, dm/s/d $28/45/66; @ ⛾) Beyond the welcoming garden is a cute cottage where rooms are named after classic Kiwiana (the jandal, Buzzy Bee...). The garage has been converted into a convivial lounge, with wood-fired stove, table tennis, pool table, music, books and games; free bikes for guest use.

Annie's Nirvana Lodge
HOSTEL $

(☑ 03-525 8766; www.nirvanalodge.co.nz; 25 Motupipi St; dm $28, d $60-66; @ ⛾) Tidy, homely YHA hostel: dorms in the main house, and four doubles at the bottom of the secluded courtyard garden, which is filled with timber furniture hewn by the friendly owner. Fluffy the cat is hanging in there and is a hirsute hit with guests.

Golden Bay Holiday Park
HOLIDAY PARK $

(☑ 03-525 9742; www.goldenbayholidaypark.co.nz; Tukurua Rd; unpowered/powered sites $41/45, cabins d/tr $70/105; @ ⛾) Eighteen kilometres north of Takaka with an unpopulated beach right out front, this gem of a park has acres of grass, graceful shade trees and hedgerows, easily atoning for tight communal facilities. There are tidy, family-friendly cabins for budget travellers, and luxury beach houses sleeping up to four ($270 to $350).

Golden Bay Motel
MOTEL $$

(☑ 03-525 9428, 0800 401 212; www.goldenbay-motel.co.nz; 132 Commercial St; d $100-145; ⛾) It's golden, alright: check out the paint job. Clean, spacious, self-contained units with decent older-style fixtures and decent older-style hosts. The rear patios overlook a lush green garden.

Adrift
COTTAGES $$$

(☑ 03-525 8353; www.adrift.co.nz; Tukurua Rd; d $250-500; @ ⛾) ⬤ Adrift on a heavenly bed of beachside bliss is what you'll be in one of these five cottages dotted within beautifully landscaped grounds, right on the beach. Tuck into your breakfast hamper, then self-cater in the fully equipped kitchen, dine on the sunny deck, or soak in the spa bath.

🍴 Eating & Drinking

Top Shop
DAIRY $

(9 Willow St; snacks $2-9; ⏱ 6am-7pm Mon-Fri, 7.30am-6pm Sat & Sun) A dairy, tearoom and takeaway at the entrance to town with high-rating pies.

Fresh Choice
SUPERMARKET $

(13 Willow St; ⏱ 8am-7pm) Stock up while you can.

Dangerous Kitchen
CAFE $$

(46a Commercial St; meals $14-28; ⏱ 9am-late Mon-Sat; ⬤) ⬤ Dedicated to Frank Zappa ('In the kitchen of danger, you can feel like a stranger'), DK serves largely healthy, good-value fare such as felafel, pizza, spicy-bean burritos, fresh pasta, great baking and juices. Mellow and laid-back, with a sun-trap courtyard out back and people-watching out front.

★ Mussel Inn
PUB $$

(www.mussellinn.co.nz; 1259 SH60, Onekaka; all-day menu $5-18, dinner $23-30; ⏱ 11am-late, closed Jul-Aug) You will find one of NZ's most beloved brewery-taverns halfway between Takaka and Collingwood. The Mussel Inn is rustic NZ at its most genuine, complete with creaking timbers, a rambling beer garden with a brazier, live music, and hearty, homemade food. Sup a handle or two of 'Captain Cooker', a brown beer brewed naturally with manuka, or the delicious 'Bitter Ass'.

Brigand
CAFE, BAR $$

(www.brigand.co.nz; 90 Commercial St; meals $16-35; ⏱ 11am-late Mon-Sat) Beyond the gates you'll find good food such as sandwiches, chowder and meaty mains served in a relaxed atmosphere. A garden bar and great baking feature, too. Equally important, the Brigand is a mainstay of the local entertainment scene with regular live music, and popular shake-a-leg open mike Thursdays.

Roots Bar
BAR

(www.rootsbar.co.nz; 1 Commercial St; ⏱ 4.30pm-late Wed-Sun; ⛾) This popular dance-music-focused joint has decent beer on tap, a quality sound system, lively evenings, and a garden bar with the odd tree root and bedecked Bay resident lending colour.

Paul's Coffee Cart   CAFE
(Takaka Library car park; ⊗ 8am-1pm Mon-Sat) The dude with the tunes does the best brew in town from his cart tucked into the library car park.

☆ Entertainment

Village Theatre   CINEMA
(www.villagetheatre.org.nz; 32 Commercial St; adult/child $12.50/7) Demonstrating, yet again, provincial NZ's appetite for quality movies.

ⓘ Information

DOC Office (✆ 03-525 8026; www.doc.govt.nz; 62 Commercial St; ⊗ 1-3pm Mon-Fri) Information on Abel Tasman and Kahurangi National Parks, the Heaphy Track, Farewell Spit and Cobb Valley. Sells hut passes.

Golden Bay Visitor Centre (✆ 03-525 9136; www.goldenbaynz.co.nz; Willow St; ⊗ 10am-4pm Mon-Fri, to 2pm Sat & Sun) A friendly little centre with all the necessary information, including the indispensible official tourist map. Bookings and DOC passes.

ⓘ Getting There & Around

Golden Bay Air (✆ 0800 588 885, 03-525 8725; www.goldenbayair.co.nz) Flies at least once and up to four times daily between Wellington and Takaka.

Golden Bay Coachlines (✆ 03-525 8352; www.gbcoachlines.co.nz) Departs from Takaka on Golden Bay and runs through to Collingwood (25 minutes), the Heaphy Track (one hour), Totaranui (one hour), and over the hill to Motueka (1¼ hours) and Nelson (2¼ hours).

Pohara

POP 350

About 10km northeast of Takaka is pint-sized Pohara, a beachy village with a population that quadruples over summer. It has more flash holiday homes than other parts of Golden Bay, but an agreeable air persists nonetheless, aided by decent food and lodging, and a beach that at low tide is as big as Heathrow's runway. Look out for **Golden Bay Blokarts** (778 Abel Tasman Dr).

Pohara lies close to the northern gateway of Abel Tasman National Park. The largely unsealed road into the park passes **Tarakohe Harbour** (Pohara's working port), followed by **Ligar Bay**. It's worth climbing to the Abel Tasman lookout as you pass by.

The next settlement along is **Tata Beach**, where **Golden Bay Kayaks** (✆ 03-525 9095; www.goldenbaykayaks.co.nz; half-day guided tours adult/child $85/35, freedom hire half-/full day $90/110) offers freedom rental of kayaks and stand-up paddle boards, as well as guided trips (including multiday) into Abel Tasman National Park.

Signposted from the Totaranui Rd at **Wainui Bay** is a leafy walk to the best cascade in the bay: **Wainui Falls**. It's a one-hour return trip, but you could easily take longer by dipping a toe or two in the river.

🛏 Sleeping & Eating

Pohara Beach Top 10 Holiday Park   HOLIDAY PARK $
(✆ 03-525 9500, 0800 764 272; www.poharabeach.com; 809 Abel Tasman Dr; campsites from $20, cabins & units $61-164; @ 🗣) Wow, what a big 'un! On a long grassy strip between the dunes and the main road, this place has a primo location – but in summer it can feel more like a suburb than the seaside. Beaut cabins abound. General store and takeaway on site.

Sans Souci Inn   LODGE, RESTAURANT $$
(✆ 03-525 8663; www.sanssouciinn.co.nz; 11 Richmond Rd; s/d $90/115, self-contained unit from $160, mains $32-35; ⊗ closed Jul–mid-Sep; 🗣) 🖉 Sans Souci means 'no worries' in French, and this will be your mantra too after staying in one of the seven Mediterranean-flavoured, mud-brick rooms. Guests share a plant-filled, mosaic bathroom that has composting toilets, and an airy lounge and kitchen opening out onto the semi-tropical courtyard. Dinner in the on-site restaurant (bookings essential) is highly recommended; breakfast by request.

Ratanui   LODGE $$
(✆ 03-525 7998; www.ratanuilodge.com; 818 Abel Tasman Dr; d $155-269; @ 🗣 ☳) This boutique lodge is a contender for NZ's most romantic, with Victorian grandeur inside, and colourful cottage garden out the front. In addition to elegant rooms, there are myriad sensual stimulators such as swimming pool, massage service, cocktails and a candelabra-lit restaurant (open to the public; bookings required). Free bikes, too.

Penguin Café & Bar   PUB $$
(www.penguincafe.co.nz; 818 Abel Tasman Dr; lunch $13-22, dinner $20-33; ⊗ 10am-late Nov-Apr, 4pm-late Mon-Wed & 11am-late Thu-Sun May-Oct) A popular locals' hang-out, this well-run spot sports a large garden suited to sundowners and thirst-quenchers on sunny days. There's an open fire inside for the odd inclement

> **DON'T MISS**
>
> ## FAREWELL SPIT
>
> Bleak, exposed and positively sci-fi, **Farewell Spit** is a wetland of international importance and a renowned bird sanctuary – the summer home of thousands of migratory waders, notably the godwit (which flies all the way from the Arctic tundra), Caspian terns and Australasian gannets. The 35km beach features colossal, crescent-shaped dunes, from where panoramic views extend across Golden Bay and a vast low-tide salt marsh. Walkers can explore the first 4km of the spit via a network of tracks (see DOC's *Farewell Spit* brochure), but beyond that point access is via tours, scheduled according to tide.
>
> The human hub of the spit is the visitor centre-cum-cafe where there's plenty of parking. It's a convenient spot to write a postcard over a coffee, especially on an inclement day.
>
> **Farewell Spit Eco Tours** (☑ 03-524 8257, 0800 808 257; www.farewellspit.com; Tasman St, Collingwood; tours $120-155) Operating for nearly 70 years, Paddy and his expert guides run tours ranging from two to 6½ hours, departing from Collingwood, taking in the spit, lighthouse, and up to 20 species of bird which may include gannets and godwits. Expect ripping yarns aplenty.
>
> **Farewell Spit Nature Experience** (☑ 03-524 8992, 0800 250 500; www.farewellspit-tours.com; Pakawau; tours $120-145) This air-conditioned operator runs a four-hour tour departing from Farewell Spit Visitor Centre, and a six-hour option leaving from the Old School Cafe, Pakawau.

day. Chow down on belly-filling bar snacks, and look out for local seafood specials come dinner time.

❶ Getting There & Away

Golden Bay Coachlines (☑ 03-525 8352; www.gbcoachlines.co.nz) Runs daily from Takaka to Pohara (15 minutes) on the way to Totaranui.

Collingwood & Around

Far-flung Collingwood (population 250) is the last town in this part of the country, and has a real end-of-the-line vibe. It's busy in summer, though for most people it's simply a launch pad for the Heaphy Track or trips to Farewell Spit.

The **Collingwood Museum** (Tasman St; admission by donation; ⊘10am-4pm) fills a tiny, unstaffed corridor with a quirky collection of saddlery, Maori artefacts, moa bones, shells and old typewriters, while the **Aorere Centre** next door houses multimedia presentations, including the works of the wonderful pioneer photographer, Fred Tyree.

No Collingwood visit would be complete without visiting **Rosy Glow** (54 Beach Rd; chocolates $3-5; ⊘10am-5pm Sat-Thu). Chocoholics: this is your cue. Don't miss it!

A foray to Farewell Spit is essential. From there, follow the signs to **Whariariki Beach** (6km unsealed road, then a 20-minute walk through Puponga Farm Park). It's a wild introduction to the West Coast, with mighty dune formations, looming rock islets just offshore and a seal colony at its eastern end. As inviting as a swim here may seem, be warned that there are strong undertows.

Befitting a frontier, this is the place to saddle up: head to **Cape Farewell Horse Treks** (☑ 03-524 8031; www.horsetreksnz.com; McGowan St, Puponga; ⊘treks from $75). Treks in this wind-blown country range from 1½ hours (to Pillar Point) to three hours (to Whariariki Beach), with longer (including overnight) trips by arrangement.

On the road to Whariariki Beach you'll pass Whariariki Beach Holiday Park (p92), a pretty, young campground with a pleasant communal building.

🛏 Sleeping & Eating

There's little in the way of refreshment round these parts, so keep some cheese and crackers up your sleeve.

⭐ **Innlet Backpackers & Cottages** HOSTEL $ (☑ 027 891 7728, 03-524 8040; www.theinnlet.co.nz; Collingwood-Puponga Rd, Pakawau; campsites from $23, dm/d $31/73, cabins from $83; @ 🤶) ☕ This absolute charmer is 10km from Collingwood on the way to Farewell Spit. The main house has elegant backpacker rooms, and there are various campsites and self-contained options, including a cottage that sleeps six. Explore the local area on a bike or kayak, or venture out for a bushwalk on the property.

Somerset House HOSTEL $

(☏03-524 8624; www.backpackerscollingwood. co.nz; 10 Gibbs Rd, Collingwood; dm/s/d incl breakfast $30/46/72; ⊗closed Jun-Sep; @ 🛜) A small, low-key hostel in a bright, historic building on a hill with views from the deck. Get tramping advice from the knowledgeable owners, who offer track transport, free bikes and kayaks, and freshly baked bread for breakfast.

Wharariki Beach Holiday Park HOLIDAY PARK $

(☏03-524 8507; www.whararikibeachholidaypark. co.nz; campsites from $18, dm $25) Right next to the Wharariki Beach track trailhead – perfectly located for those who want a sunset walk – this simple campsite offers basic facilities in a pretty setting. There are horses over the fence, and fowl rambling through the grounds – avoid this place if peacock poo is an issue for you.

Old School Cafe CAFE $$

(1115 Collingwood-Puponga Rd, Pakawau; mains $14-31; ⊗4pm-late Thu-Fri, 11am-late Sat & Sun) These folks get an A for effort by providing honest food to an unpredictable flow of passing trade. What it lacks in imagination (steak, pizza and even a shrimp cocktail), it more than makes up for with arty ambience, a garden bar and a welcoming disposition.

❶ Getting There & Away

Golden Bay Coachlines (☏03-525 8352; www. goldenbaycoachlines.co.nz) Runs twice daily from Takaka to Collingwood (25 minutes).

Kahurangi National Park

Kahurangi – 'blue skies' in one of several translations – is the second-largest of NZ's national parks, and also one of its most diverse. Its most eye-catching features are geological, ranging from windswept beaches and sea cliffs, to earthquake-shattered slopes and moraine-dammed lakes, and the smooth, strange karst forms of the interior tableland.

Around 85% of the 4520-sq-km park is forested, with beech prevalent, along with rimu and other podocarps. In all, more than 50% of all NZ's plant species can be found in the park, including more than 80% of its alpine plant species. Among the park's 60 birds species are great spotted kiwi, kea, kaka and whio (blue duck). There are creepy cave weta, weird beetles and a huge, leggy spider, but there's also a majestic and an-

cient snail known as Powelliphanta – something of a (slow) flag bearer for the park's animal kingdom. If you like a field trip filled with plenty that's new and strange, Kahurangi National Park will certainly satisfy.

The best-known walk in Kahurangi is the **Heaphy Track**. The more challenging **Wangapeka** and remote **Leslie-Karamea** are less frequented, but these form just part of a 650km network of tracks. Excellent full-day and overnight walks can be had in the **Cobb Valley** and **Mt Arthur/Tablelands**. See www.doc.govt.nz for detailed information on all Kahurangi tracks.

Heaphy Track

The Heaphy Track is one of the most popular tracks in the country. A Great Walk in every sense, it traverses diverse terrain – dense native forest, the mystical Gouland Downs, secluded river valleys, and beaches dusted in salt-spray and fringed by nikau palms.

Although quite long, the Heaphy is well cut and benched, making it easier than any other extended tramp found in Kahurangi National Park. That said, it may still be found arduous, particularly in unfavourable weather.

By walking from east to west, most of the climbing is done on the first day, and the scenic beach walk is saved for the end, a fitting and invigorating grand finale.

The track is open to mountain bikers from May to September. Factoring in distance, remoteness and the possibility of bad weather, this epic journey is only suited to well-equipped cyclists with advanced riding skills. A good port of call for more information is the Quiet Revolution Cycle Shop (p88) in Takaka.

A strong tramper could walk the Heaphy in three days, but most people take four or five days. For a detailed track description, see DOC's *Heaphy Track* brochure.

Estimated walking times:

ROUTE	DURATION (HR)
Brown Hut to Perry Saddle Hut	5
Perry Saddle Hut to Gouland Downs Hut	2
Gouland Downs Hut to Saxon Hut	1½
Saxon Hut to James Mackay Hut	3
James Mackay Hut to Lewis Hut	3½
Lewis Hut to Heaphy Hut	2½
Heaphy Hut to Kohaihai River	5

Bookings & Transport

Seven designated **Great Walk huts** ($32) lie along the track, which have bunks and a kitchen area, heating, flush toilets and washbasins with cold water. Most but not all have gas rings; a couple have lighting. There are also nine **Great Walk campsites** ($14), plus the beachside **Kohaihai Campsite** (www.doc.govt.nz; $6) at the West Coast trailhead. The two day shelters are just that; overnight stays are not permitted.

As the Heaphy is a Great Walk, all huts and campsites must be booked in advance year-round. Bookings can be made online through **Great Walks Bookings** (☑ 0800 694 732; www.greatwalks.co.nz) or at DOC visitor centres, nationwide. In person, the best spot for detailed Heaphy Track information and bookings is the DOC counter at the Nelson i-SITE (p78). Closer to the Golden Bay end of the track, hut tickets, bookings and other track information can be obtained from the DOC office (p90) or Visitor Centre (p90) in Takaka. See also www.heaphytrack.com, and DOC's *Heaphy Track* brochure.

The two road ends of the Heaphy Track are an almost unfathomable distance apart: 463km to be precise. From Takaka, you can get to the Heaphy Track (via Collingwood) with **Golden Bay Coachlines** (☑ 03-525 8352; www.gbcoachlines.co.nz; $33; ⊘ one hour. **Heaphy Bus** (☑ 0272 221 872, 0800 128 735; www.theheaphybus.co.nz) offers a round-trip shuttle service: drop off and pick up from Kohaihai ($110), and other on-demand local track transport. **Heaphy Track Help** (☑ 03-525 9576; www.heaphytrackhelp.co.nz) offers car relocations ($200 to $300, depending on the direction and time), food drops, shuttles and advice.

The Kohaihai trailhead is 15km from the small town of Karamea. **Karamea Express** (☑ 03-782 6757; info@karamea-express.co.nz) departs from the shelter at 1pm and 2pm for Karamea from October to the end of April ($15).

Flights between Karamea and Takaka are offered by **Adventure Flights Golden Bay** (☑ 03-525 6167, 0800 150 338; www.adventureflightsgoldenbay.co.nz; Takaka Airfield), from $185 per person (up to four people); **Golden Bay Air** (☑ 0800 588 885; www.goldenbayair.co.nz) from $169 per person; and **Helicopter Charter Karamea** (☑ 03-782 6111; www.karameahelicharter.co.nz), which will take up to three people for $750.

☞ Tours

Bush & Beyond GUIDED HIKE
(☑ 03-528 9054; www.bushandbeyond.co.nz) Offers various tramping trips, ranging from Mt Arthur or Cobb Valley day walks ($220) through to a guided six-day Heaphy Track package ($1749).

Kahurangi Guided Walks GUIDED HIKE
(☑ 03-525 7177; www.kahurangiwalks.co.nz) Small-group adventures such as five-day Heaphy tramps ($1500) and various one-day trips, including Abel Tasman and the Cobb (from $170).

Nelson Lakes National Park

Nelson Lakes National Park surrounds two lakes – Rotoiti and Rotoroa – fringed by sweet-smelling beech forest with a backdrop of greywacke mountains. Located at the northern end of the Southern Alps, and with a dramatic glacier-carved landscape, it's an awe-inspiring place to get up on high.

Part of the park, east of Lake Rotoiti, is classed as a 'mainland island' where a conservation scheme aims to eradicate introduced pests (possums, stoats) and regenerate native flora and fauna. It offers excellent tramping, including short walks, lake scenery and one or two sandflies... The park is flush with bird life, and is famous for brown-trout fishing.

🏃 Activities

Many spectacular walks allow you to appreciate this rugged landscape, but before you tackle them, stop by the DOC Visitor Centre (p94) for maps, track/weather updates and to pay your hut or camping fees.

The five-hour **Mt Robert Circuit Track** starts south of St Arnaud and circumnavigates the mountain. The optional side trip along Robert Ridge offers staggering views into the heart of the national park. Alternatively, the **St Arnaud Range Track** (five hours return), on the east side of the lake, climbs steadily to the ridgeline adjacent to Parachute Rocks. Both tracks are strenuous, but reward with jaw-dropping vistas of glaciated valleys, arête peaks and Lake Rotoiti. Only attempt these tramps in fine weather. At other times they are both pointless (no views) and dangerous.

There are also plenty of shorter (and flatter) walks from Lake Rotoiti's Kerr Bay and the road end at Lake Rotoroa. These and the longer day tramps are described in DOC's *Walks in Nelson Lakes National Park* pamphlet ($2).

The fit and well-equipped can embark upon longer tramps such as the **Lake Angelus Track**. This magnificent two-to-three-day tramp follows Robert Ridge to Lake Angelus, where you can stay at the fine Angelus Hut (adult/child $20/10) for a night or two before returning to St Arnaud via one of three routes. Pick up or download DOC's *Angelus Hut Tracks & Routes* pamphlet ($2) for more details.

🛏️ Sleeping & Eating

★ **DOC Campsites**   CAMPSITE $
(☑03-521 1806; www.doc.govt.nz) Near the Lake Rotoiti shore, the hugely popular Kerr Bay campsite has powered sites, toilets, hot showers, laundry and a kitchen shelter (unpowered/powered $10/15). Three kilometres from St Arnaud, the unpowered West Bay campsite ($6) has the bare necessities and is open in summer only. Bookings are essential over the Christmas and Easter holidays.

Travers-Sabine Lodge   HOSTEL $
(☑03-521 1887; www.nelsonlakes.co.nz; Main Rd; dm/d $26/62; @🛜) This modern hostel is a great base for outdoor adventure, being a short walk to Lake Rotoiti, inexpensive, clean and comfortable. It also has particularly cheerful technicolour linen in the dorms, doubles and a family room. The owners are experienced adventurers themselves, so tips come as standard; tramping equipment available for hire.

Nelson Lakes Motels   MOTEL $$
(☑03-521 1887; www.nelsonlakes.co.nz; Main Rd; d $120-130; @🛜) These log cabins and newer board-and-batten units offer all the creature comforts, including kitchenettes and Sky TV. Bigger units sleep up to six.

Alpine Lodge   LODGE $$
(☑03-521 1869; www.alpinelodge.co.nz; Main Rd; d $155-205; @🛜) Trying its darnedest to create an alpine atmosphere, this lodge has a range of accommodation, the pick of which are the split-level doubles with mezzanine bedroom, spa and pine timberwork aplenty. The adjacent backpacker lodge (dorm/double $29/69) is spartan but clean and warm, and hires mountain bikes. The in-house res-

taurant is snug, with mountain views and good food (meals $10 to $29). Long may the Sunday-night barbecue continue.

Tophouse Historic Guesthouse   HISTORIC HOTEL $$
(☑03-521 1848, 0800 544 545; www.tophouse. co.nz; 68 Tophouse Rd; s/d incl breakfast $115/175) Nine kilometres from St Arnaud, this 1887 hotel retells fireside tales, tall and true. Refreshments inlude Devonshire teas, soup and sandwiches (lunch $10 to $18), and dinner by arrangement, plus there's NZ's smallest bar and a garden with mountain views. Bed and breakfast is offered in old-fashioned rooms within the hotel, and chalets out the back sleep up to four (doubles $110, per extra person $20).

St Arnaud Alpine Village Store   SUPERMARKET, TAKEAWAY
(⊙8am-6pm, takeaways 4.30-7.30pm Fri & Sat, daily Dec-Feb) The settlement's only general store sells groceries, petrol, beer and possum-wool socks. Mountain-bike hire per half-/full day is $20/40. It has tramping food, sandwiches and pies, with fish and chips cranking up on weekends and daily in peak season ($6 to $10).

ℹ️ Information

DOC Visitor Centre (☑03-521 1806; www. doc.govt.nz; View Rd; ⊙8am-4.30pm, to 5pm in summer) Happily proffers park information (weather, activities) and hut passes, plus displays on park ecology and history.

ℹ️ Getting There & Around

Nelson Lakes Shuttles (☑03-521 1900, 021 490 095; www.nelsonlakesshuttles.co.nz) runs thrice-weekly scheduled services between Nelson and the national park from December to April (Monday, Wednesday and Friday; $45), and on-demand the rest of the year. It will also collect/drop off at Kawatiri Junction on SH63, to meet other bus services heading between Nelson and the West Coast, and offer services from St Arnaud through to Picton and Blenheim. Try also **Trek Express** (☑027 222 1872, 0800 128 735; www.trekexpress.co.nz), which regularly plies this route.

Rotoiti Water Taxis (☑021 702 278; www. rotoitiwatertaxis.co.nz) runs to/from Kerr Bay and West Bay to Lakehead Jetty ($100, up to four people). Kayaks, canoes and rowboats can also be hired from $40 per half-day; fishing trips and scenic lake cruises by arrangement.

The West Coast

Best Short Walks

➤ Scotts Beach (p104)

➤ Charming Creek Walkway
(p103)

➤ Denniston Plateau (p100)

➤ Lake Matheson (p124)

Best Places
to Stay

Old Slaughterhouse (p103)

Beaconstone Eco Lodge
(p105)

Theatre Royal Hotel (p112)

Okarito Campground (p117)

Why Go?

Hemmed in by the wild Tasman Sea and the Southern Alps, the West Coast is like nowhere else in New Zealand.

The far extremities of the coast have a remote, end-of-the-road feel, from sleepy Karamea surrounded by farms butting up against Kahurangi National Park, to the southern end of State Hwy 6, gateway to New Zealand's World Heritage areas. In between is an alluring combination of wild coastline, rich wilderness, and history in spades.

Built on the wavering fortunes of gold, coal and timber, the stories of Coast settlers are hair-raising. A hardy and individual breed, they make up less than 1% of NZ's population, scattered around almost 9% of its land area.

Travellers tend to tick off the 'must see' sights of Punakaiki Rocks, and Franz Josef and Fox Glaciers. Deviate from the trail even a short way, however, and be awed by the spectacles that await you alone.

When to Go

➡ During summer the coast road gets relatively busy, particularly with campervan traffic.

➡ May to September can be warm and clear, with fewer crowds and cheaper accommodation.

➡ The West Coast has serious rainfall (around 5m annually) but still sees as much sunshine as Christchurch.

➡ That said, there's little point trying to dodge the drops on a visit to the Coast – just bring a raincoat and keep your fingers crossed.

➡ No matter what time of year, backcountry trampers should check conditions with local Department of Conservation (DOC) office staff. Rivers can prove seriously treacherous.

The West Coast Highlights

1 Exploring the limestone forms and forest of the **Oparara Basin** (p104)

2 Getting wet 'n' wild on the mighty **Buller River** (p97)

3 Delving into the golden past around **Reefton** (p98)

4 Marvelling at nature's beautiful fury at **Punakaiki's** (p106) Pancake Rocks

5 Having a wheely good time on the **West Coast Wilderness Trail** (p111)

6 Hunting out authentic local greenstone in the galleries of **Hokitika** (p112)

7 Admiring the turquoise waters of **Hokitika Gorge** (p112)

8 Kayaking through the bird-filled channels of **Okarito Lagoon** (p116)

9 Flying high into the Southern Alps via **Franz Josef** (p118) and **Fox Glaciers** (p122)

10 Reaching the end of the line on the scenic and historical highway from **Haast** to **Jackson Bay** (p126)

ⓘ Getting There & Around

Air New Zealand (☎ 0800 737 000; www.airnz.
co.nz) flies between Westport and Wellington,
and Hokitika and Christchurch.

Coaches and shuttle transport – while not very
frequent – are reliable, and reach pretty much
everywhere you might like to go including Nelson,
Christchurch and Queenstown. Major and extensive networks are operated by **Atomic Travel**
(☎ 03-349 0697, 0508 108 359; www.atomic-
travel.co.nz), **InterCity** (☎ 03-365 1113; www.
intercity.co.nz) and **Naked Bus** (www.nakedbus.
com), while **West Coast Shuttle** (☎ 03-768 0028,
0274 927 000; www.westcoastshuttle.co.nz) runs
a daily service between Greymouth and Christchurch. Local shuttle operators go here and there.

The *TranzAlpine* (p108), one of the world's great
train journeys, links Greymouth and Christchurch.

BULLER REGION

Coming from the east, Murchison is the
gateway to the northern West Coast. From
there, State Hwy 6 snakes through Buller
Gorge, a journey that could easily take a day
or two by the time you've taken a rafting or
jetboating trip, explored Lyell, and stopped
at other interesting sites along the way.

Your big decision is which way to head
when you reach the forks at Inangahua. Continuing west along SH6 through the Lower
Buller Gorge will lead you to Westport, the
gateway to the far north. Head south from
Inangahua on SH69 and you skip Punakaiki
but reach Reefton, where you can either
head west to the coast at Greymouth, or east
over the Lewis Pass to Hanmer Springs. You
can also cut directly through to the Lewis
Pass via SH65, 10km west of Murchison.

Murchison & Buller Gorge

Murchison (population 490), 125km southwest of Nelson and 95km east of Westport,
lies on the 'Four Rivers Plain'. In fact there
aren't just four but multitudinous rivers,
the mightiest being the Buller, which runs
alongside the town. White-water sports and
trout fishing are popular here, while the surrounding forested hills dish up adventure
for the landlubbers.

◉ Sights & Activities

Ask at the Murchison **visitor centre**
(☎ 03-523 9350; www.nelsonnz.com; 47 Waller
St; ◷ 10am-6pm Oct-May, reduced hours Apr-Sep)

for a copy of the *Murchison District Map*,
which features local walks, such as the Skyline, Six Mile and Johnson Creek tracks, plus
mountain-bike rides. Staff can also hook you
up with trout-fishing guides.

Murchison Museum   MUSEUM
(60 Fairfax St; admission by donation; ◷ 10am-4pm)
This museum showcases all sorts of local
memorabilia, the most interesting of which
relate to the 1929 and 1968 earthquakes.

Wild Rivers Rafting   RAFTING
(☎ 050 846 7238; www.wildriversrafting.co.nz; 2hr
rafting adult/child $130/85) White-water raft-
ing with Bruce and Marty on the particularly exciting Earthquake Rapids section of
the beautiful Buller River (good luck with
'gunslinger' and the 'pop-up toaster'!).

Ultimate Descents   RAFTING
(☎ 03-523 9899, 0800 748 377; www.rivers.co.nz;
38 Waller St; 2hr rafting $130, half-day kayaking
$125) Offers white-water rafting and kay-
aking trips on the Buller, including half-
day, gentler family excursions (adult/child
$115/95). Helirafting trips by arrangement
from their new base in Murchison.

Natural Flames Experience   ECO TOUR
(☎ 0800 687 244; www.naturalflames.co.nz; adult/
child $85/65) An enjoyable, informative half-
day 4WD and bushwalking tour through

ESSENTIAL WEST COAST

Eat Whitebait, bought from an old-
timer's back door at an honest price

Drink The only roast on the coast, Ka-
watiri Coffee

Read Eleanor Catton's 2013 Man
Booker Prize–winning novel, *The Luminaries*, set around Hokitika

Listen to Karamea's laid-back community radio station on 107.5FM; you can
even spin your own tunes

Watch *Denniston Incline* on YouTube,
then imagine sitting in the wagon on
the way down

Festival Go bush-food crazy at Hokitika's Wildfoods Festival (p114)

Go Green At West Coast Wildlife Centre
(p118) – fluffy kiwi chicks! Too cute!

Online www.westcoastnz.com; www.
buller.co.nz; www.glaciercountry.co.nz

Area code ☎ 03

remote valleys and beech forest to a hot spot amongst the trees and ferns, where natural gas seeping out of the ground has been burning since 1922. Boil a billy on the flames and cook pancakes before returning to civilisation.

Buller Gorge Swingbridge BRIDGE

(📞0800 285 537; www.bullergorge.co.nz; SH6; bridge crossing adult/child $5/2; ⏰8am-7pm Dec-Apr, 9am-5pm May-Nov) About 14km west of Murchison is NZ's longest swingbridge (110m), across which lie short walks taking in the White Creek Faultline, epicentre of the 1929 earthquake. Coming back, ride the 160m Cometline Flying Fox, either seated (adult/child $30/15) or 'Supaman' ($45, or tandem adult/child $30/15).

Buller Canyon Jet JETBOATING

(📞03-523 9883; www.bullercanyonjet.co.nz; SH6; adult/child $95/50; ⏰Sep-Apr) Launching from Buller Gorge Swingbridge is one of NZ's most scenic and best-value jetboat trips – 40 minutes of ripping through the beautiful Buller with a good-humoured captain.

🛏 Sleeping & Eating

Murchison has a few cafes, a couple of grocery stores, and a butchery curing notable bacon.

Kiwi Park Motels
& Holiday Park MOTEL, HOLIDAY PARK $

(📞03-523 9248, 0800 228 080; www.kiwipark. co.nz; 170 Fairfax St; unpowered/powered sites from $20/25, cabins $65-85, motels $140-225; @🛜) This leafy park on the edge of town has plenty of accommodation options, from a campervan and tent area graced with mature trees, through to basic cabins, and roomy motels nestled amongst the blooms. Cheery hosts and a menagerie of friendly farm animals make this one happy family.

MAORI NZ: THE WEST COAST

For Maori, the river valleys and mountains of the West Coast were the traditional source of highly prized *pounamu* (greenstone), carved into tools, weapons and adornments. View the *pounamu* exhibit at Hokitika Museum (p112) to polish your knowledge of the precious rock before admiring the classy carvings created by the town's artists.

Lazy Cow HOSTEL $

(📞03-523 9451; www.lazycow.co.nz; 37 Waller St; dm $30, d $74-90; @🛜) It's easy to be a lazy cow here, with all the comforts of home including cosy bedrooms and a sunny backyard. Guests are welcomed with free muffins or cake, and there are freshly cooked evening meals available on evenings when the hosts aren't running their popular onsite Cow Shed (⏰6-9pm Thurs-Sat) restaurant.

Commercial Hotel HOTEL $

(📞03-523 9696; www.commercialhotel.co.nz; cnr Waller & Fairfax Sts; s/d/tr $40/75/100; ⏰8am-8.30pm; @🛜) This sunny corner pub with super street-appeal meets required standards in its dining room, and features a bar with a pool table, appealing outdoor tables, and solid pub grub (mains $14 to $29). Down the checkerboard-and-crimson hallway is a series of cheap but charming bedrooms sharing bathrooms and a cupboard-sized kitchen.

Murchison Lodge B&B $$

(📞03-523 9196, 0800 523 9196; www.murchison-lodge.co.nz; 15 Grey St; s incl breakfast $150-210, d incl breakfast $175-235; ⏰closed May-Aug; 🛜) 🐾 Surrounded by native trees, this B&B is within a short walk of the Buller River; the owners' friendly dog will probably accompany you. Attractive timber features, quality artwork and charming hosts add to the comfortable feel. Home-reared bacon and eggs for breakfast, plus evening meals by arrangement.

ℹ Information

There is no ATM in town; the postal agency is on Fairfax St.

The Murchison Visitor Centre (p97) has info on local activities and transport.

ℹ Getting There & Away

Buses passing through Murchison between the West Coast and Nelson/Picton are **InterCity** (📞03-365 1113; www.intercity.co.nz) and **Naked Bus** (www.nakedbus.com), both of which stop at Beechwoods Cafe on Waller St, as does **Trek Express** (📞0272 221 872, 0800 128 735; www.trekexpress.co.nz), which runs frequently between Nelson and the Wangapeka/Heaphy Tracks during the peak tramping season.

Reefton

POP 1030

For generations, Reefton's claims to fame have been mining and its early adoption of the electricity grid and street lighting.

Hence the tagline, 'the city of light'. Today, however, it's a different story, one which starts – improbably – with the building of the world-class Roller Park, which attracts stunt-lovers from all corners of NZ. To quote a local, 'it's more than we deserve'. We disagree. If this many volunteers and sponsors are prepared to build such an edgy civic amenity in a town that still looks like the set of *Bonanza,* we suggest there's something a little bit special about this crazy little town.

◎ Sights & Activities

With loads of crusty old buildings situated within a 200-metre radius, Reefton is a fascinating town for a stroll. To find out who lived where and why, undertake the short **Heritage Walk** outlined in the *Historic Reefton* leaflet ($1), available from the i-SITE (p100), from where you can also collect the free *Reefton* leaflet detailing other short walks including the **Bottled Lightning Powerhouse Walk** (40 minutes).

Surrounding Reefton is the 2060-sq-km **Victoria Forest Park** (NZ's largest forest park), which sports diverse flora and fauna as well as hidden historic sites such as the old goldfields around Blacks Point. Starting (or ending) at Blacks Point, the enjoyable **Murray Creek Track** takes five hours round trip.

Other tramps in the Forest Park include the three-day **Kirwans** or two-day **Big River Track**, both of which can be traversed on a mountain bike. Pick up the free *Reefton Mountain Biking ('the best riding in history')* leaflet for more information; bikes can be hired from **Reefton Sports Centre** (☑03-732 8593; 56 Broadway; bike hire per day $30), where you can also inquire about the legendary trout fishing in the environs.

Blacks Point Museum   MUSEUM
(Blacks Point, SH7; adult/child/family $5/3/12; ◎9am-noon & 1-4pm Wed-Fri & Sun, 1-4pm Sat Oct-Apr, plus school holidays during winter) Housed in an old church 2km east of Reefton on the Christchurch road, this museum is crammed with prospecting paraphernalia. Just up the driveway is the still-functional **Golden Fleece Battery** (adult/child $1/free; ◎1-4pm Wed & Sun Oct-Apr), used for crushing gold-flecked quartz. The Blacks Point walks also start from here.

Bearded Mining Company   HISTORIC BUILDING
(Broadway; admission by donation; ◎9am-2pm) Looking like a ZZ Top tribute band, the fellas hangin' at this high-street mining hut are

champing at the bit to rollick your socks off with tales tall and true. If you're lucky you'll get a cuppa from the billy.

Waiuta   HISTORIC SITE
(www.waiuta.org.nz; off SH7) A once-burgeoning gold town abandoned in 1951 after the mineshaft collapsed, remote Waiuta is one of the West Coast's most famous ghost towns, complete with a big old rusty boiler, an overgrown swimming pool, stranded brick chimneys and the odd intact cottage, which face off against mother nature who has sent in the strangleweed. Spread over a square kilometre or so of plateau, surrounded by lowland forest and looking out towards the Southern Alps, Waiuta is a very satisfying place for an amble. To get to there, drive 23km south of Reefton on SH7 to the signposted turn-off from where it's another 17km, the last half of which is unsealed, winding and narrow in places. Ask at local i-SITEs for more information and maps.

☞ Tours

Reefton Gold Mine Tours   CULTURAL TOUR
(☑027 442 4777, 03-732 8497; www.reeftongold. co.nz) Dig deeper into Reefton on a two-hour heritage tour ($25) taking in town highlights. The Gold Mine Tour (adult/child/family $55/30/120) visits the local mine, where you'll get views over the pit-edge and see plenty of huge machinery in action. Book at the i-SITE or the Broadway Tearooms.

🍴 Sleeping & Eating

It's slim pickings on the food front in Reefton, with self-catering or a night down the pub the safest bets.

Old Nurses Home   GUESTHOUSE $
(☑03-732 8881; www.reeftonaccommodation. co.nz; 104 Shiel St; s/d $55/80; @ ☏) This stately old building is warm and comfortable, with noteworthy communal areas including a pretty garden and patio. Bedrooms are clean and airy with comfy beds.

Reefton Motor Camp   HOLIDAY PARK $
(☑03-732 8477; reeftonmotorcamp@xtra.co.nz; 1 Ross St; sites from $15, cabin d $45) On the Inangahua River and a minute's walk to Broadway, this older style camp sits beside a big green sports field and shady fir trees.

Lantern Court Motels   MOTEL $$
(☑03-732 8574, 0800 526 837; www.lanterncourtmotel.co.nz; 63 Broadway; old units d $95-120, new units d $145-170; ☏) This heritage hotel offers great

value, with self-catering options for everyone from singles to family groups, while the well-assimilated motel block next door offers all mod cons with a nod to classical styling.

Broadway Tearooms
BAKERY $

(31 Broadway; snacks $3-8, meals $10-20; ⊗5am-5pm) This joint gets by far the most day-time traffic, being a civilised place for a spot of lunch, and to pick up a fresh loaf or a packet of shortbread. Middle-of-the-road meals range from egg breakfasts to a whitebait lunch. Survey the high street from al fresco tables, or peruse the cute cruet set collection indoors.

Wilson's Hotel
PUB $$

(32 Broadway; mains $13-30; ⊗11am-11pm) A solid town pub pleasing all, from smokin' youth through to soup-slurping pensioners. Meat and three veg dominate the menu, but it's all hearty and homemade. Occasional bands and DJs raise the excitement level to somewhere under fever pitch.

❶ Information

The **Reefton i-SITE** (☐ 03-732 8391; www.reefton.co.nz; 67 Broadway; ⊗9am-5pm Mon-Fri, 10am-3pm Sat & Sun) has helpful staff, and a compact re-creation of the Quartzopolis Mine (gold coin entry). There's internet at the library, which doubles as the postal agency.

❶ Getting There & Away

East West Coaches (☐ 03-789 6251; www.eastwestcoaches.co.nz) stops in Reefton every day except Saturday on the run between Westport (1¼ hours) and Christchurch (3¾ hours).

Westport & Around

POP 5600

The port of Westport made its fortune in coal mining, and coal still makes a considerable contribution to keeping the town stoked up. Beyond some respectable hospitality, the town contains little of prolonged interest, but makes a good base for exploring the fascinating coast north to Karamea, Oparara and the Heaphy Track.

◉ Sights & Activities

Westport is good for a stroll – the i-SITE can direct you to the **Millenium Walkway** and **North Beach Reserve**. The most thrilling adventure in the area is cave rafting with Norwest Adventures (p101), although mountain biking is gaining momentum as a popular pastime among local and visiting

backcountry adventurers. The folk at Habitat Sports (p102) offer bike hire, maps and advice.

Coaltown Museum
MUSEUM

(www.coaltown.co.nz; 123 Palmerston St; adult/child $15/7; ⊗9am-5pm Mon-Fri, 10am-4pm Sat & Sun) Re-opened in 2013, the new-look Coaltown Museum retells the same old yarns of hard times, but this time with well-scripted display panels alongside an excellent selection of photographs, surrounding relics of local industries and general pioneer ephemera. The Denniston displays are a highlight.

Denniston Plateau
HISTORIC SITE

(www.doc.govt.nz) Nine kilometres inland and 600m above sea level, Denniston was once NZ's largest coal producer, with 1500 residents in 1911. By 1981 there were eight. Its claim to fame was the fantastically steep Denniston Incline, an engineering marvel enabling the cartage of coal wagons down a 45-degree hillside.

Denniston is fascinating, its ghostly remains brought to life with excellent interpretive displays. The *Denniston Rose Walking Tour* brochure ($2 from DOC and Westport Library; also available as an app) may lead keen readers to the local bookshop to buy Jenny Pattrick's evocative novels set in these parts. The **Denniston Mine Experience** (☐ 0800 881 880; www.denniston.co.nz; Denniston; 2hr tour adult/child $95/65) guided tours ride the 'gorge express' train into the historic Banbury mine for what is a slightly spooky but intriguing underground adventure.

The plateau can be reached via the Denniston Bridle Track (three hours up, two down), which follows sections of the Incline. Skilled mountain bikers should speak to the folks at Westport's Habitat Sports (p102) about maps and bike hire.

Cape Foulwind
Walkway & Seal Colony
WALKING, WILDLIFE

Poor old Abel Tasman. The first European to sight the Cape, in 1642, he named it Clyppygen Hoek (Rocky Point) but was eclipsed by James Cook in 1770 who clearly found it less than pleasing.

Today, on a good day, the Cape Foulwind Walkway (1½ hours return) makes for a wonderful amble. It traverses rolling hills between Lighthouse Rd at Omau in the north, and picturesque Tauranga Bay in the south, known for its surfing (and a cafe well worth visiting if it's open).

Towards the southern end is the seal colony where – depending on the season – up to 200 NZ fur seals dot the rocks below the coastal path. Further north the walkway passes a replica astrolabe (a navigational aid) and lighthouse. At Omau, at the walk's northern end, is the Star Tavern (p102), a good place for a pit-stop.

Cape Foulwind is well signposted from Westport, 13km to Omau and 16km to Tauranga Bay.

Old Ghost Road
TRAMPING, CYCLING

(www.oldghostroad.org.nz) One of the most ambitious of NZ's new cycle trails, the 80km Old Ghost Road follows a historic byway started in the 1870s but never completed when the gold rush petered out. Finally completed after an epic build, the spectacular track traverses native forests, tussock tops, river flats and valleys.

The southern end of the track is at **Lyell**, 50 minutes' drive (62km) east of Westport along the scenic Buller Gorge (SH6). The DOC campsite and day walks here have long been popular, with visitors drawn in by readily accessible historic sites including a graveyard secreted in the bush. The northern trailhead is at **Seddonville** (p103), 45 minutes' drive (50km) north of Westport off SH67, from where the track sidles along the steep-sided and utterly stunning Mokihinui River. Joining the two ends is a spectacular alpine section, with views from sunrise to sunset.

The track is dual use. Advanced mountain bikers can complete it in 2 to 3 days, while walkers are best to allow five. There are six huts along the way, all of which need to be booked in advance. The track can also be explored in day trips from either end, with both offering a satisfying adventure.

This track is brand-spanking new, and is only just bedding down, so check the website for the latest news, and visit Murchison and Westport i-SITEs for advice on transport and bookings.

Norwest Adventures
CAVING, RAILWAY

(☑03-788 8168, 0800 116 686; www.caverafting.com; SH6, Charleston) From its monolithic new base (with cafe) at Charleston, 26km south of Westport, this friendly bunch run 'Underworld' cave-rafting trips ($175, four hours) into the glow-worm-filled Nile River Caves. Glow without the flow (no rafting) is $110 per person. Tours begin with a fun rainforest railway ride, available separately (adult/child $20/15, 1½ hours). The Adventure Cav-

ing trip ($340, five hours) includes a 40m abseil into Te Tahi *tomo* (hole) with rock squeezes, waterfalls, prehistoric fossils and trippy cave formations.

🛏 Sleeping

Bazil's Hostel
HOSTEL $

(☑03-789 6410; www.bazils.com; 54 Russell St; dm $28, d without/with bathroom $68/90) Funky Bazil's is managed by sporty, well-travelled locals who run their own surf school (three-hour lesson $70; board and suit hire per day $30) and offer mountain-bike hire, free kayaks and hook-ups with other local activities. Bazil's thoughtfully corrals its tour-bus clientele into their own area, leaving indie travellers peace and quiet in the many mural-painted corners.

Trip Inn
HOSTEL $

(☑03-789 7367, 0800 737 773; www.tripinn.co.nz; 72 Queen Street; dm $27-29, d $74; @ 🛜) Westport's stately hostel option is a grand 150-year-old villa with mature gardens. There's a variety of tidy rooms within, plus more in an annexe, and voluminous communal areas.

Westport Holiday Park
HOLIDAY PARK $

(☑03-789 7043; www.westportholidaypark.co.nz; 31 Domett St; campsites from $34, d $98-145) What it lacks in landscaping it makes up for in consistent maintenance of its basic communal facilities and affordable A-frame 'chalets'. Fifteen minutes' walk to town; minigolf course out front.

Seal Colony Top 10 Holiday Park
HOLIDAY PARK $

(☑050 893 7876, 03-789 8002; www.top10westport.co.nz; 57 Marine Pde, Carters Beach; sites from $38, units $70-145; @ 🛜) Right on Carters Beach and conveniently located 4km from Westport and 12km to Tauranga Bay, this no-frills outfit offers a full range of facilities of a more-than-acceptable standard. A good option for tourers seeking a clean and peaceful stop-off, and perhaps even a swim.

Buller Court Motel
MOTEL $$

(☑03-789 7979; www.bullercourtmotel.co.nz; 253 Palmerston St; d $125-175, q $195-215; 🛜) One of many main-road options, this older-style complex is tastefully decorated and impresses with an away-from-the-road aspect and small but private grassy gardens.

Omau Settlers Lodge
LODGE $$

(☑03-789 5200; www.omausettlerslodge.co.nz; 1054 Cape Rd; r incl breakfast $135-155; 🛜) Close to Cape Foulwind and across the road from the excellent Star Tavern, these contemporary and stylish units offer rest, relaxation and satisfying continental breakfasts. Rooms have kitchenettes, but a shared kitchen and dining room offers a chance to socialise. A hot tub surrounded by bush maximises the take-it-easy quotient.

Archer House   B&B $$
(📞 0800 789 877, 03-789 8778; www.archerhouse. co.nz; 75 Queen St; d incl breakfast $185-225; @ 🛜) This beautiful 1890 heritage home sleeps up to eight in three rooms with their own bathrooms, all sharing no fewer than three lounges, plus peaceful gardens. Lovely hosts, complimentary sherry and generous continental breakfast make this Westport's most refined accommodation option.

🍴 Eating & Drinking

Westport has more than its fair share of pubs and other places to eat, with good odds on for decent espresso, and two big supermarkets for stocking up.

PR's Cafe   CAFE $
(124 Palmerston St; meals $12-19; ⊙ 8am-4.30pm Mon-Fri, 8am-3pm Sat & Sun; 🛜) Low-key signage betrays the impressive effort by savvy PR's with its cabinet full of sharp sandwiches and pastries, and a counter groaning under the weight of amazing cakes (red velvet, Dutch apple) and cookies. An all-day menu delivers carefully composed, modern cafe meals such as salmon omelette with dill aioli, spanakopita, and seasonal specials.

Porto Bello   BAR, RESTAURANT $$
(62 Palmerston St; meals $16-32; ⊙ 5pm-late) Roman columns and renaissance artwork give this place a classical feel, but the food has its roots firmly in the US of A. Craft beer on tap, $16.50 steak special, burgers with pickles, pizza and pork ribs keep the punters happy, as does occasional live music.

Star Tavern   PUB
(6 Lighthouse Rd, Omau; meals $9-30) A motto of 'arrive as strangers, leave as friends' is backed up at this rural tavern handily positioned near Cape Foulwind. It dishes up generously proportioned grub in its old-fashioned dining room, a warm welcome, pool and a jukebox in its unprepossessing public bar, and relaxation in the garden. Proper hospitality, that's what this is.

ℹ️ Information

The major banks are along Palmerston St. There's free wi-fi at the **Westport Library** (87 Palmerston St).

Buller Hospital (📞 03-788 9030; Cobden St)

Department of Conservation Office (DOC; 📞 03-788 8008; www.doc.govt.nz; 72 Russell St; ⊙ 8am-noon & 2-4.30pm Mon-Fri) DOC bookings and information can be gained from the i-SITE. For curly questions visit this field office.

Post Office (cnr Brougham & Palmerston Sts)

Westport i-SITE (📞 03-789 6658; www.coaltown.co.nz; 123 Palmerston St; ⊙ 9am-5pm Mon-Fri, 10am-4pm Sat & Sun) Information on local tracks, walkways, tours, accommodation and transport. Self-help terminal for DOC information and hut/track bookings. See also www.westcoastnz.com.

ℹ️ Getting There & Around

AIR

Air New Zealand (📞 0800 737 000; www. airnewzealand.co.nz) has up to three flights per day to/from Wellington.

BUS

Westport is a stop on the daily Nelson to Fox Glacier runs of **InterCity** (📞 03-365 1113; www. intercity.co.nz). Travel time to Nelson is 3½ hours, to Greymouth 2¼ hours, and to Franz Josef six hours. **Naked Bus** (www.nakedbus. com) runs the same route three times per week. Buses leave from the i-SITE.

East West Coaches (📞 03-789 6251; www. eastwestcoaches.co.nz) operates a service through to Christchurch, via Reefton and the Lewis Pass, every day except Saturday, departing from the Caltex Petrol Station.

Karamea Express (📞 03-782 6757; info@ karamea-express.co.nz) links Westport and Karamea (two hours) Monday to Friday May to September, plus Saturday from October to April, departing from the i-SITE.

Trek Express (📞 0272 221 872, 0800 128 735; www.trekexpress.co.nz) passes through Westport on its frequent high-season tramper transport link between Nelson and the Wangapeka/ Heaphy Tracks.

BICYCLE

Hire bikes and obtain advice from **Habitat Sports** (📞 03-788 8002; www.habitatsports. co.nz; 234 Palmerston St; half-day bike hire $35; ⊙ 9am-5pm Mon-Fri, 9am-1pm Sat).

CAR

Hire some wheels at **Wesport Hire** (📞 03-789 5038; wesporthire@xtra.co.nz; 294 Palmerston St).

TAXI
Buller Taxis (☑ 03-789 6900) can take you to/from the airport (around $20).

Westport to Karamea

North along SH67, the road is pressed against the rocky shoreline by verdant hills. If you're driving all the way up to Karamea, fill your tank in Westport as it's 98km to the next petrol station.

The first town beyond Westport is **Waimangaroa**, with a shop worth a stop for a homemade pie and ice cream. Here you'll also find the turn-off to the Denniston Plateau (p100), which can be surveyed in as little as an hour.

Sleepy **Granity** is 30km north of Westport. Little happens here save the passing of flouro-vested mine workers heading up to **Stockton**, NZ's largest operational coal mine, which is located 8km inland.

The next coastal cluster is **Ngakawau**, shortly followed by **Hector** where stands a monument to Hector's dolphins, NZ's smallest, although you'll be lucky to see them unless your timing is impeccable.

Around 1km north of Hector is a rather special hostel nestled high on the hill amongst native bush, with epic views of the Tasman Sea. The **Old Slaughterhouse** (☑ 027 529 7640, 03-782 8333; www.oldslaughterhouse.co.nz; dm $32-36, d $80; ☺ sometimes closed Jun-Oct) 🍃, built mainly from recycled timbers, is dotted with great art and eclectic furniture, and has tranquil communal areas ideal for contemplation. The steep, 10-minute walk up the hill is well worth the effort and bolsters the off-the-grid charm.

In these parts you'll find the **Charming Creek Walkway**. One of the best day-walks on the Coast, this all-weather trail (six hours return) follows an old coal line through the Ngakawau River Gorge. Along its length are rusty relics galore, tunnels, a suspension bridge and waterfall, and lots of interesting plants and geological formations. Ask a local about transport if you don't want to walk it both ways.

You can start the walkway at Ngakawau, where you'll find the **Charming Creek B&B** (☑ 03-782 8007; www.bullerbeachstay.co.nz; Ngakawau; d incl breakfast $139-169; 🛜). The rooms are indeed charming, and there's a driftwood-fired hot tub right by the sea where the self-contained 'Beach Nest' bach sleeps 3 to 4 ($95 to $135, minimum two-night stay). Ask about the two-night walking package, which includes dinners and a picnic lunch.

The northern trailhead for the walkway is 10km beyond **Seddonville**, a small bush town on the Mokihinui River where **Seddonville Holiday Park** (☑ 03-782 1314; 108 Gladstone St; campsites per person $10) offers respectable camping in the grounds of the old school. This small dot on the map is about to get slightly bigger, being the northern trailhead for the spectacular new Old Ghost Road (p101).

At the Mokihinui River mouth, 3km off the highway, is the not-so-gentle **Gentle Annie Beach**, and salty **Gentle Annie Coastal Enclave** (☑ 0274 188 587, 03-782 1826; www.gentleannie.co.nz; De Malmanche Rd, Mokihinui; sites from $12, s/d/tr from $25/50/75, cabins $130; 🛜) where there are campsites, a lodge, a range of self-contained accommodation and the Cowshed Gallery & Cafe. There are also bush walks, a maze on a look-out point, and glow-worms nearby.

Between Mokihinui and Little Wanganui the road meanders over the thickly forested **Karamea Bluff**, affording expansive views of the Tasman Sea. It's worth stopping to do the **Lake Hanlon** walk (30 minutes return) on the Karamea side of the hill.

Karamea & Around

The relaxed town of Karamea (population 380) considers itself the West Coast's 'best kept secret', but those who've visited tend to boast about its merits far and wide. An end-of-the-road town it may well be, but it still has a bit of the 'hub' about it, servicing the end (or start) of the Heaphy and Wangapeka Tracks, and the magical Oparara Basin. With a friendly climate, and a take-it-easy mix of locals and chilled-out imports, the Karamea area is a great place to jump off the well-trodden tourist trail for a few lazy days.

◉ Sights & Activities

Hats off to the Karamea community who have established the very pleasant **Karamea Estuary Walkway**, a long-as-you-like stroll bordering the estuary and Karemea River. It features plenty of birdlife and is best walked at sunset. Ask a local for directions, follow your nose, or pick up a leaflet from the Karamea Information & Resource Centre (p105). While you're there, pick up the free *Karamea* brochure, which details other walks, including **Big Rimu** (45 minutes return), Flagstaff (one hour return) and the Zig Zag (one hour return).

Longer walks around Karamea include the Fenian Track (four hours return) leading to Cavern Creek Caves and Adams Flat, where there's a replica gold-miner's hut; and the first leg of the Wangapeka Track to Belltown Hut. The Wangapeka Track is a four-to-six-day backcountry trip suitable for experienced trampers only.

Other local activities include swimming, fishing, whitebaiting, kayaking and mountain biking. Your best bet for advice on these is to ask a local and use common sense – especially when it comes to the watery stuff. Flexible and friendly Karamea Outdoor Adventures (✆03-782 6181; www.karameaadventures.co.nz; Bridge St; guided kayak/riverbug trips from $60, kayak hire 2hr $30, bike hire 2hr $30) offers guided and freedom kayaking and riverbug trips on four West Coast rivers, plus mountain-bike hire, and advice on local excursions.

Heaphy Track

The West Coast road ends 14km from Karamea at Kohaihai, the western trailhead (and most commonly, the finish point) of the Heaphy Track, where there's also a DOC campsite (Department of Conservation; adult/child $6). A day walk or overnight stay can readily be had from here. Walk to Scotts Beach (1½ hours

return), or go as far as the fabulous new Heaphy Hut (huts/campsites $32/14) (five hours) and stay a night or two before returning.

This section can also be mountain-biked, as can the whole track (two to three days) from May to September; ask at Westport's Habitat Sports (p102) for bike hire and details.

Helicopter Charter Karamea (✆03-782 6111; www.karameahelicharter.co.nz; 79 Waverley St) can fly up to three people through to the northern trailhead in Golden Bay for $750; ask about other possible drop-off/pick-up points and bike transfers.

For detailed information on negotiating the Heaphy Track, see p92, or check out www.heaphytrack.com.

🛏 Sleeping & Eating

Cafes and restaurants are thin on the ground around these parts, so stock up at Karamea's Four Square and keep an eye out for 'open' signs.

Karamea Domain Camp   CAMPSITE $
(✆03-782 6069; www.karamea.org.nz; Waverley St; sites 1/2 people unpowered $12/16, powered $13/18) In the middle of the (ahem) action, this very simple town camp lines up pitches along the edge of the sportsfield, with the cute old Plunket Rooms refashioned into communal facilities – simple kitchen and

---

DON'T MISS

OPARARA VALLEY

To quote a local: 'if this were anywhere else, there'd be hordes streaming in.' Too true. Lying within Kahurangi National Park, the Oparara Basin is a natural spectacle of the highest order – a hidden valley concealing wonders such as limestone arches and strange caves within a thick forest of massive, moss-laden trees that tower over an undergrowth of Dr Seuss-esque form in every imaginable hue of green. Excellent information panels can be perused at the main car park and picnic area.

The valley's signature sight is the 200m-long, 37m-high Oparara Arch, spanning the picturesque Oparara River – home to the super-cute, rare blue duck (whio) – which wends alongside the easy walkway (45 minutes return). The smaller but no less stunning Moria Gate Arch (43m long, 19m high) is reached via a simply divine forest loop walk (1½ hours) which also passes the Mirror Tarn.

Just a 10-minute walk from the second car park are the Crazy Paving & Box Canyon Caves. Take your torch to enter a world of weird subterranean shapes and rare, leggy spiders. Spiders, caves, darkness... sound like fun?

Beyond this point are the superb Honeycomb Hill Caves & Arch, accessible only by guided tours (3-/5-hour tours $95/150) run by the Karamea Information & Resource Centre. Ask about other guided tours of the area, and also about transport for the Oparara Valley Track, a rewarding five-hour independent walk through ancient forest, along the river, popping out at the Fenian Walk car park.

To drive to the valley from Karamea, travel 10km along the main road north and turn off at McCallum's Mill Rd where signposts will direct you a further 14km up and over into the valley along a road that is winding, gravel, rough in places and sometimes steep.

lounge, and adequate bathrooms and bunk-rooms (per person $13).

Karamea Holiday Park HOLIDAY PARK $
(☑03-782 6758; www.karamea.com; Maori Point Rd; sites d powered/unpowered $32/28, cabins $30-50, d $86-89; @🔊) A simple, old-fashioned camp alongside the estuary in bush surrounds, 3km south of Karamea village. The classic weatherboard cabins are clean and well maintained.

Rongo Backpackers HOSTEL $
(☑03-782 6667; www.rongobackpackers.com; 130 Waverley St; sites from $20, dm $30-32, d $75; @🔊)
🌿 Part neo-hippie artists' haven and part organic vegie garden, this rainbow-coloured hostel even has its own community radio station (107.5 FM, www.karamearadio.com). Popular with long-term guests who often end up working within – either tending the garden or as de facto DJs. Every fourth night is free.

Karamea Farm Baches CABINS $
(☑03-782 6838; www.karameafarmbaches.com; 17 Wharf Rd; d/tr/q $95/120/145; @🔊) 🌿 Pushing reuse/recycle to the limit, these seven 1960s self-contained bachs are the real McCoy, right down to cobwebby corners and frayed bedspreads. If you dig organic gardening, friendly dogs and colourful hosts, this will win you over.

Karamea River Motels MOTEL $$
(☑03-782 6955; www.karameamotels.co.nz; 31 Bridge St; r $125-169; 🔊) The smart rooms at this modern, rural motel range from studios to two-bedroom units. Features include long-range views, barbecues and lush gardens complete with lily pond.

Last Resort LODGE $$
(☑03-782 6617, 0800 505 042; www.lastresort.co.nz; 71 Waverley St; s $50, d $97-155, q $195; @🔊) This iconic, rambling and rustic resort has had its ups and downs, but is currently riding a wave of friendly local hosts, accommodation upgrades and a general tidy up. Scope the joint with espresso or a beer in the cafe or bar (meals $9 to $25) or take the plunge into a range of rooms, from simple doubles to family suites hallmarked by extensive use of local timbers.

★**Karamea Village Hotel** PUB $$
(www.karameahotel.co.nz; cnr Waverley & Wharf Sts; meals $9-29; ⊙11am-11pm) Here lie simple pleasures and proper hospitality: a game of pool, a pint of ale, and a hot roast dinner followed by an old-fashioned pudding.

ⓘ Information

Karamea Information & Resource Centre
(☑03-782 6652; www.karameainfo.co.nz; Market Cross; ⊙9am-5pm Mon-Fri, 10am-1pm Sat & Sun, shorter hours off-peak) This excellent, community-owned centre has the local low-down, internet access, maps and DOC hut tickets. It also doubles as the petrol station.

ⓘ Getting There & Away

Karamea Express (☑03-782 6757; info@karamea-express.co.nz) links Karamea and Westport ($35, two hours, 7.40am Monday to Friday May to September, plus Saturdays from October to April). It also services Kohaihai twice daily during peak summer, and other times on demand. Wangapeka transport is also available.

Heaphy Bus (☑03-540 2042, 0800 128 735; www.theheaphybus.co.nz), based in Nelson, also runs between both ends of the Heaphy, as well as the Wangapeka.

Fly from Karamea to Takaka with **Helicopter Charter Karamea** (☑03-782 6111; www.karameahelicharter.co.nz; 79 Waverley St), **Golden Bay Air** (☑0800 588 885; www.goldenbayair.co.nz) or **Adventure Flights Golden Bay** (☑03-525 6167, 0800 150 338; www.adventureflightsgoldenbay.co.nz) for around $190 per person, then walk back on the Heaphy Track; contact the Information & Resource Centre for details.

Rongo Backpackers run track and town transport including services to Heaphy, Wangapeka, Oparara Basin and Westport on demand.

THE GREAT COAST ROAD

There are fine views all the way along this beautiful stretch of SH6, although its most famous attractions are the geologically fascinating Pancake Rocks at Punakaiki. Fill up in Westport if you're low on petrol and cash – there's no fuel until Runanga, 92km away, and the next ATM is in Greymouth.

Westport to Punakaiki

Set on 42 serene hectares, 17km south of Westport, the solar-powered, energy-efficient **Beaconstone Eco Lodge** (☑027 431 0491; www.beaconstoneecolodge.co.nz; Birds Ferry Rd; dm $28-31, d $70-74; ⊙Oct-May; 🔊) 🌿 is a bushy retreat with touches of Americana cool. Inside are cosy beds and a laid-back communal area, while beyond the doorstep are bush walks leading to peaceful river swimming holes. There's only room for 14, so booking is recommended.

Jack's Gasthof (☎03-789 6501; www.jacks-gasthof.co.nz; SH6; mains $12-28; ☉from 11am Oct-Apr) is 21km south of Westport on the Little Totara River, where Berliners Jack and Petra run their eternally popular pizzeria with adjacent bar improbably bejewelled with a disco ball. Avail yourself of campsites (from $6) and a basic room ($50) if you require a sleepover.

For a true taste of the region's gold mining past, swing into **Mitchell's Gully Gold Mine** (www.mitchellsgullygoldmine.co.nz; SH6; adult/child $10/free; ☉9am-5pm), 22km south of Westport, where you'll meet a pioneer's descendants and explore the family mine. There are interesting tales, relics, tunnels and railtracks, plus a giant waterwheel and the odd trap-door spider.

The next stop is **Charleston**, 26km south of Westport. It's hard to believe it now, but this place boomed during the 1860s gold rush, with 80 hotels, three breweries and hundreds of thirsty gold-diggers staking claims along the Nile River. There's not much left now except a motel, campground, a clutch of local houses and the brilliant Norwest Adventures (p101) with whom you can explore some utterly amazing hidden treasures.

From here to Punakaiki is a staggeringly beautiful panorama of lowland pakihi scrub and lush green forest alongside a series of bays dramatically sculpted by relentless ocean fury. Drive as slowly as the traffic behind you will allow.

Punakaiki & Paparoa National Park

Located midway between Westport and Greymouth is Punakaiki, a small settlement beside the rugged 380-sq-km Paparoa National Park. For most travellers it's a quick stop for coffee and a squiz at the Pancake Rocks, which is a shame because there's excellent tramping and other wild adventures, and plenty of accommodation.

◎ Sights

Paparoa National Park is blessed with high cliffs and empty beaches, a dramatic mountain range, crazy limestone river valleys, diverse flora, and a profusion of birdlife, including weka and the Westland petrel, a rare sea bird which nests only here.

Pancake Rocks NATURAL FEATURE
Punakaiki is famous for its fantastic Pancake Rocks and blowholes. Through a layering-weathering process called stylobedding the Dolomite Point limestone has formed into what looks like piles of thick pancakes. Aim for high tide (tide times are posted at the visitor information centre) when the sea surges into caverns and booms menacingly through blowholes. See it on a wild day and be reminded that Mother Nature really is the boss. An easy 15-minute walk loops from the highway out to the rocks and blowholes.

Activities

Tramps around Punakaiki include the **Truman Track** (30 minutes return) and the **Punakaiki–Porari Loop** (3½ hours), which goes up the spectacular limestone Pororari River gorge before popping over a hill and coming down the bouldery Punakaiki River to rejoin the highway.

Surefooted types can embark on the **Fox River Cave Walk** (three hours return), 12km north of Punakaiki and open to amateur explorers. BYO torch and sturdy shoes.

Other tramps in the national park are detailed in the DOC *Paparoa National Park* pamphlet ($1), and include the **Inland Pack Track** (two to three days), a route established by miners in 1866 to bypass difficult coastal terrain.

As many of Paparoa's inland walks are susceptible to river flooding it is vital that you obtain updates from the DOC visitor centre (p107) in Punakaiki before you depart.

Punakaiki Canoes KAYAKING
(☎03-731 1870; www.riverkayaking.co.nz; SH6; canoe hire 2hr/full day $40/60, family rates available) This outfit rents canoes near the Pororari River bridge, for gentle, super-scenic paddling for all abilities.

Punakaiki Horse Treks HORSE RIDING
(☎03-731 1839; www.pancake-rocks.co.nz; SH6; 3hr ride $160; ☉Nov-May) Punakaiki Horse Treks, based at Hydrangea Cottages, conducts equine outings in the Punakaiki Valley, with river crossings, finishing at the beach.

⊨ Sleeping & Eating

There's good news and bad news. The good news is that there's ample accommodation in Punakaiki. The bad news is that there's no grocery shop or petrol, and that the sole cafe may well fail to please. The tavern down the road, however, remains a consistently good performer. Keep it up, Team Pub!

★ **Punakaiki Beach Hostel**   HOSTEL $
(☑ 03-731 1852; www.punakaikibeachhostel.co.nz;
4 Webb St; campsites per person $20, dm/s/d
$28/54/75; @ 🌐) A laid-back hostel with a
sea-view verandah, just a short walk from
Pancake Rocks. Co-operative owners have
been-there-done-that and know exactly
what you want: a clean hostel with good
beds, great communal facilities, and staff
who smile because they mean it. The cutesy,
virtually-on-the-beach Sunset Cottage ($115)
is well worth a splurge.

Punakaiki Beach Camp   HOLIDAY PARK $
(☑ 03-731 1894; www.punakaikibeachcamp.co.nz; 5
Owen St; campsites per person powered/unpowered
$20/17, d $48-92; 🌐) With a backdrop of sheer
cliffs, this salty, beachside park with good
grass is studded with clean, old-style cabins and shipshape amenities. A classic Kiwi
coastal campground.

Te Nikau Retreat   HOSTEL $
(☑ 03-731 1111; www.tenikauretreat.co.nz; 19 Hart-
mount Pl; sites from $18, dm $28, d $75-90, cabins
from $96; @ 🌐) 🛇 Relax, restore and explore
at this unconventional property consisting
of numerous buildings nestled into their
own rainforest nooks, just a short walk to
the beach. There are rooms in the main
building, several cute cabins, and the larger
Nikau Lodge sleeping up to 9.

Hydrangea Cottages   COTTAGES $$
(☑ 03-731 1839; www.pancake-rocks.co.nz; SH6; d
$140-310; 🌐) On a hillside overlooking the
Tasman, these five standalone and mostly
self-contained cottages (largest sleeping up
to seven) are built from salvaged timber and
river stones. It's a classy but relaxed enclave,
with splashes of colourful mosaic and pretty
cottage gardens. The owners also run the
horse-trekking stables.

Punakaiki Tavern   PUB $$
(www.punakaikitavern.co.nz; SH6; mains $19-33;
⊙ 8am-late; 🌐) Whether it's breakfast, lunch
or dinner, this pub does decent portions
of honest food served in comfortable surrounds. Most nights the punters are a mix
of local and international, so there's ample
opportunity for conversation and friendly
debate over the rules of pool.

❶ Information

The **Paparoa National Park visitor information
centre and i-SITE** (☑ 03-731 1895; www.doc.
govt.nz; SH6; ⊙ 9am-5pm Oct-Nov, to 6pm Dec-
Mar, to 4.30pm Apr-Sep) has info on the park and
track conditions, and handles bookings for attractions and accommodation including hut tickets.

An online directory of local activities and operators is maintained by **Punakaiki Promotions**
(www.punakaiki.co.nz).

❶ Getting There & Away

InterCity (☑ 03-365 1113; www.intercity.co.nz)
travels daily north to Westport (45 minutes), and
south to Greymouth (45 minutes) and Fox Glacier
(five hours). **Naked Bus** (www.nakedbus.com)
runs to the same destinations three days a week.
Both companies stop long enough for passengers to admire the Pancake Rocks.

Punakaiki to Greymouth

The highway from Punakaiki to Greymouth
is flanked by white-capped waves and rocky
bays on one side, and the steep, bushy
Paparoa Ranges on the other.

At **Barrytown**, 17km south of Punakaiki,
Steve and Robyn run **Barrytown Knifemak-
ing** (☑ 03-731 1053, 0800 256 433; www.barry-
townknifemaking.com; 2662 SH6, Barrytown; classes
$150; ⊙ closed Mon), where you can make your
own knife – from hand-forging the blade to
crafting a handle from native rimu timber.
The day-long course features lunch, archery,
axe-throwing and a stream of entertainingly
bad jokes from Steve. Bookings essential, and
transport from Punakaiki can be arranged.

With a rainforest backdrop and coastal
views, **Ti Kouka House** (☑ 03-731 1460;
www.tikoukahouse.co.nz; 2522 SH6, Barrytown; d
incl breakfast $305; 🌐) further amazes with
its splendid architectural design, recycled
building materials, and sculptural artwork
both inside and out. It's an excellent B&B
with three luxurious rooms.

Breakers (☑ 03-762 7743; www.breakers.
co.nz; 1367 SH6, Nine Mile Creek; d incl breakfast
$215-365; @ 🌐), 14km north of Greymouth,
is one of the best-kept secrets on the coast.
Beautifully appointed en suite rooms over-
look the sea, with fine surfing opportunities at hand for the intrepid. The hosts are
sporty, friendly and have a nice dog.

Two kilometres south is **Rapahoe**, 12km
shy of Greymouth. This tiny seaside settlement is the northern trailhead for the enjoyable Point Elizabeth Walkway (p108). Should
you require refreshment before or after your
walk, call in to the **Rapahoe Hotel** (1 Beach
Rd; mains $12-29), a simple country pub offer-
ing warm hospitality and a good feed of fish
and chips in a picturesque location.

GREYMOUTH REGION

Bookending NZ's most famous alpine pass and sitting more or less halfway along the West Coast highway, the Greymouth area provides easy access to the attractions north and south as well as offering a decent smattering of diversions within its boundaries.

Greymouth

POP 8900

Welcome to the 'Big Smoke', crouched at the mouth of the imaginatively named Grey River. The West Coast's largest town has gold in its veins, and today its fortunes still ebb and flow with the tide of mining, although dairy farming and tourism top up the coffers. The town is well geared for travellers, offering all the necessary services and the odd tourist attraction, the most famous of which is Shantytown.

◉ Sights & Activities

Shantytown MUSEUM
(www.shantytown.co.nz; Rutherglen Rd, Paroa; adult/child/family $31.50/15.50/74; ⏰8.30am-5pm) Eight kilometres south of Greymouth and 2km inland from SH6, Shantytown recreates a 1860s gold-mining town, complete with steam-train rides, post office, pub and Rosie's House of Ill Repute. There's also gold panning, a flying fox, sawmill, a gory hospital and 10-minute holographic movies in the Princess Theatre.

★ Left Bank Art Gallery GALLERY
(www.leftbankarts.org.nz; 1 Tainui St; admission by donation; ⏰10am-4pm daily) This 90-year-old former bank houses contemporary NZ jade carvings, prints, paintings, photographs and ceramics. The gallery also fosters and supports a wide society of West Coast artists.

History House Museum MUSEUM
(www.history-house.co.nz; 27 Gresson St; adult/child $6/2; ⏰10am-4pm Mon-Fri) This museum documents Greymouth's pre-1920 history with an impressive collection of photographs.

TranzAlpine TRAIN TOUR
(✆03-341 2588, 0800 872 467; www.kiwirailscenic.co.nz; adult/child one way from $99/69; ⏰departs Christchurch 8.15am, Greymouth 1.45pm) The *TranzAlpine* is one of the world's great train journeys, traversing the Southern Alps between Christchurch and Greymouth, from the Pacific Ocean to the Tasman Sea, passing through Arthur's Pass National Park. En route is a sequence of dramatic landscapes, from the flat, alluvial Canterbury Plains, through narrow alpine gorges, an 8.5km tunnel, beech-forested river valleys, and alongside a lake fringed with cabbage trees. The 4½-hour journey is unforgettable, even in bad weather (if it's raining on one coast, it's probably fine on the other).

Monteith's Brewing Co BREWERY
(✆03-768 4149; www.monteiths.co.nz; cnr Turumaha & Herbert Sts; ⏰10.30am-7.30pm) The original Monteith's brewhouse may simply be brand HQ for mainstream product largely brewed elsewhere, but it still delivers heritage in spades through its excellent-value tour (one hour, $20, includes generous samples; three to five tours per day). The flash tasting-room-cum-bar is now Greymouth's most exciting watering hole (tasty snacks $7 to $18) – shame it shuts up shop so early.

Floodwall Walk WALKING
Take a 10-minute riverside stroll along Mawhera Quay, or keep going for an hour or so, taking in the fishing harbour, breakwater and Blaketown Beach, which leads on to the West Coast Wilderness Trail (p111). Other local walks (most inclined towards mining heritage sites) are detailed in the free Greymouth map and brochure, available from the i-SITE (p110).

Point Elizabeth Walkway WALKING
Accessible from Dommett Esplanade in Cobden, 6km north of Greymouth, this enjoyable walkway (three hours return) skirts around a richly forested headland in the shadow of the Rapahoe Range to an ocean lookout, before continuing on to the northern trailhead at Rapahoe (12km from Greymouth) – small town, big beach, friendly local pub.

Kea Heritage Tours GUIDED TOUR
(✆0800 532 868; www.keatours.co.nz) Kea operates high-quality shuttle-bus tours with well-informed guides, and visits coast sites and those beyond. Short tours include the half-day Punakaiki Tour ($115), and the day-long Twin Glaciers ($295). Myriad other options include a multiday exploration of the Maori greenstone trails.

⊨ Sleeping

Global Village HOSTEL $
(✆03-768 7272; www.globalvillagebackpackers.co.nz; 42 Cowper St; sites per person $18, dm/d/tr/q $28/70/96/120; @🛜) A collage of African and Asian art is infused with a passion-

Greymouth

ate travellers' vibe here. Free kayaks – the Lake Karoro wetlands reserve is just metres away – and mountain bikes are on tap, and relaxation comes easy with a spa, sauna, barbecue and fire pit.

Noah's Ark Backpackers HOSTEL $
(📱03-768 4868, 0800 662 472; www.noahs. co.nz; 16 Chapel St; sites per person $17, dm/s/d $27/54/68; @🖾) Originally a monastery, colourful Noah's has eccentric animal-themed rooms, a sunset-worthy balcony and quiet back garden with a spa pool. Mountain bikes and fishing rods are provided free of charge.

Ardwyn House B&B $
(📱03-768 6107; ardwynhouse@hotmail.com; 48 Chapel St; s/d incl breakfast from $60/90; 🖾) This old-fashioned B&B nestles amid steep gardens on a quiet dead-end street. Mary, the well-travelled host, cooks a splendid breakfast.

**Greymouth Seaside
Top 10 Holiday Park** MOTEL, HOLIDAY PARK $
(📱03-768 6618, 0800 867 104; www.top10greymouth.co.nz; 2 Chesterfield St; sites $40-46, cabins $60-125, motel r $110-374; @🖾) Well positioned for sunset walks on the adjacent beach and 2.5km south of the town centre, this large park has various tent and camper-

Greymouth

van sites as well as accommodation ranging from simple cabins to deluxe seaview motels – arguably the flashest units in town. A shipshape stop for every budget.

**Greymouth Kiwi
Holiday Park & Motels** MOTEL, HOLIDAY PARK $
(📱03-762 6768, 0800 101 222; www.southbeach. co.nz; 318 Main South Rd; sites $30-35, d $50-130; @🖾) This low-rise complex offers a range of cheap, no-frills accommodation, sandwiched

between the (busy) highway and the beach, 6km south of town.

Paroa Hotel   HOTEL $$
(☑03-762 6860, 0800 762 6860; www.paroa.co.nz; 508 Main South Rd, Paroa; d $128-140; ☎) Opposite the Shantytown turn-off, this family-owned hotel (60 years and counting) has spacious units sharing a large lawned garden next to the beach. The notable bar and restaurant dishes up warm hospitality (mains $18 to $32) in the form of roast, pavlova, and beer, amid local clientele.

✖ Eating & Drinking

Greymouth has a decent daytime cafe scene, but come evening some of the best food will be found at pubs on the town fringe and beyond.

DP:One Cafe   CAFE $
(104 Mawhera Quay; meals $7-23; ☺8am-8pm Mon-Fri, 9am-5pm Sat & Sun; ☎) A stalwart of the Greymouth cafe scene, this hip joint serves great espresso, along with good-value grub. Groovy tunes, wi-fi, a relaxed vibe and quayside tables make this a welcoming spot to linger.

Freddy's Cafe   CAFE $
(115 Mackay St; snacks $4-7, meals $8-18; ☺8am-5pm) Don't miss the doorway because upstairs the restrained-retro Freddy's beckons with good espresso, all-day hot meals (pancakes, seafood chowder, pasta) alongside an appealing selection of cabinet food. The likes of vegetarian quiche can be rounded off with several different chocolate options, including the venerable afghan biscuit.

Ali's Eating & Drinking   CAFE $$
(9 Tainui St; mains $12-27; ☺8am-10pm Mon-Sat, to 3pm Sun) Painted in warm orange and adorned with local art, conservative but comfortable Ali's serves honest all-day food of global bent such as laksa, pasta, steak and whitebait, with lovely homemade desserts such as Knickerbocker Glory.

❶ Information

Free town and regional maps are available at the i-SITE. Major banks huddle around Mackay and Tainui Sts. There's internet access at the i-SITE and **library** (18 Albert St; ☎).

Greymouth i-SITE (☑03-768 5101, 0800 473 966; www.greydistrict.co.nz; Railway Station, 164 Mackay St; ☺9am-5pm Mon-Fri, 9.30am-4pm Sat & Sun; ☎) The helpful crew at the railway station can assist with all manner of advice and bookings, including those for DOC huts and walks. See also www.westcoastnz.com.
Grey Base Hospital (☑03-768 0499; High St)
Post Office (36 Tainui St)

❶ Getting There & Around

Combined with the i-SITE in the railway station, the **West Coast Travel Centre** (☑03-768 7080; www.westcoasttravel.co.nz; Railway Station, 164 Mackay St; ☺9am-5pm Mon-Fri, 10am-4pm Sat & Sun; ☎) books local and national transport and offers luggage storage.

BUS
All buses stop outside the railway station.
InterCity (☑03-365 1113; www.intercity.co.nz) has daily buses north to Westport (two hours) and Nelson (six hours), and south to Franz Josef Glacier (3½ hours). **Naked Bus** (www.nakedbus.com) runs the same route three days a week. Both companies offer connections to destinations further afield.
Atomic Travel (☑03-349 0697, 0508 108 359; www.atomictravel.co.nz) passes Greymouth on its daily Nelson to Franz Josef service (and onward to Queenstown), as well as running across Arthur's Pass to Christchurch. **West Coast Shuttle** (☑03-768 0028, 0274 927 000; www.westcoastshuttle.co.nz) also runs a daily service between Greymouth and Christchurch.

CAR
Several car-hire company desks are located within the railway station. Local companies include **Alpine West** (☑03-768 4002, 0800 257 736; www.alpinerentals.co.nz; 11 Shelley St) and **NZ Rent-a-Car** (☑03-768 0379; www.nzrenta-car.co.nz; 170 Tainui St).

TAXI
Greymouth Taxis (☑03-768 7078)

Blackball

Around 25km upriver of Greymouth sits the ramshackle town of Blackball – established in 1866 to service gold diggers; coal mining kicked in between 1890 and 1964. The National Federation of Labour (a trade union) was conceived here, born from influential strikes in 1908 and 1931. This story is retold in historical displays on the main road.

Alongside you will find the hub of the town, **Formerly the Blackball Hilton** (☑03-732 4705, 0800 425 225; www.blackballhilton.co.nz; 26 Hart St; s/d with continental breakfast $55/110), where you can collect a copy of the helpful 'Historic Blackball' map. This official Historic Place has memorabilia galore, hot meals, cold beer, heaps of afternoon sun, and a host of rooms oozing the charm of yesteryear; it was named so after a certain global hotel chain got antsy when its name was appropriated.

Competing with the Hilton in the fame stakes is the **Blackball Salami Co** (www. blackballsalami.co.nz; 11 Hilton St; ⊙8am-4pm Mon-Fri, 9am-2pm Sat), manufacturer of tasty salami and sausages ranging from chorizo to black pudding.

Blackball's other claim to fame is as the southern end of the **Croesus Track**, a two-day historic goldfields route that clambers over a knob to reach Barrytown. Visit DOC's website for details.

Lake Brunner

Lying inland from Greymouth, **Lake Brunner** (www.golakebrunner.co.nz) can be reached via the SH7 turn-off at Stillwater, a journey of 39km. It can also be reached from the south via Kumara Junction.

One of many lakes in the area, Brunner is a tranquil spot for bushwalks, bird-spotting and various watersports including boating and fishing. Indeed, the local boast is that the lake and Arnold River are 'where the trout die of old age', which implies that the local fish are particularly clever or the fisherfolk are somewhat hopeless. Greymouth i-SITE can hook you up with a guide. Head to the marina to undertake one or all of several pretty short walks.

Moana is the main settlement, home to numerous accommodation options of which the best is **Lake Brunner Country Motel**

(☑03-738 0144; www.lakebrunnermotel.co.nz; 2014 Arnold Valley Rd; sites from $30, cabins $60-70, cottages d $135-145; ☎), 2km from the lake. It features cabins, cottages and campervan sites tucked into native plantings through park-like grounds, while tenters can enjoy the lush grassy camping field down the back. This is proper peace and quiet, unless you count birdsong and the bubbling of the spa pool.

Moana also has a couple of places to eat including a cafe opposite the station where the *TranzAlpine* train pulls in. There's also food at the petrol station, and the local pub, which is trending upward.

Kumara

POP 310

Thirty kilometres south of Greymouth, near the western end of Arthur's Pass (SH73), Kumara was yet another busy gold-rush town that ground to a halt, leaving behind a thin posse of flinty folk who have kept the town going to this day. And all to the greater good, for were it not for the Kumarians there would be no starting point for the **Coast to Coast** (www.coasttocoast.co.nz), NZ's most famous multisport race. Held each February, the strong, the brave and the totally knackered run-cycle-ride-kayak-bike a total of 243km all the way across the mountains to Christchurch, with top competitors dusting it off in just under 11 hours.

Having manned the starting gate with sterling hospitality for 30 years, this tiny town is well-oiled to cope with yet more sporty visitors, namely people cycling the

---

WORTH A TRIP

A CYCLE ON THE WILD SIDE

Officially opened in 2013, the 120km **West Coast Wilderness Trail** (www.westcoastwildernesstrail.co.nz) is one of around two dozen new **NZ Cycle Trails** (www.nzcycletrail.com). Stretching from Greymouth to Hokitika (with plans to extend it further south to Ross), the gently graded track follows a mix of gold-rush trails, water races, logging tramways and historic railway lines, as well as forging new routes cross-country. Along the way it reveals outstanding landscapes of dense rainforest, glacial rivers, lakes and wetlands, with views all the way from the snow-capped mountains of the Southern Alps to the wild Tasman Sea.

The full shebang is a good four days of riding but, like many of the new cycle trails, it can easily be sliced up into sections of various lengths, catering to every ability and area of interest. The leg from Milltown to Kumara is shaping up as an excellent day ride, taking four to six hours and finishing at the resplendent Theatre Royal Hotel (p112).

Bike hire, transport and advice is available from the major setting-off points. In Hokitika, contact **Wilderness Trail Shuttle** (☑021 263 3299, 03-755 5042; www.wildernesstrailshuttle.co.nz) and in Greymouth try the folks at **West Coast Rail Trail** (☑03-768 6649, 0800 946 543; www.westcoastrailtrail.com).

West Coast Wilderness Trail (p111), which passes through the town. Anticipating their arrival is the show-stopping **Theatre Royal Hotel** (☑03-736 9277; www.theatreroyalhotel.co.nz; 81 Seddon St, SH73, Kumara; mains $22-42, d incl breakfast $135-290; ☺10am-late; ☞), the fully restored highway stop that has kicked Kumara well and truly into the 21st century with its civilised bar, classy dining room, and sumptuous upstairs rooms styled after local personalities of old. The attention to detail in furnishings and heritage displays is simply wonderful. Stop in to enjoy some of the best food on the coast (fish and chips, local game, pizza and delicate cakes) or just pull in for a drink and a yarn with the locals.

Should you be to-ing or fro-ing over Arthur's Pass, consider staying at **Jacksons Retreat** (☑03-738 0474; www.jacksonsretreat.co.nz; Jacksons, SH73; sites from $35; @☞) ✈, 33km west of Arthur's Pass Village. Set upon 15 sloping acres with exceptional views over the Taramakau River, it offers stacks of excellent amenities for campervanner and tenter alike.

WESTLAND

The bottom third or so of the West Coast is known as Westland, a mix of farmland and rainforest backed by the Southern Alps, which pop straight up in a neck-cricking fashion. This region is most famous for its glaciers.

Hokitika

POP 3000

Popular with history buffs and the setting for numerous NZ novels – including the 2013 Man Booker Prize–winning *The Luminaries* by Eleanor Catton – Hokitika's riches come in many forms. Founded on gold, today the town is the stronghold of indigenous *pounamu* (greenstone), which jostles for attention amid many other arts and crafts, drawing rafts of visitors to the town's wide open streets.

☉ Sights & Activities

Hokitika is a great base for walking and cycling. Download or collect a copy of DOC's brochure *Walks in the Hokitika Area* ($1), and visit **Hokitika Cycles & Sports World** (☑03-755 8662; www.hokitikasportsworld.co.nz; 33 Tancred St; bike hire per day $55) for cycle hire and advice on tracks including the West Coast Wilderness Trail (p111).

★**Hokitika Museum**   MUSEUM
(www.hokitikamuseum.co.nz; 17 Hamilton St; adult/child $5/2.50; ☺10am-5pm) Housed in the imposing Carnegie Building (1908), this is an exemplary provincial museum, with intelligently curated exhibitions presented in a clear, modern style. Highlights include the fascinating *Whitebait!* exhibition, and the *Pounamu* room – the ideal primer before you hit the galleries looking for greenstone treasures.

Sunset Point   LOOKOUT
(Gibson Quay) A spectacular vantage point at any time of day, this is – as the name suggests – the primo place to watch the light fade away. Surfers, seagulls, and fish and chips: *this* is New Zealand.

Hokitika Heritage Walk   WALK
Pick up the 50-cent leaflet from the i-SITE and wander the old wharf precinct. Another brochure details the **Hokitika Heritage Trail**, a 11km (two to three hour) loop taking in historic sites and interesting town views.

Glowworm Dell   NATURAL FEATURE
Just north of town, a short stroll from SH6 leads to a Glowworm Dell, an easy opportunity to enter the other-wordly home of NZ's native fungus gnat larvae (so not even a worm at all). An information panel at the entrance will further illuminate your way.

Lake Kaniere   LAKE
(www.doc.govt.nz) Lying at the heart of a 70-sq-km scenic reserve, beautiful Lake Kaniere is 8km long, 2km wide, 195m deep, and also quite cool, as you'll discover if you swim. You may, however, prefer simply to camp or picnic at **Hans Bay** (www.doc.govt.nz), or undertake one of numerous walks in the surrounds, ranging from the 15-minute Canoe Cove Walk to the seven-hour return gut-buster up Mt Tuhua. The historic **Kaniere Water Race Walkway** (3½ hours one way) forms part of the new West Coast Wilderness Trail.

Hokitika Gorge   GORGE
(www.doc.govt.nz) A picturesque 35km drive leads to Hokitika Gorge, a ravishing ravine with unbelievably turquoise waters coloured by glacial 'flour'. Point and shoot the scene from every angle via the short forest walkway and swingbridge. The gorge is well signposted from Stafford St (past the dairy factory). En route, you will pass **Kowhitirangi**, the

Hokitika

Hokitika

◎ Top Sights
1 Hokitika Museum.....................................C2

◎ Sights
2 Hokitika Craft Gallery............................C2
3 Hokitika Glass Studio.............................C1
4 Sunset Point...A2
5 Tectonic Jade..C1
6 Waewae Pounamu..................................C2

◎ Activities, Courses & Tours
7 Bonz 'N' Stonz..C2
8 Hokitika Heritage Walk..........................B2

◎ Sleeping
9 Teichelmann's B&B................................C2

◎ Eating
10 Dulcie's Takeaways...............................B2
11 Fat Pipi Pizza..C1
12 New World...C1
13 Stumpers Cafe & Bar C1
14 Sweet Alice's Fudge
     Kitchen...C1

◎ Drinking & Nightlife
15 West Coast Wine Bar.............................C1

◎ Shopping
16 Hokitika Cycles & Sports
     World...C1

ite of NZ's first mass-murder and a massive 2-day manhunt (immortalised in the 1982 classic film *Bad Blood*). A poignant roadside monument lines up the farmstead site through a stone shaft.

Galleries

Art and craft galleries are a strong spoke in Hoki's wheel, and you could easily spend a day spinning around the lot. There are plenty of opportunities to meet the artists, and in some studios you can watch them at

work. Be aware that some galleries sell jade imported from Europe and Asia, as precious local *pounamu* (greenstone) is not surrendered lightly by the wilds.

Bonz 'N' Stonz   CARVING
(www.bonz-n-stonz.co.nz; 16 Hamilton St; full-day workshop $85-180) Design, carve and polish your own *pounamu*, bone or paua masterpiece, with tutelage from Steve. Prices vary with materials and design complexity. Bookings recommended.

Hokitika Craft Gallery
GALLERY

(www.hokitikacraftgallery.co.nz; 25 Tancred St) The town's best one-stop-shop, this co-op show-cases a wide range of local work including *pounamu*, jewellery, textiles, ceramics and woodwork.

Jagosi Jade
GALLERY

(🖉 03-755 6243; 246 Sewell St) Aden Hoglund carves traditional and modern Maori pieces from local stone; will make to order.

Tectonic Jade
GALLERY

(www.tectonicjade.com; 67 Revell St) This welcoming gallery is a great spot to view and buy local *pounamu*, carved by the talented Rex Scott.

Waewae Pounamu
GALLERY

(www.waewaepounamu.co.nz; 39 Weld St) This stronghold of NZ *pounamu* displays traditional and contemporary designs in its large, main-road gallery.

Hokitika Glass Studio
GALLERY

(www.hokitikaglass.co.nz; 9 Weld St) Glass art covering a continuum from garish to glorious; watch the blowers at the furnace on weekdays.

🕼 Tours

Wilderness Wings
SCENIC FLIGHTS

(🖉 0800 755 8118; www.wildernesswings.co.nz; Hokitika Airport; flights from $285) Offers scenic flights over Hokitika, and further afield to Aoraki/Mt Cook and the glaciers.

⚝ Festivals & Events

Driftwood & Sand
ART

(www.driftwoodandsand.co.nz) During a week in January, flotsam and jetsam is fashioned into a surprising array of arty, crafty and daft sculpture on Hokitika beach.

Wildfoods Festival
FOOD

(www.wildfoods.co.nz) Held in early March, this festival attracts thousands of curious and brave gourmands who eat a whole lot of things they would usually flee from or flick from their hair. Legendary fun; book early.

🛏 Sleeping

★ Drifting Sands
HOSTEL $

(🖉 03-755 7654; www.driftingsands.co.nz; 197 Revell St; sites from $16, dm/s/d $30/60/78; @ 🛜) Access to the beach from the back garden and this hostel's family-home feel make it our pick of Hoki's budget accommodation. The cheery, fastidious owner and crisp bedlinens don't hurt either.

Shining Star Beachfront Accommodation
HOLIDAY PARK, MOTEL $

(🖉 03-755 8921, 0800 744 646; www.shiningstar.co.nz; 16 Richards Dr; sites per person unpowered/powered $16/20, d $95-175; @ 🛜) Attractive and versatile beachside spot with everything from camping to classy self-contained seafront units. Kids will love the menagerie including pigs and alpacas straight from Dr Doolittle's appointment book. Parents might prefer the spa and sauna ($15 for two).

Birdsong
HOSTEL $

(🖉 03-755 7179; www.birdsong.co.nz; SH6; dm/s $30/60, d without/with bathroom $79/94; @ 🛜) Located 2.5km north of town, this bird themed hostel has sea views and a homely atmosphere. Free bikes, handy beach access and hidden extras will entice you into extending your stay.

Annabelle Motel
MOTEL $

(🖉 050 854 9494, 03-755 8160; www.annabellemotel.co.nz; 214 Weld St; s $130, d $140-190; 🛜) Less than 1km from the Hoki clock tower, prett

---

WHITEBAIT FEVER

On even the swiftest of visits to the Coast, you are sure to come across a little whitebait or two, whether being sold from Womble's back door, in a pattie sandwich, in museums, or in tales tall and true. These tiny, transparent fish are the young of some of NZ's precious native fish, including inanga, kokopu, smelt and even eels. Strangely enough, they all look and taste the same.

Commanding up to $80 a kilo round these parts (and much more elsewhere), competition is tough to net the elusive fish. The season runs from August to November, when riverbanks and fishing stands are busy from Karamea to Haast.

The classic pattie recipe involves little more than an egg, and is accompanied by a wedge of lemon, although some would say that mint sauce is the best embellishment. The *Whitebait!* exhibition at Hokitika Museum (p112) will give you some idea as to what all the fuss is about.

Annabelle is away from beach and town action but well located for peace and convenience. Tip-top units, decorated in green garden hues with plush furnishings, meet all middle-of-the-road modern standards.

Stations Inn   MOTEL **$$**
(☑ 03-755 5499; www.stationsinnhokitika.co.nz; Blue Spur Rd; d $170-300; ☏) Five minutes' drive from town, high upon rolling hills that overlook the distant ocean, this modern motel complex has plush units featuring king-sized beds and spa bath. With a patio, pond and waterwheel out front, the ambient on-site restaurant (mains $30 to $45; open from 5pm Tuesday to Saturday) specialises in venison, beef and lamb, with petit fours and cheese for afters.

Teichelmann's B&B   B&B **$$$**
(☑ 03-755 8232; www.teichelmanns.co.nz; 20 Hamilton St; d $235-255; ☏) Once home to surgeon, mountaineer and professional beard-cultivator Ebenezer Teichelmann, this is now a charming B&B. All rooms have their own bathrooms, including the more private Teichy's Cottage, in the garden oasis out back.

✖ Eating & Drinking

Dulcie's Takeaways   FISH & CHIPS **$**
(cnr Gibson Quay & Wharf St; fish & chips $6-11; ☺11am-9pm) Net yourself some excellent ush 'n' chups (try the turbot or blue cod), then scoff them straight from the paper at Sunset Point – a Hokitika highlight.

Sweet Alice's Fudge Kitchen   SWEETS **$**
(27 Tancred St; ☺10am-5pm) Treat yourself with a slice of Alice's all-natural, handmade fudge ($7), a real fruit ice cream, or a bag of boiled lollies – or maybe all three.

New World   SUPERMARKET **$**
(116 Revell St; ☺8am-8pm) If you're heading south, this is your last proper supermarket before Wanaka, 426km away!

★ Fat Pipi Pizza   PIZZERIA **$$**
(89 Revell St; pizzas $20-30; ☺noon-9pm Tue-Sun, 4-9pm Mon; ☛) Vegetarians, carnivores and everyone in between will be salivating for the pizza (including a whitebait version) made right before your eyes. Lovely cakes, honey buns and Benger juices, too. Best enjoyed in the garden bar.

Stumpers Cafe & Bar   CAFE, BAR **$$**
(2 Weld St; lunch $10-22, dinner $18-36; ☺7am-late) There's something for everyone here, at any time of the day. In the evening you'll find meaty mains, along with a whole host of locals meeting up for a pint and a game of pool.

West Coast Wine Bar   WINE BAR
(108 Revell St; ☺3-8pm Sun-Thu, 3pm-late Fri & Sat) Upping Hoki's sophistication factor, this weeny joint with a cute garden bar pours all sorts of deliciousness, and plates up a little nibble. Fine wines to go.

❶ Information

Banks can be found on Weld and Revell Sts. There's free wi-fi at the **library** (20 Sewell St; ☺9.30am-5.30pm Mon-Fri, 10am-1pm Sat).
Hokitika i-SITE (☑ 03-755 6166; www.hokitika.org; 36 Weld St; ☺8.30am-6pm Mon-Fri, 9am-6pm Sat & Sun) One of NZ's best i-SITEs offers extensive bookings including all bus services. Also holds DOC info, although you'll need to book online or at DOC Visitor Centres further afield. See also www.westcoastnz.com.
Post Office (Revell St)
Westland Medical Centre (☑ 03-755 8180; 54a Sewell St; ☺8.30am-10pm)

❶ Getting There & Around

AIR

Hokitika Airport (www.hokitikaairport.co.nz; Airport Dr, off Tudor St) is 1.5km east of the centre of town. **Air New Zealand** (www.airnz.co.nz) has four flights daily to/from Christchurch.

BUS

InterCity (☑ 03-365 1113; www.intercity.co.nz) buses depart from Tancred St daily for Greymouth (45 minutes), Nelson (seven hours) and Franz Josef Glacier (two hours). **Naked Bus** (www.nakedbus.com) services the same destinations three times a week, with both companies offering connections to destinations further afield.

CAR

There are several car-hire branches at Hokitika Airport. **Hokitika Airport Car Rental** (☑ 0800 556 606; www.hokitikaairportcarhire.co.nz) offers online price comparisons, or enquire and book at the i-SITE.

TAXI

Hokitika Taxis (☑ 03-755 5075)

Hokitika to Westland Tai Poutini National Park

From Hokitika it's 140km south to Franz Josef Glacier. Most travellers fast forward without stopping, but there are some satisfying stopping points for the inclined. Intercity and Naked buses stop along this stretch of SH6.

Lake Mahinapua

On the highway eight kilometres south of Hokitika is the car park for the **Mahinapua Walkway** (two hours one way), a wonderful walk along an old logging tramway with relics and a diverse range of forest. (It's an even better bike ride.) Two kilometres further on is the entrance to **Lake Mahinapua Scenic Reserve**, with a picnic area, DOC campsite and several short walks.

Five kilometres further on is a signposted turn-off to the **West Coast Treetops Walkway** (☑050 887 3386, 03-755 5052; www.treetopsnz.com; 1128 Woodstock-Rimu Rd; aduld/child $38/15; ◷9am-5pm), a further 2km away. This steel walkway – 450 metres long and 20m off the ground – offers an unusual perspective on the rainforest canopy, featuring many old rimu and kamahi. The highlight is the 40m high tower, from which there are extensive views across Lake Mahinapua, the Southern Alps, and Tasman Sea. There's a cafe and souvenir shop in the information centre which also has a large sun-drenched patio.

Ross

Ross, 30km south of Hokitika, is where the unearthing of NZ's largest gold nugget (the 2.772kg 'Honourable Roddy') caused a kerfuffle in 1907. The **Ross Goldfields Heritage Centre** (www.ross.org.nz; 4 Aylmer St; ◷9am-4pm Dec-Mar, to 2pm Apr-Nov) displays a replica Roddy, along with a scale model ($2) of the town in its shiny years.

The **Water Race Walk** (one hour return) starts near the museum, passing old gold-diggings, caves, tunnels and a cemetery. Try **gold panning** by hiring a pan from the information centre ($10) and head to Jones Creek to look for Roddy's great, great grandnuggets.

Established in 1866, the **Empire Hotel** (19 Aylmer St; meals $15-25) is one of the West Coast's hidden gems, the bar (and many of its patrons) testament to a bygone era. Breathe in the authenticity, along with a whiff of woodsmoke, over a pint and an honest meal.

Hari Hari

About 22km south of Lake Ianthe, Hari Hari is where swashbuckling Australian aviator Guy Menzies crash-landed his trusty biplane into a swamp after completing the first solo trans-Tasman flight from Sydney, in 1931. Read all about it and view a replica of his plane at a commemorative park at the southern end of town.

The **Hari Hari Coastal Walk** (www.doc.govt.nz) (2¾ hours) is a low-tide loop along the Poerua and Wanganui Rivers through bogs, estuaries and a swamp forest. The walk starts 20km from SH6, the last 8km unsealed; follow the signs from Wanganui Flats Rd. Tide times are posted at the Pukeko Tearooms, which serves decent food and coffee.

Should you need a sleepover, **Flaxbush Motels** (☑03-753 3116; www.flaxbushmotels.co.nz; SH6; d $65-120; ☎) has characterful cabins and units covering a wide range of budgets. It also has a friendly disposition towards birds (ducks and peacocks in particular), and a willingness to negotiate room rates for longer stays.

Whataroa

Near Whataroa, 35km south of Hari Hari, is the **Kotuku Sanctuary**, NZ's only nesting site for the kotuku (white heron), which roosts here between November and February. The only way to visit the nesting site is with **White Heron Sanctuary Tours** (☑03-753 4120, 0800 523 456; www.whiteherontours.co.nz; SH6, Whataroa; adult/child $120/55; ◷4 tours daily late Sep-Mar) on an enjoyable 2½-hour tour involving a gentle jetboat ride and short boardwalk to a viewing hide. Seeing the scores of birds perched in the bushes is a magical experience. A scenic rainforest tour without the herons is available year-round for the same price.

The tour people also run the **Sanctuary Tours Motel** (☑03-753 4120, 0800 523 456; www.whiteherontours.co.nz; SH6; cabins $65-75; d $110-135), with basic cabins with shared bathrooms ($10 extra for bedlinen), and enthusiastically painted motel units.

Glacier Country Scenic Flights (☑03 753 4096, 0800 423 463; www.glacieradventures.co.nz; SH6, Whataroa; flights $195-435) offers a range of scenic flights and helihikes, lifting off from Whataroa Valley. These guys give you more mountain-gawping for your buck than many of the operators flying from the glacier townships.

Okarito

Fifteen kilometres south of Whataroa is the turn-off to the Forks, branching west for 13km to the magical seaside hamlet of Okarito (population 30ish). It sits alongside **Okarito Lagoon**, the largest unmodified wetland in NZ and a superb place for spot ting birds including rare kiwi and the majestic kotuku. Peaceful Okarito has no shops and limited visitor facilities, so stock up and book up before you arrive.

◉ Sights & Activities

From a car park on the Strand you can begin the easy **Wetland Walk** (20 minutes), a longer walk to **Three Mile Lagoon** (2¾ hours return), and a jolly good puff up to **Okarito Trig** (1½ hours return), which rewards the effort with spectacular Southern Alps and Okarito Lagoon views (weather contingent).

Andris Apse Wilderness Gallery   GALLERY
(☑ 03-753 4241; www.andrisapse.com; 109 The Strand) Okarito is home to world-class landscape photographer Andris Apse. His precisely composed gallery showcases his beautiful works, printed on site and available to purchase, as are infinitely more affordable books. Ring ahead to check it's open, or look for the sandwich board at the end of the driveway.

Okarito Nature Tours   KAYAKING
(☑ 050 865 2748, 03-753 4014; www.okarito.co.nz; kayak half-/full day $60/70; ☎) Hires out kayaks for paddles into the lagoon and up into the luxuriant rainforest channels where all sorts of birds hang out. Guided tours are available (from $85), while overnight rentals ($85) allow experienced paddlers to explore further afield. There's excellent espresso and wi-fi in the welcoming office/lounge.

Okarito Boat Tours   WILDLIFE TOUR
(☑ 03-753 4223; www.okaritoboattours.co.nz) Okarito Boat Tours runs bird-spotting lagoon tours, the most fruitful of which is the 'early bird' (7.30am, 1½ hours, $70). Other worthy options include the one-hour sightseeing tour (2.30pm, $45), and the two-hour nature tours (9am and 11.30am, $85). Cheery, longtime Okaritians Paula and Swade can also fix you up with accommodation in the village.

Okarito Kiwi Tours   WILDLIFE TOUR
(☑ 03-753 4330; www.okaritokiwitours.co.nz; 3hr tours $75) Runs nightly expeditions to spot the rare bird (95% success rate) with an interesting education along the way. Numbers are limited to eight, so booking is recommended.

🛏 Sleeping

★ Okarito Campground   CAMPSITE $
(off Russell St; sites adult/child $12.50/free) Okarito Campground is a breezy patch of community-managed greenery complete with kitchen and hot showers ($1). Gather driftwood from the beach for the fire-pit, or build your bonfire on the beach while the sun goes down. No reservations necessary.

Okarito Beach House   HOSTEL, LODGE $
(☑ 03-753 4080; www.okaritobeachhouse.com; The Strand; dm $28, d $60-100; ☎) The Okarito Beach House has a variety of accommodation. The weathered, self-contained 'Hutel' ($100) is worth every cent. The Summit Lodge has commanding views and the best dining-room table you've ever seen.

WESTLAND TAI POUTINI NATIONAL PARK

The biggest highlights of the Westland Tai Poutini National Park are the Franz Josef and Fox glaciers. Nowhere else at this latitude do glaciers come so close to the ocean. The glaciers' staggering development is largely due to the West Coast's ample rain; snow falling in the glaciers' broad accumulation zones fuses into clear ice at 20m depth, then surges down the steep valleys.

Some say Franz Josef is the superior ice experience, and, while it's visually more impressive, the walk to Fox is shorter, more interesting and often gets you closer to the ice. Both glacier faces are roped off to prevent people being caught in icefalls and river surges. The danger is very real – in 2009 two tourists were killed after being hit by falling ice when they ventured too close. The only way to get close to or on to the ice safely is on a guided tour.

Beyond the glaciers, the park's lower reaches harbour deserted Tasman Sea beaches, rising up through colour-splashed podocarp forests to NZ's highest peaks. Diverse and often unique ecosystems huddle next to each other in interdependent ecological sequence. Seals frolic in the surf as deer sneak through the forests. The resident endangered bird species include kakariki, kaka and rowi (the Okarito brown kiwi), as well as kea, the South Island's native parrot. Kea are inquisitive and endearing, but feeding them threatens their health.

Heavy tourist traffic often swamps the twin towns of Franz and Fox, 23km apart. Franz is the more action-packed of the two, while Fox has a more subdued alpine charm. From December to February, visitor numbers can get a little crazy in both, so consider travelling in the shoulder seasons: September/October and March/April.

Franz Josef Glacier

The early Maori knew Franz Josef as Ka Roimata o Hine Hukatere (Tears of the Avalanche Girl). Legend tells of a girl losing her lover who fell down from the local peaks, and her flood of tears freezing into the glacier. The glacier was first explored by Europeans in 1865, with Austrian Julius Haast naming it after the Austrian emperor. The glacier car park is 5km from Franz Josef village; the primary viewpoint is a 40-minute walk from there.

◎ Sights & Activities

★ **West Coast Wildlife Centre**   WILDLIFE
(www.wildkiwi.co.nz; cnr Cron & Cowan Sts; day pass adult/child/family $30/18/80, with backstage pass $50/30/125; 🖥) 🐾 This feel-good attraction ticks all the right boxes (exhibition, cafe, retail, wi-fi), then goes a whole lot further by actually breeding the rowi – the rarest kiwi in the world. The day pass is well worthwhile by the time you've viewed the conservation, glacier and heritage displays, and hung out with real, live kiwi in their ferny enclosure. The additional backstage pass into the incubating and chick-rearing area is a rare opportunity to learn how a species can be brought back from the brink of extinction, and a chance to go ga-ga over what may be the cutest babies on the planet.

Independent Walks

A rewarding alternative to driving to the glacier car park is the richly rainforested **Te Ara a Waiau Walkway/Cycleway**, starting from near the fire station at the south end of town. It's a one-hour walk (each way) or half that by bicycle (available for hire from Across Country Quad Bikes, p121, or the YHA, p121).

Several glacier viewpoints are accessed from the car park, including **Sentinel Rock** (20 minutes return) and the **Ka Roimata o Hine Hukatere Walk** (1½ hours return), leading you to the terminal face (read the signs; respect the barriers).

GLACIERS FOR DUMMIES

During the last ice age (15,000 to 20,000 years ago) Westland's twin glaciers reached the sea. In the ensuing thaw they may have crawled back even further than their current positions, but in the 14th century a mini ice age caused them to advance to their greatest modern-era extent around 1750, and the terminal moraines from this time are still visible.

If you get rained in during your time in glacier country, here are a few glacier-geek conversation starters for the pub.

Ablation zone Where the glacier melts.

Accumulation zone Where the ice and snow collects.

Bergschrund A large *crevasse* in the ice near the glacier's starting point.

Blue ice As the accumulation zone (*névé*) snow is compressed by subsequent snowfalls, it becomes *firn* and then *blue ice*.

Calving The process of ice breaking away from the glacier terminal face.

Crevasse A crack in the glacial ice formed as it crosses obstacles while descending.

Firn Partly compressed snow en route to becoming *blue ice*.

Glacial flour Finely ground rock particles in the milky rivers flowing off glaciers.

Icefall When a glacier descends so steeply that the upper ice breaks into a jumble of ice blocks.

Kettle lake A lake formed by the melt of an area of isolated dead ice.

Moraine Walls of debris formed at the glacier's sides (*lateral moraine*) or end (*terminal moraine*).

Névé Snowfield area where *firn* is formed.

Seracs Ice pinnacles formed, like *crevasses*, by the glacier rolling over obstacles.

Terminal The final ice face at the bottom of the glacier.

Other longer walks include the **Douglas Walk** (one hour return), off the Glacier Access Rd, which passes moraine from the 1750 advance, and **Peter's Pool**, a small kettle lake. The **Terrace Track** (30 minutes return) is an easy amble over bushy terraces behind the village, with Waiho River views. Two good rainforest walks, **Tatare Tunnels** and **Callery Gorge Walk** (both around 1½ hours return), start from Cowan St.

The rougher **Roberts Point Track** (five hours return) heads off from the Douglas swing bridge (access via the Douglas Walk). The **Alex Knob Track** (eight hours return) runs from the Glacier Access Rd to the 1303m peak of Alex Knob. Look forward to three glacier lookouts and views to the coast (cloud cover permitting). Both Roberts Point and Alex Knob are suitable only for well-equipped and experienced trampers.

Check out the glacier in the morning or evening, before the cloud cover sets in or after it lifts. Expect fewer tour buses as well.

Pick up a copy of DOC's excellent *Glacier Region Walks* booklet ($2) which provides maps and illuminating background reading.

Guided Walks & Helihikes

Small group walks with experienced guides (boots, jackets and equipment supplied) are offered by **Franz Josef Glacier Guides** (☑03-752 0763, 0800 484 337; www.franzjosef-glacier.com; 6 Main Rd). Both standard tours require helicopter transfers to and from the ice: the 'Ice Explorer' ($325) is bookended by a four-minute flight, with around three hours on the ice; the easier 'Heli Hike' ($429) explores higher reaches of the glacier, requiring a 10-minute flight with around two hours on the ice. Taking around three hours, the 'Glacier Valley Walk' ($75) follows the Waiho River up to the moraine, offering a chance to get beyond the public barriers for close up views of the ice. All trips are $10–30 cheaper for children.

Aerial Sightseeing

Forget sandflies and mozzies. The buzzing you're hearing is a swarm of aircraft in the skies around the glaciers and just beyond in the realm of Aoraki/Mt Cook. A common heliflight ($200–230) is 20 minutes long, and goes to the head of Franz Glacier with a snow landing up top. A 'twin glacier' flight – taking in Fox as well as Franz in around 30 minutes – costs in the region of $300, with a full-monty 40-minute trip (swooping around Aoraki/Mt Cook) from $400. Fares for chil-

dren under 15 are between 60% and 70% of the adult price. Shop around: most operators are situated on the main road in Franz Josef.

Air Safaris SCENIC FLIGHTS
(☑03-752 0716, 0800 723 274; www.airsafaris.co.nz) Franz' only fixed-wing flyer offers a 30-minute 'twin glacier' ($250) and 50-minute 'grand traverse' ($340).

Fox & Franz Josef Heliservices SCENIC FLIGHTS
(☑03-752 0793, 0800 800 793; www.scenic-flights.co.nz)

Glacier Helicopters SCENIC FLIGHTS
(☑03-752 0755, 0800 800 732; www.glacierheli-copters.co.nz)

Helicopter Line SCENIC FLIGHTS
(☑03-752 0767, 0800 807 767; www.helicopter.co.nz)

Mountain Helicopters SCENIC FLIGHTS
(☑03-752 0046, 0800 369 432; www.mountain-helicopters.co.nz)

Other Activities

Glacier Country Kayaks KAYAKING
(☑03-752 0230, 0800 423 262; www.glacierkay-aks.com; 46 Cron St; 3hr kayak $105, 4hr kayak & walk $145) Take a guided kayak trip on Lake Mapourika (7km north of Franz), with fascinating commentary, birdlife, mountain views, a serene channel detour, and an additional bushwalk on offer. Go in the morning for better conditions. Ask about family trips, freedom rental and stand-up paddle-board hire.

Glacier Hot Pools HOT POOLS
(www.glacierhotpools.co.nz; 63 Cron St; adult/child $25/18; ⊙1-9pm) Skilfully embedded into pretty rainforest greenery on the edge of town, this stylish outdoor hot-pool complex is perfect après-hike or on a rainy day. Communal pools, private ones ($42.50 per 45 minutes) and massage also available.

Skydive Franz SKYDIVING
(☑03-752 0714, 0800 458 677; www.skydivefranz.co.nz; Main Rd) Claiming NZ's highest jump (18,000ft, 80 seconds freefall, $559), this company also offers 15,000ft for $419, and 12,000ft for $319. With Aoraki/Mt Cook in your sights, this could be the most scenic jump you ever do.

Eco-Rafting RAFTING
(☑03-755 4254, 0508 669 675; www.ecorafting.co.nz; family trip adult/child $135/110, 7hr trip $450)

Franz Josef Glacier & Village

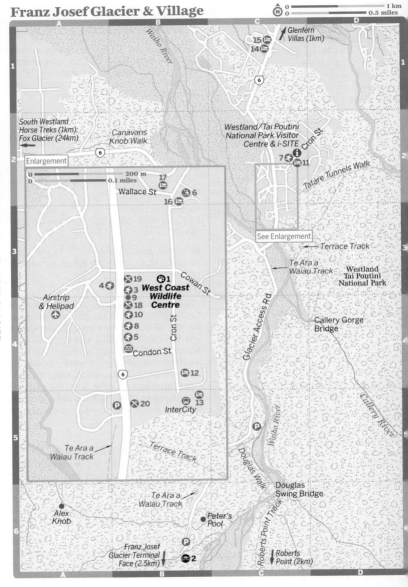

Rafting adventures throughout the coast, from gentle, family trips to the seven hour 'Grand Canyon' trip on the Whataroa River with its towering granite walls. Includes a 15-minute helicopter ride.

South Westland Horse Treks   HORSE RIDIN (☎ 03-752 0223, 0800 187 357; www.horsetreknz com; Waiho Flats Rd; 2hr trek $99) Located 5kn west of town, this trekking company run one- to six-hour equine excursions across farmland and remote beaches.

Franz Josef Glacier & Village

◎ **Top Sights**
1 West Coast Wildlife Centre.................... B3

◎ **Sights**
2 Sentinel Rock B6

⊕ **Activities, Courses & Tours**
Across Country Quad Bikes ....(see 3)
3 Air Safaris B3
4 Fox & Franz Josef Heliservices............. A3
5 Franz Josef Glacier Guides.................... B4
6 Glacier Country Kayaks B2
Glacier Helicopters ....(see 3)
7 Glacier Hot Pools C2
8 Helicopter Line....................................... B4
9 Mountain Helicopters............................. B4

10 Skydive Franz.. B4

⊜ **Sleeping**
11 58 on Cron.. C2
12 Chateau Franz B4
13 Franz Josef Glacier YHA......................... B5
14 Franz Josef Top 10 Holiday Park........... C1
15 Holly Homestead...................................... C1
16 Rainforest Retreat................................... B2
17 Te Waonui Forest Retreat....................... B2

⊗ **Eating**
18 Four Square B4
19 Landing Bar & Restaurant....................... B3
20 Picnics.. B5

THE WEST COAST FRANZ JOSEF GLACIER

Glacier Valley Eco Tours   GUIDED TOUR
(☑ 03-752 0699, 0800 999 739; www.glaciervalley.
co.nz) Offers leisurely three- to eight-hour
walking tours around local sights ($70 to
$160), packed with local knowledge. Glacier
shuttle service ($12.50 return).

Across Country Quad Bikes   QUAD BIKING
(☑ 03-752 0123, 0800 234 288; www.acrosscountry-
quadbikes.co.nz; Air Safaris Bldg, SH6) Four-
wheeled outings, rockin' and rollin' through
the rainforest (two hours, rider/passenger
$160/70). Mountain-bike hire available
(half-/full day $25/40).

🛏 Sleeping

Franz Josef Glacier YHA   HOSTEL $
(☑ 03-752 0754; www.yha.co.nz; 2-4 Cron St; dm
$23-30, s $57, d $85-110; @ 🛜) This tidy hostel
has warm, spacious communal areas, family rooms, free sauna, on-site bike hire and
a booking desk for transport and activities.
It has 130 beds, but you'll still need to book
ahead.

**Franz Josef Top 10
Holiday Park**   HOLIDAY PARK $
(☑ 03-752 073, 0800 467 8975; www.franz-
joseftop10.co.nz; 2902 Franz Josef Hwy; campsites
$40-45, d $65-165; @ 🛜) This spacious holiday
park, 1.5km from the township, has shipshape facilities and more sleeping options
than you can shake a stick at. Tenters are
well catered for with sunny, free-draining
grassy sites away from the road, looking out
over farm paddocks.

Chateau Franz   HOSTEL $
(☑ 03-752 073, 0800 728 3728; www.sircedrics.
co.nz; 8 Cron St; dm $23-33, d $50-110; @ 🛜)

This ramshackle enclave of dorms and mo-
telesque units offers a decent bolthole, with
respectable beds and enticing extras such as
a spa pool, free soup and unlimited internet.
Worn but welcoming communal areas include a sunny patio, two kitchens, and den
with a wood burner.

Rainforest Retreat   HOSTEL, HOLIDAY PARK $$
(☑ 03-752 0220, 0800 873 346; www.rainfor-
estretreat.co.nz; 46 Cron St; sites $39, dm $28-32,
d $85-220; @ 🛜) This capacious enterprise
packs plenty of options into its forested
grounds, the pick of which are the 'huts',
'houses' and 'lodges' nestled in the bush.
Campervans enjoy similar privacy but lose
out on high-use communal facilities, as do
backpackers who may well arrive on a large
tour bus. The on-site Monsoon Bar has a
low top shelf, lively atmosphere and decent
meals ($22 to $32).

58 on Cron   MOTEL $$
(☑ 03-752 0627, 0800 662 766; www.58oncron.
co.nz; 58 Cron St; d $175-245; 🛜) Lacking imagi-
nation in both name and decor, these motel
units nevertheless impress with their comfort, cleanliness, mod cons and considerate
attitude to guests.

★ Glenfern Villas   APARTMENT $$$
(☑ 03-752 005, 0800 453 6334; www.glenfern.
co.nz; SH6; d $230-289; 🛜) A handy 3km out
of the tourist hubbub, these delightful one-
and two-bedroom villas sit amid groomed
grounds with private decks surveying moun-
tain scenery. Top-notch beds, full kitchens,
bike hire and family-friendly facilities
strongly suggest 'holiday', not 'stop-off'.

Holly Homestead
B&B **$$$**

(☑03-752 0299; www.hollyhomestead.co.nz; SH6; d $265-430; @ ⬤) Guests are welcomed with fresh home baking at this wisteria-draped 1926 B&B. Choose from three characterful en suite rooms or a suite, all of which share a deck perfect for that sundowner. Children over 12 welcome.

Te Waonui Forest Retreat
HOTEL **$$$**

(☑03-752 0555, 0800 696 963; www.tewaonui. co.nz; 3 Wallace St; s/d from $579/699; @ ⬤) Franz' top-end hotel appears earthy and unflashy, with the inside following suit in natural, textured tones brightened by bold, zippy carpet. It offers a classy package of porter service, degustation dinners (included, along with breakfast, in the price) and a snazzy bar, along with luxurious rooms in which you'll sleep like a log. All have a deck facing into the forest.

✖ Eating

Expect to have numerous dining choices, but be prepared that they might not set your culinary world on fire; some menus haven't changed since the last ice age.

Picnics
BAKERY **$**

(SH6; snacks $3-7; ⊙8am-5pm) Follow the bright pink sandwich boards to this cracking little bakery. Heaps of good-value ready-to-scoff goods, including epic pasties suitable for bagging for a picnic lunch, or heating up later at dinner time. Other enticements include fresh bread and 'donut Saturday'.

Landing Bar & Restaurant
PUB **$$**

(www.thelandingbar.co.nz; SH6; mains $20-40; ⊙7.30am-late; ⬤) This busy but well-run pub offers an inordinately huge menu of crowd-pleasing food such as burgers, steaks and pizza. The patio – complete with sunshine and gas heaters – is a good place to warm up after a day on the ice.

Four Square
SUPERMARKET

(SH6; ⊙7.45am-9.30pm) Mr Four Square comes to the party, big time.

ⓘ Information

Wi-fi is available at most accommodation providers and several eating joints. There's an ATM on the main street, and the postal agency is located at **Glacier Motors** (SH6).

Franz Josef Health Centre (☑03-752 0700, 0800 7943 2584; 97 Cron St; ⊙9am-4pm Mon-Fri) South Westland's main medical centre.

Westland/Tai Poutini National Park Visitor Centre & i-SITE (☑03-752 0796; www.doc. govt.nz; Cron St; ⊙8.30am-6pm summer, 8.30am-5pm winter) Regional DOC office with good exhibits, weather information and track updates; the i-SITE desk books major nation-wide transport except the Interislander. See also www.glaciercountry.co.nz.

ⓘ Getting There & Around

The bus stop is opposite the Four Square supermarket.

InterCity (☑03-365 1113; www.intercity. co.nz) has daily buses south to Fox Glacier (35 minutes) and Queenstown (eight hours); and north to Nelson (10 hours). Some services can also be booked via Atomic Travel (p97). Book at the DOC Visitor Centre or YHA. **Naked Bus** (www.nakedbus.com) services the same routes three times a week. Both provide connections to destinations further afield.

Glacier Valley Shuttle (☑03-752 0699, 0800 999 739; www.glaciervalley.co.nz) runs scheduled shuttle services to the glacier car park (return trip $12.50).

Fox Glacier

Fox is smaller and quieter than Franz Josef, with a farmy feel and more open aspect. Beautiful Lake Matheson is a highlight, as are the historic sites and the beach itself down at Gillespies Beach.

⊙ Sights & Activities

Glacier Valley Walks

It's 1.5km from Fox Village to the glacier turn-off, and a further 2km to the car park, which you can reach under your own steam via **Te Weheka Walkway/Cycleway**, a pleasant rainforest trail starting just south of the Bella Vista motel. It's just over an hour each way to walk, or 30 minutes to cycle (leave your bikes at the car park – you can't cycle on the glacier walkways). Hire bikes from Westhaven (p124).

From the car park, the terminal face is 30 to 40 minutes' walk. How close you can get to it depends on conditions. Obey all signs: this place is dangerously dynamic.

Short walks near the glacier include the **Moraine Walk** (over a major 18th-century advance) and **Minnehaha Walk**. The **River Walk** extends to the **Chalet Lookout Track** (1½ hours return) leading to a glacier lookout. The fully accessible **River Walk Lookout Track** (20 minutes return) starts from the Glacier View Road car park and allows

Fox Glacier & Village

people of all abilities the chance to view the glacier.

Pick up a copy of DOC's excellent *Glacier Region Walks* booklet ($2) which provides maps and illuminating background reading.

Fox Glacier Guiding GUIDED WALK
(☑ 03-751 0825, 0800 111 600; www.foxguides. co.nz; 44 Main Rd) Guided walks (equipment provided) are organised by Fox Glacier Guiding. Half-day walks cost $132/105 per adult/child; full-day walks are $185. Helihikes cost $399/369 per adult/child, while a day-long introductory ice-climbing course costs $320 per adult. Note that age restrictions vary depending on the trip. There are also easygoing two-hour interpretive walks to the glacier (adult/child $49/35). Longer guided helihike adventures are also available.

Fox Glacier & Village

Activities, Courses & Tours
Fox & Franz Josef Heliservices ....(see 1)
1 Fox Glacier Guiding C2
2 Glacier Helicopters C2
3 Helicopter Line C2
4 Mountain Helicopters C3
5 Skydive Fox Glacier C1

Sleeping
6 Fox Glacier Lodge A1
7 Fox Glacier Top 10 Holiday Park A1
8 Rainforest Motel A1
9 Westhaven C2

Eating
10 Last Kitchen C2

Shopping
11 Fox Glacier General Store C2
12 Fox Glacier Motors C2

THE WEST COAST FOX GLACIER

THE WEST COAST FOX GLACIER

Other Walks

Lake Matheson
LAKE

The famous 'mirror lake' can be found about 5km down Cook Flat Rd. Wandering slowly (as you should), it will take 1½ hours to complete the circuit. At the far end – on a clear day – you may, just *may*, get the money shot, but failing that you can buy a postcard at the excellent gift store by the car park. The best time to visit is early morning, or when the sun is low in the late afternoon, although the presence of the Matheson Cafe means that any time is a good time.

Gillespies Beach
BEACH

Follow Cook Flat Rd for its full 21km (unsealed for the final 12km) to the remote black-sand Gillespies Beach, site of an old mining settlement. Various interesting walks can be had from here, from a five-minute zip to the old miners' cemetery, to the 3½-hour return walk to Galway Beach where seals are wont to haul out. Don't disturb their lazing about. On the way there or back, stop at the signposted **Peak View Picnic Area** to spin the dial and determine exactly which mountain you're looking at.

Skydiving & Aerial Sightseeing

With Fox Glacier's backdrop of Southern Alps, rainforest and ocean, it's hard to imagine a better place to get high. Costs at Fox parallel those at Franz Josef, as does healthy competition, which sees all heli-operators lined up on the main road.

Skydive Fox Glacier
SKYDIVING

(☑ 03-751 0080, 0800 751 0080; www.skydivefox.co.nz; Fox Glacier Airfield, SH6) Eye-popping scenery abounds on leaps from 16,000ft ($399) or 12,000ft ($299). The airfield is conveniently located three minutes' walk from the centre of town.

Fox & Franz
Josef Heliservices
SCENIC FLIGHTS

(☑ 03-751 0866, 0800 800 793; www.scenic-flights.co.nz)

Glacier Helicopters
SCENIC FLIGHTS

(☑ 03-751 0803, 0800 800 732; www.glacierhelicopters.co.nz; SH6)

Helicopter Line
SCENIC FLIGHTS

(☑ 03-752 0767, 0800 807 767; www.helicopter.co.nz; SH6)

Mountain Helicopters
SCENIC FLIGHTS

(☑ 03-751 0045, 0800 369 423; www.mountainhelicopters.co.nz)

🛏 Sleeping

★Fox Glacier Top 10 Holiday Park
HOLIDAY PARK $

(☑ 03-751 0821, 0800 154 366; www.fghp.co.nz; Kerrs Rd; sites per person from $20, s/d $70, cabins & units $70-215; @ 🖭) This park has options to suit all budgets, from well-draining tent sites and gravel campervan sites, to lodge rooms and upscale motel units. Shipshape amenities include a splendid communal kitchen/dining room, and a playground for the kids.

Rainforest Motel
MOTEL $$

(☑ 03-751 0140, 0800 724 636; www.rainforest-motel.co.nz; 15 Cook Flat Rd; d $115-145; 🖭) Rustic log cabins on the outside with neutral decor on the inside. Epic lawns for running around on or simply enjoying the mountain views. A tidy, good-value option.

Westhaven
MOTEL $$

(☑ 03-751 0084, 0800 369 452; www.thewesthaven.co.nz; SH6; d $145-185; @ 🖭) These architecturally precise suites are a classy combo of corrugated steel and local stone amid burnt-red and ivory walls. The deluxe king rooms have spa baths, and there are bikes to hire for the energetic (half-/full day $20/40).

Fox Glacier Lodge
B&B, MOTEL $$$

(☑ 03-751 0888, 0800 369 800; www.foxglacierlodge.com; 41 Sullivan Rd; d $195-225; 🖭) Beautiful timber adorns the exterior and interior of this attractive property, imparting a mountain chalet vibe. Similarly woody self-contained mezzanine units with spa baths and gas fires are also available.

Reflection Lodge
B&B $$$

(☑ 03-751 0707; www.reflectionlodge.co.nz; 14 Cook Flat Rd; d $210; 🖭) The gregarious hosts of this ski-lodge-style B&B go the extra mile to make your stay a memorable one. Blooming gardens complete with Monet-like pond and alpine views seal the deal.

🍴 Eating & Drinking

Fox would be a total stodge-fest were it not for a duo of notably good cafes.

Last Kitchen
CAFE $$

(cnr Sullivan Rd & SH6; lunch $10-20, dinner $22-32; ⊙ noon-late) Making the most of its sunny corner location with outside tables, the Last Kitchen is a relatively elegant option offering contemporary à la carte cafe fare such as halloumi salad, five-spice pork belly and genuinely gourmet burgers. It lacks exten sive counter food, but will satisfy for coffee and cake, and fine wine and nibbles.

★ **Matheson Cafe** MODERN NZ **$$**
(☑ 03-751 0878; www.lakematheson.com; Lake Matheson Rd; breakfast & lunch $9-20, dinner $17-33; ◷ 8am-late Nov-Mar, 8am-4pm Apr-Oct) Near the shores of Lake Matheson, this cafe does everything right: sharp architecture that maximises inspiring mountain views, strong coffee, craft beers and upmarket fare ranging from smoked salmon breakfast bagels, to slow-cooked lamb followed by berry crumble. Next door is the ReflectioNZ Gallery stocking quality, primarily NZ-made art and souvenirs.

ⓘ Information

Activity operators and accommodation providers are well-oiled at providing information on local services (and usually a booking service), but you can also find online info courtesy of the **Fox Glacier Tourism Promotions Group** (www.foxglaciertourism.co.nz) and at www.glaciercountry.co.nz. There's an ATM at **Fox Glacier General Store** (◷ 8am-8pm), the last one until Wanaka-headed south. **Fox Glacier Motors** (SH6) is your last chance for fuel before Haast, 120km away.

DOC South Westland Weheka Area Office (☑ 03-751 0807; SH6; ◷ 10am-2pm Mon-Fri) This is no longer a general visitor-information centre, but has the usual DOC information, hut tickets and weather/track updates.

Fox Glacier Guiding (☑ 03-751 0825, 0800 111 600; www.foxguides.co.nz; SH6) Books Intercity and Atomic buses, and provides postal and currency-exchange services.

Fox Glacier Health Centre (☑ 03-751 0836, 0800 7943 2584; SH6) Clinic opening hours are displayed at the centre, or ring the 0800 number for assistance from the Franz Clinic.

ⓘ Getting There & Around

Most buses stop outside the Fox Glacier Guiding building.

InterCity (☑ 03-365 1113; www.intercity.co.nz) runs two buses a day north to Franz Josef (40 minutes), the morning bus continuing to Nelson (11 hours). Daily southbound services run to Queenstown (7½ hours). Some services can also be booked via Atomic Travel (p97).

Naked Bus (www.nakedbus.com) runs three times a week north along the coast all the way through to Nelson, and south to Queenstown.

Fox Glacier Shuttles (☑ 0800 369 287), staffed by the inimitable Murray, will drive you around the area from Franz Josef to the Copland Valley, and including Lake Matheson, Gillespies Beach and the glaciers. Look for him parked up opposite Fox Glacier Motors.

SOUTH TO HAAST

From Fox Glacier it's a 120km (two-hour) drive to Haast, along a scenic stretch of highway chopped through lowland forest and occasional pasture, with views inland to sheer-sided valleys and intermittent but grand views seaward.

About 26km south of Fox Glacier, along SH6, is the **Copland Valley** trailhead, the western end of the **Copland Track**. It's a six-to-seven-hour tramp to legendary **Welcome Flat** where thermal springs bubble just metres from the door of DOC's **Welcome Flat Hut** (adult/child $15/7.50). Unsurprisingly, the hut and its adjacent campsite are extremely popular, with a warden in attendance, so both must be booked in advance either online or in person at DOC visitor centres.

Lake Moeraki, 31km north of Haast, is a rippling fishing lake. At its southern end is one of NZ's best ecolodges, **Wilderness Lodge Lake Moeraki** (☑ 03-750 0881; www.wildernesslodge.co.nz; SH6; d incl breakfast & dinner $700-1000; ☎) ✿. In a verdant setting on the edge of a river channel, it offers comfortable rooms and four-course dinners, but the real delight here are the outdoor activities, such as kayak trips and coastal walks, guided by people with conservation in their blood.

About 5km south of Lake Moeraki is the much-photographed **Knights Point**, where the Haast road was eventually opened in 1965. Stop here if humanly possible.

Ship Creek, 15km north of Haast, is a terrific place to stretch the legs, boasting two fascinating walks with interesting interpretive panels: the **Dune Lake Walk** (30 minutes return), which is all sand dunes and stunted forest, leading to a surprising view, and the unsurprisingly swampy **Kahikatea Swamp Forest Walk** (20 minutes return).

If you haven't had your fill of whitebait yet, call into the **Curly Tree Whitebait Company** (◷ 10am-5pm), 10km north of Haast at the Waita River bridge. Exemplary whitebait patties for $8, plus bait to go at the market price.

HAAST REGION

The Haast region is a major wilderness area. The area's kahikatea and rata forests, wetlands, sand dunes, seal and penguin colonies, birdlife and sweeping beaches ensured its inclusion in the Southwest New Zealand (Te Wahipounamu) World Heritage Area.

Haast

Some 120km south of Fox Glacier, Haast crouches around the mouth of the wide Haast River in three distinct pockets: Haast Junction, Haast Village and Haast Beach. As well as being a handy stop for filling the tank and tummy, it's also the gateway to some spectacular scenery which can be explored in various ways, down to the end of the line at Jackson Bay. Pick up or download a copy of DOC's brochure *Walks and Activities in the Haast Area* ($2) to survey the options.

If you're heading north, check your fuel gauge as Haast petrol station is the last one before Fox Glacier.

Sleeping

Haast Beach Holiday Park   HOLIDAY PARK $
(☑03-750 0860, 0800 843 226; www.haastpark. com; 1348 Jackson Bay Rd, Haast Beach; sites from $34, dm $25, d $45-110) Well worth the 14km drive south of Haast Junction, this old dear dishes up just enough charm, with its clean and tidy facilities that range from basic cabins to self-contained units, and a pleasant campers' block with comfortable lounge and views from the deck. The Hapuka Estuary Walk is across the road, and it's a 20-minute walk to an epic beach.

Haast River Top 10   HOLIDAY PARK $
(☑03-750 0020, 0800 624 847; www.haasttop10. co.nz; SH6, Haast Village; sites unpowered/powered $38/42, d $110-155; @ 🛜) This highwayside

---

WORTH A TRIP

JACKSON BAY ROAD

From Haast Junction, the road most travelled is SH6, upwards or across. But there is another option, and that is south... to the end of the line.

The road to Jackson Bay is quiet and intensely scenic. Towered over by Southern Alps, the farms on the flat and the settlements dotted between them stand testament to some of the hardiest souls who ever attempted settlement in NZ. Up until the 1950s, the only way to reach Haast overland was via bush tracks from Hokitika and Wanaka. Supplies came by a coastal shipping service that called every couple of months or so.

Besides the ghosts and former glories, which make an appearance here and there, there's plenty to warrant a foray down to Jackson Bay.

Near Okuru is the **Hapuka Estuary Walk** (20 minutes return), a winding boardwalk that loops through a sleepy wildlife sanctuary with good interpretation panels en route.

Five kilometres further south (19km south of Haast Junction) is where you'll find the base for **Waiatoto River Safaris** (☑03-750 0780, 0800 538 723; www.riversafaris.co.nz; Jackson Bay Rd; adult/child $199/139; ⊙ trips 10am, 1pm & 4pm), which offers a hair-tousling two-hour jetboat trip upriver into the mountains, then down to the sea, with plenty of natural- and human-history stories along the way.

The road continues west to **Arawhata Bridge**, where a turn-off leads to the **Ellery Creek Walkway**, 3.5km away. This pleasant amble through mossy beech forest (1½ hours return) leads to **Ellery Lake**, where a picnic bench encourages lunch with perhaps a skinny dip for afters.

It's less than an hour's drive from Haast town to the fishing hamlet of **Jackson Bay**, the only natural harbour on the West Coast. Migrants arrived here in 1875 under a doomed settlement scheme, their farming and timber-milling aspirations mercilessly shattered by never-ending rain and the lack of a wharf, not built until 1938. Those families who stayed turned their hands to largely subsistence living.

With good timing you will arrive when the **Cray Pot** (☑03-750 0035; fish & chips $17-29; ⊙ noon-4pm) is open. This place is just as much about the dining room (a caravan) and location (looking out over the bay) as it is about the honest seafood, including a good feed of fish and chips, crayfish, chowder or whitebait. Ask a local to confirm current opening times.

Walk off your fries on the **Wharekai Te Kou Walk** (40 minutes return) to Ocean Beach, a tiny bay that hosts pounding waves and some interesting rock formations, or the longer (three to four hour) **Smoothwater Bay Track**, nearby.

holiday park has a hangar for its amenities block, a bit of a style winner save for the lack of a door. (Waiter, there's a sandfly in my soup.) Motel units are light, spacious and enjoy great views when the weather's kind.

Haast Lodge   LODGE **$**

(☑ 03-750 0703, 0800 500 703; www.haastlodge. com; Marks Rd, Haast Village; sites from $16, dm $25, d/tw $55-65, units d $98-130; @ 🛜) Covering all accommodation bases, Haast Lodge offers clean, well-maintained facilities which include a pleasant communal area for lodge-users and campervanners, and tidy motel units at the Aspiring Court next door.

Collyer House   B&B **$$**

(☑ 03-750 0022; www.collyerhouse.co.nz; Cuttance Rd, Okuru; d $180-250; @ 🛜) This gem of a B&B has thick bathrobes, quality linen, beach views and a sparkling host who cooks a terrific breakfast. This all adds up to make Collyer House a comfortable, upmarket choice. Follow the signs off SH6 for 12km down Jackson Bay Rd.

✖ Eating & Drinking

Okoto Espresso   CAFE **$**

(Haast Village; snacks $2-10) Look out for the rusty hut being towed by the orange Landrover. Where you find it you'll encounter excellent coffee, smoothies and whitebait fritters.

Haast Foodcentre   SUPERMARKET **$**

(Pauareka Rd) This small supermarket stocks sufficient provisions for meal-making, along with fried takeaways and coffee.

Hard Antler   PUB **$$**

(Marks Rd, Haast Village; dinner $20-30; ☺ dining 11am-9pm) This display of deer antlers is enough to give you the horn. So is the general ambience of this big, bold pub. Plain, meaty food on offer.

ℹ Information

The DOC Haast Visitor Information Centre (☑ 03-750 0809; www.doc.govt.nz; cnr SH6 & Jackson Bay Rd; ☺ 9am-6pm Nov-Mar, to 4.30pm Apr-Oct) has town and backcountry information and has a landline for DIY accommodation and activity bookings. The all-too-brief

Haast landscape film *Edge of Wilderness* (adult/child $3/free) screens in the theatrette.

General regional information and visitor services listings can be found on the online directory administered by **Haast Promotions** (www.haastnz.com).

ℹ Getting There & Away

InterCity (☑ 03-365 1113; www.intercity.co.nz) buses stop at the visitor information centre on their daily runs between the West Coast and Queenstown. **Naked Bus** (www.nakedbus.com) also passes through three times a week.

Haast Pass Highway

Early Maori travelled this route between Central Otago and the West Coast in their quest for *pounamu,* naming it Tioripatea, meaning 'Clear Path'. The first party of Europeans to make the crossing may well have been led by the German geologist Julius von Haast, in 1863 – hence the name of the pass, river and township – but evidence suggests that Scottish prospector Charles Cameron may have pipped Haast at the post. It was clearly no mean feat, for such is the terrain that the Haast Pass Highway wasn't opened until 1965.

Heading inland from Haast towards Wanaka (145km, 2½ hours), the highway (SH6) snakes alongside the Haast River, crossing the boundary into Mt Aspiring National Park shortly after you hit fourth gear. The further you go, the narrower the river valley becomes, until the road clambers around sheer-sided valley walls streaked with waterfalls and scarred by rock slips. Princely sums are involved in keeping this highway clear, and even so it sets plenty of traps for unwary drivers.

Stop to admire the scenery, availing yourself of the many signposted lookouts and short walkways such as **Fantail** and **Thunder Creek** falls. These are detailed in DOC's booklet *Walks along the Haast Highway* ($2), but sufficient detail is provided at the trailheads.

The highway tops out at the 563m pass mark, shortly after which you will reach food and fuel at Makarora. Oh, hello Otago!

Christchurch & Canterbury

Best Places to Eat

➡ Pegasus Bay (p161)

➡ Cornershop Bistro (p145)

➡ C1 Espresso (p143)

➡ Saggio di Vino (p144)

➡ Addington Coffee Co-op (p144)

Best Places to Stay

➡ Double Dutch (p155)

➡ Maison de la Mer (p155)

➡ Chalet Boutique Motel (p173)

➡ Halfmoon Cottage (p155)

Why Go?

Nowhere in New Zealand is changing and developing as fast as post-earthquake Christchurch, and visiting the country's second-largest city as it's being rebuilt and reborn is both interesting and inspiring.

A short drive from Christchurch's dynamic re-emergence, Banks Peninsula conceals hidden bays and beaches – a backdrop for wildlife cruises with a sunset return to the attractions of Akaroa. To the north are the vineyards of the Waipara Valley and the family-holiday ambience of Hanmer Springs. Westwards, the well-ordered farms of the Canterbury Plains morph quickly into the dramatic wilderness of the Southern Alps.

Canterbury's summertime attractions include tramping along the braided rivers and alpine valleys around Arthur's Pass and mountain biking around the turquoise lakes of the Mackenzie Country. During winter, the attention switches to the skifields. Throughout the seasons, Aoraki/Mt Cook, the country's tallest peak, stands sentinel over this diverse region.

When to Go

➡ Canterbury is one of NZ's driest regions, as moisture-laden westerlies from the Tasman Sea dump their rainfall on the West Coast before hitting the eastern South Island. Visit from January to March for hot and settled summer weather and plenty of opportunities to get active amid the region's spectacular landscapes.

➡ It's also festival time in Christchurch with January's World Buskers Festival and the Ellerslie International Flower Show in March.

➡ Hit the winter slopes from July to October at Mt Hutt or on Canterbury's smaller club ski fields.

ℹ️ Getting There & Around

AIR

Christchurch's international airport is the South Island's main hub. Air New Zealand flies here from 15 domestic destinations, while Jetstar has flights from Auckland, Wellington and Queenstown. Air New Zealand also flies between Timaru and Wellington.

BUS

Christchurch is the hub for coaches and shuttles heading up the coast as far as Picton, down the coast to Dunedin (and on to Te Anau), through the Alps to Greymouth and across country to Queenstown.

TRAIN

The *TranzAlpine* service connects Christchurch and Greymouth, and the *Coastal Pacific* chugs north to Picton, with ferry connections across Cook Strait to the North Island.

CHRISTCHURCH

POP 342,000

Welcome to a vibrant city in transition, coping creatively with the aftermath of NZ's second-worst natural disaster. Traditionally the most English of NZ cities, Christchurch's heritage heart was all but hollowed out following the 2010 and 2011 earthquakes that left 186 people dead.

Punts still glide gently down the Avon River, and the Botanic Gardens and Hagley Park remain some of NZ's finest public spaces. But in the empty lots and abandoned buildings left in the wake of the earthquakes, interesting art projects have sprung up, and clever, creative people are slowly starting to make things happen. Each new opening and restoration is greeted with enthusiasm by a grateful public, frustrated by the pace of the rebuild and eager to see what shape their future city will take.

If you're worried that your interest in post-earthquake Christchurch may seem in poor taste, don't be. Locals are genuinely keen to welcome sensitive visitors back to their city – and despite the heartache, they're the first to acknowledge how fascinating it all is.

History

The first people to live in what is now Christchurch were moa hunters, who arrived around 1250. Immediately prior to colonisation, the Ngai Tahu tribe had a small

seasonal village on the banks of the Avon called Otautahi.

When British settlers arrived in 1880 it was an ordered Church of England project; the passengers on the 'First Four Ships' were dubbed by the British press 'the Canterbury Pilgrims'. Christchurch was meant to be a model of class-structured England in the South Pacific, not just another scruffy colonial outpost. Churches were built rather than pubs, the fertile farming land was deliberately placed in the hands of the gentry, and wool made the elite of Christchurch wealthy.

In 1856 Christchurch officially became NZ's first city, and a very English one at that. Town planning and architecture assumed a close affinity with the 'Mother Country' and English-style gardens were planted, earning it the nickname, the 'Garden City'. To this day, Christchurch in spring is a glorious place to be.

👁 Sights

👁 City Centre

⭐ **Botanic Gardens** GARDENS
(Map p136; www.ccc.govt.nz; Rolleston Ave; ⏰7am-8.30pm Oct-Mar, to 6.30pm Apr-Sep) FREE
Strolling through these blissful 30 riverside hectares of arboreal and floral splendour is a

---

ESSENTIAL CANTERBURY

Eat Salmon spawned in the shadow of NZ's tallest mountains

Drink NZ's best craft beer at Pomeroy's Old Brewery Inn (p145)

Read *Old Bucky & Me*, a poignant account of the 2011 earthquake by Christchurch journalist Jane Bowron

Listen to Scribe's *The Crusader* (2003), still the best shout-out to the region, with a name that references Canterbury's Super Rugby team

Watch *Heavenly Creatures*, Sir Peter Jackson's best film not involving hobbits, set in Christchurch

Go green At the ecofriendly Okuti Garden (p155) on Banks Peninsula

Online www.christchurchnz.com, www.mtcooknz.com

Area code ☎03

Christchurch & Canterbury Highlights

1 Supporting the exciting rebuilding and re-emergence of **Christchurch** (p129)

2 Meandering through Christchurch's beautiful **Botanic Gardens** (p129), either on foot or punting along the Avon River

3 Marvelling at the otherworldly views of the Mackenzie Country and the powdery blueness of Lake Tekapo from atop **Mt John** (p172)

4 Taking a soothing soak at **Hanmer Springs Thermal Pools** (p158)

5 Admiring Banks Peninsula's surf-bitten edges from Summit Rd before descending to

Francophile **Akaroa** (p150) for an ooh-la-la dinner

6 Tramping in the shadow of NZ's highest peak in **Aoraki/Mt Cook National Park** (p174)

7 Enjoying a lazy lunch at **Pegasus Bay winery** (p161) before careering around the vineyards of the Waipara Valley

consummate Christchurch experience. Gorgeous at any time of the year, it's particularly impressive in spring when the rhododendrons, azaleas and daffodil woodland are in riotous bloom. There are thematic gardens to explore, lawns to sprawl on, and a playground adjacent to the **Botanic Gardens Information Centre** (Map p136; ⊙9am-4pm Mon-Fri, 10.15am-4pm Sat & Sun).

Guided walks ($10) depart at 1.30pm (mid-September to April) from the Canterbury Museum, or you can tour around the gardens in the **Caterpillar train** (☑0800 88 22 23; www.gardentours.co.nz; adult/child $18/9; ⊙11am-3pm).

Hagley Park
PARK

(Map p136; Riccarton Ave) Wrapping itself around the Botanic Gardens, Hagley Park is Christchurch's biggest green space, stretching for 165 hectares. Riccarton Ave splits it in two and the Avon River snakes through the north half. It's a great place to stroll, whether on a foggy autumn morning or on a warm spring day, when the cherry trees lining Harper Ave are in flower. Joggers make the most of the tree-lined avenues, year-round.

★ Canterbury Museum
MUSEUM

(Map p136; ☑03-366 5000; www.canterburymuseum.com; Rolleston Ave; ⊙9am-5pm) **FREE** Yes, there's a mummy and dinosaur bones, but the highlights of this museum are more local and more recent. The Maori galleries contain some beautiful *pounamu* (greenstone) pieces, while Christchurch Street is an atmospheric walk through the colonial past. The reproduction of Fred & Myrtle's gloriously kitsch Paua Shell House embraces Kiwiana at its best, and kids will enjoy the interactive displays in the Discovery Centre (admission $2). Hour-long guided tours commence at 3.30pm on Tuesday and Thursday.

Arts Centre
HISTORIC BUILDINGS

(Map p136; www.artscentre.org.nz; 2 Worcester Blvd) Dating from 1877, this enclave of Gothic Revival buildings was originally Canterbury College, the forerunner of Canterbury University. The college's most famous alumnus was the father of nuclear physics Lord Ernest Rutherford, the NZ physicist who first split the atom in 1917 (that's him on the $100 bill).

You'll have to be content to admire the architecture from the street, as the complex was badly damaged in the earthquakes. Some parts are scheduled to reopen at the end of 2015, but the whole restoration is expected to take 10 years.

Quake City   MUSEUM
(Map p136; www.quakecity.co.nz; 99 Cashel St; adult/child $10/free; ⊙10am-6pm) One of the new must-sees of Christchurch, this little museum tells the story of the earthquakes through photography, video footage and various artefacts, including bits fallen off the Cathedral and the statue of the 'founder of Canterbury' John Robert Godley that toppled from its perch in the square. Most affecting of all is the film featuring locals telling their own stories from that fateful day.

★ Cathedral Square   SQUARE
(Map p136) Christchurch's historic hub sits at the heart of the grid of streets that delineate the devastated city centre. At its centre (at the time of writing, at least) is what remains

of ChristChurch Cathedral. Built in 1881, this much-loved icon of the city has become emblematic of the battle between those who seek to preserve what remains of Christchurch's heritage, the fiscal pragmatists, and those ideologically inclined to things new.

The February 2011 earthquake brought down the Gothic church's 63m-high spire, leaving only the bottom half of the tower. Subsequent earthquakes in June 2011 and December 2011 destroyed the cathedral's prized stained-glass rose window. Despite the nave remaining largely intact, the deconstruction and demolition of the cathedral was announced in March 2012 by the Anglican Diocese. Heritage advocates launched court proceedings to prevent the demolition, and at the time of writing, cases were still pending.

Other heritage buildings around Cathedral Sq were also badly damaged, but one modern landmark left unscathed is the 18m-high metal sculpture *Chalice,* designed by Neil Dawson. It was erected in 2001 to commemorate the new millennium.

Gap Filler   OUTDOORS
(www.gapfiller.org.nz) With so much empty space around the city, this organisation is doing its best to fill it with interesting things. Installations range from whimsical bits of art, to moving memorials to earthquake victims,

CHRISTCHURCH & CANTERBURY CHRISTCHURCH

Christchurch

⊚ Sights
1 Riccarton House & Bush........................ A2

⊕ Activities, Courses & Tours
2 Bone Dude B1
3 Gondola...C4

⊜ Sleeping
4 Anselm House A2
5 Arena Motel... A2
6 Christchurch Top 10................................A1
7 Elm Tree House.......................................A1
8 Fendalton House..................................... A2
9 Haka Lodge...C2
10 Jailhouse.. A2
11 Le Petit Hotel.. D3
12 Lorenzo Motor Inn.................................. A2
13 Merivale Manor A1
14 Old Countryhouse...................................B2
15 Roma on Riccarton................................. A2
Sumner Bay Motel.........................(see 11)

⊗ Eating
16 Addington Coffee Co-op A2
Bamboozle ....(see 11)
17 Bodhi Tree A1

18 Burgers & Beers Inc...............................B2
Christchurch Farmers'
Market.. (see 4)
Cornershop Bistro.........................(see 11)
19 Edesia.. A2
20 Gustav's...C3
21 Holy Smoke...C3
22 Kinji..A1
Mosaic by Simo ....(see 16)
23 Under the Red Verandah.......................B2

⊖ Drinking & Nightlife
The Brewery...................................(see 20)
Volstead Trading Company.........(see 15)

⊗ Entertainment
24 AMI Stadium A2
Court Theatre ....(see 16)
25 Dux Live A2
Hollywood Cinema .... (see 11)
26 Hoyts Riccarton....................................... A2

⊜ Shopping
Sunday Artisan Market.................. (see 4)
The Tannery...................................(see 20)
Westfield Riccarton......................(see 26)

CHRISTCHURCH IN...

Two Days

After breakfast at **C1 Espresso**, take some time to walk around the ruined and regenerating city centre, visit **Quake City** and wander through **Cathedral Square**. Make your way to the **Arts Centre** and put together your own informal lunch at **Canterbury Cheesemongers**. After lunch, visit the excellent **Canterbury Museum** and take a walk through the lovely **Botanic Gardens**. That evening, explore the Victoria St dining and drinking strip.

Start day two at the **Addington Coffee Co-op** and then head up to the gondola for the views and a walk at the top. Continue on to Lyttelton for lunch before returning to the city for a punt on the **Avon River**. Head out to Sumner for a late-afternoon swim or a stroll, then stop for dinner and catch a flick at the **Hollywood Cinema**.

Four Days

Follow the two-day itinerary, then head to Akaroa to explore its wildlife-rich harbour, and Banks Peninsula's beautiful outer bays. On day four, visit **Orana Wildlife Park** and then finish the day at the **Tannery** in Woolston.

to a minigolf course scattered around different abandoned lots. There are pianos to play, books to read and giant chess pieces to manoeuvre. One of the larger projects is the **Pallet Pavilion** (Map p136; www.palletpavilion. com; cnr Kimore & Durham Sts; 🕾), a large cafe-bar–performance space demarcated by blue-painted storage pallets.

Things are changing constantly, so check out the Gap Map on the website, or simply wander the streets and see what you can find.

Transitional Cathedral CHURCH
(Map p136; www.christchurchcathedral.co.nz; 234 Hereford St; suggested donation $5; ⊙9am-5pm) Universally known as the Cardboard Cathedral due to the 98 cardboard tubes used in its construction, this interesting structure serves as both the city's temporary Anglican cathedral and as a concert venue. Designed by Japanese 'disaster architect' Shigeru Ban, the entire building was built in 11 months.

◉ Suburbs

Riccarton House & Bush GARDENS, FOREST
(Map p132; www.riccartonhouse.co.nz; 16 Kahu Rd, Riccarton) **FREE** Historic Riccarton House (1856) has been closed to the public since the earthquakes but hundreds still head to the pretty grounds for the Saturday Farmers Market (p145) and Sunday Artisan Market (p147). Just behind the main house, cute little **Deans Cottage** is the oldest building on the Canterbury Plains, dating from 1843.

Even more venerable is the small patch of predator-free bush behind the cottage.

Enclosed by a vermin-proof fence, this is the last stand of kahikatea floodplain forest in Canterbury. Kahikatea is NZ's tallest native tree, growing to heights of 60m; the tallest trees here are a mere 30m and around 300 to 600 years old. A short loop track heads through the heart of the forest.

International
Antarctic Centre EDUCATION CENTRE
(📞0508 736 4846; www.iceberg.co.nz; 38 Orchard Rd, Christchurch Airport; adult/child $39/19; ⊙9am-5.30pm) Part of a huge complex built for the administration of the NZ, US and Italian Antarctic programs, this centre gives visitors the opportunity to see penguins and learn about the icy continent. Attractions include the Antarctic Storm chamber, where you can get a taste of -18°C wind chill.

The 'Xtreme Pass' (adult/child $59/29) includes the '4D theatre' (a 3D film with moving seats and a water spray) and rides on a Hägglund all-terrain amphibious Antarctic vehicle. An optional extra is the Penguin Backstage Pass (adult/child $25/15), which takes visitors behind the scenes of the Penguin Encounter.

A free shuttle departs from outside the Canterbury Museum on the hour from 10am to 4pm, and from the Antarctic Centre on the half-hour.

Orana Wildlife Park ZOO
(www.oranawildlifepark.co.nz; McLeans Island Rd, McLeans Island; adult/child $28/9; ⊙10am-5pm) Orana describes itself as an 'open range zoo' and you'll know what they mean if you opt

to jump in the cage for the lion encounter (an additional $35). There's an excellent, walk-through native-bird aviary, a nocturnal kiwi house, and a reptile exhibit featuring tuatara. Most of the 80-hectare grounds are devoted to Africana, including rhinos, giraffes, zebras, lemurs and cheetahs.

Willowbank Wildlife Reserve ZOO
(www.willowbank.co.nz; 60 Hussey Rd, Northwood; adult/child $28/11; ⊙9.30am-7pm Oct-Apr, to 5pm May-Sep) 🍴 About 10km north of the central city, Willowbank focuses on native NZ critters (including kiwis), heritage farmyard animals and hands-on enclosures with wal-labies, deer and lemurs. There's also a re-created Maori village. In the evening this is the setting for the **Ko Tane** (www.kotane.co.nz; adult/child $135/68; ⊙5.30pm) cultural experience, which includes a traditional Maori welcome, cultural performance and *hangi* (earth oven) meal.

🏃 Activities
Boating
Antigua Boat Sheds BOATING, KAYAKING
(Map p136; ☎03-366 6768; www.boatsheds.co.nz; 2 Cambridge Tce; ⊙7am-5pm) Dating from 1882, the photogenic green-and-white Antigua

THE CANTERBURY EARTHQUAKES

Christchurch's seismic nightmare began at 4.35am on 4 September 2010. Centred 40km west of the city, a 40-second, 7.1-magnitude earthquake jolted Cantabrians from their sleep, and caused widespread damage to older buildings in the central city. Close to the quake's epicentre in rural Darfield, huge gashes erupted amid grassy pastures and the South Island's main railway line was bent and buckled. Because the tremor struck in the early hours of the morning when most people were home in bed, there were no fatalities, and many Christchurch residents felt that the city had dodged a bullet.

Fast forward to 12.51pm on 22 February 2011, when central Christchurch was busy with shoppers and workers enjoying their lunch break. This time the 6.3-magnitude quake was much closer, centred just 10km southeast of the city and only 5km deep. The tremor was significantly more extreme, and many locals report being flung violently and almost vertically into the air. The peak ground acceleration exceeded 1.8, almost twice the acceleration of gravity.

When the dust settled after 24 traumatic seconds, NZ's second-largest city had changed forever. The towering spire of the iconic ChristChurch Cathedral lay in ruins; walls and verandahs had cascaded down on shopping strips; and two multistorey buildings had pancaked. Of the 185 deaths (across 20 nationalities), 115 occurred in the six-storey Canterbury TV building, where many international students at a language school were killed. Elsewhere, the historic port town of Lyttelton was badly damaged; roads and bridges were crumpled; and residential suburbs in the east were inundated as a process of rapid liquefaction saw tonnes of oozy silt rise from the ground.

In the months that followed literally hundreds of aftershocks rattled the city's traumatised residents (and claimed one more life), but the resilience and bravery of Cantabrians quickly became evident. From the region's rural heartland, the 'Farmy Army' descended on the city, armed with shovels and food hampers. Social media mobilised 10,000 students, and the Student Volunteer Army became a vital force for residential clean-ups in the city's beleaguered eastern suburbs. Heartfelt aid and support arrived from across NZ, and seven other nations sent specialised urban-search-and-rescue teams.

The impact of the events of a warm summer's day in early 2011 will take longer than a generation to resolve. Entire streets and neighbourhoods in the eastern suburbs have had to be abandoned, and Christchurch's heritage architecture is irrevocably damaged. Three years after the quake, families in some parts of the city were still living in substandard accommodation, waiting for insurance claims to be settled. Around 80% of the buildings within the city centre's famed four avenues have been or are due to be demolished, and at the time of writing the empty blocks are an eerie sight, leaving much of the city centre looking like a giant car park.

Plans for the next 20 years of the city's rebuild include a compact, low-rise city centre, large green spaces, and parks and cycleways along the Avon River. It's estimated that the total rebuild and repair bill could reach $40 billion.

Central Christchurch

Papanui Rd
40

Bealey Ave
20

Carlton Mill Rd

Harper Ave

Avon River

Park Tce

13
38
Dublin St
19
Dorset St
35

Victoria St

39

Montreal St

43
42

North Hagley Park

6

Lake Albert

Lake Victoria

Park Tce
26

Cranmer Sq

Chester St W

P

5 DOC

Armagh St

Rolleston Ave

Christ's College

24

Gloucester St

17

12

Canterbury 2 Museum

11

Christchurch i-SITE

1

Botanic Gardens

4

31
33

Montreal St

Worcester Blvd

Cambridge Tce

Hereford St

Cashel St

Bridge of Remembrance

Riccarton Ave

Christchurch Hospital

10

Cambridge Tce

Avon River

Oxford Tce

32

South Hagley Park

St Asaph St

Hagley Ave

Stewart St

Antigua St

Montreal St

Durham St S

Lincoln Rd

Moorhouse Ave
37

Central Christchurch

Boat Sheds hires out row boats ($35), kayaks ($12), Canadian canoes ($35) and bikes (adult/child $10/5); all prices are per hour. There's also an excellent cafe.

Punting on the Avon BOATING
(Map p136; www.punting.co.nz; 2 Cambridge Tce; adult/child $25/12; ⊙9am-6pm Oct-Mar, 10am-4pm Apr-Sep) 🧭 The Antigua Boat Sheds are the starting point for half-hour punting trips through the botanical gardens. Relax in a flat-bottomed boat while a strapping lad in Edwardian clobber, armed with a long pole, does all the work. Other boats depart from the **Worcester St bridge** (Map p136) and punt through the ruined city centre.

Swimming & Surfing
Despite having separate names for different sections, it's one solid stretch of sandy beach that spreads north from the estuary of the Avon and Heathcliff rivers. Closest to the city centre is **New Brighton**, with a dis-

tinctive pier reaching 300m out to sea and a pedestrian mall lined with phoenix palms. On either side, **South New Brighton** and **North Beach** are quieter options, as is **Waimairi**, further north.

Smaller but prettier **Sumner** is at the foot of the Port Hills, on the south side of the estuary. With good eateries, accommodation and an art-house cinema, it's an easy place to visit and a relaxing place to stay, only 12km from the city centre.

Further east around the headland, isolated **Taylors Mistake** has the cleanest water of any Christchurch beach and some good surfing breaks. Beginners should stick to Sumner or New Brighton.

Walking
The i-SITE has up-to-date information on walks around Christchurch. Some popular tracks, particularly around the Port Hills, were closed at the time of writing due to

rock falls and instability following the earth-quakes, so it's vital to check the current situation before setting off (search www.ccc.govt.nz with the keywords 'Port Hills').

For great views of the city, take the walk-way from the **Sign of the Takahe** on Dyers Pass Rd. The various 'Sign of the...' places in this area were originally roadhouses built during the Depression as rest stops. This walk leads up to the **Sign of the Kiwi** through Victoria Park and then along Summit Rd to Scotts Reserve, with several look-out points along the way.

You can walk to Lyttelton on the **Bridle Path** (1½ hours), which starts at Heathcote Valley (take bus 28). The **Godley Head Walkway** (two hours return) begins at Taylors Mistake, crossing and recrossing Summit Rd, and offers beautiful views on a clear day.

Cycling

Christchurch has more cyclists than any other NZ city, due to its flatness and over 330km of on- and off-road cycleways. These are detailed on the city council's website (www.ccc.govt.nz), which also has updates on the current status of mountain-bike tracks through the Port Hills.

The 49km **Little River Railtrail** (www.littleriverrailtrail.co.nz) links the Christchurch suburb of Hornby to the Banks Peninsula hamlet of Little River. A couple of small sections traverse roads without cycle lanes, although this is only temporary. Join the trail 20km from Little River at Motukarara for the best of the ride.

City Cycle Hire   BICYCLE RENTAL
(☑03-377 5952; www.cyclehire-tours.co.nz; bike half/full day $25/35, mountain bike half/full day $30/45) Offers door-to-door delivery of on- and off-road city bikes and touring bikes. They'll also meet you with a bike at the top of the gondola if you fancy a 16km descent ($70 including gondola ride; 1½ hours).

Natural High   BICYCLE RENTAL
(☑03-982 2966; www.naturalhigh.co.nz; 690a Harewood Rd, Harewood; per day/week from $50/175) Rents touring and mountain bikes, and can assist with guided and self-guided bicycle touring through Canterbury and the South Island.

Vintage Peddler Bike Hire Co BICYCLE RENTAL
(Map p136; ☑03-365 6530; www.thevintagepeddler.co.nz; 16 Bealey Ave; per hour/day $15/30) Take to two retro wheels on these funky vintage bicycles. Helmets, locks and local knowledge are all supplied.

Other Activities

Gondola   CABLE CAR
(Map p132; www.gondola.co.nz; 10 Bridle Path Rd; return adult/child $25/12; ◷10am-5pm) Take a ride to the top of Mt Cavendish (500m) on this 945m cable car for wonderful views over the city, Lyttelton, Banks Peninsula and the Canterbury Plains. At the top there's a cafe and the child-focused *Time Tunnel* ride through historical scenes. You can also walk to Cavendish Bluff Lookout (30 minutes return) or the Pioneer Women's Memorial (one hour return).

Tram   TRAM
(☑03-377 4790; www.tram.co.nz; adult/child $10/free) Prior to the earthquakes, historic trams operated on a 2.5km inner-city loop. Limited services resumed in late 2013, heading between New Regent St and Canterbury Museum (35 minutes), but the route will expand as the rebuild continues.

Bone Dude   COURSE
(Map p132; ☑03-385 4509; www.thebonedude.co.nz; 153 Marshland Rd, Shirley; from $60; ◷1-4pm Mon-Fri, 10am-1pm Sat) Creative types should consider booking a session with the Bone Dude, who'll show you how to carve your own bone pendant (allow three hours). Sessions are limited to eight participants, so book ahead.

Garden City Helicopters   SCENIC FLIGHT
(☑03-358 4360; www.helicopters.net.nz; 20min $199) Flights above the city and Lyttelton let you observe the impact of the earthquake and the rebuilding efforts.

ⓘ WELCOME ABOARD COMBOS

Welcome Aboard (☑03-365 8282; www.welcomeaboard.co.nz) is the company that runs the punting, tram, gondola and Botanic Garden caterpillar tours, as well as Thrillseekers Adventures in Hanmer Springs. A baffling array of combo tickets is available which will save you some money if you're considering doing more than one activity. It also operates the six-hour Grand Tour (adult/child $119/69), which includes all four Christchurch-based activities and a stop in Sumner.

☞ **Tours**

Discovery Tours   BUS TOUR
(☑0800 372 879; www.discoverytravel.co.nz; tours from $130) Excursions to Akaroa, Aoraki/Mt Cook, Hanmer Springs, Kaikoura and the Waipara Valley wine region. The Arthur's Pass tour (adult/child $355/178) packs the *TranzAlpine* train, jetboating and a farm tour into one action-packed day.

Hassle Free Tours   BUS TOUR
(☑03-385 5775; www.hasslefree.co.nz) Explore Christchurch on an open-top double-decker bus (adult/child $29/15). Regional options include a 4WD alpine safari, jetboating on the Waimakariri River, and visiting the location of Edoras from the *Lord of the Rings* trilogy.

Red Bus Rebuild Tour   BUS TOUR
(☑0800 500 929; www.redbus.co.nz; adult/child $29/15) Commentaries focus on the past, present and future of earthquake-damaged sites in the city centre. Tours take 90 minutes and include video footage of the former streetscape.

Christchurch Sightseeing Tours   BUS TOUR
(☑0508 669 660; www.christchurchtours.co.nz; tours from $75) City tours, plus further-afield detours to Akaroa, Hanmer Springs and the Waipara wine region.

Christchurch Bike Tours   CYCLING
(☑0800 733 257; www.chchbiketours.co.nz; 2/4hr $50/160) Informative, two-hour tours loop around the city daily, heading to the Farmers Market on Saturday mornings. Also available is a four-hour gourmet food tour ending with a three-course lunch. Tours leave from the Antigua Boat Sheds.

Christchurch Segway Tours   CYCLING
(☑027 542 1887; www.urbanwheels.co.nz; per person $190) Two-hour two-wheeled guided tours through the city centre, Hagley Park and Riccarton.

Hiking Guys   TOUR
(☑09-281 4481; www.hikingguys.co.nz; adult/child $445/223) Day trips incorporating the *TranzAlpine* train and tramping around Arthur's Pass. Multiday trips also available.

Christchurch Personal Guiding Service   WALKING TOUR
(Map p136; ☑03-383 2495; Rolleston Ave; tours $15; ⊙1pm daily) Nonprofit organisation offering informative two-hour city walks. Buy tickets and join tours at the i-SITE or at the red-and-black kiosk nearby.

South Pacific Motorcycle Tours DRIVING TOUR
(☑03-312 0066; www.motorbiketours.co.nz) ✐ Jump on a hog for a fully guided or self-guided multiday road trip.

★🎪 **Festivals & Events**

Check www.bethere.co.nz for a comprehensive listing of festivals and events.

Garden City SummerTimes   MUSIC
(www.summertimes.co.nz) Say g'day to summer at a huge array of outdoor events between December and March.

World Buskers Festival   PERFORMING ARTS
(www.worldbuskersfestival.com) National and international talent entertain passers-by for 10 days in mid-January. Check the website for locations – and don't forget to put money in the hat.

Festival of Flowers   FLORAL
(www.festivalofflowers.co.nz) A blooming spectacle around Christchurch's heritage gardens for three weeks in February.

Ellerslie Flower Show   FLORAL
(www.ellerslieflowershow.co.nz) Hagley Park comes alive in late February/early March with NZ's biggest flower show.

Christchurch Arts Festival   PERFORMING ARTS
(www.artsfestival.co.nz) Midwinter arts extravaganza over a month from mid-August, celebrating music, theatre and dance.

Festa   ARCHITECTURE
(www.festa.org.nz) The spotlight is shone on Christchurch's post-earthquake 'transitional architecture' over Labour Weekend in October.

NZ Cup & Show Week   HORSE RACING
(www.nzcupandshow.co.nz) Includes the NZ Cup horse race, fashion shows, fireworks and the centrepiece A&P Show, where the country comes to town. Held over a week in November.

🛏 **Sleeping**

🏘 **City Centre**

Chester Street Backpackers   HOSTEL $
(Map p136; ☑03-377 1897; www.chesterst.co.nz; 148 Chester St E; dm/tw/d $32/68/70; @🛜) This relaxed wooden villa is painted in bright colours and has a large library in the sunny front room. The friendly house cat is a regular guest at hostel barbecues. It's popular; book ahead.

Dorset House
HOSTEL $

(Map p136; ✆03-366 8268; www.dorsethouse.co.nz; 1 Dorset St; dm/s $39/90, d $105-110; ⓟ@🕸) 🏊 Built in 1871, this wooden villa has a sunny deck, a large regal lounge with a log fire, a pool table, and beds instead of bunks. It's a short stroll to Hagley Park.

Around the World Backpackers
HOSTEL $

(Map p136; ✆03-365 4363; www.aroundtheworld.co.nz; 314 Barbadoes St; dm $30, d $76-80; ⓟ@🕸) We love AtW's friendly vibe, Kiwiana decor and sunny back garden (complete with hammocks and a barbecue). Ask about the 'Love Shack' if you're visiting with the closest of travelling companions.

Foley Towers
HOSTEL $

(Map p136; ✆03-366 9720; www.backpack.co.nz/foley.html; 208 Kilmore St; dm $30-33, d with/without bathroom $78/72; ⓟ@🕸) Sheltered by well-established trees, Foley Towers provides well-maintained rooms encircling quiet garden-trimmed courtyards. Dorms sleep six in three sets of bunks, or there are share rooms containing three single beds.

Vagabond Backpackers
HOSTEL $

(Map p136; ✆03-379 9677; www.vagabondhostel.co.nz; 232 Worcester St; dm $26-30, s $53, d $60-70; ⓟ@🕸) This old place is reminiscent of a big shared house. There's an appealing garden, and the grungy ambience is matched with prices that are cheaper than most.

★ Pomeroy's on Kilmore
B&B $$

(Map p136; ✆03-374 3532; www.pomeroysonkilmore.co.nz; 282 Kilmore St; r $145-195; ⓟ🕸) Even if this cute wooden cottage wasn't the sister and neighbour of Christchurch's best craft-beer pub, it would still be one of our favourites. Three of the five elegantly furnished rooms open on to a sunny garden and rates include a self-serve continental breakfast.

Focus Motel
MOTEL $$

(Map p136; ✆03-943 0800; www.focusmotel.com; 344 Durham St N; r $150-200; ⓟ🕸) Sleek and centrally located, this friendly motel offers studio and one-bedroom units with big-screen TVs, iPod docks, kitchenettes and super-modern decor. There's a guest barbecue and laundry, and pillowtop chocolates sweeten the deal.

CentrePoint on Colombo
MOTEL $$

(Map p136; ✆03-377 0859; www.centrepointoncolombo.co.nz; 859 Colombo St; r/apt from $165/190; ⓟ🕸) The friendly Kiwi-Japanese management have imbued this centrally located motel with style and comfort. Little extras like stereos, blackout curtains and spa baths (in the deluxe rooms) take it to the next level.

Colombo in the City
MOTEL $$

(Map p136; ✆03-366 8775; www.motelcolombo.co.nz; 863 Colombo St; d $170-190, apt $190-290; ⓟ@🕸) Colombo's attractive units are equipped with Sky TV, CD players, double-glazed windows and spa baths. Options range from studios to two-bedroom apartments.

Heritage Christchurch
HOTEL $$$

(Map p136; ✆03-983 4800; www.heritagehotels.co.nz; 28-30 Cathedral Sq; ste $235-440; 🕸) 🏊 Standing grandly on Cathedral Sq while all around is in ruins, the 1909 Old Government Building owes its survival to a thorough strengthening when it was converted to a hotel in the 1990s. After a three-year post-earthquake restoration its spacious suites are more elegant than ever. All have full kitchens.

Orari B&B
B&B $$$

(Map p136; ✆03-365 6569; www.orari.co.nz; 42 Gloucester St; s $175-235, d $195-255; ⓟ🕸) Orari is an 1893 home that has been simply updated with light-filled, pastel-toned rooms and inviting guest areas, as well as a lovely front

CHRISTCHURCH & CANTERBURY CHRISTCHURCH

CHRISTCHURCH FOR CHILDREN

There's no shortage of kid-friendly sights and activities in Christchurch. If family fun is a priority, consider planning your travels around NZ's biggest children's festival, **KidsFest** (www.kidsfest.org.nz). It's held every July and is chock-full of shows, workshops and parties. The annual World Buskers Festival (p140) is also bound to be a hit.

For picnics and open-air frolicking, visit the Botanic Gardens (p129); there's a playground beside the cafe, and little kids will love riding on the Caterpillar train. Extend your nature-based experience with a wildlife encounter at Orana Wildlife Park (p134) or the Willowbank Wildlife Reserve (p135), or get them burning off energy in a rowboat or kayak from the Antigua Boatsheds (p138). Fun can be stealthily combined with education at the International Antarctic Centre (p134) and the Discovery Centre at Canterbury Museum (p132).

If the weather's good, hit the beaches at Sumner or New Brighton.

garden. A neighbouring block, constructed in a sympathetic style, contains five three-bedroom apartments.

The George HOTEL $$$
(Map p136; ☎ 03-379 4560; www.thegeorge.com; 50 Park Tce; r $295-315, ste $472-630; P@🛜) 🅿
The George has 53 handsomely decorated rooms within a 1970s-looking building on the fringe of Hagley Park. Discreet staff attend to every whim, and ritzy features include huge TVs, luxury toiletries and glossy magazines.

Classic Villa B&B $$$
(Map p136; ☎ 03-377 7905; www.theclassicvilla. co.nz; 17 Worcester Blvd; s $179, d $289-389, ste $489; P🛜) 🅿 Pretty in pink, this 1899 house is one of Christchurch's most elegant accommodation options. Rooms are trimmed with antiques and Turkish rugs, and the Mediterranean-style breakfast is a shared social occasion.

Eliza's Manor HOTEL $$$
(Map p136; ☎ 03-366 8584; www.elizas.co.nz; 82 Bealey Ave; r $235-345; P🛜) 🅿 An infestation of teddy bears has done little to dint the heritage appeal of this large 1861 mansion. Wisteria curls around weatherboards, while inside the rooms are spacious and frilly.

🛏 Merivale

Merivale Manor MOTEL $$
(Map p132; ☎ 03-355 7731; www.merivalemanor. co.nz; 122 Papanui Rd; d $145-180; P🛜) A gracious 19th-century Victorian mansion is the hub of this elegant motel, with units both in the main house and in the more typically motel-style blocks lining the drive. Accommodation ranges from studios to two-bedroom apartments.

Elm Tree House B&B $$$
(Map p132; ☎ 03-355 9731; www.elmtreehouse. co.nz; 236 Papanui Rd; r/ste $265/295; P🛜) Built in the 1920s, elegant Elm Tree House has six stylish rooms and suites, a dining area leading to sunny rose gardens, and a spacious, wood-lined guests' lounge with a working Wurlitzer jukebox.

🛏 Fendalton

Anselm House B&B $$
(Map p132; ☎ 03-343 4260; www.anselmhouse. co.nz; 34 Kahu Rd; r $190; P🛜) When we visited, post-earthquake repairs were continuing on this architecturally interesting home, but

guests were still able to stay in the blissful 'river room', gazing over the gurgling Avon. Hopefully the 'rococo room' will be back up-and-running during the lifetime of this book

Fendalton House B&B $$
(Map p132; ☎ 03-343 1661; www.fendaltonhouse. co.nz; 28a Kotare St; r $165; P🛜) There's only one guest room available at this friendly, homestay-style B&B amid the pleasant streets of leafy Fendalton. Rates include a cooked breakfast and free wi-fi.

🛏 Riccarton

Lorenzo Motor Inn MOTEL $$
(Map p132; ☎ 03-348 8074; www.lorenzomotor-lodge.co.nz; 36 Riccarton Rd; units $159-239; P🛜) There's a Mediterranean vibe to this trim two-storey motel – the best of many on the busy Riccarton Rd strip. Units range from studio to two-bedroom apartments and some have spa baths and little balconies.

Roma on Riccarton MOTEL $$
(Map p132; ☎ 03-341 2100; www.romaonriccar-ton.com; 38 Riccarton Rd; d $158-230; P🛜) It may be the mirror image of neighbouring Lorenzo, but they're completely separate businesses. Like its twin, the units are all thoroughly modern, ranging from studios to two-bedroom apartments.

🛏 Addington

Jailhouse HOSTEL $
(Map p132; ☎ 03-982 7777; www.jail.co.nz; 338 Lincoln Rd; dm $32-35, tw/d $89/92; @🛜) From 1874 to 1999 this was Addington Prison; it's now one of Christchurch's most appealing and friendly hostels. Private rooms are a bit on the small side – they don't call them cells for nothing.

Arena Motel MOTEL $$
(Map p132; ☎ 03-338 4579; www.arenamotel.co.nz; 30 Whiteleigh Ave; d $135-185; P🛜) Within walking distance of the railway station and the increasingly hip Addington strip, the Arena has tidy modern units with kitchenettes, ranging in size from studios to two-bedroom apartments.

🛏 Sumner

Le Petit Hotel HOTEL $$
(Map p132; ☎ 03-326 6675; www.lepetithotel.co.nz; 16 Marriner St; d $155; P@🛜) Relaxed coffee-and-croissant breakfasts, friendly owners

and the close proximity to Sumner beach and some of Christchurch's best restaurants make this a definite *'oui'* from us. Get in early and request an upstairs room with a view.

Sumner Bay Motel MOTEL $$
(Map p132; ☑ 03-326 5969; www.sumnermotel. co.nz; 26 Marriner St; d $159-185; ℗) The studio, one- and two-bedroom units at this striking, contemporary complex all have either balconies or courtyards, plus quality furnishings and Sky TV. Two-bedroom units contain full kitchens; the rest have kitchenettes.

Other Suburbs

Haka Lodge HOSTEL $
(Map p132; ☑ 03-980 4252; www.hakalodge.com; 518 Linwood Ave, Woolston; dm/d/apt $32/79/170; ☎) Sprawled across three floors of a modern suburban house, Haka Lodge is one of Christchurch's newest hostels. Rooms are spotless and colourful, and end-of-day treats include a comfy lounge and bird-filled garden.

Old Countryhouse HOSTEL $
(Map p132; ☑ 03-381 5504; www.oldcountryhouse-nz.com; 437 Gloucester St, Linwood; dm $35-37, d with/without bathroom $102/92; ℗@☎) Spread between three separate villas, 1km east of Latimer Sq, this chilled-out hostel has handmade wooden furniture, a reading lounge and a lovely garden filled with native ferns. A spa pool and sauna heat things up.

Christchurch Top 10 HOLIDAY PARK $
(Map p132; ☑ 03-352 9176; www.christchurchtop10. co.nz; 39 Meadow St, Papanui; sites $39-50, unit with/without bathroom from $94/76; ℗@☎☒) ✈ It could do with some freshening up, but this is the best of Christchurch's holiday parks. Accommodation ranges from sites to simple cabins and motel units, and there's an indoor pool, games rooms and a playground for the kids.

Airport Gateway MOTEL $$
(☑ 03-358 7093; www.airportgateway.co.nz; 45 Roydvale Ave, Burnside; d $155-195; ℗@☎) Handy for those early flights, this large motel has a variety of rooms with good facilities. A 24-hour airport transfer is available at no extra charge. The newer block is very comfortable and good value.

Eating

Following the February 2011 earthquake, many restaurants were forced to abandon their damaged buildings and move to the suburbs. As a result you'll find some real treats lurking in unlikely blocks of neighbourhood shops. Key dining precincts are Victoria St (to the northwest of the City Centre), Addington, Riccarton, Merivale and the beachside suburb of Sumner.

City Centre

★ C1 Espresso CAFE $
(Map p136; www.c1espresso.co.nz; 185 High St; mains $10-19; ⊙7am-10pm; ☎) ✈ Resurrected from the rubble, C1 has reopened better than ever in a grand former post office that somehow escaped the cataclysm. Recycled materials fill the interior (Victorian oak panelling, bulbous 1970s light fixtures) and tables spill onto a little square. The food, coffee and service are excellent too.

Black Betty CAFE $
(Map p136; www.blackbetty.co.nz; 163 Madras St; mains $10-20; ⊙8am-4pm; ☎) Infused with aromas from Switch Espresso's roasting operation, Black Betty's industrial-chic warehouse is a popular destination for students from nearby CPIT. Attractions include all-day breakfasts, excellent counter food and the best of NZ wine and craft beers.

Vic's Cafe & Bake CAFE $
(Map p136; www.vics.co.nz; 132 Victoria St; mains $11-18; ⊙7.30am-4.30pm) Pop in for a robust breakfast on the big shared tables or linger over lunch on the front terrace. Otherwise grab baked goodies and still-warm artisan bread for a DIY riverside picnic.

Canterbury Cheesemongers DELI $
(Map p136; www.cheesemongers.co.nz; rear, 301 Montreal St; sandwiches $5-8; ⊙9am-5pm Tue-Sat) Pop in to buy artisan cheeses, or craft your own sandwich by combining freshly baked sourdough bread and ciabatta with a whole cheese shop of dairy goodies. Coffee and juices complete a good-value lunch.

Beat Street CAFE $
(Map p136; 324 Barbadoes St; mains $10-19; ⊙7am-5pm Sun-Tue, to 10pm Wed-Sat; ☑) Welcome to the grungy hub of Christchurch cafe-cool. Free range this and organic that combine with terrific eggy breakfasts, gourmet pies and robust coffee. Look out for open mic music and poetry nights.

Dose CAFE, JAPANESE $
(Map p136; www.cafedose.co.nz; 77 Tuam St; mains $7-19; ⊙7.30am-4pm Mon & Tue, to late Wed-Sat)

Excellent coffee and superior counter food combine here with toasted bagels and what may just be Christchurch's best eggs Benedict. In the evenings Dose morphs into an *izakaya* bar with tasty grilled skewers and ice-cold Japanese beer.

King of Snake
ASIAN $$

(Map p136; ☎03-365 7363; www.kingofsnake.co.nz; 145 Victoria St; mains $24-37; ⊙11am-3.30pm Mon-Fri, 5.30-10pm daily) Dark wood, gold tiles and purple skull-patterned wallpaper fill this so-hip-right-now restaurant and cocktail bar with just the right amount of sinister opulence. The adventurous menu gainfully plunders the cuisines of Asia – from India to Korea – to delicious, if pricey, effect.

Fiddlesticks
RESTAURANT, BAR $$

(Map p136; ☎03-365 0533; www.fiddlesticksbar. co.nz; 48 Worcester Blvd; mains $20-40; ⊙9am-late) Sidle into slick Fiddlesticks and seat yourself in either the more formal dining room or in the glassed-in patio attached to the curvy cocktail bar. Food ranges from soups and beautifully presented salads to fancy meat pies and Angus steaks.

Lotus Heart
VEGETARIAN $$

(Map p136; www.thelotusheart.co.nz; 363 St Asaph St; mains $13-22; ⊙7.30am-3pm Tue-Sun & 5-9pm Fri & Sat; ⌖) ✐ Run by students of Sri Chimnoy, this vegetarian eatery serves curry, pizza, wraps, freshly squeezed organic juices and filled pita pockets. Organic, vegan and gluten-free options abound, and there's an interesting gift shop onsite.

50 Bistro
EUROPEAN $$

(Map p136; ☎03-371 0250; www.thegeorge.com; 50 Park Tce; breakfast $17-22, lunch $20-24, dinner $20-37; ⊙6.30am-late; ⌖) The more casual restaurant at the George is a bustling affair, serving savvy local twists on classic bistro flavours. Try the Nifty 50 lunch menu – $29 for soup and a main dish.

Himalayas
INDIAN $$

(Map p136; ☎03-377 8935; www.himalayas.co.nz; 830a Colombo St; lunch $9-14, dinner $18-24; ⊙11.30am-2pm Tue-Fri & 5pm-late Tue-Sun; ⌖) Himalayas' stylish dining room showcases lots of subcontinental favourites, including vegetarian options like the creamy *dal makhani* (black lentils cooked with aromatic spices). The *kadhai* chicken is studded with chilli, ginger and coriander – perfect with a cold beer.

★ Saggio di Vino
EUROPEAN $$$

(Map p136; ☎03-379 4006; www.saggiodivino. co.nz; 179 Victoria St; mains $35-42; ⊙5-10pm) Despite the Italian name, the menu has a heavy French accent at this elegant restaurant, which is quite possibly Christchurch's best. Expect delicious takes on terrine, duck *confit* and Café de Paris steak, and a well-laden cheese trolley to finish you off.

✕ Addington

★ Addington Coffee Co-op
CAFE $

(Map p132; www.addingtoncoffee.org.nz; 297 Lincoln Rd; mains $6-19; ⊙7.30am-4pm Mon-Fri, 9am-4pm Sat & Sun; ⌖⌖) One of Christchurch's biggest and most bustling cafes is also one of its best. A compact stall selling organic cotton T-shirts jostles for attention with delicious cakes, gourmet pies and the legendary house breakfasts. An onsite laundromat completes the deal for busy travellers.

Luciano Espresso Bar
CAFE $

(Map p136; www.facebook.com/LucianoEspresso; 76 Moorhouse Ave; mains $10-21; ⊙7am-4.30pm) 'Christchurch's best coffee' is the claim, and we're not about to argue. Order from the interesting selections on the menu or peruse the drool-inducing items on the counter. Slick decor distracts from the incessant traffic outside.

Mosaic by Simo
MOROCCAN $

(Map p132; www.simos.co.nz; 300 Lincoln Rd; tapas & mains $8-19; ⊙9am-9pm Mon-Sat) This delicafe is popular for its takeaway *bocadillos* (grilled wraps filled with a huge selection of Middle Eastern and African-inspired fillings, sauces and toppings). Other tasty offerings include sauteed calamari, spicy *merguez* sausages and tagines.

Edesia
EUROPEAN $$$

(Map p132; ☎03-943 2144; www.edesia.co.nz; 12 Show Pl; lunch $25-29, dinner $38-43; ⊙11.30am-3pm Mon-Wed, 8.30am-3pm Thu & Fri, 8.30am-1pm Sat, 5.30-10pm daily) Ignore the office-park location; Edesia's version of fine dining is worth seeking out. The dinner menu includes innovative spins on local venison and lamb, while lunch includes pasta and salads. After work it morphs into a cosy bar for local desk jockeys.

✕ Woolston

Gustav's
RESTAURANT, BAR $$

(Map p132; ☎03-389 5544; www.gustavs.co.nz; The Tannery, Garlands Rd, Woolston; tapas $10-14, mains

$28-33; ⏱11am-late) Hexagonal oak tables and vintage wallpaper add a touch of Edwardian class, while live jazz and the clatter of diners sharing dishes creates a convivial hubbub. Local meat and seafood features prominently, although the flavours are international.

Holy Smoke   CAFE, DELI **$$**
(Map p132; www.holysmoke.co.nz; 650 Ferry Rd, Woolston; mains $12-19; ⏱7am-4.30pm Tue-Sat) Here's your chance to get acquainted with the unique character of *manuka* (NZ tea tree). At this friendly deli-cafe it's used to smoke everything from bacon to salmon, which then make their way into cooked breakfasts and counter food.

Sumner

⭐ **Cornershop Bistro**   FRENCH **$$**
(Map p132; ☑03-326 6720; www.cornershopbistro.co.nz; 32 Nayland St, Sumner; lunch $17-21, dinner $27-35; ⏱10am-3pm Fri-Sun, 5.30-10pm Wed-Sun) Classic dishes such as *coq au vin* are expertly executed at this superior French-style bistro which never forgets it's in a relaxed beachside suburb. Spend longer than you planned to linger over brunch.

Bamboozle   ASIAN **$$**
(Map p132; ☑03-326 7878; www.facebook.com/bamboozlerestaurant; 6 Wakefield St; mains $18-29; ⏱5-10pm Tue-Sat) Asian fusion is the name of the game at stylish Bamboozle, where talented chefs conjure up innovative spins on traditional dishes. Leave room for one of Christchurch's best crème brûlées.

Other Suburbs

Christchurch Farmers' Market   MARKET **$**
(Map p132; www.christchurchfarmersmarket.co.nz; 16 Kahu Rd, Riccarton; ⏱9am-noon Sat) Held in the pretty grounds of Riccarton House, this excellent farmers market offers a tasty array of organic fruit and vegies, South Island cheeses and salmon, local craft beer and ethnic treats.

Kinji   JAPANESE **$$**
(Map p132; ☑03-359 4697; www.kinjirestaurant.com; 279b Greers Rd, Bishopdale; mains $16-18; ⏱5.30-10pm Mon-Sat) The destruction of its central city premises sparked a move to a tucked-away suburban site for this acclaimed Japanese restaurant. Fortunately its loyal clientele has followed, making bookings essential. Tuck into the likes of sashimi and ginger squid but save room

for the green-tea tiramisu, a surprising highlight.

Under the Red Verandah   CAFE **$$**
(Map p132; www.utrv.co.nz; cnr Tancred & Worcester Sts, Linwood; mains $10-20; ⏱7.30am-4pm;) A post-earthquake change of premises has done nothing to dint UTRV's popularity with Christchurch foodie types. Take a seat under said verandah and tuck into baked goodies, oaty pancakes and corn fritters.

Bodhi Tree   BURMESE **$$**
(Map p132; ☑03-377 6808; www.bodhitree.co.nz; 399 Ilam Rd, Bryndwr; dishes $13-18; ⏱6-10pm Tue-Sat; 🖉) Bodhi Tree has been wowing locals with the subtle flavours of Burmese cuisine for more than a decade. The starter-sized dishes feature exceptionally fresh ingredients and are designed to be shared. Standouts include *le pet thoke* (pickled tea-leaf salad) and *ciandi thoke* (grilled eggplant).

Burgers & Beers Inc   BURGERS **$$**
(Map p132; www.burgersandbeersinc.co.nz; 355 Colombo St, Sydenham; burgers $13-18; ⏱11am-late) Quirkily named gourmet burgers – try the Woolly Sahara Sand Hopper (Moroccan-spiced lamb with lemon yoghurt) or the Shagged Stag (venison with tamarillo and plum chutney) – and an ever-changing selection of Kiwi craft beers give you reason to head south.

🍷 Drinking & Nightlife

🍷 City Centre

Pomeroy's Old Brewery Inn   PUB
(Map p136; www.pomspub.co.nz; 292 Kilmore St; ⏱3-11pm Tue-Thu, noon-11pm Fri-Sun) Welcoming Pomeroy's is the city's hoppy hub for fans of NZ's rapidly expanding craft-beer scene. A wide range of guest taps showcase brews from around the country. There's regular live music, and the attached Victoria's Kitchen does great pub food (mains $22 to $26).

Carlton   BAR
(Map p136; www.carltonbar.co.nz; 1 Papanui Rd, Merivale; ⏱11am-midnight Sun-Wed, to 2am Thu-Sat) The rebuilt Carlton's ultramodern look includes old planning maps plastered to the walls and visual references to the shipping containers out of which it operated when the historic Carlton pub collapsed. The upstairs deck is a prime spot on a sunny afternoon.

Revival
BAR

(Map p136; www.revivalbar.co.nz; 94 Victoria St; ☺4-9pm Mon & Tue, to midnight Wed, to 3am Thu-Sun) 🍴 Revival is the hippest of Christchurch's container bars, with regular DJs and a funky lounge area dotted with a quirky collection of automotive rear ends and vintage steamer trunks.

Tequila Mockingbird
BAR, RESTAURANT

(Map p136; www.tequilamockingbird.co.nz; 98 Victoria St; shared plates $8-24; ☺11.30am-late Mon-Fri, 5pm-late Sat & Sun) If the awesome name's not enough to lure you through the door of this upmarket Latin bar-restaurant, then perhaps the Caribbean-inflected cocktails, nifty decor and late-night DJs will. The food's excellent too.

Monday Room
WINE BAR

(Map p136; www.themondayroom.co.nz; 367 Moorhouse Ave; ☺8am-late Mon-Fri, 10am-late Sat & Sun) Part cafe, part restaurant and part wine bar, the versatile Monday Room is the kind of place to hang out at any time. Occupying a restored heritage building, the funky interior is a background for interesting brunch and lunch options; later in the day, tapas, craft beers, cocktails and live musicians take centre stage.

🍷 Suburbs

★ The Brewery
BREWERY

(Map p132; www.casselsbrewery.co.nz; 3 Garlands Rd, Woolston; ☺7am-late) An essential destination for beer-loving travellers, the Cassels & Sons brewery crafts its beer using a wood-fired brew kettle, resulting in big, bold beers. Tasting trays are available for the curious and the indecisive, live bands perform most nights, and the food – including wood-fired pizzas – is top-notch, too.

Volstead Trading Company
BAR

(Map p132; www.volstead.co.nz; 55 Riccarton Rd, Riccarton; ☺4-11pm Mon-Sat) Comfy old sofas from your last student flat combine with quirky murals and interesting craft beers in this very cool shabby-chic bar. If you're peckish, dig into popcorn, nachos and toasted sandwiches.

☆ Entertainment

For live music and club listings, see www.christchurchmusic.org.nz or www.mukuna.co.nz. Also look out for the *Groove Guide* magazine in cafes.

Court Theatre
THEATRE

(Map p132; ☑03-963 0870; www.courttheatre.org.nz; Bernard St, Addington) Christchurch's original Court Theatre was an integral part of the city's Arts Centre but was forced to relocate to this warehouse after the earthquakes. The new premises are much more spacious; it's a great venue to see popular international plays and works by NZ playwrights.

Dux Live
LIVE MUSIC

(Map p132; www.duxlive.co.nz; 363 Lincoln Rd, Addington) One of the kingpins of the live-music scene, this intimate 250-capacity space has gigs most nights.

darkroom
LIVE MUSIC

(Map p136; www.facebook.com/darkroom.nz; 336 St Asaph St; ☺5pm-late Wed-Sun) A hip combination of live-music venue and bar, darkroom has lots of Kiwi beers and great cocktails. Live gigs are frequent – and frequently free.

AMI Stadium
STADIUM

(Rugby League Park; Map p132; www.crfu.co.nz; 95 Jack Hinton Dr, Addington) Following the destruction of AMI Stadium at Lancaster Park, the traditional home of rugby union and cricket in Christchurch, the Canterbury Rugby Union have shifted its home games to Rugby League Park (confusingly now also known as AMI Stadium due to sponsorship rights). The Crusaders play here from late February to July in the Super Rugby tournament, while from July to September Canterbury plays in NZ's domestic rugby championship.

Alice Cinematheque
CINEMA

(Map p136; ☑03-365 0615; www.aliceinvideoland.co.nz; 209 Tuam St; adult/child $16/12) There are only 38 seats at this Egyptian-themed art-house cinema, attached to the excellent Alice in Videoland specialty video and DVD store.

Hollywood Cinema
CINEMA

(Map p132; www.hollywoodcinema.co.nz; 28 Marriner St; adult/child $16/10) Mainly art-house and foreign-language flicks in the seaside suburb of Sumner.

Hoyts Riccarton
CINEMA

(Map p132; www.hoyts.co.nz; Westfield Riccarton, Riccarton Rd; adult/child $16.50/11.50) Hollywood blockbusters screen at Christchurch's most central multiplex.

Shopping

City Centre

Re:START Mall   MALL
(Map p136; www.restart.org.nz; Cashel Mall;
⏱10am-5pm; 🐾) This colourful labyrinth
of shops based in shipping containers was
the first retail activity in the Christchurch
CBD after the earthquakes. With a couple of
decent cafes and a good selection of stores,
it's a pleasant place to stroll. Note that
Re:START is only intended to be temporary,
so it may disappear at any time.

Ballantynes   DEPARTMENT STORE
(Map p136; www.ballantynes.com; cnr Colombo &
Cashel Sts; ⏱9am-5pm) A venerable Christchurch department store selling men's and
women's fashions, cosmetics, travel goods and
specialty NZ gifts. Fashionistas should check
out the Contemporary Lounge upstairs.

New Regent St   MALL
(Map p136; www.newregentstreet.co.nz) A forerunner to the modern mall, this pretty little stretch of pastel Spanish Mission–style
shops was described as NZ's most beautiful
street when it was completed in 1932. Fully
restored post-earthquake, it's once again a
pleasant place to stroll and peruse the tiny
galleries, gift shops and cafes.

Suburbs

★ The Tannery   SHOPPING CENTRE
(Map p132; www.thetannery.co.nz; 3 Garlands Rd,
Woolston; ⏱10am-5.30pm Mon-Sat, to 4pm Sun)
In a city mourning the loss of its heritage,
this post-earthquake conversion of a Victorian tannery couldn't be more welcome. The
19th-century industrial buildings have been
chooshed up with period-style tiles, wrought
iron and stained glass, and filled with boutique stores selling everything from books
to fashion to surfboards. Bored partners of
frenzied shoppers can slink off for a drink
in The Brewery or Gustav's (p144). Alice in
Videoland is planning to open two cinemas
here.

Westfield Riccarton   MALL
(Map p132; www.westfield.co.nz; Riccarton Rd,
Riccarton; ⏱9am-6pm Sat-Wed, to 9pm Thu &
Fri) Since the earthquakes, shopping in
Christchurch has largely been focused on
the city's suburban malls. The most conven-
ient for visitors is this megamall, west of the
city centre. As well as a huge selection of

fashion, homeware and entertainment outlets, there's a cinema multiplex, a supermarket and 22 food outlets.

Sunday Artisan Market   MARKET
(Map p132; 16 Kahu Rd, Riccarton; ⏱11am-2pm
Sun) Held in the leafy grounds of Riccarton
House, this small market combines local
arts-and-crafts vendors with gourmet food
stalls and live music.

🛈 Information

MEDIA

Cityscape (www.cityscape-christchurch.co.nz)
Quarterly entertainment and events magazine
available in inner-city cafes and retailers.
Check the website for updates on new openings
around town.

The Press (www.stuff.co.nz/the-press/)
Christchurch's newspaper, published Monday
to Saturday. Friday's edition has entertainment
listings.

MEDICAL SERVICES

24 Hour Surgery (☎03-365 7777;
www.24hoursurgery.co.nz; cnr Bealey Ave &
Colombo St) No appointment necessary.

Christchurch Hospital (☎03-364 0640,
emergency dept 03-364 0270; www.cdhb.govt.
nz; 2 Riccarton Ave) Has a 24-hour emergency
department.

Urgent Pharmacy (☎03-366 4439; cnr Bealey
Ave & Colombo St; ⏱6-11pm Mon-Fri, 9am-
11pm Sat & Sun) Located beside the 24 Hour
Surgery.

TOURIST INFORMATION

Airport i-SITE (☎03-353 7774; www.christ-
churchnz.com; ⏱7.30am-7pm)

Christchurch i-SITE (Map p136; ☎03-379
9629; www.christchurchnz.com; Botanic Gardens, Rolleston Ave; ⏱8.30am-5pm, extended
in summer)

DOC (Department of Conservation; Map p136;
☎03-379 4082; www.doc.govt.nz; Botanic
Gardens Information Centre, Armagh St; ⏱9am-
4pm Mon-Fri, 10.15am-4pm Sat & Sun) Information on South Island national parks and walks.

Visitor Kiosk (Map p136; Cathedral Sq;
⏱9.30am-5pm)

USEFUL WEBSITES

CERA (www.cera.govt.nz) The Canterbury
Earthquake Recovery Authority has the low-
down on rebuild plans and status updates.

Christchurch & Canterbury Tourism (www.
christchurchnz.com) Official tourism website
for the city and region.

Christchurch City Council (www.christchurch.
org.nz) The city council's official website.

Neat Places (www.neatplaces.co.nz) A local blogger's authoritative view of the best of Christchurch's shopping, eating and drinking.

ⓘ Getting There & Away

AIR

Christchurch Airport (CHC; ☏ 03-358 5029; www.christchurchairport.co.nz; Durey Rd) is the South Island's main international gateway (see the transport chapter for international flights). The newly modernised and expanded airport has excellent facilities, including baggage storage, hire-car counters, ATMs, foreign-exchange offices and an i-SITE visitor information centre.

The following are the domestic airlines flying from Christchurch and the destinations that they serve:

Air New Zealand (☏ 0800 737 000; www.air-newzealand.co.nz) Air New Zealand–operated flights head to/from Auckland, Wellington, Dunedin and Queenstown. Code-share flights with smaller regional airlines head to/from Blenheim, Hamilton, Hokitika, Invercargill, Napier, Nelson, New Plymouth, Palmerston North, Paraparaumu, Rotorua and Tauranga.

Jetstar (☏ 0800 800 995; www.jetstar.com) Flies to/from Auckland, Wellington and Queenstown.

BUS

The following services stop outside the Canterbury Museum on Rolleston St, unless otherwise stated. Enquire at the i-SITE about seasonal ski shuttles.

Akaroa French Connection (☏ 0800 800 575; www.akaroabus.co.nz; one way/return $25/45) Daily service to Akaroa.

Akaroa Shuttle (☏ 0800 500 929; www.akaroashuttle.co.nz; one way/return $35/50) Heads to Akaroa daily, increasing to twice daily from November to April.

Atomic Shuttles (☏ 03-349 0697; www.atomictravel.co.nz) Destinations include Picton ($35, 5¼ hours), Greymouth ($45, 3¾ hours), Timaru ($25, 2½ hours), Dunedin ($30 to $35, 5¾ hours) and Queenstown ($50, seven hours).

Budget Buses & Shuttles (☏ 03-615 5119; www.budgetshuttles.co.nz; ⊗ Mon-Sat) Offers a door-to-door shuttle to Geraldine ($57) and Timaru ($47), along with cheaper scheduled runs (from $27).

Hanmer Connection (☏ 0800 242 663; www.hanmerconnection.co.nz; one way/return $30/50) Daily bus to/from Hanmer Springs via Amberley and Waipara.

InterCity (☏ 03-365 1113; www.intercity.co.nz) The most reliable of the coach services, with the most extensive network. The main bus stop is on Armagh St, between New Regent and Manchester Sts. Coaches head to Picton (from $26, 5¼ hours), Timaru (from $28, 2½ hours), Dunedin (from $40, six hours) and Queenstown (from $55, eight to 11 hours) twice daily; and to Te Anau (from $61, 10¾ hours) daily.

Knightrider (☏ 03-342 8055; www.knightrider.co.nz) Has a bus departing from 118 Bealey Ave most evenings, heading to Timaru ($38, three hours), Oamaru ($43, four hours), Moeraki ($47, five hours) and Dunedin ($50, six hours).

Naked Bus (www.nakedbus.com; prices vary; ☏) Destinations include Picton (4½ to 5¾ hours), Kaikoura (1½ hours), Dunedin (six hours), Wanaka (7½ hours) and Queenstown (eight hours).

West Coast Shuttle (☏ 03-768 0028; www.westcoastshuttle.co.nz) Buses stop outside Central Station on Tuam St, heading to/from Springfield ($30, 1¼ hours), Arthur's Pass ($40, 2¾ hours) and Greymouth ($53, four hours).

TRAIN

Christchurch railway station (☏ 03-341 2588; www.kiwirailscenic.co.nz; Troup Dr, Addington; ⊗ ticket office 6.30am-3pm) is the terminus for two highly scenic train journeys. At the time of writing there was a free shuttle from city-centre accommodation to the station, although this may not continue; enquire at the i-SITE or ask your accommodation provider.

The *Coastal Pacific* runs daily from October to April departing from Christchurch at 7am and arriving at Picton at 12.13pm ($79 to $159). Other stops include Waipara ($59, 56 minutes), Kaikoura ($49 to $69, three hours) and Blenheim ($79 to $159, 4¾ hours). It then departs Picton at 1pm, returning to Christchurch at 6.21pm.

The *TranzAlpine* is widely considered one of the best train journeys in the world. It operates year-round with a daily train between Christchurch and Greymouth ($99 to $198, 4½ hours) via Springfield ($89, one hour), Arthur's Pass ($89, 2½ hours) and Lake Brunner ($99 to $198, 3½ hours).

ⓘ Getting Around

TO/FROM THE AIRPORT

Christchurch Airport is only 10km from the city centre but a **taxi** between the two can cost a hefty $45 to $65. Alternatively, the airport is well served by **public buses** (www.metroinfo.co.nz). Bus 3 heads through Riccarton (25 minutes) to the central bus station (35 minutes) and on to Sumner (70 minutes). Bus 29 heads through Fendalton (10 minutes) to the bus station (30 minutes). Both services cost $8 and run every half-hour from roughly 7am to 11pm.

MAORI NZ: CANTERBURY

Only 14% of Maori live on the South Island but of those, half of them live in Canterbury. The first major tribe to become established here were Waitaha, who were subsequently conquered and assimilated into the Ngati Mamoe tribe in the 16th century. In the following century, they in turn were conquered and subsumed by Ngai Tahu (www.ngaitahu. iwi.nz), a tribe that has its origins in the East Coast of the North Island.

In 1848 most of Canterbury was sold to the crown under an agreement which stipulated that an area of 10 acres per person would be reserved for the tribe; less than half of that actually was. With so little land left to them, Ngai Tahu were no longer able to be self-sufficient and suffered great financial hardship. It wasn't until 1997 that this injustice was addressed, with the tribe receiving an apology from the crown and a settlement valued at $170 million. Part of the deal was the official inclusion of the Maori name for the most spiritually significant part of the tribe's ancestral land: Aoraki/Mt Cook.

Today, Ngai Tahu is considered to be one of Maoridom's great success stories, with a reputation for good financial management, sound cultural advice and a portfolio including property, forestry, fisheries and many high-profile tourism operations.

There are many ways to engage in Maori culture in Canterbury. Artefacts can be seen at Canterbury Museum (p132), Akaroa Museum (p152), Okains Bay Maori & Colonial Museum (p152) and South Canterbury Museum (p170). Willowbank Wildlife Reserve (p135) has a replica Maori village and an evening cultural show. Further south in Timaru, the Te Ana Maori Rock Art Centre (p169) has interactive displays and arranges tours to see centuries-old work in situ.

as the others (Arthur's and Haast) and the forest isn't as dense either. Mainly it's comprised of beech (red and silver) and kowhai trees growing along river terraces.

The area has some interesting tramps, passing through beech forest with a backdrop of snowcapped mountains, lakes, and alpine tarns and rivers. Popular tracks include the **St James Walkway** (66km; three to five days) and the paths through **Lake Sumner Forest Park**; see the Department of Conservation (DOC) pamphlet *Lake Sumner & Lewis Pass* ($2). Subalpine conditions apply, so make sure you sign the intentions books at the huts.

Maruia Springs (☑03-523 8840; www. maruiasprings.co.nz; SH7; d $179-199; ☺pools 8am-7.30pm; @☎) is a small, Japanese-style hot-spring resort on the banks of the Maruia River, 7km west of Lewis Pass, with elegant minimalist accommodation, a cafe-bar and a Japanese restaurant (breakfast and dinner only). In the thermal pools (adult/child $20/9, free for guests), water with black mineral flakes of 'hot spring flowers' is pumped into a gender-segregated traditional Japanese bathhouse and outdoor rock pools. It's a magical setting during a winter snowfall, but mind the sandflies in summer. Massages (30/60 minutes $48/90) and private spa houses (45 minutes $26) are available.

From Lewis Pass the highway wiggles east for 62km before reaching the turn-off to Hanmer Springs.

Hanmer Springs
POP 843

Ringed by sculpted mountains, Hanmer Springs is the main thermal resort on the South Island. It's a pleasantly low-key spot to indulge yourself, whether soaking in hot pools, dining out or being pampered in the spa complex. In case that all sounds too soporific, fear not; there are plenty of family-friendly activities on offer, including a few to get the adrenaline pumping.

◉ Sights & Activities

Wai Ariki Farm Park FARM, ZOO
(☑03-315 7772; www.waiariki-farmpark.co.nz; 108 Rippingale Rd; adult/child $12/6; ☺10am-4pm Tue-Sun, daily during school holidays) With more animals than Dr Dolittle's Facebook page, Wai Ariki is a great spot for kids. Llamas, Tibetan yaks, deer, rabbits, guinea pigs and goats all feature, and many of the critters can be hand-fed; horse treks for the young ones are also available (from $50). For mum and dad there's a licensed cafe and craft gallery.

★ **Hanmer Springs Thermal Pools** SPA
(📞 03-315 0000; www.hanmersprings.co.nz; 42
Amuri Ave; adult/child $20/10, locker $2; ⏰ 10am-
9pm) 🏊 Maori legend has it that these springs
formed as a result of embers from Mt Ngauruhoe in the North Island falling from the sky.
The main pool complex consists of a series
of large pools of various temperatures, along
with smaller landscaped rock pools, a freshwater 25m lap pool with a whirlpool attached,
private thermal pools ($30 per 30 minutes)
and a cafe. Kids of all ages will love the wa-
terslides and speedy superbowl ride ($10).

The adjacent **Spa** (📞 0800 873 529, 03-315
0029; www.hanmerspa.co.nz; ⏰ 10am-7pm) has
massage and beauty treatments from $75.
Entry to the pools is discounted to $12 if you
partake of the spa's facilities.

Hanmer Forest Park WALKING
Walkers and mountain bikers will find plenty of room to move within the 130 sq km expanse of forest abutting the town. The easy
Woodland Walk starts 1km up Jollies Pass
Rd and goes through Douglas fir, poplar and
redwood stands. It joins the Majuba Walk,
which leads to Conical Hill Lookout and
then heads back towards town (1½ hours).
The i-SITE stocks a *Forest Park Walks* booklet and a mountain-bike trail map (both $3).

Thrillseekers Adventures ADVENTURE SPORTS
(📞 03-315 7046; www.thrillseekers.co.nz; Hanmer
Springs Rd) Bungy off a 35m-high bridge
($169), jetboat the Waiau Gorge (adult/
child $115/60), white-water raft (Grade II
to III) down the Waiau River (adult/child
$149/79) or get dirty on a quad-bike (adult/
child $149/99). The Thrillseekers Adventure
centre is next to the bridge near the turn-
off from SH7 but there's a **booking office**
(📞 03-315 7346; www.thrillseekers.co.nz; Conical
Hill Rd; ⏰ 9am-5pm) in town (which also has
free internet terminals).

Hanmer Springs
Adventure Centre ADVENTURE SPORTS
(📞 03-315 7233; www.hanmeradventure.co.nz; 20
Conical Hill Rd; ⏰ 8.30am-5pm) Offers quad-
biking (from $129), mountain-bike shuttles
to the top of Jack's Pass ($115), clay-shooting
($35) and archery ($35). It also books local
tours and rents mountain bikes (per hour/
day from $19/45), fishing rods (per day $29)
and ski/snowboard gear.

Hanmer Springs Ski Area SKIING
(📞 027 434 1806; www.skihanmer.co.nz; day pass
adult/child $60/30) Only 17km from town via
an unsealed road, this small complex has
runs to suit all levels of ability. The Adventure
Centre provides shuttles during the season.

Hanmer Springs

Hanmer Springs ⊕ 0 ▬▬ 100 m / 0 ▬▬ 0.05 miles

MOLESWORTH STATION

Filling up 180 mountainous sq km between Hanmer Springs and Blenheim, Molesworth Station is NZ's largest farm, with the country's largest cattle herd (up to 10,000). It's also an area of national ecological significance and the entire farm is now administered by **DOC** (Department of Conservation; ☑03-572 9100; www.doc.govt.nz).

Visits are usually only possible when the Acheron Rd through the station is open from November to early April (weather permitting; check with DOC or at the Hanmer Springs i-SITE). The 207km drive from Hanmer Springs north to Blenheim on this narrow, unsealed backcountry road takes around six hours; note that the gates are only open from 7am to 7pm, and overnight camping (adult/child $6/3) is permitted in certain areas (no open fires allowed). Pick up DOC's *Molesworth Station* brochure from the i-SITE or download it from their website.

Molesworth Heritage Tours (☑03-315 7401; www.molesworth.co.nz; tours $198-750; ☉Oct-May) leads 4WD coach trips to the station from Hanmer Springs. Day tours include a picnic lunch, but there's also a five-hour 'no frills' option. From the Blenheim side, **Molesworth Tours** (☑03-572 8025; www.molesworthtours.co.nz) offers one- to four-day all-inclusive heritage and 4WD trips ($190 to $1835), as well as four-day fully supported (and catered) mountain-bike adventures ($1450).

Mt Lyford Alpine Resort   SKIING
(☑03-315 6178, snow-phone 03-366 1220; www.mtlyford.co.nz; day pass $70/35) This skifield is 60km from Hanmer, off the Inland Rd to Kaikoura.

🛌 Sleeping

Hanmer Backpackers   HOSTEL $
(☑03-315 7196; www.hanmerbackpackers.co.nz; 41 Conical Hill Rd; sites from $16, dm $28, with/without bathroom s $71/61, d $74/64; ☏) The town's original backpackers is a cosy, wood-lined haven with friendly, well-travelled Dutch/Japanese hosts. Well-maintained shared social areas and free fruit, coffee and (occasionally) home-baking all add further big ticks.

Rosie's   B&B $
(☑03-315 7095; www.rosiesbandbhanmer.co.nz; 9 Cheltenham St; tw $85-95, d with/without bathroom 130/95) Rosie has left the building but the hospitality continues at this homely hostel-like B&B. Most rooms share bathrooms. Rates include a continental breakfast and crummy toasted croissants.

Jack in the Green   HOSTEL $
(☑03-315 5111; www.jackinthegreen.co.nz; 3 Devon St; site/dm $20/29, d with/without bathroom 86/70; @☏) This charming old converted home is a 10-minute walk from the centre. Large rooms (no bunks), relaxing gardens and a lovely lounge area are the main drawcards. For extra privacy, book a garden 'chalet' with an en suite.

Kakapo Lodge   HOSTEL $
(☑03-315 7472; www.kakapolodge.co.nz; 14 Amuri Ave; dm $28, d with/without bathroom $90/66; @☏) The YHA-affiliated Kakapo has a roomy kitchen and lounge, chill-busting underfloor heating and a 1st-floor deck. Bunk-free dorms (some with bathrooms) are joined by a motel-style unit ($100) with its own TV and cooking facilities.

Hanmer Springs Top 10   HOLIDAY PARK $
(☑03-315 7113; www.hanmerspringstop10.co.nz; Bath St; sites $36-46, unit with/without bathroom from $95/78; @☏) This family-friendly park is just a few minutes' walk from the pools. Kids will love the playground and the trampoline. Take your pick from basic cabins (BYO everything) to two-bedroom motel units with everything supplied.

★ Woodbank Park Cottages   COTTAGES $$
(☑03-315 5075; www.woodbankcottages.co.nz; 381 Woodbank Rd; d $200) These two matching cottages in a woodland setting are around 10 minutes' drive from Hanmer, but feel a million miles away. Decor is crisp and modern, bathrooms and kitchens are well appointed and wooden decks come equipped with gas barbecues and rural views.

Chalets Motel   MOTEL $$
(☑03-315 7097; www.chaletsmotel.co.nz; 56 Jacks Pass Rd; d $135-180; ☏) Soak up the mountain views from these tidy, reasonably priced, free-standing wooden chalets, set on the slopes behind the town centre. All have full kitchens and the more expensive units have spa baths.

Tussock Peak Motor Lodge   MOTEL $$
(☑03-315 5191; www.tussockpeak.co.nz; 2 Leamington St; d $150-165; ☎) Modern, spotless and central, Tussock Peak has colourful decor and friendly service that's a cut above other motels on Hanmer's main drag. Units come in studio, one- and two-bedroom incarnations, and some have spa baths and balconies.

Scenic Views   MOTEL $$
(☑03-315 7419; www.hanmerscenicviews.co.nz; 2 Amuri Ave; d $140-220; ☎) An attractive timber-and-stone complex with modern studios (one with an outdoor spa pool) and two- and three-bedroom apartments. Mountain views come as standard.

Cheltenham House   B&B $$$
(☑03-315 7545; www.cheltenham.co.nz; 13 Cheltenham St; r $235-280; ☎) This large 1930s house has room to fit a billiard table and grand piano, as well as four art-filled suites in the main house and two in cosy garden cottages. Cooked gourmet breakfasts are delivered to the rooms and wine is served in the evening.

St James   APARTMENTS $$$
(☑03-315 5225; www.thestjames.co.nz; 20 Chisholm Cres; apt $190-365; ☎) Luxuriate in a schmick modern apartment with all the mod cons, including an iPod dock and a kitchen with the latest Fisher & Paykel appliances. Sizes range from studios to two-bedroom apartments.

✖ Eating & Drinking

Hanmer Springs Bakery   BAKERY $
(16 Conical Hill Rd; ⏱6am-4pm) In peak season, queues stretch out the door for this humble bakery's meat pies and salmon bagels.

Malabar   ASIAN $$
(☑03-315 7745; www.malabar.co.nz; 5 Conical Hill Rd; lunch $10-22, dinner $28-33; ⏱5-10pm Sun-Fri, 11.30am-10pm Sat) This elegant eatery presents Asian cuisine from Beijing to Bangalore, although the emphasis is more on the Indian. All dishes are designed to be shared. A limited takeaway menu of Indian, Chinese and Thai favourites is also available.

Powerhouse Cafe   CAFE $$
(☑03-315 5252; www.powerhousecafe.co.nz; 8 Jacks Pass Rd; brunch $15-23, dinner $36; ⏱7.30am-3pm daily, 6-10pm Sat; ☎) Power up with a huge High Country breakfast or a Highland Fling caramelised whisky-sodden

porridge. Return for a burger, laksa or curry platter for lunch, and pop back again on Saturday evening when it morphs into a bistro.

Coriander's   INDIAN $$
(☑03-315 7616; www.corianders.co.nz; Chisholm Cres; mains $14-22; ⏱11.30am-2pm Mon-Fri 5-10pm daily; ✐) Spice up your life at this brightly painted North Indian restaurant. It's a beef-free zone, but there are plenty of tasty lamb, chicken and seafood dishes to choose from, and a particularly good vegetarian selection.

★Chantellini's   FRENCH $$$
(☑03-315 7667; www.chantellinis.com; 11 Jollies Pass Rd; mains $36-39; ⏱6-10pm Mon-Sat) Tucked away behind the main street, this quiet oasis offers a winning combination of classic French cooking, generous portions and charming service. Chandeliers and black drapes create an elegant ambience.

No. 31   MODERN NZ $$$
(☑03-315 7031; 31 Amuri Ave; mains $32-39 ⏱5.30-11pm Tue-Sun) It's complicated, sophisticated modern fare that's on offer in this pretty wooden cottage, but unlike many of its ilk, the serves here are quite substantial. The upmarket ambience befits the prices the paper napkins don't.

Monteith's Brewery Bar   PUB
(www.mbbh.co.nz; 47 Amuri Ave; ⏱9am-11pm) The best pub in town features lots of different Monteith's beers and tasty tucker from cooked breakfasts ($12 to $17), to bar snacks ($10 to $17) to full meals ($23 to $35). Live musicians kick off from 4pm Sundays.

❶ Information

Hurunui i-SITE (☑03-315 0000; www.visithanmersprings.co.nz; 42 Amuri Ave; ⏱10am-5pm) Books transport, accommodation and activities.

❶ Getting There & Away

The **main bus stop** is near the corner of Amuri Ave and Jacks Pass Rd.

Hanmer Connection (☑0800 242 663; www.hanmerconnection.co.nz; one way/return $30/50) Daily bus to/from Christchurch via Waipara and Amberley.

Hanmer Tours & Shuttle (☑03-315 7418; www.hanmertours.co.nz) Runs shuttles to/from Waipara ($20), Amberley ($20), Christchurch city centre ($30) and Christchurch Airport ($40).

Waipara Valley

Conveniently stretched along SH1 near the Hanmer Springs turn-off, this resolutely rural area makes for a tasty pitstop en route to Christchurch. The valley's warm dry summers followed by cool autumn nights have proved a winning formula for growing grapes, olives, hazelnuts and lavender. Since vines were planted in 1982, it has swiftly built its reputation as a producer of riesling, chardonnay and pinot noir, and the valley's wineries now produce over 250,000 cases annually.

To explore the valley's bounty fully, pick up a copy of the Waipara Valley Map (or download it from www.waiparawine.co.nz) or visit www.foodandwinetrail.co.nz. Otherwise, you'll spot several of the big players from the highway. The area's two main towns are tiny Waipara and slightly larger Amberley, although the latter is just outside the main wine-growing area.

The annual **Waipara Wine & Food Festival** (www.waiparawineandfood.co.nz) is held in March.

🛏 Sleeping

Waipara Sleepers HOSTEL $
(☑03-314 6003; www.waiparasleepers.co.nz; 12 Glenmark Dr, Waipara; sites from $20, dm $25, s $35-45, d $55-65; @ 🛜) Train tragics will appreciate this unusual hostel, where you can bunk down in converted carriages and cook your own meals in the 'station house'. The facilities are fairly basic and you'll need to bring your own sleeping bag for the dorm room.

🍴 Eating & Drinking

Pukeko Junction CAFE, DELI $
(www.pukekojunction.co.nz; 458 Ashworths Rd (SH1); mains $10-19; ⊙9am-4.30pm) One of the most popular roadside pitstops, this cafe-cum-giftstore in Leithfield (south of Amberley) serves delicious baked goods including gourmet sausage rolls and lamb shank pies. As well as arts and crafts, the store stocks a good selection of local wine.

Nor'wester CAFE $$
(www.norwestercafe.co.nz; 95 Carters Rd (SH1); breakfast $9-21, lunch $18-26, dinner $20-39; ⊙9am-late) Bluster into this old wooden villa on the main street of Amberley for great coffee, yummy muffins and a whole variety of

cooked meals, ranging from pizza and pasta to bistro-style meals in the evening.

Brew Moon CAFE, BREWERY $$
(www.brewmooncafe.co.nz; 150 Ashworths Rd (SH1); mains $16-28; ⊙10am-late) Just south of Amberley on SH1, Brew Moon crafts six different beers along with seasonal brews; sample four of them for $16. The menu stretches from cooked breakfast to gourmet pizza, pasta and daily fish specials.

Waipara Hills WINERY, CAFE $$
(www.waiparahillswines.co.nz; 780 Glasnevin Rd (SH1); mains $23-27; ⊙tastings 10am-5pm, restaurant 10am-3pm) Hard to miss in an impressive edifice immediately south of Waipara, this winery produces an excellent Gewürztraminer, as well as the more common valley varietals. The cafe serves leisurely lunches on the terrace, and in summer the winery hosts occasional big-name concerts (see www.adayonthegreen.com.au).

Waipara Springs WINERY, CAFE $$
(www.waiparasprings.co.nz; SH1; mains $20-27; ⊙11am-5pm; 🕿) Slightly north of Waipara township, this is one of the valley's oldest vineyards. The attached cafe serves platters and bistro-style lunches.

⭐**Pegasus Bay** RESTAURANT, WINERY $$$
(☑03-314 6869; www.pegasusbay.com; Stockgrove Rd; mains $38-45; ⊙restaurant noon-4pm, tastings 10am-5pm) It's fitting that Waipara Valley's premier winery should have the loveliest setting and one of Canterbury's best restaurants. Beautiful gardens set the scene but it's the contemporary NZ menu that steals the show, taking advantage of superb local produce and recommending wines to match.

ℹ Getting There & Away

The *Coastal Pacific* train from Christchurch to Picton stops at Waipara. Wine tours are available from several Christchurch-based companies.
Hanmer Connection (☑0800 242 663; www.hanmerconnection.co.nz) Heads to Hanmer Springs ($20, 50 minutes) and Christchurch ($20, 1¼ hours).
Hanmer Tours & Shuttle (☑03-315 7418; www.hanmertours.co.nz) Runs shuttles to/from Hanmer Springs ($20), Christchurch city centre ($15) and Christchurch Airport ($25).
InterCity (☑03-365 1113; www.intercity.co.nz) Coaches head to/from Picton (from $24, 4½ hours), Blenheim (from $22, four hours), Kaikoura (from $13, 1¾ hours) and Christchurch (from $10, one hour) twice daily.

CENTRAL CANTERBURY

While the dead-flat agricultural heartland of the Canterbury Plains blankets the majority of the region, there's plenty of interest for travellers in the west, where the Southern Alps soar to snowy peaks. Here you'll find Canterbury's best ski fields and some brilliant wilderness walks.

Unusually for NZ, the most scenic routes avoid the coast, and most items of interest can be accessed from one of two spectacular roads: the Great Alpine Highway (SH73), which barrels from Christchurch across the plains and into the mountains, and the Inland Scenic Route (SH72), which skirts the dividing line between the two.

Selwyn District

Named after NZ's first Anglican bishop, this largely rural district has swallowed an English map book and regurgitated place names such as Lincoln, Darfield and Sheffield to punctuate this green and pleasant land. Yet any illusions of Albion are quickly dispelled by the looming presence of the snow-capped Southern Alps, providing a rugged retort to 'England's mountains green'.

Selwyn's numerous ski fields may not be the country's most glamorous but they provide plenty of thrills for rampant ski bunnies. Porters (p39) is the main commercial field, but club fields include Mt Olympus (p40), Mt Cheeseman (p39), Broken River (p39), Craigieburn Valley (p39) and Temple Basin (p39).

The highly scenic Great Alpine Highway pierces the heart of the district on its journey between Christchurch and the West Coast. Before it leaves the Canterbury Plains, it passes through the little settlement of Springfield (population 219), which is distinguished by two notable monuments. One honours Rewi Alley (1897–1987), a local lad who became a great hero of the Chinese Communist Party, and surely the only party member to be offered a knighthood (he declined, naturally, but accepted companionship of the Queen's Service Order); for more about his fascinating life, stop to read the information panels.

The other monument is a giant pink-iced doughnut, originally erected to promote *The Simpsons Movie* but now a permanent feature – one can only imagine what Alley would make of it.

Heading west from Springfield, the landscape starts expanding until the highway is hidden within the mountainous folds of the Torlesse and Craigieburn Ranges. Just when you think it couldn't get more spectacular, views open up across the braided Waimakariri River.

Arthur's Pass village (www.arthurspass. com; population 62) is 4km from the pass of the same name. At 900m, it's NZ's highest-altitude settlement and a handy base for tramps, climbs and skiing. To say that it rains a lot up here is an understatement.

Maori used this pass to cross the Southern Alps long before its 'discovery' by Arthur Dobson in 1864. The Westland gold rush created the need for a dependable crossing over the Alps from Christchurch, and the coach road was completed within a year. Later, the coal and timber trade demanded a railway, duly completed in 1923.

⦿ Sights & Activities

Castle Hill   LANDMARK
The jagged limestone outcrops of Castle Hill loom above the highway, roughly 33km from Springfield, looking surprisingly reminiscent of an ancient ruin. Unsurprisingly, this area is a favourite of rock climbers and boulderers. Scenes from *The Chronicles of Narnia* were filmed in the area.

Cave Stream Scenic Reserve   CAVE
(www.doc.govt.nz) Near Broken River Bridge, 2km past Castle Hill, it's well worth stopping to take a look at the large circular outlet of this 594m-long cave, even if you're not planning to explore its depths. If a one-hour walk in waist-deep cold water through the pitch-black cave sounds appealing, take all the necessary precautions (check the water level and take a helmet, at least one light source per person, spare batteries etc); for details, pick up DOC's *Cave Stream Scenic Reserve* pamphlet. It's recommended that you walk up the outlet end and exit via the fixed ladder beside the 3m waterfall at the inlet.

Craigieburn Forest Park   FOREST
(www.doc.govt.nz) Beech forest covers the lower slopes and valleys of this mountainous area, giving way to tussock and alpine scrub on the peaks. You may spot some South Island edelweiss, kārearea (NZ falcons) and kea (native parrots). The Craigieburn Range has several peaks over 2000m and is one of NZ's best skiing areas, with slopes that suit advanced skiers. Ski fields include Mt

Cheeseman, Broken River and Craigieburn Valley. The DOC website lists numerous day walks (pick up a copy of the *Craigieburn Forest Park Day Walks* pamphlet), longer tramps and mountain-bike tracks to suit intermediate to advanced riders.

Arthur's Pass National Park   NATIONAL PARK
(www.doc.govt.nz) In 1923 this vast (1143 sq km) alpine wilderness became the South Island's first national park. Day tramps offer endless views of snowcapped peaks, many of them over 2000m; the highest is Mt Murchison (2400m). DOC's *Discover Arthur's Pass* booklet details dozens of walks as well as backcountry huts and camping areas. The newest track is the **Arthur's Pass Walkway**, a safe and reasonably easy track from the village to the Dobson Memorial at the summit of the pass (2½ hours return).

Other options include the **Devils Punchbowl walking track** (one hour return) to a 131m waterfall, and the steep walk to beautiful views at **Temple Basin ski field** (three hours return). The **Bealey Spur track** (four to five hours return) offers expansive views of the Waimakariri River valley and surrounding mountains. The pleasant **Dobson Nature Walk** (30 minutes return) is best from November to February when the alpine flowers are blooming.

Fit trampers might like to tackle the **Avalanche Peak track** (eight hours return). Longer tramps with superb alpine backdrops include the **Goat Pass track** (two days) and the longer and more difficult **Harman Pass** and **Harpers Pass tracks**. These tracks require previous tramping experience as flooding can make the rivers dangerous and the weather is extremely changeable; ask DOC first. For specific information on weather conditions see www.softrock.co.nz.

Rubicon Horse Treks   HORSE RIDING
(☑ 03-318 8886; www.rubiconvalley.co.nz; 534 Rubicon Rd) Operating from a sheep farm 6km from Springfield, Rubicon offers hour-long farm treks ($50), two-hour river, valley or sunset rides ($85), and six-hour mountain trail rides ($250).

🛌 Sleeping

🛏 Springfield to Bealey

Smylies Accommodation   HOSTEL $
(☑ 03-318 4740; www.smylies.co.nz; 5653 West Coast Rd, Springfield; dm/s/d $30/50/70; @ 🛜) 🌊

This welcoming YHA-associated hostel has a large communal kitchen and a vast book and DVD library. There's also a handful of self-contained motel units ($85 to $160) and a three-bedroom cottage ($220). In winter, packages including ski-equipment rental and ski-field transport are on offer.

Flock Hill Lodge   MOTEL, HOSTEL $$
(☑ 03-318 8196; www.flockhill.co.nz; Great Alpine Hwy, Craigieburn Valley; dm/d $31/155; @ 🛜) In a tranquil spot close to Craigieburn Forest Park and Lake Pearson, this high-country sheep station has a cosy bar-restaurant, comfortable two-bedroom motel units and large cottages with kitchenettes. Unfussy backpackers can stay in rustic shearers' quarters.

Wilderness Lodge   LODGE $$$
(☑ 03-318 9246; www.wildernesslodge.co.nz; Cora Lynn Rd, Bealey; s $450-699 d $700-1160; 🛜) For an absolute middle-of-nowhere atmosphere, this alpine lodge hidden within a beech forest on a 24-sq-km sheep station takes some beating. The standalone studios with private spa baths feel even more remote. Rates include breakfast, dinner and guided activities, but even then they seem inflated.

🛏 Arthur's Pass

Camping is possible near the basic **public shelter** (adult/child $6/3) opposite DOC, where there's running water, a sink, tables and toilets. You can also camp for free at **Klondyke Corner**, 8km south of Arthur's Pass, where perks are limited to a toilet and stream water for boiling.

Mountain House YHA   HOSTEL $
(☑ 03-318 9258; www.trampers.co.nz; 83 Main Rd; sites $22, dm $27-31, s/d/unit $74/86/145; @ 🛜) Straddling the highway in the centre of the village, this excellent complex includes a well-kept hostel, two upmarket motel units and two three-bedroom cottages with log fires ($340). Campers will need to take their chances with the kleptomaniacal keas.

Arthur's Pass Village B&B   B&B $$
(☑ 021 394 776; www.arthurspass.org.nz; 72 School Tce; d $100; 🛜) 🌊 This former railway cottage is now a cosy B&B, complete with an open fire, free-range bacon and eggs and homebaked bread for breakfast, and the company and conversation of the interesting owners. Home-cooked dinners are also available ($35). The two guest bedrooms share a bathroom.

Arthur's Pass Alpine Motel   MOTEL **$$**
(✐ 03-318 9233; www.apam.co.nz; 52 Main Rd; d
$125-145; 🐾) On the southern approach to
the village, this older-style motel has simple
units, some with gas fires. If you're snowed in
there's a good DVD library and satellite TV.

🍴 Eating

Famous Sheffield Pie Shop   BAKERY **$**
(www.sheffieldpieshop.co.nz; 51 Great Alpine Hwy,
Sheffield; pies $4-5; ⊘ 7.30am-4pm) This road-
side bakery in the quiet Canterbury Plains
hamlet of Sheffield turns out some of the
region's best meat pies. There are more than
20 different varieties on offer, along with
filled rolls, sweet things and surprisingly
good coffee.

Arthur's Pass Store & Cafe   CAFE **$**
(85 Main Rd, Arthur's Pass; mains $5-15; ⊘ 8am-
5pm; 🐾) Sells sandwiches, burgers, pies
and breakfasts, alongside petrol and basic
groceries.

Wobbly Kea   CAFE, BAR **$$**
(www.wobblykea.co.nz; 108 Main Rd, Arthur's Pass;
breakfast $10-17, mains $23-25; ⊘ 9am-8pm)
Breakfast at the Wobbly Kea is a local tradition designed to set you up for the most
active of days. At night, this friendly cafe-bar
serves steak, curry, pasta and pizza. Takeaway pizza ($29) is also available.

ℹ Information

DOC Arthur's Pass Visitor Centre (✐ 03-318
9211; www.doc.govt.nz; 80 Main Rd; ⊘ 8.30am-
4.30pm) Has displays on the park, including
a short video on the history of Arthur's Pass.
Staff also provide information and advice on
suitable tramps and on the park's changeable
weather. You can purchase route guides and
detailed topographical maps, and hire locator
beacons (highly recommended). Computers
are provided for you to log your tramping intentions on the AdventureSmart website (www.
adventuresmart.org.nz).

ℹ Getting There & Away

BUS
Atomic Shuttles (✐ 03-349 0697; www.
atomictravel.co.nz) From Arthur's Pass a bus
heads to/from Christchurch ($35, 2½ hours),
Springfield ($35, one hour), Lake Brunner
($30, 50 minutes) and Greymouth ($35, 1¼
hours).
West Coast Shuttle (✐ 03-768 0028; www.
westcoastshuttle.co.nz) Buses stopping at
Arthur's Pass head to/from Christchurch ($40,

2¾ hours), Springfield ($30, one hour) and
Greymouth ($30, 1¾ hours).

CAR
Make sure you check your petrol before you
leave Springfield (or Hokitika or Greymouth if
you're travelling in the other direction). There's
a pump at Arthur's Pass Store but it's expensive
and only operates from 8am until 5pm.

TRAIN
TranzAlpine (✐ 0800 872 467; www.kiwirail-
scenic.co.nz; all fares $89) One train in each
direction stops in Arthur's Pass, heading to/
from Springfield (1½ hours) and Christchurch
(2½ hours), or Lake Brunner (one hour) and
Greymouth (two hours).

Methven
POP 1330

Methven is busiest in winter, when it fills up
with snow bunnies heading to nearby Mt
Hutt. At other times tumbleweeds don't quite
blow down the main street – much to the
disappointment of the wannabe gunslingers
arriving for the raucous October rodeo. Over
summer it's a low-key and affordable base for
trampers, bikers and fisher-folk.

Dominating the town centre, two giant
historic pubs glower at each other across the
main street. Despite the rivalry between the
Blue Pub and the Brown Pub (it's actually
beige, but don't tell them that), they're
surprisingly similar.

🏃 Activities

Ask at the i-SITE about walking trails,
horse riding, mountain biking, fishing, clay-
shooting, archery, golfing, scenic helicopter
flights and jetboating through the nearby
Rakaia Gorge.

Methven Heliski   SKIING
(✐ 03-302 8108; www.methvenheli.co.nz; Main St;
5-run day trips $975; ⊘ Jul-Sep) Trips include
guide service, safety equipment and lunch.

Black Diamond Safaris   SKIING
(✐ 027 450 8283; www.blackdiamondsafaris.co.nz;
⊘ May-Oct) Provides access to uncrowded
club ski fields by 4WD. Prices start at $100
for 4WD transport and safety equipment
only, while $275 includes a lift pass, guiding
and lunch.

Aoraki Balloon Safaris   BALLOONING
(✐ 03-302 8172; www.nzballooning.com; flights
$385) Early morning combos of snowcapped
peaks and a breakfast with bubbly.

Skydiving NZ   SKYDIVING
(☑ 03-302 9143; www.skydivingnz.com; Pudding Hill Airfield) Offers tandem jumps from 12,000ft ($335) and 15,000ft ($440).

Big Al's Snow Sports   EQUIPMENT RENTAL
(☑ 03-302 8003; www.bigals.co.nz; The Square, Main St; mountain bikes per hr/day from $15/45) In winter the focus is ski and snowboard gear, while in summer Big Al turns his attention to mountain biking. Ask for a map of Mt Hutt Bike Park (near the bottom of Mt Hutt Skifield Access Rd) which has 26 tracks ranging from kid-friendly to extreme.

🛏 Sleeping

Some accommodation is closed in summer, but the following are open year-round. During the ski season, it pays to book well ahead, especially for budget accommodation. We've listed summer prices; expect them to rise in winter.

Alpenhorn Chalet   HOSTEL $
(☑ 03-302 8779; www.alpenhorn.co.nz; 44 Allen St; dm $30, d $65-85; @🖵) This small, inviting home has a conservatory housing an indoor garden and a spa pool. A log fire, free internet and complimentary espresso coffee seal the deal. Bedrooms are spacious and brightly coloured, with lots of warm, natural wood. Some of the doubles have en-suite bathrooms.

Redwood Lodge   HOSTEL $
(☑ 03-302 8964; www.redwoodlodge.co.nz; 3 Wayne Pl; s $50-60, d $90; @🖵) Despite being a BBH member there are no dorms at this charming family-friendly hostel. En-suite doubles have their own TVs, and there's a large shared lounge and kitchen. Bigger rooms can be reconfigured to accommodate families.

Big Tree Lodge   HOSTEL $
(☑ 03-302 9575; www.bigtreelodge.co.nz; 25 South Belt; dm $35-40, r $75, apt $120-160; @🖵) Once a vicarage, this relaxed hostel has bunk-free dorms and wood-trimmed bathrooms. Tucked just behind is Little Tree Studio, a self-contained unit sleeping up to four people.

Snow Denn Lodge   HOSTEL $
(☑ 03-302 8999; www.methvenaccommodation.co.nz; cnr McMillan & Bank Sts; dm $25, d with/without bathroom $80/70; @🖵) Spread over two identical large wooden buildings, this modern YHA-associated lodge has appealing dining and living areas, including

large kitchens. Prices include breakfast and equipment hire (bikes, golf clubs, fishing gear etc). A bit more attention to scrubbing the bathrooms would lift it up the list.

Whitestone Cottages   RENTAL HOUSES $$$
(☑ 021 179 0257; www.whitestonecottages.co.nz; 3016 Methven Hwy; house $210-350) For those mid-holiday moments when you just want to spread out, cook a meal, do your laundry and have your own space, these four large free-standing houses on the edge of town are just the ticket. Each sleeps six in two en-suite bedrooms.

🍴 Eating & Drinking

Aqua   JAPANESE $
(112 Main St; mains $11-17; ⏰5-9pm Jan-Oct) Dive into this tiny relaxed restaurant where kimono-clad waitresses serve *yakisoba* (fried noodles), *ramen* (noodle soup) and *izakaya*-style dishes (small plates to share over drinks) to grateful guests. Top it off with sesame or green-tea ice cream.

Cafe 131   CAFE $
(131 Main St; meals $10-20; ⏰7.30am-5pm; 🖵) Polished timber and leadlight windows lend warmth and style to this smart eatery. The menu extends to all-day breakfasts, good-value platters, soup, pasta and sandwiches, but beer and wine takes over later in the day. It's also the town's de facto internet cafe.

Cafe Primo   CAFE $
(38 McMillan St; meals $7-18; ⏰7.30am-4pm) Sandwiched in and around the souvenir

> **DON'T MISS**
>
> ## MT HUTT SKI AREA
>
> Canterbury's premier ski field, Mt Hutt (p39) has the largest skiable area of any of NZ's commercial fields (365 hectares), with its longest run stretching for 2km. Half of the terrain is suitable for intermediate skiers, with a quarter each for beginners and advanced. Usually the season runs from mid-June to mid-October.
>
> The skifield is only 26km from Methven but in wintry conditions the drive takes about 40 minutes; allow two hours from Christchurch. **Methven Travel** (☑03-302 8106, 0800 684 888; www.methventravel.co.nz) runs mountain buses in season ($20).

teaspoons and Buzzy Bee bookends of this secondhand shop are tasty cakes, panini and legendary bacon and egg sandwiches. You'll also unearth Methven's best coffee.

Blue Pub   PUB
(www.thebluepub.co.nz; Barkers Rd; mains $20-35; 🛜) Drink at the bar crafted from a huge slab of native timber, or tuck into robust meals in the quieter cafe. Afterwards, challenge the locals to a game of pool or watch the rugby on the big screen.

☆ Entertainment

Cinema Paradiso   CINEMA
(🖉 03-302 1957; www.cinemaparadiso.co.nz; Main St; adult/child $15/10) Quirky cinema with an arthouse skew.

ℹ Information

Medical Centre (🖉 03-302 8105; The Square, Main St; ⊙8.30am-5.30pm)
Methven i-SITE (🖉 03-302 8955; www. amazingspace.co.nz; 160 Main St; ⊙7.30am-6pm Jul-Sep, 9am-5pm Mon-Fri, 10am-3pm Sat & Sun Oct-Jun; 🛜) The information centre is housed in the Heritage Centre, which also includes a cafe, art gallery (free) and the hands-on *NZ Alpine & Agriculture Encounter* (adult/child $18/10).

ℹ Getting There & Around

Methven Travel (🖉 03-302 8106; www. methventravel.co.nz) Runs shuttles between Methven and Christchurch Airport ($42) three to four times a week, increasing to three times daily in the ski season.

Mt Somers

The small settlement of Mt Somers sits on the edge of the Southern Alps, beneath the mountain of the same name. The biggest drawcard to the area is the **Mt Somers track** (30km), a one- to two-day hike circling the mountain, linking the popular picnic spots of Sharplin Falls and Woolshed Creek. Trail highlights include volcanic formations, Maori rock drawings, deep river canyons and botanical diversity. The route is subject to sudden weather changes, so precautions should be taken.

There are two DOC huts on the track: Pinnacles Hut and Woolshed Creek Hut (adult/child $15/7.50). Hut tickets and information are available at the **Mt Somers General Store** (61 Pattons Rd; ⊙8am-6pm).

🛏 Sleeping & Eating

Mt Somers Holiday Park   HOLIDAY PARK $
(🖉 03-303 9719; www.mountsomers.co.nz; Hoods Rd; sites $18-32, cabin with/without bathroom $80/55) This small, friendly and well-maintained park offers both powered and unpowered sites. Ensuite cabins are fully made up, but you'll need to bring your own linen (or hire it) for the standard cabins.

Stronechrubie   CHALETS, RESTAURANT $$
(🖉 03-303 9814; www.stronechrubie.co.nz; cnr Hoods Rd & SH72; d $120-160, mains $33-38; ⊙restaurant 6.30-9pm Wed-Sat; 🛜) Comfortable chalets ranging in size from studio to two-bedroom are scattered across bird-filled gardens at this oddly named lodge. The intimate restaurant showcases local produce such as beef, lamb, venison and duck.

SOUTH CANTERBURY

After crossing the Rangitata River into South Canterbury, SH1 and the Inland Scenic Route (SH72) narrow to within 8km of each other at the quaint town of Geraldine. Here you can choose to take the busy coastal highway through the port city of Timaru (and on to Oamaru and Dunedin), or continue inland on SH79 into the Mackenzie Country, the expansive high ground from which NZ's tallest peaks rise above powder blue lakes. Most travellers pick the latter.

The Mackenzie Basin is a wild, tussock-strewn bowl at the foot of the Southern Alps, carved out by ancient glaciers. It takes its name from the legendary James 'Jock' McKenzie, who ran his stolen flocks in this then-uninhabited region in the 1840s. When he was finally caught, other settlers realised the potential for grazing in this seemingly inhospitable land and followed in his footsteps.

Director Sir Peter Jackson made the most of this rugged and untamed landscape while filming the *Lord of the Rings* films.

Peel Forest

Tucked away between the foothills of the Southern Alps and the Rangitata River (well signposted from SH72), the Peel Forest is among NZ's most important remnants of indigenous podocarp (conifer) forest. Many of the totara, kahikatea and matai trees here are hundreds of years old and are home to an abundance of bird life including riflemen, kereru (wood pigeons), bellbirds, fantails and grey warblers. One example of totara on the Big Tree Walk (30 minutes return) is 31m tall, has a circumference of 9m and is over 1000 years old. There are also trails to Emily Falls (1½ hours return), Rata Falls (two hours return) and Acland Falls (one hour return); pick up the *Peel Forest Park* brochure ($2) from Peel Forest Store.

A road from nearby Mt Peel sheep station leads to Mesopotamia, the run of English writer Samuel Butler in the 1860s. His experiences here partly inspired his famous satire *Erewhon* ('nowhere' backwards, almost).

Sights & Activities

St Stephen's Church   CHURCH
Sitting in a pretty glade right next to the general store, this gorgeous little Anglican church (1885) has a warm wooden interior and some interesting stained glass. Look for St Francis of Assisi surrounded by NZ flora and fauna (get the kids to play spot-the-tuatara).

Peel Forest Horse Trekking   HORSE RIDING
(☑ 03-696 3703; www.peelforesthorsetrekking.co.nz; 1hr/2hr/half-day/full day $55/110/220/380) Ride through lush forest on short stints or multiday treks ($982 to $1623, minimum four people). Accommodation packages are available in conjunction with Peel Forest Lodge.

Rangitata Rafts   RAFTING
(☑ 0800 251 251; www.rafts.co.nz; Rangitata Gorge Rd; ☺ Sep-May) Head out for an exhilarating three-hour trip through Grade V rapids in the Rangitata Gorge ($208, minimum age 15), or start further down the Rangitata River for a gentler two-hour journey through Grade II rapids ($165, minimum age six).

Hidden Valleys   RAFTING
(☑ 03-696 3560; www.hiddenvalleys.co.nz; ☺ Sep-May) They may be based in Peel Forest but this crew doesn't limit itself to rafting the Rangitata. Multiday expeditions head to the Waimakariri, Waiau, Landsborough, Grey and Waiatoto Rivers, peaking with a five-day trip down the Clarence (near Kaikoura). Short, child-friendly trips on the Rangitata River are also available (adult/child $200/180).

Sleeping & Eating

DOC Camping Ground   CAMPSITE $
(☑ 03-696 3567; www.peelforest.co.nz; sites per adult/child $18/8.50, cabins $50-80) Beside the Rangitata River, about 3km beyond the Peel Forest Store, this excellent campground is equipped with basic two- to four-berth cabins (bring your own sleeping bag), hot showers and a kitchen. Check in at the store.

Peel Forest Lodge   LODGE $$$
(☑ 03-696 3703; www.peelforestlodge.co.nz; d $350, additional people $40; ☎) Would-be Davy Crocketts with champagne tastes will love this beautiful log cabin hidden in the forest. There are four rooms sleeping eight people, but they only take one booking at a time, so you and your posse will have the place to yourselves. It's fully self-contained, but meals can be arranged.

Peel Forest Store   CAFE, SELF-CATERING $$
(☑ 03-696 3567; www.peelforest.co.nz; lunch $13-15, dinner $24-30; ☺ 9am-5.30pm Sun-Thu, to 8.30pm Fri & Sat) Your one-stop-shop for groceries, takeaway food and internet access also runs the camping ground and the attached cafe-bar. Cooked meals include burgers, pizza and steaks.

Geraldine
POP 2420
Consummately Canterbury in its dedication to English-style gardening, pretty Geraldine has a village vibe and an active arts scene. In spring, duck behind the war memorial on Talbot St to the River Garden Walk, where green-fingered locals have gone completely bonkers planting azaleas and rhododendrons.

Sights

Vintage Car & Machinery Museum   MUSEUM
(178 Talbot St; adult/child $10/free; ☺ 9.30am-4pm daily Oct-May, 10am-4pm Sat & Sun Jun-Sep) You don't have to be a rev-head to enjoy this vintage car collection. The oldest is a 1907 De Dion-Bouton but the most impressive is a gleaming, fully restored 1926 Bentley. There's also a purpose-built Daimler used for the 1954 royal tour, plus some very nice Jags, 1970s muscle cars and all sorts of farm machinery.

1066 – A Medieval Mosaic   GALLERY
(www.1066.co.nz; 10 Wilson St; ☺ 10am-4pm) FREE One can only marvel at the obsessive-compulsion behind this 42m re-creation of the Bayeux Tapestry, painted onto a backdrop made from two-million steel bits sourced from discarded industrial knitting machine parts. Just as impressive are the bespoke mathematical puzzles and games for sale. And if you're feeling chilly, the world's biggest woollen jersey is also on display.

Geraldine Historical Museum   MUSEUM
(5 Cox St; ⊙10am-3pm Mon-Sat, 12.30-3pm Sun)
FREE Occupying the photogenic Town
Board Office building (1885), this cute little
museum tells the town's story with an eclectic mix of exhibits including old photos,
a wedding dress and a pump organ (which
you're welcome to play).

🏃 Activities

Big Rock Canyons   CANYONING
(📞03-693 8904; www.bigrockcanyons.co.nz; ⊙Nov-
Apr) Offers slippy, slidey day-long adventures
in the Kaumira Canyon ($260), as well as five
others of varying degrees of difficulty.

Skydiving Kiwis   SKYDIVING
(📞0800 359 549; www.skydivingkiwis.com; 1 Brodie Rd) Kiwis aren't so great at flying but we
expect they're quite good at plummeting.
Strap yourself to the human version for a
6000ft ($235), 9000ft ($285) or 12,000ft
($335) leap. Flights depart from Rangitata
Island Airport, 21km east of Geraldine.

🛏 Sleeping

Rawhiti House   HOSTEL $
(📞03-693 8252; www.rawhitibackpackers.co.nz;
27 Hewlings St; dm/s/d $32/50/72; @ 🛜) On a
hillside on the edge of town, this former maternity hospital is now a sunny and spacious
hostel with good communal areas, comfortable rooms and sparkling bathrooms. Bikes
are available to borrow.

Geraldine Kiwi Holiday Park   HOLIDAY PARK $
(📞03-693 8147; www.geraldineholidaypark.co.nz;
39 Hislop St; sites $33-36, units with/without bath-
room from $80/50; @ 🛜) 🐾 This top-notch
holiday park is set amid well-established
trees across the road from a grassy park. Besides budget cabins and motel units, there's
a TV room and playground.

Scenic Route Motor Lodge   MOTEL $$
(📞03-693 1700; www.motelscenicroute.co.nz; 28
Waihi Tce; d $135-140; 🛜) There's a vague herit-
age feel to this stone-and-timber motel, but
the modern units have double-glazing, flat-
screen TVs and broadband internet. Larger
studios have spa baths.

🍴 Eating

Four Peaks Plaza at the corner of Talbot and
Cox Sts has a bakery, deli, cafes and the Talbot
Forest cheese shop. Every Saturday during
summer the town kicks into organic action
with a **farmers market** (⊙9am-12.30pm).

Verde   CAFE $
(45 Talbot St; mains $11-18; ⊙9am-4pm) Down
the lane beside the old post office and en-
veloped in beautiful gardens, this excellent
cafe is easily the best of Geraldine's eateries.
It's just a shame that it's not open for dinner.

Coco   SWEETS, CAFE $
(www.coco-geraldine.co.nz; 10 Talbot St; truffles $2;
⊙10am-5pm) For a quality sugar rush, visit
Coco for handmade choccies, designer teas,
coffee, hot chocolate and cake.

☆ Entertainment

Geraldine Cinema   CINEMA
(📞03-693 8118; www.facebook.com/GeraldineCin-
ema; Talbot St; adult/child $10/8) Snuggle in to
watch a Hollywood favourite or an art-house
surprise. There's also occasional live music,
usually with a folk, blues or country spin.

ℹ Information

Geraldine Visitor Centre (📞03-693 1006;
www.southcanterbury.org.nz; cnr Talbot & Cox
Sts; ⊙10am-3pm)

ℹ Getting There & Away

Atomic Shuttles (📞03-349 0697; www.atomic-
travel.co.nz) Daily buses to/from Christchurch
($30, two hours), Lake Tekapo (from $21, 1¼
hours), Twizel ($25, two hours), Cromwell ($35,
4¼ hours) and Queenstown ($35, five hours).

Budget Buses & Shuttles (📞03-615 5119;
www.budgetshuttles.co.nz; ⊙Mon-Sat) Offers
a door-to-door shuttle to Christchurch ($57),
along with a cheaper scheduled run ($47).

InterCity (📞03-365 1113; www.intercity.co.nz)
Daily coaches head to/from Christchurch
(from $32, 2¼ hours), Lake Tekapo (from $21,
1¼ hours), Mt Cook Village (from $38, three
hours), Cromwell (from $40, 4¾ hours) and
Queenstown (from $42, 5¾ hours).

Timaru

POP 26,900

The port city of Timaru is a handy stopping-
off point halfway between Christchurch and
Dunedin. Many travellers prefer to kick on
85km further south to the smaller, more
charming Oamaru, but Timaru has a few
worthy attractions of its own. The town's
name comes from the Maori name Te Maru,
meaning 'The Place of Shelter'. No permanent
settlement existed here until 1839, when the
Weller brothers set up a whaling station.
The *Caroline,* a sailing ship that transported
whale oil, gave the picturesque bay its name.

Timaru

◉ Sights

Caroline Bay Park   PARK, BEACH

(Marine Pde) Ranging from a formal
Edwardian-style park below the cliffs of the
Bay Hill, to a large lawn, to an extensive dune
system and then the beach, Caroline Bay is
Timaru's favourite locale. The formal section includes a soundshell, a war memorial
and the 1000 romantic blooms, arbours and
water features of the **Trevor Griffiths Rose
Garden** FREE. Hector's dolphins are regular visitors to the bay and you may be lucky
enough to spot a seal, sea lion or a penguin
on the beach; if you do, keep your distance.

Te Ana Maori Rock Art Centre   MUSEUM
(☏03-687 7372; www.teana.co.nz; 2 George St;
adult/child admission $20/10, tour $125/50;
⊙10am-3pm) Passionate Ngai Tahu guides
bring this innovative multimedia exhibition
about Maori rock paintings to life. You can

Timaru

also take a three-hour excursion (departing 2pm, November to April) to see isolated rock art in situ; prior booking is essential.

South Canterbury Museum MUSEUM
(www.timaru.govt.nz/museum; Perth St; admission by donation; ⊙10am-4.30pm Tue-Fri, 1.30-4.30pm Sat & Sun) Historical and natural artefacts of the region are displayed here. Highlights include the Maori section and a replica of the aeroplane designed and flown by local pioneer aviator and inventor Richard Pearse. It's speculated that his mildly successful attempts at manned flight came before the Wright brothers' famous achievement in 1903.

Aigantighe Art Gallery GALLERY
(www.timaru.govt.nz/art-gallery; 49 Wai-iti Rd; ⊙10am-4pm Tue-Fri, noon-4pm Sat & Sun) FREE One of the South Island's largest public galleries, this 1908 mansion houses an important collection of NZ, Pacific and European art from the past four centuries. Local luminaries featured include Frances Hodgkins, Colin McCahon and Ralph Hotere. The gallery's Gaelic name means 'at home' and is pronounced 'egg-and-tie'. If the gallery's closed, take time to explore the sculpture garden.

Timaru Botanic Gardens GARDENS
(cnr King & Queen Sts; ⊙8am-dusk) FREE Established in 1864, these gardens feature ponds, a conservatory, an aviary and a collection of roses and native tree ferns. The gardens are south of the centre; enter from Queen St.

Sacred Heart Basilica CHURCH
(7 Craigie Ave, Parkside) Roman Catholic with a definite emphasis on the Roman, this beautiful neoclassical church (1911) impresses with multiple domes, Ionian columns and richly coloured stained glass. Its architect, Francis Petre, also designed the large basilicas in Christchurch (now in ruins) and Oamaru. Inside, there's an art nouveau feel to the plasterwork, which includes intertwined floral and sacred heart motifs. There are no set opening hours; try the side door.

★ Festivals & Events

Timaru Festival of Roses CULTURAL
(www.festivalofroses.co.nz) Three days of public and private garden displays in late November.

Christmas Carnival MUSIC
(www.carolinebay.org.nz) Held from 26 December to mid-January at Caroline Bay, this fun festival (inaugurated in 1912) includes concerts, events and carnival rides.

🛏 Sleeping

Timaru Top 10 Holiday Park HOLIDAY PARK $
(☎03-684 7690; www.timaruholidaypark.co.nz; 154a Selwyn St, West End; sites $38-42, unit with/without bathroom from $92/62; @ 🖵) 🐾 Tucked away in the suburbs, this excellent holiday park has clean, colourful amenities and a golf course nearby that's included in the tariff.

Pleasant View B&B $$
(☎03-686 6651; www.pleasantview.co.nz; 2 Moore St, Waimataitai; s $99-115, d $129-145; 🖵) Spot Hector's dolphins over breakfast from this modern clifftop house overlooking Caroline Bay. Both rooms are very comfortable, but only one gets the views. No matter, the large guest lounge has them in abundance, as well as a Nespresso machine and a mammoth TV.

Sefton Homestay B&B $$
(☎03-688 0017; www.seftonhomestay.co.nz; 32 Sefton St, Seaview; r/ste $125/135; 🖵) Set back behind a pretty garden, this imposing heritage house has two guest rooms: one with an en suite, and a larger bedroom with an adjoining sunroom and a bathroom across the hall. Swap travel stories over a glass of port in the guest sitting room.

Panorama Motor Lodge MOTEL $$
(☎03-688 0097; www.panorama.net.nz; 52 The Bay Hill; units from $135; 🖵) The rooms in this hilltop motel are modern and well appointed. If you're given a choice of an ocean view or a spa unit, opt for the view; there's a communal spa pool and sauna in the complex anyway.

🍴 Eating & Drinking

Arthur St Café CAFE $
(8 Arthur St; mains $9-19; ⊙7am-5.30pm Mon-Fri, 9am-3pm Sat) Excellent coffee and cruisy Kiwi dub is always a good way to ease into the day. Decked out with retro furniture, Timaru's funkiest eatery offers quiches, bagels and locally famous breakfasts. There's also occasional live music with an alternative and folkie spin.

Zest PIZZERIA, CAFE $$
(☎03-688 8313; www.zestrestaurant.co.nz; 4a Elizabeth St; lunch $15-20, dinner $19-29; ⊙10am-10pm) Neapolitans might sniff at the non-traditional toppings, but the Greek and Hawaiian pizzas served in this converted church hall have plenty of fans. The menu is rounded out with a crowd-pleasing line-up of curry, pasta, schnitzel, steak and salad.

from Europe; and red deer, also European. Summertime brings into bloom the Mt Cook lily, a large mountain buttercup, and mountain daisies, gentians and edelweiss.

⊙ Sights

DOC Aoraki/Mt Cook Visitor Centre
INTERPRETATION CENTRE

(☑03-435 1186; www.doc.govt.nz; 1 Larch Grove; ⊙8.30am-4.30pm) FREE As well as being the font of all knowledge about tramping routes and weather conditions, DOC's visitor centre has excellent displays on local flora, fauna and history, as well as videos and a sunken garden showcasing a historic mountain hut. Most activities can be booked here.

Sir Edmund Hillary Alpine Centre
MUSEUM

(www.hermitage.co.nz; The Hermitage; adult/child $20/10; ⊙7am-8.30pm Oct-Mar, 8am-7pm Apr-Sep) This multimedia museum opened just three weeks before the January 2008 death of the man widely regarded as the greatest New Zealander of all time. Sir Ed's commentary tracks were recorded only a few months before he died. As well as memorabilia and displays about mountaineering, there's a domed digital planetarium (showing four different digital presentations) and a cinema (screening four documentaries, including the *Mt Cook Magic* 3D movie and a fascinating 75-minute film about Sir Ed's conquest of Mt Everest).

Tasman Glacier
GLACIER

At 27km long and up to 3km wide, the Tasman is the largest of NZ's glaciers, but it's melting fast, losing hundreds of metres from its length each year. It is also melting from the top down, shrinking around 150m in depth since it was first surveyed in 1891. In its lower section the melts have exposed rocks, stones and boulders, which form a solid unsightly mass on top of the ice. Despite this considerable melt, at its thickest point the ice is still estimated to be over 600m deep.

Tasman Lake, at the foot of the glacier, only started to form in the early 1970s and now stretches to 7km. The ongoing effects of climate change are expected to extend it to 16km within the next 20 years. The lake is covered by a maze of huge icebergs which are continuously being sheared off the glacier's terminal face. On 22 February 2011 the Christchurch earthquake caused a 1.3km long, 300m high, 30-million-tonne chunk of ice to break off, causing 3.5m waves to roll into the tourist boats on the lake at the time (no one was injured).

In the glacier's last major advance (17,000 years ago), the glacier crept south far enough to carve out Lake Pukaki. A later advance did not reach out to the valley sides, so there's a gap between the outer valley walls and the lateral moraines of this later advance. The unsealed Tasman Valley Rd, which branches off Mt Cook Rd 800m south of the village, travels through this gap. From the Blue Lakes shelter, 8km along the road, the Tasman Glacier View Track (40 minutes return) leads to a viewpoint on the moraine wall, passing the Blue Lakes on the way.

🏃 Activities

Tramping & Climbing

Various easy walks from the Hermitage area are outlined in brochures available from DOC. Longer walks are only recommended for those with mountaineering experience, as conditions at higher altitudes are severe and the tracks dangerous. If you intend staying at any of the park's huts, it's essential to register your intentions at the DOC visitor centre and pay the hut fee. Intentions cards are also recommended for longer day walks.

For the experienced, there's unlimited scope for climbing, but regardless of your skills, take every precaution – more than 200 people have died in climbing accidents here. The bleak *In Memoriam* book in the visitor information centre begins with the first death on Aoraki/Mt Cook in 1907, and since then more than 70 climbers have died on the peak.

Highly changeable weather is typical here: Aoraki/Mt Cook is only 44km from the coast and weather conditions rolling in from the Tasman Sea can mean sudden storms. Unless you're experienced in such conditions, don't climb anywhere without a guide.

Check with the park rangers before attempting any climb and always heed their advice. Fill out a climbers-intentions card before starting out – so rangers can check on you if you're overdue coming out – and sign out again when you return. The visitor centre also hires locator beacons (per three days/week $30/40).

Walkers can use the public shelter (⊙8am-7pm Oct-Apr, to 5pm May-Sep) in the village, which has running water, toilets and coin-operated showers. Note that this shelter cannot be used for overnight stays.

Hooker Valley Track
TRAMPING

Perhaps the best of the day walks, this track (three hours return from the village) heads up the Hooker Valley and crosses three

Aoraki/Mt Cook National Park

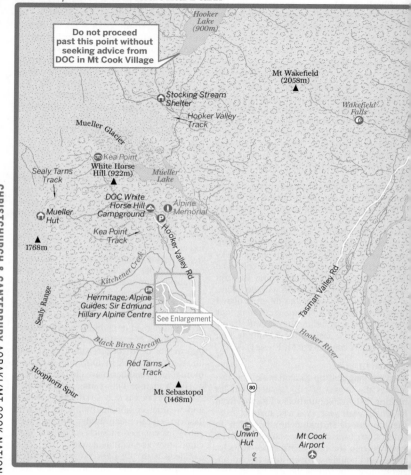

Do not proceed past this point without seeking advice from DOC in Mt Cook Village

Hooker Lake (900m)

Mt Wakefield (2058m)

Wakefield Falls

Stocking Stream Shelter

Hooker Valley Track

Mueller Glacier

Kea Point

White Horse Hill (922m)

Sealy Tarns Track

Mueller Lake

DOC White Horse Hill Campground

Alpine Memorial

Mueller Hut

Kea Point Track

1768m

Kitchener Creek

Hermitage; Alpine Guides; Sir Edmund Hillary Alpine Centre

See Enlargement

Sealy Range

Black Birch Stream

Hoophorn Spur

Red Tarns Track

Mt Sebastopol (1468m)

Hooker Valley Rd

Tasman Valley Rd

Hooker River

80

Unwin Hut

Mt Cook Airport

swing bridges to the Stocking Stream and the terminus of the Hooker Glacier. After the second swing bridge, Aoraki/Mt Cook totally dominates the valley, and you'll often see icebergs floating in Hooker Lake.

Kea Point Track   TRAMPING
The trail to Kea Point (two hours return from the village) is lined with native plants and ends at a platform with excellent views of Aoraki/Mt Cook, the Hooker Valley and the ice faces of Mt Sefton and the Footstool. Despite the name, you're no more likely to see a kea here than in other parts of the park.

Sealy Tarns Track   TRAMPING
The walk to Sealy Tarns (three to four hours return) branches off the Kea Point Track and continues up the ridge to Mueller Hut (dorm $36), a comfortable 28-bunk hut with gas, cooking facilities and longdrop toilets.

Alpine Recreation   TRAMPING, CLIMBING
(☎ 03-680 6736, 0800 006 096; www.alpinerecreation.com) Based in Lake Tekapo, Alpine Recreation organises high-altitude guided treks, as well as mountaineering courses and ski touring. Also on offer are guided ascents of Aoraki/Mt Cook, Mt Tasman and other peaks.

Snow Sports

Alpine Guides　　　　　　　　SNOW SPORTS
(✆03-435 1834; www.alpineguides.co.nz) Skiing, touring, heliskiing, guided climbs and mountaineering courses. Its store in the Hermitage sells travel clothing, outdoor and mountaineering gear, and rents ice axes, crampons, daypacks and sleeping bags.

Southern Alps Guiding　　　　　SNOW SPORTS
(✆03-435 1890; www.mtcook.com; Old Mountaineers, 3 Larch Grove Rd) From June to October heliskiers can head up Tasman Glacier for a 10km to 12km downhill run ($830 to $870).

Private guiding is also available, as well as three- to four-hour helihiking trips on Tasman Glacier year-round ($450).

Other Activities

Glentanner Horse Trekking　　　HORSE RIDING
(✆03-435 1855; www.glentanner.co.nz; 1/2/3hr ride $70/90/150; ☉Nov-Apr) Leads guided treks on a high-country sheep station with options suited to all levels of experience.

Glacier Sea-Kayaking　　　　　　KAYAKING
(✆03-435 1890; www.mtcook.com; per person $145; ☉Oct-Apr) Guided trips head out on the terminal lake of the Tasman or the Mueller Glacier. There are usually icebergs to negotiate, but if this is your prime reason for taking the trip, it pays to check in advance whether there actually are any. Because of the danger of ice carving from the ends of the glaciers, you can only admire them and the larger icebergs from a distance. Expect to spend about an hour on the water; book at the Old Mountaineers Cafe.

Big Sky　　　　　　　　　　　STARGAZING
(✆0800 686 800; www.hermitage.co.nz; adult/child $60/30, planetarium only $24/12) NZ's southern sky is introduced by a 45-minute presentation in the Alpine Centre's digital planetarium, before participants venture outside to study the real deal with telescopes, binoculars and an astronomy guide. If the weather's not cooperating, the experience is confined to the planetarium.

🕭 Tours

Tasman Valley 4WD & Argo Tours　　TOUR
(✆0800 686 800; www.mountcooktours.co.nz; adult/child $75/38) Offers a 90-minute Argo (8WD all-terrain vehicle) tour checking out the Tasman Glacier and its terminal lake. Expect plenty of alpine flora and an interesting commentary along the way. Book online or at the Hermitage hotel activities desk.

Glacier Explorers　　　　　　　BOAT TOUR
(✆03-435 1641; www.glacierexplorers.com; adult/child $145/70) Head out on the terminal lake of the Tasman Glacier onboard a custom-built MAC boat and get up close and personal with 300-year-old icebergs. Book at the activities desk at the Hermitage.

Helicopter Line　　　　　　　SCENIC FLIGHTS
(✆03-435 1801; www.helicopter.co.nz) From Glentanner Park, the Helicopter Line offers 20-minute Alpine Vista flights ($230), an exhilarating 35-minute flight over the Ben

DON'T MISS

ALPS 2 OCEAN CYCLE TRAIL

Hoping to give the Otago Central Rail Trail a ride for its money, this new mountain-biking route stretches from Mt Cook Village to Oamaru, via Twizel, Lake Ohau Lodge, Omarama, Otematata, Kurow and Duntroon. While there are some quite long sections on SH83, about 40% of the trail is offroad. It's mainly downhill too, descending 780m over its 300km course.

The route is split into eight sections which can be tackled individually or consecutively as a four- to six-day ride. The official start involves an expensive helicopter trip over the Tasman River, so you might like to pick up the trail later at the southern end of Lake Pukaki.

See www.alps2ocean.com for more.

Ohau Range ($345) and a 40-minute Mountains High flight over the Tasman Glacier and alongside Aoraki/Mt Cook ($425). All feature snow landings.

Mount Cook Ski Planes SCENIC FLIGHTS
(☑ 03-430 8034; www.mtcookskiplanes. com) Based at Mt Cook Airport, offering 40-minute (adult/child $405/295) and 55-minute (adult/child $530/405) flights, both with snow landings. Flightseeing without a landing is a cheaper option; try the 25-minute Mini Tasman trip (adult/child $275/255) or 45-minute Alpine Wonderland (adult/child $370/275).

🛏 Sleeping

Accommodation is more expensive in Mt Cook Village than in Twizel, but the thrill of waking up so close to the mountains is worth the additional expense.

Mt Cook YHA HOSTEL $
(☑ 03-435 1820; www.yha.co.nz; 4 Bowen Dr; dm $37, d $118; @ 🐾) 🖉 Handsomely decked out in pine, this excellent hostel has a free sauna, drying room, log fires and DVDs. Rooms are clean and warm, although some are a tight squeeze (particularly the twin bunk rooms).

**DOC White Horse Hill
Campground** CAMPSITE $
(☑ 03-435 1186; Hooker Valley Rd; site per adult/ child $10/5) Located 2km up the Hooker Valley from Aoraki/Mt Cook village, this self-registration campsite doesn't have elec-

tricity or cooking facilities but it does have running water, toilets and an abundance of blissful views. It's also perfectly positioned for tackling various walking tracks.

Glentanner Park Centre HOLIDAY PARK
(☑ 03-435 1855; www.glentanner.co.nz; Mt Coo' Rd; sites $19-22, dm $29, unit with/without bath room from $160/80; @ 🐾) 🖉 On the northern shore of Lake Pukaki, 22km south of the village, this is the nearest fully equipped campground to the national park. Facilitie include various cabins and motel units, bunk room and a restaurant.

Unwin Hut HOSTEL $
(☑ 03-435 1100; www.alpineclub.org.nz; Mt Coo' Rd; dm adult/child $30/15; 🐾) About 3.5km before the village, this lodge belongs to the New Zealand Alpine Club (NZAC). Member get preference, but beds are usually avail able for climbing groupies. There are basi bunks (bring your own linen), and a bi common room with a fireplace and kitchen

Aoraki/Mt Cook Alpine Lodge LODGE $
(☑ 03-435 1860; www.aorakialpinelodge.co.nz Bowen Dr; d $164-189; @) This modern lodge has comfortable en-suite rooms and a huge lounge and kitchen area. The superb moun tain views from the barbecue area will have you arguing for the privilege of grilling the sausages for dinner.

Aoraki Court Motel MOTEL $$
(☑ 03-435 1111; www.aorakicourt.co.nz; 26 Bowe Dr; d $205-295) While it wouldn't command these prices elsewhere, this clump of new motel units is very good indeed. Featur wallpaper sharpens up the decor, and th tiled bathrooms have designery touches Some units have spa baths but all hav kitchenettes and gee-golly mountain views.

Hermitage HOTEL $$
(☑ 03-435 1809; www.hermitage.co.nz; Terrace R r $239-599; @ 🐾) Completely dominating M Cook Village, this famous hotel offers fan tastic mountain views. While the corridor in some of the older wings can seem a lit tle hospital-like, all of the rooms have bee renovated to a high standard. As well as th hotel, the Hermitage offers motel rooms an well-equipped A-frame chalets.

🍴 Eating & Drinking

Old Mountaineers CAFE, BAR $
(www.mtcook.com; Bowen Dr; breakfast $10-15, lunc $15-26, dinner $18-35; ⏰ 10am-9pm daily Nov-Ap

Tue-Sun May & Jul-Oct; 🤖) 🍴 A good-value alternative to the eateries at the Hermitage, this large eatery provides mountain views through picture windows or from outside tables in summer. As well as cooked breakfasts, it delivers top-notch burgers, pizza, pasta and salad. Linger to study the old black-and-white pics and mountaineering memorabilia.

Panorama MODERN NZ **$$$**
(📞0800 686 800, 03-435 1809; www.hermitage. co.nz; Terrace Rd; mains $34-40; ⊙6-10pm) The Hermitage's signature restaurant is by far the best of the hotel's dining options, which include a buffet restaurant and a lacklustre cafe. The sophisticated fare is well matched to wonderful views and interesting mid-20th-century architecture.

Chamois Bar & Grill PUB
(www.mountcookbackpackers.co.nz; Bowen Dr; ⊙4pm-late) Upstairs in Mt Cook Backpacker Lodge, in the heart of the village, this large bar offers pub grub, a pool table, a big-screen TV and the occasional live gig.

ℹ Information

The DOC visitor centre (p175) is the best source of local information. The nearest ATM and supermarket are in Twizel.

ℹ Getting There & Away

The village's small airport only serves aerial sightseeing companies. Some of these may be willing to combine transport to the West Coast (ie Franz Josef) with a scenic flight, but flights are heavily dependent on weather.

If you're driving, fill up at Lake Tekapo or Twizel. There is petrol at Mt Cook, but it's expensive and involves summoning an attendant from the Hermitage (for a fee).

Cook Connection (📞0800 266 526; www.cook-connect.co.nz) Shuttle services to Lake Tekapo ($35, 1½ hours) and Twizel ($25, one hour).

InterCity (📞03-365 1113; www.intercity.co.nz) Daily coaches head to/from Christchurch (from $67, 5¼ hours), Geraldine (from $38, three hours), Lake Tekapo, (from $30, 1½ hours), Cromwell (from $59, 2¾ hours) and Queenstown (from $64, four hours). They stop at the YHA and the Hermitage, both of which handle bookings.

Twizel

POP 1140

It wasn't long ago that New Zealanders maligned Twizel. The forest-ringed town just south of Lake Pukaki was built in 1968 to serve ice construction of the nearby hydroelectric power station, and was due to be abandoned in 1984 when the project was completed. Now Twizel's residents are having the last laugh as new lakeside subdivisions have been built to take advantage of the area's relaxed lakes-and-mountains lifestyle. Accommodation, eateries, petrol and groceries are all better value in Twizel than Mt Cook Village.

⊙ Sights & Activities

Nearby Lake Ruataniwha is popular for rowing, boating and windsurfing. Fishing in local rivers, canals and lakes is also big business; ask at the information centre about local guides.

Kaki Visitor Hide WILDLIFE RESERVE
(📞03-435 3124; adult/child $20/10; ⊙9.30am & 4.30pm late Oct-Apr) The rare kaki (black stilt) is found only in NZ, and a breeding program is aiming to increase the population at the Ahuriri Conservation Park. It's possible to get a close-up look at these elusive birds by booking a one-hour guided tour through the information centre. Tours depart from the centre, but you'll need your own transport.

👉 Tours

OneRing Tours TOUR
(📞0800 213 868; www.lordoftheringstour.com) How often do you get the opportunity to charge around like a mad thing weilding replica *LOTR* gear? Not often enough! Tours head onto the sheep station used for the location of the Battle of the Pelennor Fields and include lots of information about the filming. Choose between a two-hour version (adult/child $84/45), a truncated one-hour option (adult/child $64/35) and an adults-only twilight tour, enjoying beer, wine and nibbles as the sun sets over Gondor ($115).

Helicopter Line SCENIC FLIGHTS
(📞03-435 0370; www.helicopter.co.nz; Pukaki Airport, Harry Wigley Dr) Flight options include the hour-long Aoraki/Mt Cook Discovery ($640), the 45-minute Southern Alps Experience ($520), the 35-minute Alpine Scenic Flight ($345) and the 25-minute Alpine Express ($265). All but the shortest guarantee snow landings.

🛏 Sleeping

Twizel Holiday Park HOLIDAY PARK **$**
(📞03-435 0507; www.twizelholidaypark.co.nz; 122 Mackenzie Dr; sites from $34, dm $30, units $95-215; 🤖) Offers green, flower-filled grounds

RUATANIWHA CONSERVATION PARK

Taking in a large chunk of the space between Lake Pukaki and Lake Ohau, this 368 sq km protected area includes the Ben Ohau Range and various valleys and beech forests. The numerous walks in this vast expanse are detailed in DOC's *Ruataniwha Conservation Park* pamphlet (available online). There are also five good mountain-bike tracks.

DOC huts and camping areas are scattered throughout the park, but for a more comfortable stay, try **Lake Ohau Lodge** (✆ 03-438 9885; www.ohau.co.nz; Lake Ohau Rd; s $101-180, d $107-205) ✿, idyllically sited on the western shore of the rower-friendly lake. Accommodation includes everything from budget rooms with shared facilities, to upmarket rooms with decks and mountain views. The lodge is the wintertime service centre for the Ohau Ski Field (p39). In summer it's a quieter retreat. DB&B packages are available.

and accommodation in a refurbished maternity hospital. There are a few en-suite cabins, a bunkroom and room for tents and campervans. The modern, self-contained cottages are particularly good value.

★ Omahau Downs   B&B **$$**
(✆ 03-435 0199; www.omahau.co.nz; SH8; s/d $115/135, cottage $125-225; ⊙ closed Jun-Aug; ⊛) This farmstead, 2km north of Twizel, has two cosy, self-contained cottages (one sleeping up to six), and a lodge with sparkling, modern rooms and a deck looking out at the Ben Ohau Range. An essential experience is a moonlit, wood-fired outdoor bath ($20).

Mountain Chalets   MOTEL, HOSTEL **$$**
(✆ 03-435 0785; www.mountainchalets.co.nz; Wairepo Rd; dm $28, d $110-130; ⊛) Wooden ceilings add a rustic quality to these cosy, well-equipped, self-contained A-frame chalets, available as studio, one- and two-bedroom units. There's also a small, laid-back lodge that's perfect for backpackers.

Heartland Lodge   B&B **$$$**
(✆ 03-435 0008; www.heartland-lodge.co.nz; 19 North West Arch; apt $160, s $230-260, d $270-300; ⊛) Built on the leafy outskirts of town, this large modern house has a surfeit of space,

translating to a large wraparound living area downstairs and spacious guest rooms above. Prices include cooked breakfasts, unless you're staying in 'the retreat', a separate apartment with its own kitchenette.

✗ Eating & Drinking

★ Shawty's   CAFE, BAR **$$**
(✆ 03-435 3155; www.shawtys.co.nz; 4 Market Pl; brunch $12-20, dinner $29-34; ⊙ 8.30am-3pm Mon & Tue, 8.30am-late Wed-Sun Apr-Oct, to late daily Nov-Mar; ⊛) Cool beats and craft beers create a mood that's surprisingly sophisticated for Twizel. Big breakfasts and gourmet pizza ($14 to $18) are a good way to start and end an active day amid the surrounding alpine vistas. The adjacent Grappa Lounge has DJs and live music in summer.

Poppies Cafe   CAFE **$$**
(✆ 03-435 0848; www.poppiescafe.com; 1 Benmore Pl; brunch $10-20, dinner $23-35; ⊙ 10am-3pm & 5.30-9pm; ⊛) Lunch showcases the likes of gourmet pies, burgers and pasta, while dinner features more substantial fare; excellent pizzas ($20 to $24) occupy a tasty middle ground. It's located on the outskirts of town near the Mackenzie Country Inn.

Jasmine Thai Café   THAI **$$**
(1 Market Pl; lunch $12, dinner $18-22; ⊙ noon-2pm Tue-Sat & 5-9pm daily) The zesty and zingy flavours of your favourite Southeast Asian beach holiday have travelled well to get this far inland. Alcohol is BYO, so grab a few cold beers from the Four Square supermarket to ease Jasmine's authentic Thai heat.

ℹ Information

Twizel Information Centre (✆ 03-435 3124; Market Pl; ⊙ 8.30am-5pm Mon-Fri, 11am-2pm Sat & Sun)

ℹ Getting There & Away

Atomic Shuttles (✆ 03-349 0697; www.atomic travel.co.nz) Daily buses to/from Christchurch ($35, 3¾ hours), Geraldine ($25, two hours), Lake Tekapo ($20, 40 minutes), Cromwell ($30, 2¼ hours) and Queenstown ($30, 3¼ hours).

Cook Connection (✆ 0800 266 526; www.cookconnect.co.nz) Shuttle services to Mt Cook Village ($25, one hour).

InterCity (✆ 03-365 1113; www.intercity.co.nz) Daily coaches head to/from Christchurch (from $40, 5¼ hours), Lake Tekapo (from $13, 50 minutes), Mt Cook Village (from $32, one hour), Cromwell (from $29, two hours) and Queenstown (from $35, three hours).

Dunedin & Otago

Best Places to Eat

➡ Riverstone Kitchen (p190)

➡ Fleur's Place (p191)

➡ The Shed at Northburn Station (p212)

➡ Pitches Store (p208)

➡ Otago Farmers' Market (p198)

Best Places to Stay

➡ Burn Cottage Retreat (p212)

➡ Pitches Store (p208)

➡ Dunstan House (p211)

➡ Pen-y-bryn Lodge (p189)

Why Go?

Otago has attractions both urban and rural, ranging from quirky towns to world-class wineries and some of the country's most accessible wildlife. Its historic heart is Dunedin, home to a vibrant student culture and arts scene. From the town's stately Edwardian train station, catch the famous Taieri Gorge Railway inland, and continue on two wheels along the craggily scenic Otago Central Rail Trail.

Those seeking colonial New Zealand can soak up the frontier atmosphere of gold-rush towns such as Clyde, St Bathans, Naseby and cute-as-a-button Ophir. For wildlife, head to the Otago Peninsula, where penguins, albatross, sea lions and seals are easily sighted. Seaside Oamaru has a wonderful historic precinct, resident penguin colonies and a quirky devotion to Steampunk culture.

Unhurried and overflowing with picturesque scenery, Otago is generous to explorers who are after a more leisurely style of holiday.

When to Go

➡ February and March have settled, sunny weather (usually...), and the juicy appeal of fresh apricots, peaches and cherries.

➡ At Easter, hook yourself a Southern Man at the Middlemarch Singles Ball, or drown your sorrows at the Clyde Wine & Food Festival.

➡ Take to two wheels on the Otago Central Rail Trail during the quieter months of May and December.

➡ In November watch the pros battle it out on the Highlands Motorsport Park, then ride graciously into the past on a penny farthing bicycle at Oamaru's Victorian Heritage Celebrations.

Dunedin & Otago Highlights

❶ Experiencing a heritage past, and a possible Steampunk future, in kooky **Oamaru** (p183)

❷ Peering at penguins, admiring albatross and staring at seals on **Otago Peninsula** (p203)

❸ Exploring New Zealand's southern heritage in quaint backcountry villages such as **Ophir** (p208) and **Naseby** (p207)

❹ Taste-testing some of the planet's best pinot noir in the wineries scattered around **Cromwell** (p211)

❺ Sampling local beers and listening out for local bands in

the bars and cafes of **Dunedin** (p192)

❻ Cycling through lonely vistas of brown and gold along the **Otago Central Rail Trail** (p206)

❼ Winding through gorges, alongside canyons and across tall viaducts on the snaking **Taieri Gorge Railway** (p196)

ⓘ Getting There & Around

Air New Zealand (☑ 0800 737 000; www.airnewzealand.co.nz) flies from Dunedin to Christchurch, Wellington and Auckland, and **Jetstar** (☑ 0800 800 995; www.jetstar.com) flies to Auckland. The only train services are heritage trips from Dunedin to Middlemarch and Dunedin to Palmerston. The main bus routes follow SH1 or SH8.

WAITAKI DISTRICT

The broad, braided Waitaki River provides a clear dividing line between Otago and Canterbury to the region's north. The Waitaki Valley is a direct but less-travelled route from the Southern Alps to the sea, featuring freaky limestone formations, Maori rock paintings and ancient fossils. The area is also one of NZ's newest winemaking regions, and a major component of the new Alps 2 Ocean Cycle Trail (p178) that links Aoraki/Mt Cook National Park to Oamaru on the coast. The district's main town, Oamaru, is a place of penguins and glorious heritage architecture.

Omarama

POP 267

At the head of the Waitaki Valley, Omarama is surrounded by mountain ranges and fabulous landscapes. Busy times in this sleepy place include the rodeo (28 December) and the sheepdog trials (March).

◎ Sights & Activities

Clay Cliffs Paritea   LANDMARK
This bizarre moonscape is the result of two million years of erosion on layers of silt and gravel that were exposed along the active Ostler fault line. The cliffs are on private land; before setting out, pay the $5 vehicle admission fee at Omarama Hot Tubs. To get to the area, head north from town for 4km on SH8, turn left onto Quailburn Rd, and then turn left after 4km onto unsealed Henburn Rd.

Wrinkly Rams   FARM
☑ 03-438 9751; www.thewrinklyrams.co.nz; 24 Omarama Ave; adult/child $20/10) A regular stop for our buses, Wrinkly Rams stages 30-minute shearing and sheepdog shows, including lamb-feeding in season. Phone ahead to tag along with a tour group, or book your own one-off show. Attached is one of Omarama's better **cafes** (mains $7-25; ⊙7am-4.30pm; ☏).

Omarama Hot Tubs   SPA
(☑ 03-438 9703; www.hottubsomarama.co.nz; 29 Omarama Ave; per 1-/2-/3-/4-person tub $45/80/105/120, pod 75/140/180/200; ⊙11am-late) If your legs are weary after mountain biking or tramping, or you just want to cosy up with your significant other, these private, wood-fired hot tubs could be just the ticket. The concept is Japanese, but with the surrounding mountain ranges, the lakeside setting and a pristine night sky, you could only be on the South Island of NZ.

Choose between a 90-minute soak in a tub (each has its own dressing room) or a two-hour session in a 'wellness pod', which includes a sauna. The chemical-free glacier and snow-melt water is changed after each booking, and the used water is recycled for irrigation. Therapeutic massages (30/60 minutes $60/100) and beauty treatments are also available.

Glide Omarama   GLIDING
(☑ 03-438 9555; www.glideomarama.com) The area's westerlies and warm summer thermals allow for world-class gliding over the hills and spectacular Southern Alps, and a national gliding meet is held here in December or January. This crew offers lessons and scenic flights ranging from 30 minutes ($325) to three hours ($640).

ESSENTIAL OTAGO

Eat Cheese from Oamaru's Whitestone factory

Drink Central Otago pinot noir

Read Owls Do Cry by Oamaru's Janet Frame

Listen to Tally Ho! Flying Nun's Greatest Bits, a 2011 compilation marking the 30th anniversary of Dunedin's iconic record label

Watch In My Father's Den (2004), set in Central Otago

Festival Oamaru's Victorian Heritage Celebrations in late November

Go green Tiptoe down to Otago Peninsula beaches in search of yellow-eyed penguins

Online www.dunedinnz.com, www.centralotagonz.com

Area code ☑ 03

DUNEDIN & OTAGO OMARAMA

🛏 Sleeping & Eating

Buscot Station   FARMSTAY, HOSTEL $
(☑ 027 222 1754; SH8; site/dm/s/d $10/25/43/61)
For a completely different and uniquely
Kiwi experience, grab a room in the homely
farmhouse attached to a huge sheep and cattle station, or a bed in the large dormitory
out the back. Look for it on SH8, 10km north
of Omarama.

Omarama Top 10   HOLIDAY PARK $
(☑ 03-438 9875; www.omaramatop10.co.nz; SH8;
sites $34-39, unit with/without bathroom $110/55;
@🛜) This streamside holiday park is a
peaceful green space to camp in. Standard
cabins are compact, but larger en suite and
self-contained motel units are available.

Ladybird Hill   WINERY $$
(www.ladybirdhill.co.nz; 1 Pinot Noir Ct; mains $6-
32; ⊙10am-4pm Thu-Sun Aug-Jun) Sure, you
can do it the easy way and simply order a
leisurely lunch from the menu. Or you can
grab a rod, catch a salmon from the well-
stocked ponds and wait until it's prepared,
smoked and served to your table ($37, which
feeds two to three adults). Other attractions
include a kids' playground and walking
tracks through the hillside vineyard.

ℹ Information

Omarama Hot Tubs doubles as the information
office, and can assist with accommodation and
transport information. See www.discoveroma-
rama.co.nz for more information.

MAORI NZ: OTAGO

The early Maori history of Otago echoes
that of Canterbury (p157), with Ngai
Tahu the dominant tribe at the time the
British arrived. One of the first parcels
of land that Ngai Tahu sold was called
the Otago block, a 1618-sq-km parcel
of land which changed hands in 1844
for £2400. The name Otago reflects the
Ngai Tahu pronunciation of Otakou, a
small village on the far reaches of the
Otago Peninsula, where there's still a
marae (Maori meeting place).

Dunedin's Otago Museum (p195)
has the finest Maori exhibition in the
South Island, including an ornately
carved *waka taua* (war canoe) and
finely crafted *pounamu* (greenstone).
Maori rock art can still be seen in situ in
the Waitaki Valley.

ℹ Getting There & Away

InterCity (☑ 03-471 7143; www.intercity.co.nz)
Daily coaches head to/from Christchurch (from
$42, 5¾ hours), Mt Cook Village (from $32, 1¼
hours), Twizel (from $13, 19 minutes), Cromwell
(from $23, 1½ hours) and Queenstown (from
$32, 2½ hours).

Atomic Shuttles (☑ 03-349 0697; www.
atomictravel.co.nz) Services stop in Omarama
for a break before continuing on to Christchurch
($35, four hours), Lake Tekapo ($20, one hour),
Twizel ($20, 20 minutes), Cromwell ($25, 1½
hours) and Queenstown ($30, 2¼ hours).

Waitaki Valley

Wine, waterskiing and salmon-fishing are
just some of the treats on offer along this
little-travelled route. Coming from Omarama
SH83 passes an array of arrestingly blue
lakes, each abutted by a hydroelectric power
station. For a scenic detour along the north
bank, leave the highway at Otematata and
cross over the huge Benmore Dam, then cross
over Aviemore Dam to rejoin the highway.

A succession of sleepy little heartland
towns line the highway, peppered with rus-
tic heritage bank buildings and pubs. One
of the most appealing is tiny lost-in-time
Kurow (population 302), the home town
of World Cup–winning All Blacks captain
Richie McCaw. From almost-as-cute Dun-
troon (population 90), adventurous (and
appropriately insured) drivers can take the
unsealed road over Danseys Pass to Naseby.

Although they've got a long way to go to
attain the global reputation that their col-
leagues on the other side of the mountains in
Central Otago enjoy, a few winemaking pio-
neers in Waitaki Valley are making wine that
international experts are taking notice of.

👁 Sights

👁 Kurow

**Kurow Heritage
& Information Centre**   MUSEUM
(☑03-436   0950;   www.kurow.org.nz;   SH83;
⊙9.30am-4pm Mon-Fri) FREE While Richie Mc-
Caw might get all the attention these days,
Kurow's other famous son was Arnold Nord-
meyer (1901–1989), a Labour Party leader
who was one of the key architects of NZ's
welfare and public-health system. His mem-
ory is honoured in this interesting commu-
nity museum, which jokingly refers to itself
as the National Museum of Social Security.

Limelight Cinema CINEMA
☑03-434 1070; www.limelightcinema.co.nz; 239 Thames St; adult/child $15/10) Cheaper on Tuesdays.

❶ Information

Oamaru i-SITE (☑03-434 1656; www.visit-oamaru.co.nz; 1 Thames St; ⊙10am-4pm; 🛜) Mountains of information including details on local walking trips and wildlife, plus daily penguin-viewing times are posted here. There's also bike hire (per day $40) and an interesting 40-minute DVD on the history of the town.

Oamaru Whitestone Civic Trust (☑03-434 6385; www.historicoamaru.co.nz; 2 Harbour St; ⊙10am-4pm) Vintage B&W photos of Oamaru's heritage, maps, information and walking tours of the historic precinct.

❶ Getting There & Away

Most buses and shuttles depart from the **Lagonda Tearooms** (191 Thames St; ⊙9am-4.30pm). Both the tearooms and the i-SITE take bookings.

Atomic Shuttles (☑03-349 0697; www.atomictravel.co.nz) Daily buses to/from Christchurch ($30, 3¾ hours), Timaru ($20, 1¼ hours) and Dunedin ($20, 1¾ hours).

Coast Line Tours (☑03-434 7744; www.coastline-tours.co.nz) Shuttles to/from Dunedin ($30) with a detour to Dunedin airport possible.

InterCity (☑03-471 7143; www.intercity.co.nz) Two daily coaches to/from Christchurch (from $21, 4¼ hours), Timaru (from $14, one hour), Moeraki (from $11, 30 minutes) and Dunedin (from $14, 40 minutes), and one to Te Anau (from $29, 6½ hours).

Knightrider (www.knightrider.co.nz) Has a bus most nights to/from Christchurch ($43, four hours), Christchurch airport ($48, 3¾ hours), Timaru ($28, 1¼ hours), Moeraki ($25, one hour) and Dunedin ($33, two hours).

Naked Bus (☑0900 625 33; www.nakedbus.com; prices vary) Daily buses head to/from Christchurch (3¾ hours), Timaru (1¼ hours), Moeraki (35 minutes) and Dunedin (1¾ hours).

Moeraki

The name Moeraki means 'sleepy sky', which should give you some clue as to the pace of life in this little fishing village. You might be surprised to learn that this was one of the first European settlements in NZ, with a whaling station established here in 1836. Since then, Moeraki has nurtured the creation of several national treasures, from Frances Hodgkins' paintings to Keri Hulme's *The Bone People*, and Fleur Sullivan's cooking.

Apart from Fleur's eponymous restaurant, the main attraction is the collection of large spherical boulders scattered along a beautiful stretch of beach like a kid's giant discarded marbles. The famed **Moeraki Boulders** (Te Kaihinaki) lie just off SH1, a kilometre north of the Moeraki turn-off. Try to time your visit with low tide.

It's a pleasant 45-minute walk along the beach from the village to the boulders. Head in the other direction on the Kaiks Wildlife Trail and you'll reach a cute old wooden lighthouse. You might even spot yellow-eyed penguins and fur seals (be sure to keep your distance).

🛏 Sleeping & Eating

Olive Grove Lodge & Holiday Park HOSTEL $
(☑03-439 5830; www.olivebranch.co.nz; SH1, Waianakarua; sites/dm $12/31, d with/without bathroom $85/75) 🌿 Nestled in a loop of the Waianakarua River, 12km north of the Moeraki turn-off, this organic farm offers both bucolic camping sites and a colourful lodge with a sunny communal lounge. Kids will love the playground and highland cattle; parents will love the spa, eco lifestyle, organic vegies and peaceful vibe.

Moeraki Village Holiday Park HOLIDAY PARK $
(☑03-439 4759; www.moerakivillageholidaypark.co.nz; 114 Haven St; sites $32, unit with/without bathroom $100/60; @🛜) Occupying a small field above the road into town, this complex offers powered sites, basic cabins (bring your own linen) and fully equipped motel units.

Moeraki Beach Motel MOTEL $$
(☑03-439 4862; www.moerakibeachmotels.co.nz; cnr Beach & Haven Sts; d from $105) The four split-level units at this motel aren't about to win any design awards, but they are spacious. Each has a full kitchen and a balcony.

★Fleur's Place SEAFOOD $$$
(☑03-439 4480; www.fleursplace.com; Old Jetty, 169 Haven St; mains $32-42; ⊙9.30am-late Wed-Sun) There's a rumble-tumble look about it, but this timber hut houses one of the South Island's best seafood restaurants. Head for the upstairs deck and tuck into fresh chowder, tender muttonbird and other ocean bounty. Bookings are strongly recommended.

❶ Getting There & Away

All of the buses on the Oamaru–Dunedin run stop on SH1 by the Moeraki turn-off. From here it's a 2km walk into the centre of the village.

DUNEDIN

POP 121,000

Two words immediately spring to mind when Kiwis think of their seventh-largest city: 'Scotland' and 'students'. The 'Edinburgh of the South' is immensely proud of its Scottish heritage, never missing an opportunity to break out the haggis and bagpipes on civic occasions.

In fact, the very name Dunedin is derived from the Scottish Gaelic name for Edinburgh: Dùn Èideann. The first permanent European settlers, two shiploads of pious, hard-working Scots, arrived at Port Chalmers in 1848, and included the nephew of Scotland's favourite son, Robbie Burns. A statue of the poet dominates the Octagon, the city's civic heart, and the city even has its own tartan.

If there were a tenuous link between the Scottish and the students that dominate Dunedin in term time, it would probably be whisky. The country's oldest university provides plenty of student energy to sustain the local bars, and in the 1980s it even spawned its own internationally influential indie music scene, with Flying Nun Records and the 'Dunedin sound'.

Dunedin is an easy place in which to while away a few days. Weatherboard houses ranging from stately to ramshackle pepper its hilly suburbs, and bluestone Victorian buildings punctuate the compact city centre. It's a great base for exploring the wildlife-rich Otago Peninsula, which officially lies within the city limits.

⊙ Sights

★**Toitu Otago Settlers Museum**   MUSEUM
(Map p194; www.toituosm.com; 31 Queens Gardens; ⊙10am-4pm Fri-Wed, to 8pm Thu;) FREE Storytelling is the focus of this excellent interactive museum. The engrossing Maori section is followed by a large gallery where floor-to-ceiling portraits of Victorian-era

Dunedin & the Otago Peninsula

settlers stare out from behind their whiskers and lace; click on the terminal to learn more about the individuals that catch your eye. Other displays include a re-created passenger-ship cabin, an awesome car collection and a room devoted to the underground stars of Flying Nun Records.

★ **Railway Station**   HISTORIC BUILDING
(Map p194; Anzac Ave) Featuring mosaic-tile floors and glorious stained-glass windows, Dunedin's striking bluestone railway station (built between 1903 and 1906) claims to be NZ's most-photographed building. Head upstairs for the **NZ Sports Hall of Fame** (Map p194; www.nzhalloffame.co.nz; Dunedin Railway Station; adult/child $5/2; ⊙10am-4pm), a small museum devoted to the nation's obsession, and the **Art Station** (Map p194; www.otagoartsociety.co.nz; ⊙10am-4pm), the local Art Society's gallery and shop.

Dunedin Public Art Gallery   GALLERY
(Map p194; www.dunedin.art.museum; 30 The Octagon; ⊙10am-5pm; 🛜) **FREE** Explore NZ's art scene at this expansive and airy gallery. Only a fraction of the collection is displayed at any given time, with most of the space given over to often-edgy temporary shows.

Speight's Brewery   BREWERY
(Map p194; 📞03-477 7697; www.speights.co.nz; 200 Rattray St; adult/child $25/10; ⊙noon, 2pm, 4pm & 6pm Jun-Sep, plus 5pm & 7pm Oct-May) Speight's has been churning out beer on this site since the late 1800s. The 90-minute tour offers samples of six different brews, and there's an option to combine a tour with a

DUNEDIN & OTAGO DUNEDIN

Central Dunedin

0 — 500 m
0 — 0.25 miles

No 7 Balmac (600m)

858 George St (250m);
Leith Valley Touring
Park (1.5km); Mt Cargill-
Bethunes Gully Walkway (6km)

Dunedin Botanic Garden (800m);
Arden Street House (1.5km);
Baldwin St (2.2km);
Mt Cargill (8km)

Luna (400m);
Roslyn Apartments
(600m)

Eureka (150m)

Dunedin Botanic
Garden (1km)

Forsyth Barr Stadium
(1km); Port Chalmers
(12km)

InterCity
(500m)

St Kilda (3km);
St Clair (4km);
Dunedin (27km)

Manor Pl

DUNEDIN & OTAGO DUNEDIN

Olveston 1

Town Belt

Queens Dr

London St

Royal Tce

Cobden St

Heriot Row

Queen St

Pitt St

George St

Knox Church

Otago Museum 2

Great King St

Union St

Albany St

Frederick St

Castle St

Great King St

Hanover St

St Andrew St

Moray Pl

Filleul St

Haddon Pl

Cargill St

York Pl

Stuart St

Tennyson St

Rattray St

Elm Row

Bishops Rd

St Joseph's
Cathedral

St Paul's
Cathedral

The
Octagon

Dunedin
i-SITE

First
Church of
Otago

DOC
Visitor
Centre

Cumberland St

Anzac Ave

Ward St

**Railway
Station**

Dunedin 7

Mason St

**Toitu Otago
Settlers
Museum** 4

Queens
Gardens

MacLaggan St

Broadway

Princes St

Rattray St

Water St

Wills St

Graham St

High St

Hope St

Stafford St

Liverpool St

Jetty St

Crawford St

Vogel St

Cumberland St

Wharf St

Otago Harbour

Birch St

Central Dunedin

DUNEDIN & OTAGO DUNEDIN

meal at the neighbouring Ale House (lunch/dinner $55/61).

★ **Olveston** HOUSE
(Map p194; ☑ 03-477 3320; www.olveston.co.nz; 42 Royal Tce; adult/child $19/9.50; ☉ tours 9.45am, 10.45am, noon, 1.30pm, 2.45pm & 4pm) Although it's a youngster by European standards, this spectacular 1906 mansion provides a wonderful window into Dunedin's past. Until 1966 it was the family home of the wealthy Theomin family, notable patrons of the arts who were heavily involved with endowing the Public Art Gallery.

This artistic bent is evident in Olveston's grand interiors, which include works by Charles Goldie and Frances Hodgkins (a family friend). A particular passion was Japanese art, and the home is liberallly peppered with exquisite examples. The family

was Jewish, and the grand dining table is set up as if for Shabbat dinner.

Entry is via fascinating guided tours; it pays to book ahead. There's also a pretty little garden to explore.

★ **Otago Museum** MUSEUM
(Map p194; www.otagomuseum.govt.nz; 419 Great King St; admission by donation; ☉ 10am-5pm) The centrepiece of this august institution is *Southern Land, Southern People,* showcasing Otago's cultural and physical past and present, from geology and dinosaurs to the modern day. The *Tangata Whenua* Maori gallery houses an impressive *waka taua* (war canoe), wonderfully worn old carvings, and some lovely *pounamu* (greenstone) weapons, tools and jewellery.

Other major galleries include *Pacific Cultures, People of the World* (including the requisite mummy), *Nature, Maritime* and

WORTH A TRIP

TAIERI GORGE RAILWAY

With narrow tunnels, deep gorges, winding tracks, rugged canyons and more than a dozen stone and wrought-iron viaduct crossings (up to 50m high), the scenic **Taieri Gorge Railway** (Map p194; ☎03-477 4449; www.taieri.co.nz; departs Dunedin Railway Station, Anzac Ave; ⊙office 8.30am-5pm Mon-Fri, to 3pm Sat-Sun) consistently rates highly with visitors.

The four-hour return trip aboard 1920s heritage coaches travels to Pukerangi (one way/return $59/89), 58km away. Some trains carry on to Middlemarch (one way/return $71/107) – which is particularly handy for those cycling the Otago Central Rail Trail – or you can opt for a train-coach trip to Queenstown (one way $139).

the *Animal Attic*. The hands-on *Discovery World* (adult/child $10/5) is mainly aimed at kids, although the tropical forest, filled with colourful live butterflies, is an all-ages treat.

Check the timing of the daily guided tours ($12) and free gallery talks on the website.

Dunedin Botanic Garden GARDENS
(Map p192; www.dunedinbotanicgarden.co.nz; cnr Great King St & Opoho Rd; ⊙dawn-dusk) **FREE**
Dating from 1863, these 22 peaceful, grassy and shady hectares include rose gardens, rare natives, a four-hectare rhododendron dell, glasshouses, a playground and a cafe. Kids love tootling about on the Community Express 'train' (adult/child $3/1).

Baldwin St STREET
(Map p192) The world's steepest residential street (or so says the *Guinness Book of World Records*), Baldwin St has a gradient of 1 in 2.86 (19°). From the city centre, head 2km north up Great King St to where the road branches sharp left to Timaru. Get in the right-hand lane and continue straight ahead. This becomes North Rd, and Baldwin St is on the right after 1km.

🏃 Activities

Swimming & Surfing

St Clair and St Kilda are both popular swimming beaches (though you need to watch for rips at St Clair). Both have consistently good left-hand breaks, and you'll also find good surfing at Blackhead further south, and at Aramoana on Otago Harbour's North Shore.

Moana Pool SWIMMING
(Map p194; 60 Littlebourne Rd, Roslyn; adult/child $6/3; ⊙6am-10pm Mon-Fri, 7am-7pm Sat & Sun) This indoor pool complex has waterslides, wave machines, a spa and a gym.

St Clair Hot Salt Water Pool SWIMMING
(Map p192; Esplanade, St Clair; adult/child $5.70/2.60; ⊙7am-7pm Oct-Mar) This heated outdoor pool sits on the western headland of St Clair Beach.

Esplanade Surf School SURFING
(☎0800 484 141; www.espsurfschool.co.nz; 1½hr group lessons $60, private instruction $120) Operating from a van parked at St Clair Beach in summer (call at other times), this experienced crew provides equipment and lessons.

Walking & Cycling

The **Otago Tramping and Mountaineering Club** (www.otmc.co.nz) organises weekend day and overnight tramps, often to the Silver Peaks Reserve north of Dunedin. Nonmembers are welcome, but must contact trip leaders beforehand.

Tunnel Beach Walkway WALKING
(Tunnel Beach Rd, Blackhead) This short but extremely steep track (15 minutes down, 30 back up) accesses a dramatic stretch of coast where the wild Pacific has carved sea stacks, arches and unusual formations out of the limestone. It takes its name from a hand-hewn stone tunnel at the bottom of the track, which civic father John Cargill had built to give his family access to secluded beachside picnics. Strong currents make swimming here dangerous.

The track is 7km southwest of central Dunedin. Head south on Princes St and continue as it crosses under the motorway and then a railway bridge. Turn right at the next traffic lights onto Hillside Rd and follow it until the end, then make a quick left then right onto Easther Cres. Stay on this road for 3.5km (it changes name several times) and then look for Tunnel Beach Rd on the left.

Mt Cargill-Bethunes Gully Walkway WALKING
Yes, it's possible to drive up 676m Mt Cargill, but that's not the point. The track (3½ hours return) starts from Norwood St, which is accessed from North Rd. From Mt Cargill, a trail continues to the 10-million-year-old, lava-formed Organ Pipes and, after another

half hour, to Mt Cargill Rd on the other side of the mountain.

Cycle World BICYCLE RENTAL

(Map p194; ☑ 03-477 7473; www.cycleworld.co.nz; 67 Lower Stuart St; per day $40; ⊗ 8.30am-6pm Mon-Fri, 10am-3pm Sat & Sun) Rents out bikes, performs repairs and has mountain-biking information.

🕝 Tours

Tasty Tours TOUR

(☑ 03-453 1455; www.tastytours.co.nz; adult/child from $99/59) Tuck into local seafood, cheese, chocolate and beer on specialised foodie tours.

Back to Nature Tours BUS TOUR

(☑ 0800 286 000; www.backtonaturetours.co.nz) The full-day Royal Peninsula tour (adult/child $189/125) heads to points of interest around Dunedin before hitting the Otago Peninsula. Stops include Larnach Castle's gardens (castle entry is extra), a pub lunch, Penguin Place and the Royal Albatross Centre. There's also a half-day option which visits various bays and beaches (adult/child $79/55) and another tackling the Lovers Leap and Chasm tracks (adult/child $89/55). Tours depart from Port Chalmers, Dunedin i-SITE and centrally located accommodation.

First City Tours BUS TOUR

(adult/child $25/15; ⊗ buses depart the i-SITE 9am, 10.30am, 1pm & 2.30pm) Double-decker bus tours loop around the city, stopping at the Otago Museum, Speight's, Botanic Gardens and Baldwin St.

Walk Dunedin WALKING TOUR

(☑ 03-434 3300; www.toituosm.com; 2hr walk $30; ⊗ 10am) History-themed strolls around the city organised by the Settlers Museum. They depart from the i-SITE.

🛏 Sleeping

🛏 City Centre

Hogwartz HOSTEL $

(Map p194; ☑ 03-474 1487; www.hogwartz.co.nz; 77 Rattray St; dm $29, s $60, d with/without bathroom from $80/64, apt $110-165; @ 🛜) The Catholic bishop's residence from 1872 to 1999, this beautiful building is now a fascinating warren of comfortable and sunny rooms, many with harbour views. The old coach house and stables have recently been converted into swankier en suite rooms and apartments.

Chalet Backpackers HOSTEL $

(Map p194; ☑ 03-479 2075; www.chaletbackpackers.co.nz; 296 High St; dm/s/d $29/43/66; @ 🛜) The kitchen of this rambling old building is big, sunny and festooned with flowers, and there's also a compact garden, pool table, piano and rumours of a ghost. There are no en suite rooms but some have handbasins.

315 Euro MOTEL $$

(Map p194; ☑ 03-477 9929; www.eurodunedin.co.nz; 315 George St; d $160-200; P 🛜) This sleek complex is accessed by an unlikely-looking alley off Dunedin's main retail strip. Choose from modern studios or larger one-bedroom apartments with full kitchens. Double glazing keeps George St's irresistible buzz at bay.

Dunedin Palms Motel MOTEL $$

(Map p194; ☑ 03-477 8293; www.dunedinpalmsmotel.co.nz; 185-195 High St; units $155-250; P 🛜) A mercifully short stroll up from the city centre, the Palms has smartly renovated studio, one- and two-bedroom units arrayed around a central car park.

Fletcher Lodge B&B $$$

(Map p194; ☑ 03-477 5552; www.fletcherlodge.co.nz; 276 High St; s $295-500, d $335-595, apt $650-775; P @ 🛜) Originally home to one of NZ's wealthiest industrialists, this gorgeous red-brick mansion is just minutes from the city, but the secluded gardens feel wonderfully remote. Rooms are elegantly trimmed with antique furniture and ornate plaster ceilings.

Brothers Boutique Hotel HOTEL $$$

(Map p194; ☑ 03-477 0043; www.brothershotel.co.nz; 295 Rattray St; d $170-395; P 🛜) Rooms in this 1920s Christian Brothers residence have been refurbished beyond any monk's dreams, while still retaining many unique features. The chapel room ($320) includes the original arched stained-glass windows. There are great views from the rooftop units.

🛏 North Dunedin

Kiwi's Nest HOSTEL $

(Map p194; ☑ 03-471 9540; www.kiwisnest.co.nz; 597 George St; dm $28, s with/without bathroom $60/45, d $80/70, apt $95; @ 🛜) This wonderfully homely two-storey house has a range of tidy centrally heated rooms, some with en suites, fridges and kettles. Plus it's a flat walk to the Octagon – something few Dunedin hostels can boast.

858 George St
MOTEL **$$**

(Map p192; ☑03-474 0903; www.858george-streetmotel.co.nz; 858 George St; units $135-280; 🅿🛜) 🖉 Cleverly designed to blend harmoniously with the neighbourhood's two-storey Victorian houses, this top-quality motel complex has units ranging in size from studios to two bedrooms. Each has a terrace or small balcony.

Bluestone on George
APARTMENTS **$$$**

(Map p194; ☑03-477 9201; www.bluestonedunedin.co.nz; 571 George St; apt $190-235; 🅿🛜) If you're expecting an imposing old bluestone building, think again: this four-storey block couldn't be more contemporary. The elegant studio units are decked out in muted tones, with kitchenettes, laundry facilities and tiny balconies.

🛏 St Clair

Majestic Mansions
APARTMENTS **$$**

(Map p192; ☑03-456 5000; www.st-clair.co.nz; 15 Bedford St; apt $139-210; 🅿🛜) One street back from St Clair beach, this venerable 1920s apartment block has been thoroughly renovated, keeping the layout of the original little flats but sprucing them up with feature wallpaper and smart furnishings.

Hotel St Clair
HOTEL **$$$**

(Map p192; ☑03-456 0555; www.hotelstclair.com; 24 Esplanade; r $205-255, ste $370; 🅿🛜) Soak up St Clair's surfy vibe from the balcony of your chic room in this contemporary medium-rise hotel. All but the cheapest have ocean views, and the beach is only metres from the front door.

🛏 Other Suburbs

Leith Valley Touring Park
HOLIDAY PARK **$**

(Map p192; ☑03-467 9936; www.leithvalleytouringpark.co.nz; 103 Malvern St, Woodhaugh; sites $38, units with/without bathroom from $92/49; 🅿@🛜) 🖉 This holiday park is surrounded by native bush studded with walks, glow-worm caves and a small creek. Self-contained modern motel units are spacious, and tourist flats are smaller but have a more rustic feel (linen required).

Roslyn Apartments
APARTMENTS **$$**

(Map p192; ☑03-477 6777; www.roslynapartments.co.nz; 23 City Rd, Roslyn; 1-/2-bedroom apt $195/330; 🅿🛜) Modern decor and brilliant city and harbour views are on tap at these apartments, just a short walk from Roslyn's

eating strip. Leather furniture and designe kitchens add a touch of class.

Arden Street House
B&B **$**

(Map p192; ☑03-473 8860; www.ardenstreethouse.co.nz; 36 Arden St, North East Valley; s $75, d with/without bathroom $130/120; 🅿@🛜) With crazy artworks, an organic garden, charming hosts and a porthole in the bathroom, this 1930s hilltop house makes a wonderfully eccentric base. To get here from the city, drive up North Rd, turn right into Glendining Av and then left into Arden St.

🍴 Eating

Inexpensive Asian restaurants are clustered along George St; most do takeaways. Uphill from the Octagon, Roslyn has good restaurants and cafes, and the beachy ambience of St Clair is great for a lazy brunch.

🍴 City Centre

★ Otago Farmers Market
MARKET

(Map p194; www.otagofarmersmarket.org.nz; Dunedin Railway Station; ⊙8am-12.30pm Sat) This thriving market is all local, all edible (or drinkable) and mostly organic. Grab falafel or espresso to sustain you while you browse and stock up on fresh meats, seafood, veggies and cheese for your journey. Also pick up some locally brewed Green Man organic beer. Sorted.

The Good Oil
CAFE

(Map p194; 314 George St; mains $9-17; ⊙7.30am-4pm) This sleek little cafe is Dunedin's top spot for coffee and cake. If you're still waking up, kick-start the day with imaginative brunches such as kumara hash with hot smoked salmon.

Circadian Rhythm
VEGAN, VEGETARIAN

(Map p194; www.circadianrhythm.co.nz; 72 St Andrew St; mains $9-13; ⊙11am-9pm Mon-Sat; 🖉) Specialising in organic curries, felafels and stir-fries, this meat-free cafe is also a music venue, with jazz on Friday nights from 5.30pm. Dunedin's Emerson's and Green Man beers are both available, so you don't have to be *too* healthy.

Best Cafe
FISH & CHIPS

(Map p194; www.facebook.com/bestcafedunedin; 30 Stuart St; takeaways $6-10, mains $10-23; ⊙11am-2.30pm & 5-8pm Mon-Sat) Serving up fish and chips since 1932, this local stalwart has its winning formula down pat, complete with vinyl tablecloths, hand-cut chips and curls of butter on white bread. If there are a few of you, try the 'Old School' platter ($43).

Velvet Burger   BURGERS **$**
(Map p194; www.velvetburger.co.nz; 150 Stuart St; mains $9-16; ☺11.30am-late) Well positioned for the postbeer crowd, Velvet Burger's gourmet offerings are an excellent alcohol sop, especially the mammoth Goneburger (beef, chicken *and* bacon). There's another VB (Map p194) at 375 George St (same hours).

Modaks Espresso   CAFE, BAR **$**
(Map p194; 337-339 George St; mains $9-16; ☺7.30am-4pm; ☒) This funky little place with brick walls, mismatched Formica tables and couches for slouching is popular with students and those who appreciate chilled-out reggae while they nurse a pot of tea. Plump toasted bagels warm the insides in winter.

Saigon Van   VIETNAMESE **$**
(Map p194; 66 St Andrew St; mains $9-19; ☺11.30am-2pm & 5-9pm Tue-Sun) The decor looks high-end Asian, but the food is definitely budget-friendly. Try the combination spring rolls and a bottle of Vietnamese beer to re-create lazy nights in Saigon. The bean-sprout-laden *pho* (noodle soup) and salads are also good.

Etrusco at the Savoy   ITALIAN **$$**
(Map p194; ☎03-477 3737; www.etrusco.co.nz; 8a Moray Pl; mains $17-21; ☺5.30pm-late) NZ has very few dining rooms to match the Edwardian elegance of the Savoy, with its moulded ceilings, stained-glass crests, brass chandeliers, green Ionian columns and fabulously over-the-top lamps. Pizza and pasta might seem like an odd fit, but Etrusco's deliciously rustic dishes absolutely hold their own.

Nova Cafe   CAFE **$$**
(Map p194; ☎03-479 0808; www.novadunedin.co.nz; 29 The Octagon; breakfast $15-18, lunch $18-24, dinner $18-34; ☺7am-11pm Mon-Fri, 8.30am-10pm Sat & Sun) Not surprisingly, this extension of the art gallery has a stylish look about it. Start the day with the interesting breakfast selections, dabble in some Asian flavours for lunch, then finish the day with bistro-style grills and a glass of wine.

Miga   KOREAN **$$**
(Map p194; ☎03-477 4770; www.migadunedin.co.nz; 4 Hanover St; mains $16-39; ☺11am-2pm & 5-10pm Mon-Sat) Settle into a booth at this attractive brick-lined eatery, and order claypot rice or noodle dishes from the extensive menu. Otherwise go for broke and cook a Korean barbecue right at your table.

Scotia   MODERN SCOTTISH **$$**
(Map p194; ☎03-477 7704; www.scotiadunedin.co.nz; 199 Stuart St; mains $18-32; ☺4pm-late Tue-Sun) Occupying a cosy heritage townhouse, Scotia toasts all things Scottish with a wall full of single-malt whisky and hearty fare such as smoked salmon and Otago hare. The two Scottish Robbies – Burns and Coltrane – look down approvingly on a menu that also includes haggis and whisky-laced pâté.

Paasha   TURKISH **$$**
(Map p194; www.paasha.co.nz; 32 St Andrew St; lunch $12-20, dinner $21-34) Authentic Turkish kebabs, dips and salads are faithfully created at this long-running Dunedin favourite. It's a top place for takeaways, and most nights the spacious and warm interior is filled with groups drinking Efes beer and sharing heaving platters of tasty Ottoman goodness.

Izakaya Yuki   JAPANESE, BAR **$$**
(Map p194; 29 Bath St; dishes $5-10; ☺noon-2pm Mon-Fri, 5pm-2.30am daily; ☎☒) Cute and cosy, with a huge array of small dishes on which to graze, Yuki is a lovely spot for supper or a relaxed, drawn-out Japanese meal. Make a night of it with sake or Asahi beer, sushi and sashimi, and multiple plates of *kushiyaki* (grilled skewers).

JUST GIVE ME THE COFFEE & NO ONE WILL GET HURT

Dunedin has some excellent coffee bars in which you can refuel and recharge.

Fix (Map p194; 15 Frederick St; ☺Mon-Sat) Wage slaves queue at the pavement window every morning, while students and others with time on their hands relax in the courtyard. Fix doesn't serve food, but you can bring along your own.

Mazagran Espresso Bar (Map p194; 36 Moray Pl; ☺8am-6pm Mon-Fri, 10am-2pm Sat) The godfather of Dunedin's coffee scene, this compact wood-and-brick coffee house is the source of the magic bean for many of the city's restaurants and cafes.

Strictly Coffee (Map p194; www.strictlycoffee.co.nz; 23 Bath St; ☺7.30am-4pm Mon-Fri) Stylish retro coffee bar hidden down grungy Bath St. Different rooms provide varying views and artworks to enjoy while you sip and sup.

Plato
MODERN NZ $$$

(Map p194; ☎ 03-477 4235; www.platocafe.co.nz; 2 Birch St; brunch $16-22, dinner $32-33; ⊙ 11am-2pm Sun, 6pm-late daily) The kooky decor (including collections of toys and beer tankards) gives little indication of the seriously good food on offer at this relaxed eatery by the harbour. Seafood features prominently in a menu full of international flavours.

Two Chefs Bistro
FRENCH $$$

(Map p194; www.twochefsbistro.com; 121 Stuart St; mains $34-37; ⊙ noon-3pm Fri, 6-10pm daily) French bistro dishes flirt with Asian and North African flavours on the plate, while high ceilings and dark wood conjure up a romantic ambience. The service is the opposite of French stereotypes: delightful but not always efficient. Save room for dessert.

North Dunedin

Everyday Gourmet
CAFE, DELI $

(Map p194; www.everydaygourmet.net.nz; 466 George St; mains $7-16; ⊙ 8am-5pm) Apart from cooked breakfasts, most of the goodies beckon from the counter of this excellent bakery-style cafe and deli. It's light, bright and extremely popular, with a good selection of magazines and newspapers.

Governor's
CAFE $$

(Map p194; 438 George St; mains $10-19; ⊙ 7am-4pm) Popular with students, Governor's does a nice line in early-morning pancakes and other light meals. If you're feeling a little off the pace after the previous night, a strong coffee and a mixed grill are just what the doctor ordered.

Other Suburbs

No 7 Balmac
CAFE $$

(Map p192; ☎ 03-464 0064; www.no7balmac.co.nz; 7 Balmacewen Rd, Maori Hill; brunch $15-25, dinner $28-37; ⊙ 7am-late Mon-Fri, 8.30am-late Sat, 8.30am-5pm Sun) We wouldn't recommend walking to this sophisticated cafe at the top of Maori Hill; luckily it's well worth the price of a cab. The fancy fare stretches to the likes of venison pie and dry-aged beef. If you're on a diet, avoid eye contact with the sweets cabinet.

Starfish
CAFE, BAR $$

(Map p192; ☎ 03-455 5940; www.starfishcafe.co.nz; 7/240 Forbury Rd, St Clair; brunch $14-20, dinner $20-30; ⊙ 7am-5pm Sun-Tue, to late Wed-Sat) Starfish is the coolest creature in the growing restaurant scene at St Clair Beach. Pop out on a weekday to score an outside table, and tuck into gourmet pizza and wine. Dinner is a more sophisticated beast.

Luna
MODERN NZ $$$

(Map p192; ☎ 03-477 2227; www.lunaroslyn.co.nz; 314 Highgate, Roslyn; lunch $14-25, dinner $34-37; ⊙ noon-late) Make the trek to Roslyn for an inventive menu and outstanding harbour views in this glass-encased hilltop pavilion; ask for a window seat when you book. A more relaxed option is a drink in the classy bar, accompanied by selections from the 'Luna Bites' menu.

🍷 Drinking & Nightlife

Mou Very
BAR

(Map p194; www.facebook.com/MouVeryBar; 357 George St; ⊙ 7am-12.30pm) Welcome to one of the world's smallest bars – it's only 1.8m wide, but is still big enough to host regular DJs, live bands and poetry readings. There are just six bar stools, so patrons spill out into an adjacent laneway. By day, it's a handy caffeine-refuelling spot.

Albar
BAR

(Map p194; 135 Stuart St; ⊙ 11am-late) This former butcher is now a bohemian little bar attracting maybe the widest age range in Dunedin. Most punters are drawn by the many single-malt whiskies, interesting tap beers and cheap-as-chips bar snacks ($6 to $9).

Di Lusso
COCKTAIL BAR

(Map p194; www.dilusso.co.nz; 117 Stuart St; ⊙ 4pm-3am Mon-Sat) Upmarket and designery with wood panelling, chandeliers and a backlit drinks display, Di Lusso serves seriously good cocktails. DJs play from Thursday to Saturday.

Carousel
COCKTAIL BAR

(Map p194; www.carouselbar.co.nz; upstairs 141 Stuart St; ⊙ 5pm-late Tue-Sat) Tartan wallpaper, a roof deck and great cocktails leave the dressed-up clientele looking pleased to be seen somewhere so deadly cool. DJs spin deep house until late on the weekends, and there's live jazz on Friday evenings.

Stuart St Mac's Brewbar
BAR

(Map p194; www.stuartst.co.nz; 12 The Octagon; ⊙ 10am-late) Nelson's Mac's brewery is making a strike deep into Speights' territory in the form of this funky bar right on the Octagon. It's the sunniest spot for an afternoon drink, and after the sun sets there's often live music.

Speight's Ale House PUB
(Map p194; www.thealehouse.co.nz; 200 Rattray St; ☺11.30am-late) Busy even in the nonuniversity months, the Ale House is a favourite of strapping young lads in their cleanest dirty shirts. It's a good spot to watch the rugby on TV and to try the full range of Speight's beers.

Pequeno COCKTAIL BAR
(Map p194; www.pequeno.co.nz; behind 12 Moray Pl; ☺5pm-late Mon-Fri, 7pm-late Sat & Sun) Down the alleyway opposite the Rialto cinema, Pequeno attracts a sophisticated crowd with leather couches, a cosy fireplace and an excellent wine and tapas menu. Music is generally laid-back and there's live jazz on Fridays.

Tonic BAR
(Map p194; www.tonicbar.co.nz; 138 Princes St; ☺4pm-late Tue-Fri, 6pm-late Sat) Limited-release Kiwi craft beers, single-malt whiskies and good cocktails appeal to a different crowd than Dunedin's numerous student pubs. Antipasto plates, cheeseboards and pizza are good reasons to stay for another drink.

Urban Factory CLUB
(Map p194; www.urbanfactory.co.nz; 101 Great King St; ☺10pm-3am) The hippest of NZ's touring bands, regular DJ sessions and carefully crafted cocktails.

Pop CLUB
(Map p194; downstairs, 14 The Octagon; ☺10pm-late Wed-Sat) Pop serves Dunedin's best martinis and prides itself on seriously good DJs playing funk and house.

☆ **Entertainment**

Metro Cinema CINEMA
(Map p194; ☎03-471 9635; www.metrocinema.co.nz; Moray Pl; adult/student $13/12) Within the town hall, Metro shows art-house and foreign flicks.

Rialto Cinemas CINEMA
(Map p194; ☎03-474 2200; www.rialto.co.nz; 11 Moray Pl; adult/child $16/10) Blockbusters and art-house flicks. Rates often cheaper on Tuesdays.

Fortune Theatre THEATRE
(Map p194; ☎03-477 8323; www.fortunetheatre.co.nz; 231 Stuart St) The world's southernmost professional theatre company has been staging dramas, comedies, pantomimes, classics and contemporary NZ productions for almost 40 years. Shows are performed – watched over by the obligatory theatre ghost – in a Gothic-style old Wesleyan church.

Sammy's LIVE MUSIC
(Map p194; 65 Crawford St) Dunedin's premier live-music venue draws an eclectic mix of genres from noisy-as-hell punk to chilled reggae and gritty dubstep. It's the venue of choice for visiting Kiwi bands and up-and-coming international acts.

Forsyth Barr Stadium STADIUM
(Map p192; www.forsythbarrstadium.co.nz; 130 Anzac Ave) Constructed for the 2011 Rugby World Cup, this is the only major stadium in NZ with a fully covered roof. It's the home ground for the Highlanders Super 15 rugby team (www.thehighlanders.co.nz) and the Otago rugby team (www.orfu.co.nz).

🛍 **Shopping**

George St is Dunedin's main shopping strip.

Gallery De Novo ARTS & CRAFTS
(Map p194; www.gallerydenovo.co.nz; 91 Stuart St; ☺9.30am-5.30pm Mon-Fri, 10am-3pm Sat & Sun) This interesting, contemporary fine-art gallery is worth a look, whether you're likely to invest in a substantial piece of Kiwi art or not.

Stuart St Potters Cooperative ARTS & CRAFTS
(Map p194; 14 Stuart St; ☺10am-5pm Mon-Fri, 9am-3pm Sat) Locally designed and made pottery and ceramic art.

Bivouac Outdoor OUTDOOR EQUIPMENT
(Map p194; www.bivouac.co.nz; 171 George St; ☺9am-5.30pm Mon-Fri, 10am-4pm Sat & Sun) Clothing, footwear and rugged gear.

University Book Shop BOOKS
(Map p194; www.unibooks.co.nz; 378 Great King St; ☺8.30am-5.30pm Mon-Fri, 11am-3pm Sat & Sun) Dunedin's best bookshop, with lots of Maori, Pacific and NZ titles.

ℹ **Information**

MEDICAL SERVICES

Dunedin Hospital (☎03-474 0999, emergency department 0800 611 116; www.southerndhb.govt.nz; 201 Great King St)

Urgent Doctors & Accident Centre (☎03-479 2900; www.dunedinurgentdoctors.com; 95 Hanover St; ☺8am-11.30pm) There's also a late-night pharmacy next door.

TOURIST INFORMATION

DOC Visitor Centre (Department of Conservation; Map p194; ☎03-477 0677; www.doc.govt.nz; 1st fl, 77 Stuart St; ☺8.30am-5pm Mon-Fri) Information and maps on regional walking tracks, Great Walks bookings and hut tickets.

Dunedin i-SITE (Map p194; ☑03-474 3300; www.isitedunedin.co.nz; 26 Princes St; ⊙8.30am-5pm)

Getting There & Away

AIR

For information on international flights, see p335. Domestic options include the following:

Air New Zealand (☑0800 737 000; www.airnewzealand.co.nz) Flies to/from Auckland, Wellington and Christchurch.

Jetstar (☑0800 800 995; www.jetstar.com) Flies to/from Auckland.

BUS

Buses and shuttles leave from the Dunedin Railway Station, except where we've noted otherwise.

Alpine Connexions (☑03-443 9120; www.alpineconnexions.co.nz) Shuttles head to/from Alexandra ($40), Clyde ($40), Cromwell ($45), Queenstown ($45) and Wanaka ($45), as well as key stops on the Otago Central Rail Trail.

Atomic Shuttles (☑03-349 0697; www.atomictravel.co.nz) To/from Christchurch (from $30, 5¾ hours), Oamaru ($20, 1¾ hours), Cromwell ($30, 3¾ hours), Wanaka ($35, 4½ hours) and Invercargill ($37, 3¼ hours).

Catch-a-Bus (☑03-449-2024; www.catcha-bus.co.nz) Door-to-door shuttle between Dunedin and Cromwell stopping at Otago Central Rail Trail towns along the way. Bikes can be transported.

Coast Line Tours (☑03-434 7744; www.coastline-tours.co.nz) Shuttles to Oamaru ($30) depart from the Octagon; detours to Dunedin airport and Moeraki can be arranged.

InterCity (Map p192; ☑03-471 7143; www.intercity.co.nz; 7 Halsey St) Coaches to/from Christchurch (from $40, six hours) and Oamaru (from $14, 40 minutes) twice daily, and Cromwell (from $20, 3¼ hours), Queenstown (from $22, 4¼ hours) and Te Anau (from $37, 4½ hours) daily.

Knightrider (☑03-342 8055; www.knightrider.co.nz) Has a bus most nights to/from Christchurch ($50, six hours), Christchurch Airport ($55, 5½ hours), Timaru ($44, 3¼ hours), Moeraki ($33, 1¼ hours) and Oamaru ($33, two hours).

TRAIN

Two interesting train journeys start at Dunedin's railway station (p193): the Taieri Gorge Railway (p196) and the **Seasider** (www.seasider.co.nz; 1-way/return $59/89). The latter journeys up the coast to Palmerston and back.

Getting Around

TO & FROM THE AIRPORT

Dunedin Airport (DUD; ☑03-486 2879; www.flydunedin.com; Airport Rd, Momona) is 27km southwest of the city. A standard taxi ride between the city and the airport costs $80 to $90. There is no public bus service. For door-to-door shuttles, try **Kiwi Shuttles** (☑03-487 9790; www.kiwishuttles.co.nz; per 1/2/3/4 passengers $20/36/48/60) or **Super Shuttle** (☑0800 748 885; www.supershuttle.co.nz; per 1/2/3/4 passengers $25/35/45/55).

BUS

Dunedin's **GoBus** (☑03-474 0287; www.orc.govt.nz; adult fare $2-6.70) network extends across the city. It's particularly handy for getting to St Clair, St Kilda, Port Chalmers and as far afield as Portobello on the Otago Peninsula. Buses run regularly during the week, but services are greatly reduced (or nonexistent) on weekends and holidays.

CAR

The big rental companies all have offices in Dunedin, and inexpensive local outfits include **Get Away** (☑03-489 7614; www.getawaycarhire.co.nz) and **Driven Rentals** (☑03-453 6576; www.drivenrentals.co.nz).

TAXI

Dunedin Taxis (☑03-477 7777; www.dunedin-taxis.co.nz)

Otago Taxis (☑03-477 3333)

AROUND DUNEDIN

Port Chalmers & Around

POP 1370

Little Port Chalmers is only 13km out of Dunedin but it feels a world away. Somewhere between working class and bohemian, Port Chalmers has a history as a port town but has increasingly attracted Dunedin's arty types. Dunedin's best rock-and-roll pub, **Chick's Hotel** (Map p192; 2 Mount St; ⊙4pm-1am Wed-Sun) is an essential after-dark destination, and daytime attractions include a few raffish cafes, design stores and galleries.

◉ Sights & Activities

Traditional rock climbing (nonbolted) is popular at Long Beach and the cliffs at Mihiwaka, both accessed via Blueskin Rd north of Port Chalmers.

🛏 Sleeping

Peter's Farm Lodge   LODGE $

(☑ 03-444 9811; www.petersfarm.co.nz; 113 Tregonning Rd, Waipiata; per person $55) Set on a sheep farm 13km south of Ranfurly, this rustic 1882 farmhouse offers comfy beds, hearty barbecue dinners ($25) and free pick-ups from the rail trail. Kayaks, fishing rods and gold pans are all available, so it's worth staying a couple of nights. Further beds are available in neighbouring Tregonnings Cottage (1882).

Hawkdun Lodge   MOTEL $$

(☑ 03-444 9750; www.hawkdunlodge.co.nz; 1 Bute St; s/d from $125/175; 🖥) 🖋 This smart new boutique motel is the best option in the town centre by far. Each unit has a kitchenette with a microwave, but travelling chefs can flex their skills in the guest kitchen and on the barbecue. Rates include a continental breakfast.

Kokonga Lodge   B&B $$$

(☑ 03-444 9774; www.kokongalodge.co.nz; 33 Kokonga-Waipiata Rd; r $285; @🖥) 🖋 Just off SH87 between Ranfurly and Hyde, this upmarket rural property offers six contemporary en suite rooms, one of which housed Sir Peter Jackson when he was filming *The Hobbit* in the area. The Rail Trail passes nearby.

ℹ Getting There & Away

Trail Journey's **Catch-a-Bus** (☑ 03-449 2024; www.catchabus.co.nz) shuttle passes through Ranfurly on its way between Cromwell and Dunedin.

Naseby

POP 120

Cute as a button, surrounded by forest and dotted with 19th-century stone buildings, Naseby is the kind of small town where life moves slowly. That the town is pleasantly obsessed with the fairly insignificant world of NZ curling indicates there's not much else going on. It's that lazy small-town vibe, along with good mountain-biking and walking trails through the surrounding forest, that make Naseby an interesting place to stay for a couple of days.

🏃 Activities

Maniototo Curling International   CURLING

(☑ 03-444 9878; www.curling.co.nz; 1057 Channel Rd; per 1½hr adult/family $30/80; ☺10am-5pm) All year round you can shimmy after curling stones at the indoor ice rink; tuition is available. In winter there's also an outdoor ice rink to skate around.

Naseby Ice Luge   SNOW SPORTS

(☑ 03-444 9270; www.lugenz.com; 1057 Channel Rd; adult/child $30/25; ☺Jun-Aug) Hurtle 360m down a hillside on a wooden sled. Bookings are recommended.

🛏 Sleeping & Eating

Royal Hotel   PUB $

(☑ 03-444 9990; www.naseby.co.nz; 1 Earne St; dm $40, r with/without bathroom $100/70; 🖥) The better of the town's historic pubs, the 1863 Royal Hotel sports the royal coat of arms and what just might be NZ's most rustic garden bar. Rooms are simple but spotless, and the meals are good too (mains $25 to $30).

Naseby Lodge   APARTMENTS $$

(☑ 03-444 8222; www.nasebylodge.co.nz; cnr Derwent & Oughter Sts; 1-/2-bedroom apt $170/260; 🖥) Constructed of environmentally friendly straw-bale walls sheathed in rustic corrugated iron, these free-standing modern apartments are smart and spacious, with fully equipped kitchens and underfloor heating in the bathrooms. There's also a good restaurant on site.

Old Doctor's Residence   B&B $$$

(☑ 03-444 9775; www.olddoctorsresidence.co.nz; 58 Derwent St; r/ste $275/325; 🖥) 🖋 Old doctors take note: this is how to reside! Sitting behind a pretty garden, this gorgeous 1870s house offers two luxurious guest rooms and a lounge where wine and nibbles are served of an evening. The suite has a sitting room and an en suite bathroom (with a fabulous make-up desk). The smaller room's bathroom is accessed from the corridor.

Black Forest Café   CAFE $

(☑ 03-444 9820; 7 Derwent St; mains $10-17; ☺9am-4pm) Fresh baking and good coffee feature at this cafe. Inside, stone walls, bright colours and warm polished wood create a pleasant ambience. The wide-ranging menu includes bagels, panini and creamy smoothies made from Central Otago fruit.

ℹ Information

Ernslaw One Forestry Office (☑ 03-444 9995; www.ernslaw.co.nz/naseby-recreational-area; 34 Derwent St) Administers the 500-hectare recreation reserve within the privately owned

Naseby Forest. Call in for maps of walking tracks and mountain bike trails.

Naseby Information & Crafts (☏03-444 9961; Derwent St; ☺11am-2pm Sun, Mon & Fri, to 4pm Sat)

❶ Getting There & Away

The Ranfurly–Naseby Rd leaves SH85 4km north of Ranfurly. There's no public transport and cyclists should factor in a 12km detour from the Rail Trail. From Naseby, you can wind your way on unsealed roads northeast through spectacular scenery to Danseys Pass and through to Duntroon in the Waitaki Valley.

St Bathans

A worthwhile 17km detour north from SH85 heads into the foothills of the imposing Dunstan Mountains and on to diminutive St Bathans. This once-thriving gold-mining town of 2000 people is now home to only half a dozen permanent residents living amid a cluster of cutesy 19th-century buildings.

The **Blue Lake** is an accidental attraction: a large hollow filled with amazingly blue water that has run off abandoned gold workings. Walk along the sculpted cliffs to the lookout for a better view of the alien landscape (one hour return).

The **Vulcan Hotel** (☏03-447 3629; stbathans.vulcanhotel@xtra.co.nz; Loop Rd; r per person $60) is an atmospheric (and famously haunted) spot to drink, eat or stay in. Considering St Bathans' tiny population, you'll find the bar here pretty busy on a Friday night as thirsty shearers from around the valley descend en masse. Further accommodation is available at the nearby **St Bathans Jail & Constable's Cottage** (☏0800 555 016; www.stbathansnz.co.nz; $145-340).

Lauder, Omakau & Ophir

Separated by 8km of SH85, tiny **Lauder** and larger **Omakau** (population 250) are good stops if you're a hungry Rail-Trailer with a sore bum and in need of a feed and a bed. However, the area's real gem is adorable **Ophir** (population 50), 2km from Omakau across the Manuherikia River.

Gold was discovered here in 1863 and the town swiftly formed, adopting the name of the biblical place where King Solomon sourced his gold. By 1875, the population hit over 1000 but when the gold disappeared, so did the people. Ophir's fate was sealed when

the railway bypassed it in 1904, leaving its main street trapped in time.

The most photogenic of its many heritage buildings is the still-functioning 1886 **post office** (www.historic.org.nz; Swindon St; ☺9am-noon Mon-Fri). At the far end of the town, the sealed road ends at the 1870s wooden-planked **Dan O'Connell Bridge**, a bumpy but scenic crossing which continues via a gravel road to SH85.

Ophir lays claim to the country's largest range of temperatures: from −21.6°C to 35°C (Alexandra, just up the road, once recorded a temperature of 38°C).

🛏 Sleeping & Eating

Muddy Creek Cutting B&B $$
(☏03-447 3682; www.muddycreekcutting.co.nz; SH85, Lauder; per person $80) Art fills the walls of this charmingly restored 1930s mudbrick farmhouse, with five bedrooms that share two bathrooms. Dinners with a local, organic spin are also available ($55 per person).

Omakau Commercial Hotel PUB $$
(☏03-447 3715; www.omakauhotel.co.nz; 1 Harvey St, Omakau; s with/without bathroom from $79/55, d from 109/105; 🖥) There's an old-fashioned ambience to this venerable pub, where good-value rooms, excellent food and local company are all on tap. The bedrooms don't have televisions or kettles, but these are available in the guest lounge downstairs.

Chatto Creek Tavern HOTEL $$
(☏03-447 3710; www.chattocreektavern.co.nz; 1544 SH85, Chatto Creek; dm/s/d without bathroom $50/90/120) Dating from 1886, this attractive stone hotel sits right beside the Rail Trail and highway, 10km southwest of Omakau. Pop in for a whitebait fritter (in season) or steak sandwich, or rest your weary calf muscles in a dorm bed or double room. Rates include breakfast.

★**Pitches Store** B&B, RESTAURANT $$$
(☏03-447 3240; www.pitches-store.co.nz; 45 Swindon St, Ophir; r $250, brunch $9-19, dinner $33-35; ☺restaurant 10am-late daily Nov-May, 11am-late Fri-Mon Jun-Oct) Formerly a general store and butcher, this heritage building has been sensitively transformed into six elegant guest rooms and a humdinger of a restaurant. Exposed-stone walls may speak of the past but the menu is stridently contemporary.

Stationside Cafe CAFE $
(Lauder-Matakanui Rd, Lauder; mains $8-18; ☺7am-5pm Oct-Apr) Home baking and coun-

ry cooking are showcased at this great little railside place. Options include healthy salads, sandwiches, soups and pasta.

Muddy Creek Cafe CAFE $
2 Harvey St, Omakau; mains $8-16; ⊗8.30am-7pm Mon-Sat, 10am-7pm Sun) Take a break from the Rail Trail at this friendly spot festooned with old radios. Cafe treats include all-day breakfasts, pasta, pies and ice cream, or you can grab a burger or fish and chips from the takeaway counter.

Alexandra

POP 4800

Unless you've come especially for the Easter Bunny Hunt or September's NZ Merino Shearing Championships, the main reason to visit unassuming Alexandra is mountain biking. It's the biggest Rail Trail settlement by far, offering more eating and sleeping options than the rest of the one-horse (or fewer) towns on the route. It's also the start of the brand-new Roxburgh Gorge Trail.

Alex, as it's known to the locals, marks the southeastern corner of the acclaimed Central Otago wine region. Of the dozen wineries in the immediate vicinity, only a handful are open for tastings. These are detailed on the *Central Otago Wine Map*, available from the i-SITE (p210).

⊙ Sights & Activities

Walkers and mountain bikers will love the old gold trails weaving through the hills; collect maps from the i-SITE. The **Alexandra–Clyde 150th Anniversary Walk** (12.8km, three hours one way) is a riverside trail that's fairly flat with ample resting spots and shade.

Central Stories MUSEUM
(www.centralstories.com; 21 Centennial Ave; admission by donation; ⊗10am-4pm) Central Otago's history of gold-mining, winemaking, orcharding and sheep farming is covered in this excellent regional museum which shares a building with the i-SITE.

Roxburgh Gorge Trail MOUNTAIN BIKING
(www.roxburghgorge.co.nz) Opened to considerable fanfare in 2013, this well-constructed cycling and walking track was intended to connect Alexandra to Roxburgh Dam. As access through some of the farmland in the middle section wasn't successfully negotiated, riding the 'full trail' requires prearranging a 13km ferry trip ($95) through

the local information centres. Once you add on the noncompulsory track-maintenance fee ($25), it makes it a very expensive trail indeed. An alternative is to make a return trip from each end: Alexandra–Doctors Point (20km return) or Roxburgh Dam–Shingle Peak (22km return). Note, parts of the trail are rated Grade III and are not recommended for those under 15 years.

From Roxburgh Dam you can continue on the **Clutha Gold Trail** (www.cluthagold.co.nz), an easier 73km track which follows the Clutha through Roxburgh to Beaumont and then heads to Lawrence. The same maintenance fee covers both tracks.

Altitude Bikes BICYCLE RENTAL
(☑03-448 8917; www.altitudeadventures.co.nz; 88 Centennial Ave; per day from $25) Rents bikes and organises logistics for riders on the Otago Central, Clutha Gold and Roxburgh Gorge trails.

Clutha River Cruises BOAT TOUR
(☑03-449 3173; www.clutharivercruises.co.nz; adult/child $90/45; ⊗11am & 2pm Oct-May) Explore the scenery and history of the region on a 2½-hour boat trip; book at the i-SITE.

🛏 Sleeping

Marj's Place HOSTEL $
(☑03-448 7098; www.marjsplace.co.nz; 5 Theyers St; dm $25-30, s/d $40/70; @🖥) The standard varies widely between the three neighbouring houses that comprise Marj's sprawling 'place'. The 'homestay' has private rooms, a Finnish sauna and a spa bath. It's much nicer, not to mention cleaner, than the 'backpackers', which is let mainly to seasonal workers.

Quail Rock B&B $$
(☑03-448 7224; www.quailrock.co.nz; 5 Fairway Dr; s/d from $100/150) Perched high above town, this very comfortable B&B offers equal servings of privacy and mountain views. Homemade preserves give breakfast a unique touch, and dinners are also available. And yes, quail are often seen scratching around the rocks in the garden.

🍴 Eating

Tin Goose Cafe CAFE $
(www.thetingoosecafe.com; 22 Centennial Ave; $8-16; ⊗6am-5pm) Start the day with a cooked breakfast and then return for home-style baking and superior counter food, including interesting salads.

WORTH A TRIP

ROXBURGH

Heading south from Alexandra, SH8 winds along rugged, rock-strewn hills above the Clutha River as it passes Central Otago's famous orchards. In season, roadside fruit stalls sell just-picked stone fruit, cherries and berries. En route are a scattering of small towns, many dating from gold-rush days.

Thirteen kilometres south of Alexandra, **Speargrass Inn** (✆ 03-449 2192; www.speargrassinn.co.nz; 1300 Fruitlands-Roxburgh Rd (SH8), Fruitlands; d $180; ☜) has three units in attractive gardens. The original 1869 building houses a charming **cafe** (lunch $18-21, dinner $20-31; ⊙ 9am-4pm Mon & Thu, 9am-7pm Fri-Sun). It's a good place to stop for coffee and cake, and stock up on tasty homemade preserves and chutneys.

Further south, the Clutha broadens into **Lake Roxburgh**, with a large hydroelectric power station at its terminus, before rushing past Roxburgh itself (population 522). Call into the friendly **Visitor Information Centre** (✆ 03-446 8920; www.centralotagonz.com; 120 Scotland St; ⊙ 9am-5pm daily Nov-Mar, Mon-Fri Apr-Oct) for information on mountain biking, water sports and seasonal fruit-picking work in the surrounding apple and stone-fruit orchards.

Another source of fruit-picking contacts is **Villa Rose Backpackers** (✆ 03-446 8761; www.villarose.co.nz; 79 Scotland St; dm $30, d with/without bathroom $105/80; ☜). This lovely old bungalow has spacious dorm rooms, comfortable self-contained units and a huge modern kitchen.

Before you leave Roxburgh, drop into **Jimmy's Pies** (✆ 03-444-8596; 143 Scotland St; pies $4-6; ⊙ 7.30am-5pm Mon-Fri), renowned across the South Island since 1959. If you're at a loss as to which meaty pastry to choose, try the apricot chicken – you're in orchard country after all.

Continuing south from Roxburgh, the road passes through Lawrence and the Manuka Gorge Scenic Reserve, a scenic route through wooded hills and gullies. SH8 joins SH1 near Milton.

Red Brick　　　　　　　　EUROPEAN $$$
(✆ 03-448 9174; www.redbrickrestaurant.co.nz; off Limerick St; dinner $32-33; ⊙ 4.30pm-late Tue-Sun) Housed in what was Alexandra's first bakery, Red Brick is positioned beside a shoppers' car park, the last place you'd expect to find such sophisticated Modern European cooking. Most ingredients and wines are locally sourced.

ⓘ Information

Alexandra i-SITE (✆ 03-448 9515; www.centralotagonz.com; 21 Centennial Ave; ⊙ 9am-5pm; ☜) Pick up a free map of this very spread-out town.

ⓘ Getting There & Away

Atomic Shuttles (✆ 03-349 0697; www.atomictravel.co.nz) A daily bus heads to/from Dunedin ($30, 2¼ hours), Roxburgh ($15, 30 minutes), Cromwell ($15, 50 minutes) and Wanaka ($20, 1¾ hours).

Alpine Connexions (✆ 03-443 9120; www.alpineconnexions.co.nz) Shuttles head to/from Dunedin ($40), Clyde ($15), Cromwell ($24), Queenstown ($35) and Wanaka ($35), as well as key stops on the Otago Central Rail Trail.

InterCity (✆ 03-471 7143; www.intercity.co.nz) A daily coach heads to/from Dunedin (from $21, three hours), Roxburgh (from $14, 34 minutes), Clyde (from $15, nine minutes), Cromwell (from $18, 24 minutes) and Queenstown (from $22, 1½ hours).

Clyde

POP 1020

Much more charming than his buddy Alex 8km down the road, Clyde looks more like a 19th-century gold-rush film set than a real town. Set on the banks of the emerald-green Clutha River, **Clyde** (www.clyde.co.nz) retains a friendly, small-town feel, even when holidaymakers arrive in numbers over summer. It's also one end of the Otago Central Rail Trail (see p206).

◉ Sights & Activities

Clyde Historical Museums　　　　MUSEUM
(5 Blyth St; admission by donation; ⊙ 2-4pm Tue-Sun Sep-Apr) The main building showcases Maori and Victorian exhibits and provides information about the Clyde Dam. Large exhibits (machinery, horse-drawn carts etc)

are housed in the Herb Factory complex at 2 Fraser St.

Trail Journeys   BICYCLE RENTAL
(☑03-449 2150; www.trailjourneys.co.nz; 16 Springvale Rd; ☉tours Sep-Apr) Right by the Rail Trailhead, Trail Journeys rents bikes from \$40 per day) and arranges cycling tours, baggage transfers and shuttles. It also has a depot in Middlemarch.

Festivals & Events

Clyde Wine & Food Festival   WINE, FOOD
(www.promotedunstan.org.nz) Showcases the region's produce and wines on Easter Sunday.

Sleeping

Clyde gets crammed with Rail Trailers in February and March, so book in advance.

Post Master's House   B&B $
(☑03-449 2488; www.postofficecafeclyde.co.nz; Blyth St; d with/without bathroom \$125/95) Antique furnishings are dotted around the large and lovely rooms in this pretty stone cottage. Two of the three rooms share an en suite bathroom; the third has its own.

★ Dunstan House   B&B $$
(☑03-449 2295; www.dunstanhouse.co.nz; 29 Sunderland St; s \$95, d with/without bathroom from \$160/120; ☉Oct-Apr; ☎) This restored late-Victorian balconied inn has lovely bar and lounge areas, and rooms decorated in period style. The less expensive rooms share bathrooms but are just as comfortable and atmospheric.

Oliver's   B&B $$$
(☑03-449 2600; www.oliverscentralotago.co.nz; Hollaway Rd; d \$205-345; ☎) Oliver's fills an 1860s merchant's house and stone stables with luxurious rooms decked out with old maps, heritage furniture and claw-foot baths. Most rooms open onto a secluded garden courtyard.

Eating

Bank Cafe   CAFE $
(www.bankcafe.co.nz; 31 Sunderland St; \$9-15; ☉9am-4pm) Grab a table inside or out and tuck into cakes, slices, waffles and delicious burgers. The robust takeaway sandwiches are perfect for lunch on two wheels.

Post Office Café & Bar   CAFE $$
(www.postofficecafeclyde.co.nz; 2 Blyth St; mains 15-32; ☉10am-9pm) Clyde's 1899 post office houses a popular restaurant famous for its garden tables and hearty food. There are loads of nooks and crannies conducive to newspaper perusing.

🛍 Shopping

Central Gourmet Galleria   FOOD
(www.centralone.co.nz; 27 Sunderland St; ☉10am-5pm daily Aug-May, Tue-Sat Jun & Jul) Stocks a selection of award-winning local wines, many of which you won't find anywhere else. There are also plenty of Central Otago foodie treats such as jams and chutneys.

ℹ Getting There & Away

InterCity (☑03-471 7143; www.intercity.co.nz) A daily coach heads to/from Dunedin (from \$19, 3¼ hours), Roxburgh (from \$12, 44 minutes), Alexandra (from \$15, nine minutes), Cromwell (from \$10, 14 minutes) and Queenstown (from \$13, 1½ hours).

Alpine Connexions (☑03-443 9120; www.alpineconnexions.co.nz) Shuttles head to/from Dunedin (\$40), Alexandra (\$15), Cromwell (\$24), Queenstown (\$35) and Wanaka (\$35), as well as key stops on the Otago Central Rail Trail.

Cromwell & Around

POP 4150

Cromwell has a charming lakeside historic precinct, a great weekly farmers market and perhaps the South Island's most over-the-top 'big thing' – a selection of giant fruit by the highway.

It's also at the very heart of the prestigious Central Otago wine region (www.cowa.org.nz), known for its extraordinarily good pinot noir and, to a lesser extent, riesling, pinot gris and chardonnay. The Cromwell Basin – which stretches from Bannockburn, 5km southwest of Cromwell, to north of Lake Dunstan – accounts for over 70% of Central Otago's total wine production. Pick up the *Central Otago Wine Map* for details of upwards of three dozen local wineries.

◉ Sights & Activities

Old Cromwell Town   HISTORIC BUILDING
(www.oldcromwell.co.nz) When the Clyde Dam was completed in 1992, it flooded the original Cromwell village including the town centre, 280 homes, six farms and 17 orchards. Many historic buildings were disassembled before the flooding and have since been rebuilt in a pedestrianised precinct

beside Lake Dunstan. While some have been set up as period pieces (stables and the like), others house some good cafes, galleries and interesting shops. In summer there's an excellent weekly **farmers market** (⊘9am-1pm Sun Nov-Feb) and monthly **craft market** (10am-2pm every 3rd Sun Nov-Feb).

Highlands Motorsport Park   MOTOR SPORTS
(☑03-445 4052; www.highlands.co.nz; cnr SH6 & Sandflat Rd; ⊘10am-5pm) Transformed from a paddock into a topnotch 4km racing circuit in just 18 months, this revheads' paradise hosted its first major event in 2013 – the inaugural three-day Highlands 101, now scheduled to take place every November.

Outside of the big events, budding speed freaks can start out on the go-karts ($35 per 10 minutes) before taking a 200km/h ride in the Highlands Taxi ($75 for two people), completing three laps of the circuit as a passenger in a Porsche GT3 ($295), or having a go at the wheel of a Suzuki Swift GT3 ($295).

If you'd prefer a less racy experience, the **National Motorsport Museum** (adult/child $20/8) showcases racing cars and displays about Kiwi racing legends such as Bruce McLaren, Possum Bourne, Emma Gilmour and Scott Dixon. Plus there's free minigolf.

Goldfields Jet   JETBOATING
(☑03-445 1038; www.goldfieldsjet.co.nz; adult/child $95/49) Zip through the Kawarau Gorge on a 40-minute jetboat ride.

⎋ Tours

Central Otago Motorcycle Hire   TOUR
(☑03-445 4487; www.comotorcyclehire.co.nz; 271 Bannockburn Rd; per day from $185) The sinuous and hilly roads of Central Otago are perfect for negotiating on two wheels. This crew hires bikes and advises on improbably scenic routes. They also offer guided Gravel 'n' Gold trail-bike tours (from $195) and extended road tours (from $575).

**Bannockburn Historic
Goldfields Tours**   WALKING TOUR
(☑03-445 1559; www.bannockburngold.co.nz; per person $15-29) Informative tours exploring Bannockburn's gold-mining heritage.

🛏 Sleeping

Cromwell Top 10   HOLIDAY PARK $
(☑03-445 0164; www.cromwellholidaypark.co.nz; 1 Alpha St; sites $40-42, units with/without bathroom $105/75; @ 🛜) The size of a small European

nation and packed with cabins and self contained units of various descriptions, all set in tree-lined grounds.

★**Burn Cottage Retreat**   RENTAL HOUSE $
(☑03-445 3050; www.burncottageretreat.co.nz; 168 Burn Cottage Rd; d $195-200; 🛜) Set amongst walnut trees and gardens 3km northwest of Cromwell, Burn Cottage has three luxury self-contained cottages with classy decor, spacious kitchens and modern bathrooms. B&B accommodation is available in the main house.

Carrick Lodge   MOTEL $
(☑03-445 4519; www.carricklodge.co.nz; 10 Barry Ave; d $135-160; @ 🛜) One of Cromwell's more stylish motels, Carrick's spacious, modern units are just a short stroll from the main shopping complex. Executive units have spa baths and views over the golf course.

✗ Eating & Drinking

Grain & Seed Café   CAFE
(Melmore Tce; meals $10-14; ⊘9am-4pm) Set in a beautiful stone building that was once Jolly's Grain Store, this cute cafe serves up big, delicious, inexpensive meals. Grab an outside table beside the lake.

★**The Shed at
Northburn Station**   MODERN NZ $
(☑03-445 1743; www.northburn.co.nz; 45 Northburn Station Rd; mains $25; ⊘10.30am-4.30pm) Outside tables take advantage of lake and mountain views at this acclaimed winery restaurant, 5km from Cromwell on the eastern side of Lake Dunstan. The seasonal menu consists of only a handful of dishes done exceptionally well.

Armando's Kitchen   CAFE $
(71 Melmore Tce; breakfast $10-17, lunch $17-22; ⊘9.30am-4pm daily Dec-Mar, Tue-Sun Apr-Nov) Old Cromwell Town is best enjoyed from the heritage verandah of Armando's Kitchen with an espresso or gourmet ice cream in hand. The homemade pasta, pizza, pies and cakes are all excellent.

Mt Difficulty   MODERN NZ $$
(☑03-445 3445; www.mtdifficulty.co.nz; 73 Felton Rd, Bannockburn; platters $19-28, mains $35-36; ⊘tastings 10.30am-4.30pm, restaurant noon-4pm) As well as making our favourite pinot noir, Mt Difficulty is a lovely spot for a leisurely lunch looking down over the valley. Desserts are particularly decadent.

ℹ Information

Cromwell i-SITE (☎ 03-445 0212; www.
centralotagonz.com; 47 The Mall; ⊙9am-5pm)
Stocks the *Walk Cromwell* brochure, covering local mountain-bike and walking trails,
including the nearby gold-rush ghost town of
Bendigo.

ℹ Getting There & Away

Alpine Connexions (☎ 03-443 9120; www.
alpinecoachlines.co.nz) Scheduled shuttles to/
from Clyde ($24, 20 minutes), Alexandra ($24,
35 minutes), Queenstown ($25, one hour) and
Wanaka ($25, 45 minutes).

Atomic Shuttles (☎ 03-349 0697; www.
atomictravel.co.nz) Daily buses head to/from
Queenstown ($15, 50 minutes), Alexandra ($15,
50 minutes), Roxburgh ($25, 1¼ hours), Dun-
edin ($30, 3¾ hours) and Christchurch ($40,
5¼ hours).

Catch-a-Bus (☎ 03-449 2024; www.catcha-
bus.co.nz) Bike-friendly shuttles to Clyde (20
minutes), Alexandra (30 minutes), Ranfurly (1¾
hours), Middlemarch (2¾ hours) and Dunedin
(3¾ hours).

InterCity (☎ 03-471 7143; www.intercity.co.nz)
There are four daily coaches to Queenstown
(from $10, one hour), and one to Fox Glacier
(from $44, 6½ hours), Christchurch (from $40,
4¾ hours), Alexandra (from $18, 24 minutes)
and Dunedin (from $20, 3¼ hours).

Naked Bus (www.nakedbus.com; prices vary)
Buses head to/from Queenstown, Wanaka,
Twizel, Tekapo and Christchurch.

Queenstown & Wanaka

Best Places to Eat

➡ Francesca's Italian Kitchen (p247)

➡ La Rumbla (p240)

➡ Bistro Gentil (p247)

➡ Botswana Butchery (p230)

➡ Fergbaker (p229)

Best Places to Stay

➡ Riversong (p246)

➡ The Dairy (p228)

➡ Altamont Lodge (p245)

➡ Arrowtown Lodge (p239)

➡ Wanaka Bakpaka (p245)

Why Go?

With a cinematic background of mountains and lakes, and a 'what can we think of next?' array of adventure activities, it's little wonder Queenstown tops the itineraries of many travellers.

Slow down slightly in Wanaka – Queenstown's less flashy cousin – which also has good restaurants, bars and outdoor adventures on tap. With Mt Aspiring National Park nearby, you're only a short drive from true New Zealand wilderness.

Slow down even more in Glenorchy, an improbably scenic reminder of what Queenstown and Wanaka were like before the adventure groupies moved in. Negotiate the Greenstone and Routeburn Tracks for extended outdoor thrills, or kayak the upper reaches of Lake Wakatipu.

Across in historic Arrowtown, consider the town's gold-mining past over a chilled wine or dinner in a cosy bistro. The following day there'll be plenty more opportunities to dive back into Queenstown's action-packed whirlwind.

When to Go

➡ The fine and settled summer weather from January to March is the perfect backdrop to Queenstown's active menu of adventure sports and outdoor exploration. March also brings the Gibbston Wine & Food Festival to Queenstown Gardens.

➡ Easter sees an inundation of mountain bikers for the Queenstown Bike Festival.

➡ In late June the Queenstown Winter Festival celebrates the coming of the ski season. From June to August, the slopes surrounding Queenstown and Wanaka are flush with an international crew of ski and snowboard fans.

➡ Spring thaws herald Wanaka Fest in October.

ℹ Getting There & Around

Domestic flights head to Queenstown from Auckland, Wellington and Christchurch; for international services, see the Transport chapter. Queenstown is also the main bus hub, with services radiating out to the West Coast (via Wanaka and Haast Pass), Christchurch, Dunedin (via Central Otago), Invercargill and Te Anau. Wanaka also has services to Christchurch and Dunedin.

QUEENSTOWN

POP 12,500

Surrounded by the soaring indigo heights of the Remarkables and framed by the meandering coves of Lake Wakatipu, it's little wonder that Queenstown is a show-off. No-one's ever visited and said, 'I'm bored'. Looking like a small town, but displaying the energy of a small city, Queenstown wears its 'Global Adventure Capital' badge proudly, and most visitors take the time to do crazy things they've never done before.

A new Queenstown is also emerging, with a cosmopolitan restaurant and arts scene, excellent vineyards and five international-standard golf courses. Go ahead and jump off a bridge or out of a plane, but take time to slow down and experience Queenstown without the adrenaline. At the very least, find a lakeside bench at dusk and immerse yourself in one of NZ's most beautiful views.

Queenstown is well used to visitors with international accents, so expect great tourist facilities but also big crowds, especially in summer and winter. Autumn (March to May) and spring (October to November) are slightly quieter, but Queenstown is a true year-round destination.

The town's restaurants and bars are regularly packed with a mainly young crowd that really know how to holiday. If you're a more private soul, drop in to see what all the fuss is about, but then get out and about by exploring the sublime wilderness further up the lake at Glenorchy.

History

The region was deserted when the first Pakeha (white person) arrived in the mid-1850s, although there is evidence of previous Maori settlement. Sheep farmers came first, but after two shearers discovered gold on the banks of the Shotover River in 1862, a deluge of prospectors followed.

Queenstown & Wanaka Highlights

❶ Doing things you've only dreamed about in **Queenstown** (p217), the adrenaline-rush capital of NZ

❷ Soaking up the sophisticated small-town vibe and sublime lake views of **Wanaka** (p241)

❸ Relaxing and dining in **Arrowtown** (p237) after a day's mountain biking and gold panning

❹ Walking the peaceful **Routeburn Track** (p234), arguably the best of NZ's Great Walks.

❺ Exploring the upper reaches of Lake Wakatipu from sleepy **Glenorchy** (p233) by horseback, kayak or jetboat

❻ Restraining the urge to yodel as you stroll through the sublime Matukituki Valley on the **Rob Roy Glacier Track** (p244)

❼ Partying the night away among a multitude of accents on a **Queenstown bar-hop** (p231)

Queenstown Region

Queenstown Region

Within a year Queenstown was a mining town with streets, permanent buildings and a population of several thousand. It was declared 'fit for a queen' by the NZ government, hence Queenstown was born. Lake Wakatipu was the principal means of transport, and at the height of the boom there were four paddle steamers and 30 other craft plying the waters.

By 1900 the gold had petered out and the population was a mere 190. It wasn't until the 1950s that Queenstown became a popular holiday destination.

◎ Sights

Lake Wakatipu
LAK
Shaped like a perfect cartoon thunderbolt this gorgeous lake has a 212km shoreline and reaches a depth of 379m (the average depth is over 320m). Five rivers flow into it but only one (the Kawarau) flows out, making it prone to sometimes quite dramatic floods

If the water looks clean, that's because it is. Scientists have rated it as 99.9% pure – making it the second-purest lake water in the world. In fact, you're better off dipping your glass in the lake than buying bottled water. It's also very cold. That beach by Marine Pde may look tempting on a scorching day, but trust us – you won't want to splash about in water that hovers around 10°C year-round. Because cold water increases the risk of drowning, local bylaws require the wearing of life jackets in all boats under 6m, including kayaks, on all of the district's lakes.

Maori tradition sees the lake's shape as the burnt outline of the evil giant Matau sleeping with his knees drawn up. Local lad Matakauri set fire to the bed of bracken on which the giant slept in order to rescue his beloved Manata, a chief's daughter who was kidnapped by the giant. The fat from Matau's body created a fire so intense that it burnt a hole deep into the ground.

★ Queenstown Gardens   PARK
(Map p220; Park St) Set on its own little tongue of land framing Queenstown Bay, this pretty park was laid out by those garden-loving Victorians as a place to promenade. The clothes may have changed (they've certainly shrunk), but people still flock to this leafy peninsula to stroll, picnic and laze about. Less genteel types head straight for the frisbee golf course (p222).

Other highlights of the park include an ice-skating rink, skateboard park, lawn-bowling club, tennis courts, mature exotic trees (including large sequoias and some fab monkey puzzles by the rotunda) and a rose garden. There's also a memorial to Captain Robert Scott (1868–1912), leader of the doomed South Pole expedition, which includes an engraving of his moving final message.

St Peter's Anglican Church   CHURCH
(Map p224; www.stpeters.co.nz; 2 Church St) This pretty wood-beamed stone building (1932) has an impressive organ and colourful stained glass. Take a look at the eagle-shaped cedar lectern, carved and donated in 1874 by Ah Tong, a Chinese immigrant.

Underwater World   VIEWPOINT
(Map p224; www.kjet.co.nz; main jetty; adult/child $5/3; ⊙8.30am-5pm) Six giant windows showcase life under the lake in this reverse aquarium (the people are behind glass). Large brown trout abound, and look out for freshwater eels and scaup (diving ducks),

which cruise right past the windows – especially when the coin-operated food-release box is triggered.

Kiwi Birdlife Park   BIRD SANCTUARY
(Map p224; www.kiwibird.co.nz; Brecon St; adult/child $42/21; ⊙9am-5pm, shows 11am & 3pm) These 5 acres are home to 10,000 native plants, tuatara and scores of birds, including kiwi, kea, moreporks, parakeets and extremely rare black stilts. Stroll around the aviaries, watch the conservation show, and tiptoe quietly into the darkened kiwi houses.

★ Skyline Gondola   CABLE CAR
(Map p220; www.skyline.co.nz; Brecon St; adult/child return $27/16) Hop aboard for fantastic views. At the top there's the inevitable cafe, restaurant, souvenir shop and observation deck, as well as the Queenstown Bike Park (p221) and Skyline Luge (p222). At night there are Maori culture shows from Kiwi Haka (p232) and stargazing tours (including gondola adult/child $79/39).

Walking trails include a loop track through the Douglas firs (30 minutes return). The energetic (or frugal) can forgo the gondola and hike to the top on the Tiki Trail (p218).

🏃 Activities

A baffling array of activities is offered by a baffling number of shops in the town centre. It's even more confusing due to the fact that some shops change their name from winter to summer, some run multiple activities from the same shop, and some activities

---

ESSENTIAL QUEENSTOWN & WANAKA

Eat A leisurely lunch at a vineyard restaurant

Drink One of the surprising seasonal brews by Wanaka Beerworks' (p241)

Read *Walking the Routeburn Track* by Philip Holden for a wander through the history, flora and fauna of this tramp

Listen to The silence as you kayak blissfully around Glenorchy and Kinloch

Watch *Top of the Lake*, the Jane Campion–directed TV series set around the top of Wakatipu

Online www.queenstownnz.co.nz; www.lakewanaka.co.nz

Area code 🖉 03

MAORI NZ: QUEENSTOWN & WANAKA

The same transition from moa-hunter to Waitaha, to Ngati Mamoe to Ngai Tahu rule took place here as in other parts of the South Island. Lake Wakatipu is shrouded in legend, and sites to its north were highly valued sources of greenstone.

The Ngai Tahu *iwi* (tribe) owns Shotover Jet (p219) and Dart River Jet Safaris (p235), the latter of which involves a cultural component. Other cultural insights are offered by Kiwi Haka (p232), who perform nightly atop the gondola, and Million Dollar Cruise's Maori culture trips (p222).

are branded differently but are actually the same thing. Several places call themselves information centres, but only the i-SITE (p232) is the true, independent, official information centre.

If you're planning on tackling several activities, various combination tickets are available, including those offered by **Queenstown Combos** (☑03-442 7318; www.combos.co.nz).

Tramping & Climbing

Pick up the *Wakatipu Walks* brochure ($5) from the Department of Conservation (DOC) for local tramping tracks ranging from easy one-hour strolls to tough eight-hour slogs.

Queenstown Hill Walkway TRAMPING
(Map p220) The strenuous trek up 900m Queenstown Hill takes two to three hours return. Access is from Belfast Tce.

Ben Lomond Track TRAMPING
(Map p220) The track to the summit of Ben Lomond (1748m, six to eight hours return) is a steep tramp requiring a high-level of fitness and shouldn't be underestimated. Snow and ice can make it even more difficult; in winter check at DOC or the i-SITE before setting out. It starts by following the Tiki Trail from Lomond Ave.

Tiki Trail WALKING
(Map p220) The hour-long walk up to the top of the gondola is not particularly scenic, but the views at the top are excellent. You can access the track from either Brecon St or Lomond Ave.

Guided Nature Walks WALKING
(☑03-442 7126; www.nzwalks.com; adult/child from $105/65) Excellent walks in the Queenstown area, including a *Walk & Wine* option and snowshoeing in winter.

Ultimate Hikes TRAMPING
(Map p224; ☑03-450 1940; www.ultimatehikes.co.nz; 9 Duke St; ☺8am-6pm Nov-Apr) ⌀ Offers day walks on the Routeburn Track (adult/child $169/85) and the Milford Track (adult/child $295/95) from Queenstown. Or you can do the multiday tracks in their entirety, staying in Ultimate Hikes' own staffed lodges rather than DOC huts, where hot meals and en suite bathrooms await (Routeburn/Milford from $1225/1930).

Climbing Queenstown ROCK CLIMBING
(☑03-450 2119; www.climbingqueenstown.com; from $149) Rock climbing, via ferrata (climbing with fixed metal rungs, rails, pegs and cables) and alpine trekking led by qualified guides.

Bungy & Swings

AJ Hackett Bungy BUNGY JUMPING
(Map p224; ☑03-450 1300; www.bungy.co.nz; The Station, cnr Camp & Shotover Sts) The bungy originators now operate bungy from three sites in the Queenstown area, with giant swings available at two of them. It all started at the historic 1880 Kawarau Bridge (Map p216; adult/child $180/130), 23km from Queenstown (transport included). In 1988 it became the world's first commercial bungy site, offering a 43m leap over the river.

The closest to Queenstown are the Ledge Bungy (Map p220; adult/child $180/130) and Ledge Swing (Map p220; adult/child $150/100) at the top of the Skyline Gondola; the leap is only 47m, but it's 400m above town. In winter you can even leap into the dark.

Last but most pant-wetting is the Nevis Bungy (per person $260) – the highest bungy in Australasia. 4WD buses will transport you from the Kawarau Bridge site onto private farmland where you can jump from a specially constructed pod, 134m above the Nevis River. The Nevis Swing (solo/tandem $320/180) starts 160m above the river and cuts a 300-degree arc across the canyon on a rope longer than a rugby field – yes, it's the world's biggest swing.

Shotover Canyon Swing EXTREME SPORTS
(Map p224; ☑03-442 6990; www.canyonswing.co.nz; booking office 35 Shotover St; per person

$215, additional swings $35) Be released loads of different ways – backwards, in a chair, upside down. From there it's a 60m free fall and a wild swing across the canyon at 150km/h.

White-Water Rafting & Sledging

Queenstown Rafting   RAFTING
(Map p224; 03-442 9792; www.rafting.co.nz; 35 Shotover St; rafting/helirafting $199/285) Rafts year-round on the choppy Shotover River (Grade III to V) and calmer Kawarau River (Grade II to III). Trips take four to five hours with two to three hours on the water. Helirafting trips are an exciting alternative. Participants must be at least 13 years old and weigh more than 40kg. If you book through other rafting companies such as **Extreme Green** (03-442 8517; www.nzraft.com; rafting/helirafting $195/279) and **Challenge** (0800 423 836, 03-442 7318; www.raft.co.nz; rafting/helirafting $195/279), you'll end up on the same trips.

Family Adventures   RAFTING
(03-442 8836; www.familyadventures.co.nz; adult/child $179/120) Gentler (Grade I to II) trips on the Shotover suitable for children three years and older. Operates in summer only.

Serious Fun   EXTREME SPORTS
(03-442 5262; www.riversurfing.co.nz; per person $195) The only company to surf the infamous Chinese Dogleg section of the Kawarau River, on what's basically a glorified boogie board.

Frogz   EXTREME SPORTS
(03-441 2318; www.frogz.co.nz; per person $195) Steer buoyant sleds on the rapids and whirlpools of the Kawarau River.

Jetboating

Skippers Canyon Jet   JETBOATING
(03-442 9434; www.skipperscanyonjet.co.nz; Skippers Rd; adult/child $129/79) Incorporates a 30-minute blast through the narrow gorges of the remote **Skippers Canyon** (Map p216), on the upper reaches of the Shotover River. The three-hour return trips (picking up from Queenstown accommodation) also cover the region's gold-mining history.

Shotover Jet   JETBOATING
(03-442 8570; www.shotoverjet.com; Gorge Rd, Arthurs Point; adult/child $129/69) Half-hour trips through the rocky Shotover Canyons, with lots of thrilling 360-degree spins.

K Jet   JETBOATING
(Map p224; 03-409 0000; www.kjet.co.nz; adult/child $119/69) One-hour trips on the Kawarau and Lower Shotover Rivers, leaving from the main jetty.

Skydiving, Gliding & Parasailing

NZone   SKYDIVING
(Map p224; 03-442 5867; www.nzone.biz; 35 Shotover St; 9000-15,000ft jumps $269-439) Jump out of a perfectly good airplane – with a tandem skydiving expert.

G Force Paragliding   PARAGLIDING
(Map p220; 03-441 8581; www.nzgforce.com; per person $199) Tandem paragliding from the

QUEENSTOWN & WANAKA QUEENSTOWN

QUEENSTOWN IN...

Two Days

Start your day at **Vudu Cafe & Larder** before either hitting the slopes or heading to Shotover St to book your adrenaline-charged activities. Ride the **Skyline Gondola** to get the lay of the land and have a go on the **luge**. Head out on the **Skippers Canyon Jet** and then wind down with a walk through **Queenstown Gardens** to capture dramatic views of the **Remarkables** at dusk. Have a sunset drink at **Pub on Wharf** before dinner at **Botswana Butchery** and an evening of bar-hopping.

The next day fuel up at **Fergbaker** before devoting the morning to snowboarding, bungy jumping, skydiving or white-water rafting. Spend the afternoon on two wheels, either at the **Queenstown Bike Park** or touring around the **Gibbston** wineries. Have dinner at **Public** before hitting the bars.

Four Days

Follow the two-day itinerary, then head to **Arrowtown** to wander the **Chinese settlement** and browse the shops. The following day, drive along the shores of Lake Wakatipu to tiny **Glenorchy**. Have lunch at the **Glenorchy Cafe** and then drive to the trailhead of the **Routeburn Track** for a short tramp.

Queenstown

N

0 — 500 m
0 — 0.25 miles

Queenstown Hill Recreation Reserve

Villa del Lago (200m)

Frankton Rd

Walking Track to Frankton

Frankton Arm

Belfast Tce

Edinburgh Dr

Panorama Tce

Upr Suburb St

Dublin St

The Terrace

16
21

Lwr Suburb St

11

Kent St

York St

12

Adelaide St

Hallenstein St

Melbourne St

Sydney St

Frankton Rd

Hobart St

8

Ballarat St

20

Anderson Heights

19

Stanley St

Coronation Dr

13

Park St

Turner St

Weaver St

17

Park St

Gorge Rd

23

Shotover St

Robins Rd

18

22

6

4

9

Hamilton Rd

See Central Queenstown Map (p224)

Steamer Wharf

Queenstown Gardens

1

Brecon St

Skyline Gondola

2

Lake St

14

Queenstown Bay

TSS Earnslaw Route

Bob's Peak

5
7

10

Lake ESP

Brunswick St

St Omer Park

15

Lake Wakatipu

Evergreen Lodge (2.2km)

Lomond Ave

Thompson St

11

Fernhill (1km); VKnow (1km)

Queenstown

op of the gondola or from Coronet Peak
9am departures are $20 cheaper).

Coronet Peak

Tandem PARAGLIDING, HANG GLIDING
(☎0800 467 325; www.tandemparagliding.com;
from $189) Offering spectacular take-offs
from Coronet Peak, with free pick-ups from
Queenstown accommodation.

Skytrek PARAGLIDING, HANG GLIDING
(☎0800 759 873; www.skytrek.co.nz; from $190)
Soar on tandem flights from Coronet Peak;
transfers included.

Queenstown Paraflights PARASAILING
(Map p224; ☎0800 225 520; www.paraflights.
co.nz; solo/tandem per person $159/129) Float
100m above the lake as you're pulled behind
a boat. Departs from the main pier.

Elevation Paragliding School PARAGLIDING
(☎0800 359 444; www.elevation.co.nz; instruction
from $240) Learn the paragliding ropes and
graduate to four solo flights.

Mountain Biking

With the opening of the Queenstown Bike
Park, the region is now firmly established as
an international focus for the sport. If you're
in town for a while, consider joining the
Queenstown Mountain Bike Club (www.
queenstownmtb.co.nz).

The **Queenstown Trail** – more than
100km in total – links five scenic smaller
trails showcasing Queenstown, Arrowtown,
Gibbston, Lake Wakatipu and Lake Hayes.
The trail is suitable for cyclists of all levels

Queenstown Bike Park MOUNTAIN BIKING
(Map p220; ☎03-441 0101; www.queenstown-
bikepark.co.nz; Skyline; half-/full day $60/85;
☉10am-6pm Sep-Nov, Mar & Apr, to 8pm Dec-Feb)
Thirteen different trails – from easy (green)
to extreme (double black) – traverse Bob's
Peak high above the lake. Once you've descended on two wheels, simply jump on
the gondola and do it all over again. The
best trail for novice riders is the 6km-long
Hammy's Track, which is studded with lake
views and picnic spots. BYO bike.

Vertigo Bikes MOUNTAIN BIKING
(Map p224; ☎03-442 8378; www.vertigobikes.
co.nz; 4 Brecon St; rental half-/full day from $39/59)
If you're serious about getting into mountain biking QT-style, Vertigo is an essential
first stop. Options include skills training
clinics (from $149), guided sessions in the
Queenstown Bike Park ($159), downhill
rides into Skippers Canyon (two runs $159)
and Remarkables helibiking ($399).

Fat Tyre Adventures MOUNTAIN BIKING
(☎0800 328 897; www.fat-tyre.co.nz; tours from
$229) Tours cater to different abilities, with
day tours, multiday tours, helibiking and
singletrack riding. Bike hire and trail snacks
are included.

Outside Sports BICYCLE RENTAL
(Map p224; ☎03-441 0074; www.outsidesports.
co.nz; 36-38 Shotover St) One-stop shop for
bike rentals and trail information. It also
sells outdoor gear and rent skis and snow-
boards in winter.

QUEENSTOWN & WANAKA QUEENSTOWN

Queenstown Bike Hire   BICYCLE RENTAL
(Map p224; 03-442 6039; 28 Church St; 9am-dark) Best for tandems (per hour $30) and lakefront bike rides (per hour/day $14/38). It also hires kayaks, scooters, cars and snow chains.

Skiing & Snowboarding

Queenstowners have two excellent ski fields to choose between in the Remarkables (p39) and Coronet Peak (p37), and when they fancy a change of scenery, there's always Cardrona and Treble Cone (p39) near Wanaka. Coronet Peak is the only field to offer night skiing, which is an experience not to be missed.

The ski season generally lasts from around June to September. Tune into 99.2FM from 6.45am to 9am to hear snow reports. In winter the shops are full of ski gear for purchase and hire; Outside Sports (p221) is a reliable option.

Even outside of the main season, heli-skiing is an option for cashed-up serious skiers; try Over The Top Helicopters (p223), **Harris Mountains Heli-Ski** (03-442 6722; www.heliski.co.nz; from $825), or **Southern Lakes Heliski** (03-442 6222; www.heliskinz.com; from $820).

Other Activities

It would be impractical to list absolutely every activity on offer in Queenstown. If you're interested in golf, minigolf, sailing or diving, enquire at the i-SITE.

Skyline Luge   LUGE
(Map p220; 03-441 0101; www.skyline.co.nz; Skyline; 1/2/3/5 rides incl gondola $36/39/45/50; 10am-dusk) Ride the gondola to the top, then hop on a three-wheeled cart to ride the 800m track. Nail the 'scenic' run once and you're allowed on the advanced track with its banked corners and tunnel.

Queenstown Ice Arena   ICE SKATING
(Map p220; 03-441 8000; www.queenstownicearena.co.nz; 29 Park St; entry incl skate hire $15; 10am-

5pm Sun-Thu, to 9.30pm Fri & Sat Apr-Oct) Slip-slide around the rink or watch a game of ice hockey

Ziptrek Ecotours   ZIPLINE
(Map p220; 03-441 2102; www.ziptrek.com Skyline) Incorporating a series of ziplines (flying foxes), this harness-clad thrill ride takes you from treetop to treetop high above Queenstown. Ingenious design and eco-friendly values are a bonus. Choose from the two-hour four-line 'Moa' tour (adult/child $129/79) or the gnarlier three-hour six-line 'Kea' option ($179/129).

Canyoning.co.nz   CANYONING
(03-441 3003; www.canyoning.co.nz) Half-day trips in the nearby 12-Mile Delta Canyon ($185) or the remote Routeburn Valley ($250)

XD Dark Ride   GAMING
(Map p224; 03-441 8080; 1/7 Earl St; session $30; 11am-late) Shoot up zombies or Wild West outlaws in the equivalent of a bi-screen multiplayer computer game, with 3D vision surround sound and multisensory seats Great fun for a rainy day.

Stu Dever Fishing Charters   FISHING
(027 433 3052; www.fishing-queenstown.co.nz 2hr adult/child $120/60) Salmon and trout fishing from the 34ft launch *Chinook*.

Frisbee Golf   FRISBEE
(Map p220; www.queenstowndiscgolf.co.nz; Queenstown Gardens) FREE A series of 18 tree-mounted chain baskets set among the trees; local sport stores sell frisbees and scorecards.

Tours
Lake Cruises

TSS Earnslaw   BOAT TOUR
(Map p224; 0800 656 501; www.realjourneys.co.nz; Steamer Wharf, Beach St; tours from $55 The stately, steam-powered TSS *Earnslaw* celebrated a centenary of continuous service in 2012. Once the lake's major mean of transport, now its ever-present cloud of black soot seems a little incongruous in such a pristine setting. Climb aboard for the standard 1½-hour Lake Wakatipu tour (adult/child $55/22) or take a 3½-hour excursion to the high-country **Walter Peak Farm** (Map p216; adult/child $68/20) for sheep shearing demonstrations and sheep-dog performances (adult/child $75/22).

Million Dollar Cruise   BOAT TOUR
(Map p224; 03-442 9770; www.milliondollarcruise.co.nz; tours 11am, 2pm & 4pm) Good-value

This pretty little hostel sits on a quiet hillside west of the town centre, ruled over by Jimmy the cat. There are no bunks but no en suite bathrooms either. You won't believe the views from the deck.

Nomads
HOSTEL $

(Map p224; ☑ 03-441 3922; www.nomadshostels. com; 5 Church St; dm $28-37, r $110-135; @ 🛜) With a prime location near Queenstown's nightlife, this massive hostel has facilities galore including its own minicinema, en suite rooms, massive kitchens and an on-site travel agency. It even sweetens the deal with free breakfast and dinner.

Creeksyde Top 10
HOLIDAY PARK $

(Map p220; ☑ 03-442 9447; www.camp.co.nz; 54 Robins Rd; campsites $49-52, d $77, units with/ without bathroom $128/89; P @ 🛜) In a garden setting, this pretty spot has accommodation ranging from basic tent sites to self-contained motel units. Quirky touches include oddball sculptures and an ablutions block disguised as a medieval oast house.

Hippo Lodge
HOSTEL $

(Map p220; ☑ 03-442 5785; www.hippolodge.co.nz; 4 Anderson Heights; campsites $20, dm $29-30, s $42, d with/without bathroom from $90/70; P @ 🛜) Homely and slightly shabby, this relaxed hostel has a student-flat vibe, although it's a lot cleaner than that implies. The views come with a correspondingly high number of stairs.

Bumbles
HOSTEL $

(Map p220; ☑ 03-442 6298; www.bumblesback-packers.co.nz; cnr Lake Esplanade & Brunswick St; campsites/dm/r $20/30/65; P @ 🛜) Enjoying a prime lakeside location, this popular wee hive has colourful decor and a supremely laid-back vibe. The 10 beds are split between one private room and one dorm, and there's limited space for tents and campervans.

Black Sheep Lodge
HOSTEL $

(Map p220; ☑ 03-442 7289; www.blacksheeppackers.co.nz; 13 Frankton Rd; dm $29, d $75-85; P @ 🛜) This place keeps younger social types happy with a spa pool, frisbees and a truckload of DVDs. There are also plenty of private nooks and crannies for escaping with your favourite book. Rooms share bathrooms.

Last Resort
HOSTEL $

(Map p224; ☑ 03-442 4320; www.tlrqtn.com; 6 Memorial St; dm $30; @ 🛜) Supercentral, this smaller hostel is reached across a tiny brick-and-timber bridge traversing a bubbling brook in the backyard. The setting is lovely but the facilities could do with an upgrade.

Southern Laughter
HOSTEL $

(Map p224; ☑ 03-441 8828; www.sircedrics.co.nz; 4 Isle St; dm $26-29, r with/without bathroom $80/70; P 🛜) Lame jokes cover the walls of this sprawling old-school hostel. The rooms are fine but the bathrooms are a little shabby. Free veggie soup and a spa pool are added benefits.

Amity Lodge
MOTEL $$

(Map p220; ☑ 03-442 7288; www.amitylodge.co.nz; 7 Melbourne St; units from $170; P 🛜) In a quiet street around a five-minute walk up from the town centre, this angular white block

QUEENSTOWN & WANAKA QUEENSTOWN

REMEMBER, YOU'RE ON HOLIDAY...

Here's our pick of the best experiences to slow down, recharge, and remind your body that there's more to the travelling life than scaring yourself silly.

➡ Onsen Hot Pools (p240) has private Japanese-style hot tubs with mountain views. Book ahead and one will be warmed up for you.

➡ To reboot your system after a few days of skiing, biking and jetboating, ease into in-room massage and spa treatments with the **Mobile Massage Company** (☑ 0800 426 161; www.queenstownmassage.co.nz; 1hr from $115; ⊙ 9am-9pm).

➡ Slow down even more by checking into **Hush Spa** (Map p224; ☑ 03-442 9656; www. hushspa.co.nz; 1st fl, 32 Rees St; 30/60min massage from $70/125; ⊙ 9am-9pm Tue-Fri, to 7pm Sat) for a massage, hot-rock therapy or a pedicure.

➡ For truly world-class spa treatments, make the short trek to Millbrook near Arrowtown, where the **Spa at Millbrook** (Map p216; ☑ 03-441 7017; www.millbrook.co.nz; Malaghans Rd; treatments from $230) has been rated one of the world's best.

➡ Catch a water taxi across the lake to **Eforea: Spa at Hilton** (Map p216; ☑ 03-450 9416; www.queenstownhilton.com; Hilton Queenstown, Peninsula Rd; treatments from $120).

has renovated one- and two-bedroom units and friendly owners. The triple glazing is more about keeping out the cold than noise.

Coronation Lodge
LODGE $$

(Map p220; 03-442 0860; www.coronationlodge. co.nz; 10 Coronation Dr; d $165-185; P 🛜) Right beside Queenstown Gardens, this tidy block has basement parking, plush bed linen, wooden floors and Turkish rugs. Larger rooms have kitchenettes.

Alexis Queenstown
MOTEL $$

(Map p220; 03-409 0052; www.alexisqueenstown.co.nz; 69 Frankton Rd; unit from $155; P 🛜) This modern hillside motel is an easy 10-minute walk from town along the lakefront. The pleasant self-contained units have thoughtful extras such as stereos and robes, along with beaut lake views.

Queenstown Motel Apartments
MOTEL $$

(Map p220; 03-442 6095; www.qma.co.nz; 62 Frankton Rd; unit from $125; P @ 🛜) This well-run spot has a mixture of newer units with smart decor, and older, cheaper 1970s-style units. There's a handy on-site laundry, and the lake and mountain views are uniformly great – even from the cheaper accommodation.

Lomond Lodge
LODGE $$

(Map p224; 03-442 8235; www.lomondlodge. com; 33 Man St; d $145-169; P @ 🛜) A makeover has modernised Lomond Lodge's cosy decor. Share your on-the-road stories with fellow travellers around the garden barbecue. Larger family apartments ($299 for up to four people) are also available.

★ The Dairy
BOUTIQUE HOTEL $$$

(Map p224; 03-442 5164; www.thedairy.co.nz; 10 Isle St; s $435-465, d $465-495; P @ 🛜) 🏵 Once a corner store, the Dairy is now a luxury B&B with 13 rooms packed with classy touches like designer bed linen, silk cushions and luxurious mohair rugs. Rates include cooked breakfasts and freshly baked afternoon teas.

Eichardt's Private Hotel
BOUTIQUE HOTEL $$$

(Map p224; 03-441 0450; www.eichardtshotel. co.nz; 1-3 Marine Pde; apt $1250-1900, r $1700-1950; P 🛜) Dating from 1867, this restored hotel enjoys an absolute lakefront location. Each of the five giant suites has a fireplace, king-sized bed, heated floor, lake-sized bath tub and lake views. Four nearby apartments are equally luxurious.

Queenstown Park
BOUTIQUE HOTEL $$$

(Map p220; 03-441 8441; www.queenstown-parkhotel.co.nz; 21 Robins Rd; r $295-395; P 🛜) 🏵 White curtains billow over beds decked out in luxurious linen at this very chic 16-room hotel. The 'Remarkables rooms' have balconies facing over a park to the mountain range (there aren't any lake views). The gondola-facing rooms are smaller but have courtyards; all have kitchenettes.

Historic Stone House
APARTMENTS $$$

(Map p220; 03-442 9812; www.historicstone-house.co.nz; 47 Hallenstein St; apt from $225; P 🛜) Formerly the mayor's digs, this lovely stone building (1874) has been converted into a three-bedroom apartment, with an additional one-bedroom unit in a wooden extension and another in an elevated building behind it. Inside, modern kitchens and bathrooms meld with antique furniture, while outside there are established gardens and a spa pool.

Chalet Queenstown B&B
B&B $$$

(Map p220; 03-442 7117; www.chaletqueenstown.co.nz; 1 Dublin St; s/d $195/245; P 🛜) The seven perfectly appointed rooms at this stylish B&B are decked out with flat-screen TVs, interesting original artworks and quality bed linen. All have balconies with views; get in early and request one looking over the lake.

🛏 Surrounds

Shotover Top 10 Holiday Park
HOLIDAY PARK $

(03-442 9306; www.shotoverholidaypark.co.nz; 70 Arthurs Point Rd, Arthurs Point; campsites $38, units with/without bathroom from $100/65; P @ 🛜) 🏵 High above the Shotover River, this family-friendly park with brand-new motel units is 10 minutes' drive from the hustle and bustle of Queenstown. Fall out of your campervan straight onto the famous Shotover Jet.

Little Paradise Lodge
LODGE $$

(Map p216; 03-442 6196; www.littleparadise. co.nz; Glenorchy-Queenstown Rd, Mt Creighton; dm $45, r with/without bathroom $140/120) Wonderfully eclectic, this slice of arty paradise is the singular vision of the Swiss/Filipina owners. Each rustic room features wooden floors, quirky artwork and handmade furniture. Outside the fun continues with a back-to-nature swimming hole and well-crafted walkways through beautiful gardens.

Wakatipu Grill   EUROPEAN $$$
(Map p216; ☎ 03-450 9400; www.queenstown-hilton.com; Hilton Queenstown, Peninsula Rd, Kelvin Heights; mains $34-52; ☺ 4pm-late Wed-Sun) The Hilton sprawls along the lakeside by the Kawarau River outlet, and part of the fun of visiting its signature restaurant is the 8km water-taxi ride. The grill menu stretches to Fred Flintstone–sized Angus T-bones but would-be Wilmas can opt for freshly shucked oysters, pasta or French-influenced fish, lamb and duck dishes.

Gantley's   FRENCH $$$
(☎ 03-442 8999; www.gantleys.co.nz; 172 Arthurs Point Rd, Arthurs Point; mains $37-44; ☺ 6-10pm) Gantley's French-influenced menu and highly regarded wine list justify the 7km journey from Queenstown. The atmospheric dining experience is showcased in a stone-and-timber building, built in 1863 as a wayside inn. If you feel like splurging, try the six-course *degustation* ($90).

🍷 Drinking & Nightlife

Drinking is almost a competitive sport in Queenstown, and there's a good range of options for after-dark carousing. Live music and clubbing are a nightly affair, and even on Monday and Tuesday nights you should have no problem finding a bar open until 4am.

A couple of outfits run organised pub crawls, where a wristband buys you a riotous night of discounted drinks, giveaways and games along the way; look for the ads in hostels and bars around town.

Ballarat Trading Company   PUB
(Map p224; www.ballarat.co.nz; 7-9 The Mall; ☺ 11am-late) Stuffed bears, rampant wall-mounted ducks and a re-created colonial general store – there's really no competition for the title of Queenstown's most eclectic decor. Beyond the grab bag of infuences, Ballarat is quite a traditional spot, with gleaming beer taps, sports on TV, occasional lapses into 1980s music and robust meals.

Zephyr   BAR
(Map p224; 1 Searle Lane; ☺ 8pm-4am) Queenstown's coolest indie rock bar is located – as all such places should be – in a grungy basement off a back lane.

Pub on Wharf   PUB
(Map p224; www.pubonwharf.co.nz; 88 Beach St; ☺ 10am-late; 🛜) Ubercool interior design combines with handsome woodwork and lighting fit for a hipster hideaway. Fake sheep heads reinforce that you're still in NZ, and Mac's beers on tap, scrummy nibbles and a decent wine list make this a great place to settle in for the evening. There's live music nightly.

Monty's   PUB
(Map p224; www.montysbar.co.nz; 12 Church St) On warm summer days, the patio at this Monteith's Brewery 'concept bar' is prime real estate. Bands crank up from Thursday to Sunday night.

New Zealand Wine Experience   WINE BAR
(Map p224; ☎ 03-409 2226; www.winetastes.com; 14 Beach St; ☺ 10.30am-10pm) Here's something different: load up cash on a smart card and then help yourself to tasting pours or glasses of over 90 NZ wines dispensed through an automated gas-closure system. There's also a whisky corner, and cheese platters are available.

Bardeaux   WINE BAR
(Map p224; Eureka Arcade, Searle Lane; ☺ 4pm-4am) This small, low-key, cavelike wine bar is all class. Under a low ceiling are plush leather armchairs and a fireplace made from Central Otago schist. The wine list is extraordinary, with the price of several bottles reaching four digits.

Atlas Beer Cafe   BAR
(Map p224; www.atlasbeercafe.com; Steamer Wharf, Beach St; ☺ 10am-2am) Perched at the end of Steamer Wharf, this pint-sized bar specialises in beers from Dunedin's Emerson's Brewery and regular guest beers from further afield. The small but tasty food menu includes tapas.

Searle Lane   BAR
(Map p224; www.searlelane.co.nz; 15 Church St; ☺ 11am-late) Pool tables, lunch specials and shared rotisserie chickens make this a top spot for getting to know any new arrivals at your hostel. Free-flowing beer and well-mixed cocktails will help things along.

Barmuda   COCKTAIL BAR
(Map p224; Searle Lane; ☺ 3pm-late) A huge open fire makes Barmuda's walled-in courtyard an inviting space, even in cooler weather.

Surreal   BAR
(Map p224; www.surrealbar.co.nz; 7 Rees St; ☺ noon-late; 🛜) The big attraction at this otherwise average bar is the roof terrace – a wonderfully hidden-away spot for an alfresco drink. Later in the evening DJ-inspired goings-on kick off and the dance floor comes to life. Tuesday is open-mic night.

QUEENSTOWN & WANAKA QUEENSTOWN

Debajo   CLUB
(Map p224; www.facebook.com/Debajoqueenstown;
Cow Lane; ⊙10pm-4am) The perennial end-of-
night boogie spot – house and big beat gets
the dance floor heaving till closing time.

Tardis Bar   BAR
(Map p224; www.tardisbar.com; Skyline Arcade,
20 Cow Lane) A good dance bar with regular
DJs playing hip-hop, drum 'n' bass and dub.
Like Dr Who's phone booth, it's surprisingly
roomy inside.

World Bar   BAR
(Map p224; www.theworldbar.co.nz; 27 Shotover St;
⊙4pm-late) Before it was destroyed by fire
in 2013, the World Bar was Queenstown's
legendary party hub. At the time of writing, ambitious rebuilding plans were well
underway and we're hoping it will reopen
before this book hits the shelves. If not, the
same crew is running **The Find** (Map p224; 53
Shotover St) as a pop-up gap-filler, just down
the road.

☆ Entertainment

Pick up the *Source* (www.facebook.com/
SourceNZ), a free monthly flyer with a gig
guide and events listings.

Kiwi Haka   TRADITIONAL DANCE
(Map p220; ☑03-441 0101; www.skyline.co.nz;
Skyline; adult/child excl gondola $39/26) For a
traditional Maori cultural experience, head
to the top of the gondola. There are three
30-minute shows nightly; bookings are
essential.

Reading Cinemas   CINEMA
(Map p224; ☑03-442 9990; www.readingcinemas.
co.nz; 11 The Mall; adult/child $17/11) Discounts
on Tuesdays.

🛍 Shopping

★ Vesta   ARTS & CRAFTS
(Map p224; www.vestadesign.co.nz; 19 Marine Pde;
⊙10.30am-5.30pm) Showcasing really cool
NZ-made art and craft, Vesta is full of interesting prints, paintings, glass art and
gifts. It's housed in Williams Cottage (1864),
Queenstown's oldest home. It's worth visiting just to check out the 1930s wallpaper
and 1920s garden.

Kapa   ARTS & CRAFTS
(Map p224; www.kapa.co.nz; 29 Rees St; ⊙10am-
8pm) Quirky and eclectic NZ design infused
with a healthy dose of contemporary Maori
culture.

Fetch   CLOTHING
(Map p224; www.fetchnz.com; 34 Shotover St;
⊙10am-6pm) Grab a uniquely Kiwi hand-
screened T-shirt or create your own design
as a wearable souvenir of the time you
bungied, mountain-biked and ziplined to
adventure-sports nirvana.

Kathmandu   OUTDOOR EQUIPMENT
(Map p224; www.kathmandu.co.nz; 88 Beach St;
⊙10am-6pm) A well-known and good-quality
NZ-founded chain selling tents, sleeping
bags, rugged backpacks, active footwear and
stylish adventure clothing.

Small Planet Sports   OUTDOOR EQUIPMENT
(Map p224; www.smallplanetsports.com; 17 Shot-
over St; ⊙9am-7pm Oct-May, 8am-9pm Jun-Sep)
New and used outdoor equipment. There's
also a cheaper **outlet store** (Map p224; 23
Beach St) in town.

Arts & Crafts Market   MARKET
(Map p224; www.marketplace.net.nz; Earnslaw
Park; ⊙9.30am-3.30pm Sat) Locally crafted
gifts and souvenirs, on the lakefront beside
Steamer Wharf.

ℹ Information

DOC Visitor Centre (Department of Conservation; Map p224; ☑03-442 7935; www.doc.govt.
nz; 38 Shotover St; ⊙8.30am-5pm) Backcountry Hut Passes and weather and track updates;
on the mezzanine floor above Outside Sports.
Head here to pick up confirmed bookings for
the Routeburn Track.

Queenstown i-SITE (Map p224; ☑03-442 4100;
www.queenstown-vacation.com; cnr Shotover &
Camp Sts; ⊙8.30am-7pm) Friendly and informa-
tive (but perpetually frantic), the staff can help
with bookings and information on Queenstown,
Gibbston, Arrowtown and Glenorchy.

ℹ Getting There & Away

AIR

For information on international flights, see
the Transport chapter. Both **Air New Zealand**
(☑0800 737 000; www.airnewzealand.co.nz)
and **Jetstar** (☑0800 800 995; www.jetstar.
com) fly to Queenstown from Auckland, Wellington and Christchurch.

BUS

Most buses and shuttles stop on Athol St or opposite the i-SITE; check when you book.
Alpine Connexions (☑03-443 9120; www.
alpinecoachlines.co.nz) Shuttles head to/from
Cardrona ($35), Wanaka ($35), Cromwell ($25),
Alexandra ($35) and Dunedin ($45), as well as
key stops on the Otago Central Rail Trail.

Atomic Shuttles (☎03-349 0697; www.atomictravel.co.nz) Daily bus to Cromwell ($15, 50 minutes), Omarama ($30, 2¼ hours), Twizel ($30, 3¼ hours), Lake Tekapo ($30, 3¾ hours) and Christchurch ($50, seven hours).

Connect Wanaka (www.connectabus.com) Heads to/from Wanaka twice daily ($35, 1½ hours).

InterCity (Map p224; ☎03-442 4922; www.intercity.co.nz) Daily coaches to/from Wanaka (from $17, 1½ hours), Franz Josef (from $62, eight hours), Dunedin (from $22, 4¼ hours) and Invercargill ($48, three hours), and twice daily to Christchurch (from $55, eight to 11 hours).

Naked Bus (www.nakedbus.com) Two buses to Wanaka (1¼ hours) daily; one to Cromwell (one hour); Franz Josef (six hours) and Christchurch (nine hours); and less frequent services to Te Anau (2¾ hours). Prices vary.

Kiwi Discovery (p224) also offers mountain and trailhead transport.

Info & Track Centre (☎03-442 9708; www.infotrack.co.nz; 37 Shotover St; ⏰7.30am-8pm) During the Great Walks season, this agency provides transfers to the trailheads for the Routeburn, Greenstone and Caples, and Rees-Dart Tracks.

NZSki Snowline Express (www.nzski.com; return $15) During the ski season shuttles depart from outside the Snow Centre on Duke St every 20 minutes from 8am until 11.30am, heading to both Coronet Peak and the Remarkables. Buses return as they fill up, from 1.30pm onwards. They also leave on the hour from 4pm to 7pm for night skiing at Coronet Peak, returning on the half hour from 5.30pm to 9.30pm.

Trackhopper (☎021-187 7732; www.trackhopper.co.nz; from $230, plus fuel costs) Offers a handy car-relocation service from either end of the Routeburn, Greenstone and Caples and Rees-Dart Tracks.

❶ Getting Around

TO/FROM THE AIRPORT

Queenstown Airport (ZQN; Map p216; ☎03-450 9031; www.queenstownairport.co.nz; Sir Henry Wrigley Dr, Frankton) is 7km east of the town centre.

Connnectabus (☎03-441 4471; www.connectabus.com) route 11 runs to to the airport from Camp St every 15 minutes from 6.50am to 11pm (adult/child $8/5). There are also services to Arrowtown and Wanaka.

Super Shuttle (☎0800 748 885; www.supershuttle.co.nz; fare $16) picks up and drops off in Queenstown.

Queenstown Taxis (☎03-450 3000; www.queenstown.bluebubbletaxi.co.nz) and **Green**

Cabs (☎0508 447 336; www.greencabs.co.nz) charge around $35.

PUBLIC TRANSPORT

Connnectabus (☎03-441 4471; www.connectabus.com) has various colour-coded routes, reaching as far as Sunshine Bay, Fernhill, Arthurs Point, Frankton and Arrowtown. A day pass (adult/child $20/12) allows travel on the entire network. Pick up a route map and timetable from the i-SITE. Buses leave from Camp St.

AROUND QUEENSTOWN

Glenorchy & Around

POP 360

Set in achingly beautiful surroundings, postage-stamp-sized Glenorchy is the perfect low-key antidote to Queenstown. An expanding range of adventure operators will get you active on the lake and in nearby mountain valleys by kayak, horse or jetboat, and if you prefer to strike out on two legs, the mountainous region at the northern end of Lake Wakatipu is the setting for some of the South Island's finest tramps.

Those with sturdy wheels can explore the superb valleys north of Glenorchy. Paradise lies 15km northwest of town, just before the start of the Dart Track (p234). Keep your expectations low: Paradise is just a paddock, but the gravel road there runs through beautiful farmland fringed by majestic mountains. You might recognise it from *The Lord of the Rings (LOTR)* movies as the approach to both Isengard and Lothlorien.

🎣 Activities

Almost all organised activities offer shuttles to and from Queenstown for a small surcharge. Other activities on offer include farm tours, fly-fishing, guided photography tours and cookery classes; enquire at the Queenstown i-SITE (p232).

Tramping

DOC's *Head of Lake Wakatipu* and *Wakatipu Walks* brochures (both $5) detail day walks taking in the Routeburn Valley, Lake Sylvan, Dart River and Lake Rere. Two of the best short tracks are the Routeburn Nature Walk (one hour), at the start of the Routeburn Track, and the Lake Sylvan tramp (one hour 40 minutes).

Before setting out on any of the longer tramps, call into DOC in Queenstown (p232) or **Te Anau** (📞 03-249 7924; www.doc.govt.nz; cnr Lakefront Dr & Te Anau-Manapouri Rd; ⏰8.30am-4.30pm, to 6pm 9 Dec-16 Mar) for the latest track conditions and to purchase detailed maps. Another good resource is Lonely Planet's *Tramping in New Zealand*.

For track snacks or meals, stock up on groceries in Queenstown. Track transport is at a premium during the summer Great Walks season (late October to March); try to book in advance. Many of the local accommodation providers offer trailhead transport; see p233 for services from Queenstown.

★ Routeburn Track   TRAMPING

(www.doc.govt.nz; huts/campsites Nov-Apr $54/18, May-Oct $15/5) Passing through a huge variety of landscapes with fantastic views, the 32km-long, two- to four-day Routeburn Track is one of the most popular rainforest/subalpine tracks in NZ. It's one of NZ's nine designated 'Great Walks', and many trampers rate it as the very best.

Increased pressure on the track has necessitated the introduction of an online booking system in the Great Walks season, which covers all huts and campsites on the route. You'll then need to call into the DOC Visitor Centre in either Queenstown or Te Anau to collect actual tickets, either the day before or on the day of departure. Outside of the season, bookings aren't required but you'll still need to visit one of the DOC centres to purchase your hut and campsite tickets.

The Routeburn track remains open in winter. However, to traverse the alpine section after the snow falls is not recommended for casual trampers, as winter mountaineering skills are required. There are 32 avalanche paths across the section between Routeburn Falls hut and Howden hut, and the avalanche risk continues through to spring. Always check conditions with DOC.

The track can be started from either end. Many people travelling from Queenstown try to reach the **Divide** in time to catch the bus to Milford and connect with a cruise on the sound. En route, you'll take in breathtaking views from **Harris Saddle** and the top of nearby **Conical Hill**, from where you can see waves breaking at Martins Bay. From **Key Summit**, there are panoramic views of the Hollyford Valley and the Eglinton and Greenstone River Valleys.

There are car parks at both ends of the track, but they're unattended, so don't leave any valuables in your car.

ROUTE	ESTIMATED WALKING TIME (HR)
Routeburn Shelter to Flats Hut	1½-2½
Flats Hut to Falls Hut	1-1½
Falls Hut to Mackenzie Hut	4½-6
Mackenzie Hut to Howden Hut	3-4
Howden Hut to the Divide	1-1½

Greenstone & Caples Tracks   TRAMPING

(huts adult/child $15/5) Following meandering rivers through peaceful valleys, these tracks form a loop that many trampers stretch out into a moderate four- or five-day tramp. Basic huts en route are Mid Caples, Upper Caples, McKellar and Greenstone; Backcountry Hut Passes must be purchased in advance.

Both tracks meet up with the Routeburn Track; you can either follow its tail end to the Divide or (if you've prebooked) pursue it back towards Glenorchy. From McKellar Hut you can tramp two or three hours to Howden Hut on the Routeburn Track, which is an hour from the Divide.

Access to the Greenstone and Caples Tracks is from Greenstone Wharf; nearby you'll find unattended parking.

ROUTE	ESTIMATED WALKING TIME (HR)
Greenstone Wharf to Mid Caples Hut	2-3
Mid Caples Hut to Upper Caples Hut	2-3
Upper Caples Hut to McKellar Hut	5-8
McKellar Hut to Greenstone Hut	5-7
Greenstone Hut to Greenstone Wharf	3-5

Rees-Dart Track   TRAMPING

(huts/campsites $15/5) This is a difficult, demanding four- to five-day circular route from the head of Lake Wakatipu, taking you through valleys and over an alpine pass, with the possibility of a side trip to the Dart Glacier if you're suitably equipped and experienced. Access by vehicle is possible as far as Muddy Creek on the Rees side, from where it's six hours to Shelter Rock Hut.

Most people go up the Rees track first and come back down the Dart. Backcountry Hut Passes must be purchased in advance for the three basic DOC huts (Shelter Rock, Daleys Flat and Dart).

ROUTE	ESTIMATED WALKING TIME (HR)
Muddy Creek to Shelter Rock Hut	6-8
Shelter Rock Hut to Dart Hut	4-6
Dart Hut to Daleys Flat Hut	5-7
Daleys Flat Hut to Paradise	6-8

Horse Riding

Dart Stables HORSE RIDING
(☏ 03-442 5688; www.dartstables.com; Coll St) Options include a two-hour 'River Wild' ride ($135) and a 1½-hour 'Ride of the Rings' trip ($175) for Hobbity types. If you're really keen, consider the overnight two-day trek with a sleepover in Paradise ($705).

High Country Horses HORSE RIDING
(☏ 03-442 9915; www.high-country-horses.co.nz; Priory Rd) Offers many choices, ranging from an hour-long 'Rees River Ride' ($80) to overnight and multiday treks.

Other Activities

Dart River Jet Safaris JETBOATING
(☏ 03-442 9992; www.dartriver.co.nz; adult/child $219/119; ⊙ departs 9am & 1pm) Journeys into the heart of the Dart River wilderness, including a short walk through the beech forest and a 4WD trip. The round trip from Glenorchy takes three hours. You can also combine a jetboat ride with a river descent in an inflatable three-seater 'funyak' (adult/child $319/219). Prices include Queenstown pick-ups.

Skydive Paradise SKYDIVING
(☏ 03-442 8333; www.skydiveparadise.co.nz; Glenorchy airport; 12,000-15,000ft jump $335-409) Tandem skydiving above some of the planet's most spectacular scenery.

QUEENSTOWN & WANAKA GLENORCHY & AROUND

LOCAL KNOWLEDGE

THE REES VALLEY

Acclaimed NZ film-maker Jane Campion, whose 2013 TV series *Top of the Lake* was filmed in the region, reflects on her connection to the Rees Valley.

'As many times a year as I can, I travel to a holiday hut up the Rees Valley, at the top end of Lake Wakatipu. I love the lake, the majesty of the surrounding mountains, the good weather in the basin, the walks, the rivers, the end-of-the-world feeling and the laconic people who live nearby. Everyone who has visited me up here is infected by the ready magic of the landscape and the sensation of worldly troubles dissolving. Lake Sylvan is one of many good bush walks in the area – a fairly short walk for this scale of landscape, but the intimacy of being inside the bush immediately gives you a sense of delight. Recently the lake has been high and is phenomenal to swim in.'

☞ Tours

Ultimate Hikes   WALKING TOUR
(☎03-450 1940; www.ultimatehikes.co.nz; ⊙Nov–mid-Apr) If you fancy comfort while adventuring, Ultimate Hikes offers a three-day guided tramp on the Routeburn (from $1225); a six-day Grand Traverse, combining walks on the Routeburn and Greenstone Tracks (from $1660); and the Classic, an eight-day tour combining the Routeburn and Milford Tracks (from $3155). All trips include meals and accommodation in Ultimate's own comfortable huts. It also offers a one-day Routeburn Encounter ($169).

Glenorchy Base   WALKING TOUR
(☎03-409 0960; www.glenorchybase.co.nz; half-/full day from $350/420) Specialises in guided walks around the Glenorchy area. Highlights include bird-watching around Lake Sylvan and a Routeburn Track day walk.

Private Discovery Tours   DRIVING TOUR
(☎03-442 2299; www.rdtours.co.nz) Half-day 4WD tours head through a high-country sheep station in a remote valley between Mts Earnslaw and Alfred (adult/child $185/92). Full-day tours include LOTR sites around Paradise (adult/child $295/150). Prices include pick-up from Queenstown.

🛏 Sleeping & Eating

Kinloch Lodge   LODGE, CAFE $
(☎03-442 4900; www.kinlochlodge.co.nz; Kinloch Rd; dm $35, d with/without bathroom from $140/85; @🖥) 🅿 Across Lake Wakatipu from Glenorchy (26km by road; five minutes by boat), this wonderfully remote 1868 lodge rents mountain bikes, offers guided kayaking and provides transfers to tramping trailheads. The Heritage Rooms are small but stylish, with shared bathrooms. Rooms in the YHA-associated hostel are comfy and colourful, and there's a post-tramp hot tub. The excellent cafe-bar is open for lunch year-round and for à la carte dinners in summer and set dinners in winter.

DOC Kinloch Campsite   CAMPSITE $
(www.doc.govt.nz; Kinloch Rd; adult/child $6/3) Right by the lake and Kinloch Lodge, this standard DOC campsite has toilets, a barbecue and pure lake water for drinking. Head to the lodge for hot showers ($6) and meals.

Mt Earnslaw Motels   MOTEL $$
(☎03-442 6993; mtearnslaw@xtra.co.nz; 89 Oban St, Glenorchy; r $120; 🖥) Springtime flowers enliven the gardens of this unassuming but tidy seven-room motel. The well-priced units have comfy recliners, small kitchens and large beds, but won't win any awards for style.

Glenorchy Lake House   B&B $$$
(☎03-442 7084; www.glenorchylakehouse.co.nz; Mull St, Glenorchy; r $325-380; 🖥) After a day's tramping, recharge in the spa pool of this lakefront B&B. Other little luxuries include Egyptian cotton sheets, flat-screen TVs and nice toiletries. Transfers to the Routeburn and Greenstone Tracks are available.

Glenorchy Cafe   CAFE $$
(Mull St, Glenorchy; mains $10-20, pizzas $25; ⊙9am-5pm Sun-Wed, to 9pm Thu-Sat Jan-Apr, 10am-5pm Sun-Fri, to 9pm Sat May-Dec) Grab a sunny table out the back of this cute little cottage and tuck into cooked breakfasts, sandwiches and soup. Head inside at night to partake in pizza and beer underneath the oddball light fixtures.

Glenorchy Hotel   PUB $$
(☎03-442 9902; www.glenorchy-nz.co.nz; Mull St, Glenorchy; mains $15-29) The rooms are crappy but the front garden of the local pub isn't a bad spot for a beer or filling meal.

films. Every screening in the main theatre has an intermission – the perfect opportunity to tuck into a tub of gourmet ice cream.

ℹ Information

Arrowtown Visitor Information Centre (☑ 03-442 1824; www.arrowtown.com; 49 Buckingham St; ⊗ 8.30am-5pm) Shares premises with the Lake District Museum & Gallery.

ℹ Getting There & Away

Connectabus (☑ 03-441 4471; www.connectabus.com) runs regular services (7.45am to 11pm) on its No 10 route from Frankton to Arrowtown. From Queenstown, you'll need to catch a No 11 bus to the corner of Frankton and Kawarau Rds, and change there. The only direct service is the double-decker bus heading out on the first Arrowtown Legends Tour (p239) of the day, which departs Queenstown at 9.30am ($8).

WANAKA

POP 6480

Which is better, Queenstown or Wanaka? That's the perennial question around these parts and one which doesn't have an easy answer. It's hard to say which is more beautiful – both have blissful lake and mountain settings. Ditto, the jury's out as to which offers better skiing and tramping opportunities.

The main difference is in size, scale and buzz. Unlike its amped-up sibling across the Crown Range, Wanaka retains a laid-back, small-town feel. It's definitely not a sleepy hamlet anymore though, and new restaurants and bars are adding a veneer of sophistication. And while it doesn't have quite the same range of adrenaline-inducing activities on offer, Wanaka is no slacker on the outdoor-adventure front. Importantly, it's also cheaper.

◉ Sights

Puzzling World AMUSEMENT PARK

(www.puzzlingworld.com; 188 Wanaka Luggate Hwy/SH84; adult/child $18/12; ⊗ 8.30am-5.30pm) A 3D Great Maze and lots of fascinating brain-bending visual illusions to keep people of all ages bemused, bothered and bewildered. It's en route to Cromwell, 2km from town.

National Transport & Toy Museum MUSEUM

(www.wanakatransportandtoymuseum.com; 851 Wanaka Luggate Hwy/SH6; adult/child $15/5; ⊗ 8.30am-5pm) Small armies of Smurfs, Star Wars figurines and Barbie dolls share billing with dozens of classic cars and a mysteriously

acquired MiG jet fighter in this vast collection, which fills four giant hangers near the airport. There are around 30,000 items in total, including plenty of toys you're bound to remember from rainy childhood afternoons.

Wanaka Beerworks BREWERY

(www.wanakabeerworks.co.nz; SH6; tours & tasting $10; ⊗ tastings 11am-4pm, tours 2pm Thu-Tue) Somewhat incongruously attached to the toy museum, this small brewery's two main beers (Cardrona Gold lager and Brewski pilsner) are complemented by seasonal brews. Dave the owner is a real-deal Belgian brewing supremo.

Warbirds & Wheels MUSEUM

(www.warbirdsandwheels.com; Wanaka Airport, 11 Lloyd Dunn Av; adult/child $20/5; ⊗ 9am-5pm) Dedicated to NZ combat pilots, the aircraft they flew and the sacrifices they made, this museum features Hawker Hurricanes, a de Havilland Vampire and lots of shiny, beautifully restored classic cars. Grab a bite to eat and fire up the jukebox in the retro diner.

Rippon WINERY

(www.rippon.co.nz; 246 Mt Aspiring Rd; ⊗ noon-4.30pm Jul-Apr) Along with just about the best view of any NZ winery, Rippon has great wine too. To save fights as to who's going to be the designated driver, take a 2km stroll along the lakeside and look out for the track up the hill from the end of Sargood Dr.

⚡ Activities

Wanaka is the gateway to Mt Aspiring National Park and to the Treble Cone (p39), Cardrona (p249), Harris Mountains and Pisa Range Ski Areas.

Tramping

For walks close to town, including various lakeside walks, pick up the DOC brochure *Wanaka Outdoor Pursuits* ($3.50). The short climb to the top of **Mt Iron** (527m, 1½ hours return) reveals panoramic views.

To the north of Wanaka, the usually unpeopled **Minaret Burn Track** (six to seven hours) in the Mt Alta Conservation Area is suitable for walking and mountain biking. After about two to three hours, a track heads down to **Colquhouns Beach**, a great swimming spot.

Aspiring Guides MOUNTAINEERING, SKIING

(☑ 03-443 9422; www.aspiringguides.com; L1, 99 Ardmore St) With over 20 years of alpine experience, this crew offers a multitude of options, including guided wilderness tramping (three to eight days); mountaineering

Wanaka

Wanaka

Activities, Courses & Tours
1 Aspiring Guides D3
2 Cardrona Alpine Resort Booking
   Office D3
3 Lakeland Adventures D3
4 Outside Sports D3
5 Thunderbikes D3
6 Wanaka Golf Club C2
7 Wanaka Kayaks C3

Sleeping
8 Archway Motels C1
9 Asure Brookvale B1
10 Criffel Peak View C1
11 Harpers B3
12 Lakeside B1
13 Matterhorn South B2
14 Mountain View Backpackers C1
15 Wanaka View Motel B2
16 YHA Wanaka Purple Cow B2

Eating
17 Bistro Gentil C3
18 Boaboa Food Company D3
19 Federal Diner D3

20 Francesca's Italian Kitchen D3
21 Kai Whakapai D3
22 Red Star C1
23 Relishes Cafe D3
24 Ritual D3
25 Soulfood B1
26 Spice Room D3
27 The Landing B1
   Yohei .... (see 4)

Drinking & Nightlife
28 Barluga & Woody's C1
29 Gin & Raspberry D3
   Lalaland .... (see 1)
30 Opium B1

Entertainment
31 Cinema Paradiso B2

Shopping
32 Chop Shop D3
33 Gallery Thirty Three D3
34 MT Outdoors D3
   Picture Lounge .... (see 4)

and ice-climbing courses; guided ascents of Mt Aspiring, Aoraki/Mt Cook and Mt Tasman; and off-piste skiing (one- to five-day backcountry expeditions).

**Alpinism
& Ski Wanaka**   MOUNTAINEERING, SKIING
(📞 03-442 6593; www.alpinismski.co.nz; from $135;
Guided day walks and overnight tramps, and

more full-on mountain assaults, courses and ski touring.

Adventure Consultants MOUNTAINEERING
(☑ 03-443 8711; www.adventureconsultants.com; 5 days from $4100) Offers two-days excursions on Brewster Glacier ($890) and three-day trips in Gillespies Pass ($1250) in Mt Aspiring National Park, as well as longer treks, ascents (Mts Aspiring, Tutoko, Tasman and Aoraki/Mt Cook) and mountaineering courses.

Rock Climbing

Excellent rock climbing can be found at Hospital Flat – 25km from Wanaka towards Mt Aspiring National Park.

Basecamp Wanaka ROCK CLIMBING
(☑ 03-443 1110; www.basecampwanaka.co.nz; 50 Cardrona Valley Rd; adult/child $20/17; ☺noon-8pm Mon-Fri, 10am-6pm Sat & Sun) Before you hit the mountains, learn the ropes on climbing walls.

Wanaka Rock Climbing ROCK CLIMBING
(☑ 03-443 6411; www.wanakarock.co.nz) Introductory rock-climbing course (half-/full day $140/210), a half-day abseiling intro ($140), and bouldering and multipitch climbs for the experienced.

Mountain Biking

Hundreds of kilometres of tracks and trails in the region are open to mountain bikers. Pick up the DOC brochure *Wanaka Outdoor Pursuits* ($3.50), describing mountain-bike rides ranging from 2km to 24km, including the **Deans Bank Loop Track** (12km).

One particularly scenic new route is the **Newcastle Track** (12km), which follows the raging blue waters of the Clutha River from the Albert Town Bridge to Red Bridge. You can make it a 30km loop by joining the **Upper Clutha River Track** at Luggate.

Thunderbikes BICYCLE RENTAL
(☑ 03-443 2558; www.thunderbikes.co.nz; 16 Helwick St; ☺9am-5pm) Hires bikes (half-/full day from $20/35) and carries out repairs. It is located inside the Board House, which also rents ski and snowboard gear in season, and sells outdoorsy clothes.

Outside Sports BICYCLE RENTAL
(www.outsidesports.co.nz; Spencer House Mall, 23 Dunmore St; ☺9am-6pm) Rents (half-/full day from $35/55), repairs and sells bikes, along with snow-sports equipment and clothing.

Other Activities

Deep Canyon CANYONING
(☑ 03-443 7922; www.deepcanyon.co.nz; canyoning from $220; ☺Oct-Apr) Loads of climbing, walking and waterfall-abseiling through confined, wild gorges.

Skydive Lake Wanaka SKY DIVING
(☑ 03-443 7207; www.skydivewanaka.com; skydiving from $329) Jump from 12,000ft or go the whole hog with a 15,000ft leap and 60 seconds of freefall.

Wanaka River Journeys JETBOATING, WALKING
(☑ 03-443 4416; www.wanakariverjourneys.co.nz; adult/child $229/119) ✐ Combination bush walk (50 minutes) and jetboat ride in the gorgeous Matukituki Valley.

Wanaka Kayaks KAYAKING
(☑ 0800 926 925; www.wanakakayaks.co.nz; from per hour $12; ☺9am-6pm Dec-Mar) Rents kayaks ($14 per hour), stand-up paddle boards ($18 per hour), and catamarans ($60 per hour), and offers guided paddle-powered tours of the lake (half/full day $75/149). It's on the lakefront, opposite 163 Ardmore St.

Wanaka Paragliding PARAGLIDING
(☑ 0800 359 754; www.wanakaparagliding.co.nz; tandem $199) Count on around 20 minutes soaring on the summer thermals around Treble Cone.

Hatch FISHING
(☑ 03-443 8446; www.hatchfishing.co.nz; 2 adults half-/full day $490/750) Lakes Wanaka and Hawea and the surrounding rivers have excellent trout fishing. Hatch offers guided fly-fishing, with the option of accessing remote spots by helicopter or jetboat.

Pioneer Rafting RAFTING
(☑ 03-443 1246; www.ecoraft.co.nz; half-day adult/child $145/85, full day $195/105) Raft on the high-volume Clutha, with Grade II to III rapids, gold panning and bird-watching.

Wanaka Golf Club GOLF
(☑ 03-443 7888; www.wanakagolf.co.nz; Ballantyne Rd; green fees $60) A spectacular 18-hole course.

☞ Tours
Scenic Flights

U-Fly SCENIC FLIGHTS
(☑ 03-445 4005; www.u-flywanaka.co.nz; flights from $199) Scratch 'flying a plane' off the bucket list on a scenic flight over Mt Aspiring National Park. Don't fret, there are dual

MT ASPIRING NATIONAL PARK

Verdant valleys, alpine meadows, unspoiled rivers, more than 100 glaciers and sheer mountains make **Mt Aspiring National Park** (www.doc.govt.nz) an outdoor enthusiast's paradise. Protected as a national park in 1964, and later included in the Southwest New Zealand (Te Wahipounamu) World Heritage Area, the park now blankets 3555 sq km along the Southern Alps, from the Haast River in the north to its border with Fiordland National Park in the south. Lording it over all is colossal Mt Aspiring (Tititea; 3033m), the highest peak outside the Aoraki/Mt Cook area.

While the southern end of Mt Aspiring National Park near Glenorchy includes better known tramps such as the Routeburn (p234), Greenstone and Caples (p234) and Rees-Dart (p234) Tracks, there are plenty of blissful short walks and more demanding multiday tramps in the Matukituki Valley, close to Wanaka; see the Department of Conservation (DOC) brochure *Matukituki Valley Tracks* ($2).

The dramatic **Rob Roy Glacier Track** (two to four hours return) takes in glaciers, waterfalls and a swing bridge. It's a moderate walk, but some parts are quite steep. The **West Matukituki Valley Track** goes on to Aspiring Hut (four to five hours return; peak/off-peak $25/20 per night), a scenic walk over mostly grassy flats. For overnight or multiday tramps offering great views of Mt Aspiring, continue up the valley to Liverpool Hut (at an elevation of 1000m; $15 per night) and French Ridge Hut (at 1465m; $20 per night).

Many of these tramps are prone to snow and avalanches and can be treacherous. It is extremely important to consult DOC in Wanaka (p250) and to purchase hut tickets before heading off. You should also register your intentions on www.adventuresmart.org.nz.

Tracks are reached from Raspberry Creek at the end of Mt Aspiring Rd, 50km from Wanaka. The road is unsealed for 30km and involves nine ford crossings; it's usually fine in a 2WD, except in very wet conditions (check at DOC).

controls ready to take over at a moment's notice – they're not completely insane.

Classic Flights SCENIC FLIGHTS
(☑03-443 4043; www.classicflights.co.nz; flights from $249) 🖉 Runs sightseeing flights in a vintage Tiger Moth or Waco biplane. 'Biggles' goggles and flowing silk scarf provided.

Wanaka Helicopters HELICOPTER
(☑03-443 1085; www.wanakahelicopters.co.nz) Options range from 15-minute tasters ($95) to two-hour-plus trips to Milford Sound ($995).

Aspiring Helicopters HELICOPTER
(☑03-443 7152; www.aspiringhelicopters.co.nz) Take a 20-minute flight ($170) or a 2½-hour trip to Milford Sound ($1250); in-between options include Mt Aspiring.

Alpine Helicopters HELICOPTER
(☑03-443 4000; www.alpineheli.co.nz) Options range from a 20-minute flight ($185) to the four-hour Fiordland Heli Traverse ($7500 for up to six).

Wanaka Flightseeing SCENIC FLIGHTS
(☑03-443 8787; www.flightseeing.co.nz) Spectacular flyovers of Mt Aspiring ($240), Aoraki/Mt Cook ($435) and Milford Sound ($490).

Other Tours

Adventure Wanaka CRUISE, FISHING
(☑03-443 6665; www.adventurewanaka.com) Offers lake cruises and fishing trips in an 8m launch.

Lakeland Adventures CRUISE, KAYAKING
(☑03-443 7495; www.lakelandadventures.co.nz; Log Cabin, 100 Ardmore St) Has two-hour trips to Stevensons Island (adult/child $95/55) and a three-hour trip to Mou Waho island (adult/child $165/55); both include guided nature walks and morning or afternoon tea. Otherwise you can hire a kayak ($15 per hour) and paddle your way to Ruby Island.

Also offers one-hour jetboat trips across the lake (adult/child $109/55) and water taxis to the start of the Minaret Burn track ($75).

Eco Wanaka Adventures TRAMPING, CRUISE
(☑03-443 2869; www.ecowanaka.co.nz; half-/full day from $105/170) 🖉 Guided tours include a full-day trek to the Rob Roy glacier ($250), a four-hour cruise and walk on Mou Waho island, and a full-day cruise-4WD combo ($390).

Wanaka Bike Tours MOUNTAIN BIKING
(☑0800 862 453; www.wanakabiketours.co.nz; tours from $99) Guided trips including heli-biking options.

Ridgeline Adventures DRIVING TOUR
(📞0800 234 000; www.ridgelinenz.com; tours from $140) Explore the wilderness surrounding Wanaka on a 4WD nature safari.

Funny French Cars DRIVING TOUR
(📞027 386 6932; www.funnyfrenchcars.co.nz) Ride in a classic Citroen around Central Otago wineries (per person $165), up into the hills for a picnic lunch (per person $150), or tour the highlights of Wanaka (per car per hour $80).

★✿ Festivals & Events

Warbirds over Wanaka AIRSHOW
(📞03-443 8619, 0800 496 920; www.warbirdsoverwanaka.com; Wanaka Airport; 3-day adult/child $190/45) Held every second Easter (even-numbered years), this incredibly popular international airshow attracts upwards of 50,000 people. Tickets for the first day only cost $65/15 per adult/child, the second and third days are $90/15 each.

Rippon Festival MUSIC
(www.ripponfestival.co.nz) Held every second year in early February (even-numbered years) at the lakeside Rippon Vineyard. Big-name Kiwi acts headline with a variety of styles represented, including R&B, reggae, rock, pop and punk.

Wanaka Fest CARNIVAL
(www.wanakafest.co.nz) This four-day event in mid-October has the feel of a small-town fair. Street parades, live music, wacky competitions and fine regional produce get the locals saying g'day to the warmth of spring.

🛏 Sleeping

In summer, and especially around New Year, prices and demand increase considerably. During winter, the town receives an influx of international snowboarders.

Wanaka

⭐ **Altamont Lodge** LODGE $
(📞03-443 8864; www.altamontlodge.co.nz; 121 Mt Aspiring Rd; s/d without bathrooms $49/79; 🛜) At the quiet end of town, Altamont has tidy little rooms which share bathrooms and a spacious, well-equipped kitchen. Natural wood gives it a ski-lodge ambience, while the spa pool and roaring fire in the lounge will warm you up postslopes.

⭐ **Wanaka Bakpaka** HOSTEL $
(📞03-443 7837; www.wanakabakpaka.co.nz; 117 Lakeside Rd; dm $28-29, d with/without bathroom

$90/70; @🛜) An energetic husband-and-wife team run this friendly hostel above the lake with just about the best views in town. Amenities are top shelf and the onto-it staff consistently offer a red-carpet welcome to weary travellers. It's worth considering paying a bit extra for the en suite double with the gorgeous views.

YHA Wanaka Purple Cow HOSTEL $
(📞03-443 1880; www.yha.co.nz; 94 Brownston St; dm $31-34, d with/without bathroom from $95/81; @🛜) 🍃 In the top echelons of NZ YHAs, the Purple Cow offers a range of shared and private rooms, including some with en suites in a newer building out the back. Best of all is the large lounge, with commanding lake and mountain views, and a wood stove.

Aspiring Campervan & Holiday Park HOLIDAY PARK $
(📞03-443 7766; www.campervanpark.co.nz; Studholme Rd; campsites $20-25, s/d $25/60, units with/without bathroom from $75/65; @🛜) Grassy sites for tents and campervans, lots of trees, and pretty views add up to a relaxing spot. Facilities include a barbecue area with gas heaters, and free wi-fi, spa pool and sauna. Older-style motel units have all been renovated, and the newest budget cabins are warm and cosy with wooden floors.

Matterhorn South HOSTEL $
(📞03-443 1119; www.matterhornsouth.co.nz; 56 Brownston St; dm $28-35, d with/without bathroom from $115/80; @🛜) Split between two buildings – the 'lodge' and the slightly rougher-around-the-edges 'backpackers' – this friendly spot has clean, good-value dorms and private rooms. Each has its own kitchen and lounge, and the garden is a great place to relax after a day's adventuring.

Mountain View Backpackers HOSTEL $
(📞03-443 9010; www.wanakabackpackers.co.nz; 7 Russell St; dm $27-29, d $68; 🅿@🛜) This colourfully renovated and characterful house features a manicured lawn and warm, comfortable rooms. Fire up the barbecue after a busy day's exploring. Handy features include a drying room and off-street parking.

Criffel Peak View B&B $$
(📞03-443 5511; www.criffelpeakview.co.nz; 98 Hedditch St; s $130, d $160-165, apt $270) Situated in a quiet cul-de-sac, this excellent B&B has three rooms sharing a large lounge with a log fire and a sunny wisteria-draped deck. The charming hostesses live in a separate

house behind, which has a self-contained two-bedroom apartment attached.

Harpers B&B $$
(☏ 03-443 8894; www.harpers.co.nz; 95 McDougall St; tw/d $140/160) The garden (with pond and waterfall no less...) is a labour of love for the retiree owners at this quiet, homely B&B. Legendary breakfasts are served on a sunny deck with expansive views. You'd be wise to factor a leisurely second cup of breakfast coffee into your day's plans.

Wanaka View Motel MOTEL $$
(☏ 03-443 7480; www.wanakaviewmotel.co.nz; 122 Brownston St; units $120-195; 🐾) The refurbished Wanaka View has five apartments with Sky TV, spa baths, full kitchens and lake views; the largest has three bedrooms. There's also a comfortable studio unit tucked around the back, which is cheaper but doesn't have a kitchen or view.

Archway Motels MOTEL $$
(☏ 03-443 7698; www.archwaymotels.co.nz; 64 Hedditch St; units from $120; 🐾) This older motel with clean and spacious units and chalets is a short uphill walk from the town centre. Friendly and helpful owners, new flat-screen TVs, and cedar hot tubs with mountain views make Archway great value in a sometimes-expensive town. Check online for good off-peak discounts.

Asure Brookvale MOTEL $$
(☏ 03-443 8333; www.brookvale.co.nz; 35 Brownston St; d $150-180; 🐾🏊) At this older-style motel with studio and family units, the patios open onto a grassy lawn edged by a gently flowing creek. There's also a barbecue, hot tub and swimming pool.

Lakeside APARTMENTS $$$
(☏ 03-443 0188; www.lakesidewanaka.co.nz; 7 Lakeside Rd; apt $295-795; 🐾🏊) 🌿 Luxuriate in a modern apartment in a prime position overlooking the lake, right by the town centre. All have three bedrooms but can be rented with only one or two bedrooms open. The swimming pool is a rarity in these parts and an appealing alternative to the frigid lake on a sweltering day.

Wanaka Homestead LODGE $$$
(☏ 03-443 5022; www.wanakahomestead.co.nz; 1 Homestead Close; d $269, cottages $399-499; @🐾) 🌿 Wooden interiors, oriental rugs and local artwork punctuate this boutique lodge, which has won awards for its eco-friendly approach. Despite the focus on green good deeds, it's still luxurious, with underfloor heating and an under-the-stars hot tub. Choose from rooms in the main lodge or in self-contained cottages.

🛏 Albert Town

⭐**Riversong** B&B $$
(☏ 03-443 8567; www.riversongwanaka.co.nz; 5 Wicklow Tce; d $160-190; 🐾) Across from the Clutha River in nearby Albert Town, Riversong has two guest bedrooms in a lovely weatherboard house. The well-travelled owner has a fabulous nonfiction library. If you can tear yourself away from the books, there's excellent trout fishing just metres away.

Wanaka Alpine Lodge B&B, APARTMENTS $$$
(☏ 03-443 5355; www.wanakaalpinelodge.co.nz; 114 Albert Town-Lake Hawea Rd; r $259-289, apt $390; 🐾) Guests in the four spacious, modern bedrooms are pampered with home baking, an evening glass of wine and a cedar hot tub. It's slightly out of town, but the young owners will lend you a mountain bike to get around on and even chauffeur you in for dinner.

🍴 Eating

Boaboa Food Company FAST FOOD $
(www.facebook.com/boaboafc; 137 Ardmore St; mains $10-18; ⊙10am-9pm) Fancy burgers (spiced pulled pork, high-country salmon, porterhouse steak) are the mainstay of this white-tiled takeway bar, but it also does fish and chips and fried chicken. There are only a handful of high tables, but the lakefront beckons.

Kai Whakapai CAFE, BAR $
(cnr Helwick & Ardmore Sts; brunch $7-18, dinner $17-22; ⊙7am-11pm) An absolute Wanaka institution, Kai (the Maori word for food) is the place to be for a liquid sundowner accompanied by a massive sandwich or pizza. Locally brewed Wanaka Beerworks beers are on tap and there are Central Otago wines as well.

Red Star BURGERS $
(26 Ardmore St; burgers $10-17; ⊙11.30am-11pm; 🍴) Red Star spoils diners with a menu featuring inventive ingredients and 22 different burgers. Everybody is catered for – even vegetarians, who get a show-stopping three choices.

Soulfood ORGANIC, CAFE $
(www.soulfoodwanaka.co.nz; 74 Ardmore St; mains $10-15; ⊙8am-6pm Mon-Fri, to 4pm Sat & Sun; 🍴)

It's not soul food in the African American sense; rather this little organics store offers a healthy range of id-affirming soups, pizza, pasta and muffins. Not everything's strictly vegetarian, with wild venison and free-range bacon breaking the spell. Juices and smoothies are suitably virtuous, but coffee's limited to the plunger variety.

Yohei SUSHI $
(Spencer House Mall, 23 Dunmore St; mains $12-15; ⊙8am-5.30pm; 🛜🍴) Tucked away in a shopping arcade, this funky Japanese-inspired eatery does interesting local spins on sushi (how about venison?), and superlative juices and smoothies. There's also a good range of vego options and free wi-fi with any $4 purchase.

⭐**Francesca's Italian Kitchen** ITALIAN $$
(☑03-443 5599; www.fransitalian.co.nz; 93 Ardmore St; mains $20-25; ⊙noon-3pm & 5.30pm-late) Ebullient expat Francesca has brought the big flavours and easy conviviality of an authentic Italian family trattoria to Wanaka in the form of this stylish and perennially busy eatery. Even simple things like pizza, pasta and polenta chips are exceptional. She also runs a pizza cart from the New World car park.

Florence's Foodstore & Cafe CAFE $$
(www.florencesfoodstore.co.nz; 71 Cardrona Valley Rd; mains $16; ⊙8.30am-4pm) Wood, corrugated iron and jute-cladding create a rustic feel for this edge-of-town gourmet providore. Call in for the region's prettiest salmon Benedict, as well as French-style pastries and delicious ham-and-cheese baguettes.

Relishes Cafe CAFE $$
(☑03-443 7538; www.relishescafe.co.nz; 99 Ardmore St; brunch $11-20, dinner $31-35; ⊙7am-10pm) A cafe by day with good breakfast and lunch options, this place transforms itself at night into a sophisticated restaurant with a good wine list. Try the free-range pork belly or Aoraki salmon, and toast the lakefront setting with a glass of Central Otago's finest.

Spice Room INDIAN $$
(☑03-443 1133; www.spiceroom.co.nz; 43 Helwick St; mains $21-25; ⊙5.30-10pm; 🍴) The combination of an authentic curry, crispy garlic naan and cold beer is a great way to recharge after a day's snowboarding or tramping. Beyond the spot-on renditions of all your subcontinental favourites, the Spice Room springs a few surprises, with starters including a zingy scallops masala salad.

Ritual CAFE $$
(18 Helwick St; mains $10-20; ⊙9am-5pm) A classic 21st-century Kiwi cafe, Ritual is smart but not too trendy, gay-friendly but family-friendly too, and filled to the gills with delicious food. The counter positively groans under the weight of tasty salads, slices and scones.

Federal Diner CAFE $$
(www.federaldiner.co.nz; 47 Helwick St; mains $9-21; ⊙7am-4pm; 🛜) Tucked away in a back lane, this cosmopolitan cafe delivers robust breakfasts, excellent coffee and chunky gourmet sandwiches. Try the 'Roaster Coaster' with slow-roasted pork shoulder and apple sauce on ciabatta. Service is sometimes chaotic.

⭐**Bistro Gentil** FRENCH $$$
(☑03-443 2299; www.bistrogentil.co.nz; 76a Golf Course Rd; mains $30-42; ⊙11.30am-2pm Sat & Sun, 5-9pm Wed-Sun, extended Dec-Feb) Lake views, fabulous NZ art, oodles of wines by the glass and delicious modern French cuisine – Gentil ticks plenty of boxes for a memorable night out. On a balmy night, request an outside table.

The Landing MODERN NZ $$$
(☑03-443 5099; www.thelandinglakewanaka.co.nz; L1, 80 Ardmore St; mains $29-39; ⊙5-10pm) Local beef, lamb and salmon is served in innovative ways in this upmarket upstairs restaurant at the apex of the main streets. The beautifully presented dishes do well to compete with the spectacular lake views.

🍷 **Drinking & Nightlife**

Barluga & Woody's BAR
(Post Office Lane, 33 Ardmore St; ⊙4pm-2.30am) The tucked-away Post Office Lane complex is Wanaka's coolest drinking destination – despite the lack of lake views. Sharing both a courtyard and owners, these neighbouring bars operate more or less in tandem, especially when there's a DJ event on. Barluga's leather armchairs and retro wallpaper bring to mind a refined gentlemen's club. Wicked cocktails and killer back-to-back beats soon smash that illusion. Woody's plays the role of the younger brother, with pool tables and indie sounds.

Lalaland COCKTAIL BAR
(www.lalalandwanaka.co.nz; L1, 99 Ardmore St; ⊙3pm-2am) Keep a watchful eye on the lake or sink into a comfy chair at this little, low-lit, completely over-the-top cocktail palace/bordello. The young barmeister-owner truly

knows his stuff, concocting elixirs to suit every mood. Entry is via the rear stairs.

Gin & Raspberry COCKTAIL BAR
(www.ginandraspberry.co.nz; L1, 155 Ardmore St; ⊙4pm-late) If you're in the swing for bling, this lush bar offers gilded mirrors, sparkling chandeliers, a piano and a central fireplace. Classic movies provide a backdrop to classic cocktails (including seven different martinis), and the occasional live band fires things up.

Opium CLUB
(L1, 68 Ardmore St; ⊙9pm-late Wed-Sun) An Asian-themed club with DJs and occasional live music. It's popular in winter with the snowboarder crowd, but in summer the lakefront bars are busier.

☆ Entertainment

Cinema Paradiso CINEMA
(✆03-443 1505; www.paradiso.net.nz; 72 Brownston St; adult/child $15/9) Stretch out on a comfy couch or in an old Morris Minor at this Wanaka institution, screening the best of Hollywood and art-house flicks. At intermission the smell of freshly baked cookies wafts through the theatre, although the homemade ice cream is just as alluring.

Ruby's CINEMA
(✆03-443 6901; www.rubyscinema.co.nz; 50 Cardrona Valley Rd; adult/child $19/13) Channelling a lush New York or Shanghai vibe, this hip-art-house-cinema-meets-chic-cocktail-bar is a real surprise in outdoorsy Wanaka. Luxuriate in the huge cinema seats, or chill out in the red-velvet lounge with craft beers, classic cocktails and sophisticated bar snacks. You'll find Ruby's concealed within the Basecamp Wanaka building on the outskirts of town.

🛍 Shopping

Picture Lounge PHOTOGRAPHY
(www.thepicturelounge.co.nz; Spencer House Mall, 23 Dunmore St) Showcases large-format art shots, mainly of local landscapes.

Chop Shop CLOTHING
(www.chop.co.nz; Pembroke Mall) The best coffee in town and a natty range of locally designed beanies and cool T-shirts for the discerning snowboarder.

Gallery Thirty Three ARTS & CRAFTS
(www.gallery33.co.nz; 33 Helwick St; ⊙10am-5pm) Pottery, glass and jewellery from local artists.

MT Outdoors OUTDOOR EQUIPMENT
(www.mtoutdoors.co.nz; 17 Dunmore St; ⊙9am-6pm) Rents and sells rock-climbing, mountaineering, camping and tramping gear.

ℹ Information

Lake Wanaka i-SITE (✆03-443 1233; www.lakewanaka.co.nz; 103 Ardmore St; ⊙8.30am-5.30pm) Extremely helpful but always busy.

Mt Aspiring National Park Visitor Centre (DOC; ✆03-443 7660; www.doc.govt.nz; Ardmore St; ⊙8.30am-5pm daily Nov-Apr, Mon-Sat May-Oct) In an A-framed building on the edge of the town centre, this Department of Conservation centre takes hut bookings and offers advice on tracks and conditions. There's a small display on Wanaka geology, flora and fauna.

Wanaka Medical Centre (✆03-443 7811; www.wanakamedical.co.nz; 23 Cardrona Valley Rd; ⊙8am-6pm Mon-Fri, 9am-noon & 4-6pm Sat & Sun) Patches up adventure-sports mishaps.

ℹ Getting There & Away

Alpine Connexions (✆03-443 9120; www.alpinecoachlines.co.nz) Links Wanaka with Queenstown, Cromwell, Alexandra, Dunedin and the Rail Trail towns of Central Otago. It also has shuttles to Wanaka Airport, the Mt Aspiring trailheads and Lake Hawea in summer, and Cardrona and Treble Cone in winter.

Atomic Shuttles (✆03-349 0697; www.atomictravel.co.nz) Daily bus to/from Dunedin ($35, 4½ hours) via Cromwell ($15, 50 minutes), Alexandra ($20, 1¾ hours) and Roxburgh ($30, 2¼ hours).

Connectabus (✆0800 405 066; www.connectabus.com) 1-way/return $35/65) Handy twice-daily service linking Wanaka with Queenstown airport (1¼ hours) and Queenstown (1½ hours). Free pick-up from most accommodation.

InterCity (✆03-442 4922; www.intercity.co.nz) Coaches depart from outside the Log Cabin on the lakefront, with daily services to Cromwell (from $10, 44 minutes), Queenstown (from $17, 1½ hours), Lake Hawea (from $10, 24 minutes), Makarora (from $12, 1¾ hours) and Franz Josef (from $43, 6½ hours).

Naked Bus (www.nakedbus.com) Services to Queenstown, Cromwell, Franz Josef, Lake Tekapo and Christchurch. Prices vary.

ℹ Getting Around

Adventure Rentals (✆03-443 6050; www.adventurerentals.co.nz; 20 Ardmore St) Hires cars and 4WDs.

Yello (✆03-443 5555; www.yello.co.nz) Taxis and shuttles.

AROUND WANAKA

Cardrona

The cute hamlet of Cardrona reached its zenith in the 1870s at the height of the gold rush, when its population numbered over a thousand. Now it's a sleepy little place which wakes up with a jolt for the ski season.

With views of foothills and countless snowy peaks, the Crown Range Road from Cardrona to Queenstown is one of the South Island's most scenic drives. At 1076m, it's the highest sealed road in NZ. It passes through tall, swaying tussock grass in the Pisa Conservation Area (Map p216), which has several short walking trails. There are some great places to stop and drink in the view, particularly at the Queenstown end of the road before you start the switchback down towards Arrowtown. However, the road is narrow and winding, and needs to be tackled with care in poor weather. In winter it's sometimes closed after heavy snows, and you'll often need snow chains for your wheels.

Activities

Cardrona Alpine Resort   SKIING

Map p216; 03-443 7341; www.cardrona.com; off Cardrona Valley Rd; day pass adult/child $99/51; 9am-4pm Jul-Sep) Well-organised and professional, this 345-hectare ski field offers runs to suit all abilities (25% beginners, 50% intermediate, 25% advanced) at elevations ranging from 1670m to 1860m. In season it operates a booking office (03-443 7411; 18 Dunmore St) in Wanaka where you can buy ski passes and book Yello shuttles (return adult/child $35/28).

Snow Farm New Zealand   SKIING

Map p216; 03-443 7542; www.snowfarmnz. com; off Cardrona Valley Rd; day pass adult/child $40/20) In winter this is home to fantastic cross-country skiing, snowshoeing, sledding and dog-sled tours, with over 40km of groomed trails. Lessons and ski hire are available.

Backcountry Saddle
Expeditions   HORSE RIDING

Map p216; 03-443 8151; www.backcountrysaddles.co.nz; Crown Range Rd; adult/child $85/65) Runs horse treks through the Cardrona Valley on Appaloosa horses.

Sleeping & Eating

Cardrona Hotel   PUB $$

(03-443 8153; www.cardronahotel.co.nz; Crown Range Rd; d $185; bar 10am-2am) Après-ski, this iconic hotel really comes into its own. This classic southern pub first opened its doors in 1863, and today you'll find a good restaurant (mains $20 to $32) and a great garden bar. The lovingly restored rooms have snug, country-style furnishings and patios opening onto the garden (expect some noise on summer nights).

Getting There & Away

Ski shuttles are offered by Alpine Connexions (03-443 9120; www.alpinecoachlines.co.nz), Yello (03-443 5555; www.yello.co.nz) and Ridgeline Adventures (p245) in Wanaka, and Kiwi Discovery (p224) in Queenstown.

Lake Hawea

POP 2180

The small town of Lake Hawea, 15km north of Wanaka, sits near the dam at the southern end of its 141-sq-km namesake. Separated from Lake Wanaka by a narrow isthmus called the Neck, blue-grey Lake Hawea is 35km long and 410m deep, and home to trout and landlocked salmon. The lake was raised 20m in 1958 to facilitate the power stations downriver.

Sleeping & Eating

Lake Hawea Holiday Park   HOLIDAY PARK $

(03-443   1767;   www.haweaholidaypark.co.nz; SH6; campsites $16-34, units with/without bathroom $130/60; @) On the lakeshore, this spacious and peaceful old-fashioned holiday park is a favourite of fishing and boating enthusiasts. Units range from a block of basic cabins with brightly painted doors to motel units and cottages.

Lake Hawea Hotel   HOTEL $$

(03-443 1224; www.lakehawea.co.nz; 1 Capell Ave; dm/d $30/180, lunch $11-27, dinner $19-32;) It's looking a little shabby from the outside, but the rooms have been refurbished and have unbeatable views across the lake. The complex includes a large bar and restaurant with equally stellar vistas.

Getting There & Away

InterCity (03-442 4922; www.intercity. co.nz) Coaches stop at the dam (SH6) daily, heading to/from Queenstown (from $20, two hours), Cromwell (from $14, 1¼ hours), Wanaka (from $10, 24 minutes), Makarora (from $10, 1¼ hours) and Franz Josef (from $40, six hours).

Makarora

POP 40

Remote Makarora is the last frontier before you cross Haast Pass and enter the wild West Coast – and it certainly feels that way. Aside from the tour buses passing through, it feels wonderfully remote.

🏃 Activities

Tramping

Short tramps in this secluded area include the **Bridal Track** (1½ hours one way, 3.5km), from the top of Haast Pass to Davis Flat, and the **Blue Pools Walk** (30 minutes return), where you may see huge rainbow and brown trout.

Longer tramps go through magnificent countryside but shouldn't be undertaken lightly. Changeable alpine and river conditions mean you must be well prepared; consult with DOC before heading off. Its *Tramping in the Makarora Region* brochure ($2) is a worthwhile investment.

Gillespie Pass   TRAMPING
The three-day Gillespie Pass loop tramp goes via the Young, Siberia and Wilkin Valleys. This is a high pass with avalanche danger in winter and spring. With a jetboat ride down the Wilkin to complete it, this rates as one of NZ's most memorable tramps.

Wilkin Valley Track   TRAMPING
The Wilkin Valley Track heads off from Kerin Forks Hut – at the top of the Wilkin River – and on to Top Forks Hut and the picturesque Lakes Diana, Lucidus and Castalia (one hour, 1½ hours and three to four hours respectively from Top Forks Hut). Jetboats go to Kerin Forks, and a service goes across the Young River mouth when the Makarora floods. Another option is to use the High River Route from the Blue Pools (7km and two hours). Enquire at Wilkin River Jets or DOC.

Other Activities

Siberia Experience   ADVENTURE TOUR
(☑03-443 4385; www.siberiaexperience.co.nz; adult/child $310/287) ✎ This thrill-seeking extravaganza combines a 25-minute scenic small-plane flight, a three-hour bush walk through a remote mountain valley and a half-hour jetboat trip down the Wilkin and Makarora Rivers in Mt Aspiring National Park. It's possible to arrange transfers from Wanaka.

Wilkin River Jets   JETBOATING
(☑03-443 8351; www.wilkinriverjets.co.nz) A superb 50km, one-hour jetboating trip (adult/child $110/57) into Mt Aspiring National Park, following the Makarora and Wilkin Rivers. It's cheaper than Queenstown options and it can be combined with a helicopter ride.

Southern Alps Air   SCENIC FLIGHTS
(☑0800 345 666, 03-443 4385; www.southernalpsair.co.nz) ✎ Trip to Aoraki/Mt Cook and the glaciers (adult/child $435/275), Milford Sound flyovers ($405/255) and Milford fly-cruise combos ($490/305).

ℹ Information

DOC Visitor Centre (☑03-443 8365; www.doc.govt.nz; SH6; ⊙8am-5pm daily Dec-Mar, Mon-Fri Nov & Apr) Call in to check conditions and routes before undertaking any wilderness tramps. The nearest DOC camping grounds (adult/child $6/3) are on SH6 at Cameron Flat, 10km north of Makarora, and at Boundary Creek, 18km south of Makarora on the shores of Lake Wanaka.

Makarora Tourist Centre (☑03-443 8372; www.makarora.co.nz; 5944 Haast Pass-Makarora Rd/SH6; ⊙8am-8pm) A large complex incorporating a cafe, bar, shop, information centre, camping ground, bunk house and self-contained units.

ℹ Getting There & Away

InterCity (☑03-442 4922; www.intercity.co.nz) Daily coaches to/from Queenstown (from $24, 3½ hours), Cromwell (from $19, 2½ hours), Wanaka (from $12, 1¾ hours), Lake Hawea (from $10, 1¼ hours) and Franz Josef (from $36, 4¾ hours).

Wings & Water Te Anau   SCENIC FLIGHTS
(📞03-249 7405; www.wingsandwater.co.nz; Lakefront Dr) Ten-minute local flights (adult/child $95/55), and longer flights over the Kepler Track and Doubtful and Milford Sounds (from $225).

Luxmore Jet   JETBOATING
(📞0800 253 826; www.luxmorejet.com; adult/child $99/49) One-hour trips on the Upper Waiau River (aka the River Anduin).

Short Walks & Bike Rides

Te Anau's **Lakeside Track** makes for a delightful stroll in either direction – north to the marina and around to the Upukerora River (around an hour return), or south past the National Park Visitor Centre and on to the control gates and start of the Kepler Track (50 minutes). Hire bikes and obtain cycle-track maps from Outside Sports (p256) or **Te Anau Bike Hire** (7 Mokonui St; mountain bikes per hour/day from $12/30; ⊙from 10am Sep-Apr).

Day tramps in the national park are readily accessible from Te Anau. **Kepler Water Taxi** (📞03-249 8364; stevsaunders@xtra.co.nz; 1-way/return $25/50) will scoot you over to Brod Bay from where you can walk to Mt Luxmore (seven to eight hours) or back along the Lakeside Track to Te Anau (two to three hours). During summer, **Trips & Tramps** (📞0800 305 807, 03-249 7081; www.tripsandtramps.com; ⊙Oct-Apr) offers small-group, guided tramps on the Kepler and Routeburn, amongst other tracks. Real Journeys (p265) runs guided day tramps (adult/child $195/127, November to mid-April) along an 11km stretch of the Milford Track. A number of day walks can also be completed by linking with regular bus services run by **Tracknet** (📞0800 483 262; www.tracknet.net).

For self-guided adventures, pick up DOC's *Fiordland National Park Day Walks* brochure ($2) from Te Anau i-SITE or Fiordland National Park Visitor Centre or download it at www.doc.govt.nz.

🛏 Sleeping

Accommodation can get booked out in the peak season (December to February). Book early if possible.

Bob & Maxines   HOSTEL $
(📞03-249 7429; bob.anderson@woosh.co.nz; 20 Paton Pl, off Oraka St; dm $33, d $86-100; 🛜) Only 2.5km out of town, off the Te Anau–Milford Hwy, this relaxed and modern hostel gets rave reviews for the big mountain vistas from the communal lounge. Warm up beside the woodburner, cook up a storm in the well-equipped kitchen, or just chill out. Free bikes and wi-fi.

Rosie's Backpacker & Homestay   HOSTEL $
(📞03-249 8431; www.rosiesbackpackers.co.nz; 23 Tom Plato Dr; dm/d $33/78; ⊙closed Jun-Jul; @🛜) You're immediately made to feel part of the family in this smart and intimate homestay, a short walk north of the town centre.

Te Anau YHA Hostel   HOSTEL $
(📞03-249 7847; www.yha.co.nz; 29 Mokonui St; dm $27-32, d $84-92; @🛜) This centrally located, modern hostel has great facilities and comfortable, colourful rooms. Play volleyball in the grassy backyard, crank up the barbecue or get cosy by the fire in the lounge.

Barnyard Backpackers   HOSTEL $
(📞03-249 8006; www.barnyardbackpackers.com; 80 Mt York Rd, off SH95; dm $29-31, d $76; @) On a deer farm 8km south of town, this rustic communal building and its collection of bunk-free, en suite log cabins sit on a view-laden hillside. The main lodge is great for playing pool or sitting around the toasty fireplace.

Te Anau Lakeview Holiday Park   HOLIDAY PARK $
(📞03-249 7457, 0800 483 262; www.teanauholidaypark.co.nz; 77 Manapouri-Te Anau Hwy; sites per person from $17, dm/s $28/36, units $70-260; @🛜) This 22-acre, grassy lakeside holiday park has plenty of room to pitch your tent or park your van. It also has a wide range of accommodation from basic dorms and singles through to tidy cabins and motels, and rather swanky Marakura Apartments with enviable lake and mountain views. Friendly staff will hook you up with local activities and transport.

Te Anau Top 10 Holiday Park   HOLIDAY PARK $
(📞03-249 7462, 0800 249 746; www.teanautop10.co.nz; 128 Te Anau Tce; sites per person from $20, units $75-166; @🛜) Near the town and lake with private sites, a playground, spa bath, bike hire, a barbecue area and modern kitchen facilities. Well-priced cabins and units run from basic to fancy.

Keiko's Cottages B&B   B&B $$
(📞03-249 9248; www.keikos.co.nz; 228 Milford Rd; d $165-195; ⊙closed Jun-Aug; 🛜) The private, self-contained cottages here are lovely, and surrounded by Japanese-style gardens. A Japanese breakfast in the morning and a bamboo-bordered hot tub in the evening are worthy extras.

Te Anau Lodge B&B B&B $$$

(📞03-249 7477; www.teanaulodge.com; 52 Howden St; d $240-350; @ 🤶) The former 1930s-built Sisters of Mercy Convent, relocated to a grand location just north of town, is a heavenly accommodation option. Sip your complimentary wine in a chesterfield in front of the fire, retire to your spa before collapsing on a king-size bed, then awaken to a fresh, delicious breakfast in the old chapel.

✖ Eating

★ Miles Better Pies PIES $

(cnr Town Centre & Mokonui St; pies $5-7) The bumper selection includes venison, lamb and mint, and fruit pies. There are a few pavement tables, but sitting beside the lake is nicer.

Mainly Seafood FISH & CHIPS $

(www.mainlyseafood.co.nz; 106 Town Centre; fish & chips $7-11, burgers $8-14; ⏰10am-8.30pm) Commendable fish and chips, and burgers with homemade patties – yippee! Massage chair ($2) for if the queue stresses you out.

Fresh Choice Supermarket SUPERMARKET $

(5 Milford Cres; ⏰7am-9pm) A decent-sized supermarket right in the middle of town.

Sandfly Cafe CAFE $$

(9 The Lane; breakfast & lunch $7-18; ⏰7am-4.30pm; 🤶) Clocking the most local votes for the town's best espresso, simple but satisfying Sandfly is a top spot to enjoy an all-day breakfast, soup, pie or sweet treat, while listening to cruisy music or sunning yourself on the lawn.

Ristorante Pizzeria Da Toni ITALIAN $$

(📞03-249 4305; 1 Milford Cres; pizzas $23-25, mains $20-29; ⏰4-10pm Mon-Fri, noon-10pm Sat & Sun; 📶) This rather utilitarian space is *bella*-fied by red gingham tablecloths, the odd splash of Roman and Venetian art and excellent, authentic Italian fare. Wood-fired pizzas with simple, high-quality toppings and homemade pastas are the stars of the show, supported by fine $10 desserts, thoughtful service and a baroque soundtrack.

★ Redcliff Cafe RESTAURANT $$$

(www.theredcliff.co.nz; 12 Mokonui St; mains $31-39; ⏰4-10pm) Housed in a replica old settler's cottage, relaxed Redcliff offers generous fine dining in a convivial atmosphere backed by sharp service. The predominantly locally sourced food is truly terrific: try the wild venison or hare. Kick off or wind it up with a drink in the rustic front bar, which often hosts live music.

🍷 Drinking & Entertainment

Fat Duck BAR

(124 Town Centre; ⏰8.30am-late; 🤶) This corner bar with alfresco seating is a sound choice for a pint or two of Mac's. Marginally trendy gastropub style is reflected in fair modern fare (breakfast $13 to $20, dinner $22 to $39).

Ranch Bar & Grill PUB

(www.theranchbar.co.nz; 111 Town Centre) Popular with locals for its generous pub meals, head here for a quality Sunday roast dinner ($15) and daily happy hour from 8pm to 9pm.

Moose PUB

(www.themoose.co.nz; 84 Lakefront Dr) Head to this waterfront bar for late-afternoon beer and bar snacks on the patio. Plain all-day meals range from $20 to $35.

Fiordland Cinema CINEMA

(📞03-249 8812; www.fiordlandcinema.co.nz; 7 The Lane; 🤶) In between back-to-back showings of the excellent *Ata Whenua* (adult/child $10/5), essentially a 32-minute advertisement for Fiordland scenery, Fiordland Cinema serves as the local movie house. The adjacent Black Dog Bar is the town's most sophisticated watering hole.

🔒 Shopping

Bev's Tramping Gear Hire OUTDOOR EQUIPMENT

(📞03-249 7389; www.bevs-hire.co.nz; 16 Homer St; ⏰9am-noon & 5.30-7pm, closed Sun mornings) Lovely Bev walks the talk, hires tramping and camping equipment, and sells Back Country dehydrated meals. From May to October, only open by prior arrangement.

Outside Sports OUTDOOR EQUIPMENT

(www.outsidesports.co.nz; 38 Town Centre; ⏰9am-5pm) Tramping and camping equipment for sale, or hire, plus bike rental (half-/full day $30/50).

ℹ Information

Fiordland i-SITE (📞03-249 8900; www.fiordland.org.nz; 85 Lakefront Dr; ⏰8.30am-5.30pm) Activity, accommodation and transport bookings.

Fiordland Medical Centre (📞03-249 7007; 25 Luxmore Dr; ⏰8am-5.30pm Mon-Fri, to noon Sat)

Fiordland National Park Visitor Centre (DOC; 📞03-249 0200; www.doc.govt.nz; cnr Lakefront Dr & Te Anau-Manapouri Rd; ⏰8.30am-4.30pm) Can assist with Great Walks bookings, general hut tickets and information, with the bonus of a natural-history display and a shop stocking essential topographical maps for backcountry trips.

Post Office (100 Town Centre; ⊘8.30am-5.30pm Mon-Fri, 9.30am-5pm Sat) In bookshop.

Real Journeys (☑0800 656 501; www.real-journeys.co.nz; Lakefront Dr; ⊘9am-5pm) Booking office for local tours and activities.

Rosco's Milford Kayaks (☑0800 476 726; www.roscosmilfordkayaks.com; 72 Town Centre; ⊘9am-5pm) Booking office for active pursuits.

Southern Discoveries (☑0800 264 536; www.southerndiscoveries.co.nz; Lakefront Dr; ⊘9am-5pm) Booking office for local tours and activities.

❶ Getting There & Away

InterCity (☑03-471 7143; www.intercity.co.nz) has daily bus services between Te Anau and Queenstown (2½ hours), Invercargill (2½ hours) and Dunedin (4¾ hours). Buses depart outside Kiwi Country on Miro St.

Bottom Bus (☑03-477 9083; www.travel-headfirst.com)is a hop-on, hop-off bus service linking Te Anau to Queenstown, Invercargill and Milford Sound (1½ hours). **Naked Bus** (www.nakedbus.com) links Te Anau with Queenstown, Invercargill and Milford Sound.

Te Anau-based **Tracknet** (☑0800 483 262; www.tracknet.net) runs regular services north to Queenstown and south to Invercargill, as well as servicing tramping trailheads and Milford Sound.

Around Te Anau

Te Anau is the gateway to two Great Walks – the Kepler and Milford – and the less visited but equally worthy Hollyford. Detailed information can be found in Lonely Planet's *Hiking & Tramping New Zealand* guide, and from the helpful folk at the Fiordland National Park Visitor Centre, where you can also register your intentions via the Adventuresmart website (www.adventuresmart.org.nz).

Kepler Track

Opened in 1988 to relieve pressure on the Milford and Routeburn, the Kepler is one of NZ's best-planned tracks and now one of its most popular: a moderately strenuous 60km

Kepler Track

loop beginning and ending at the Waiau River control gates at southern end of Lake Te Anau. It features an all-day tramp across the mountaintops taking in incredible panoramas of the lake, the Jackson Peaks and the Kepler Mountains. Along the way it traverses rocky ridges, tussock lands and peaceful beech forest.

The route can be covered in four days, staying in the three huts, although it is possible to reduce the tramp to three days by continuing past Moturau Hut and leaving the track at Rainbow Reach swing bridge. However, spending a night at Moturau Hut on the shore of Lake Manapouri is an ideal way to end this tramp. The track can also be walked in either direction, although the most popular is Luxmore–Iris Burn–Moturau.

The alpine sections require a good level of fitness and may be closed in winter, although this is a heavily weather-dependent track at any time of year.

Estimated walking times:

DAY	ROUTE	TIME
1	Fiordland National Park Visitor Centre to control gates	45min
1	Control gates to Brod Bay	1½hr
1	Brod Bay to Luxmore Hut	3½-4½hr
2	Luxmore Hut to Iris Burn Hut	5-6hr
3	Iris Burn Hut to Moturau Hut	5-6hr
4	Moturau Hut to Rainbow Reach	1½-2hr
4	Rainbow Reach to control gates	2½-3½hr

Bookings & Transport

The Kepler is a Great Walk. Between late October and mid-April you must obtain a Great Walk pass (hut per night $54) for the huts. Passes must be obtained in advance, and it will pay to book early, either online via DOC's **Great Walks Bookings** (☎0800 694 732; www.greatwalks.co.nz) or in person at a DOC visitor centre. In the off-season the huts revert to backcountry Serviced huts ($15). There are campsites at Brod Bay and near Iris Burn Hut (Great Walks season $15, out of season free).

The recommended map for this tramp is 1:60,000 *Parkmap 335-09 (Kepler Track)*.

Conveniently, the track begins under an hour's walk from the Fiordland National Park Visitor Centre, via the lakeside track alongside the Manapouri–Te Anau Rd (SH95). There's a car park and shelter at the control gates. **Tracknet** (☎0800 483 262; www.tracknet.net) runs shuttles to the trailhead ($6) and offers secure parking.

Kepler Water Taxi (☎03-249 8364; stevsaunders@xtra.co.nz) offers early-morning boat services across Lake Te Anau to Brod Bay ($25), slicing 1½ hours off the first day's tramp.

Milford Track

The best-known track in NZ and routinely touted as 'the finest walk in the world', the Milford is an absolute stunner, complete with rainforest, deep glaciated valleys, a glorious alpine pass surrounded by towering peaks, and powerful waterfalls including the legendary Sutherland Falls, one of the loftiest in the world. All these account for its popularity: more than 14,000 trampers complete the 54km-long track each year.

During the Great Walks season, the track can only be walked in one direction, starting from Glade Wharf. You must stay at Clinton Hut the first night, despite it being only one hour from the start of the track, and you must complete the trip in the prescribed three nights and four days. This is perfectly acceptable if the weather is kind, but when the weather turns sour you'll still have to push on across the alpine Mackinnon Pass and may miss some rather spectacular views. It's all down to the luck of the draw.

During the Great Walk season, the track is also frequented by guided tramping parties, which stay at cosy, carpeted lodges with hot showers and proper food. If that sounds appealing, contact **Ultimate Hikes** (☎03-450 1940, 0800 659 255; www.ultimatehikes.co.nz; 5-day tramp $1930-2095), the only operator permitted to run guided tramps of the Milford.

The track is covered by NewTopo map *Milford Track* 1:55,000, and 1:70,000 *Parkmap 335-01 (Milford Track)*.

Estimated walking times:

DAY	ROUTE	TIME
1	Glade Wharf to Glade House	20min
1	Glade House to Clinton Hut	1hr
2	Clinton Hut to Mintaro Hut	5-6hr
3	Mintaro Hut to Dumpling Hut	6-7hr
3	Side trip to Sutherland Falls	1½hr return
4	Dumpling Hut to Sandfly Point	5½-6hr

Milford Track

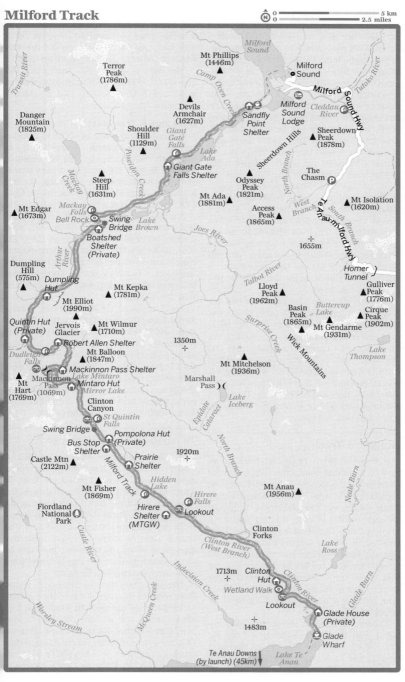

N 0 — 5 km
0 — 2.5 miles

Milford Sound

Transit River

Terror Peak (1786m) ▲

Mt Phillips (1446m) ▲

Milford Sound

Milford Sound Hwy

Camp Oven Creek

Cleddau River

Devils Armchair (1627m) ▲

Sandfly Point Shelter

Milford Sound Lodge

Sheerdown Peak (1878m) ▲

Danger Mountain (1825m) ▲

Shoulder Hill (1129m) ▲

Giant Gate Falls

Lake Ada

Giant Gate Falls Shelter

Sheerdown Hills

The Chasm

Poseidon Creek

Steep Hill (1631m) ▲

Odyssey Peak (1821m) ▲

Mt Ada (1881m) ▲

Mt Isolation (1620m) ▲

Mackay Creek

Mt Edgar (1673m) ▲

Mackay Falls Bell Rock

Swing Bridge

Lake Brown

Joes River

Access Peak (1865m) ▲

North Branch

West Branch

Te Anau–Milford Hwy

South Branch

+ 1655m

Homer Tunnel

Gulliver Peak (1776m) ▲

Boatshed Shelter (Private)

Talbot River

Cirque Peak (1902m) ▲

Dumpling Hill (575m) ▲

Dumpling Hut

Arthur River

Mt Kepka (1781m) ▲

Lloyd Peak (1962m) ▲

Buttercup Lake

Basin Peak (1865m) ▲

Mt Gendarme (1931m) ▲

Mt Elliot (1990m) ▲

Surprise Creek

Wick Mountains

Lake Thompson

Quintin Hut (Private)

Jervois Glacier

Mt Wilmur (1710m) ▲

Robert Allen Shelter

+ 1350m

Dudleigh Falls

Mt Balloon (1847m) ▲

Mt Mitchelson (1936m) ▲

Mackinnon Pass Shelter

Mackinnon Pass (1069m)

Marshall Pass) (

Mintaro Hut

Lake Mintaro

Mirror Lake

Mt Hart (1769m) ▲

Clinton Canyon

Lake Iceberg

St Quintin Falls

Swing Bridge

Pompolona Hut (Private)

Epidote Cataract

North Branch

Bus Stop Shelter

Prairie Shelter

+ 1920m

Castle Mtn (2122m) ▲

Milford Track

Hidden Lake

Mt Fisher (1869m) ▲

Hirere Falls

Lookout

Mt Anau (1956m) ▲

Fiordland National Park

Hirere Shelter (MTGW)

Castle River

Clinton Forks

Lake Ross

Neale Burn

Clinton River (West Branch)

+ 1713m

Clinton Hut

Clinton River

Indecision Creek

Wetland Walk

Glade Burn

McQueen Creek

Lookout

Glade House (Private)

+ 1483m

Glade Wharf

Worsley Stream

Te Anau Downs (by launch) (45km)

Lake Te Anau

Bookings & Transport

The Milford Track is a Great Walk. Between late October and mid-April, you need a Great Walk pass ($162) to cover your three nights in the huts. Passes must be obtained in advance (book early to avoid disappointment), either online via DOC's **Great Walks Bookings** (☑0800 694 732; www.greatwalks. co.nz) or in person at a DOC visitor centre. In the off-season the huts revert to Serviced ($15), and the track can be walked in any time frame you like. This makes the month or so either side of the Great Walks season a great time to tramp, weather dependent.

The track starts at Glade Wharf, at the head of Lake Te Anau, accessible by a 1½-hour boat trip from Te Anau Downs, 29km from Te Anau on the road to Milford Sound. The track finishes at Sandfly Point, a 15-minute boat trip from Milford Sound village from where you can return by road to Te Anau, around two hours away. You will be given options to book the above connecting transport online, at the same time as you book your hut tickets.

To book your own transport, your best bet is to contact **Tracknet** (☑0800 483 262; www. tracknet.net), which offers round-trip packages and secure parking at its Te Anau base. There are other options for transport to and from the track, including a float-plane hop from Te Anau to Glade Wharf with **Wings & Water Te Anau** (☑03-249 7405; www.wingsandwater.co.nz). Te Anau i-SITE and the Fiordland National Park Visitor Centre can advise on options to best suit you.

Hollyford Track

The five-day, 58km Hollyford Track is an easy to moderate tramp through the lower Hollyford – the longest valley in Fiordland National Park – to remote Martin's Bay. Track upgrades and improved transport services, combined with the fact that it's a low-level tramp achievable year-round, have resulted in more trampers discovering the splendid mountain and lake vistas, beautiful forest, extensive birdlife and magical coast that make the Hollyford so special. Even so, the track averages only 4000 trampers a year, making it a good option for those in search of solitude.

The track is basically one way (unless combined with the super-challenging Pyke–Big Bay Route), with the majority of trampers turning tail at Martins Bay and retracing their steps, or flying out from the airstrip at the bay. If possible, spend an extra day in the bay, where you can view a seal colony and get a sneaky peak at a penguin, if you're lucky. This will more than make up for the misdeeds of the most demonic sandflies in NZ.

The best maps for this tramp are NZ-Topo50 *CB09 (Hollyford), CA09 (Alabaster)* and *CA08 (Milford Sound)*. DOC produces a Hollyford Track brochure.

Bookings & Transport

Trampers have the use of six DOC huts on the track, ranging from Serviced ($15) to Standard ($5). Camping ($5) is permitted next to the huts, although sandflies will prevent this being remotely enjoyable. Tickets should be obtained in advance online from DOC visitor centres.

Shuttles services for the Hollyford trailhead are **Tracknet** (☑0800 483 262; www. tracknet.net) and **Trips & Tramps** (☑03-249 7081, 0800 305 807; www.tripsandtramps.com). Nine kilometres (two hours' walk) shy of the trailhead is Gunn's Camp, a good bolthole before or after the feat with car storage and transfers available.

Fly Fiordland (☑0800 359 346; www.fly-fiordland.com) flies out of the Martins Bay airstrip, and Milford Sound for $160 per person (minimum two people), while jetboat trips along Lake McKerrow are offered by **Hollyford Track** (☑03-442 3000, 0800 832 226; www. hollyfordtrack.com), which also runs excellent three-day guided trips on the Hollyford staying at private huts/lodges and ending with a scenic flight to Milford Sound ($1895).

Te Anau–Milford Highway

The 119km road from Te Anau to Milford (SH94) offers the most easily accessible experience of Fiordland. Head out from Te Anau early (8am) or later in the morning (11am) to avoid the tour buses heading for midday sound cruises. Fill up with petrol in Te Anau before setting off, and note that chains must be carried on avalanche-risk days from May to November (there will be signs on the road); these can be hired from most service stations in Te Anau.

The trip takes two to 2½ hours if you drive straight through, but take time to stop and experience the majestic landscape. Pull off the road and explore the many viewpoints and nature walks en route. Pick up DOC'S *Fiordland National Park Day Walks* brochure ($2) from Te Anau i-SITE or Fiordland National Park Visitor Centre or download it at www.doc.govt.nz. The brochure also details the 10 basic DOC campsites ($6 per person) along the highway. All are scenic but also popular with sandflies.

The first part of the road meanders through rolling farmland atop the lateral moraine of the glacier that once gouged out Lake Te Anau. At the 29km mark the road passes Te Anau Downs, where an easy 45-minute return walk leads through forest to Lake Mistletoe, a small glacier-formed lake.

The road then heads into the Eglinton Valley, at first pocketed with sheepy pasture, then reaching deeper wilderness immersion as it crosses the boundary into Fiordland National Park. The knobby peaks, thick beech forest, lupin-lined river banks and grassy meadows are a grand sight indeed.

Just past the Mackay Creek campsite (at 51km) are great views to Pyramid Peak (2295m) and Ngatimamoe Peak (2164m) ahead. The boardwalk at Mirror Lakes (at 58km) takes you through beech forest and wetlands, and on a calm day the lakes reflect the mountains across the valley.

At 63km is Knob's Flat (☏ 03-249 9122; www.knobsflat.co.nz; sites per person $15, d $130-150), which has six self-contained units catering to trampers and anglers but perfect for those who appreciate the simple things in life such a cosy room with a view. And boy, do these units have views. Unpowered sites cater to those who want back-to-nature camping with the relative luxuries of hot showers and a kitchen with a fridge and gas cookers.

At the 77km mark is Cascade Creek and Lake Gunn. This area was known to Maori as O Tapara, and a stopover for parties heading to Anita Bay in search of *pounamu* (greenstone). The Lake Gunn Nature Walk (45 minutes return) loops through tall red beech forest ringing with bird calls, with side trails leading to quiet lakeside beaches.

At 84km the vegetation changes as you pass across the Divide, the lowest east–west pass in the Southern Alps. The roadside shelter here is used by trampers either finishing or starting the Routeburn, Greenstone or Caples Tracks, with bus services pulling in and out with regularity. From here you can embark on a marvellous two-hour return walk along the start of the Routeburn, climbing up through beech forest to the alpine tussockland of Key Summit. On a good day the views of the Humboldt and Darran mountains are sure to knock your socks off, and the nature walk around the boggy tops and stunted beech is a great excuse to linger.

From the Divide, the road falls into the beech forest of the Hollyford Valley (stop at Pop's View for a great outlook) and there's a worthwhile detour off SH94 down the Lower Hollyford to Gunn's Camp, 8km along the unsealed road leading to the Hollyford Track, a further 9km away, where you will also find the track to Humboldt Falls (30 minutes return).

Also known as Hollyford Camp, Gunn's Camp (www.gunnscamp.org.nz; Lower Hollyford Valley Rd; camping per person $15, dm $25, cabins $65, bed linen extra $5) is a stronghold of colourful pioneer legends – of ridiculously difficult road-building, and of Davey Gunn, the hard-core bushman who drove stock then guided tourists through the valley for 25 years before falling off his horse and drowning in 1950. This 1930s public-works camp has a small shop and museum (adult/child $2/free), as well as original cabins with coal/wood-fired stoves, one newer bunk-room and a similarly modern communal kitchen-lounge. Payment is by cash or credit cards only, and the electricity generator gets switched off at 10pm.

Back on the main road to Milford, the road climbs through the cascade-tastic valley to the Homer Tunnel, 101km from Te Anau and framed by a spectacular, high-walled, ice-carved amphitheatre. Begun as a relief project in the 1930s and finally opened to motor traffic in 1954, the tunnel is one way, with the world's most alpine set of traffic lights to direct traffic. Dark, magnificently rough-hewn and dripping with water, the 1270m-long tunnel emerges at the other end at the head of the spectacular Cleddau Valley. Any spare 'wows' might pop out about now. Kea (alpine parrots) hang around the tunnel looking for food from tourists, but don't feed them as it's bad for their health.

About 10km before Milford, the wheelchair- and pram-friendly Chasm Walk (20 minutes return) is well worth a stop. The forest-cloaked Cleddau River plunges through eroded boulders in a narrow chasm, creating deep falls and a natural rock bridge. From here, watch for glimpses of Mt Tutoko (2746m), Fiordland's highest peak, above the beech forest just before Milford.

Milford Sound/Piopiotahi

POP 114

The first sight of Milford Sound is stunning. Sheer rocky cliffs rise out of still, dark waters, and forests clinging to the slopes sometimes relinquish their hold, causing a 'tree avalanche' into the waters. The spectacular, photogenic 1692m-high Mitre Peak rises dead ahead.

Milford Sound receives about half a million visitors each year, many of them crammed into the peak months (January and February). Some 14,000 arrive by foot, via the Milford Track which ends at the sound. Many more drive from Te Anau, but most arrive via the multitude of bus tours. But don't worry: out on the water all this humanity seems tiny compared to nature's vastness.

◎ Sights & Activities

The clue is in the name: Milford Sound is all about the water, and the landforms that envelop it. It's enough to make you go misty-eyed, as an average annual rainfall of 7m fuels innumerable cascading waterfalls. The unique ocean environment – caused by freshwater sitting atop warmer seawater – replicates deep-ocean conditions, encouraging the activity of marine life such as dolphins, seals and penguins. Getting out on the water is a must.

One of the best perspectives you can get of Milford Sound is from a kayak, dwarfed by the cliffs. Two operators can get you out on the water, both of which have booking offices in Te Anau.

Rosco's Milford Kayaks KAYAKING
(☑0800 476 726, 03-249 8500; www.roscosmilfordkayaks.com; 72 Town Centre, Te Anau; trips $99-255) Guided, tandem-kayak trips including the 'Morning Glory' ($189), a challenging paddle the full length of the fiord to Anita Bay, and the easier 'Stirling Sunriser' ($189), which ventures beneath the 151m-high Stirling Falls. Among many other options are trips 'your grandmother could do', and kayak-walk combos on the Milford Track.

Fiordland Wilderness Experiences KAYAKING
(☑03-249-7700, 0800 200 434; www.seakayakfiordland.co.nz; Sandy Brown Rd, Te Anau; per person $145; ☺Sep-Apr) Offers guided six-hour trips on Milford Sound, with four to five hours on the water.

Descend Scubadiving DIVING
(☑0800 337 2363; www.divemilfordsound.co.nz; ex Te Anau/Milford $349/299) Offering a chance to see marine life unique to the Fiordland marine reserve (including a multitude of corals), Descend runs day trips with four hours' cruising on Milford Sound (7m alloy cat), with two dives along the way. Transport, equipment, lunch, hot drinks and snack supplied.

☞ Tours

A cruise on Milford Sound is Fiordland's most accessible experience, as evident from the slew of cruise companies located in the flash **cruise terminal** (☺8am-5.15pm Oct-Apr, 9am-4.15pm May-Sep), a 10-minute walk from the cafe and car park.

Each cruise company claims to be quieter, smaller, bigger, cheaper, or in some way preferable to the rest. What really makes a difference is the timing of the cruise. Most bus tours aim for 1pm sailings so if you avoid that time of day there'll be less people on the boat (and on the road). With some companies you get a better price on cruises outside rush hour, too.

If you're particularly keen on wildlife, ask whether there'll be a nature guide on board. It's wise to book ahead regardless. You generally need to arrive 20 minutes before departure. Most companies offer coach transfers from Te Anau for an additional cost. Day trips from Queenstown make for a very long 13-hour day.

All the cruises visit the mouth of the sound, just 15km from the wharf, poking their prow into the choppy waves of the Tasman Sea. The shorter cruises visit less of the en route 'highlights', which include Bowen Falls, Mitre Peak, Anita Bay and Stirling Falls.

Only visitable on boat trips run by Milford Sound Cruises and Mitre Peak Cruises, **Milford Discovery Centre** (adult/child $36/18; ☺9am-3.45pm) is a five-storey, largely submerged Deep Underwater Observatory offering a chance to view deep-water corals, tube anemones and bottom-dwelling sea perch.

Real Journeys BOAT TOUR
(☑0800 656 501, 03-249 7416; www.realjourneys.co.nz; adult/child from $70/22) Milford's biggest operator runs various trips including the popular 1¾-hour scenic cruise (adult $70 to $93, child $22). The nature cruise (2½ hours, adult $85 to $95, child $22) hones in on wildlife with a specialist nature guide providing commentary. Overnight cruises are also available, on which you can kayak

can assist with maps and heritage trails, as well accommodation.

Just along the road in an insanely turquoise building that has been various forms of eatery since 1891, **Mrs Clark's Café** (108 Palmerston St; meals $12-25; ⊙7am-4pm; 🛜) serves thoroughly contemporary and delicious daytime food (beaut baking!) alongside ace espresso and craft beer.

The **South Coast Environment Centre** (www.sces.org.nz; 154 Palmerston St) has a good range of organic groceries and is the local WWOOF agent.

Invercargill

POP 49,900

This flat and somewhat featureless town tends to inspire ambivalence in its visitors, yet it satisfies all key requirements as a pit stop between the Catlins, Stewart Island/Rakiura and Fiordland. Moreover, it sports some handsome buildings, a notable craft brewery, a decent dining scene, a few arty bits and pleasant open spaces.

👁 Sights & Activities

The streets of Invercargill boast a slew of historic buildings and other features which can be discovered with the *Invercargill Heritage Trail* brochure. The *Short Walks* brochure details various walks in and around the town, including several around **Sandy Point** butting out on to the Oreti River. **Oreti Beach**, 10km to the southwest of town, is a nice spot for a walk or swim.

Southland Museum & Art Gallery   GALLERY
(www.southlandmuseum.com; Queens Park, 108 Gala St; admission by donation; ⊙9am-5pm Mon-Fri, 10am-5pm Sat & Sun) Invercargill's cultural hub has permanent displays on Southland's natural and human history, recounting plenty of fascinating tales around maritime exploits in particular. Be sure to view 'Beyond the Roaring Forties' if you're headed to Stewart Island/Rakiura. The art-gallery area hosts exhibitions from contemporary local arts spliced with occasional international shows.

The museum's rock stars are undoubtedly the tuatara, NZ's unique lizardlike reptiles, unchanged for 220 million years. If the slow-moving, 100-years-old-and-counting patriarch Henry is any example, they're not planning to do much for the next 220 million years either. Feeding time is 4pm on Fridays; outside opening hours they can be viewed through windows at the rear of the pyramid.

If you're a fan of motorcyclist Burt Munro's speedy achievements as captured in *The World's Fastest Indian* (2005), make a beeline for the museum's short but sweet display then follow up with a visit to **E Hayes & Sons** (www.ehayes.co.nz; 168 Dee St) hardware store where you can see his famous motorbike in the flesh. Further evidence of Southland's petrolheadism will manifest in the next few years in the world's finest truck museum. We kid you not – we've eyeballed the exhibits already.

Anderson Park Art Gallery   GALLERY
(McIvor Rd; admission by donation; ⊙gallery 10am-5pm, gardens 8am-dusk) In a 1925 Georgian-style manor, this excellent gallery contains works from many NZ artists. The landscaped gardens are studded with trees and trails, and include a children's playground and *wharepuni* (sleeping house). The gallery is 7km north of the city centre; follow North Rd then turn right into McIvor Rd.

Invercargill Brewery   BREWERY
(www.invercargillbrewery.co.nz; 72 Leet St; ⊙10am-6pm) NZ's great southern brewery has 20 taps for flagon-fills plus a bottled section of its own brews and guests'. Pop in for a tasting, or the 45-minute daily tour at 1pm ($15). Our favourites are the crisp Biman Pilsner and the chocolatey Pitch Black stout.

Queens Park   PARK
Wander around the half-wild, half-tamed Queens Park – a whopping 81 hectares of trees, plant collections, playing fields, ponds, children's playground and even a Wonderland castle.

🛏 Sleeping

Many places will store luggage for guests heading to Stewart Island/Rakiura. Motels cluster along Hwy 1 East (Tay St) and Hwy 6 North (North Rd).

Southern Comfort Backpackers   HOSTEL $
(📞03-218 3838; coupers@xtra.co.nz; 30 Thomson St; dm $28, s $58-66, d$68-74; @🛜) This large, lovely old house offers a well-equipped kitchen and TV-free lounge (hooray!) as well as colourful rooms including spacious doubles. Pick herbs from the peaceful gardens: you'd hardly know you were five minutes' walk from town. Cash only.

Invercargill

Invercargill

Tuatara Backpackers HOSTEL $
(☑ 03-214 0954; www.tuataralodge.co.nz; 30-32 Dee St; dm $25-29, d $69-80; @ 🛜) The town's largest hostel has heaps of basic rooms stacked three floors high in a central city building. If natural light is big on your hit list, ask for a room without the gloom. The ground-floor cafe doubles as a traveller hub, and the Bluff bus for Stewart Island/Rakiura stops just outside.

Invercargill Kiwi Holiday Park HOLIDAY PARK $
(☑ 03-235 8031, 0800 234 600; www.invercargill-kiwihp.co.nz; 352 Lorneville-Dacre Rd; sites per person $19, units d $60-120; @ 🛜) 🍃 Plenty of person-ality is packed into this well-set-out holiday park surrounded by farmland. Homely units feature lovingly preserved and enhanced retro style, while the new 'Barn' communal camping facilities block is one of the nicest we've seen. Rural relaxation, grassy sites, a playground and friendly animals – what a charmer. Around 10km north of Invercargill centre, east of the Lorneville roundabout.

Invercargill Top 10 Holiday Park HOLIDAY PARK $
(☑ 03-218 9032, 0800 486 873; www.invercargilltop10.co.nz; 77 McIvor Rd; sites from $20, units $78-150; @ 🛜) A particularly attractive option for

motel- and cabin-dwellers, this leafy park 6.5km north of town also has pleasant sites and smart communal facilities.

Bushy Point Fernbirds   HOMESTAY $$
(📞03-213 1302; www.fernbirds.co.nz; 197 Grant Rd, Otatara; s/d incl breakfast $140/150; @ 🛜)
🐾 Two friendly corgis are among the hosts at this eco-aware homestay set on the edge of 4.5 hectares of private forest reserve and wetlands. Fernbirds is very popular with birding types, so booking ahead is essential. It's five minutes' drive from central Invercargill, and rates include a guided walk in the reserve.

★**Victoria Railway Hotel**   HISTORIC HOTEL $$
(📞0800 777 557, 03-218 1281; www.hotelinvercargill.com; cnr Leven & Esk Sts; d $145-195; @ 🛜)
For a hit of 19th-century heritage, the plush and individually styled en suite rooms and swanky guests' areas in this grand old refurbished hotel fit the bill. Partake of breakfast or dinner in the elegant dining room, or a locally brewed ale in the cosy house bar. Singles and twins should inquire about bargain rooms.

388 Tay   MOTEL $$
(📞03-217 3881, 0508 388 829; www.388taymotel.co.nz; 388 Tay St; d $125-160; 🛜) Modern and spacious units and a friendly welcome are standard at this well-run spot that's a standout along Invercargill's Tay St motel alley.

✖ Eating

Seriously Good Chocolate Company CAFE $
(147 Spey St; ⊙8am-5pm Mon-Fri, 9am-2pm Sat) This sweet little cafe specialises in artisan chocolates (around $2.50 each), which can be nibbled alongside espresso, or spirited away in lovely gift boxes. Our seriously good recommendation is the ginger. And the hard caramel. And the rocky road...

Turkish Kebabs   TURKISH $
(29 Esk St; kebabs from $10; ⊙10am-10pm; 🍴) Generously proportioned felafel, meaty kebabs and mixed plates are served up in a pleasant dining space or available to take away. Other ethnic take-out joints lie nearby.

Colonial Bakery   BAKERY $
(25a Gala St; snacks $2-8; ⊙7.30am-5pm Tue-Fri, to 3pm Sat & Sun) Euro goods such as baguettes, croissants and seedy Swiss-style breads nudge their way into a line of Kiwi classics such as fruit buns, meat pies and the ridiculous cheese roll.

Three Bean Café   CAFE $
(73 Dee St; meals $11-20; ⊙7am-4pm Mon-Fri, 8am-2.30pm Sat) This main-street cafe prides itself on good coffee then matches the promise with carefully prepared snacks such as savoury pies and delightful lemon cake, and more substantial meals such as soup, salad and burgers. Helpful staff get our thumbs up, too.

★**Batch**   CAFE $$
(173 Spey St; meals $10-20; ⊙7am-4pm) Large shared tables, a relaxed beachy ambience, and top-notch coffee and smoothies add up to the cafe regularly being voted Southland's best. Delicious counter food includes bagels and brownies, and a smallish wine and beer list partners healthy lunch options. Open for platters on Friday nights, until 7.30pm.

Rocks   CAFE $$
(📞03-218 7597; www.shop5rocks.com; Courtville Pl, 101 Dee St; lunch $12-25, dinner $21-37; ⊙10am-2pm & 5pm-late Tue-Sat) Tucked away in a shopping arcade, this stylish candlelit bar with exposed brick and burgundy walls boasts fine dining at reasonable prices. Lunch highlights include belly pork open sandwiches, pastas and salads, while stars of the extended evening menu are venison in blueberry sauce and the Sicilian fish bowl.

Buster Crabb   RESTAURANT $$
(www.bustercrabb.co.nz; 326 Dee St; lunch mains $16-27, dinner mains $24-39; ⊙10.30am-late) Inexplicably named after a British navy frogman who went missing in 1956, Buster Crabb, housed in a spacious heritage villa, is one of Invercargill's best dining experiences. Local workers crowd in for lunchtime salads, roasts, burgers and platters; come evenings the char grill gets fired up for meaty mains like rib-eye wrapped in bacon.

🍸 Drinking & Entertainment

Kiln   BAR †
(www.thekiln.co.nz; 7 Don St; mains $30-35; ⊙11am-late) Invercargill's best gastropub is also its most stylish, with trendy wallpaper and muted lighting from oversized lampshades. Food worth the wait comes in epic portions and runs a well-honed gamut from mussels and caesar salad, to fish and chips or a joint of meat to share between friends. Thursday $15 steak and live music Friday.

WORTH A TRIP

GORE

Around 66km northeast of Invercargill, Gore is the proud 'home of country music' in NZ, with the annual **Gold Guitar Week** (www.goldguitars.co.nz) in late May and early June ensuring the town's accommodation is booked out for at least 10 days per year. For the other 355 days, good reasons to stop include a notable art gallery, a neat little museum and the chance to view vintage aeroplanes.

Sharing the same building, the **Hokonui Moonshine Museum** (www.hokonuiwhiskey.com; admission $5; ☺8.30am-5pm Mon-Fri, 9.30am-4pm Sat, 1-4pm Sun) and **Gore Historical Museum** (admission by donation) combine to celebrate Gore's proud history of fishing, farming and illegal distilleries. Admission to the Moonshine Museum includes a wee dram of the local liquid gold.

The outstanding **Eastern Southland Gallery** (☑03-208 9907; www.esgallery.co.nz; 14 Hokonui Dr; admission by donation; ☺10am-4.30pm Mon-Fri, 1-4pm Sat & Sun) – aka the 'Goreggenheim' – in Gore's century-old former public library houses a hefty collection of NZ art including a large Ralph Hotere collection. The amazing John Money Collection combines indigenous folk art from West Africa and Australia with works by iconic New Zealand artist Rita Angus.

Croydon Aircraft Company (www.croydonaircraft.com; 1558 Waimea Hwy, SH94; admission $10; ☺9.30am-4.30pm Mon-Fri, 11am-3pm Sat & Sun), 16km along SH94 towards Queenstown, restores vintage aircraft. Inside a viewing hangar (admission $10) several gems can be seen including a rare Dragonfly. Flights are also offered in a 1930s Tiger Moth biplane ($95/220 for 10/30 minutes). The adjacent **Moth** (www.themoth.co.nz; 1558 Waimea Hwy, SH94; lunch $12-26, dinner $27-45) is a bright and breezy place for a meal.

See www.gorenz.com for more on Gore.

Louie's BAR
(142 Dee St; mains $20-30; ☺11.30am-late Tue-Sat) This cosy downtown bar is an enjoyable place to while away an evening, snuggled into a sofa or nook or fireside. Soak up fine beer, wine and spirits with tapas-style food ($13 to $17) or tuck into a main course ($30 to $32). Expect chilled-out music; occasional live gigs.

Tillermans Music Lounge LIVE MUSIC
(16 Don St; ☺open on gig nights) The saviour of Southland's live-music fans, Mr Tillerman's venue hosts everything from thrash to flash, with a battered old dance floor to show for it. Visit the fun downstairs Vinyl Bar, which is open more regularly, to find out what's coming up and put in your request for Roxy Music.

ℹ Information

DOC office (☑03-211 2400; www.doc.govt.nz; 7th fl, 33 Don St; ☺8.30am-4.30pm Mon-Fri) Call in for DOC-related information and maps only if the i-SITE fails you or if you can't get to a DOC visitor centre.

Invercargill i-SITE (☑03-211 0895; www. invercargillnz.com; Queens Park, 108 Gala St; ☺8am-5pm Mon-Fri, to 4pm Sat & Sun) Sharing the Southland Museum & Art Gallery building, the i-SITE can help with all general enquiries including DOC tracks, and is a god-send if you're stuck for Stewart Island/Rakiura or Catlins accommodation options .

Post office (51 Don St; ☺8.30am-5.30pm Mon-Fri, 9am-1pm Sat)

ℹ Getting There & Away

AIR

Air New Zealand flights link Invercargill to Christchurch (one hour) and onward, several times a day.

BUS

Buses leave from the Invercargill i-SITE, where you can also book your tickets. Travel time to Dunedin is four hours, Te Anau three hours, Queenstown four hours, and Christchurch 10 hours.

Atomic Shuttles (☑03-349 0697, 0508 108 359; www.atomictravel.co.nz) To Dunedin and Christchurch via Gore.

InterCity (☑03-471 7143; www.intercity.co.nz) To Te Anau and Queenstown, and Dunedin and Christchurch via Gore.

Naked Bus (www.nakedbus.com) To Queenstown, and Dunedin and Christchurch via Gore.

Tracknet (☑0800 483 262; www.tracknet.net) To Te Anau and Queenstown.

❶ Getting Around

Invercargill Airport (☎ 03-218 6367; www. invercargillairport.co.nz; 106 Airport Ave) is 3km west of central Invercargill. The door-to-door **Airport Shuttle** (☎ 03-214 3434) costs $5 to $10 from the city centre to the airport; more for residential pick-up. By taxi it's around $22; try **Blue Star Taxis** (☎ 03-217 7777).

Bluff

POP 1791

Bluff is Invercargill's port, 27km south of the city. It's also home to NZ's only aluminum smelter, but the main reason folk come here is to catch the ferry to Stewart Island/Rakiura or to pose for photos beside the **Stirling Point signpost**, which signifies that you've reached the furthest southern reaches of NZ. Sorry to disappoint you, but you haven't, for despite the oft-quoted phrase 'from Cape Reinga to Bluff' and the fact that SH1 terminates at Stirling Point, the South Island's southernmost point is Slope Point in the Catlins, with Stewart Island/Rakiura and remote dots of rock lying even further south. But let's not let the facts get in the way of a good story...

Salty tales abound round these parts, as evident in the small **Bluff Maritime Museum** (☎ 03-212 7534; 241 Foreshore Rd; adult/child $2/free; ⊙10am-4.30pm Mon-Fri, 1-5pm Sat & Sun), complete with century-old oyster boat and steam engine. It also houses interesting displays on Bluff history. The *Bluff Heritage Trail* brochure will guide you around local points of interest.

Oysters are Bluff's most famous export, celebrated during the **Bluff Oyster & Food Festival** (www.bluffoysterfest.co.nz) held annually around May. Buy fresh oysters in season from late March to late August from **Fowlers Oysters** (Ocean Beach Rd; ⊙9am-5pm Mar-Aug) on the way into town on the left.

Near the Four Square supermarket, **Stella's** (64 Gore St; ⊙7am-3pm) is your best bet for a coffee before braving the ferry crossing to Stewart Island/Rakiura. The muttonbird pie might prove a questionable decision.

For more information see www.bluff.co.nz.

The Catlins

The most direct route between Invercargill and Dunedin is via SH1. The pastoral scenery is pretty, but not as spectacular as the SH92 route via the Catlins coast. The Catlins is an enchanting region, combining lush farmland, native forests, usual coastal landmarks and empty beaches, bushwalks and wildlife-spotting opportunities. On a clear summer's day it is a beauty to behold. In the face of an Antarctic southerly it's an entirely different kettle of fish. Good luck.

Public transport is limited to the **Bottom Bus** (☎ 03-477 9083; www.travelheadfirst.com), which travels swiftly through from Dunedin three days a week. By far the best way to explore the area is with your own wheels. It's a slow-going route, with plenty of winding bits, narrows, gravel sections and optional detours, but this is *all* about the journey, rather than the destination. Allow a few days if at all possible, and make sure you have on hand the *Southern Scenic Route* brochure and the purple *Catlins* brochure and map, which detail every dot. The yellow heritage-trail pamphlet is also worth hunting down.

Flora & Fauna

The Catlins is a wonderful place for independent wildlife-watching. Fur seals and sea lions laze along the coast, while in spring migratory southern right whales are occasionally spotted. Dolphins are also frequent visitors.

Unlike much of Southland, tall kahikatea, totara and rimu forests still exist in the Catlins. Prolific birdlife includes the wonderfully noisy tui, and you'll also see kereru (NZ pigeons). Among many other birds are the endangered yellow-eyed penguin and the rare mohua (yellowhead).

🏃 Activities

Catlins Wildlife Trackers   WILDLIFE TOUR
(☎ 03-415 8613, 0800 228 5467; www.catlins-ecotours.co.nz) ✔ Based near Papatowai and running since 1990, Catlins Wildlife Trackers offers customised guided walks and tours with a focus on ecology. If you want to see the beloved mohua, penguins, sea lions or other wildlife, Mary and Fergus will track them down for you. Their fully guided three-night/two-day package costs $800, including all food, accommodation and transport.

Catlins River-Wisp Loop Track   TRAMPING
(www.doc.govt.nz) Opened in 2013, this 24km loop comprises two 12km sections: the low-level, well-formed Catlins River Walk (five to six hours), and the Wisp Walk (four to five hours), a higher-altitude tramp with a side trip to Rocky Knoll boasting great views and subalpine vegetation. The routes can be

The Catlins

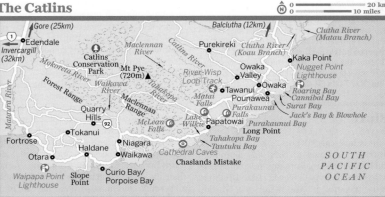

walked in either direction as one long day, divided over two days, or split into shorter sections accessed via various entry/exit points. The main access is via Catlins Valley Road, south of Owaka.

Catlins Surf School SURFING
(☑ 03-246 8552; www.catlins-surf.co.nz) Located in Porpoise Bay, the Catlins Surf School runs 90-minute surfing lessons for $50. The occasional group of dolphin spectators is free of charge. If you're already confident on the waves, hire a board and wetsuit (very necessary) for three hours ($40). Owner Nick also offers tuition in stand-up paddleboarding (two hours, $75).

Catlins Horse Riding HORSE RIDING
(☑ 027 269 2904, 03-415 8368; www.catlinshorse-riding.co.nz; 41 Newhaven Rd, Owaka; 1/2/3hr rides $60/100/150) Explore the idiosyncratic coastline and landscapes on four legs with Catlins Horse Riding. Learners treks and the full gallop available.

ℹ️ Information

The i-SITEs in Invercargill and Balclutha have lots of Catlins information. On the road, you'll pass two information centres: the small Catlins Info Centre in Owaka or even smaller **Waikawa Information Centre** (☑ 03-246 8464; waikawamuseum@hyper.net.nz; Main Rd; ⊙10am-5pm). Online, see www.catlins.org.nz and www.catlins-nz.com.

The Catlins has no banks and limited options for eating out and grocery shopping. There's an ATM at the Four Square supermarket in Owaka, and petrol stations (hours can be irregular) in Fortrose, Papatowai and Owaka.

Invercargill to Papatowai

Heading east and south from Invercargill, SH92 enters the Catlins region at **Fortrose**. Take the turn-off here towards Waipapa Point and use the coastal route via Haldane, Waikawa and Niagara (where you rejoin SH92).

The **Waipapa Point lighthouse** dates from 1884, three years after the wreck of SS *Tararua*. Information panels recount the terrible tale, in which 131 people lost their lives. Tiptoe through the sea lions to survey the beach.

Follow the signs to **Slope Point**, the South Island's true southerly point. A 20-minute walk across farmland leads to a signpost designating this landmark in underwhelming fashion. The views more than make up for it, not only of the ocean but of the chunky rocks tumbling down to meet it. The track is closed in September and October for lambing.

Further east at **Curio Bay**, fossilised Jurassic-age trees are visible for four hours either side of low tide. Yellow-eyed penguins waddle ashore here an hour or so before sunset. Do the right thing and keep your distance. Backing on to Curio is **Porpoise Bay**, a popular travellers' stop with numerous accommodation options. Blue penguins nest in the dunes and in summer Hector's dolphins come here to rear their young. Whales are occasional visitors, and fur seals and sea lions may also be seen. There's safe swimming on the beach, and an excellent surf school.

The next civilised stop is **Waikawa**, which has a small museum, information centre, some accommodation and a takeway. Keep on trucking to **McLean Falls**. The car park is 4km off the highway, with the falls themselves a 40-minute return walk through tree ferns and rimu.

Cutting back 150m into cliffs, the huge, arched **Cathedral Caves** (www.cathedralcaves. co.nz; adult/child $5/1) are only accessible for two hours either side of low tide (tide timetables are posted on the website, at the highway turn-off and at visitor facilities). From SH92 it's 2km to the car park, then a ferny 15-minute walk down to the beach – rather stunning in itself – and a further five minutes to the caves.

Around 6km further east, an easy forest walk leads to the dark peaty waters of **Lake Wilkie** (20 minutes return). Bellbirds may ring. Another 1km further along the highway, a short gravel road leads to sweeping **Tautuku Bay**, which can also be viewed from on high at the **Florence Hill Lookout** just before the descent into Papatowai.

The must-see in **Papatowai** is the **Lost Gypsy Gallery** (☑ 03-415 8908; SH92; ☺ 10am-5pm Thu-Tue, closed May-Sept; ☎). Fashioned from remaindered bits and bobs, artist Blair Sommerville's intricately crafted automata are wonderfully irreverent. The bamboozling collection in the bus (free entry) is a teaser for the carnival of creations through the gate ($5 entry, children under 12 not allowed). The buzz, bong and bright lights of the organ are bound to tickle your ribs. Espresso caravan and wi-fi on site.

Papatowai has a couple of short walks, a picnic spot at the mouth of the Tahakopa River, a handful of accommodation options and a general store selling petrol.

🛏 Sleeping

SLOPE POINT

Slope Point Backpackers　　　HOSTEL $
(☑ 03-246 8420; www.slopepoint.co.nz; 164 Slope Point Rd; sites per person from $12, dm $22-27, d $47, unit $87; @☎) This rural property has modern dorms and rooms, along with a great-value self-contained unit. There are grassy tent pitches and gravel sites for campervans, and the owners' children are always keen to show off the working farm. Board games, puzzles and loads of magazines take the place of TV.

CURIO BAY

Curio Bay Holiday Park　　　HOLIDAY PARK $
(☑ 03-246 8897; valwhyte@hotmail.com; 601 Curio Bay Rd; sites unpowered/powered 2 people $20/30) Tucked into an outcrop between Curio and Porpoise Bays, within easy walking distance to both, this camp offers private campsites hidden in a sea of tall flax. It's a truly beautiful place to camp, despite seriously ancient amenities. Long-promised upgrades are apparently in the pipeline. Guided nature walks are available.

Lazy Dolphin Lodge　　　HOSTEL $
(☑ 03-246 8579; www.lazydolphinlodge.co.nz; 529 Curio Bay Rd; dm/d/tw $35/76/76; @☎) This perfect hybrid of seaside holiday home and hostel is looking totally swell. Light and airy bedrooms sport cheerful linen, and there are two kitchens and lounges. The upstairs area is king for its deck overlooking Porpoise Bay.

Curio Bay Boutique Studios　　　APARTMENTS $$
(☑ 03-246 8797; www.curiobay.co.nz; 501 Curio Bay Rd; d $160-200) Three plush units are on offer here – one apartment attached to the hosts' house, and two similar down the road. All are self-contained, decorated in rustic, beachy style, with big windows and sun-drenched decks right next to the beach. A larger cottage is good for groups. Lovely options offering a touch of romance.

Catlins Beach Cottages　　　RENTAL HOUSE $$
(☑ 03-246 8552; www.catlins-surf.co.nz; houses $110-190) A range of self-contained cottages and houses around Curio Bay can be rented through Catlins Surf School. One-night rentals are fine, and it's a good option for travelling families or groups of up to six.

WAIKAWA

Penguin Paradise Holiday Lodge　　　HOSTEL $
(☑ 03-246 8552; www.catlins-surf.co.nz; 612 Niagara-Waikawa Rd; dm/d/tw $28/60/60) Laid-back backpackers in a heritage cottage in Waikawa village near the estuary. Special deals combine one night's accommodation and a 90-minute surf lesson ($75).

Waikava Harbourview　　　RENTAL HOUSE $$
(☑ 03-246 8866; www.southcatlins.co.nz; 14 Larne St; d $130-170) Waikava Harbourview is a four-bedroom house that's a good option for families or a group; up to 10 people can be accommodated. Opened in 2009, the newer one- and two-bedroom Harakeke and Toi Tois units are also good value.

MCLEAN FALLS

Catlins Kiwi Holiday Park   HOLIDAY PARK $
(☑ 03-415 8338; www.catlinsnz.com; SH92; sites
from $20, cabins s/d $50/74, units $135-195; @ ☎)
Formerly known as McLean Falls Holi-
day Park, this modern holiday park offers
personality-packed accommodation ranging from cute cabins to smart family motels.
Tenters get the more ambient of the camping
options; all share good communal amenities.
Hop along to the on-site **Whistling Frog Cafe**
for some of the Catlins' best food.

PAPATOWAI

Hilltop   LODGE $
(☑ 03-415 8028; www.hilltopcatlins.co.nz; 77 Tahakopa Valley Rd; dm $34, d $85-100) High on a hill
1.5km out of town, with native forest at the
back door and surrounded by a sheep farm,
these two shipshape cottages command
spectacular views of the Tahakopa Valley
and coast. Rent by the room or the whole
house; the en suite double is the pick of a
very nice bunch.

Catlins Mohua Park   COTTAGES $$
(☑ 03-415 8613, 0800 228 5467; www.catlinsmohua-
park.co.nz; 744 Catlins Valley Rd; d $120-200) ✿
Situated on the edge of a peaceful 14-hectare
nature reserve (7km off the highway), these
four luxurious self-contained cottages are the
perfect base for exploration, although with
such interesting mixed forest and birdlife on
the doorstep, you may well just want to sit
still for a bit. The owners have other accom-
modation options available at Papatowai.

✕ Eating

You'll find roadside takeaways in Waikawa
and Papatowai. The Papatoawi general store
has a limited range of groceries.

Whistling Frog Café & Bar   CAFE $$
(☑ 03-415 8338; www.whistlingfrogcafe.com; SH92,
McLeans Falls; mains $20-32; ⊙ 8.30am-9pm; ☎)
✿ Colourful and fun, the Frog has a serious
approach to food and drink, offering craft
beer on tap (happy hour 4.30pm to 6pm)
and a refreshingly cosmopolitan menu.
We're talking a seriously rich steak-and-ale
pie with gourmet fries and a side salad with
blueberry dressing and candied nuts. Or
duck salad with blue cheese and rocket. Rib-
bit! Located at the Catlins Kiwi Holiday Park.

Niagara Falls Café   CAFE $$
(www.niagarafallscafe.co.nz; 256 Niagara-Waikawa
Rd, Niagara; lunch mains $13-27, dinner $23-35;

⊙ 8am-10pm; ☎ ✍) Located in an old school-
house, this is a friendly spot to linger over
coffee and a scone, or tuck into homemade
meals from breakfast through dinner. Tasty
lamb burgers are sandwiched into freshly
baked bread, and there's blue cod and chow-
der as well as plenty of vegetarian options.
Bask in the grassy garden with a local craft
beer or fine wine.

Papatowai to Balclutha

From Papatowai, follow the highway north
to **Matai Falls** (a 30-minute return walk)
on the Maclennan River, then head south-
east on the signposted road to the tiered
Purakaunui Falls (20 minutes return). Both
falls are reached via cool, dark forest walks
through totara and tree fern.

Continue along the gravel road from
Purakaunui Falls to the 55m-deep **Jack's
Blowhole**. In the middle of a paddock 200m
from the sea but connected by a subterrane-
an cavern, this huge cauldron was named af-
ter Chief Tuhawaiki, nicknamed Bloody Jack
for his cussin'. It's a fairly brisk 30-minute
walk each way.

Owaka is the Catlins' main town (popula-
tion a hefty 303), bolstered by the **Catlins
Info Centre & Owaka Museum** (adult/child
$5/free; ⊙ 9.30am-1pm & 1.30-4.30pm Mon-Fri
10am-4pm Sat & Sun), which houses displays
on local history. The Catlins' reputation
as a shipwreck coast is explained in video
presentations. A petrol station, Four Square
supermarket with an ATM, and several run-
of-the-mill places to eat make Owaka a use-
ful spot for stocking up before moving on.

Pounawea, 4km east, is a beautiful ham-
let on the edge of the Catlins River Estuary.
Just across the inlet is **Surat Bay**, notable
for the sea lions that lie around the beach
between here and **Cannibal Bay**, an hour's
beach walk away.

Heading north from Owaka, detour off
SH92 to **Nugget Point** and walk out to the
lighthouse. This is the king of the Catlins
viewpoints, made all the more interesting
by the wave-thrashed cliffs, toothy nug-
gets, seals and sea lions lolling about below.
There's also plenty of birdlife, such as soar-
ing shearwaters and spoonbills huddling in
the lea of the breeze.

Just shy of the Nugget Point car park is
the car park for **Roaring Bay**, where a well
placed hide allows you to see yellow-eyed
penguins coming ashore (best two hours be-
fore sunset). Obey all signs: as you can see

this is a pretty precarious existence. If you don't have your own transport, nightly **twilight tours** (✆0800 525 278; www.catlins.co.nz; per person $30) are run by the folks at Nugget View & Kaka Point Motels.

From Nugget Point the road loops back through the little township of **Kaka Point**, which has a surfy swimming beach, several accommodation options and a waterfront pub. The road continues north from here to Balclutha.

🛏 Sleeping & Eating

You won't starve along this stretch, as there are numerous food stops dotted along the highway. However, an investment in cheese and crackers may save you being smothered in chips.

OWAKA & PURAKAUNUI

DOC Camping Grounds CAMPSITE $
(www.doc.govt.nz; adult/child $6/3) There are DOC camping grounds at Purakaunui Bay and inland at Tawanui.

POUNAWEA

Pounawea Motor Camp HOLIDAY PARK $
(✆03-415 8483; www.catlins-nz.com/pounawea-motor-camp; Park Lane; sites from $30, units $50-80; ☎) Right on the estuary and next to a precious remant of native forest, this small park is best suited to tenters and campervanners who share a dated kitchen but smart bathrooms with the dwellers of some musty cabins. Tall trees and birdsong are the key features here.

Pounaewa Grove Motel MOTEL $$
(✆03-415 8339; www.pounaweagrove.co.nz; 5 Ocean Grove; d $130; ☎) If you're looking for modern units with big, comfy beds, plush textiles, flat-screen TVs and sharp bathrooms, this four-unit studio complex will tick all the boxes. If you're looking for room to swing a cat, it will need to be a small one.

SURAT BAY

★ Newhaven Holiday Park HOLIDAY PARK $
(✆03-415 8834; www.newhavenholiday.com; Newhaven Rd; sites unpowered/powered $32/35, units $66-120; ☎) Sitting on the estuary edge at the gateway to the Surat Bay beach walk, this delightful little holiday park has nice sites with good communal facilities, along with cheerful cabins and three self-contained flats. Play with the giant chess set or lounge around on the lawn.

NUGGET & KAKA POINTS

Kaka Point Camping Ground HOLIDAY PARK $
(✆03-412 8801; www.kakapointcamping.co.nz; 39 Tarata St; sites per person unpowered/powered $14.50/16, cabins s/d $30/56; ☎) Cabins are basic but functional, and there are grassy hedged areas for campers. Bushwalks delve into the surrounding forest, and it's a short, though steep, stroll downhill to the beach and village.

Nugget Lodge LODGE $$
(✆03-412 8783; www.nuggetlodge.co.nz; Nugget Rd; d $175; ☎) Sitting on a seaside knoll on the road south to the lighthouse are two modern bach-style self-contained units – one with balcony, one with private garden. It's worth including the lodge's huge continental breakfast ($12.50 per person) with freshly baked bread and homemade muesli. If you're lucky you might spy a couple of resident sea lions lolling on the beach below you.

Nugget View & Kaka Point Motels MOTEL $$
(✆0800 525 278; www.catlins.co.nz; 11 Rata St; d $95-200; ☎) A veritable minivillage of motel options ranging from good-value older units through to more modern ones with spa baths. All except one have a sea-view verandah. The friendly owners also operate day tours of the Catlins, and twilight tours ($30 per person) to view Nugget Point and the penguin colony at Roaring Bay.

Point Café & Bar PUB $$
(58 Esplanade; meals $13-30) Prop yourself at the driftwood bar for a cool beer, play pool or grab a window seat for a sea view. Takeaways and ice creams are available at the attached store – $10 will get you burger and a scoop of hokeypokey ice cream.

Stewart Island/Rakiura

Travellers who undertake the short jaunt to Stewart Island/Rakiura will be rewarded with a warm welcome from both the local kiwi and the local Kiwis. NZ's 'third' island is a good place to spy the country's shy, feathered icon in the wild, and the close-knit community of Stewart Islanders (population 381) are relaxed hosts. If you're staying on the island for just a few days, don't be too surprised if most people quickly know who you are and where you came from – especially if you mix and mingle over a beer at

Stewart Island (North)

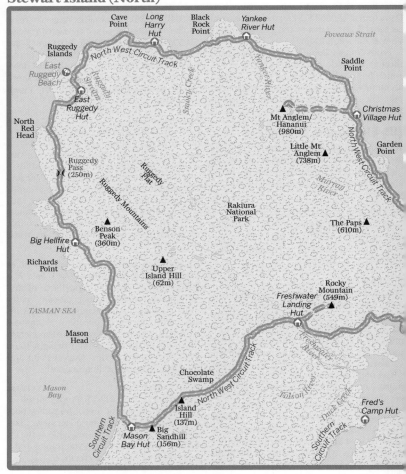

NZ's southernmost pub, in the main settlement of Oban.

The island offers up plenty of active adventure including kayaking, and tramping the Great Walk or other tramps in Rakiura National Park which makes up 85% of the land area. As well as beautiful coastal and inland scenery, a major impetus for such excursions is birdlife. Stewart Island/Rakiura is a bird sanctuary of international repute, and even the most amateur of spotters will likely be distracted by the constant – and utterly glorious – squawking, singing and flitting of feathery flocks.

History

Stewart Island's Maori name is Rakiura (Glowing Skies), and you only need to catch a glimpse of a spectacular blood-red sunset or the aurora australis to see why. According to myth, NZ was hauled up from the ocean by Maui, who said, 'Let us go out of sight of land, far out in the open sea, and when we have quite lost sight of land, then let the anchor be dropped'. The North Island was the fish that Maui caught, the South Island his canoe and Rakiura was the anchor – Te Punga o te Waka o Maui.

In June 1864 Stewart and the adjacent islets were bought from local Maori for £6000. Early industries were sealing, timber-milling, fish-curing and shipbuilding, with a short-lived gold rush towards the end of the 19th century. Today the island's economy is dependent on tourism and fishing.

Flora & Fauna

With an absence of mustelids (ferrets, stoats and weasels) and large areas of intact forest, Stewart Island/Rakiura has one of the largest and most diverse bird populations of anywhere in NZ. Even in the streets of Oban the air resonates with birds such as tui, bellbirds and kaka, which share their island home with weka, kakariki, fernbirds, robins and Rakiura tokoeka/kiwi. There are also plenty of shore- and seabirds including dotterels, shags, mollymawks, prions, petrels and albatross, as well as the sooty shearwater which is seen in large numbers during breeding season. Ask locals about the evening parade of penguins on a small beach near the wharf; and *please* – don't feed the birds. It's bad for them.

Exotic animals include two species of deer, the red and the Virginia (whitetail), introduced in the early 20th century, as were brush-tailed possums, which are now numerous throughout the island and destructive to the native bush. Stewart Island/Rakiura also has NZ fur seals, NZ sea lions, elephant seals and occasionally leopard seals that visit the beaches and rocky shores.

Beech, the tree that dominates much of NZ, is absent from Stewart Island/Rakiura. The predominant lowland bush is podocarp forest, with exceptionally tall rimu, miro, totara and kamahi forming the canopy. Because of mild winters, frequent rainfall and porous soil, most of the island is a lush forest, thick with vines and carpeted in deep green ferns and mosses.

⊙ Sights

★Ulva Island   ISLAND
A tiny paradise covering only 250 hectares, Ulva Island/Te Wharawhara is a great place to see lots of birds. Established as a bird sanctuary in 1922, it remains one of Stewart Island/Rakiura's wildest corners – 'a rare taste of how NZ once was and perhaps could be again', according to DOC. The island was declared rat free in 1997 and three years later

There is evidence that parts of Rakiura were occupied by moa hunters as early as the 13th century. The titi (muttonbird or sooty shearwater) on adjacent islands were an important seasonal food source for the southern Maori.

The first European visitor was Captain Cook. Sailing around the eastern, southern and western coasts in 1770 he mistook it for the bottom end of the South Island and promptly named it South Cape. In 1809 the sealing vessel *Pegasus* circumnavigated Rakiura and named it after its first officer, William Stewart.

FIORDLAND & SOUTHLAND STEWART ISLAND/RAKIURA

Oban

was chosen as the site to release endangered South Island saddlebacks. Today the air is alive with birdsong, which can be appreciated on walking tracks in the island's northwest as detailed in *Ulva: Self-Guided Tour* ($2), available from the DOC visitor centre. Many paths intersect amid beautiful stands of rimu, miro, totara and rata. Any water-taxi company will run you to the island from Golden Bay wharf, with scheduled services run by **Ulva Island Ferry** (☑03-219 1013; return adult/child $20/10; ☺ departs 9am, noon & 4pm; returns noon, 4pm & 6pm). To get the most out of Ulva Island, go on a tour with Ulva's Guided Walks (p279).

Rakiura Museum   MUSEUM
(Ayr St; adult/child $2/50c; ☺10am-1.30pm Mon-Sat, noon-2pm Sun) Historic photographs are stars of this small museum focused on local natural and human history, and featuring Maori artifacts, whaling gear and household items.

Presbyterian Church   CHURCH
(Kamahi Rd) This wooden church has perched on a knoll overlooking the bay since 1904. One local wagers that shipwrights had a hand in its building: 'some of the joints are a pleasure to behold.'

🏃 Activities

Rakiura National Park protects 85% of the island, making it a mecca for trampers and bird-watchers. There are plenty of tracks on which to explore the wilderness, ranging from short, easy trails readily accessible on foot from Oban, to the epic North West Circuit, one of NZ's most legendary backcountry tramps.

Numerous operators offer guided tours: walking, driving, boating and by air, most focusing on wildlife with history slotted in. Independent walkers have plenty to choose from; visit Rakiura National Park Visitor Centre for details on local tramps, long and short, and huts along the way. The trails in DOC's *Stewart Island/Rakiura Short Walks* pamphlet ($2) would keep you busy for several days, and a bit less if you hire a bike from the Red Shed to fast-track the road sections. Longer tramps can also be shortened and indeed enhanced via an air hop with **Rakiura Helicopters** (☑ 03-219 1155; www.rakiurahelicopters.co.nz), or Stewart Island Flights (p282), which works with Rakiura Charters to offer the fulfilling day-long or overnight **Coast to Coast** cross-island hike. Both air operators offer scenic flights.

If you haven't ever sea-fished, or just fancy it, this is the place, for NZ boasts no better fishers. Oh, and the answer to the question of swimming is definitely yes: yes, it is possible, and yes, you will probably freeze your nuts off.

Day Walks

Observation Rock
WALKING

This short but quite sharp 15-minute climb reaches the Observation Rock lookout where there are panoramic views of Paterson Inlet, Mount Anglem and Mount Rakeahua. The trail is clearly marked from the end of Leonard Rd, off Ayr St.

Ackers Point
WALKING

This three-hour return walk features an amble around the bay to a bushy track passing the historic **Stone House** (built 1835) at **Harrald Bay** before reaching **Ackers Point Lighthouse** where there are wide views of Foveaux Strait and the chance to see blue penguins and a colony of titi.

Overnight Tramps

Rakiura Track
TRAMPING

(www.doc.govt.nz) One of NZ's nine Great Walks, the 39km, three-day Rakiura Track is a peaceful and leisurely loop which sidles around beautiful beaches before climbing over a 250m-high forested ridge and traversing the sheltered shores of Paterson Inlet/Whaka a Te Wera. It passes sites of historical interest and introduces many of the common sea- and forest birds of the island.

Rakiura Track is actually only 32km long, but adding in the road sections at either end bumps it up to 39km, conveniently forming a circuit from Oban. It's a well-defined circuit requiring a moderate level of fitness, suitable for tramping year-round. Being a Great Walk, it has been gravelled to eliminate most of the mud for which the island is infamous.

There are two Great Walk huts ($22) en route, which need to be booked in advance, either via **Great Walks Bookings** (☑ 0800 694 732; www.greatwalks.co.nz) or in person at the national park visitor centre. There is a limit of two consecutive nights in any one hut. Camping ($6) is permitted at the Standard campsites near the huts, and also at Maori Beach.

North West Circuit Track
TRAMPING

(www.doc.govt.nz) The North West Circuit Track is Stewart Island/Rakiura's legendary tramp, a demanding coastal epic around a remote and natural coastline featuring isolated beaches, sand dunes, birds galore and miles of mud. It's 125km and takes 10 to 12 days, although there are several options for shortening it involving boats and planes.

The track begins and ends in Oban. There are well-spaced huts along the way, all of which are Standard ($5) except for two Great Walk Huts ($22) which must be booked in advance. A North West Circuit Pass ($35) provides for a night in each of the backcountry huts. Detailed information and essential topographical maps are available from DOC; and do register your intentions at the Adventuresmart website (www.adventuresmart.org.nz) as this is no easy walk in the park.

👉 Tours

Ulva's Guided Walks
WALKING TOUR

(☑ 03-219 1216; www.ulva.co.nz) Focused firmly on birding and guided by expert naturalists, these excellent half-day tours ($125; transport included) explore Ulva Island. Book at the Fernery. If you're a mad-keen twitcher, look for the Birding Bonanza trip ($400) on Ulva's website.

Stewart Island Experience
GUIDED TOUR

(☑ 03-219 0056, 0800 000 511; www.stewartisland-experience.co.nz; ⊕ 12 Elgin Tce) Runs 2½-hour Paterson Inlet cruises (adult/child $90/22) via Ulva Island; 1½-hour minibus tours of Oban and the surrounding bays ($45/25); and 2½-hour marine-life nature cruises with semisubmersible viewing ($90/45).

Bravo Adventure Cruises
BIRD-WATCHING

(☑ 03-219 1144; www.kiwispotting.co.nz) Departing around sunset, Bravo runs small-group kiwi-spotting tours ($140) on a scenic reserve reached by a 30-minute boat trip and involving gentle walking through forest and on a beach.

SPOTTING A KIWI: A BRUSH WITH THE GODS

Stewart Island/Rakiura is one of the few places on earth where you can spot a kiwi in the wild. Considered the king of the forest by Maori, the bird has been around for 70 million years and is related to the now-extinct moa. Brown feathers camouflage the kiwi against its bush surroundings and a nocturnal lifestyle means spying a kiwi in the wild is a challenge. This is compounded by Stewart Island/Rakiura's fickle weather, with tours sometimes cancelled – allow a few nights on the island if you're desperate for a sighting.

As big as a barnyard chicken and estimated to number around 20,000 birds, the Stewart Island/Rakiura brown kiwi (*Apteryx australis lawryi*, also known as the tokoeka) is larger in size, longer in the beak and thicker in the legs than its northern cousins. They are also the only kiwi active during daylight hours, and birds may be seen around sunrise and sunset foraging for food in grassed areas and on beaches where they mine sandhoppers under washed-up kelp. If you spot one, keep silent, and stay still and well away. The birds' poor eyesight and single-mindedness in searching for food will often lead them to bump right into you.

Rakiura Charters   BOAT TOUR, FISHING
(☑ 0800 725 487, 03-219 1487; www.rakiuracharters.co.nz; adult/child from $100/70) The most popular outing on the *Rakiura Suzy* is the half-day fishing cruise which stops in at the historic Whalers' Base. Trips can be tailored to suit timing and interests, such as wildlife-spotting and tramping.

Leask Bay Fishing Charters   FISHING
(☑ 027 828 1147, 03-219 1391; www.leaskbaycharters.co.nz; per person $80, min 2 people) Go handlining with Andy on his family heirloom, the 110-year-old *Rawhiti*. Eat your catch for lunch on the morning trip; take it away for dinner on the afternoon trip.

Lo Loma Fishing Charters   FISHING
(☑ 027 393 8362, 03-219 1141) Join Squizzy Squires on the *Lo Loma* for a fun handlining fishing trip.

Phil's Sea Kayak   KAYAKING
(☑ 03-219 1444, 027 444 2323; trips from $79) Stewart Island/Rakiura's only kayaking guide, Phil runs trips on Paterson Inlet tailored for all abilities which include Ulva Island and sandy beaches, with sightings of wildlife along the way. Watch for good weather and give him a bell.

Ruggedy Range
Wilderness Experience   BIRD-WATCHING
(☑ 0274 784 433, 03-219 1066; www.ruggedyrange.com; Main Rd) Nature-guide Furhana runs small-group guided walks including half- and full-day trips to Ulva Island ($120/185), and overnight trips to see kiwi in the wild ($525).

🛏 Sleeping

Finding accommodation can be difficult, especially in the low season when many places shut down. Booking ahead is highly recommended. The island has many holiday homes, which are often good value and offer the benefit of self-catering, which is especially handy if you do a spot of fishing (although many impose a two-night minimum stay or charge a surcharge for one night). Invercargill i-SITE and the Stewart Island Experience Red Shed can help you book such rentals. See also www.stewartisland.co.nz.

⭐ **Jo & Andy's B&B**   B&B $
(☑ 03-219 1230; jariksem@clear.net.nz; cnr Morris St & Main Rd; s $60, d & tw $90; @ 🛜) A great option for budget travellers, this cosy blue home squeezes in twin, double and single rooms. A big breakfast of muesli, fruit and homemade bread prepares you for the most active of days. Jo and Andy are splendid company and there's hundreds of books in the weather packs up.

Bunkers Backpackers   HOSTEL $
(☑ 03-219 1160; www.bunkersbackpackers.co.nz; 13 Argyle St; dm/d $32/76; ☺ closed mid-Apr–mid-Oct; @ 🛜) A converted wooden villa houses Stewart Island/Rakiura's most promising hostel option, which is somewhat squeezed but offers the benefits of a sunny garden and inner village location.

Stewart Island Backpackers   HOSTEL $
(☑ 03-219 1114; www.stewartislandbackpackers.com; cnr Dundee & Ayr Sts; sites $20, dm/d $35/70; 🛜) The island's biggest backpackers has an

adequate offering of rooms with up to four beds in a dorm, many of which face onto a courtyard. Somewhat shabby on last inspection, the communal lounge and kitchen are adequate and there's a barbecue area which traps some decent sun. There are terraced, grassy tents sites behind the lodge.

Stewart Island Lodge   LODGE $$
(☑ 03-219 0085; www.stewartislandlodge.co.nz; Nichol Rd; d incl breakfast $195; @ 🖥) On a hill overlooking the bay, five minutes' walk to town, this grand lodge has six comfortable en suite rooms. Shared facilities include a sunny balcony, lounge and dining patio for partaking of the continental breakfast or your own meals prepared in the guest kitchen. As it's owned by Stewart Island Experience, enquire about island tours and transport.

Latt 47   RENTAL HOUSE $$
(☑ 03-219 1330; john.barry@clear.net.nz; 12a Excelsior Rd; d $180) This modern hillside house sleeps up to four. Debbie can also hook you up with other suitable Stewart Island/Rakiura accommodation.

Bay Motel   MOTEL $$
(☑ 03-219 1119; www.baymotel.co.nz; 9 Dundee St; d $175-200; 🖥) Modern, comfortable units with lots of light and views over the harbour. Some rooms have spa baths, all have kitchens and two are wheelchair-accessible. When you've exhausted the island's bustling after-dark scene, Sky TV's on hand for on-tap entertainment.

Kaka Retreat   MOTEL $$$
(☑ 03-219 1252; www.kakaretreat.co.nz; 7 Miro Cres; d $230-256; @ 🖥) These studio units are among the island's best, with plush interiors, flash bathrooms and private verandahs, although kitchen facilities are scant. Two older-style but smart fully self-contained units offer good value for up to six people.

Port of Call B&B   B&B, RENTAL HOUSE $$$
(☑ 0272 244 4722, 03-219 1394; www.portofcall.co.nz; Leask Bay Rd; s/d incl breakfast $320/385) Take in ocean views, relax before an open fire, or explore an isolated beach. Port of Call is 2km southwest of Oban, near Acker's Point. Two cosy self-contained options are available – The Bach, near the B&B ($250), and Hunter Cottage ($190) in Oban. All have a two-night minimum stay, and guided walks and water-taxi trips can also be arranged.

Observation Rock Lodge   LODGE $$$
(☑ 027 444 1802, 03-219 1444; www.observationrocklodge.co.nz; 7 Leonard St; d standard/deluxe package $395/780; 🖥) Secluded in bird-filled bush with views south to Golden Bay, Annett and Phil's delightful lodge has two stylish, luxurious rooms with private decks and shared lounge. Guided activites, sauna, hot tub and Annett's gourmet meals are inclusive in the deluxe package (breakfast and dinner) or by arrangement as additions to the standard B&B rate.

🍴 Eating

Bird on a Pear   CAFE $
(meals $10-18; ⊙ 7am-3.30pm) Upstairs on the wharf with Halfmoon Bay views, the Bird is a bright and breezy spot to enjoy a cooked breakfast, lunch or coffee and fresh home baking.

Four Square   SUPERMARKET $
(Elgin Tce; ⊙ 7.30am-7pm) Beyond a good selection of the usual groceries, this shop stocks sandwiches, blue cod and a few surprises besides.

Stewart Island Smoked Salmon   FISH $
(www.siss.co.nz; Miro Cres) If you're a fan of freshly smoked salmon, pop up to the smokehouse to see if anyone's in. This sweet, hot-smoked fish is a tasty treat for a picnic or pasta.

★ South Sea Hotel   PUB $$
(www.stewart-island.co.nz; 26 Elgin Tce; mains $16-30; ⊙ 7am-9pm; 🖥) Welcome to one of NZ's classic pubs, complete with stellar cod and chips, beer by the quart, civilised cafe ambience in the dining room, and plenty of friendly banter in the public bar. Great at any time of day (or night), but try to wash up for the Sunday-night quiz – an unforgettable, fun slice of island life hosted by Quizmistress Vicki. Basic rooms available (double $90 to $115) and studio motels out back ($165).

**Church Hill Restaurant
& Oyster Bar**   CAFE, BAR $$$
(☑ 03-219 1123; www.churchill.co.nz; 36 Kamahi Rd; lunch $14-28, dinner $36-48; ⊙ lunch noon-2.30pm, dinner from 5.30pm) During summer this heritage villa's sunny deck provides hilltop views, and in cooler months you can get cosy inside beside the open fire. Big on local seafood, highlights include oysters and smoked salmon, prepared in refined modern style, followed by excellent desserts such as fig and pear sticky pudding. Dinner bookings advisable.

☆ Entertainment

Bunkhouse Theatre   CINEMA
(☑027 867 9381; Main Rd; $10; ☺screenings 2pm & 4pm) Oban's comfy little theatre screens the quirky, cute 40-minute film *A Local's Tail,* which provides an entertaining overview of Stewart Island/Rakiura history and culture. Jaffas and DIY popcorn.

🛍 Shopping

Fernery   ART & CRAFTS
(www.thefernerynz.com; Main Rd; ☺10.30am-5pm, reduced hours in winter) A delightful store stocking local art, craft, cards and books.

Glowing Sky   CLOTHING
(www.glowingsky.co.nz; Elgin Tce; ☺10am-5pm) Hand-printed T-shirts with Maori designs and NZ-made merino clothing.

ℹ Information

Stewart Island/Rakiura has no banks. There's an ATM in the Four Square which has a mind of its own; credit cards are accepted for most activities. Wi-fi is available at the South Sea Hotel and most accommodation. Mobile phone service is limited to Telecom (027) numbers.

The best place for information on the mainland is Invercargill i-SITE. Online, see www.stewartisland.co.nz.

Post office (Elgin Tce; ☺8am-6pm Mon-Fri, 9am-5pm Sat & Sun) At Stewart Island Flights.

Rakiura National Park Visitor Centre (☑03-219 0008; www.doc.govt.nz; Main Rd; ☺8am-5pm Jan-Mar, reduced hours Apr-Dec) Stop in to obtain information on short walks and overnight tramps, as well as hut bookings and passes, topographical maps, books, and a few tramping essentials such as insect repellent and wool socks. Information displays introduce Stewart Island/Rakiura's flora and fauna, while a video library provides entertainment and education (a good rainy day Plan B). Register your intentions here via Adventuresmart.

Stewart Island Experience Red Shed
(☑03-219 0056, 0800 000 511; www.stewartislandexperience.co.nz; 12 Elgin Tce; ☺7.30am-6.30pm) Conveniently located next to the wharf, the helpful crew at the Red Shed can hook you up with nearly everything on and around the island including accommodation,

guided tours, boat trips, bikes, scooters and rental cars.

Stewart Island Health Centre (☑03-219 1098; Argyle St; ☺10am-12.30pm) Has 24-hour on-call service.

ℹ Getting There & Away

AIR
Stewart Island Flights (☑03-218 9129; www.stewartislandflights.com; Elgin Tce; adult/child 1 way $117.50/75, return $203/118) Flies between the island and Invercargill three times daily, with good standby and over-60s discounts.

BOAT
Stewart Island Experience (☑0800 000 511, 03-212 7660; www.stewartislandexperience.co.nz; Main Wharf) The passenger-only ferry runs between Bluff and Oban (adult/child $75/38 one way) up to four times daily (reduced in winter). Book a few days ahead in summer. The crossing takes one hour and can be a rough ride. The company also runs a shuttle between Bluff and Invercargill (adult/child $24/12) with pick-ups and drop-offs in Invercargill at the i-SITE, Tuatara Backpackers and Invercargill Airport. Cars and campervans can be stored in a secure car park at Bluff for an additional cost.

A shuttle also runs between Bluff and Queenstown (adult/child $73/36), and Bluff and Te Anau (adult/child $73/36) with pick-up and drop-off at the Real Journeys offices.

ℹ Getting Around

Water taxis offer pick-ups and drop-offs to remote parts of the island – a handy service for trampers. The taxis also service Ulva Island (return $25).

Aihe Eco Charters & Water Taxi (☑03-219 1066; www.aihe.co.nz)

Rakiura Water Taxi (☑027 354 9991, 0800 725 487; www.rakiurawatertaxi.co.nz)

Stewart Island Water Taxi & Eco Guiding
(☑03-219 1394, 0800 469 283; www.stewartislandwatertaxi.co.nz)

Rakiura Helicopters can also provide remote access.

Rent a scooter (per half-/full day from $60/70) or a car (per half-/full day from $65/95) from Stewart Island Experience.

Understand the South Island

The South Island Today

New Zealand has had a bad run on the disaster front in recent years, between devastating earthquakes and a mining tragedy, not to mention the usual storms, droughts, drownings, sinkings and suchlike that make headline news. The global financial crisis hasn't helped either, with money troubles well and truly trickling down to ground level. Despite this, a typically plucky New Zealand public has turned to the sporting arena – and increasingly the arts – to put a smile on its dial.

Top Films

The Hobbit trilogy (Sir Peter Jackson; 2012–14)
Lord of the Rings trilogy (Sir Peter Jackson; 2001–03)
The Piano (Jane Campion; 1993)
Whale Rider (Niki Caro; 2002)
Once Were Warriors (Lee Tamahori; 1994)

Etiquette

Rugby Try to feign some enthusiasm. If in doubt, mumble 'forward pass' or 'offside'.
Possums Don't express any affection for the tree-munching possum.
Australanders Be sure never to mistake a New Zealander for an Australian.
Dinnertime In Maori culture, sitting on a table is bad manners.

Top Books

The Luminaries (Eleanor Catton; 2013)
Mister Pip (Lloyd Jones; 2007)
Live Bodies (Maurice Gee; 1998)
The 10pm Question (Kate De Goldi; 2009)
The Collected Stories of Katherine Mansfield (2007)
Bone People (Keri Hulme; 1984)

Shaky Isles

New Zealand may be a long way away from just about everywhere, but it is not immune to the vagaries of the global economy. In September 2010, just as the country was edging out of its worst recession in 30 years, a magnitude 7.1 earthquake struck near Christchurch, the nation's second-largest city. The damage was extensive but miraculously no lives were lost, partly because the earthquake occurred in the early hours of the morning when people were in their beds.

Then, in the early afternoon of 22 February 2011, a magnitude 6.3 earthquake struck Christchurch. This time, 185 people lost their lives. Numerous buildings, already weakened by the September 2010 quake and its aftershocks, were damaged beyond repair and had to be demolished completely.

The city's rebuild has been slow; the city centre didn't re-open fully until mid-2013. Cantabrians, however, have displayed admirable resilience and innovation, helping Christchurch to re-emerge as one of NZ's most exciting cities. Fringe suburbs have been reinvigorated, such as Woolston ('Coolston') and Addington, while a cardboard (yes cardboard!) cathedral has been brought into the fold. The city was named by Lonely Planet as one of the world's top 10 cities in *Best in Travel 2013*.

Christchurch isn't the only place to be awarded such a plaudit, with the South Island's West Coast named one of the world's must-visit regions in *Best in Travel 2014*. This is a timely boost for a region still reeling in the aftermath of one of NZ's worst disasters – the loss of 29 men in the Pike River coalmine explosions in November 2010. This national tragedy further pushed the bounds of the country's emotional and economic resilience.

The nation's nerves were jangled yet again in July and August 2013 as a swarm of moderate earthquakes struck the top of the South Island. Widely felt in the capital, they served as a seismic reminder that New Zealanders do indeed live on the shaky isles.

Reasons to be Cheerful

Christchurch's recovery and rebuild is still a major preoccupation, producing good news and bad stories in equal measure. On one hand it is testing relationships between the citizens and government agencies, as tough decisions are made about fix-ups and payouts. On the other, Christchurch's recovery reinforces Kiwis' perceptions of themselves as 'battlers' with strong communities and civic pride.

New Zealanders have little difficulty in finding something to feel proud about. While the All Blacks remain a foundation – not only for their sporting achievements but as figureheads for 'brand NZ' – the depth of Kiwi talent ranges far beyond the rugby pitch. Following the All Blacks' success at the 2011 Rugby World Cup, this featherweight country punched well above its weight at the 2012 London Olympics. Claiming six gold medals, Team NZ gave traditional rival and sporting giant Australia a run for its money as it only managed to win one more. Other Kiwi sporting stars making their mark around the globe include young golfing sensation Lydia Ko, NBA rookie Steve Adams, IndyCar speedster Scott Dixon, and Valerie Adams, the greatest female shot putter the world has ever seen.

While Sir Peter Jackson holds his position as a heavyweight in cinema with his blockbusting adaptations of *The Hobbit,* another major player has thrown his hat into the ring. Canadian director James Cameron has set up a rural home base near Wellington and will create the *Avatar* sequels in the capital, bringing substantial investment and cementing NZ's reputation as a world-class filmmaking destination.

Pop pundits are also taking note of new Kiwi stars, with Grammy Award–winning Lorde (she of *Pure Heroine,* one of *Rolling Stone*'s albums of 2013) and Kimbra (of Goyte's 2012 smash-hit *Somebody That I Used to Know*) making huge impressions. Pages are also being turned on the international literary scene, as evidenced by Cantabrian Eleanor Catton. She claimed one of the world's most coveted publishing accolades in 2013, the Man Booker Prize, with her voluminous historical novel *The Luminaries* – only the second New Zealander to do so.

POPULATION: **1.04 MILLION**

AREA: **151,215 SQ KM**

GDP GROWTH: **1.4% (2013)**

INFLATION: **1.4% (2013)**

UNEMPLOYMENT: **6.2% (2013)**

if the South Island were 100 people

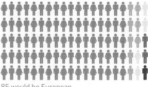

85 would be European
8 would be Maori
4 would be Asian
2 would be Pacific Islanders
1 would be other

Where they live
(% of New Zealanders)

64 — North Island
20 — South Island

10 — Australia
4 — Rest of the World
2 — Travelling

population per sq km

NORTH ISLAND   SOUTH ISLAND   AUSTRALIA

👤 ≈ 3 people

History

by James Belich

New Zealand's history is not long, but it is fast. In less than a thousand years these islands have produced two new peoples: the Polynesian Maori and European New Zealanders. The latter are often known by their Maori name, 'Pakeha' (though not all like the term). NZ shares some of its history with the rest of Polynesia, and with other European settler societies, but has unique features as well. It is the similarities that make the differences so interesting, and vice versa.

Making Maori

One of New Zealand's foremost modern historians, James Belich has written a number of books on NZ history and hosted the TV documentary series *The New Zealand Wars*.

Despite persistent myths, there is no doubt that the first settlers of NZ were the Polynesian forebears of today's Maori. Beyond that, there are a lot of question marks. Exactly where in east Polynesia did they come from – the Cook Islands, Tahiti, the Marquesas? When did they arrive? Did the first settlers come in one group or several?

Some evidence, such as the diverse DNA of the Polynesian rats that accompanied the first settlers, suggests multiple founding voyages. On the other hand, only rats and dogs brought by the founders have survived, not the more valuable pigs and chickens. The survival of these cherished animals would have had high priority, and their failure to be successfully introduced suggests fewer voyages.

NZ seems small compared with Australia, but it is bigger than Britain, and very much bigger than other Polynesian islands. Its regions vary wildly in environment and climate. Prime sites for first settlement were warm coastal gardens for the food plants brought from Polynesia (kumara or sweet potato, gourd, yam and taro); sources of workable stone for knives and adzes; and areas with abundant big game.

For a thorough overview of NZ history from Gondwanaland to today, visit www.history-nz.org.

NZ has no native land mammals apart from a few species of bat, but 'big game' is no exaggeration: the islands were home to a dozen species of moa (a large flightless bird), the largest of which weighed up to 240kg, about twice the size of an ostrich. There were also other species of flightless birds and large sea mammals such as fur seals, all unaccustomed to being hunted.

TIMELINE	AD 1000 –1200	1642	1769
	Possible date of the arrival of Maori in NZ. Solid archaeological evidence points to about AD 1200, but much earlier dates have been suggested for the first human impact on the environment.	First European contact: Abel Tasman arrives on an expedition from the Dutch East Indies (Indonesia) to find the 'Great South Land'. His party leaves without landing, after a sea skirmish with Maori.	European contact recommences with visits by James Cook and Jean de Surville. Despite some violence, both communicate with Maori. This time NZ's link with the outside world proves permanent.

For people from small Pacific islands, this was like hitting the jackpot. The first settlers spread far and fast, from the top of the North Island to the bottom of the South Island within the first 100 years. High-protein diets are likely to have boosted population growth.

By about 1400, however, with big-game supply dwindling, Maori economics turned from big game to small game – forest birds and rats – and from hunting to gardening and fishing. A good living could still be made, but it required detailed local knowledge, steady effort and complex communal organisation, hence the rise of the Maori tribes. Competition for resources increased, conflict did likewise, and this led to the building of increasingly sophisticated fortifications, known as *pa*. Vestiges of *pa* earthworks can still be seen around the country (on the hilltops of Auckland, for example).

The Maori had no metals and no written language (and no alcoholic drinks or drugs). But their culture and spiritual life was rich and distinctive. Below Ranginui (sky father) and Papatuanuku (earth mother) were various gods of land, forest and sea, joined by deified ancestors over time.

The mischievous demigod Maui was particularly important. In legend, he vanquished the sun and fished up the North Island before meeting his death between the thighs of the goddess Hine-nui-te-po in an attempt to conquer the human mortality embodied in her. Maori traditional performance art, the group singing and dancing known as *kapa haka,* has real power, even for modern audiences. Visual art, notably woodcarving, is something special – 'like nothing but itself', in the words of 18th-century explorer-scientist Joseph Banks.

Rumours of late survivals of the giant moa bird abound, but none have been authenticated. So if you see a moa in your travels, photograph it – you'll have just made the greatest zoological discovery of the last 100 years.

THE MORIORI & THEIR MYTH

One of NZ's most persistent legends is that Maori found mainland NZ already occupied by a more peaceful and racially distinct Melanesian people, known as the Moriori, whom they exterminated. This myth has been regularly debunked by scholars since the 1920s, but somehow hangs on.

To complicate matters, there were real 'Moriori', and Maori did treat them badly. The real Moriori were the people of the Chatham Islands, a windswept group about 900km east of the mainland. They were, however, fully Polynesian, and descended from Maori – 'Moriori' was their version of the same word. Mainland Maori arrived in the Chathams in 1835, as a spin-off of the Musket Wars, killing some Moriori and enslaving the rest. But they did not exterminate them.

The mainland Moriori remain a myth.

1772	1790s	1818–36
Marion du Fresne's French expedition arrives; it stays for some weeks at the Bay of Islands. Relations with Maori start well, but a breach of Maori *tapu* (sacred law) leads to violence.	Whaling ships and sealing gangs arrive in the country. Relations are established with Maori, with Europeans depending on the contact for essentials such as food, water and protection.	Intertribal Maori 'Musket Wars' take place: tribes acquire muskets and win bloody victories against tribes without them. The war tapers off in 1836, probably due to the equal distribution of weapons.

→ Captain Cook statue

DANITA DELIMONT/GETTY IMAGES ©

Enter Europe

NZ became an official British colony in 1840, but the first authenticated contact between Maori and the outside world took place almost two centuries earlier in 1642, in Golden Bay at the top of the South Island. Two Dutch ships sailed from Indonesia, to search for southern land and anything valuable it might contain. The commander, Abel Tasman, was instructed to pretend to any natives he might meet 'that you are by no means eager for precious metals, so as to leave them ignorant of the value of the same'.

When Tasman's ships anchored in the bay, local Maori came out in their canoes to make the traditional challenge: friends or foes? Misunderstanding this, the Dutch challenged back, by blowing trumpets. When a boat was lowered to take a party between the two ships, it was attacked. Four crewmen were killed. Tasman sailed away and did not come back; nor did any other European for 127 years. But the Dutch did leave a name: 'Nieuw Zeeland' or 'New Sealand'.

Contact between Maori and Europeans was renewed in 1769, when English and French explorers arrived, under James Cook and Jean de Surville. Relations were more sympathetic, and exploration continued, motivated by science, profit and great power rivalry. Cook made two more visits between 1773 and 1777, and there were further French expeditions.

Unofficial visits, by whaling ships in the north and sealing gangs in the south, began in the 1790s. The first mission station was founded in 1814, in the Bay of Islands, and was followed by dozens of others: Anglican, Methodist and Catholic. Trade in flax and timber generated small European–Maori settlements by the 1820s. Surprisingly, the most numerous category of Western visitor was probably American. New England whaling ships favoured the Bay of Islands for rest and recreation; 271 called there between 1833 and 1839 alone. To whalers, 'rest and recreation' meant sex and drink. Their favourite haunt, the little town of Kororareka (now Russell) was known to the missionaries as 'the hellhole of the Pacific'. New England visitors today might well have distant relatives among the local Maori.

One or two dozen bloody clashes dot the history of Maori–European contact before 1840 but, given the number of visits, interracial conflict was modest. Europeans needed Maori protection, food and labour, and Maori came to need European articles, especially muskets. Whaling stations and mission stations were linked to local Maori groups by intermarriage, which helped keep the peace. Most warfare was between Maori and Maori: the terrible intertribal 'Musket Wars' of 1818–36. Because Northland had the majority of early contact with Europe, its Ngapuhi tribe acquired muskets first. Under their great general Hongi

The Ministry for Culture & Heritage's history website (www.nzhistory.net.nz) is an excellent source of info on NZ history.

HISTORY ENTER EUROPE

ABEL TASMAN

Abel Tasman named NZ Statenland, assuming it was connected to Staten Island near Argentina. It was subsequently named after the province of Zeeland in Tasman's Holland.

1837	1840	1844	1858
Possums are introduced to New Zealand from Australia. Brilliant.	Starting at Waitangi in the Bay of Islands on 6 February, around 500 chiefs countrywide sign the Treaty of Waitangi to 'settle' sovereignty once and for all. NZ becomes a nominal British colony.	Young Ngapuhi chief Hone Heke challenges British sovereignty, first by cutting down the British flag at Kororareka (now Russell), then by sacking the town itself. The ensuing Northland war continues until 1846.	The Waikato chief Te Wherowhero is installed as the first Maori King.

CAPTAIN JAMES COOK

If aliens ever visit earth, they may wonder what to make of the countless obelisks, faded plaques and graffiti-covered statues of a stiff, wigged figure gazing out to sea from Alaska to Australia, from NZ to North Yorkshire, from Siberia to the South Pacific. James Cook (1728–79) explored more of the earth's surface than anyone in history, and it's impossible to travel the Pacific without encountering the captain's image and his controversial legacy in the lands he opened to the West.

For a man who travelled so widely, and rose to such fame, Cook came from an extremely pinched and provincial background. The son of a day labourer in rural Yorkshire, he was born in a mud cottage, had little schooling, and seemed destined for farm work – and for his family's grave plot in a village churchyard. Instead, Cook went to sea as a teenager, worked his way up from coal-ship servant to naval officer, and attracted notice for his exceptional charts of Canada. But Cook remained a little-known second lieutenant until, in 1768, the Royal Navy chose him to command a daring voyage to the South Seas.

In a converted coal ship called *Endeavour,* Cook sailed to Tahiti, and then became the first European to land at NZ and the east coast of Australia. Though the ship almost sank after striking the Great Barrier Reef, and 40% of the crew died from disease and accidents, the *Endeavour* limped home in 1771. On a return voyage (1772–75), Cook became the first navigator to pierce the Antarctic Circle and circle the globe near its southernmost latitude, demolishing the myth that a vast, populous and fertile continent surrounded the South Pole. Cook criss-crossed the Pacific from Easter Island to Melanesia, charting dozens of islands between. Though Maori killed and cooked 10 sailors, the captain remained sympathetic to islanders. 'Notwithstanding they are cannibals,' he wrote, 'they are naturally of a good disposition.'

On Cook's final voyage (1776–79), in search of a northwest passage between the Atlantic and Pacific, he became the first European to visit Hawaii, and coasted America from Oregon to Alaska. Forced back by Arctic pack ice, Cook returned to Hawaii, where he was killed during a skirmish with islanders who had initially greeted him as a Polynesian god. In a single decade of discovery, Cook had filled in the map of the Pacific and, as one French navigator put it, 'left his successors with little to do but admire his exploits'.

But Cook's travels also spurred colonisation of the Pacific, and within a few decades of his death, missionaries, whalers, traders and settlers began transforming (and often devastating) island cultures. As a result, many indigenous people now revile Cook as an imperialist villain who introduced disease, dispossession and other ills to the Pacific (hence the frequent vandalising of Cook monuments). However, as islanders revive traditional crafts and practices, from tattooing to *tapa* (traditional barkcloth), they have turned to the art and writing of Cook and his men as a resource for cultural renewal. For good and ill, a Yorkshire farm boy remains the single most significant figure in the shaping of the modern Pacific.

Tony Horwitz is a Pulitzer Prize–winning reporter and nonfiction author.
In researching Blue Latitudes (or Into the Blue), Tony travelled the Pacific –
'boldly going where Captain Cook has gone before'.

1860–69	1861	1863–64	1868–72
First and Second Taranaki wars, starting with the controversial swindling of Maori land by the government at Waitara, and continuing with outrage over the confiscation of more land as a result.	Gold discovered in Otago by Gabriel Read, an Australian prospector. As a result, the population of Otago climbs from less than 13,000 to over 30,000 in six months.	Waikato Land War. Up to 5000 Maori resist an invasion mounted by 20,000 imperial, colonial and 'friendly' Maori troops. Despite surprising successes, Maori are defeated and much land is confiscated.	East Coast war. Te Kooti, having led an escape from his prison on the Chatham Islands, leads a holy guerrilla war in the Urewera region. He finally retreats to establish the Ringatu Church.

Hika, Ngapuhi then raided south, winning bloody victories against tribes without muskets. Once they acquired muskets, these tribes saw off Ngapuhi, but also raided further south in their turn. The domino effect continued to the far south of the South Island in 1836. The missionaries claimed that the Musket Wars then tapered off through their influence, but the restoration of the balance of power through the equal distribution of muskets was probably more important.

Europe brought such things as pigs (at last) and potatoes, which benefited Maori, while muskets and diseases had the opposite effect. The negative effects have been exaggerated, however. Europeans expected peoples like the Maori to simply fade away at contact, and some early estimates of Maori population were overly high – up to one million. Current estimates are between 85,000 and 110,000 for 1769. The Musket Wars killed perhaps 20,000, and new diseases did considerable damage too (although NZ had the natural quarantine of distance: infected Europeans usually recovered or died during the long voyage, and smallpox, for example, which devastated native Americans, did not make it here). By 1840, the Maori had been reduced to about 70,000, a decline of at least 20%. Maori bent under the weight of European contact, but they certainly did not break.

Similarities in language between Maori and Tahitian indicate close contact in historical times. Maori is about as similar to Tahitian as Spanish is to French, despite the 4294km separating these island groups.

Making Pakeha

By 1840, Maori tribes described local Europeans as 'their Pakeha', and valued the profit and prestige they brought. Maori wanted more of both, and concluded that accepting nominal British authority was the way to get them. At the same time, the British government was overcoming its reluctance to undertake potentially expensive intervention in NZ. It too was influenced by profit and prestige, but also by humanitarian considerations. It believed, wrongly but sincerely, that Maori could not handle the increasing scale of unofficial European contact. In 1840, the two peoples struck a deal, symbolised by the treaty first signed at Waitangi on 6 February that year.

The Treaty of Waitangi now has a standing not dissimilar to that of the Constitution in the US, but is even more contested. The original problem was a discrepancy between British and Maori understandings of it. The English version promised Maori full equality as British subjects in return for complete rights of government. The Maori version also promised that Maori would retain their chieftainship, which implied local rights of government. The problem was not great at first, because the Maori version applied outside the small European settlements. But as those settlements grew, conflict brewed.

In 1840, there were only about 2000 Europeans in NZ, with the shanty town of Kororareka (now Russell) as the capital and biggest settlement.

Scottish influence can still be felt in NZ, particularly in the south of the South Island. NZ has more Scottish pipe bands per capita than Scotland itself.

1886–87

Tuwharetoa tribe gifts the mountains of Ruapehu, Ngauruhoe and Tongariro to the government to establish the world's fourth national park.

1893

NZ becomes the first country in the world to grant the vote to women, following a campaign led by Kate Sheppard, who petitioned the government for years.

RAIMUND LINKE/GETTY IMAGES ©

➔ Mt Tongariro, Tongariro National Park

By 1850, six new settlements had been formed with 22,000 settlers between them. About half of these had arrived under the auspices of the New Zealand Company and its associates. The company was the brainchild of Edward Gibbon Wakefield, who also influenced the settlement of South Australia. Wakefield hoped to short-circuit the barbarous frontier phase of settlement with 'instant civilisation', but his success was limited. From the 1850s, his settlers, who included a high proportion of upper-middle-class gentlefolk, were swamped by succeeding waves of immigrants that continued to wash in until the 1880s. These people were part of the great British and Irish diaspora that also populated Australia and much of North America, but the NZ mix was distinctive. Lowland Scots settlers were more prominent in NZ than elsewhere, for example, with the possible exception of parts of Canada. NZ's Irish, even the Catholics, tended to come from the north of Ireland. NZ's English tended to come from the counties close to London. Small groups of Germans, Scandinavians and Chinese made their way in, though the last faced increasing racial prejudice from the 1880s, when the Pakeha population reached half a million.

The Waitangi Treaty Grounds, where the Treaty of Waitangi was first signed in 1840, is now a tourist attraction for Kiwis and non-Kiwis alike. Each year on 6 February Waitangi hosts treaty commemorations and protests.

Much of the mass immigration from the 1850s to the 1870s was assisted by the provincial and central governments, which also mounted large-scale public works schemes, especially in the 1870s under Julius Vogel. In 1876, Vogel abolished the provinces on the grounds that they were hampering his development efforts. The last imperial governor with substantial power was the talented but Machiavellian George Grey, who ended his second governorship in 1868. Thereafter, the governors (governors-general from 1917) were largely just nominal heads of state; the head of government, the premier or prime minister, had more power. The central government, originally weaker than the provincial governments, the imperial governor and the Maori tribes, eventually exceeded the power of all three.

The Maori tribes did not go down without a fight, however. Indeed, their resistance was one of the most formidable ever mounted against European expansion, comparable to that of the Sioux and Seminole in the US. The first clash took place in 1843 in the Wairau Valley, now a wine-growing district. A posse of settlers set out to enforce the myth of British control, but encountered the reality of Maori control. Twenty-two settlers were killed, including Wakefield's brother, Arthur, along with about six Maori. In 1845, more serious fighting broke out in the Bay of Islands, when Hone Heke sacked a British settlement. Heke and his ally Kawiti baffled three British punitive expeditions, using a modern variant of the traditional *pa* fortification. Vestiges of these innovative earthworks can still be seen at Ruapekapeka (south of Kawakawa). Governor Grey claimed victory in the north, but few were convinced at the time. Grey

TREATY OF WAITANGI

1901	1908	1914–18	1931
NZ politely declines the invitation to join the new Commonwealth of Australia.	NZ physicist Ernest Rutherford is awarded the Nobel Prize in chemistry for 'splitting the atom', investigating the disintegration of elements and the chemistry of radioactive substances.	NZ's contribution to WWI is staggering for a country of just over a million people: about 100,000 NZ men serve overseas. Some 60,000 become casualties, mostly in France.	Napier earthquake kills 131 people.

had more success in the south, where he arrested the formidable Ngati Toa chief Te Rauparaha, who until then wielded great influence on both sides of Cook Strait. Pakeha were able to swamp the few Maori living in the South Island, but the fighting of the 1840s confirmed that the North Island at that time comprised a European fringe around an independent Maori heartland.

In the 1850s, settler populations and aspirations grew, and fighting broke out again in 1860. The wars burned on sporadically until 1872 over much of the North Island. In the early years, a Maori nationalist organisation, the King Movement, was the backbone of resistance. In later years, some remarkable prophet-generals, notably Titokowaru and Te Kooti, took over. Most wars were small-scale, but the Waikato war of 1863–64 was not. This conflict, fought at the same time as the American Civil War, involved armoured steamships, ultramodern heavy artillery, telegraph and 10 proud British regular regiments. Despite the odds, the Maori won several battles, such as that at Gate Pa, near Tauranga, in 1864. But in the end they were ground down by European numbers and resources. Maori political, though not cultural, independence ebbed away in the last decades of the 19th century. It finally expired when police invaded its last sanctuary, the Urewera Mountains, in 1916.

'Kaore e mau te rongo – ake, ake!' (Peace never shall be made – never, never!) War chief Rewi Maniapoto in response to government troops at the battle of Orakau, 1864.

Welfare & Warfare

From the 1850s to the 1880s, despite conflict with Maori, the Pakeha economy boomed on the back of wool exports, gold rushes and massive overseas borrowing for development. The crash came in the 1880s, when NZ experienced its Long Depression. In 1890, the Liberals came to power, and stayed there until 1912, helped by a recovering economy. The Liberals were NZ's first organised political party, and the first of several governments to give NZ a reputation as 'the world's social laboratory'. NZ became the first country in the world to give women the vote in 1893, and introduced old-age pensions in 1898. The Liberals also introduced a long-lasting system of industrial arbitration, but this was not enough to prevent bitter industrial unrest in 1912–13. This happened under the conservative 'Reform' government, which had replaced the Liberals in 1912. Reform remained in power until 1928, and later transformed itself into the National Party. Renewed depression struck in 1929, and the NZ experience of it was as grim as any. The derelict little farmhouses still seen in rural areas often date from this era.

In 1935, a second reforming government took office: the First Labour government, led by Michael Joseph Savage, easily NZ's favourite Australian. For a time, the Labour government was considered the most socialist

'I believe we were all glad to leave New Zealand. It is not a pleasant place. Amongst the natives there is absent that charming simplicity...and the greater part of the English are the very refuse of society.' Charles Darwin, referring to Kororareka (Russell), in 1860.

1935–49	1936	1939–45	1948
First Labour government in power, under Michael Savage. This government creates NZ's pioneering version of the welfare state, and also takes some independent initiatives in foreign policy.	NZ aviatrix Jean Batten becomes the first aviator to fly solo from Britain to NZ.	NZ troops back Britain and the Allied war effort during WWII; from 1942 around 100,000 Americans arrive to protect NZ from the Japanese.	Maurice Scheslinger invents the Buzzy Bee, NZ's most famous children's toy.

government outside Soviet Russia. But, when the chips were down in Europe in 1939, Labour had little hesitation in backing Britain.

NZ had also backed Britain in the Boer War (1899–1902) and WWI (1914–18), with dramatic losses in WWI in particular. You can count the cost in almost any little NZ town. A central square or park will contain a memorial lined with names – more for WWI than WWII. Even in WWII, however, NZ did its share of fighting: around 100,000 New Zealanders fought in Europe and the Middle East. NZ, a peaceful-seeming country, has spent much of its history at war. In the 19th century it fought at home; in the 20th, overseas.

To find out more about the New Zealand Wars, visit www. newzealand wars.co.nz.

HISTORY WELFARE & WARFARE

LAND WARS

Five separate major conflicts made up what are now collectively known as the New Zealand Wars (also referred to as the Land Wars or Maori Wars). Starting in Northland and moving throughout the North Island, the wars had many complex causes, but *whenua* (land) was the one common factor. In all five wars, Maori fought both for and against the government, on whose side stood the Imperial British Army, Australians and NZ's own Armed Constabulary. Land confiscations imposed on the Maori as punishment for involvement in these wars are still the source of conflict today, with the government struggling to finance compensation for what are now acknowledged to have been illegal seizures.

Northland war (1844–46) 'Hone Heke's War' began with the famous chopping of the flagpole at Kororareka (now Russell) and 'ended' at Ruapekapeka (south of Kawakawa). In many ways, this was almost a civil war between rival Ngapuhi factions, with the government taking one side against the other.

First Taranaki war (1860–61) Starting in Waitara, the first Taranaki war inflamed the passions of Maori across the North Island.

Waikato war (1863–64) The largest of the five wars. Predominantly involving Kingitanga, the Waikato war was caused in part by what the government saw as a challenge to sovereignty. However, it was land, again, that was the real reason for friction. Following defeats such as Rangiriri, the Waikato people were pushed entirely from their own lands, south into what became known as the King Country.

Second Taranaki war (1865–69) Caused by Maori resistance to land confiscations stemming from the first Taranaki war, this was perhaps the war in which the Maori came closest to victory, under the brilliant, one-eyed prophet-general Titokowaru. However, once he lost the respect of his warriors (probably through an indiscretion with the wife of one of his warriors), the war too was lost.

East Coast war (1868–72) Te Kooti's holy guerrilla war.

Errol Hunt

1953	1973	1974	1981
New Zealander Edmund Hillary, with Tenzing Norgay, 'knocks the bastard off'; the pair become the first men to reach the summit of Mt Everest.	Fledgling Kiwi prog-rockers Split Enz enter a TV talent quest... finishing second to last.	Pacific Island migrants who have outstayed visas ('overstayers') are subjected to Dawn Raids by immigration police under Robert Muldoon and the National government. These raids continue until the early 1980s.	Springbok rugby tour divides the nation. Many New Zealanders show a strong anti-apartheid stance by protesting the games. Others feel sport and politics shouldn't mix, and support the tour going ahead.

Better Britons?

British visitors have long found NZ hauntingly familiar. This is not simply a matter of the British and Irish origin of most Pakeha. It also stems from the tightening of NZ links with Britain from 1882, when refrigerated cargoes of food were first shipped to London. By the 1930s, giant ships carried frozen meat, cheese and butter, as well as wool, on regular voyages taking about five weeks one way. The NZ economy adapted to the feeding of London, and cultural links were also enhanced. NZ children studied British history and literature, not their own. NZ's leading scientists and writers, such as Ernest Rutherford and Katherine Mansfield, gravitated to Britain. This tight relationship has been described as 'recolonial', but it is a mistake to see NZ as an exploited colony. Average living standards in NZ were normally better than in Britain, as were the welfare and lower-level education systems. New Zealanders had access to British markets and culture, and they contributed their share to the latter as equals. The list of 'British' writers, academics, scientists, military leaders, publishers and the like who were actually New Zealanders is long. Indeed, New Zealanders, especially in war and sport, sometimes saw themselves as a superior version of the British – the Better Britons of the south. The NZ–London relationship was rather like that of the American Midwest and New York.

'Recolonial' NZ prided itself, with some justice, on its affluence, equality and social harmony. But it was also conformist, even puritanical. Until the 1950s, it was technically illegal for farmers to allow their cattle to mate in fields fronting public roads, for moral reasons. The 1953 American movie, *The Wild One,* was banned until 1977. Sunday newspapers were illegal until 1969, and full Sunday trading was not allowed until 1989. Licensed restaurants hardly existed in 1960, nor did supermarkets or TV. Notoriously, from 1917 to 1967, pubs were obliged to shut at 6pm. Yet the puritanical society of Better Britons was never the whole story. Opposition to Sunday trading stemmed, not so much from belief in the sanctity of the Sabbath, but from the belief that workers should have weekends too. Six o'clock closing was a standing joke in rural areas, notably the marvellously idiosyncratic region of the South Island's West Coast. There was always something of a Kiwi counterculture, even before imported countercultures took root from the 1960s.

There were also developments in cultural nationalism, beginning in the 1930s but really flowering from the 1970s. Writers, artists and filmmakers were by no means the only people who 'came out' in that era.

'God's own country, but the devil's own mess.' Prime Minister Richard (King Dick) Seddon, speaking on the source of NZ's self-proclaimed nickname 'Godzone'.

The Six o'clock Swill referred to the frantic after-work drinking at pubs when men tried to drink as much as possible from 5.05pm until strict closing time at 6pm.

PAUL KAY/GETTY IMAGES ©

1985	1992	1995
Rainbow Warrior is sunk in Auckland Harbour by French government agents to prevent the Greenpeace protest ship from making its intended voyage to Moruroa, where the French are conducting nuclear tests.	Government begins reparations for the Land Wars, and confirms Maori fishing rights in the 'Sealord deal'. Major settlements follow, including reparations for the Waikato land confiscations (1995).	Peter Blake and Russel Coutts win the America's Cup for NZ, sailing *Black Magic;* red socks become a matter of national pride.

➔ *Rainbow Warrior* memorial

Coming In, Coming Out

The 'recolonial' system was shaken several times after 1935, but managed to survive until 1973, when Mother England ran off and joined the Franco-German commune now known as the EU. NZ was beginning to develop alternative markets to Britain, and alternative exports to wool, meat and dairy. Wide-bodied jet aircraft were allowing the world and NZ to visit each other on an increasing scale. NZ had only 36,000 tourists in 1960, compared with more than two million a year now. Women were beginning to penetrate first the upper reaches of the workforce and then the political sphere. Gay people came out of the closet, despite vigorous efforts by moral conservatives to push them back in. University-educated youths were becoming more numerous and more assertive.

From 1945, Maori experienced both a population explosion and massive urbanisation. In 1936, Maori were 17% urban and 83% rural. Fifty years later, these proportions had reversed. The immigration gates, which until 1960 were pretty much labelled 'whites only', widened, first to allow in Pacific Islanders for their labour, and then to allow in (East) Asians for their money. These transitions would have generated major socioeconomic change whatever happened in politics. But most New Zealanders associate the country's recent 'Big Shift' with the politics of 1984.

In 1984, NZ's third great reforming government was elected – the Fourth Labour government, led nominally by David Lange and in fact by Roger Douglas, the Minister of Finance. This government adopted an antinuclear foreign policy, delighting the left, and a more-market economic policy, delighting the right. NZ's numerous economic controls were dismantled with breakneck speed. Middle NZ was uneasy about the antinuclear policy, which threatened NZ's ANZUS alliance with Australia and the US. But in 1985, French spies sank the antinuclear protest ship *Rainbow Warrior* in Auckland Harbour, killing one crewman. The lukewarm American condemnation of the French act brought middle NZ in behind the antinuclear policy, which became associated with national independence. Other New Zealanders were uneasy about the more-market economic policy, but failed to come up with a convincing alternative. Revelling in their new freedom, NZ investors engaged in a frenzy of speculation, and suffered even more than the rest of the world from the economic crash of 1987.

In the early 21st century, NZ's food, wine, film and literature are flowering as never before, and a new ethnic mix is creating something special in music. There are continuities, however – the pub, the sportsground, the bush, the beach and the bach – and they too are reasons people come here. Realising that NZ has a great culture and an intriguing history, as well as a great natural environment, will double the bang for your buck.

Wellington-born Nancy Wake (codenamed 'The White Mouse') led a guerrilla attack against the Nazis with a 7000-strong army. She had the multiple honours of being the Gestapo's most-wanted person and being the most decorated Allied servicewoman of WWII.

NZ's staunch antinuclear stance earned it the nickname 'The Mouse that Roared'.

2004	2010	2011	2013
Maori TV begins broadcasting – for the first time, a channel committed to NZ content and the revitalisation of Maori language and culture hits the small screen.	A cave-in at Pike River coalmine on the South Island's West Coast kills 29 miners.	A severe earthquake strikes Christchurch, killing 185 people and badly damaging the central business district. NZ hosts (and wins) the Rugby World Cup.	New Zealand becomes one of just 15 countries in the world to legally recognise same-sex marriage.

Environment

by Vaughan Yarwood

New Zealand is a young country – its present shape is less than 10,000 years old. Having broken away from the supercontinent of Gondwanaland (which included Africa, Australia, Antarctica and South America) in a stately geological dance some 85 million years ago, it endured continual uplift and erosion, buckling and tearing, and the slow fall and rise of the sea as ice ages came and went.

The Land

Vaughan Yarwood is a historian and travel writer who is widely published in New Zealand and internationally. He is the author of *The History Makers: Adventures in New Zealand Biography*.

Straddling the boundary of two great colliding slabs of the earth's crust – the Pacific plate and the Indian/Australian plate – to this day NZ remains the plaything of nature's strongest forces.

The result is one of the most varied and spectacular series of landscapes in the world, ranging from snow-dusted mountains and drowned glacial valleys to rainforests, dunelands and an otherworldly volcanic plateau. It is a diversity of landforms you would expect to find across an entire continent rather than a small archipelago in the South Pacific.

Evidence of NZ's tumultuous past is everywhere. The South Island's mountainous spine – the 650km-long ranges of the Southern Alps – is a product of the clash of the two plates; the result of a process of rapid lifting that, if anything, is accelerating. Despite NZ's highest peak, Aoraki/Mt Cook, losing 10m from its summit overnight in a 1991 landslide, the Alps are on an express elevator that, without erosion and landslides, would see them 10 times their present height within a few million years.

On the North Island, the most impressive changes have been wrought by volcanoes. Auckland is built on an isthmus peppered by scoria cones, on many of which you can still see the earthworks of *pa* (fortified villages) built by early Maori. The city's biggest and most recent volcano, 600-year-old Rangitoto Island, is just a short ferry ride from the downtown wharves. Some 300km further south, the classically shaped cone of snowcapped Mt Taranaki/Egmont overlooks tranquil dairy pastures.

NZ is one of the most spectacular places in the world to see geysers. Rotorua's short-lived Waimangu geyser, formed after the Mt Tarawera eruption, was once the world's largest, often gushing to a dizzying height of 400m.

But the real volcanic heartland runs through the centre of the North Island, from the restless bulk of Mt Ruapehu in Tongariro National Park northeast through the Rotorua lake district out to NZ's most active volcano, White Island, in the Bay of Plenty. Called the Taupo Volcanic Zone, this great 250km-long rift valley – part of a volcano chain known as the 'Pacific Ring of Fire' – has been the seat of massive eruptions that have left their mark on the country physically and culturally.

Most spectacular were the eruptions that created Lake Taupo. Considered the world's most productive volcano in terms of the amount of material ejected, Taupo last erupted 1800 years ago in a display that was the most violent anywhere on the planet within the past 5000 years.

You can experience the aftermath of volcanic destruction on a smaller scale at Te Wairoa (the Buried Village), near Rotorua on the shores of Lake Tarawera. Here, partly excavated and open to the public, lie the remains of a 19th-century Maori village overwhelmed when nearby Mt Tarawera erupted without warning. The famous Pink and White Terraces (one of several claimants to the popular title 'eighth wonder of the world') were destroyed overnight by the same upheaval.

But when nature sweeps the board clean with one hand she often rebuilds with the other: Waimangu Valley, born of all that geothermal violence, is the place to go to experience the hot earth up close and personal amid geysers, silica pans, bubbling mud pools, and the world's biggest hot spring. Or you can wander around Rotorua's Whakarewarewa Thermal Village, where descendants of Maori displaced by the eruption live in the middle of steaming vents and prepare food for visitors in boiling pools.

A second by-product of movement along the tectonic plate boundary is seismic activity – earthquakes. Not for nothing has NZ been called 'the Shaky Isles'. Most quakes only rattle the glassware, but one was indirectly responsible for creating an internationally celebrated tourist attraction...

In 1931 an earthquake measuring 7.9 on the Richter scale levelled the Hawke's Bay city of Napier, causing huge damage and loss of life. Napier was rebuilt almost entirely in the then-fashionable art-deco architectural style, and walking its streets today you can relive its brash exuberance in what has become a mecca for lovers of art deco.

However, the North Island doesn't have a monopoly on earthquakes. In September 2010 Christchurch was rocked by a magnitude 7.1 earthquake. Less than six months later, in February 2011, a magnitude 6.3 quake destroyed much of the city's historic heart and claimed 185 lives, making it the country's second-deadliest natural disaster. NZ's second city continues to be jostled by aftershocks as it begins to build anew.

The South Island can also see some evidence of volcanism – if the remains of the old volcanoes of Banks Peninsula weren't there to repel the sea, the vast Canterbury Plains, built from alpine sediment washed down the rivers from the Alps, would have eroded away long ago.

But in the south it is the Southern Alps themselves that dominate, dictating settlement patterns, throwing down engineering challenges and offering outstanding recreational opportunities. The island's mountainous backbone also helps shape the weather, as it stands in the path of the prevailing westerly winds which roll in, moisture-laden, from the Tasman Sea. As a result bush-clad lower slopes of the western Southern Alps are among the wettest places on earth, with an annual precipitation of some 15,000mm. Having lost its moisture, the wind then blows dry across the eastern plains towards the Pacific coast.

The North Island has a more even rainfall and is spared the temperature extremes of the South – which can plunge when a wind blows in from Antarctica. The important thing to remember, especially if you are tramping at high altitude, is that NZ has a maritime climate. This means weather can change with lightning speed, catching out the unprepared.

The ✏ icon in reviews marks places that demonstrate a commitment to sustainability. Travellers seeking other sustainable tourism operators should look for operators accredited with Qualmark Green (www.qualmark.co.nz) or listed at Organic Explorer (www.organicexplorer.co.nz).

ENVIRONMENT WILDLIFE

Wildlife

NZ may be relatively young, geologically speaking, but its plants and animals go back a long way. The tuatara, for instance, an ancient reptile unique to these islands, is a Gondwanaland survivor closely related to the dinosaurs, while many of the distinctive flightless birds (ratites) have distant African and South American cousins.

Due to its long isolation, the country is a veritable warehouse of unique and varied plants, most of which are found nowhere else. And with separation of the landmass occurring before mammals appeared on the scene, birds and insects have evolved in spectacular ways to fill the gaps.

The now extinct flightless moa, the largest of which grew to 3.5m tall and weighed over 200kg, browsed open grasslands much as cattle do today (skeletons can be seen at Auckland Museum), while the smaller kiwi still ekes out a nocturnal living rummaging among forest leaf litter for insects and worms much as small mammals do elsewhere. One of the country's most ferocious-looking insects, the mouse-sized giant weta, meanwhile, has taken on a scavenging role elsewhere filled by rodents.

As one of the last places on earth to be colonised by humans, NZ was for millennia a safe laboratory for such risky evolutionary strategies, but with the arrival first of Maori and soon after of Europeans, things went downhill fast.

Many endemic creatures, including moa and the huia, an exquisite songbird, were driven to extinction, and the vast forests were cleared for their timber and to make way for agriculture. Destruction of habitat and the introduction of exotic animals and plants have taken a terrible environmental toll and New Zealanders are now fighting a rearguard battle to save what remains.

Birds & Animals

B Heather and H Robertson's *Field Guide to the Birds of New Zealand* is a comprehensive guide for bird-watchers and a model of helpfulness for anyone even casually interested in the country's remarkable bird life.

The first Polynesian settlers found little in the way of land mammals – just two species of bat – but forests, plains and coasts found elsewhere. Largely lacking the bright plumage found elsewhere, NZ's birds – like its endemic plants – have an understated beauty that does not shout for attention.

Among the most musical is the bellbird, common in both native and exotic forests everywhere except Northland, though like many birds it is more likely to be heard than seen. Its call is a series of liquid bell notes, most often sounded at dawn or dusk.

The tui, another nectar eater and the country's most beautiful songbird, is a great mimic, with an inventive repertoire that includes clicks, grunts and chuckles. Notable for the white throat feathers that stand out against its dark plumage, the tui often feeds on flax flowers in suburban gardens but is most at home in densely tangled forest ('bush' to New Zealanders).

Fantails are commonly encountered on forest trails, swooping and jinking to catch insects stirred up by passing trampers, while pukeko, elegant swamp-hens with blue plumage and bright-red beaks, are readily seen along wetland margins and even on the sides of roads nearby – be warned, they have little road sense.

KIWI SPOTTING

A threatened species, the kiwi is also nocturnal and difficult to see in the wild, although you can do this in Okarito on the West Coast and on Stewart Island. They can, however, be observed in many artificially dark 'kiwi houses':

➡ **West Coast Wildlife Centre** (p118) Franz Josef

➡ **Orana Wildlife Park** (p134) Christchurch

➡ **Willowbank Wildlife Reserve** (p135) Christchurch

➡ **Kiwi Birdlife Park** (p217) Queenstown

If you spend any time in the South Island high country, you are likely to come up against the fearless and inquisitive kea – an uncharacteristically drab green parrot with bright-red underwings. Kea are common in the car parks of the Fox and Franz Josef Glaciers, where they hang out for food scraps or tear rubber from car windscreens.

Then there is the takahe, a rare flightless bird thought extinct until a small colony was discovered in 1948, and the equally flightless kiwi, NZ's national emblem and the nickname for New Zealanders themselves.

The kiwi has a round body covered in coarse feathers, strong legs and a long, distinctive bill with nostrils at the tip for sniffing out food. It is not easy to find them in the wild, but they can be seen in simulated environments at excellent nocturnal houses. One of the best is the Otorohanga Kiwi House, which also has other birds, including native falcons, moreporks (owls) and weka.

To get a feel for what the bush used to be like, take a trip to Tiritiri Matangi island. This regenerating island is an open sanctuary and one of the country's most successful exercises in community-assisted conservation.

Bird-Watching

The flightless kiwi is the species most sought after by bird-watchers. Sightings of the Stewart Island subspecies are common at all times of the year. Elsewhere, wild sightings of this increasingly rare nocturnal species are difficult, apart from in enclosures. Other birds that twitchers like to sight are the royal albatross, white heron, Fiordland crested penguin, yellow-eyed penguin, Australasian gannet and wrybill.

On the Coromandel Peninsula on the North Island, the Firth of Thames (particularly Miranda) is a haven for migrating birds, while the Wharekawa Wildlife Refuge at Opoutere Beach is a breeding ground of the endangered NZ dotterel. There's also a very accessible Australasian gannet colony at Muriwai, west of Auckland, and one in Hawke's Bay. On the South Island there are popular trips to observe pelagic birds out of Kaikoura, and royal albatross viewing on the Otago Peninsula.

Two good guides are the revised *Field Guide to the Birds of New Zealand,* by Barrie Heather and Hugh Robertson, and *Birds of New Zealand: Locality Guide* by Stuart Chambers.

Marine Mammal–Watching

Kaikoura, on the northeast coast of the South Island, is NZ's nexus of marine mammal–watching. The main attraction here is whale-watching, but this is dependent on weather conditions, so don't expect to just be able to rock up and head straight out on a boat for a dream encounter. The sperm whale, the largest toothed whale, is pretty much a year-round resident, and depending on the season you may also see migrating humpback whales, pilot whales, blue whales and southern right whales. Other mammals – including fur seals and dusky dolphins – are seen year-round.

Kaikoura is also an outstanding place to swim with dolphins. Pods of up to 500 playful dusky dolphins can be seen on any given day. Dolphin swimming is common elsewhere in NZ, with the animals gathering off the North Island near Whakatane, Paihia, Tauranga, and in the Hauraki Gulf, and off Akaroa on the Banks Peninsula. On the South Island, swimming with seals is possible in Kaikoura and in the Abel Tasman National Park.

Nature Guide to the New Zealand Forest, by J Dawson and R Lucas, is a beautifully photographed foray into the world of NZ's forests. Far from being drab and colourless, these lush treasure houses are home to ancient species dating from the time of the dinosaurs. This guidebook will have you reaching for your boots.

ENVIRONMENT WILDLIFE

TOWERING KAURI

When Chaucer was born this was a sturdy young tree. When Shakespeare was born it was 300 years old. It predates most of the great cathedrals of Europe. Its trunk is sky-rocket straight and sky-rocket bulky, limbless for half its height. Ferns sprout from its crevices. Its crown is an asymmetric mess, like an inverted root system. I lean against it, give it a slap. It's like slapping a building. This is a tree out of Tolkien. It's a kauri.

Joe Bennett (A Land of Two Halves) referring to the McKinney kauri in Northland

Trees

No visitor to NZ (particularly Australians!) will go for long without hearing about the damage done to the bush by that bad-mannered Australian import, the brush-tailed possum. The long list of mammal pests introduced to NZ accidentally or for a variety of misguided reasons includes deer, rabbits, stoats, pigs and goats. But the most destructive by far is the possum, 70 million of which now chew through millions of tonnes of foliage a year despite the best efforts of the Department of Conservation (DOC) to control them.

Among favoured possum food are NZ's most colourful trees: the kowhai, a small-leaved tree growing to 11m that in spring has drooping clusters of bright-yellow flowers (NZ's national flower); the pohutukawa, a beautiful coastal tree of the northern North Island which bursts into vivid red flower in December, earning the nickname 'Christmas tree'; and a similar crimson-flowered tree, the rata. Rata species are found on both islands; the northern rata starts life as a climber on a host tree (that it eventually chokes).

The few remaining pockets of mature centuries-old kauri are stately emblems of former days. Their vast hammered trunks and towering, epiphyte-festooned limbs, which dwarf every other tree in the forest, are reminders of why they were sought after in colonial days for spars and building timber. The best place to see the remaining giants is Northland's Waipoua Forest, home to three-quarters of the country's surviving kauri.

Now the pressure has been taken off kauri and other timber trees, including the distinctive rimu (red pine) and the long-lived totara (favoured for Maori war canoes), by one of the country's most successful imports – *Pinus radiata*. Pine was found to thrive in NZ, growing to maturity in just 35 years, and plantation forests are now widespread through the central North Island – the southern hemisphere's biggest, Kaingaroa Forest, lies southeast of Rotorua.

You won't get far into the bush without coming across one of its most prominent features – tree ferns. NZ is a land of ferns (more than 80 species) and most easily recognised are the mamaku (black tree fern) – which grows to 20m and can be seen in damp gullies throughout the country – and the 10m-high ponga (silver tree fern) with its distinctive white underside. The silver fern is equally at home as part of corporate logos and on the clothing of many of the country's top sportspeople.

The Department of Conservation website (www. doc.govt.nz) has useful information on the country's national parks, tracks and walkways. It also lists backcountry huts and campsites.

National Parks

A third of the country – more than 5 million hectares – is protected in environmentally important parks and reserves that embrace almost every conceivable landscape: from mangrove-fringed inlets in the north to the snow-topped volcanoes of the Central Plateau, and from the forested fastness of the Ureweras in the east to the Southern Alps' majestic mountains, glaciers and fiords. The 14 national parks, three marine

National Parks & Forest Parks

0 — 200 km
0 — 100 miles

Kaitaia

Northland
Forest Park

Whangarei

Dargaville

TASMAN
SEA

Auckland

Coromandel
Forest Park

Kaimai-Mamaku
Forest Park

Hamilton

Tauranga

Raukumara
Forest Park

Pirongia
Forest Park

Whirinaki
Forest
Park

Te Urewera
National Park

Pureora
Forest Park

Tongariro World
Heritage Area

Turangi

Gisborne

New Plymouth

Kaimanawa Forest Park

Kaweka Forest Park

Egmont National Park

Whanganui
National Park

Tongariro
National Park

Napier
Hastings

Whanganui

Ruahine
Forest Park

Palmerston North

Abel Tasman
National
Park

Tararua Forest Park

Takaka

Kahurangi National Park

WELLINGTON

Masterton

Nelson

Rimutaka Forest Park

Mt Richmond Forest Park

Aorangi Forest Park

Westport

Blenheim

Victoria Forest Park

Paparoa National Park

Nelson Lakes National Park

Lake Sumner Forest Park

Kaikoura

Hokitika

Hanmer Forest Park

Westland Tai Poutini
National
Park

Arthur's Pass National Park

Craigieburn Forest Park

Franz Josef

Fox Glacier

Mt Cook Village

Aoraki/Mt Cook National Park

Christchurch

Lake Tekapo

Peel Forest Park

Mt Aspiring
National Park

Twizel

Timaru

Fiordland
National
Park

Wanaka

Southwest New Zealand
(Te Wahipounamu)
World Heritage Area

Queenstown

Te Anau

SOUTH
PACIFIC
OCEAN

Dunedin

Balclutha

Invercargill

Catlins Forest Park

Oban

Rakiura National Park

Stewart Island (Rakiura)

Subantarctic Islands
World Heritage Area

parks and more than 30 marine reserves, along with numerous forest parks, offer huge scope for wilderness experiences, ranging from climbing, snow skiing and mountain biking to tramping, kayaking and trout fishing.

Three places are World Heritage Areas: NZ's Subantarctic Islands, Tongariro National Park and Te Wahipounamu, an amalgam of several

ENVIRONMENTAL ISSUES IN NEW ZEALAND

Employing images of untouched landscapes, Tourism New Zealand's 100% Pure marketing campaign has been critically acclaimed, and is the envy of tourism organisations worldwide. Such portrayals of a pristine environment have, however, been repeatedly rumbled in recent years as environmentalists – and the media – place NZ's 'clean green' credentials under the microscope. Mining, offshore oil and gas exploration, pollution, biodiversity loss, conservation funding cuts and questionable urban planning – there have been endless hooks for bad-news stories, and numerous reasons to protest.

A 2013 university study found that New Zealanders rate water quality as the country's most serious environmental issue. Their concern is well founded, with one-third of NZ's 425 lakes, rivers and beaches deemed unsafe for swimming; research from diverse quarters confirms that the health of NZ's waterways is in serious decline. The primary culprit is 'dirty dairying' – cow effluent leaching into freshwater ecosystems, carrying with it high levels of nitrates, as well as bacteria and parasites such as E. coli and giardia.

The dairy industry is NZ's biggest export earner, and it continues to boom with more land being converted, despite clear evidence of its detrimental effects, which include the generation of half of NZ's greenhouse gas emissions. Parliamentary Commissioner for the Environment, Jan Wright, has referred to the matter as a 'classic economy versus environment dilemma'. NZ's dominant dairy cooperative – Fonterra – has expressed a commitment to upping its game to ensure farm management practices 'preserve New Zealand's clean green image'; some farmers are indeed cleaning up their act.

There are many other threats to water and land ecosystems, including proliferation of invasive weeds and pests, with biodiversity loss continuing in parallel. The worst offenders are possums, stoats and rats, which chomp through swathes of forest and kill wildlife, particularly birds. Controversy rages at the Department of Conservation's use of 1080 poison (sodium fluoroacetate) to control these pests, despite it being sanctioned by prominent environmental groups such as Forest & Bird and the Parliamentary Commissioner for the Environment. Vehement opposition to 1080 is expressed by such diverse camps as hunters and animal-rights activists, who cite detriments such as by-kill and the poison's transmittal into waterways.

This is just one of DOC's increasing range of duties, which includes processing applications for mining within the conservation estate. Public feeling runs high on this issue, too, as demonstrated by recent ructions over opencast coalmining on the West Coast's Denniston Plateau. DOC has increasingly found itself in the thick of it; at the same time as budget cuts and major internal restructuring have left it appearing thinner on the ground.

Meanwhile, NZ's principle legislation governing the NZ environment – the 1991 Resource Management Act – is undergoing controversial reforms suspected of opening the door to further exploitation of the environment. NGOs and community groups – ever-vigilant and already making major contributions to the welfare of NZ's environment – will find plenty to keep them occupied in the years to come.

Sarah Bennett & Lee Slater

national parks in southwest NZ that boasts the world's finest surviving Gondwanaland plants and animals in their natural habitats.

Access to the country's wild places is relatively straightforward, though huts on walking tracks require passes and may need to be booked in advance. In practical terms, there is little difference for travellers between a national park and a forest park, though dogs are not allowed in national parks without a permit. Camping is possible in all parks, but may be restricted to dedicated camping grounds – check first. Permits are required for hunting (game birds), and licences are needed for inland fishing (trout, salmon); both can be bought online at www.fishandgame.org.nz.

Maori Culture

by John Huria

'Maori' once just meant 'common' or 'everyday', but now it means...let's just begin by saying that there is a lot of 'then' and a lot of 'now' in the Maori world. Sometimes the cultural present follows on from the past quite seamlessly; sometimes things have changed hugely; sometimes we just want to look to the future.

Maori today are a diverse people. Some are engaged with traditional cultural networks and pursuits; others are occupied with adapting tradition and placing it into a dialogue with globalising culture. The Maori concept of *whanaungatanga* – family relationships – is important to the culture. And families spread out from the *whanau* (extended family) to the *hapu* (subtribe) and *iwi* (tribe) and even, in a sense, beyond the human world and into the natural and spiritual worlds.

Maori are New Zealand's *tangata whenua* (people of the land), and the Maori relationship with the land has developed over hundreds of years of occupation. Once a predominantly rural people, many Maori now live in urban centres, away from their traditional home base. But it's still common practice in formal settings to introduce oneself by referring to home: an ancestral mountain, river, sea or lake, or an ancestor. There's no place like home, but it's good to be away as well.

If you're looking for a Maori experience in NZ you'll find it – in performance, in conversation, in an art gallery, on a tour...

John Huria (Ngai Tahu, Muaupoko) has an editorial, research and writing background with a focus on Maori writing and culture. He runs an editorial and publishing services company, Ahi Text Solutions Ltd (www.ahitextsolutions.co.nz).

Maori Then

Some three millennia ago people began moving eastward into the Pacific, sailing against the prevailing winds and currents (hard to go out, easier to return safely). Some stopped at Tonga and Samoa, and others settled the small central East Polynesian tropical islands.

The Maori colonisation of Aotearoa began from an original homeland known to Maori as Hawaiki. Skilled navigators and sailors travelled across the Pacific, using many navigational tools – currents, winds, stars, birds and wave patterns – to guide their large, double-hulled ocean-going craft to a new land.

The first of many was the great navigator Kupe, who arrived, the story goes, chasing an octopus named Muturangi. But the distinction of giving NZ its well-known Maori name – Aotearoa – goes to his wife, Kuramarotini, who cried out, *'He ao, he ao tea, he ao tea roa!'* (A cloud, a white cloud, a long white cloud!).

Kupe and his crew journeyed around the land, and many places around Cook Strait (between the North and South Islands), and the Hokianga in Northland still bear the names that they gave them and the marks of his passage. Kupe returned to Hawaiki, leaving from (and naming) Northland's Hokianga. He gave other seafarers valuable navigational information. And then the great *waka* (ocean-going craft) began to arrive.

Kupe's passage is marked around NZ: he left his sails (Nga Ra o Kupe) near Cape Palliser as triangular landforms; he named the two islands in Wellington Harbour Matiu and Makaro after his daughters; his blood stains the red rocks of Wellington's south coast.

The *waka* that the first setters arrived on, and their landing places, are immortalised in tribal histories. Well-known *waka* include *Takitimu, Kurahaupo, Te Arawa, Mataatua, Tainui, Aotea* and *Tokomaru*. There are many others. Maori trace their genealogies back to those who arrived on the *waka* (and further back as well).

What would it have been like making the transition from small tropical islands to a much larger, cooler land mass? Goodbye breadfruit, coconuts, paper mulberry; hello moa, fernroot, flax – and immense space (relatively speaking). NZ has over 15,000km of coastline. Rarotonga, by way of contrast, has a little over 30km. There was land, lots of it, and a flora and fauna that had developed more or less separately from the rest of the world for 80 million years. There was an untouched, massive fishery. There were great seaside mammalian convenience stores – seals and sea lions – as well as a fabulous array of birds.

The early settlers went on the move, pulled by love, by trade opportunities and greater resources; pushed by disputes and threats to security. When they settled, Maori established *mana whenua* (regional authority), whether by military campaigns, or by the peaceful methods of intermarriage and diplomacy. Looking over tribal history it's possible to see the many alliances, absorptions and extinctions that went on.

Histories were carried by the voice, in stories, songs and chants. Great stress was placed on accurate learning – after all, in an oral culture where people are the libraries, the past is always a generation or two away from oblivion.

Maori lived in *kainga,* small villages, which often had associated gardens. Housing was quite cosy by modern standards – often it was hard to stand upright while inside. From time to time people would leave their home base and go to harvest seasonal foods. When peaceful life was interrupted by conflict, the people would withdraw to *pa,* fortified dwelling places.

And then Europeans began to arrive.

Arriving for the first time in NZ, two crew members of *Tainui* saw the red flowers of the pohutukawa tree, and they cast away their prized red feather ornaments, thinking that there were plenty to be had on shore.

HOW THE WORLD BEGAN

In the Maori story of creation, first there was the void, then the night, then Rangi-nui (sky father) and Papa-tu-a-nuku (earth mother) came into being, embracing with their children nurtured between them. But nurturing became something else. Their children were stifled in the darkness of their embrace. Unable to stretch out to their full dimensions and struggling to see clearly in the darkness, their children tried to separate them. Tawhiri-matea, the god of winds, raged against them; Tu-mata-uenga, the god of war, assaulted them. Each god child in turn tried to separate them, but still Rangi and Papa pressed against each other. And then Tane-mahuta, god of the great forests and of humanity, placed his feet against his father and his back against his mother and slowly, inexorably, began to move them apart. Then came the world of light, of demigods and humanity.

In this world of light Maui, the demigod ancestor, was cast out to sea at birth and was found floating in his mother's topknot. He was a shape-shifter, becoming a pigeon or a dog or an eel if it suited his purposes. He stole fire from the gods. Using his grandmother's jawbone, he bashed the sun so that it could only limp slowly across the sky, so that people would have enough time during the day to get things done (if only he would do it again!). Using the South Island as a canoe, he used the jawbone as a hook to fish up Te Ika a Maui (the fish of Maui) – the North Island. And, finally, he met his end trying to defeat death itself. The goddess of death, Hine Nui Te Po, had obsidian teeth in her vagina (obsidian is a volcanic glass that takes a razor edge when chipped). Maui attempted to reverse birth (and hence defeat death) by crawling into her birth canal to reach her heart as she slept. A small bird – a fantail – laughed at the absurd sight. Hine Nui Te Po awoke, and crushed Maui between her thighs. Death one, humanity nil.

Maori Today

Today's culture is marked by new developments in the arts, business, sport and politics. Many historical grievances still stand, but some *iwi* (Ngai Tahu and Tainui, for example) have settled historical grievances and are major forces in the NZ economy. Maori have also addressed the decline in Maori language use by establishing *kohanga reo, kura kaupapa Maori* and *wananga* (Maori-medium preschools, schools and universities). There is now a generation of people who speak Maori as a first language. There is a network of Maori radio stations, and Maori TV is attracting a committed viewership. A recently revived Maori event is becoming more and more prominent – Matariki, or Maori New Year. The constellation Matariki is also known as Pleiades. It begins to rise above the horizon in late May or early June and its appearance traditionally signals a time for learning, planning and preparing as well as singing, dancing and celebrating. Watch out for talks and lectures, concerts, dinners, and even formal balls.

The best way to learn about the relationship between the land and the *tangata whenua* is to get out there and start talking with Maori.

Religion

Christian churches and denominations are important in the Maori world: televangelists, mainstream churches for regular and occasional worship, and two major Maori churches (Ringatu and Ratana) – we've got it all.

But in the (non–Judaeo Christian) beginning there were the *atua Maori,* the Maori gods, and for many Maori the gods are a vital and relevant force still. It is common to greet the earth mother and sky father when speaking formally at a *marae*. The gods are represented in art and carving, sung of in *waiata* (songs), invoked through *karakia* (prayer and incantation) when a meeting house is opened, when a *waka* is launched, even (more simply) when a meal is served. They are spoken of on the *marae* and in wider Maori contexts. The traditional Maori creation story is well known and widely celebrated.

The Arts

There are many collections of Maori *taonga* (treasures) around the country. Some of the largest and most comprehensive are at Wellington's Te Papa Museum and the Auckland Museum. Canterbury Museum in Christchurch also has a good collection, and Hokitika Museum has an exhibition showing the story of *pounamu* (nephrite jade, or greenstone).

You can stay up to date with what is happening in the Maori arts by reading *Mana* magazine (available from most newsagents), listening to *iwi* stations (www.irirangi.net) or weekly podcasts from Radio New Zealand (www.radionz.co.nz). Maori TV also has regular features on the Maori arts – check out www.maoritelevision.com.

See Ngahuia Te Awekotuku's *Mau Moko: The World of Maori Tattoo* (2007) for the big picture, with powerful, beautiful images and an incisive commentary.

Maori TV went to air in 2004, an emotional time for many Maori who could at last see their culture, their concerns and their language in a mass medium. Over 90% of content is NZ-made, and programs are in both Maori and English: they're subtitled and accessible to everyone. If you want to really get a feel for the rhythm and meter of spoken Maori from the comfort of your own chair, switch to Te Reo, a Maori-language-only channel.

Ta Moko

Ta moko is the Maori art of tattoo, traditionally worn by men on their faces, thighs and buttocks, and by women on their chins and lips. *Moko* were permanent grooves tapped into the skin using pigment (made from burnt caterpillar or kauri gum soot), and bone chisels: fine, sharp combs for broad work, and straight blades for detailed work. Museums in the major centres – Auckland, Wellington and Christchurch – all display traditional implements for *ta moko*.

The modern tattooist's gun is common now, but bone chisels are coming back into use for Maori who want to reconnect with tradition. Since the general renaissance in Maori culture in the 1960s, many artists have taken up *ta moko* and now many Maori wear *moko* with quiet pride and humility.

VISITING MARAE

As you travel around NZ, you will see many *marae* complexes. Often *marae* are owned by a descent group. They are also owned by urban Maori groups, schools, universities and church groups, and they should only be visited by arrangement with the owners. Some *marae* that may be visited include Huria Marae in Tauranga; Koriniti Marae on the Whanganui River Rd; Te Manuka Tutahi Marae in Wakatane; and Te Papa in Wellington.

Marae complexes include a *wharenui* (meeting house), which often embodies an ancestor. Its ridge is the backbone, the rafters are ribs, and it shelters the descendants. There is a clear space in front of the *wharenui* (ie the *marae atea*). Sometimes there are other buildings: a *wharekai* (dining hall); a toilet and shower block; perhaps even class-rooms, play equipment and the like.

Hui (gatherings) are held at *marae*. Issues are discussed, classes conducted, mile-stones celebrated and the dead farewelled. *Te reo Maori* (the Maori language) is promi-nent, sometimes exclusively so.

Visitors sleep in the meeting house if a *hui* goes on for longer than a day. Mattresses are placed on the floor, someone may bring a guitar, and stories and jokes always go down well as the evening stretches out…

The Powhiri

If you visit a *marae* as part of an organised group, you'll be welcomed in a *powhiri* (for-mal welcome). The more common ones are outlined here.

There may be a *wero* (challenge). Using *taiaha* (quarter-staff) moves, a warrior will approach the visitors and place a baton on the ground for a visitor to pick up.

There is a *karanga* (ceremonial call). A woman from the host group calls to the visitors and a woman from the visitors responds. Their long, high, falling calls begin to overlap and interweave and the visiting group walks on to the *marae atea*.

It is then time for *whaikorero* (speechmaking). The hosts welcome the visitors, the visitors respond. Speeches are capped off by a *waiata* (song), and the visitors' speaker places *koha* (gift, usually an envelope of cash) on the *marae*. The hosts then invite the visitors to *hariru* (shake hands) and *hongi* (press foreheads together). Visitors and hosts are now united and will share light refreshments or a meal.

The Hongi

Press forehead and nose together firmly, shake hands, and perhaps offer a greeting such as '*Kia ora*' or '*Tena koe*'. Some prefer one press (for two or three seconds, or longer), others prefer two shorter (press, release, press). Men and women sometimes kiss on one cheek. Some people mistakenly think the *hongi* is a pressing of noses only (awkward to aim!) or the rubbing of noses (even more awkward).

Tapu

Tapu (spiritual restrictions) and *mana* (power and prestige) are taken seriously in the Maori world. Sit on chairs or seating provided (never on tables), and walk around peo-ple, not over them. The *powhiri* is *tapu,* and mixing food and *tapu* is right up there on the offence-o-meter. Do eat and drink when invited to do so by your hosts. You needn't worry about starvation: an important Maori value is *manaakitanga* (kindness).

Depending on the area, the *powhiri* has gender roles: women *karanga* (call), men *whaiko-rero* (orate); women lead the way on to the *marae,* men sit on the *paepae* (the speakers' bench at the front). In a modern context, the debate around these roles continues.

Can visitors get involved, or even get some work done? The term *kirituhi* (skin inscriptions) has arisen to describe Maori motif–inspired modern tattoos that non-Maori can wear.

Carving

Traditional Maori carving, with its intricate detailing and curved lines, can transport the viewer. It's quite amazing to consider that it was done with stone tools, themselves painstakingly made, until the advent of iron (nails suddenly became very popular).

Some major traditional forms are *waka* (canoes), *pataka* (storage buildings), and *wharenui* (meeting houses). You can see sublime examples of traditional carving at Te Papa in Wellington, and at the following in the South Island:

➡ **Maori & Colonial Museum** (p152) A *waka taua* (war canoe) dating back to 1867; Okains Bay, Banks Peninsula.

➡ **Otago Museum** (p195) Nice old *waka* and *whare runanga* (meeting house) carvings; Dunedin.

➡ **Canterbury Museum** (p132) A magnificent *poutokomanawa* or male ancestor figure, Christchurch.

The apex of carving today is the *whare whakairo* (carved meeting house). A commissioning group relates its history and ancestral stories to a carver, who then draws (sometimes quite loosely) on traditional motifs to interpret or embody the stories and ancestors in wood or composite fibreboard.

Rongomaraeroa Marae, by artist Cliff Whiting, at Te Papa in Wellington is a colourful example of a contemporary re-imagining of a traditional art form. The biggest change in carving (as with most traditional arts) has been in the use of new mediums and tools. Rangi Kipa uses a synthetic polymer called Corian to make his *hei tiki* (figure motif worn around the neck), the same stuff that is used to make kitchen benchtops. You can check out his gallery at www.rangikipa.com.

Weaving

Weaving was an essential art that provided clothing, nets and cordage, footwear for rough country travel, mats to cover earthen floors, and *kete* (bags). Many woven items are beautiful as well as practical. Some were major works – *korowai* (cloaks) could take years to finish. Woven predominantly with flax and bird feathers, they are worn now on ceremonial occasions, a stunning sight.

Working with natural materials for the greater good of the people involved getting things right by maintaining the supply of raw material and ensuring that it worked as it was meant to. Protocols were necessary, and women were dedicated to weaving under the aegis of the gods. Today, tradition is greatly respected, but not all traditions are necessarily followed.

Flax was (and still is) the preferred medium for weaving. To get a strong fibre from flax leaves, weavers scraped away the leaves' flesh with a mussel shell, then pounded until it was soft, dyed it, then dried it. But contemporary weavers are using everything in their work: raffia, copper wire, rubber – even polar fleece and garden hoses!

The best place to experience weaving is to contact one of the many weavers running workshops. By learning the art, you'll appreciate the examples of weaving in museums even more. And if you want your own? Woven *kete* and backpacks have become fashion accessories and are on sale in most cities. Weaving is also found in dealer art galleries around the country.

MAORI CULTURE MAORI TODAY

Maori legends are all around you as you tour NZ: Maui's *waka* became today's Southern Alps; a *taniwha* (supernatural creature) formed Lake Waikaremoana in its death throes; and a rejected Mt Taranaki walked into exile from the central North Island mountain group, carving the Whanganui River.

See Hirini Moko Mead's *Tikanga Maori,* Pat and Hiwi Tauroa's *Visiting a Marae,* and Anne Salmond's *Hui* for detailed information on Maori customs.

Haka

Experiencing *haka* can get the adrenaline flowing, as it did for one Pakeha observer in 1929 who thought of dark Satanic mills: 'They looked like fiends from hell wound up by machinery'. *Haka* can be awe-inspiring; they can also be uplifting. The *haka* is not only a war dance – it is used to welcome visitors, honour achievement, express identity or to put forth very strong opinions.

Haka involve chanted words, vigorous body movements, and *pukana* (when performers distort their faces, eyes bulging with the whites showing, perhaps with tongue extended).

The well-known *haka* 'Ka Mate', performed by the All Blacks before rugby test matches, is credited to the cunning fighting chief Te Rauparaha. It celebrates his escape from death. Chased by enemies, he hid himself in a food pit. After they had left, a friendly chief named Te Whareangi (the 'hairy man' referred to in the *haka*), let him out; he climbed out into the sunshine and performed 'Ka Mate'.

In the South Island you can experience *haka* at various cultural performances including at **Ko Tane** (☑03-359 6226; www.kotane.co.nz; 60 Hussey Rd, Willowbank Wildlife Reserve; dancing, tour & dinner package adult/child $110/54; ⊙5.30pm Mon & Thu-Sat) at Willowbank in Christchurch; Maori Tours (p70) in Kaikoura and Myths & Legends Eco-tours (p57) in Picton.

But the best displays of *haka* are at the national Te Matatini National Kapa Haka Festival when NZ's top groups compete. It is held every two years, with the next festival in February 2015 to take place in Christchrch.

Contemporary Visual Art

For information on Maori arts today, check out Toi Maori www.maoriart.org.nz.

A distinctive feature of Maori visual art is the tension between traditional Maori ideas and modern artistic mediums and trends. Shane Cotton produced a series of works that conversed with 19th-century painted meeting houses, which themselves departed from Maori carved houses. Kelcy Taratoa uses toys, superheroes and pop urban imagery alongside weaving and carving design.

Of course not all Maori artists use Maori motifs. Ralph Hotere is a major NZ artist who 'happens to be Maori' (his words), and his career-long exploration of black speaks more to modernism than the traditional *marae* context.

Contemporary Maori art is by no means only about painting. Many other artists use installations as the preferred medium – look out for work by Jacqueline Fraser and Peter Robinson.

There are some great permanent exhibitions of Maori visual arts in the major centres. Both the Auckland and Christchurch Art Galleries hold strong collections, as does Wellington's Te Papa. Note that the Christchurch Art Gallery was closed for repairs after the earthquakes at the time of writing.

Contemporary Theatre

The 1970s saw the emergence of many Maori playwrights and plays, and theatre is a strong area of the Maori arts today. Maori theatre drew heavily on the traditions of the *marae*. Instead of dimming the lights and immediately beginning the performance, many Maori theatre groups began with a stylised *powhiri*, had space for audience members to respond to the play, and ended with a *karakia* or a farewell.

Taki Rua is an independent producer of Maori work for both children and adults and has been in existence for over 25 years. As well as staging its shows in the major centres, it tours most of its work – check out its website (www.takirua.co.nz) for the current offerings. Maori drama is also often showcased at the professional theatres in the main centres as well as the biennial New Zealand International Festival. Hone Kouka and Briar Grace-Smith (both have published playscripts available) have toured their works around NZ and to festivals in the UK.

Contemporary Dance

Contemporary Maori dance often takes its inspiration from *kapa haka* (cultural dance) and traditional Maori imagery. The exploration of pre-European life also provides inspiration. For example, a Maori choreographer, Moss Patterson, used *kokowai* (a body-adorning paste made from reddish clay and shark oil) as the basis of his most recent piece of the same name.

NZ's leading specifically Maori dance company is the Atamira Dance Collective (www.atamiradance.co.nz), which has been producing critically acclaimed, beautiful and challenging work since 2000. If that sounds too earnest, another choreographer to watch out for is Mika Torotoro, who happily blends *kapa haka*, drag, opera, ballet and disco into his work. You can check out clips of his work at www.mika.co.nz.

Maori Film-Making

Although there had already been successful Maori documentaries (*Patu!* and the *Tangata Whenua* series are brilliant, and available from some urban video stores), it wasn't until 1987 that NZ had its first fiction feature-length movie by a Maori director with Barry Barclay's *Ngati*. Mereta Mita was the first Maori woman to direct a fiction feature, with *Mauri* (1988). Both Mita and Barclay had highly political aims and ways of working, which involved a lengthy pre-production phase, during which they would consult with and seek direction from their *kaumatua* (elders). Films with significant Maori participation or control include the harrowing *Once Were Warriors* and the uplifting *Whale Rider*. Oscar-shortlisted Taika Waititi, of Te Whanau-a-Apanui descent, wrote and directed *Eagle vs Shark* and *Boy*.

The New Zealand Film Archive (www.filmarchive.org.nz) is a great place to experience Maori film, with most showings being either free or relatively inexpensive. It has offices in Auckland and Wellington.

Maori Writing

There are many novels and collections of short stories by Maori writers, and personal taste will govern your choices. How about approaching Maori writing regionally? Read Patricia Grace *(Potiki, Cousins, Dogside Story, Tu)* around Wellington, and maybe Witi Ihimaera *(Pounamu, Pounamu, The Matriarch, Bulibasha, The Whale Rider)* on the North Island's East Coast. Keri Hulme *(The Bone People, Stonefish)* and the South Island go together like a mass of whitebait bound in a frying pan by a single egg (ie very well). Read Alan Duff *(Once Were Warriors)* anywhere, but only if you want to be saddened, even shocked. Definitely take James George *(Hummingbird, Ocean Roads)* with you to Auckland's West Coast beaches and Northland's Ninety Mile Beach. Paula Morris *(Queen of Beauty, Hibiscus Coast, Trendy but Casual)* and Kelly Ana Morey *(Bloom, Grace Is Gone)* – hmm, Auckland and beyond? If poetry appeals you can't go past the giant of Maori poetry in English, the late, lamented Hone Tuwhare *(Deep River Talk: Collected Poems)*. Famously sounding like he's at church and in the pub at the same time, you *can* take him anywhere.

Music plays an important role in traditional and contemporary Maori culture.

MAORI CULTURE MAORI TODAY

The first NZ hip-hop song to become a hit was Dalvanius Prime's 'Poi E', which was sung entirely in Maori by the Patea Maori Club. It was the highest-selling single of 1984 in NZ, outselling all international artists.

The Kiwi Psyche

New Zealand is like that little guy at school when they're picking rugby teams – quietly waiting to be noticed, desperately wanting to be liked. Then, when he does get the nod, his sheer determination to prove himself propels him to score a completely unexpected try. When his teammates come to congratulate him he stares at the ground and mumbles, 'It was nothing, ay'.

What Makes Kiwis Tick?

In 2009 and 2010 NZ topped the Global Peace Index, earning the distinction of being rated the world's most peaceful country. In 2011 it dropped to second place behind Iceland – something to do with all those *haka* performed during the Rugby World Cup, perhaps?

While NZ is a proud little nation, Kiwis traditionally don't have time for show-offs. Jingoistic flag-waving is generally frowned upon. People who make an impression on the international stage are respected and admired, but flashy tall poppies have traditionally had their heads lopped off.

This is perhaps a legacy of NZ's early egalitarian ideals – the ones that sought to avoid the worst injustices of the 'mother country' (Britain) by breaking up large land holdings and enthusiastically adopting a 'cradle to grave' welfare state. 'Just because someone's got a bigger car than me, or bigger guns, doesn't make them better' is the general Kiwi attitude.

NZ has rarely let its size get in the way of making a point on the international stage. A founding member of the League of Nations (the precursor to the UN), it ruffled feathers between the world wars by failing to blindly follow Britain's position. It was in the 1980s, however, that things got really interesting.

A Turbulent Decade

Modern Kiwi culture pivots on the 1980s. Firstly, the unquestioned primacy of rugby union as a source of social cohesion (which rivalled the country's commitment to the two world wars as a foundation of nation-building) was stripped away when tens of thousands of New Zealanders took to the streets to protest a tour by the South African rugby side in 1981. The protestors held that the politics of apartheid not only had a place in sport, they trumped it. The country was starkly divided; there were riots in paradise. The scar is still strong enough that most New Zealanders over the age of 40 will recognise the simple phrase 'The Tour' as referring to those events.

The tour protests both harnessed and nourished a political and cultural renaissance among Maori that had already been rolling for a decade. Three years later, that renaissance found its mark when a reforming Labour government gave statutory teeth to the Waitangi Tribunal, an agency that has since guided a process of land return, compensation for past wrongs and interpretation of the Treaty of Waitangi – the 1840 pact between Maori and the Crown – as a living document.

At the same time antinuclear protests that had been rumbling for years gained momentum, with mass blockades of visiting US naval ships. In 1984 Prime Minister David Lange barred nuclear-powered or armed ships from entering NZ waters. The mouse had roared. As a result the US threw NZ out of ANZUS, the country's main strategic military alliance, which also included Australia, declaring NZ 'a friend but not an ally'.

However, it was an event in the following year that completely changed the way NZ related to the world, when French government agents launched an attack in Auckland Harbour, sinking Greenpeace's antinuclear flagship *Rainbow Warrior* and killing one of its crew. Being bombed by a country that NZ had fought two world wars with – and the muted or nonexistent condemnation by other allies – left an indelible mark. It strengthened NZ's resolve to follow its own conscience in foreign policy, and in 1987 the New Zealand Nuclear Free Zone, Disarmament, and Arms Control Act became law.

From the Boer to Vietnam Wars, NZ had blithely trotted off at the behest of the UK or US. Not anymore, as is demonstrated by its lack of involvement in the invasion of Iraq. That's not to say that the country shirks its international obligations: NZ troops continue to be deployed in peacekeeping capacities throughout the world and are currently active in Afghanistan.

If that wasn't enough upheaval for one decade, 1986 saw another bitter battle split the community – this time over the decriminalisation of homosexuality. The debate was particularly rancorous, but the law that previously incarcerated consenting gay adults was repealed, paving the way for the generally accepting society that NZ is today. In 1999 Georgina Beyer, an openly transsexual former prostitute, would win a once-safe rural seat off a conservative incumbent, and in 2013 NZ legalised same-sex marriage.

Yet while the 1980s saw the country jump to the left on social issues, simultaneously economic reforms were carried out that were an extreme step to the right (to paraphrase one-time Hamiltonian Richard O'Brien's song 'The Time Warp'). The bloated public sector was slashed, any state assets that weren't bolted to the floor were sold off, regulation was removed from many sectors, trade barriers dismantled and the power of the unions greatly diminished.

If there is broad agreement that the economy had to be restructured, the reforms carried a heavy price. The old social guarantees are not as sure. New Zealanders work long hours for lower wages than their Australian cousins would ever tolerate. Compared with other Organisation for Economic Co-operation and Development (OECD) nations, NZ family incomes are low, child poverty rates are high and the gap between rich and poor is widening.

For many, Sir Edmund Hillary, the first person to climb Mt Everest, was the consummate New Zealander: humble, practical and concerned for social justice. A public outpouring of grief followed his death in 2008.

IT'S A WOMAN'S WORLD

New Zealand is justifiably proud of being the first country in the world to give women the vote (in 1893). Kate Sheppard, the hero of the women's suffrage movement, even features on the country's $10 bill. Despite that early achievement, the real role for women in public life was modest for many years. That can hardly be said now. Since 1997 the country has had two female prime ministers and for a time in the 2000s every key constitutional position was held by a woman, including the prime minister, attorney general, chief justice, governor general and head of state – although New Zealanders can't take credit for choosing Betty Windsor for that last role. At the same time a Maori queen headed the Kingitanga (King Movement) and a woman led NZ's biggest listed corporation. Things have slipped a little since and only two of those roles are held by women – and, yes, one of those is filled by Queen Elizabeth II.

A New New Zealand

There is a dynamism about NZ today that was rare in the 'golden weather' years before the reforms. Today NZ farmers take on the world without the massive subsidies of yore, and Wellington's inner city – once virtually closed after dark by oppressive licensing laws – now thrives with great bars and restaurants.

As with the economic reforms, the 'Treaty process' of redress and reconciliation with Maori made some New Zealanders uneasy, more in their uncertainty about its extent than that it happened at all. The Maori population sat somewhere between 85,000 and 110,000 at the time of first European contact 200 years ago. Disease and warfare subsequently decimated the population, but a high birth rate sees about 15% of New Zealanders (599,000 people) identify as Maori, and that proportion is likely to grow.

The implication of the Treaty is one of partnership between Maori and the British Crown, together forging a bicultural nation. After decades of attempted cultural assimilation it's now accepted in most quarters that the indigenous culture has a special and separate status within the country's ethnic mix. For example, Maori is an official language and there is a separate electoral roll granting Maori guaranteed parliamentary seats.

Yet room has had to be found for the many New Zealanders of neither British nor Maori heritage. In each new wave of immigration there has been a tendency to demonise before gradually accepting and celebrating what the new cultures have to offer. This happened with the Chinese in the mid-19th century, Pacific Islanders in the 1970s, the Chinese again in the 1990s and, most recently, Croatians at the beginning of the 20th. That said, NZ society is more integrated and accepting than most. People of all races are represented in all levels of society and race isn't an obstacle to achievement.

For the younger generation, for whom the reformist 1980s are prehistory, political apathy is the norm today. In the 2011 general election only 75% of the population turned out to vote; for the under 30s this figure dropped to less than 64%. Perhaps it's because a decade of progressive government has given them little to kick against – unlike those politicised by the anti–Iraq War movements elsewhere. Ironically, as NZ has finally achieved its own interesting, independent cultural sensibility, the country's youth seem more obsessed with US culture than ever. This is particularly true within the hip-hop scene, where a farcical identification with American gangsta culture has developed into a worrying youth gang problem.

A Long Way From Britain

Most Kiwis (except perhaps the farmers) would probably wish it rained a little less and they got paid a little more, but it sometimes takes a few years travelling on their 'Big OE' (Overseas Experience – a traditional rite of passage) before they realise how good they've got it. In a 2012 study of the quality of life in the world's major cities, Auckland was rated third and Wellington 13th.

Despite all the change, key elements of the NZ identity are an unbroken thread, and fortune is still a matter of economics rather than class. If you are well served in a restaurant or shop, it will be out of politeness or pride in the job, rather than servility.

In country areas and on bushwalks don't be surprised if you're given a cheery greeting from passers-by, especially in the South Island. In a legacy of the British past, politeness is generally regarded as one of the highest virtues. A 'please' and 'thank you' will get you a long way. The three great exceptions to this rule are: a) on the road, where genteel Dr

Jekylls become raging Mr Hydes, especially if you have the misfortune of needing to change lanes in Auckland; b) if you don't speak English very well; and c) if you are Australian.

The latter two traits are the product of insularity and a smallness of world view that tends to disappear among Kiwis who have travelled (and luckily many do). The NZ/Australian rivalry is taken much more seriously on this side of the Tasman Sea. Although it's very unlikely that Kiwis will be rude outright, visiting Aussies must get pretty sick of the constant ribbing, much of it surprisingly ill-humoured. It's a sad truth that while most Australians would cheer on a NZ sports team if they were playing anyone other than their own, the opposite is true in NZ.

Ironically, the person responsible for the nuclear age was a New Zealander. In 1917 Ernest Rutherford was the first to split the nucleus of an atom. His face appears on the $100 note.

THE KIWI PSYCHE NUMBER-EIGHT WIRE

Number-Eight Wire

You might on your travels hear the phrase 'number-eight wire' and wonder what on earth it means. It's a catchphrase New Zealanders still repeat to themselves to encapsulate a national myth: that NZ's isolation and its pioneer stock created a culture in which ingenuity allowed problems to be solved and tools to be built from scratch. A NZ farmer, it was said, could solve pretty much any problem with a piece of number-eight wire (the gauge used for fencing on farms).

It's actually largely true – NZ farms are full of NZ inventions. One reason big offshore film and TV producers bring their projects here – apart from the low wages and huge variety of locations – is that they like the can-do attitude and ability to work to a goal of NZ technical crews. Many more New Zealanders have worked as managers, roadies or chefs for famous recording artists (everyone from Led Zeppelin and U2 to

'SO, WHAT DO YOU THINK OF NEW ZEALAND?'

That, by tradition, is the question that visitors are asked within an hour of disembarking in NZ. Sometimes they might be granted an entire day's research before being asked to pronounce, but asked they are. The question – composed equally of great pride and creeping doubt – is symbolic of the national consciousness.

When George Bernard Shaw visited for four weeks in 1934, he was deluged with what-do-you-think-of questions from newspaper reporters the length of the country. Although he never saw fit to write a word about NZ, his answers to those newspaper questions were collected and reprinted as *What I Saw in New Zealand: the Newspaper Utterances of George Bernard Shaw in New Zealand*. Yes, people really were that keen for vindication.

Other visitors were more willing to pronounce in print, including the British Liberal MP, David Goldblatt, who wrote an intriguing and prescient little book called *Democracy At Ease: a New Zealand Profile*. Goldblatt found New Zealanders a blithe people: kind, prosperous and fond of machines.

For the bon vivant Goldblatt, the attitude towards food and drink was all too telling. He found only 'the plain fare and even plainer fetch and carry of the normal feeding machine of this country' and shops catering 'in the same pedestrian fashion for a people never fastidious – the same again is the order of the day'.

Thus, a people with access to some of the best fresh ingredients on earth tended to boil everything to death. A nation strewn almost its entire length with excellent microclimates for viticulture produced only fortified plonk. Material comfort was valued, but was a plain thing indeed.

It took New Zealanders a quarter of a century more to shuck 'the same dull sandwiches', and embrace a national awareness – and, as Goldblatt correctly anticipated, it took 'hazards and misfortunes' to spur the 'divine discontent' for change.

But when it did happen, it really happened.

By Russell Brown. Brown is a journalist and manager of the Public Address blog site, www.publicaddress.net.

Madonna) than have enjoyed the spotlight themselves. Which just goes to show that New Zealanders operate best at the intersection of practicality and creativity, with an endearing (and sometimes infuriating) humility to boot.

A Sporting Chance

> No matter where you are in NZ, you're never more than 128km from the sea.

The arena where Kiwis have most sated their desperation for recognition on the world stage is sport. In 2012, NZ was ranked the most successful sporting nation per capita in the world (in 2013 it slipped to third behind Slovenia and Norway). NZ's teams are the current world champions in Rugby Union, holding both the men's and women's world cup.

For most of the 20th century, NZ's All Blacks dominated international rugby union, with one squad even dubbed 'The Invincibles'. Taking over this pastime of the British upper class did wonders for national identity and the game is now interwoven with NZ's history and culture. The 2011 Rugby World Cup victory did much to raise spirits after a year of tragedy and economic gloom.

For all rugby's influence on the culture, don't go to a game expecting to be caught up in an orgy of noise and cheering. Rugby crowds at Auckland's Eden Park are as restrained as their teams are cavalier, but they get noisier as you head south. In contrast, a home game for the NZ Warriors rugby league team at Auckland's Mt Smart Stadium is a thrilling spectacle, especially when the Polynesian drummers kick in.

Despite the everyman appeal of rugby union in NZ (unlike in the UK), rugby league retains the status of the working-class sport and support is strongest from Auckland's Maori, Polynesian and other immigrant communities. Still, taking the Rugby League World Cup off the Australians – NZ's constant arch-rivals – brought a smile to the faces of even the staunchest supporters of the rival rugby code.

> NZ is defined as a state in the Australian constitution. At the time of Australia's federation into one country it was hoped that NZ would join. On this side of the Tasman that idea proved as unpopular then as it does now.

Netball is the leading sport for women and the one in which the national team, the Silver Ferns, perpetually vies for world supremacy with the Australians – one or other of the countries has taken the world championship at every contest (except for a three-way tie in 1979).

In 2010 the All Whites, NZ's national soccer (football) squad, competed in the FIFA World Cup for the second time ever, emerging with the totally unanticipated distinction of being the only unbeaten team in the competition. They didn't win any games either, but most Kiwis were overjoyed to have seen their first ever World Cup goals and three draws. Sadly, they failed to qualify for the 2014 tournament.

Other sports in which NZ punches above its weight include sailing, rowing, canoeing, equestrian, cycling and triathlon. The most Olympic medals NZ has won have been in athletics, particularly in track and field events. Cricket is the established summer team sport, and the Black Caps national team enjoyed some good results over India and the West Indies in early 2014.

If you truly want to discover the good, the bad and the ugly of the national psyche, the sporting field isn't a bad place to start.

Arts & Music

It took a hundred years for post-colonial New Zealand to develop its own distinctive artistic identity. In the first half of the 20th century it was writers and visual artists who led the charge. By the 1970s NZ pub rockers had conquered Australia, while in the 1980s, indie music obsessives the world over hooked into Dunedin's weird and wonderful alternative scene. However, it took the success of the film industry in the 1990s to catapult the nation's creativity into the global consciousness.

Literature

In 2013 New Zealanders rejoiced when 28-year-old Eleanor Catton became only the second NZ writer to win the Man-Booker Prize, arguably the world's most prestigious award for literature. Lloyd Jones had come close in 2007 when his novel *Mister Pip* was shortlisted, but it had been a long wait between drinks since Keri Hulme took the prize in 1985. Interestingly, both Catton's epic historical novel *The Luminaries* and Hulme's haunting *The Bone People* were set on the numinous West Coast of the South Island – both books capture something of the raw and mysterious essence of the landscape.

Catton and Hulme continue in a proud line of NZ women writers, starting in the early 20th century with Katherine Mansfield. Mansfield's work began a Kiwi tradition in short fiction, and for years the standard was carried by novelist Janet Frame, whose dramatic life was depicted in Jane Campion's film of her autobiography, *An Angel at My Table*. Frame's novel *The Carpathians* won the Commonwealth Writers' Prize in 1989.

Less recognised internationally, Maurice Gee has gained the nation's annual top fiction gong six times, most recently with *Blindsight* (2005). His much-loved children's novel *Under the Mountain* (1979) was made into a seminal NZ TV series in 1981 and then a major motion picture in 2009. In 2004 the adaptation of another of his novels, *In My Father's Den* (1972), won major awards at international film festivals and is one of the country's highest-grossing films.

Maurice is an auspicious name for NZ writers, with the late Maurice Shadbolt also achieving much acclaim for his many novels, particularly those set during the NZ Wars. Try *Season of the Jew* (1987) or *The House of Strife* (1993).

A wide range of cultural events are listed on www.eventfinder.co.nz. This is a good place to find out about concerts, classical music recitals and *kapa haka* performances. For more specific information on the NZ classical music scene, see www.sounz.org.nz.

MAORI VOICES IN PRINT

Some of the most interesting and enjoyable NZ fiction voices belong to Maori writers, with Booker winner Keri Hulme leading the way. Witi Ihimaera's novels give a wonderful insight into small-town Maori life on the East Coast – especially *Bulibasha* (1994) and *The Whale Rider* (1987), which was made into an acclaimed film. Patricia Grace's work is similarly filled with exquisitely told stories of rural *marae*-centred life: try *Mutuwhenua* (1978), *Potiki* (1986), *Dogside Story* (2001) or *Tu* (2004).

MIDDLE-EARTH TOURISM

If you are one of those travellers inspired to come down under by the scenery of the *Lord of the Rings* movies, you won't be disappointed. Jackson's decision to film in NZ wasn't mere patriotism. Nowhere else on earth will you find such wildly varied, unspoiled landscapes – not to mention poorly paid actors.

You will doubtless recognise some places from the films. For example, Hobbiton (near Matamata), Mt Doom (instantly recognisable as towering Ngauruhoe) and the Misty Mountains (the South Island's Southern Alps). The visitor information centres in Wellington, Twizel or Queenstown should be able to direct you to local *LOTR* sites of interest. If you're serious about finding the exact spots where scenes were filmed, buy a copy of Ian Brodie's nerdtastic *The Lord of the Rings: Location Guidebook,* which includes instructions, and even GPS coordinates, for finding all the important places.

Cinema & TV

If you first got interested in NZ by watching it on the silver screen, you're in good company. Sir Peter Jackson's NZ-made *The Hobbit* and *Lord of the Rings* (*LOTR*) trilogies were the best thing to happen to NZ tourism since Captain Cook.

Yet NZ cinema is hardly ever easygoing. In his BBC-funded documentary, *Cinema of Unease,* NZ actor Sam Neill described the country's film industry as 'uniquely strange and dark', producing bleak, haunted work. One need only watch Lee Tamahori's harrowing *Once Were Warriors* (1994) to see what he means.

The *Listener's* film critic, Philip Matthews, makes a slightly more upbeat observation: 'Between (Niki Caro's) *Whale Rider,* (Christine Jeffs') *Rain* and *Lord of the Rings,* you can extract the qualities that our best films possess. Beyond slick technical accomplishment, all share a kind of land-mysticism, an innately supernatural sensibility'.

You could add to this list Jane Campion's *The Piano* (1993), Brad McGann's *In My Father's Den* (2004) and Jackson's *Heavenly Creatures* (1994) – all of which use magically lush scenery to couch disturbing violence. It's a land-mysticism constantly bordering on the creepy.

Even when Kiwis do humour it's as resolutely black as their rugby jerseys; check out Jackson's early splatter-fests and Taika Waititi's *Boy* (2010). Exporting NZ comedy hasn't been easy, yet the HBO-produced TV musical parody *Flight of the Conchords* – featuring a mumbling, bumbling Kiwi folk-singing duo trying to get a break in New York – has found surprising international success.

It's the Polynesian giggle-factor that seems likeliest to break down the bleak house of NZ cinema, with feel-good-through-and-through *Sione's Wedding* (2006) netting the second-biggest local takings of any NZ film.

New Zealanders have gone from never seeing themselves in international cinema to having whole cloned armies of Temuera Morrisons invading the universe in *Star Wars.* Familiar faces such as Cliff Curtis and Karl Urban seem to constantly pop up playing Mexican or Russian gangsters in action movies. Many of them got their start in long-running soap opera *Shortland St* (7pm weekdays, TV2).

Visual Arts

The NZ 'can do' attitude extends to the visual arts. If you're visiting a local's home don't be surprised to find one of the owner's paintings on the wall or one of their mate's sculptures in the back garden, pieced together

Other than 2003's winner *Return of the King, The Piano* is the only NZ movie to be nominated for a Best Picture Oscar. Jane Campion was the first Kiwi nominated for the Best Director Oscar and Peter Jackson the first to win it.

out of bits of shell, driftwood and a length of the magical 'number-eight wire'.

This is symptomatic of a flourishing local art and crafts scene cultivated by lively tertiary courses churning out traditional carvers and weavers, jewellery-makers, multimedia boffins, and moulders of metal and glass. The larger cities have excellent dealer galleries representing interesting local artists working across all media.

Not all the best galleries are in Auckland or Wellington. In the South Island, Gore's Eastern Southland Gallery (p270) has an important and growing collection.

Traditional Maori art has a distinctive visual style with well-developed motifs that have been embraced by NZ artists of every race. In the painting medium, these include the cool modernism of the work of Gordon Walters and the more controversial pop-art approach of Dick Frizzell's *Tiki* series. Likewise, Pacific Island themes are common, particularly in Auckland. An example is the work of Niuean-born Auckland-raised John Pule.

It should not be surprising that in a nation so defined by its natural environment, landscape painting constituted the first post-European body of art. John Gully and Petrus van der Velden were among those to arrive and paint memorable (if sometimes overdramatised) depictions of the land.

A little later, Charles Frederick Goldie painted a series of compelling, realist portraits of Maori, who were feared to be a dying race. Debate over the political propriety of Goldie's work raged for years, but its value is widely accepted now: not least because Maori themselves generally acknowledge and value them as ancestral representations.

From the 1930s NZ art took a more modern direction and produced some of the country's most celebrated artists including Rita Angus, Toss Woollaston and Colin McCahon. McCahon is widely regarded to have been the country's most important artist. His paintings might seem inscrutable, even forbidding, but even where McCahon lurched into Catholic mysticism or quoted screeds from the Bible, his spirituality was rooted in geography. His bleak, brooding landscapes evoke the sheer power of NZ's terrain.

ACADEMY AWARDS

The only Kiwi actors to have won an Oscar are Anna Paquin (for *The Piano*) and Russell Crowe (for *Gladiator*). Paquin was born in Canada but moved to NZ when she was four, while Crowe moved from NZ to Australia at the same age.

Music
by Gareth Shute

NZ music began with the *waiata* (singing) developed by Maori following their arrival in the country. The main musical instruments were wind instruments made of bone or wood, the most well known of which is the *nguru* (also known as the 'nose flute'), while percussion was provided by chest- and thigh-slapping.

These days, the liveliest place to see Maori music being performed is at *kapa haka* competitions in which groups compete with their own routines of traditional song and dance: track down the **Te Matatini National Kapa Haka Festival** (www.tematatini.co.nz) which happens in

GOOD LORDE!

Of course, the big news in Kiwi music recently has been the success of Lorde, a singer-songwriter from Devonport on Auckland's North Shore. Known less regally to her friends as Ella Yelich-O'Connor, Lorde cracked the number-one spot on the US Billboard charts in 2013 with her magical, schoolyard-chant-evoking hit 'Royals' – just 16 years old at the time, she was the first NZ solo artist to top the American charts. 'Royals' then went on to win the 'Song of the Year' Grammy in 2014. Her debut album *Pure Heroine* has spawned a string of hits and is selling millions of copies worldwide. Not bad for 16!

March in odd-numbered years at different venues (Christchurch in 2015).

In a similar vein, Auckland's **Pasifika Festival** (www.aucklandnz.com/pasifika) represents each of the Pacific Islands. It's a great place to see both traditional and modern forms of Polynesian music: modern hip-hop, throbbing Cook Island drums, or island-style guitar, ukulele and slide guitar.

Classical & Opera

Early European immigrants brought their own styles of music and gave birth to local variants during the early 1900s. In the 1950s Douglas Lilburn became one of the first internationally recognised NZ classical composers. More recently the country has produced a number of world-renowned musicians in this field, including opera singer Dame Kiri Te Kanawa, million-selling pop diva Hayley Westenra, composer John Psathas (who created music for the 2004 Olympic Games) and composer/percussionist Gareth Farr (who also performs in drag under the name Lilith).

Rock

New Zealand also has a strong rock scene, its most acclaimed exports being the revered indie label Flying Nun and the music of the Finn Brothers.

In 1981 Flying Nun was started by Christchurch record store owner Roger Shepherd. Many of the early groups came from Dunedin, where local musicians took the DIY attitude of punk but used it to produce a lo-fi indie-pop that received rave reviews from the likes of *NME* in the UK and *Rolling Stone* in the US. *Billboard* even claimed in 1989: 'There doesn't seem to be anything on Flying Nun Records that is less than excellent.'

Many of the musicians from the Flying Nun scene still perform live to this day, including David Kilgour (from The Clean) and Shayne Carter (from the Straitjacket Fits, and subsequently Dimmer and The Adults). The Bats are still releasing albums, and Martin Phillipps' band The Chills released a live album in 2013.

Reggae, Hip-Hop & Dance

The genres of music that have been adopted most enthusiastically by Maori and Polynesian New Zealanders have been reggae (in the 1970s) and hip-hop (in the 1980s), which has led to distinct local forms. In Wellington, a thriving jazz scene took on a reggae influence to create a host of groups that blended dub, roots, and funky jazz – most notably Fat Freddy's Drop. The national public holiday, Waitangi Day, on 6 February also happens to fall on the birthday of Bob Marley and annual reggae concerts are held on this day in Auckland and Wellington.

The local hip-hop scene has its heart in the suburbs of South Auckland, which have a high concentration of Maori and Pacific Island residents. This area is home to one of New Zealand's foremost hip-hop labels, Dawn Raid, which takes its name from the infamous early-morning house raids of the 1970s that police performed on Pacific Islanders suspected of outstaying their visas. Dawn Raid's most successful artist is Savage, who sold a million copies of his single 'Swing' after it was featured in the movie *Knocked Up*. Within New Zealand, the most well-known hip-hop acts are Scribe, Che Fu, and Smashproof (whose song 'Brother' held number one on the NZ singles charts longer than any other local act).

Gareth Shute wrote this music section. He is the author of four books, including Hip Hop Music in Aotearoa and NZ Rock 1987–2007. He is also a musician and has toured the UK, Europe and Australia as a member of The Ruby Suns and The Brunettes. He now plays in indie soul group The Cosbys.

For indie rock fans, a great source of local info is www.cheeseontoast.co.nz, which lists gigs and has band interviews and photos. For more on local hip-hop, pop and rock, check out www.thecorner.co.nz and the long-running www.muzic.net.nz.

THE BROTHERS FINN

There are certain tunes that all Kiwis can sing along to, given a beer and the opportunity. A surprising proportion of these were written by Tim and Neil Finn, many of which have been international hits.

Tim Finn first came to prominence in the 1970s group Split Enz. When the original guitarist quit, Neil flew over to join the band in the UK, despite being only 15 at the time. Split Enz amassed a solid following in Australia, NZ and Canada before disbanding in 1985.

Neil then formed Crowded House with two Australian musicians (Paul Hester and Nick Seymour) and one of their early singles, 'Don't Dream It's Over', hit number two on the US charts. Tim later did a brief spell in the band, during which the brothers wrote 'Weather With You' – a song that reached number seven on the UK charts, pushing their album *Woodface* to gold sales.

The original line-up of Crowded House played their final show in 1996 in front of 100,000 people on the steps of the Sydney Opera House (though Finn and Seymour reformed the group in 2007 and continue to tour and record occasionally). Tim and Neil have both released a number of solo albums, as well as releasing material together as the Finn Brothers.

More recently, Neil has also remained busy, organising a set of shows/releases under the name Seven Worlds Collide – a collaboration with well-known overseas musicians including Jeff Tweedy (Wilco), Johnny Marr (The Smiths) and members of Radiohead. His latest band is the Pajama Club, a collaboration with wife Sharon and Auckland musicians Sean Donnelly and Alana Skyring.

Neil's son Liam also has a burgeoning solo career, touring the US with Eddie Vedder and The Black Keys and appearing on the *Late Show with David Letterman*. Both Tim and Neil were born in the small town of Te Awamutu: the local museum has a collection documenting their work.

Dance music gained a foothold in Christchurch in the 1990s, spawning club/electronica outfit Salmonella Dub and its offshoot act, Tiki Taane. Drum 'n' bass remains popular locally and has spawned internationally renowned acts such as Concord Dawn and Shapeshifter.

New Music

Since 2000, the NZ music scene has developed new vitality after the government convinced commercial radio stations to adopt a voluntary quota of 20% local music. This enabled commercially oriented musicians to develop solid careers. Rock groups such as Shihad, The Feelers and Op-shop have thrived in this environment, as have a set of soulful female solo artists (who all happen to have Maori heritage): Bic Runga, Anika Moa, and Brooke Fraser (daughter of All Black Bernie Fraser). NZ also produced two internationally acclaimed garage rock acts over this time: the Datsuns and the D4.

Current Kiwis garnering international recognition include the incredibly gifted songstress Kimbra (who sang on Gotye's global smash 'Somebody That I Used To Know'); indie anthem atl-rockers The Naked & Famous; multitalented singer-songwriter Ladyhawke; the arty Lawrence Arabia; and the semi-psychedelic Unknown Mortal Orchestra. Aaradhna is a much-touted R&B singer currently making a splash with her album *Treble & Reverb,* which won 'Album of the Year' at the 2013 New Zealand Music Awards.

The TV show *Popstars* originated in New Zealand, though the resulting group, True Bliss, was short-lived. The series concept was then picked up in Australia, the UK and the US, inspiring the *Idol* series.

Venues

An up-to-date list of gigs in the main centres is listed at www.rip-itup.co.nz. Tickets for most events can be bought at www.ticketek.co.nz, www.ticket-master.co.nz, or, for smaller gigs, www.underthera-dar.co.nz.

Unfortunately the music scene in Christchurch was crippled by the earthquakes in late 2010 and early 2011. In the interim, a number of temporary spaces have opened up as gig venues; a full list of events can be found at www.christchurchmusic.org.nz.

Further south, many local bands tour through Queenstown during the ski season, and the spirit of the Flying Nun scene is kept alive at **Chicks Hotel** (2 Mount St) in Port Chalmers (near Dunedin).

Festivals

A number of festivals happen over summer, including the excellent Rippon Festival (p245) in February (bi-annual, even-numbered years) on the shores of Lake Wanaka. February also sees the Nelson Jazz & Blues Festival (p75), while Gore's New Zealand Golden Guitar Awards gets toes-a-tapping to a country beat during Gold Guitar Week (p270) in June.

Survival Guide

Directory A–Z

Accommodation

Across the South Island you can bed down in historic guesthouses, facility-laden hotels, uniform motel units, beautifully situated campsites, and hostels that range in character from clean-living to tirelessly party-prone.

If you're travelling during peak tourist seasons, book your bed well in advance. Accommodation is most in demand (and at its priciest) during the summer holidays from Christmas to late January, at Easter, and during winter in snowy resort towns like Queenstown. Booking ahead for accommodation in Christchurch is also advised.

Visitor information centres provide reams of local accommodation information, often in the form of folders detailing facilities and up-to-date prices; many can also make bookings on your behalf.

For listings, check out the websites of the **Automobile Association** (AA; www.aa.co.nz) and **Jasons** (www.jasons.com).

B&Bs

Bed and breakfast (B&B) accommodation across the South Island pops up in the middle of cities, in rural hamlets and on stretches of isolated coastline, with rooms on offer in everything from suburban bungalows to stately manors.

Breakfast may be 'continental' (cereal, toast and tea or coffee), 'hearty continental' (add yoghurt, fruit, home-baked bread or muffins), or a stomach-loading cooked meal (eggs, bacon, sausages...). Some B&B hosts may also cook dinner for guests and advertise dinner,

bed and breakfast (DB&B) packages.

B&B tariffs are typically in the $120 to $180 bracket (per double), though some places charge upwards of $300 per double. Some hosts cheekily charge hefty prices for what is, in essence, a bedroom in their home. Off-street parking is often a bonus in Christchurch and Dunedin. Resources include:

→ **Bed & Breakfast Book** (www.bnb.co.nz)

→ **Bed and Breakfast Directory** (www.bed-and-breakfast.co.nz)

Camping & Holiday Parks

Campers and campervan drivers alike converge upon the South Island's hugely popular 'holiday parks', slumbering peacefully in powered and unpowered sites, cheap bunk rooms (dorm rooms), cabins, and self-contained units (often called motels or tourist flats). Well-equipped communal kitchens, dining areas, and games and TV rooms often feature. In Christchurch and Dunedin, holiday parks are can be a fair way from the action, but in smaller South Island towns they can be impressively central or near lakes, beaches, rivers and forests.

The nightly cost of holiday-park camping is usually between $15 and $20 per adult, with children charged half price; powered sites are

---

SLEEPING PRICE RANGES

The following price indicators used throughout this book refer to a double room with bathroom during high season:

$ less than $100

$$ $100–$200

$$$ more than $200

Price ranges generally increase by 20% to 25% in Queenstown and Christchurch. Here you can still find budget accommodation at up to $100 per double, but midrange stretches from $100 to $240, with top-end rooms more than $240.

a couple of dollars more. Cabin/unit accommodation normally ranges from $70 to $120 per double. Unless noted otherwise, the prices we've listed for campsites, campervan sites, huts and cabins are for two people.

DOC CAMPSITES & FREEDOM CAMPING

A fantastic option for those in campervans is the 250-plus vehicle-accessible 'Conservation Campsites' run by the **Department of Conservation** (www.doc.govt.nz), with fees ranging from free (basic toilets and fresh water) to $15 per adult (flush toilets and showers). DOC publishes free brochures with detailed descriptions and instructions to find every campsite (even GPS coordinates). Pick up copies from DOC offices before you hit the road, or visit the website.

DOC also looks after hundreds of 'Backcountry Huts' and 'Backcountry Campsites' which can only be reached on foot. See the website for details. 'Great Walk' huts and campsites are also managed by DOC; see the Hiking in New Zealand chapter (p29) for info.

The South Island is so photogenic, it's tempting to just pull off the road at a gorgeous viewpoint and camp the night. But never just assume it's OK to camp somewhere: always ask a local or check with the local i-SITE, DOC office or commercial campground. If you are freedom camping, treat the area with respect. Note that if your chosen campsite doesn't have toilet facilities and neither does your campervan, it's illegal for you to sleep there (your campervan must also have an on-board grey-water storage system). Legislation allows for $200 on-the-spot fines for camping in prohibited areas, or improper disposal of waste (in cases where dumping waste could damage the

environment, fines are up to $10,000). See www.camping. org.nz for more freedom-camping tips.

Farmstays

Farmstays open the door to the agricultural side of South Island life, with visitors encouraged to get some dirt beneath their fingernails at orchards, and dairy, sheep and cattle farms. Costs can vary widely, with B&Bs generally ranging from $80 to $120. Some farms have separate cottages where you can fix your own food, while others offer low-cost, shared, backpacker-style accommodation.

➡ **Farm Helpers in NZ** (FHINZ; www.fhinz.co.nz) produces a booklet ($25) that lists around 350 NZ farms providing lodging in exchange for four to six hours' work per day.

➡ **Rural Holidays NZ** (www. ruralholidays.co.nz) lists farmstays and homestays throughout the country on its website.

Hostels

The South Island is packed to the rafters with backpacker hostels, both independent and part of large chains, ranging from small, homestay-style affairs with

a handful of beds, to refurbished hotels and towering modern structures in the big cities. Hostel bed prices listed throughout this book are nonmember rates, usually between $25 and $35 per night.

HOSTEL ORGANISATIONS

Budget Backpacker Hostels (BBH; www.bbh. co.nz) NZ's biggest hostel group with around 275 hostels. Membership costs $45 for 12 months and entitles you to stay at member hostels at rates listed in the annual (free) *BBH Backpacker Accommodation* booklet. Nonmembers pay an extra $3 per night. Pick up a membership card from any member hostel or order one online for $50; see the website for details.

YHA New Zealand (Youth Hostels Association; www.yha.co.nz) More than 50 hostels in prime NZ locations. The YHA is part of the **Hostelling International** (HI; www.hihostels.com) network, so if you're an HI member in your own country, membership entitles you to use NZ hostels. If you don't already have a home membership, you can join at major NZ YHA hostels or online for $42, valid for 12 months. Nonmembers pay an extra $3 per night.

Base Backpackers
(www.stayatbase.com) Chain with seven hostels around NZ, including South Island properties in Wanaka and Queenstown, plus affiliates in Nelson and Dundein (the Christchurch hostel is closed for post-quake repairs) . Expect clean dorms, women-only areas and party opportunities aplenty. Offers a 10-night 'Base Jumping' accommodation card for $239, bookable online.

VIP Backpackers (www.vipbackpackers.com) International organisation affiliated with around 20 NZ hostels (not BBH or YHA), mainly in the cities and tourist hot-spots. For around $61 (including postage) you'll receive a 12-month membership entitling you to a $1 discount off nightly accommodation. Join online or at VIP hostels.

Nomads Backpackers
(www.nomadsworld.com) Seven franchises in NZ with South Island locations in Abel Tasman National Park and Queenstown. Membership costs $49 for 12 months and, like VIP, offers $1 off the cost of nightly accommodation. Join at participating hostels or online.

Pubs, Hotels & Motels

➡ The least expensive form of South Island hotel accommodation is the humble pub. Pubs are often full of character (and characters), while others are grotty, ramshackle places that are best avoided, especially by women travelling solo. Check whether there's a band playing the night you're staying – you could be in for a sleepless night. In the cheapest pubs, singles/

doubles might cost as little as $30/60 (with a shared bathroom down the hall), though $50/80 is more common.

➡ At the top end of the hotel scale are five-star international chains, resort complexes and architecturally splendorous boutique hotels, all of which charge a hefty premium for their mod cons, snappy service and/or historic opulence. We quote 'rack rates' (official advertised rates) for such places, but discounts and special deals often apply.

➡ South Island towns have a glut of nondescript, low-rise motels and 'motor lodges', charging between $80 and $180 for double rooms. These tend to be squat structures skulking by highways on the edges of towns. Most are modernish (though decor is often mired in the early 2000s) and have similar facilities, namely tea- and coffee-making equipment, fridge, and TV – prices vary with standard.

Rental Accommodation

The basic Kiwi holiday home is called a 'bach' (short for 'bachelor', as they were historically used by single men as hunting and fishing hideouts); in Otago and Southland they're known as 'cribs'. These are simple self-contained cottages that can be rented in rural and coastal areas, often in isolated locations. Prices are typically $80 to $150 per night, which isn't bad for a whole house or self-contained bungalow. For more upmarket holiday

houses, expect to pay anything from $150 to $400 per double.

Resources include:

➡ www.holidayhomes.co.nz

➡ www.bookabach.co.nz

➡ www.holidayhouses.co.nz

➡ www.nzapartments.co.nz

Children

NZ's South Island is a terrific place to travel with kids: safe and affordable, with loads of playgrounds, kid-centric activities, a moderate climate and chilli-free cuisine. For helpful general tips, see Lonely Planet's *Travel with Children*.

Handy online resources for kids' activities and travel info include:

➡ www.kidzgo.co.nz

➡ www.kidspot.co.nz

➡ www.kidsnewzealand.com

➡ www.kidsfriendlynz.com

Practicalities

➡ Many motels and holiday parks have playgrounds, games and DVDs, and, occasionally, fenced swimming pools and trampolines. Cots and highchairs aren't always available at budget and midrange accommodation, but top-end hotels supply them and often provide child-minding services. Many B&Bs promote themselves as kid-free, and hostels tend to focus on the backpacker demographic, but there are plenty of hostels (including YHA) that do allow kids.

➡ For specialised childcare, try www.rockmybaby.co.nz, or look under 'babysitters' and 'child care centres' in the *Yellow Pages* directory.

➡ Check that your car-hire company can supply the right-sized seat for your child, and that the seat will be properly fitted. Some

BOOK YOUR STAY ONLINE

For more accommodation reviews by Lonely Planet authors, check out http://lonelyplanet.com/hotels. You'll find independent reviews, as well as recommendations on the best places to stay. Best of all, you can book online.

Climate

Christchurch

Nelson

Queenstown

companies legally require you to fit car seats yourself.

➡ Most Kiwis are relaxed about public breastfeeding. Alternatively, cities and major towns have public rooms where parents can go to feed a baby or change a nappy (diaper); check with the local visitor information centre, or ask a local.

➡ Kids' and family rates are often available for accommodation, tours, attraction entry fees, and air, bus and train transport, with discounts of as much as 50% off the adult rate. Note that the definition of 'child' can vary from under 12 to under 18 years; toddlers (under four years old) usually get free admission and transport.

➡ There are plenty of family-friendly restaurants in NZ with highchairs and kids'

menus. Pubs often serve kids' meals and most cafes and restaurants (with the exception of upmarket eateries) can handle the idea of child-sized portions.

➡ NZ's medical services and facilities are world-class, and goods such as formula and disposable nappies are widely available.

Customs Regulations

For the low-down on what you can and can't bring into NZ, see the **New Zealand Customs Service** (www.customs.govt.nz) website. Per-person duty-free allowances:

➡ 1125mL of spirits or liqueur

➡ 4.5L of wine or beer

➡ 200 cigarettes (or 50 cigars or 250g of tobacco)

➡ dutiable goods up to the value of $700

➡ It's a good idea to declare any unusual medicines. Tramping gear (boots, tents etc) will be checked and may need to be cleaned before being allowed in. You must declare any plant or animal products (including anything made of wood), and food of any kind. Weapons and firearms are either prohibited or require a permit and safety testing.

Discount Cards

➡ The internationally recognised **International Student Identity Card** is produced by the **International Student Travel Confederation** (ISTC; www.istc.org), and issued to full-time students aged 12 and over. It provides discounts on accommodation, transport and admission to attractions.

➡ The ISTC also produces the **International Youth Travel Card**, available to folks under 30 who are not full-time students, with equivalent benefits to the ISIC.

➡ Also similar is the **International Teacher Identity Card**, available to teaching professionals. All three of the above cards (NZ$30 each) are available online at www.isiccard.co.nz, or from student travel companies like STA Travel.

➡ The **New Zealand Card** (www.newzealandcard.com) is a $35 discount pass that'll score you between 5% and 50% off a range of accommodation, tours, sights and activities.

➡ Travellers over 60 with some form of identification (eg an official seniors card from your home country) are often eligible for concession prices.

Electricity

230-240V/50Hz

Embassies & Consulates

Most principal diplomatic representations to NZ are in Wellington, with a few in Auckland.

Australian High Commission (☏04-473 6411; www. australia.org.nz; 72-76 Hobson St, Thorndon, Wellington)

Canadian High Commission (☏04-473 9577; Lvl 11, 125 The Terrace, Wellington)

Chinese Embassy (☏04-474 9631; www.chinaembassy. org.nz; 2-6 Glenmore St, Kelburn, Wellington)

Fiji High Commission (☏04-473 5401; www.fiji.org. nz; 31 Pipitea St, Thorndon, Wellington)

French Embassy (☏04-384 2555; www.ambafrance-nz.org; 34-42 Manners St, Wellington)

German Embassy (☏04-473 6063; www.wellington. diplo.de; 90-92 Hobson St, Thorndon, Wellington)

Israeli Embassy (☏04-439 9500; http://embassies.gov. il/wellington; Lvl 13, Bayleys Building, 36 Brandon St, Wellington)

Irish Consulate (☏09-977 2252; www.ireland.co.nz; Lvl 3, Tower 1, 205 Queen St, Auckland)

Japanese Embassy (☏04-473 1540; www. nz.emb-japan.go.jp; Lvl 18, The Majestic Centre, 100 Willis St, Wellington)

Netherlands Embassy (☏04-471 6390; http:// newzealand.nlembassy.org; Lvl 10, Cooperative Bank Building, cnr Featherston & Ballance Sts, Wellington)

UK High Commission (☏04-924 2888; www.gov.uk; 44 Hill St, Thorndon, Wellington)

US Embassy (☏04-462 6000; http://newzealand. usembassy.gov; 29 Fitzherbert Tce, Thorndon, Wellington)

Food & Drink

NZ's restaurants and cafes are adept at throwing together traditional staples (lamb, beef, venison, green-lipped mussels) with Asian, European and pan-Pacific flair. Eateries themselves range from fish-and-chip shops and pub bistros to retro-styled cafes, restaurant-bars with full à la carte service and crisp-linen fine dining rooms. Tipping is not mandatory, but feel free if you've had a happy culinary experience (about 10% of the bill). For online listings check out:

➡ www.dineout.co.nz

➡ www.menus.co.nz

On the liquid front, NZ wine is world class (especially sauvignon blanc and pinot noir), and you'll be hard-pressed to find a NZ town of any size without decent espresso. NZ's craft beer scene is forever expanding, and specialist beer bars are popping up across the South Island.

Vegetarians & Vegans

Most large urban centres have at least one dedicated vegetarian cafe or restaurant: see the **Vegetarians New Zealand** (www.vegetarians. co.nz) website for listings. Beyond this, almost all restaurants and cafes offer some vegetarian menu choices (although sometimes only one or two). Many eateries also provide gluten-free and vegan options. Always check that stocks and sauces are vegetarian, too.

In this book, the vegetarian icon in Eating listings (🥄) indicates a good vegetarian selection.

Gay & Lesbian Travellers

The gay and lesbian tourism industry in NZ isn't as high-profile as it is in neighbouring Australia, but homosexual communities are prominent in Auckland and Wellington, with myriad support organisations across both islands. NZ has progressive laws protecting the rights of gays and lesbians and same-sex marriage was legalised here

---

EATING PRICE RANGES

Listings within this book are in order of author preference within their respective budget ranges. The following price indicators used throughout refer to the average price of a main course:

$ less than $15

$$ $15–$32

$$$ more than $32

in 2013. Generally speaking, Kiwis are fairly relaxed and accepting about homosexuality, but that's not to say that homophobia doesn't exist.

Resources

There are loads of websites dedicated to gay and lesbian travel in NZ. **Gay Tourism New Zealand** (www.gaytourismnewzealand.com) is a good starting point, with links to various sites. Other worthwhile queer websites include the following:

➡ www.gaynz.com
➡ www.gaynz.net.nz
➡ www.lesbian.net.nz
➡ www.gaystay.co.nz

Check the nationwide magazine *express* (www.gayexpress.co.nz) every second Wednesday for the latest happenings, reviews and listings on the NZ gay scene.

Festivals & Events

Big Gay Out (www.biggayout.co.nz) Free festival (food, drink, entertainment) held every February in Auckland.

Gay Ski Week (www.gayskiweekqt.com) Annual Queenstown snow-fest in August/September

Health

NZ is one of the healthiest countries in the world in which to travel. Diseases such as malaria and typhoid are unheard of, and the absence of poisonous snakes or other dangerous animals makes outdoor adventures here less risky than in neighbouring Australia.

Before You Go
MEDICATIONS

Bring medications in their original, clearly labelled containers. A signed and dated letter from your physician describing your medical conditions and medications (including generic names) and any requisite syringes or needles, is also wise.

TO MARKET, TO MARKET

There are more than 20 farmers markets held around the South Island. Most happen on weekends and are upbeat local affairs, where visitors can meet local producers and find fresh regional produce. Mobile coffee is usually present, and tastings are offered by enterprising and innovative stall holders. Bring a carry bag, and get there early for the best stuff! Check out www.farmersmarkets.org.nz for market locations, dates and times.

VACCINATIONS

NZ has no vaccination requirements for travellers, but the World Health Organization recommends that all travellers should be covered for diphtheria, tetanus, measles, mumps, rubella, chickenpox and polio, as well as hepatitis B, regardless of their destination. Ask your doctor for an *International Certificate of Vaccination* (or 'the yellow booklet'), which will list all the vaccinations you've received.

HEALTH INSURANCE

Health insurance is essential for all travellers. While health care in NZ is of a high standard and not overly expensive by international standards, considerable costs can be built up and repatriation can be pricey.

If your current health insurance doesn't cover you for medical expenses incurred overseas, consider extra insurance – see www.lonelyplanet.com/travel-insurance for more information. Find out in advance if your insurance plan will make payments directly to providers or reimburse you later for overseas health expenditures.

In New Zealand
AVAILABILITY & COST OF HEALTH CARE

NZ's public hospitals offer a high standard of care (free for residents). All travellers are covered for medical care resulting from accidents that occur while in NZ (eg motor-vehicle accidents, adventure-activity accidents) by the **Accident Compensation Corporation** (ACC; www.acc.co.nz). Costs incurred due to treatment of a medical illness that occurs while in NZ will only be covered by travel insurance. For more details, see www.moh.govt.nz and www.acc.co.nz.

The 24-hour, free-call **Healthline** (0800 611 116; www.health.govt.nz) offers health advice throughout NZ.

PHARMACEUTICALS

Over-the-counter medications are widely available in NZ through private chemists. These include painkillers, antihistamines and skin-care products. Some medications, such as antibiotics and the contraceptive pill, are only available via a prescription obtained from a general practitioner. If you take regular medications, bring an adequate supply and details of the generic name, as brand names differ from country to country.

INFECTIOUS DISEASES

The giardia parasite is widespread in NZ waterways: drinking untreated water from streams and lakes is not recommended. Using water filters and boiling or treating water with iodine are effective ways of preventing the disease. Symptoms consist of intermittent diarrhoea, abdominal bloating and wind. Effective treatment is available (tinidazole or metronidazole).

ENVIRONMENTAL HAZARDS

➜ Hypothermia is a significant risk, especially during winter and year-round at altitude. Mountain ranges and/or strong winds produce a high chill factor, which can cause hypothermia even in moderate temperatures. Early signs include the inability to perform fine movements (such as doing up buttons), shivering, and a bad case of the 'umbles' (fumbles, mumbles, grumbles, stumbles). To treat, minimise heat loss: remove wet clothing, add dry clothes with wind- and waterproof layers, and consume water and carbohydrates to allow shivering to build the internal temperature. In severe hypothermia, shivering actually stops; this is a medical emergency requiring rapid evacuation in addition to the above measures.

➜ NZ has exceptional surf beaches. The power of the surf can fluctuate as a result of the varying slope of the seabed at many beaches. Check with local surf-lifesaving organisations before entering the surf and be aware of your own limitations and expertise.

Insurance

➜ A watertight travel insurance policy covering theft, loss and medical problems is essential. Some policies specifically exclude designated 'dangerous activities' such as scuba diving, bungy jumping, white-water rafting, skiing and even tramping. If you plan on doing any of these things (a distinct possibility in NZ!), make sure your policy covers you fully.

➜ It's worth mentioning that under NZ law, you cannot sue for personal injury (other than exemplary damages). Instead, the country's

Accident Compensation Corporation (ACC; www. acc.co.nz) administers an accident compensation scheme that provides accident insurance for NZ residents and visitors to the country, regardless of fault. This scheme, however, does not negate the necessity for your own comprehensive travel-insurance policy, as it doesn't cover you for such things as income loss, treatment at home or ongoing illness.

➜ Consider a policy that pays doctors or hospitals directly, rather than you paying on the spot and claiming later. If you have to claim later, keep all documentation. Some policies ask you to call (reverse charges) to a centre in your home country where an immediate assessment of your problem is made. Check that the policy covers ambulances and emergency medical evacuations by air.

➜ Worldwide travel insurance is available at www.lonelyplanet.com/ travel-insurance. You can buy, extend and claim online anytime – even if you're already on the road.

Internet Access

Wi-fi & Internet Service Providers

➜ You'll be able to find wi-fi access across the country, from hotel rooms to pub beer gardens to hostel dorms. Usually you have to be a guest or customer to log on; you'll be issued with an access code. Sometimes it's free, sometimes there's a charge.

➜ The country's main telecommunications company is **Telecom New Zealand** (www.telecom.co.nz), which has wireless hotspots around the country where you can purchase prepaid access cards. Alternatively, purchase a prepaid number

from the login page at any wireless hotspot using your credit card. See Telecom's website for hotspot listings.

➜ If you've brought your palmtop or laptop, consider buying a prepay USB modem (aka a 'dongle') with a local SIM card: both Telecom and **Vodafone** (www.vodafone. co.nz) sell these from around $100. If you want to get connected via a local internet service provider (ISP), options include the following:

➜ **Clearnet** (☑0508 888 800; www.clearnet.co.nz)

➜ **Earthlight** (☑03-479 0303; www.earthlight.co.nz)

➜ **Slingshot** (☑0800 892 000; www.slingshot.co.nz)

Internet Cafes

➜ There are fewer internet cafes around these days than there were five years ago (thanks to the advent of smartphones and wi-fi) but you'll still find them in most sizable towns. Access at cafes ranges anywhere from $4 to $6 per hour.

➜ Most youth hostels have both wi-fi and computers for internet access, as do many hotels and caravan parks. Many public libraries have internet access, including wi-fi, but generally it's provided for research, not for travellers to check Facebook.

Legal Matters

➜ Marijuana is widely indulged in but is illegal: anyone caught carrying this or other illicit drugs will have the book thrown at them.

➜ Drink-driving is a serious offence and remains a significant problem in NZ. The legal blood alcohol limit is 0.08% for drivers over 20, and zero for those under 20.

➜ If you are arrested, it's your right to consult a lawyer before any formal questioning begins.

Maps

➧ NZ's **Automobile Association** (AA; ☎0800 500 444; www.aa.co.nz/travel) produces excellent city, town, regional, island and highway maps, available from its local offices. The AA also produces a detailed *New Zealand Road Atlas*. Other reliable countrywide atlases, available from visitor information centres and bookshops, are published by Hema, KiwiMaps and Wises.

➧ **Land Information New Zealand** (LINZ; www.linz. govt.nz) publishes several exhaustive map series, including street, country and holiday maps, national park and forest park maps, and topographical trampers' maps. Scan the larger bookshops, or try the nearest DOC office or visitor information centre for topo maps.

➧ Online, log onto **AA Maps** (www.aamaps.co.nz) or **Yellow Maps** (www.maps.yellowpages.co.nz) to pinpoint exact NZ addresses.

Money

ATMs & Eftpos

Branches of the country's major banks across the South Island have ATMs, but you won't find them everywhere (eg not in small towns).

Many NZ businesses use electronic funds transfer at point of sale (Eftpos), allowing you to use your bank card (credit or debit) to make direct purchases and often withdraw cash as well. Eftpos is available practically everywhere: just like an ATM, you'll need a personal identification number (PIN).

Bank Accounts

We've heard mixed reports on the subject of travellers opening bank accounts in NZ, and bank websites are vague. Some sources say opening an account is as simple as flashing a few pieces of ID; other sources say banks won't allow visitors to open an account unless the application is accompanied by proof of employment. Either way, do your homework before you arrive and be prepared to shop around to get the best deal.

Credit & Debit Cards

CREDIT CARDS

Credit cards such as Visa and MasterCard are widely accepted for everything from a hostel bed to a bungy jump, and are pretty much essential for car hire. They can also be used for over-the-counter cash advances at banks and from ATMs, but be aware that such transactions incur charges. Diners Club and American Express cards are not as widely accepted.

DEBIT CARDS

Debit cards enable you to draw money directly from your home bank account using ATMs, banks or Eftpos facilities. Any card connected to the international banking network (Cirrus, Maestro, Visa Plus and Eurocard) should work with your PIN. Fees will vary depending on your home bank; ask before you leave. Alternatively, companies such as Travelex offer debit cards with set withdrawal fees and a balance you can top-up from your personal bank account while on the road.

Currency

NZ's currency is the NZ dollar, comprising 100 cents. There are 10c, 20c, 50c, $1 and $2 coins, and $5, $10, $20, $50 and $100 notes. Prices are often still marked in single cents and then rounded to the nearest 10c when you hand over your money.

Moneychangers

Changing foreign currency or travellers cheques is usually no problem at NZ banks or at licensed moneychangers (eg Travelex) in the major cities. Moneychangers can be found in all major tourist areas, cities and airports.

PRACTICALITIES

➧ **News** Leaf through Christchurch's *The Press* newspaper or Dunedin's *Otago Daily Times*. Online see www.stuff.co.nz or www.odt.co.nz.

➧ **TV** Watch one of the national government-owned TV stations (TV One, TV2, TVNZ 6, Maori TV and the 100% Maori language Te Reo) or the subscriber-only Sky TV (www.skytv.co.nz).

➧ **Radio** Tune in to Radio NZ National for current affairs and Concert FM for classical and jazz (see www.radionz.co.nz for frequencies). Radio Hauraki (www.hauraki.co.nz) cranks out the rock, and the most impassioned talkback bubbles away on Newstalk ZB (www.newstalkzb.co.nz).

➧ **DVDs** Kiwi DVDs are encoded for Region 4, which includes Mexico, South America, Central America, Australia, the Pacific and the Caribbean.

➧ **Electrical** To plug yourself into the electricity supply (230V AC, 50Hz), use a three-pin adaptor (the same as in Australia; different to British three-pin adaptors).

➧ **Weights & measures** NZ uses the metric system.

Taxes & Refunds

The Goods and Services Tax (GST) is a flat 15% tax on all domestic goods and services. Prices in this book include GST. There's no GST refund available when you leave NZ.

Travellers Cheques

Amex, Travelex and other international brands of travellers cheques are a bit old-fashioned these days, but they're easily exchanged at banks and moneychangers. Present your passport for identification when cashing them; shop around for the best rates.

Opening Hours

Note that most attractions close on Christmas Day and Good Friday.

Shops & businesses 9am to 5.30pm Monday to Friday, and 9am to 12.30pm or 5pm Saturday. Late-night shopping (until 9pm) in larger cities on Thursday and/or Friday nights. Sunday trading in most big towns and cities.

Supermarkets 8am to 7pm, often 9pm or later in cities.

Banks 9.30am to 4.30pm Monday to Friday; some city branches also open Saturday mornings.

Post offices 8.30am to 5pm Monday to Friday; larger branches also 9.30am to 1pm Saturday. Postal desks in newsagencies open later.

Restaurants noon to 2.30pm and 6.30 to 9pm, often until 11pm Fridays and Saturdays.

Cafes 7am to 4pm or 5pm.

Pubs Noon until late; food from noon to 2pm and from 6pm to 8pm.

Post

The services offered by **New Zealand Post** (☏0800 501 501; www.nzpost.co.nz) are reliable and reasonably inexpensive. See the website for current info on national and international zones and rates, plus post office locations.

Public Holidays

NZ's main public holidays:

New Year 1 and 2 January

Waitangi Day 6 February

Easter Good Friday and Easter Monday; March/April

Anzac Day 25 April

Queen's Birthday First Monday in June

Labour Day Fourth Monday in October

Christmas Day 25 December

Boxing Day 26 December

In addition, each NZ province has its own anniversary-day holiday. The dates of these provincial holidays vary: when they fall on Friday to Sunday, they're usually observed the following Monday; if they fall on Tuesday to Thursday, they're held on the preceding Monday.

The South Island's anniversary holidays:

Southland 17 January

Nelson 1 February

Otago 23 March

South Canterbury 25 September

Marlborough 1 November

Westland 1 December

Canterbury 16 December

School Holidays

The Christmas holiday season, from mid-December to late January, is part of the summer school vacation: expect transport and accommodation to book-out in advance, and queues at tourist attractions. There are three shorter school-holiday periods during the year: from mid- to late April, early to mid-July, and mid-September to early October. For exact dates see the **Ministry of Education** (www.minedu. govt.nz) website.

Safe Travel

➡ Although it's no more dangerous than other developed countries, violent crime does happen in NZ, so it's worth taking sensible precautions on the streets at night or if staying in remote areas. Gang culture permeates some parts of the country; give any black-jacketed, insignia-wearing groups a wide berth.

➡ Theft from cars is a problem around NZ – travellers are viewed as easy marks. Avoid leaving valuables in vehicles, no matter where they're parked; you're tempting fate at tourist parking areas and trailhead car parks.

➡ Don't underestimate the dangers posed by NZ's unpredictable, ever-changing climate, especially in high-altitude areas. Hypothermia is a real risk.

GOVERNMENT TRAVEL ADVICE

The following government websites offer travel advisories and information on current hot spots:

➡ **Australian Department of Foreign Affairs** (www.smarttraveller.gov.au)

➡ **British Foreign & Commonwealth Office** (www.gov.uk/fco)

➡ **Foreign Affairs, Trade & Development Canada** (www.international.gc.ca)

➡ **US Department of State** (www.travel.state.gov)

➡ NZ has been spared the proliferation of venomous creatures found in neighbouring Australia (spiders, snakes, jellyfish...). Sharks patrol NZ waters, but rarely nibble on humans. Much greater ocean hazards are rips and undertows, which can quickly drag swimmers out to sea: heed local warnings.

➡ Kiwi roads are often made hazardous by speeding locals, wide-cornering campervans and traffic-ignorant sheep. Set yourself a reasonable itinerary and keep your eyes on the road. Cyclists take care: motorists can't always overtake easily on skinny roads.

➡ In the annoyances category, NZ's sandflies are a royal pain (the intense itching can last for months). Lather yourself with insect repellent in coastal areas, even if you're only sitting on the edge of a beach for a minute or two.

Telephone

Telecom New Zealand (www.telecom.co.nz) The country's key domestic player, with a stake in the local mobile (cell) market.

Vodafone (www.vodafone. co.nz) Mobile network option.

2 Degrees (www.2degreesmobile.co.nz) Mobile network option.

Mobile Phones

Local mobile phone numbers are preceded by the prefix ☑021, ☑022, ☑025 or ☑027. Mobile phone coverage is good in cities and towns, but can be patchy on the South Island away from urban centres.

If you want to bring your own handset and use a pre-paid service with a local SIM card, **Vodafone** is a practical option. Any Vodafone shop (found in most major towns) will set you up with a SIM card and phone number (about $40); top-ups can be

purchased at newsagencies, post offices and petrol stations practically anywhere.

Alternatively, if you don't bring your own phone from home, you can rent one from **Vodafone Rental** (www.vodarent.co.nz) priced from $5 per day (for which you'll also need a local SIM card), with pick-up and drop-off outlets at NZ's major airports. We've also had some positive feedback on **Phone Hire New Zealand** (www.phonehirenz. com), which hires out mobile phones, SIM cards, modems and GPS systems.

Local Calls

Local calls from private phones are free! Local calls from payphones cost $1 for the first 15 minutes, and $0.20 per minute thereafter, though coin-operated payphones are scarce (and if you do find one, chances are the coin slot will be gummed up); you'll generally need a phonecard. Calls to mobile phones attract higher rates.

International Calls

Payphones allow international calls, but the cost and international dialling code for calls will vary depending on which provider you're using. International calls from NZ are relatively inexpensive and subject to specials that reduce the rates even more, so it's worth shopping around – consult the *Yellow Pages* for providers.

To make international calls from NZ, you need to dial the international access code ☑00, then the country code and the area code (without the initial 0). So for a London number, you'd dial ☑00-44-20, then the number.

If dialling NZ from overseas, the country code is ☑64, followed by the appropriate area code minus the initial zero.

Long Distance Calls & Area Codes

NZ uses regional two-digit area codes for long-distance

calls, which can be made from any payphone. If you're making a local call (ie to someone else in the same town), you don't need to dial the area code. But if you're dialling within a region (even if it's to a nearby town with the same area code), you do have to dial the area code.

Information & Toll-Free Calls

Numbers starting with ☑0900 are usually recorded information services, charging upwards of $1 per minute (more from mobiles); these numbers cannot be dialled from payphones.

Toll-free numbers in NZ have the prefix ☑0800 or ☑0508 and can be called free of charge from anywhere in the country, though they may not be accessible from certain areas or from mobile phones. Telephone numbers beginning with ☑0508, ☑0800 or ☑0900 cannot be dialled from outside NZ.

Phonecards

NZ has a wide range of phonecards available, which can be bought at hostels, newsagencies and post offices for a fixed-dollar value (usually $5, $10, $20 and $50). These can be used with any public or private phone by dialling a toll-free access number and then the PIN number on the card. Shop around – rates vary from company to company.

Time

NZ is 12 hours ahead of GMT/UTC and two hours ahead of Australian Eastern Standard Time. The Chathams are 45 minutes ahead of NZ's main islands.

In summer, NZ observes daylight-saving time, where clocks are wound forward by one hour on the last Sunday in September; clocks are wound back on the first Sunday of the following April.

Toilets

Toilets in NZ are sit-down Western style. Public toilets are plentiful, and (to make a sweeping generalisation) are usually reasonably clean with working locks and toilet paper.

See www.toiletmap.co.nz for public toilet locations around the country.

Tourist Information

Tourism New Zealand

The website for the official national tourism body, **Tourism New Zealand** (www.newzealand.com), is the best place for pretrip research. Emblazoned with the hugely successful 100% Pure New Zealand branding, the site has information in several languages, including German and Japanese, and also lists Tourism New Zealand contact offices overseas (Australia, UK, USA etc).

Local Tourist Offices

Almost every South Island city or town seems to have a visitor information centre. The bigger centres stand united within the outstanding **i-SITE** (www.newzealand.com/travel/i-sites) network – around 80 info centres affiliated with Tourism New Zealand. i-SITEs have trained staff, information on local activities and attractions, and free brochures and maps. Staff can also book activities, transport and accommodation.

Bear in mind that some information centres only promote accommodation and tour operators who are paying members of the local tourist association, and that sometimes staff aren't supposed to recommend one activity or accommodation provider over another.

There's also a network of **DOC** (Department of Conservation; www.doc.govt.nz) visitor centres to help you plan activities and make bookings. DOC visitor centres – in national parks, regional centres and major cities – usually also have displays on local lore, flora, fauna and biodiversity.

Travellers with Disabilities

Kiwi accommodation generally caters fairly well for travellers with disabilities, with a significant number of hostels, hotels, motels and B&Bs equipped with wheelchair-accessible rooms. Many tourist attractions similarly provide wheelchair access, with wheelchairs often available.

Tour operators with accessible vehicles operate from most major centres. Key cities are also serviced by 'kneeling' buses (buses that hydraulically stoop down to kerb level to allow easy access), and taxi companies offer wheelchair-accessible vans. Large car-hire firms (Avis, Hertz etc) provide cars with hand controls at no extra charge (advance notice required).

Activities

Want to tackle a wilderness pathway? Pick up a copy of *Accessible Walks* by Anna and Andrew Jameson ($30 including postage), with first-hand descriptions of 100-plus South Island walks. It's available online at www.accessiblewalks.co.nz.

If cold-weather activity is more your thing, see the **Disabled Snowsports NZ** (www.disabledsnowsports.org.nz) website.

Resources

➡ **Weka** (www.weka.net.nz) Good general information, with categories including Transport and Travel.

➡ **Royal New Zealand Foundation of the Blind** (www.rnzfb.org.nz)

➡ **National Foundation for the Deaf** (www.nfd.org.nz)

➡ **Mobility Parking** (www.mobilityparking.org.nz) Info on mobility parking permits and online applications.

Visas

Visa application forms are available from NZ diplomatic missions overseas, travel agents and **Immigration New Zealand** (☎09-914 4100, 0508 558 855; www.immigration.govt.nz). Immigration New Zealand has over a dozen offices overseas; consult the website.

Visitor Visa

Citizens of Australia don't need a visa to visit NZ and can stay indefinitely (provided they have no criminal convictions). UK citizens don't need a visa either and can stay in the country for up to six months.

Citizens of another 56 countries that have visa-waiver agreements with NZ don't need a visa for stays of up to three months, provided they have an onward ticket and sufficient funds to support their stay: see the website for details. Nations in this group include Canada, France, Germany, Ireland, Japan, the Netherlands, South Africa and the USA.

Citizens of other countries must obtain a visa before entering NZ. Visas come with three months' standard validity and cost NZ$130 if processed in Australia or certain South Pacific countries (eg Samoa, Fiji) or around NZ$165 if processed elsewhere in the world.

A visitor's visa can be extended for stays of up to nine months within any 18-month period, or to a maximum of 12 months in the country. Applications are assessed on a case-by-case basis; you may need to provide proof of adequate funds to sustain you during your visit (NZ$1000 per month) plus an onward ticket establishing your intent to leave. Apply for extensions at any Immigration

New Zealand office – see the website for locations.

Work Visa & Working Holiday Scheme

WORK VISA

It's illegal for foreign nationals to work in NZ on a visitor visa, except for Australians who can legally gain work without a visa or permit. If you're visiting NZ to find work, or you already have an employment offer, you'll need to apply for a work visa, which translates into a work permit once you arrive and is valid for up to three years. You can apply for a work permit after you're in NZ, but its validity will be backdated to when you entered the country. The fee for a work visa fluctuates between NZ$230 and $360, depending on where and how it's processed (paper or online) and the type of application.

WORKING HOLIDAY SCHEME

Eligible travellers who are only interested in short-term employment to supplement their travels can take part in one of NZ's working holiday schemes (WHS). Under these schemes citizens aged 18 to 30 years from 40 countries – including Canada, France, Germany, Ireland, Japan, Malaysia, the Netherlands, Scandinavian countries, the UK and the USA – can apply for a visa. For most nationalities the visa is valid for 12 months. It's only issued to those seeking a genuine working holiday, not permanent work, so you're not supposed to work for one employer for more than three months.

Most WHS-eligible nationals must apply for this visa from within their own country; residents of some countries can apply online. Applicants must have an onward ticket, a passport valid for at least three months from the date they will leave NZ and evidence of at least NZ$4200 in accessible funds. The application fee is NZ$165 regardless of where you apply, and isn't refunded if your application is declined.

The rules vary for different nationalities, so make sure you read up on the specifics of your country's agreement with NZ at www.immigration. govt.nz/migrant/stream/ work/workingholiday.

Volunteering

NZ presents a swathe of active, outdoorsy volunteer opportunities for travellers to get some dirt under their fingernails and participate in conservation programs. Programs can include anything from tree-planting and weed removal to track construction, habitat conservation and fencing. Ask about local opportunities at any regional i-SITE visitor information centre, or check out www. conservationvolunteers.org. nz and www.doc.govt.nz/getting-involved, both of which allow you to browse for opportunities by region. Another resource is www.helpx.net, which lists volunteering opportunities on farms where you can work in exchange for accommodation.

Women Travellers

NZ is generally a very safe place for women travellers, although the usual sensible precautions apply: avoid walking alone late at night and never hitchhike alone. If you're out on the town, always keep enough money aside for a taxi back to your accommodation. Lone women should also be wary of staying in basic pub accommodation unless it looks safe and well managed. Sexual harassment is not a widely reported problem in NZ.

See www.womentravel. co.nz for more information.

Work

If you arrive in NZ on a visitor visa, you're not allowed to work for pay. If you're caught breaching this (or any other) visa condition, you could be booted back to where you came from.

If you have been approved for a WHS visa, look into the possibilities for temporary employment. There's plenty of casual work around, mainly in agriculture (fruit picking, farming, wineries), hospitality (bar work, waiting tables) or at ski resorts. Office-based work can be found in IT, banking, finance and telemarketing. Register with a local office-work agency to get started.

Seasonal fruit picking, pruning and harvesting is prime short-term work for visitors. More than 30,000 hectares of apples, kiwifruit and other fruit and veg are harvested from December to May. Rates are around $12 to $17 an hour (not much) for physically taxing toil, working in the dirt under the hot sun– turnover of workers is high. You're usually paid by how much you pick (per bin, bucket or kilogram): if you stick with it for a while, you'll get faster and fitter and can actually make some reasonable cash. Prime South Island picking locations include Nelson (Tapawera and Golden Bay), Marlborough (around Blenheim) and Central Otago (Alexandra and Roxburgh).

Winter work at ski resorts and their service towns includes bartending, waiting, cleaning, ski-tow operation and, if you're properly qualified, ski or snowboard instructing.

Resources

Backpacker publications, hostel managers and other travellers are the best sources of info on local work possibilities. **Base Backpackers** (www.stayatbase.com/ work) runs an employment service via its website, while the Notice Boards page on **Budget Backpacker Hostels** (BBH; www.bbh.co.nz) lists job vacancies in BBH hostels and a few other possibilities.

Kiwi Careers (www.careers.govt.nz) lists professional opportunities in various fields (agriculture, creative, health, teaching, volunteer work and recruitment), while **Seek** (www.seek.co.nz) is one of the biggest NZ job-search networks, with thousands of jobs listed.

Check ski-resort websites for work opportunities in the snow; in the fruit-picking/ horticultural realm, try the following websites:

➡ www.seasonalwork.co.nz

➡ www.seasonaljobs.co.nz

➡ www.picknz.co.nz

➡ www.pickingjobs.com

Income Tax

Death and taxes – no escape! For most travellers, Kiwi dollars earned in NZ will be subject to income tax, deducted from payments by employers – a process called Pay As You Earn (PAYE). Standard NZ income tax rates are 12.2% for annual salaries up to $14,000, then 19.2% up to $48,000, 31.7% up to $70,000, then 34.7% for higher incomes. A NZ Accident Compensation Corporation (ACC) scheme levy (around 2%) will also be deducted from your pay packet. Note that these rates tend to change slightly year-to-year.

If you visit NZ and work for a short time (eg on a working-holiday scheme), you may qualify for a tax refund when you leave. Complete a *Refund Application – People Leaving New Zealand IR50* form and submit it with your tax return, along with proof of departure (eg air ticket copies) to the **Inland Revenue Department** (www.ird.govt.nz). For more info, see the IRD website, or contact the **Inland Revenue Non-Resident Centre** (☎03-951 2020; nonres@ird.govt.nz; Private Bag 1932, Dunedin 9054).

IRD Number

Travellers undertaking paid work in NZ must obtain an IRD (Inland Revenue Department) number. Download the *IRD Number Application – Individual IR595* form from the **Inland Revenue Department** (www.ird.govt.nz) website. IRD numbers normally take eight to 10 working days to be issued.

Transport

GETTING THERE & AWAY

New Zealand is a long way from almost everywhere – most travellers jet in from afar. Flights, tours and rail tickets can be booked online at lonelyplanet.com/bookings.

Entering the Country

Disembarkation in NZ is generally a straightforward affair, with only the usual customs declarations and the luggage carousel scramble to endure. Under the the Orwellian title of 'Advance Passenger Screening', documents that used to be checked after you touched down in NZ (passport, visa etc) are now checked before you board your flight – make sure all your documentation is in order so that your check-in is stress-free.

Passport

There are no restrictions when it comes to foreign citizens entering NZ. If you have a current passport and visa (or don't require one), you should be fine.

Air

There are a number of competing airlines that service NZ if you're flying in from Asia, Europe or North America, though ultimately you'll still pay a lot for a flight unless you arrive from Australia. NZ's abundance of year-round activities means that airports are busy most of the time: if you want to fly at a particularly popular time of year (eg over the Christmas period), book well in advance.

The high season for flights into NZ is during summer (December to February), with slightly less of a premium on fares over the shoulder months (October/November and March/April). The low season generally tallies with the winter months (June to August), though this is still a busy time for airlines ferrying ski bunnies and powder hounds to Queenstown.

International Airports

Three South Island airports handle international flights:

Christchurch International Airport (CHC; ☑03-358 5029; www.christchurchairport.co.nz; 30 Durey Rd, Christchurch Airport)

Dunedin International Airport (DUD; ☑03-486 2879; www.dnairport.co.nz; 25 Miller Rd, Momona)

Queenstown Airport (ZQN; ☑03-450 9031; www.queenstownairport.co.nz; Sir Henry Wrigley Dr)

CLIMATE CHANGE & TRAVEL

Every form of transport that relies on carbon-based fuel generates CO_2, the main cause of human-induced climate change. Modern travel is dependent on aeroplanes, which might use less fuel per kilometre per person than most cars but travel much greater distances. The altitude at which aircraft emit gases (including CO_2) and particles also contributes to their climate change impact. Many websites offer 'carbon calculators' that allow people to estimate the carbon emissions generated by their journey and, for those who wish to do so, to offset the impact of the greenhouse gases emitted with contributions to portfolios of climate-friendly initiatives throughout the world. Lonely Planet offsets the carbon footprint of all staff and author travel.

DEPARTURE TAX

An international departure tax of NZ$25 applies when leaving three of NZ's smaller international airports (all in the North Island); Hamilton, Rotorua and the sporadically international Palmerston North. At all other airports across the country the tax has been replaced with a NZ$12.50 Passenger Service Charge (PSC), which is included in your ticket price. At Hamilton, Rotorua and Palmerston North, the departure tax must be paid separately at the airport before you board your flight (via credit card or cash). For kids under 12 it's NZ$10, and free for kids under two.

International Airlines

➡ NZ's own international carrier is **Air New Zealand** (www.airnewzealand.co.nz), which flies to runways across Europe, North America, eastern Asia and the Pacific, and has an extensive network across NZ.

➡ Winging-in from Australia, **Virgin Australia** (www.virginaustralia.com), **Qantas** (www.qantas.com.au), **Jetstar** (☑0800 800 995; www.jetstar.com) and Air New Zealand are the key players.

➡ Air New Zealand also flies in from North America, but you can head south with **Air Canada** (www.aircanada.com) and **American Airlines** (www.aa.com), too.

➡ From Europe, the options are a little broader, with **British Airways** (www.britishairways.com), **Lufthansa** (www.lufthansa.com) and **Virgin Atlantic** (www.virginatlantic.com) entering the fray, and plenty of others stopping in NZ on broader round-the-world routes.

➡ From Asia and the Pacific there are myriad options, with direct flights from China, Japan, Singapore, Malaysia, Thailand and many Pacific island nations.

Sea

➡ It's possible (though by no means easy or safe) to make your way between NZ and Australia, and some smaller Pacific islands, by hitching rides or crewing on yachts. Try asking around at harbours, marinas, and yacht and sailing clubs. Popular yachting harbours in NZ include the Bay of Islands and Whangarei (both in Northland), Auckland and Wellington. March and April are the best months to look for boats heading to Australia.

➡ From Fiji, October to November is a peak departure season to beat the cyclones that soon follow in that neck of the woods.

➡ If you're looking for something with a slower pace, plenty of passenger cruise liners stop in NZ on the South Pacific legs of their respective schedules: try **P&O Cruises** (www.pocruises.com.au) for starters.

➡ Alternatively, a berth on a cargo ship or freighter to/from NZ is a quirky way to go: check out websites such as www.freightercruises.com and www.freighterexpeditions.com.au for more info.

GETTING AROUND

Air

Those who have limited time to get between NZ's attractions can make the most of a widespread (and very reliable and safe) network of intra- and inter-island flights.

Domestic Airlines

The country's major domestic carrier, Air New Zealand, has an aerial network covering most of the country, often operating under the Air New Zealand Link moniker on less popular routes. Australia-based Jetstar also flies between the main urban areas. Between them, these two airlines carry the vast majority of domestic passengers in NZ. Beyond this, several small-scale regional operators provide services between the North Island and the South Island, to Stewart Island, and around the glaciers and mountains of the South Island. Operators include the following:

➡ **Air Chathams** (www.airchathams.co.nz) Services to the remote Chatham Islands from Wellington, Christchurch and Auckland.

➡ **Air Fiordland** (www.airfiordland.com) Services around Milford Sound, Te Anau and Queenstown.

➡ **Air New Zealand** (www.airnewzealand.co.nz) Offers flights between 30-plus domestic destinations, plus myriad overseas destinations.

➡ **Air West Coast** (www.airwestcoast.co.nz) Operates charter/scenic flights ex-Greymouth, winging over the west coast glaciers and Aoraki/Mt Cook, and stopping in Milford Sound, Queenstown and Christchurch.

→ **Air2there.com** (www.air2there.com) Connects destinations across Cook Strait, including including Paraparaumu, Wellington, Nelson and Blenheim.

→ **Golden Bay Air** (www.goldenbayair.co.nz) Flies regularly between Wellington, Nelson and Takaka in Golden Bay. Also connects to Karamea for Heaphy Track trampers.

→ **Jetstar** (www.jetstar.com) Joins the dots between key tourism centres: Auckland, Wellington, Christchurch, Dunedin and Queenstown (and flies Queenstown to Melbourne and Sydney and Christchurch to Melbourne, Sydney and the Gold Coast).

→ **Soundsair** (www.soundsair.co.nz) Numerous flights each day between Picton and Wellington, with connections to Blenheim and Nelson.

→ **Stewart Island Flights** (www.stewartislandflights.com) Flies between Invercargill and Stewart Island.

Air Passes

With discounting being the norm these days, and a number of budget airlines now serving the trans-Tasman route as well as the Pacific islands, the value of air passes isn't as red-hot as in the past.

→ Available exclusively to travellers from the USA or Canada who have bought an Air New Zealand fare to NZ from the USA or Canada, Australia or the Pacific Islands, Air New Zealand offers the good-value **New Zealand Explorer Pass**. The pass lets you fly between up to 27 destinations in NZ, Australia and the South Pacific islands (including Norfolk Island, Tonga, Vanuatu, Tahiti, Fiji, Niue and the Cook Islands). Fares are broken down into four discounted, distance-based zones: zone one flights start at US$79 (eg Auckland to Christchurch); zone two from US$109 (eg Auckland

to Queenstown); zone three from US$214 (eg Wellington to Sydney); and zone four from US$295 (eg Tahiti to Auckland). You can buy the pass before you travel, or after you arrive in NZ.

→ **Star Alliance** (www.staralliance.com) offers the sector-based **South Pacific Airpass**, valid for selected journeys within NZ, and between NZ, Australia and several Pacific islands, including Fiji, New Caledonia, Tonga, the Cook Islands and Samoa. Passes are available to nonresidents of these countries, must be issued outside NZ in conjunction with Star Alliance international tickets, and are valid for three months. A typical Sydney–Christchurch–Wellington–Auckland–Nadi pass cost NZ$1050 at the time of research.

Bicycle

Touring cyclists proliferate in NZ, particularly over summer. The country is clean, green and relatively uncrowded, and has lots of cheap accommodation (including camping) and abundant fresh water. The roads are generally in good nick, and the climate is generally not too hot or cold. Road traffic is the biggest danger: trucks overtaking too close to cyclists are a particular threat. Bikes and cycling gear are readily available to rent or buy in the main centres, as are bicycle repair shops.

By law all cyclists must wear an approved safety helmet (or risk a fine); it's also vital to have good reflective safety clothing. Cyclists who use public transport will find that major bus lines and trains only take bicycles on a 'space available' basis and charge up to $10. Some of the smaller shuttle bus companies, on the other hand, make sure they have storage space for bikes, which they carry for a surcharge.

If importing your own bike or transporting it by plane within NZ, check with the relevant airline for costs and the degree of dismantling and packing required.

See www.nzta.govt.nz/traffic/ways/bike for more bike safety and legal tips, and p42 for info on Nga Haerenga, New Zealand Cycle Trail – a network of 22 'Great Rides' across NZ.

Hire

Rates offered by most outfits for renting road or mountain bikes range from $10 to $20 per hour and $30 to $50 per day. Longer-term rentals may be available by negotiation. You can often hire bikes from your accommodation (hostels, campgrounds, etc), or rent more reputable machines from bike shops in the larger towns.

Buying a Bike

Bicycles can be readily bought in NZ's larger cities, but prices for newer models are high. For a decent hybrid bike or rigid mountain bike you'll pay anywhere from $800 to $1800, though you can get a cheap one for around $500 (but you still then need to buy panniers, helmet, lock etc, and the cost quickly climbs). Other options include the post-Christmas sales and midyear stocktakes, when newish cycles can be heavily discounted.

Boat

NZ may be an island nation but there's virtually no long-distance water transport around the country. Obvious South Island exceptions include the inter-island ferries that chug across Cook Strait between Wellington and Picton, and the passenger ferry that negotiates Foveaux Strait between Bluff and the town of Oban on Stewart Island.

If you're cashed-up, consider the cruise liners that

chug around the NZ coastline as part of broader South Pacific itineraries: **P&O Cruises** (www.pocruises.com. au) is a major player.

Bus

Bus travel in NZ is relatively easy and well-organised, with services transporting you to the far reaches of both islands (including the start/end of various walking tracks), but it can be expensive, tedious and time-consuming.

NZ's dominant bus company is **InterCity** (www. intercity.co.nz), which can drive you to just about any-where on the South Island. InterCity also has a South Island sightseeing arm called **Newmans Coach Lines** (☑09-583 5780; www. newmanscoach.co.nz), travelling between Queenstown, Christchurch and the West Coast glaciers. **Naked Bus** (www.nakedbus.com) has similar routes and remains the main competition. Both bus lines offer fares as low as $1.

Seat Classes & Smoking

There are no allocated economy or luxury classes on NZ buses (very democratic), and smoking on the bus is a definite no-no.

Reservations

Over summer, school holidays and public holidays, book well in advance on popular routes (a week or two if possible). At other times a day or two ahead is usually fine. The best prices are generally available on-line, booked a few weeks in advance.

Bus Passes

If you're covering a lot of ground, both InterCity and Naked Bus offer bus passes that can be cheaper than paying as you go, but they do of course lock you into using their respective net-works. InterCity also offers a

10% discount for YHA, ISIC, Nomands, BBH or VIP card holders, and passes are generally valid for 12 months.

NATIONWIDE PASSES

➡ **Flexipass** A hop-on/hop-off InterCity pass, allowing travel to pretty much anywhere in NZ, in any direction, including the Interislander ferry accross Cook Strait. The pass is purchased in blocks of travel time: minimum 15 hours ($119), maximum 60 hours ($449). The average cost of each block becomes cheaper the more hours you buy. You can top up the pass if you need more time.

➡ **Flexitrips** An InterCity bus-pass system whereby you purchase a specific number of bus trips (eg Auckland to Tauranga would count as one trip) in blocks of five, with or without the Cook Strait ferry trip included. Five/15/30 trip passes including the ferry cost $210/383/550 (subtract $54 if you don't need the ferry).

➡ **Aotearoa Adventurer**, **Kiwi Explorer**, **Kia Ora New Zealand** and **Tiki Tour New Zealand** Hop-on/hop-off, fixed-itinerary nationwide passes offered by InterCity. These passes link up tourist hot spots and range in price from $645 to $1219. See www.travelpass.co.nz for details.

➡ **Naked Passport** (www. nakedpassport.com) A Naked Bus pass that allows you to buy trips in blocks of five, which you can add to any time, and book each trip as needed. Five/15/30 trips cost $151/318/491. An unlimited pass costs $597 – great value if you're travelling NZ for many moons.

SOUTH ISLAND PASSES

On the South Island, Inter-City offers 11 hop-on/hop-off fixed-itinerary passes, ranging from $43 trips between Christchurch and Kaikoura,

to $583 loops around the whole island. See www.travel-pass.co.nz for details.

Shuttle Buses

As well as InterCity and Naked Bus, regional shuttle buses fill in the gaps between the smaller towns. South Island regional shuttle-bus operators include the following:

➡ **Abel Tasman Travel** (www.abeltasmantravel.co.nz) Traverses the roads between Nelson, Motueka, Golden Bay, and Kahurangi and Abel Tasman National Parks.

➡ **Atomic Shuttles** (www. atomictravel.co.nz) Has services throughout the South Island, including to Christchurch, Dunedin, Invercargill, Picton, Nelson, Greymouth/Hokitika, Te Anau and Queenstown/Wanaka.

➡ **Cook Connection** (www.cookconnect.co.nz) Triangulates between Mt Cook, Twizel and Lake Tekapo.

➡ **East West Coaches** (www.eastwestcoaches.co.nz) Offers a service between Christchurch and Westport via Reefton.

➡ **Hanmer Connection** (www.atsnz.com) Twice-daily services between Hanmer Springs and Christchurch.

➡ **Knightrider** (www. knightrider.co.nz) Runs a nocturnal service from Christchurch to Dunedin return. (David Hasselhoff is nowhere to be seen...)

➡ **Topline Tours** (www. toplinetours.co.nz) Connects Te Anau and Queenstown.

➡ **Tracknet** (www.tracknet. net) Daily track transport (Milford, Routeburn, Hollyford, Kepler etc) between Queenstown, Te Anau, Milford Sound, Invercargill, Fiordland and the West Coast.

➡ **Trek Express** (☑027 222 1872, 0800 128 735; www.trekexpress.co.nz) 4WD shuttle services to all

ROAD DISTANCES (KM)

	Aoraki/Mt Cook	Arthur's Pass	Blenheim	Christchurch	Dunedin	Franz Josef Glacier	Greymouth	Hanmer Springs	Hokitika	Invercargill	Kaikoura	Milford Sound	Nelson	Oamaru	Picton	Queenstown	Te Anau	Timaru	Wanaka
Arthur's Pass	410																		
Blenheim	635	420																	
Christchurch	330	150	310																
Dunedin	325	455	665	360															
Franz Josef Glacier	485	230	500	390	560														
Greymouth	510	95	330	250	550	180													
Hanmer Springs	460	265	260	140	490	395	215												
Hokitika	510	100	370	250	550	135	40	255											
Invercargill	440	660	870	570	210	530	710	700	665										
Kaikoura	505	290	130	185	535	540	330	135	390	745									
Milford Sound	540	840	1060	760	410	630	805	890	770	275	930								
Nelson	745	370	115	425	775	470	290	310	335	990	245	1100							
Oamaru	210	340	550	250	115	510	430	375	435	325	420	525	660						
Picton	660	450	30	340	690	530	355	290	400	900	160	1090	120	580					
Queenstown	260	565	785	480	285	355	530	610	490	190	660	290	820	290	815				
Te Anau	420	725	945	640	295	515	690	770	650	160	815	120	980	410	975	170			
Timaru	210	260	465	165	200	490	350	295	360	410	340	605	580	85	495	330	490		
Wanaka	210	510	730	430	280	285	465	555	420	245	600	345	755	230	760	70	230	275	
Westport	610	195	260	340	650	280	100	220	145	810	330	905	230	535	290	630	790	455	565

tramping tracks in the top half of the South Island.

➡ **West Coast Shuttle** (www. westcoastshuttle.co.nz) Daily bus from Greymouth to Christchurch and back.

Backpacker Buses

If you feel like clocking up some kilometres with like-minded fellow travellers, the following operators run fixed-itinerary bus tours, nationwide or on the North or South Island. Accommodation and hop-on/hop-off flexibility are often included.

➡ **Adventure Tours New Zealand** (www.adventuretours. com.au)

➡ **Bottom Bus** (☏03-477 9083; www.travelheadfirst.com)

➡ **Flying Kiwi** (www.flyingkiwi. com)

➡ **Kiwi Experience** (www. kiwiexperience.com)

➡ **Haka Tours** (www. hakatours.com)

➡ **Stray Travel** (www. straytravel.com)

Car & Motorcycle

The best way to explore NZ in depth is to have your own wheels. It's easy to hire cars and campervans at good rates. Alternatively, if you're in NZ for a few months, you might consider buying your own vehicle.

Automobile Association (AA)

NZ's **Automobile Association** (AA; ☏0800 500 444; www.aa.co.nz/travel) provides emergency breakdown services, maps and accommodation guides (from holiday parks to motels and B&Bs).

Members of overseas automobile associations should bring their membership cards – many of these bodies have reciprocal agreements with the AA.

Drivers Licences

International visitors to NZ can use their home country drivers licence – if your licence isn't in English, it's a good idea to carry a certified translation with you. Alternatively, use an International Driving Permit (IDP), which will usually be issued on the spot (valid for 12 months) by your home country's automobile association.

Fuel

Fuel (petrol, aka gasoline) is available from service stations across NZ: unless you're cruising around in something like the '70s, you'll be filling up with 'unleaded' or LPG (gas). LPG is not always stocked by rural suppliers; if you're on gas, it's safer to have dual-fuel capability. Aside from remote South Island locations like Milford Sound and Mt Cook, petrol prices don't vary much from place to place: per-litre costs at the time of research were around $2.40.

Campervan Rental

➡ Check your rear-view mirror on any far-flung NZ road and you'll probably see a shiny white campervan (aka mobile home, motor home, RV) packed with liberated travellers, mountain bikes and portable barbecues cruising along behind you.

➡ Most towns of any size have a campground or holiday park with powered sites (where you can plug your vehicle in) for around $35 per night. There are also 250-plus vehicle-accessible **Department of Conservation** (Department of Conservation; www.doc.govt. nz) campsites around NZ, ranging in price from free to $15 per adult: check the website for info.

➡ You can hire campervans from dozens of companies. Prices vary with season, vehicle size and length of rental.

➡ A small van for two people typically has a minikitchen and foldout dining table, the latter transforming into a double bed when dinner is done and dusted. Larger 'superior' two-berth vans include shower and toilet. Four- to six-berth campervans are the size of trucks (and similarly sluggish) and, besides the extra space, usually contain a toilet and shower.

➡ Over summer, rates offered by the main rental firms for two-/four-/six-berth vans start at around $160/200/290 per day for a month-long rental, dropping to as low as $45/60/90 per day during winter.

Major operators include the following:

➡ **Apollo** (☎0800 113 131, 09-889 2976; www. apollocamper.co.nz)

➡ **Britz** (☎0800 831 900, 09-255 3910; www.britz.co.nz) Also does 'Britz Bikes' (add a mountain or city bike from $13 per day).

➡ **Kea** (☎0800 520 052, 09-448 8800)

➡ **Maui** (☎0800 651 080, 09-255 3910; www.maui.co.nz)

➡ **United Campervans** (☎0800 759 919, 09-275 9919; www.unitedcampervans.co.nz)

➡ **Wilderness Motorhomes** (☎09-255 5300; www. wilderness.co.nz)

BACKPACKER VANS

Budget players in the campervan industry offer slick deals and funky (often gregariously spray-painted: Jimi Hendrix, *Where The Wild Things Are,* Sly Stone etc), well-kitted-out vehicles for backpackers. Rates are competitive (from $35/50 per day for a two-/four-berth van May to September; from $100/150 per day December to February). Operators include the following:

➡ **Backpacker Sleeper Vans** (☎0800 321 939, 03-359 4731; www.sleepervans.co.nz)

➡ **Escape Campervans** (☎0800 216 171; www. escaperentals.co.nz)

➡ **Hippie Camper** (☎0800 113 131; www.hippiecamper. co.nz)

➡ **Jucy** (☎0800 399 736, 09-374 4360; www.jucy.co.nz)

➡ **Mighty Cars & Campers** (☎0800 422 267; www. mightycampers.co.nz)

➡ **Spaceships** (☎0800 772 237, 09-526 2130; www. spaceshipsrentals.co.nz)

➡ **Wicked Campers** (☎0800 246 870, 09-634 2994; www. wickedcampers.co.nz)

Car Rental

Competition between car-rental companies in NZ is torrid, particularly in the big cities and Picton. Remember that if you want to travel far, you need unlimited kilometres. Some (but not all) companies require drivers to be at least 21 years old – ask around.

Most car-hire firms suggest (or insist) that you don't take their vehicles between islands on the Cook Strait ferries. Instead, you leave your car at either Wellington or Picton terminal and pick up another car once you've crossed the strait. This saves you paying to transport a vehicle on the ferries, and is a pain-free exercise.

INTERNATIONAL RENTAL COMPANIES

The big multinational companies have offices in most major cities, towns and airports. Firms sometimes offer one-way rentals (eg collect a car in Queenstown, leave it in Christchurch), but there are often restrictions and fees. On the other hand, an operator in Christchurch may need to get a vehicle back to Auckland and will offer an amazing one-way car relocation deal (sometimes free!).

The major companies offer a choice of either unlimited kilometres, or 100km (or so) per day free, plus so many cents per subsequent kilometre. Daily rates in main cities typically start at around $40 per day for a compact, late-model, Japanese car, and around $75 for medium-sized cars (including GST, unlimited kilometres and insurance).

➡ **Avis** (☎0800 655 111, 09-526 2847; www.avis.co.nz)

➔ **Budget** (☎0800 283 438, 09-529 7784; www.budget.co.nz)

➔ **Europcar** (☎0800 800 115; www.europcar.co.nz)

➔ **Hertz** (☎0800 654 321, 03-358 6789; www.hertz.co.nz)

➔ **Thrifty** (☎0800 737 070, 03-359 2721; www.thrifty.co.nz)

LOCAL RENTAL COMPANIES

Local rental firms dapple the *Yellow Pages*. These are almost always cheaper than the big boys – sometimes half the price – but the cheap rates may come with serious restrictions: vehicles are often older, and with less formality sometimes comes a less protective legal structure for renters.

Rentals from local firms start at around $30 per day for the smallest option. It's obviously cheaper if you rent for a week or more, and there are often low-season and weekend discounts.

Affordable, independent operators with national networks include the following:

➔ **a2b Car Rentals** (☎0800 545 000; www.a2b-carrentals.co.nz)

➔ **Ace Rental Cars** (☎0800 502 277, 09-303 3112; www.acerentalcars.co.nz)

➔ **Apex Rentals** (☎0800 939 597, 03-379 6897; www.apexrentals.co.nz)

➔ **Go Rentals** (☎0800 467 368, 09-525 7321; www.gorentals.co.nz)

➔ **Omega Rental Cars** (☎0800 525 210, 09-377 5573; www.omegarentalcars.com)

➔ **Pegasus Rental Cars** (☎0800 803 580, 03-548 2852; www.rentalcars.co.nz)

➔ **Transfercar** (☎09-630 7533; www.transfercar.co.nz) One-way relocation specialists.

Motorcycle Rental

Born to be wild? NZ has great terrain for motorcycle touring, despite the fickle weather in some regions. Most of the South Island's motorcycle-hire shops are in Christchurch, where you can hire anything from a little 50cc moped (aka nifty-fifty) to a throbbing 750cc touring motorcycle and beyond. Recommended operators (who also run guided tours) with rates from $80 to $345 per day:

➔ **New Zealand Motorcycle Rentals & Tours** (☎09-486 2472; www.nzbike.com)

➔ **Te Waipounamu Motorcycle Tours** (☎03-377 3211; www.motorcycle-hire.co.nz)

Insurance

Rather than risk paying out wads of cash if you have an accident, you can take out your own comprehensive insurance policy, or (the usual option) pay an additional fee per day to the rental company to reduce your excess. This brings the amount you must pay in the event of an accident down from around $1500 or $2000 to around $200 or $300. Smaller operators offering cheap rates often have a compulsory insurance excess, taken as a credit-card bond, of around $900.

Most insurance agreements won't cover the cost of damage to glass (including the windscreen) or tyres, and insurance coverage is often invalidated on beaches and certain rough (4WD) unsealed roads – read the fine print.

See p327 for info on NZ's **Accident Compensation Corporation** (ACC; www.acc.co.nz) insurance scheme (fault-free personal injury insurance).

Purchase

Buying a car then selling it at the end of your travels can be one of the cheapest and best ways to see NZ. Auckland is the easiest place to buy a car, followed by Christchurch: scour the hostel noticeboards. **Turners Auctions** (www.turners.co.nz) is NZ's biggest car-auction operator, with 11 locations.

LEGALITIES

➔ Make sure your prospective vehicle has a Warrant of Fitness (WoF) and registration valid for a reasonable period: see the **Land Transport New Zealand** (www.landtransport.govt.nz) website for details.

➔ Buyers should also take out third-party insurance, covering the cost of repairs to another vehicle in an accident that is your fault: try the **Automobile Association** (AA; ☎0800 500 444; www.aa.co.nz/travel). NZ's no-fault Accident Compensation Corporation scheme covers personal injury, but make sure you have travel insurance, too.

➔ If you're considering buying a car and want someone to check it out for you, various car-inspection companies inspect cars for around $150; find them at car auctions, or they will come to you. Try **Vehicle Inspection New Zealand** (VINZ; ☎0800 468 469, 09-573 3230; www.vinz.co.nz) or the AA.

➔ Before you buy it's wise to confirm ownership of the vehicle, and find out if there's anything dodgy about the car (eg stolen, or outstanding debts). The AA's **LemonCheck** (☎0800 536 662, 09-420 3090; www.lemoncheck.co.nz) offers this service ('Pry before you buy'...).

BUY-BACK DEALS

➔ You can avoid the hassle of buying/selling a vehicle privately by entering into a buy-back arrangement with a dealer. Predictably, dealers often find sneaky ways of knocking down the return-sale price, which may be 50% less than what you paid, so hiring or buying and selling a vehicle yourself (if you have the time) is usually a better bet.

Road Hazards

➡ Kiwi traffic is usually pretty light, but it's easy to get stuck behind a slow-moving truck or campervan – pack plenty of patience. There are also lots of slow wiggly roads, one-way bridges and plenty of gravel roads, all of which require a more cautious driving approach. And watch out for sheep!

➡ To check road conditions call ☑0800 444 449 or see www.nzta.govt.nz/traffic/current-conditions.

Road Rules

➡ Kiwis drive on the left-hand side of the road; cars are right-hand drive. Give way to the right at intersections.

➡ At single-lane bridges (of which there are a surprisingly large number), a smaller red arrow pointing in your direction of travel means that *you* give way.

➡ Speed limits on the open road are generally 100km/h; in built-up areas the limit is usually 50km/h. Speed cameras and radars are used extensively.

➡ All vehicle occupants must wear a seatbelt or risk a fine. Small children must be belted into approved safety seats.

➡ Always carry your licence when driving. Drink-driving is a serious offence and remains a significant problem in NZ, despite

widespread campaigns and severe penalties. The legal blood alcohol limit is 0.08% for drivers over 20, and 0% (zero!) for those under 20.

Hitching & Ride-Sharing

NZ is no longer immune from the perils of solo hitching. Those who decide to hitch are taking a small but potentially serious risk. That said, it's not unusual to see hitch-hikers along country roads.

Alternatively, check hostel noticeboards for ride-share opportunities, or have a look online at www.carpoolnz.org or www.nationalcarshare.co.nz.

Local Transport

Bus, Train & Tram

NZ's larger cities have extensive bus services but, with a few honourable exceptions, they are mainly daytime, weekday operations; weekend services can be infrequent or nonexistent. Christchurch has a free city-shuttle service and the historic tramway (now open again after the earthquake). The bigger South Island cities have late-night buses for boozy Friday and Saturday nights.

Taxi

The main cities have plenty of taxis and even small towns may have a local service.

Train

In NZ train travel is about the journey, not about getting anywhere in a hurry. **KiwiRail Scenic Journeys** (☑0800 872 467, 04-495 0775; www.tranzscenic.co.nz) operates two routes in the South Island (listed below). Reservations can be made through KiwiRail Scenic Journeys directly, or at most train stations, travel agents and visitor information centres:

➡ **Coastal Pacific** Between Christchurch and Picton.

➡ **TranzAlpine** Over the Southern Alps between Christchurch and Greymouth.

Train Passes

A KiwiRail Scenic Journeys **Scenic Journey Rail Pass** (www.kiwirailscenic.co.nz/scenic-rail-pass) allows unlimited travel on all of its rail services, including passage on the Wellington–Picton Interislander ferry. There are two types of pass, both requiring you to book your seats a minimum of 24 hours before you want to travel:

➡ **Fixed Pass** Limited duration fares for one/two/three weeks, costing $599/699/799 per adult (a little bit less for kids).

➡ **Freedom Pass** Affords you travel on a certain number of days over a 12-month period; a three-/seven-/nine-day pass costs $417/903/1161.

Language

New Zealand has three official languages: English, Maori and NZ sign language. Although English is what you'll usually hear, Maori has been making a comeback. You can use English to speak to anyone in New Zealand, but there are some occasions when knowing a small amount of Maori is useful, such as when visiting a *marae,* where often only Maori is spoken. Some knowledge of Maori will also help you interpret the many Maori place names you'll come across.

KIWI ENGLISH

Like the people of other English-speaking countries in the world, New Zealanders have their own, unique way of speaking the language. The flattening of vowels is the most distinctive feature of Kiwi pronunciation. For example, in Kiwi English, 'fish and chips' sounds more like 'fush and chups'. On the North Island sentences often have 'eh!' attached to the end. In the far south a rolled 'r' is common, which is a holdover from that region's Scottish heritage – it's especially noticeable in Southland.

MAORI

The Maori have a vividly chronicled history, recorded in songs and chants that dramatically recall the migration to New Zealand from Polynesia as well as other important events. Early missionaries were the first to record the language in a written form using only 15 letters of the English alphabet.

Maori is closely related to other Polynesian languages such as Hawaiian, Tahitian and Cook Islands Maori. In fact, New Zealand Maori and Hawaiian are quite similar, even though more than 7000km separates Honolulu and Auckland.

The Maori language was never dead – it was always used in Maori ceremonies – but over time familiarity with it was definitely on the decline. Fortunately, recent years have seen a revival of interest in it, and this forms an integral part of the renaissance of *Maoritanga* (Maori culture). Many Maori people who had heard the language spoken on the *marae* for years but had not used it in their day-to-day lives, are now studying it and speaking it fluently. Maori is taught in schools throughout New Zealand, some TV programs and news reports are broadcast in it, and many English place names are being renamed in Maori. Even government departments have been given Maori names: for example, the Inland Revenue Department is also known as Te Tari Taake (the last word is actually *take,* which means 'levy', but the department has chosen to stress the long 'a' by spelling it 'aa').

In many places, Maori have come together to provide instruction in their language and culture to young children; the idea is for them to grow up speaking both Maori and English, and to develop a familiarity with Maori tradition. It's a matter of some pride to have fluency in the language. On some *marae* only Maori can be spoken.

WANT MORE?

For in-depth language information and handy phrases, check out Lonely Planet's *South Pacific Phrasebook*. You'll find it at **shop.lonelyplanet.com**, or you can buy Lonely Planet's iPhone phrasebooks at the Apple App Store.

Pronunciation

Maori is a fluid, poetic language and surprisingly easy to pronounce once you remember to split each word (some can be amazingly long) into separate syllables. Each syllable ends in a vowel. There are no 'silent' letters.

Most consonants in Maori – *h, k, m, n, p, t* and *w* – are pronounced much the same as in English. The Maori *r* is a flapped sound (not rolled) with the tongue near the front of the mouth. It's closer to the English 'l' in pronunciation.

The *ng* is pronounced as in the English words 'singing' or 'running', and can be used at the beginning of words as well as at the end. To practise, just say 'ing' over and over, then isolate the 'ng' part of it.

The letters *wh*, when occuring together, are generally pronounced as a soft English 'f'. This pronunciation is used in many place names in New Zealand, such as Whakatane, Whangaroa and Whakapapa (all pronounced as if they begin with a soft 'f'). There is some local variation: in the region around the Whanganui River, for example, *wh* is pronounced as in the English word 'when'.

The correct pronunciation of the vowels is very important. The examples below are a rough guideline – it helps to listen carefully to someone who speaks the language well. Each vowel has both a long and a short sound, with long vowels often denoted by a line over the letter or a double vowel. We have not indicated long and short vowel forms in this book.

Vowels

a	as in 'large', with no 'r' sound
e	as in 'get'
i	as in 'marine'
o	as in 'pork'
u	as the 'oo' in 'moon'

Vowel Combinations

ae, ai	as the 'y' in 'sky'
ao, au	as the 'ow' in 'how'
ea	as in 'bear'
ei	as in 'vein'
eo	as 'eh-oh'
eu	as 'eh-oo'
ia	as in the name 'Ian'
ie	as the 'ye' in 'yet'
io	as the 'ye o' in 'ye old'
iu	as the 'ue' in 'cue'
oa	as in 'roar'
oe	as in 'toe'
oi	as in 'toil'
ou	as the 'ow' in 'how'
ua	as the 'ewe' in 'fewer'

Greetings & Small Talk

Maori greetings are becoming increasingly popular – don't be surprised if you're greeted with *Kia ora*.

Welcome!	*Haere mai!*
Hello./Good luck./ Good health.	*Kia ora.*
Hello. (to one person)	*Tena koe.*
Hello. (to two people)	*Tena korua.*
Hello. (to three or more people)	*Tena koutou.*
Goodbye. (to person staying)	*E noho ra.*
Goodbye. (to person leaving)	*Haere ra.*
How are you? (to one person)	*Kei te pehea koe?*
How are you? (to two people)	*Kei te pehea korua?*
How are you? (to three or more people)	*Kei te pehea koutou?*
Very well, thanks./ That's fine.	*Kei te pai.*

Maori Geographical Terms

The following words form part of many Maori place names in New Zealand, and help you understand the meaning of these place names. For example: Waikaremoana is the Sea (*moana*) of Rippling (*kare*) Waters (*wai*), and Rotorua means the Second (*rua*) Lake (*roto*).

a – of
ana – cave
ara – way, path or road
awa – river or valley
heke – descend
hiku – end; tail
hine – girl; daughter
ika – fish
iti – small
kahurangi – treasured possession; special greenstone
kai – food
kainga – village
kaka – parrot
kare – rippling
kati – shut or close
koura – crayfish
makariri – cold
manga – stream or tributary
manu – bird
maunga – mountain
moana – sea or lake
moko – tattoo
motu – island
mutu – finished; ended; over
nga – the (plural)

noa – ordinary; not *tapu*
nui – big or great
nuku – distance
o – of, place of...
one – beach, sand or mud
pa – fortified village
papa – large blue-grey mudstone
pipi – common edible bivalve
pohatu – stone
poto – short
pouri – sad; dark; gloomy
puke – hill
puna – spring; hole; fountain
rangi – sky; heavens
raro – north
rei – cherished possession
roa – long
roto – lake
rua – hole in the ground; two
runga – above
tahuna – beach; sandbank
tane – man
tangata – people
tapu – sacred, forbidden or taboo
tata – close to; dash against; twin islands
tawaha – entrance or opening
tawahi – the other side (of a river or lake)
te – the (singular)
tonga – south
ure – male genitals
uru – west

waha – broken
wahine – woman
wai – water
waingaro – lost; waters that disappear in certain seasons
waka – canoe
wera – burnt or warm; floating
wero – challenge
whaka... – to act as ...
whanau – family
whanga – harbour, bay or inlet
where – house
whenua – land or country
whiti – east

Here are some more place names composed of words in the list:

Aramoana – Sea *(moana)* Path *(ara)*
Awaroa – Long *(roa)* River *(awa)*
Kaitangata – Eat *(kai)* People *(tangata)*
Maunganui – Great *(nui)* Mountain *(maunga)*
Opouri – Place of *(o)* Sadness *(pouri)*
Te Araroa – The *(te)* Long *(roa)* Path *(ara)*
Te Puke – The *(te)* Hill *(puke)*
Urewera – Burnt *(wera)* Penis *(ure)*
Waimakariri – Cold *(makariri)* Water *(wai)*
Wainui – Great *(nui)* Waters *(wai)*
Whakatane – To Act *(whaka)* as a Man *(tane)*
Whangarei – Cherished *(rei)* Harbour *(whanga)*

GLOSSARY

Following is a list of abbreviations, 'Kiwi English', Maori and slang terms used in this book and which you may hear in New Zealand.

All Blacks – NZ's revered national rugby union team
ANZAC – Australia and New Zealand Army Corps
Aoraki – *Maori* name for Mt Cook, meaning 'Cloud Piercer'
Aotearoa – *Maori* name for NZ, most often translated as 'Land of the Long White Cloud'
aroha – love

B&B – 'bed and breakfast' accommodation
bach – holiday home (pronounced 'batch'); see also crib
black-water rafting – rafting or tubing underground in a cave

boozer – public bar
bro – literally 'brother'; usually meaning mate
BYO – 'bring your own' (usually applies to alcohol at a restaurant or cafe)

choice/chur – fantastic; great
crib – the name for a bach in Otago and Southland

DB&B – 'dinner, bed and breakfast' accommodation
DOC – Department of Conservation (or Te Papa Atawhai); government department that administers national parks, tracks and huts

eh? – roughly translates as 'don't you agree?'

farmstay – accommodation on a Kiwi farm
football – rugby, either union or league; occasionally soccer

Great Walks – set of nine popular tramping tracks within NZ
greenstone – jade; *pounamu*
gumboots – rubber boots or Wellingtons; originated from diggers on the gum-fields

haka – any dance, but usually a war dance
hangi – oven whereby food is steamed in baskets over embers in a hole; a *Maori* feast
hapu – subtribe or smaller tribal grouping
Hawaiki – original homeland of the *Maori*

hei tiki – carved, stylised human figure worn around the neck; also called a *tiki*

homestay – accommodation in a family house

hongi – *Maori* greeting; the pressing of foreheads and noses, and sharing of life breath

hui – gathering; meeting

i-SITE – information centre

iwi – large tribal grouping with common lineage back to the original migration from *Hawaiki*; people; tribe

jandals – contraction of 'Japanese sandals'; flip-flops; thongs; usually rubber footwear

jersey – jumper, usually woollen; the shirt worn by rugby players

kauri – native pine

kia ora – hello

Kiwi – New Zealander; an adjective to mean anything relating to NZ

kiwi – flightless, nocturnal brown bird with a long beak

Kiwiana – things uniquely connected to NZ life and culture, especially from bygone years

kiwifruit – small, succulent fruit with fuzzy brown skin and juicy green flesh; aka Chinese gooseberry or zespri

kumara – Polynesian sweet potato, a *Maori* staple food

Kupe – early Polynesian navigator from *Hawaiki*, credited with the discovery of the islands that are now NZ

mana – spiritual quality of a person or object; authority or prestige

Maori – indigenous people of NZ

Maoritanga – things *Maori*, ie *Maori* culture

marae – sacred ground in front of the *Maori* meeting house; more commonly used to refer to the entire complex of buildings

Maui – figure in *Maori* (Polynesian) mythology

mauri – life force/principle

moa – large, extinct flightless bird

moko – tattoo; usually refers to facial tattoos

nga – the (plural); see also *te*

ngai/ngati – literally, 'the people of' or 'the descendants of'; tribe (pronounced 'kai' on the South Island)

NZ – universal term for New Zealand; pronounced 'en zed'

pa – fortified *Maori* village, usually on a hilltop

Pacific Rim – modern NZ cuisine; local produce cooked with imported styles

Pakeha – *Maori* for a white or European person

Pasifika – Pacific Island culture

paua – abalone; iridescent paua shell is often used in jewellery

pavlova – meringue cake topped with cream and kiwifruit

PI – Pacific Islander

poi – ball of woven flax

pounamu – *Maori* name for *greenstone*

powhiri – traditional *Maori* welcome onto a marae

rip – dangerously strong current running away from the shore at a beach

Roaring Forties – the ocean between 40° and 50° south, known for very strong winds

silver fern – symbol worn by the *All Blacks* and other national sportsfolk on their jerseys; the national netball team is called the Silver Ferns

sweet, sweet as – all-purpose term like choice; fantastic, great

tapu – strong force in *Maori* life, with numerous meanings; in its simplest form it means sacred, forbidden, taboo

te – the (singular); see also *nga*

te reo – literally 'the language'; the *Maori* language

tiki – short for *hei tiki*

tiki tour – scenic tour

tramp – bushwalk; trek; hike

tuatara – prehistoric reptile dating back to the age of dinosaurs

tui – native parson bird

wahine – woman

wai – water

wairua – spirit

Waitangi – short way of referring to the Treaty of Waitangi

waka – canoe

Warriors – NZ's popular rugby league club, affiliated with Australia's NRL

Wellywood – Wellington, because of its thriving film industry

zorbing – rolling down a hill inside an inflatable plastic ball

Behind the Scenes

SEND US YOUR FEEDBACK

We love to hear from travellers – your comments keep us on our toes and help make our books better. Our well-travelled team reads every word on what you loved or loathed about this book. Although we cannot reply individually to your submissions, we always guarantee that your feedback goes straight to the appropriate authors, in time for the next edition. Each person who sends us information is thanked in the next edition – the most useful submissions are rewarded with a selection of digital PDF chapters.

Visit **lonelyplanet.com/contact** to submit your updates and suggestions or to ask for help. Our award-winning website also features inspirational travel stories, news and discussions.

Note: We may edit, reproduce and incorporate your comments in Lonely Planet products such as guidebooks, websites and digital products, so let us know if you don't want your comments reproduced or your name acknowledged. For a copy of our privacy policy visit lonelyplanet.com/privacy.

OUR READERS

Many thanks to the travellers who used the last edition and wrote to us with helpful hints, useful advice and interesting anecdotes:
Issy Cooper, Thais Fournier, Omar Hasan, Beverly Ladyman and Kirsty Smith

AUTHOR THANKS

Brett Atkinson

Thanks to all of the i-SITE, DOC and information centre staff who patiently answered all my questions. Cheers to the clever craft brewers of New Zealand for sustenance on the road, and to Carol for support on occasional forays via the back roads. Thanks to my fellow authors, the most professional and wittiest bunch one could aspire to work with, and huge thanks and friendship to the mighty Errol Hunt.

Sarah Bennett & Lee Slater

Thanks to everyone who helped us on the road, including RTO and visitor information centre staff, tourism operators and travellers. Special thanks to DOC staff, especially Penny McIntosh and Katrina Henderson. Big ups to everyone in-house at Lonely Planet, and to our fellow authors – Brett, Charles and Peter. Thanks also to Sarah Ewing. To all who provided a park for our camper, a fridge for the flagon, and even a feed of kaimoana on occasion: *arohanui, e hoa ma*.

Peter Dragicevich

I owe a great debt of thanks to Hamish Blennerhassett, Harry and Ngaio Tyler, and all the Tyler cousins for their help and companionship during the research of this book. But above all, I'd like to thank Errol Hunt – editor extraordinaire, all-round great guy, originator of the 'four more years' chant at the 2011 Rugby World Cup final, and the person most responsible for making the *New Zealand* guides so successful over many successive editions.

Charles Rawlings-Way

Thanks to the many generous, knowledgeable and quietly self-assured Kiwis I met on the road, especially the staff at the Palmerston North, Hastings and New Plymouth i-SITEs who flew through my questions with the greatest of ease. Huge thanks to Errol Hunt for signing me up (again), and the in-house Lonely Planet staff who schmoozed this book through production. Humongous gratitude to my tireless, witty and professional co-authors – Sarah, Peter, Brett and Lee – who infused this book with humour and local low-down. Most of all, thank you Meg, Ione and Remy for holding the fort while I was away.

ACKNOWLEDGMENTS

Climate map data adapted from Peel MC, Finlayson BL & McMahon TA (2007) 'Updated World Map of the Köppen-Geiger Climate Classification', *Hydrology and Earth System Sciences*, 11, 1633¬44.

Cover photograph: Cascade Saddle, Mt Aspiring National Park, Colin Monteath/ Corbis ©

BEHIND THE SCENES

THIS BOOK

This 4th edition of Lonely Planet's *New Zealand's South Island* guidebook was coordinated by Brett Atkinson, and researched and written by Brett, Sarah Bennett, Peter Dragicevich, Charles Rawlings-Way and Lee Slater. It includes some content from the 17th edition of the *New Zealand* guide, coordinated by Charles Rawlings-Way.

This guidebook was commissioned in Lonely Planet's Melbourne office, and produced by the following:

Commissioning Editors
Errol Hunt, Glenn van der Knijff

Destination Editor
Tasmin Waby

Product Editor
Catherine Naghten

Senior Cartographer
Diana Von Holdt

Book Designer
Wendy Wright

Assisting Editors
Nigel Chin, Samantha Forge, Jeanette Wall

Cover Researcher
Naomi Parker

Thanks to Elin Berglund, Brendan Dempsey, Ryan Evans, Larissa Frost, Anna Harris, Genesys India, Jouve India, Claire Naylor, Karyn Noble, Alison Ridgway, Eleanor Simpson, Tracy Whitmey

Index

Map Legend

Sights

- Beach
- Bird Sanctuary
- Buddhist
- Castle/Palace
- Christian
- Confucian
- Hindu
- Islamic
- Jain
- Jewish
- Monument
- Museum/Gallery/Historic Building
- Ruin
- Sento Hot Baths/Onsen
- Shinto
- Sikh
- Taoist
- Winery/Vineyard
- Zoo/Wildlife Sanctuary
- Other Sight

Activities, Courses & Tours

- Bodysurfing
- Diving
- Canoeing/Kayaking
- Course/Tour
- Skiing
- Snorkelling
- Surfing
- Swimming/Pool
- Walking
- Windsurfing
- Other Activity

Sleeping

- Sleeping
- Camping

Eating

- Eating

Drinking & Nightlife

- Drinking & Nightlife
- Cafe

Entertainment

- Entertainment

Shopping

- Shopping

Information

- Bank
- Embassy/Consulate
- Hospital/Medical
- Internet
- Police
- Post Office
- Telephone
- Toilet
- Tourist Information
- Other Information

Geographic

- Beach
- Hut/Shelter
- Lighthouse
- Lookout
- Mountain/Volcano
- Oasis
- Park
- Pass
- Picnic Area
- Waterfall

Population

- Capital (National)
- Capital (State/Province)
- City/Large Town
- Town/Village

Transport

- Airport
- Border crossing
- Bus
- Cable car/Funicular
- Cycling
- Ferry
- Metro station
- Monorail
- Parking
- Petrol station
- Subway station
- Taxi
- Train station/Railway
- Tram
- Underground station
- Other Transport

Note: Not all symbols displayed above appear on the maps in this book

Routes

- Tollway
- Freeway
- Primary
- Secondary
- Tertiary
- Lane
- Unsealed road
- Road under construction
- Plaza/Mall
- Steps
- Tunnel
- Pedestrian overpass
- Walking Tour
- Walking Tour detour
- Path/Walking Trail

Boundaries

- International
- State/Province
- Disputed
- Regional/Suburb
- Marine Park
- Cliff
- Wall

Hydrography

- River, Creek
- Intermittent River
- Canal
- Water
- Dry/Salt/Intermittent Lake
- Reef

Areas

- Airport/Runway
- Beach/Desert
- Cemetery (Christian)
- Cemetery (Other)
- Glacier
- Mudflat
- Park/Forest
- Sight (Building)
- Sportsground
- Swamp/Mangrove

Charles Rawlings-Way

Survival Guide English by birth, Australian by chance, All Blacks fan by choice: Charles's early understanding of Aotearoa was less than comprehensive (sheep, mountains, sheep on mountains...). He realised there was more to it when a wandering uncle returned with a faux-jade tiki in 1981. He wore it with pride until he saw the NZ cricket team's beige uniforms in 1982...Mt Taranaki's snowy summit, Napier's art-deco deliverance and Wanganui's raffish charm have helped him forgive: he's once again smitten with the country's phantasmal landscapes, disarming locals and determination to sculpt its own political and indigenous destiny.

Contributing Writers

Professor James Belich wrote the History chapter. James is one of NZ's pre-eminent historians and the award-winning author of *The New Zealand Wars, Making Peoples* and *Paradise Reforged*. He has also worked in TV – *New Zealand Wars* was screened in NZ in 1998.

Tony Horwitz wrote the Captain James Cook boxed text in the History chapter. Tony is a Pulitzer-winning reporter and nonfiction author. His fascination with James Cook, and with travel, took him around NZ, Australia and the Pacific while researching *Blue Latitudes* (alternatively titled *Into the Blue*), part biography of Cook and part travelogue.

John Huria (Ngai Tahu, Muaupoko) wrote the Maori Culture chapter. John has an editorial, research and writing background with a focus on Maori writing and culture. He was senior editor for Maori publishing company Huia and now runs an editorial and publishing services company, Ahi Text Solutions Ltd (www.ahitextsolutions.co.nz).

Josh Kronfeld wrote the Surfing in New Zealand boxed text in the Extreme South Island chapter. Josh is an ex–All Black flanker, whose passion for surfing NZ's beaches is legendary and who found travelling for rugby a way to surf other great breaks around the world.

Gareth Shute wrote the Music section in the Arts & Music chapter. Gareth is the author of four books, including *Hip Hop Music in Aotearoa* and *NZ Rock 1987–2007*. He is also a musician and has toured the UK, Europe and Australia as a member of the Ruby Suns and the Brunettes. He now plays in indie soul group The Cosbys.

Vaughan Yarwood wrote the Environment chapter. Vaughan is an Auckland-based writer whose books include *The History Makers: Adventures in New Zealand Biography, The Best of New Zealand: A Collection of Essays on NZ Life and Culture by Prominent Kiwis,* which he edited, and the regional history *Between Coasts: From Kaipara to Kawau*. He has written widely for NZ and international publications and is the former associate editor of *New Zealand Geographic,* for which he has also written for many years.

OUR STORY

A beat-up old car, a few dollars in the pocket and a sense of adventure. In 1972 that's all Tony and Maureen Wheeler needed for the trip of a lifetime – across Europe and Asia overland to Australia. It took several months, and at the end – broke but inspired – they sat at their kitchen table writing and stapling together their first travel guide, *Across Asia on the Cheap*. Within a week they'd sold 1500 copies. Lonely Planet was born.

Today, Lonely Planet has offices in Franklin, London, Melbourne, Oakland, Beijing and Delhi, with more than 600 staff and writers. We share Tony's belief that 'a great guidebook should do three things: inform, educate and amuse'.

OUR WRITERS

Brett Atkinson

Coordinating Author Although he now calls Auckland his hometown, Brett has been exploring the South Island for several decades. Highlights include being the first Lonely Planet author to revisit Christchurch after the earthquakes, taking the longer – and every scenic – route south through the Catlins, and tandem hang gliding above Queenstown. Brett has contributed to Lonely Planet guidebooks spanning Europe, Asia and the Pacific, and covered almost 50 countries as a food and travel writer. See www.brett-atkinson.net for his latest travels.

Sarah Bennett & Lee Slater

Marlborough & Nelson, The West Coast, Fiordland & Southland Lee and Sarah live in Wellington, but spend many months on the road each year in their small campervan, boots on board, mountain bikes on the back. Specialists in 'soft-core adventure' (tramping without crampons, kayaking without capsize), they reimagine their journeys in magazine features, and guidebooks including Lonely Planet's *Hiking & Tramping New Zealand*, four editions of *New Zealand*, as well as *The New Zealand Tramper's Handbook* and *Let's Go Camping*. Read more at www.bennettand slater.co.nz and follow on Twitter @BennettnSlater.

Peter Dragicevich

Christchurch & Canterbury, Dunedin & Otago, Queenstown & Wanaka After nearly a decade working for off-shore publishing companies, Peter's life has come full circle, returning to his home town of Auckland. As managing editor of *Express* newspaper, he spent much of the '90s writing about the local arts, club and bar scene. This is the fourth edition of the *New Zealand* guide he's worked on and, after dozens of Lonely Planet assignments, it remains his favourite gig.

Read more about Peter at:
lonelyplanet.com/members/peterdragicevich

OVER MORE
PAGE WRITERS

Published by Lonely Planet Publications Pty Ltd
ABN 36 005 607 983
4th edition – October 2014
ISBN 978 1 74220 789 6
© Lonely Planet 2014   Photographs © as indicated 2014
10 9 8 7 6 5 4 3 2
Printed in China

Although the authors and Lonely Planet have taken all reasonable care in preparing this book, we make no warranty about the accuracy or completeness of its content and, to the maximum extent permitted, disclaim all liability arising from its use.